The Letters of C. Vann Woodward

THE LETTERS OF
C. Vann Woodward

EDITED BY

Michael O'Brien

Yale
UNIVERSITY PRESS

New Haven & London

Published with assistance from the Kingsley Trust Association Publication Fund established by the Scroll and Key Society of Yale College; and from the foundation established in memory of James Wesley Cooper of the Class of 1865, Yale College.

Yale University Press books may be purchased in quantity for educational,
business, or promotional use. For information,
please e-mail sales.press@yale.edu (U.S. office) or
sales@yaleup.co.uk (U.K. office).

Designed by James J. Johnson.
Set in Bulmer type by Integrated Publishing Solutions, Grand Rapids, Michigan.
Printed in the United States of America.

Library of Congress Cataloging-in-Publication Data
Woodward, C. Vann (Comer Vann), 1908–1999.
[Correspondence]
The letters of C. Vann Woodward / edited by Michael O'Brien.
pages   cm
Includes bibliographical references and index.
ISBN 978-0-300-18534-8 (hardcover : alk. paper)   1. Woodward, C. Vann (Comer Vann),
1908–1999—Correspondence.   2. Historians—United States—Biography.   3. Southern States—
Historiography.   I. O'Brien, Michael, 1948 April 13–   II. Title.
E175.5.W66A4 2013
975'.007202—dc23
2013011897

A catalogue record for this book is available from the British Library.

This paper meets the requirements of ANSI/NISO Z39.48–1992 (Permanence of Paper).

10   9   8   7   6   5   4   3   2   1

For Steven Stowe
in friendship

Contents

Introduction

The rationale for publishing letters varies. There are a few whose letters justify publication because their author had a remarkable gift for the form, but perhaps little else. Madame de Sévigné would occasion scant interest for her quiet routines (reading, visiting a salon, listening to a nightingale) as a lesser French aristocrat of the late seventeenth century. But her letters were exquisitely good at describing her world, which contained those—the Bourbon royal family, Madame de la Fayette, La Rochefoucauld—who then cut a greater figure in the world than the widow bereft of her child, but who now seem lesser than the woman who but scribbled. There are then those who are regarded as immensely important, for sundry reasons—ruling an empire, writing an opera, or examining strange animals on the Galapagos—and who happened to write letters, not especially well, but they have been published nonetheless because every scrap of Lincoln, Mozart, and Darwin is felt to be indispensable. Next, there is a handful of those who are "truly great," as Stephen Spender would fantastically have it, in both life and letters, but these are very, very few.[1] Cicero and Voltaire certainly, Jefferson perhaps. Lastly, there are those who are significant enough that the world cares about them, whether or not they wrote an engaging epistle. If they did not, the letters stay in archives and are used only by the specialized scholar. If they did, the letters get published. This last is C. Vann Woodward's case.

1. Stephen Spender, "I think continually of those who were truly great" (1931); Stephen Spender, *Poems* (London: Faber & Faber, 1933), 45–46.

Of his significance as an American historian, there can be no doubt. There have now been several generations of scholars who have described, criticized, and contributed to fashioning the significance of Woodward. He himself was not the least of these fashioners. That significance was not a closely guarded secret. In his lifetime, there were prizes (Bancroft, Pulitzer), presidencies of scholarly organizations, and a wardrobe of honorary degrees from home and abroad. From early middle age, he taught in the best universities and wrote for the best editors, and the intellectual world noticed when he spoke. While still in his sixties, he was designated a master of his craft and, a few decades later and in his lifetime, there was an intellectual biography of him and a volume of criticism. Another such critical volume appeared posthumously to mark the fiftieth anniversary of his most important book.[2] There is a lecture series named for him, a prize, a professorial chair, and, fleetingly, a gossipy blog about academia whose witty author dubbed himself "C. Vann Winchell" and presumed that C. Vann would be as recognizable as Walter.[3] To be sure, the bubble of reputation can burst after death. This has not happened to Woodward, though his *nachleben* is yet young.

Taken all around, if one were to play the game of ranking the greatest American historians since the birth of the republic, it is probable that many cognoscenti would put him, probably not in the top ten, but perhaps in the top twenty, somewhere below Henry Adams, above Vernon Parrington, and around about Frederick Jackson Turner. If one were to play the more circumscribed game of ranking the greatest historians of the American South since the birth of the South, he would probably win hands down, at least if the voters knew what they were about.[4]

2. David M. Potter, "C. Vann Woodward," in *Pastmasters: Some Essays on American Historians*, ed. Marcus Cunliffe and Robin Winks (New York: Harper & Row, 1969), 375–407; John Herbert Roper, *C. Vann Woodward, Southerner* (Athens: University of Georgia Press, 1987); John Herbert Roper, ed., *C. Vann Woodward: A Southern Historian and His Critics* (Athens: University of Georgia Press, 1997); John B. Boles and Bethany L. Johnson, eds., *Origins of the New South Fifty Years Later: The Continuing Influence of a Historical Classic* (Baton Rouge: Louisiana State University Press, 2003).

3. The C. Vann Woodward Lectures in Southern History and Literature at Henderson State University; the C. Vann Woodward Dissertation Prize of the Southern Historical Association; the Peter V. and C. Vann Woodward professorship at Yale; the blog can be found at http://historygossip.blogspot.com/.

4. When the *Oxford American* recently asked a panel of experts to vote for the best Southern "nonfiction of all time," Woodward had three entries in the top fifteen. Apart from Flan-

   Before settling to this introduction's primary task of considering
Woodward's letters—appraising the cogency of his historical interpretations is only a tangential concern here and has been well done elsewhere—
it will be helpful to begin with a bare summary of his life, some of whose
facts will need to be elaborated later. Comer Vann Woodward was born
in the tiny village of Vanndale, northeastern Arkansas, on November 13,
1908; he was the son of a school superintendent. In 1911 or 1912, his father moved to a similar job in Arkadelphia and then, two years later, to
Morrilton (both in central Arkansas), where the younger Woodward grew
up and attended the local high school, over which his father presided. In
1926, he went to study at Henderson-Brown College in Arkadelphia, but
in 1928, when his father became dean of Emory Junior College in Oxford, Georgia, he transferred to Emory University in Atlanta, from which
he graduated with a Ph.B. in 1930. Then, for a year he taught freshman
English at the Georgia Institute of Technology, before (1931–32) completing an M.A. in political science at Columbia University. He returned to
teach at Georgia Tech until laid off in 1933, then was mostly unemployed
for a year or so, during which time he began to write a biography of
Tom Watson, the Georgia Populist. In 1934, he secured a fellowship to
pursue a doctorate in history at the University of North Carolina, from
which he graduated in 1937. He then taught at the University of Florida
(1937–39), the University of Virginia (1939–40) as a visiting professor, and
Scripps College in southern California (1940–43) as an associate professor, before taking a commission in the U.S. Navy. In 1946 he went to
Johns Hopkins University as an associate professor, becoming a full professor a year later, and he stayed in Baltimore until he moved to Yale in
1962 as Sterling Professor of History, a position from which he retired in
1977, though without leaving Connecticut, where he was to remain for
the rest of his life, which ended on December 17, 1999. In December
1937 he married Glenn Boyd MacLeod (1910–1982), and in 1943 they
had their only child, Peter Vincent, who predeceased his parents in 1969.
   Along the way, C. Vann Woodward published nine books as sole author and edited a further six, as well as producing a small number of
scholarly articles and hundreds of book reviews, all of which, cumula-

nery O'Connor (with two), he was the only author to have more than one entry: see http://
www.oxfordamerican.org/articles/2009/aug/31/best-southern-nonfiction-all-time/ (accessed
5 January 2012).

tively, transformed how the history of the American South, especially after the Civil War, was viewed. It will be useful, briefly, to describe the implication of this scholarship. Before Woodward came along, the history of the American South had been preoccupied with the colonial period, especially that history of Virginia which might explain the American Revolution and celebrate Founding Fathers, and with the era of the Civil War, understood as a regrettable catastrophe, the more catastrophic because of the sequel of Radical Reconstruction. To the events of the mid-nineteenth century, the fact of slavery was guardedly thought to be relevant, though in the hands of its most erudite historian, Ulrich B. Phillips, the institution was viewed as the defensible means by which uncivilized Africans had been made serviceable as workers for a modern America. The history of the post-Reconstruction South was little written and, when it was, understood as the worthy, if mildly frustrating, venture of a "New South"—that is, the remaking of the South in the image of Massachusetts, if with better manners and a wiser racial system. The prejudice of the historiography was that the upper and middle classes had done a good job in containing ominously unruly elements (blacks, poor whites, misguided radicals, ill-informed Northerners) and, if left in charge, would gradually improve matters. Industry would prosper, education would improve, and farmers would make a better living, and the region would serenely reassume its rightful place in the American order of things, a place that its self-evident gifts merited. This New South was "marked by a spirit of hopefulness, a belief in the future, and a desire to take a fuller part in the life of the nation."[5] Hence the extant historical literature was, for the most part, an affidavit for the established order.

Woodward turned all this on its head. To the contrary, his books suggested, Radical Reconstruction had been a worthwhile experiment in egalitarian politics, and its failure was to be regretted. The Compromise of 1877 was a squalid deal between white Northerners, anxious to retain national political power and willing to abandon inconvenient black allies, and white Southerners, keen to regain local political power and accept a federal economic patronage that confirmed the South's new status as a colonial economy. The region, black and white, after 1877 was not pulling together but was riven by savage class, racial, and economic tensions,

5. Holland Thompson, *The New South: A Chronicle of Social and Industrial Evolution* (New Haven, CT: Yale University Press, 1921), 8.

which eventually led to the system of Jim Crow for blacks and systematic disfranchisement for blacks and poorer whites alike. These tensions
occasioned the Populist revolt, a splendid challenge to the established
order that failed and, in time, occasioned a bittersweet reaction, as even
the tribunes of the disadvantaged—chief among them Tom Watson of
Georgia—turned to the vicious mendacities of racism, anti-Semitism, and
demagoguery. Progressivism did little to alter this situation but merely
tinkered: a few better schools for whites, some paved roads, a less violent and disorderly enforcement of the new racial order, and many pious
and complacent sentiments. So Woodward's was a bleak history, redeemed by two things. Firstly, poverty, military defeat, and insistent tragedy had taught Southerners a kind of wisdom about the intractability of
the human condition, which Northerners, intoxicated with success, had
not acquired. Secondly, the bastards, though they had mostly prevailed,
had not gone unchallenged. There had been "forgotten alternatives,"
dissident thinkers, discontinuities, moments that occasioned encouragement.[6] Southern history was not stable but always shifting, contingent,
and so promising, for those who wished for a more humane social order
that might fulfill "the political aspirations and deeper needs of the mass
of the people."[7]

Understanding this accomplishment has, of necessity, so far proceeded by critics reading Woodward's writings. Reading his private papers is another route, now available. But these papers have a form, mostly
shaped by Woodward himself, which alternately facilitates and constrains
what it is possible to understand.

Woodward liked to write letters and was a magpie about papers.
There are many thousands of documents, mostly in the collection of
his papers held by the Manuscripts and Archives division of the Yale
University Library, which had invited him to donate them soon after his
retirement.[8] The bulk was transferred across the street from his small and
fairly gloomy office in the Hall of Graduate Studies in the mid-1980s,

6. "Forgotten Alternatives" is the title of the first chapter of CVW, *The Strange Career of Jim
Crow* (New York: Oxford University Press, 1955).

7. CVW, *Origins of the New South, 1877–1913* (Baton Rouge: Louisiana State University
Press, 1951), 395.

8. Lawrence Dowler to CVW, 8 March 1978, C. Vann Woodward Papers, Manuscripts
and Archives, Yale University Library. All manuscripts hereinafter cited can be assumed to be
in this collection, unless otherwise specified.

with another batch in the mid-1990s. After his death, the last items were added and, in 2004, the collection, having been catalogued, was opened for the use of scholars. In all, there are ninety-six boxes, which makes his one of the largest manuscript collections of any modern American historian.[9] To a great extent, the papers seem to replicate how he kept his own files during his lifetime. There are, firstly, boxes (Series I) which contain letters to and from individuals and organizations; these are organized, first, alphabetically, and then chronologically. Series II collects his writings, arranged in groups (shorter writings, books, reviews, unpublished works, and lectures); these boxes mingle manuscripts and his correspondence with editors and friends asked to read drafts. Series III concerns "subjects" and is eclectic, while Series IV is designated "research" and is, again, eclectic (note cards, applications for research grants, correspondence with archives, copies of historical documents). Series V collects papers relevant to his time at Yale (departmental matters, letters with administrative officials, the record of his terms of employment). Series VI is dubbed "personal," by which is mostly meant family documents (including some from the nineteenth century), but also diaries, material to do with students, some job offers, photographs, and clippings.

This arrangement is somewhat unusual. It is more common for personal papers to be segregated into incoming and outgoing correspondence, arranged either alphabetically by correspondent or chronologically. At Yale, rather, the researcher comes to the evidence differently. Woodward writes and somebody replies, or he gets a letter and responds, but alphabetical quirkiness means one can jump immediately from a 1934 letter to one in 1988, from a friend in South Carolina to an organization in South Africa. This randomness is compounded because a correspondence with a given individual, or documents concerning him or her, can show up in many places. Woodward's friend and collaborator Richard Hofstadter, for example, is scattered through the papers—in Series I in the "H" folders under "Hofstadter," but also in the "O" folders, in a subset of the folders containing Woodward's correspondence with Oxford University Press about the *Oxford History of the United States*, which he coedited with Hofstadter in the 1960s. He is also in the "A" folders of Series I, under

9. Of other Yale historians whose papers are held in the Sterling Library, those of George W. Pierson come to 37 boxes, Ralph Gabriel 23, Samuel Flagg Bemis 68, and Charles M. Andrews 68. The Richard Hofstadter Papers at Columbia are in 47 boxes, the Eric McKitrick Papers in 51.

"American Historical Association." In Series II, he appears in the folders that concern Woodward's *The Burden of Southern History,* because they corresponded about the manuscript. In Series III, there is a folder that concerns Hofstadter's death, including the text of Woodward's memorial address for his friend. The upshot is that the researcher gets a large sequence of mini-correspondences and topics, a sequence which has the advantage of focusing attention on how Woodward, in a given context, dealt with individuals and organizations. The disadvantage is that development over time is obscured, as is the nature of a relationship with any given individual, when that person (less so, organizations) appears in many contexts in Woodward's life, as many of his friends, students, and colleagues necessarily did.

These are hindrances to understanding that can be readily overcome, of course. Making sure that a narrative does not duplicate an archive's arrangement of evidence is habitually one of any historian's tasks. Another problem inherent in the Woodward papers is, however, more or less insuperable. Woodward was a reserved man who disliked exposing himself to the public gaze. "I do not like to write about myself," he said to those who pried and elsewhere added, "Autobiography . . . is not a branch of literature which I have ever cultivated."[10] In principle, he thought that a historian's private life was fair game for the historian. In 1984 he said to John Herbert Roper, after reading the latter's study of Ulrich Phillips, "I was glad to see you break new ground in biography by endowing a historian with a marriage and an emotional life."[11] Woodward had, after all, begun his scholarly life as a biographer, not uninterested in the personal. Still, when it came to his own life, he preferred reticence, once published memoirs notable for their silence about himself, and purged his own papers of anything too intimate.[12] When the friend of a colleague once asked his advice on how to dispose of personal papers, exchanged between herself and the colleague, he wrote back that they ought to be destroyed. "If you can't quite bring yourself to burn them, I would suggest that you seal them and leave instructions for your attorney in your will to destroy them unopened." He added that this was his own policy about "certain correspondence of my own—things of deep personal meaning

10. CVW to Perry Curtis, 3 January 1967; CVW to Mary M. Heslin, 8 January 1965.

11. CVW to John Herbert Roper, 27 July 1984.

12. CVW, *Thinking Back: The Perils of Writing History* (Baton Rouge: Louisiana State University Press, 1986).

but strictly off the record." He explained that this was not a conflict for a historian, this destruction of the evidence of the past. "As for the 'historical record,' I have managed over the years to enjoy a comfortable relation with Clio upon the understanding with her that I tell the whole truth as I understand it regarding such history as I write. But that is with the understanding that my muse agrees that some things are not for the record, and therefore not within her province or my obligation." This was necessary because the world was full of those with few scruples, "scandal mongers" who liked repeating tittle-tattle.[13]

One cannot know reliably whether this purge arose because he had intriguing matters to conceal, or because he felt that what was private, intriguing or not, should remain private. Probably the latter. Either way, reticence could not be perfectly achieved, because he could not control what might appear in the papers of others nor could he control the fact that, when you write so many letters over so many years, you are likely to offer occasional hostages to posterity's fortune, because the boundaries between the personal and professional are necessarily porous. As he aged, he was more willing to reminisce and a few interesting documents, intentionally or not, slipped through—some of his and his wife's medical records, for example. Still, the fact remains that this volume is obliged to be a study, not of the full emotional and intellectual experience of C. Vann Woodward, but of the professional life of a historian in the mid-twentieth century and, perhaps, none the worse for that. We do not lack self-revelations from those of Woodward's era, but documents that help us understand the working life of a historian are in shorter supply.

So what is the overall shape of his epistolary oeuvre? Unsurprisingly, there is a sharp distinction between his early and later correspondence. In time Woodward would become an establishment figure par excellence and inhabit the center of American intellectual culture, insofar as it had a center. Since he became very willing to belong to and serve organizations, later there is a tremendous amount of correspondence that might be regarded as administrative. Reports on grants and manuscripts, letters suggesting nominees for prizes and honors, references for students and colleagues, and the like. Much of this was routine and of small interest, but some is very significant and each of these genres—the graduate

13. CVW to Katherine Verdery, undated (but the letter mentions the approach of Yale's tercentennial, so presumably was written in the 1990s).

student reference and the reader's report, after all, are as much genres as the haiku and the short story—deserves representation in a volume such as this. In addition, and to surprising degree, he got letters from his reading public, to whom he courteously replied, sometimes cursorily, but sometimes fully. That he was able to generate so many thousands of documents is a measure not only of his assiduity and conscientiousness, but also of his standing, as at Hopkins and Yale he had access to a secretary, to whom he dictated letters or gave handwritten drafts; he also used a Dictaphone. He sometimes typed his own letters (especially when working from home), and in both cases carbons were habitually kept. Now and again, especially for brief letters, he wrote in longhand.

The earlier correspondence is different. Though he used a typewriter at least from 1930, he composed more handwritten letters (and postcards) and, significantly, did not make carbons until the late 1930s. So the survival of this early correspondence depends more on whether the recipient kept the letter and whether, in time, it found its way to an archive. It is likely that he wrote far fewer letters, since the demands on him were fewer, and of those, few survive. As importantly, until he went to Johns Hopkins in 1946 he was fairly unimportant, as the self-important world reckons importance. Almost all his early correspondence, therefore, was with friends, overwhelmingly fellow Southerners, and never with the grandees of the Ivy League, and only a little with New York editors. Woodward had not been the son of privilege and had not attended the best universities as an undergraduate, and, though he attended Columbia University and lived in New York for a year, he did not stay on but went back to the South's familiarities and would stay there until he took a job in California in 1940. His reading was worldly, but he himself was little so, though he jauntily effected a style that impersonated worldliness.

It would be conventional to say that he was finding his way, but, in this instance, the truism is sharply relevant. As a young man, he was much at odds with his family and culture. He was, as he later put it, "a rebellious stripling" or, as he put it at the time, "perverse and rebellious."[14] His family was Methodist, seriously so. His grandfather had been a Methodist circuit rider, his uncle was a Methodist minister, and his father

14. CVW, "Morrilton Memoir," 3; CVW to Antonina Jones Hansell, 7 April 1935, Antonina Hansell Looker Papers, Southern Historical Collection, Wilson Library, University of North Carolina-Chapel Hill (hereinafter AHL).

was dean of a Methodist junior college in a town—Oxford, Georgia—where even other sorts of Protestants were an exoticism. ("I was eight years old before I even knowingly saw a Baptist, and it was the shock of my life," one resident later remembered.)[15] These were sober people who did not dance, did not drink, did not play cards, went to Sunday school, and said their prayers at meals. These pieties were not confined to religion, but to the South's customary beliefs. Woodward's mother, for instance, belonged actively to the United Daughters of the Confederacy in Arkansas.[16] But Woodward not only came to prize the cocktail before dinner but was, from as early as there are records, an atheist who would later scarcely bother to fathom the role of religion in Southern history and who, at the end, expressed a strong desire for a secular memorial service. He was also a dissident from his region's racism and sympathetic to labor unions, socialism, and communism, even to the extent that he was complacent about Stalin's ruthlessness and, when visiting Moscow in 1932, gave thought to remaining. In these impulses as a young Southerner of his generation he was fairly idiosyncratic, though he did not lack for companions in this dissidence, for his Atlanta circle in the late 1920s and early 1930s consisted of other awkward and ironical young men who wrote modernist poetry for little magazines, might be gay, and wanted to transform their suffocating world of Coca-Cola magnates, peremptory bishops, and white ambulance drivers who would leave an injured African-American to die in the street.

Most important, one difference between the young and the mature Woodward is that, while the latter built his life around the tasks of the professional historian, the former did not. At least as late as 1938, he displayed no vocation for historical scholarship and the academy. For a while, as he himself admitted, he had a "lack of direction."[17] He majored in philosophy in college, briefly studied sociology and then switched to political science for his master's degree, taught freshman English, dabbled in journalism, planned to teach English in Germany, considered writing a "panoramic picture of the Negro in America since the Civil War," tried to get a Rhodes scholarship, worked briefly for a New Deal agency, and

15. Polly Stone Buck, *The Blessed Town: Oxford, Georgia, at the Turn of the Century* (Chapel Hill, NC: Algonquin Books of Chapel Hill, 1986), 94.

16. CVW to James Loewen, 11 January 1999.

17. CVW to Glenn W. Rainey, 19 February 1931, Glenn Weddington Rainey Papers, Manuscripts, Archives, and Rare Book Library, Emory University (hereinafter GWR).

nowhere articulated a burning ambition to be a historian.[18] As he often remarked later, because he got interested in Southern demagogues in general, and Tom Watson in particular, and started to write about these topics—though more as a biographer than a historian—and could not make enough money to sustain the endeavor, he reluctantly agreed to undertake a doctorate in history, because it came with a scholarship. Part of the deal was getting a Ph.D., which he acquired with distaste, and the degree qualified him for an academic job—in the 1930s, jobs were not to be lightly disdained—which he duly took, but even when teaching at the University of Florida he did not teach much history but rather general courses in the social sciences and humanities (such as "Man and the Social World"), and found academic life so little to his taste that he toyed with giving it up.[19] But he did not, because, as he put it in 1939, "I know damned well that it is from teaching and not writing that I am going to have to make my living."[20] That is, as a young man, it was tolerably clear that he wanted to write, but he did not know what genre would suit him, what topics would hold his attention, let alone whether a professional career was possible or desirable.[21] He was not even sure whether he wished to be a Southerner. One of the more striking passages in his letters is where, writing to Daniel Boorstin in 1953, he said: "I was surprised to learn that we grew up as close together as Oklahoma and Arkansas. I do not know whether you ever shook off the Southern heritage. I set out deliberately to do so in several attempts, but I never really did. I will have to work it out some day in order to live with it."[22]

If Woodward had ended up as a novelist or poet, one would have no difficulty in understanding his trajectory, for the South—and the rest of the United States, for that matter—was full of young college graduates who started with miscellaneous writing, began to settle on a genre or

18. CVW to Glenn W. Rainey, 11 May 1931, GWR.

19. On his teaching, see Adrian H. Daane to CVW, 18 February 1991; on his discontent, see CVW to Hannah Josephson, 19 April 1954, in which he remembers that Matthew Josephson had advised CVW in 1938 not to give up academic life: "I had expressed some impatience with the academic routine and confessed a temptation to kick over the traces."

20. CVW to Glenn W. Rainey, 26 March 1939, GWR.

21. CVW to Glenn W. Rainey, 20 October 1931, GWR: "I have about decided that unless I hit upon a field that really challenges my interest, something that I can be happy in studying that I shall turn to something else besides teaching—anything."

22. CVW to Daniel J. Boorstin, 17 May 1953.

two, tried to make freelancing work but failed, and ended up taking an academic post. This was what happened to Allen Tate. Some historians have suggested that this was the trajectory of American intellectual life during the twentieth century, that the so-called public intellectuals, as well as novelists and poets, drifted into universities, for good or ill. (Good for the universities, ill for the writers and the public, some think.) It is not usual to see Woodward in this light, because most see the real Woodward as the later Woodward, so evidently rooted in the academy, and know little about the uncertain young man of the 1930s. But this perspective is helpful, because it may help to explain not only the young man but the older one, who—after a phase of careful scholarship—did act as a public intellectual, who used the university as a base.

So what do we have from these early years? Preeminent is the sustained and warm exchange of letters with Glenn Weddington Rainey. He and Woodward had become friends when undergraduates at Emory in the late 1920s, when they had belonged to a small coterie, of which the senior member had been Ernest Hartsock, poet, homosexual, little magazine editor, and musician, and the junior member "Pete" Ficklen. These were young men who read James Joyce, copied Mencken's satirical mannerisms, admired wit, and wanted to make a difference, not just aesthetically but socially. It did not work out for most of them: Hartsock died young, Ficklen ran up careless debts, and Rainey, though he married happily and became a valued English professor at Georgia Tech, never finished his doctorate and, apart from the odd piece (including poetry), published little. In time, as Woodward soared away from Atlanta and the world of freshman English, he and Rainey would drift apart, while remaining fondly reminiscent about what they had once had. But in the 1930s, if the letters are a guide, no relationship was more important to Woodward, who wrote often, needily, discursively, and brightly. Fortunately for us, they were usually apart, Rainey in Evanston working on his Northwestern doctorate and Woodward in Atlanta, or Woodward at Columbia or Chapel Hill and Rainey in Atlanta, or both in Georgia, but Woodward in Oxford and Rainey in Atlanta. So the letters buzzed backwards and forwards—about the books they were reading, the movies and people and places they saw, the girls they met, the politicians they disliked, the uncertainties they had, the plans that worked out or went astray.

Less central, but valuable, are the letters Woodward wrote to a South-

ern divorcée called Antonina Jones Hansell, known as "Nina." They had
become lovers in 1933, when they were both living in Georgia. Later,
when separated, they would write. Apart from a few letters from the late
1930s, when she had moved to New York, her side of the correspondence
has disappeared from Woodward's papers, but his letters are in her papers at the Southern Historical Collection. She was ten years older and
interested in psychology and he seems to have used her as a young man
might be expected to use an older woman and sexual partner, as a counselor, less on his intellectual career, more on his emotional life. Then,
at least, he was conscious of being too repressed and she seems to have
released some of these repressions, so these letters are among the few that
show a glimpse of Woodward's inner feelings and self-appraisal. They
also show him coming to know and marrying his wife Glenn, whom he
candidly described to Hansell, even a little after the marriage.

These two, Rainey and Hansell, occasioned most of Woodward's
significant and surviving correspondence up until 1937, when his life
changed and began to diversify. He was now a college professor and, in
Gainesville, acquired two friends who would remain important to him.
There was the political scientist-cum-historian Manning J. Dauer, whose
intellectual pertinence to Woodward was mostly early but who remained
a personal friend, one who used to send Woodward (a migrant in the
cold wastelands of the North) regular consignments of Florida oranges
and whom, thirty years later, Woodward would meet regularly for vaca-
tions in Ocean City, Maryland, where they would go deep-sea fishing.
Over the long haul, more important intellectually was William G. Carleton, political scientist, charismatic lecturer, and ebullient letter writer,
who commented shrewdly on Woodward's writings and career down the
years (though also public affairs) and acted as a blunt adviser who would
remind Woodward, in the midst of triumphs, that he was mortal. Typical
is a Carleton letter of 1961, when Woodward was about to move to Yale:
"Do not get too immersed in your career, your reputation, the activities
of being eminent, the opinions of the Establishment. Having to keep up
a reputation—or more precisely the feeling of having to keep it up, to
augment it . . . can become a terrible slavery and you will pay a price. Up
to now you have escaped this. But I see signs."[23]

In the late 1930s, too, because Woodward had published a success-

23. William G. Carleton to CVW, 18 December 1961.

ful first book, *Tom Watson: Agrarian Rebel* (1938), he came to undertake
more correspondence with editors and became known to a wider public,
including other Southern intellectuals, historians, and even a few politicians.[24] (For most of his life, however, though he usually supported liberal Democrats, by comparison with someone like Arthur Schlesinger
Jr., Woodward kept his distance from politicians and was never in danger
of ending up in a corner office of the West Wing.) Not least, he attracted
the notice of the editors of the History of the South series, who, with
much misgiving for they were conservative and staid gentlemen, invited
the young dissident to write what would eventually become *Origins of
the New South*.[25] Woodward also moved to places—Charlottesville and
Claremont—remote from most of his friends and so there was the business of keeping up. Further, with events moving quickly, more now needed
to be said about the world's politics. Woodward himself, like many of his
immediate friends, was an isolationist who mistrusted Britain and capitalism's combats and, upon his own account, was made "physically as well
as emotionally sick" when Pearl Harbor turned the prospect of war into
a reality.[26] He did not rush into uniform, did not join the U.S. Naval Reserve until 1943, saw no combat, only briefly went beyond the boundaries
of the United States, and served out a scholar's war in the Office of Naval
Intelligence in Washington, DC, where he was charged with writing accounts of naval battles, one of which became his second book, *The Battle
for Leyte Gulf* (1947).[27] Though there are a number of letters from wartime
California, in part concerned with struggles at Scripps College to defend
German faculty members, after his conscription there is, with few exceptions, a silence in his correspondence about the war itself, a silence little
broken afterwards.[28] He was not one of those historians who liked to talk
about his war, and the little that we can know—apart from a few military
documents in the Yale papers—comes from the reminiscences of others
who speak of Washington lunches and the "handsome naval lieutenant
whose bright blue eyes took in everything that was going on."[29]

24. CVW, *Tom Watson: Agrarian Rebel* (New York: Macmillan, 1938).
25. CVW, *Origins of the New South, 1877–1913*.
26. CVW to David Riesman, 15 June 1981.
27. CVW, *The Battle for Leyte Gulf* (New York: Macmillan, 1947).
28. Woodward, *Thinking Back*, 45–47, which briefly mentions the war, is not informative
about his wartime experience, just about the value of writing naval history.
29. John Morton Blum, *A Life with History* (Lawrence: University Press of Kansas, 2004), 69.

Joining the faculty at Johns Hopkins in 1946 changed much. It is, in fact, obscure how the appointment came about. It may be that, because he had spent much time in the Washington area both during the war and before, when working at the Library of Congress he had come to know Hopkins people from nearby Baltimore. Of course, *Tom Watson* had been a critical success and Hopkins had a long tradition of recruiting talented young Southerners to a university that was part Ivy league, part Southern, part Washington political. Still, it was a long step up from Scripps College, which instructed genteel young ladies amid Spanish groves, to Hopkins, whose seminars were notorious for male competitiveness, and there is evidence that the move was transformative.

As a practical matter, because the teaching load was small, he was able to make progress with *Origins of the New South*, some chapters of which he had drafted before the war, but which had been, understandably, stalled. For the first time he had graduate students, which was Hopkins's specialty and became his, and he would there begin to lose the knack, if he ever had it, of teaching undergraduates. (Though there are some early letters which speak of his pleasure in the endeavor and some later letters from ex-students which suggest that he had not been as ineffective as later legend would have it.)[30] The value of Hopkins was that it was culturally poised. It enabled him to keep and even diversify his Southern links. He became, for example, much engaged by the Southern Historical Association, whose program committee he chaired in 1949 and whose president he became in 1952, and he spent much time in encouraging and discoursing with the region's postwar intellectuals, to whom he gradually became a sort of tribune, especially after the miraculous years of 1951–55, when in swift succession he brought out *Origins of the New South* (1951), *Reunion and Reaction* (1951), and *The Strange Career of Jim Crow* (1955).[31] Equally, he acquired a whole new range of connections beyond the South, for Hopkins was a place through which the academic world passed, and was conveniently at the farthest end of the northeastern corridor. (Indeed, it is not implausible to see Woodward as a fellow traveler of the New York

30. For example, CVW to Glenn W. Rainey, 28 October 1941, GWR: "I have been pleasantly surprised at my feelings about this place [Scripps] and my work since return. . . . The main thing, I expect, has been my teaching which I feel much happier about than I did last year. I am really having a lot of fun, especially with the History of Am. Political Ideas."

31. CVW, *Reunion and Reaction: The Compromise of 1877 and the End of Reconstruction* (Boston: Little, Brown, 1951).

intellectuals, for some of his characteristic themes, usually explained as Southern in origin, are also explicable as Manhattan in origin, for New York was a place where, after 1945, he spent more time than he ever did in the South below the Potomac.) So new people appeared among his correspondents, social scientists like David Riesman, historians (not of the South) like Richard Hofstadter. He even became international, because in 1954–55 he served as the visiting Harmsworth Professor at the University of Oxford, an experience out of which he acquired no small connection with those who wrote American history in Britain and, though far less so, continental Europe. In 1953 he had also spent a semester in Tokyo, and he tried hard in the late 1950s, though unsuccessfully, to work out a similar stint in India, a place he had briefly visited as a naval courier during the war. These experiences never made him a cosmopolitan, a species he mistrusted, they just indulged his liking for travel. (This fondness was fortunate, for this was a man who spent a lot of his adult life on the road, at the end of which was a lecture to give, a conference to attend, a committee to chair, a hotel bar, and a room at the Hilton.) These foreign experiences, however, did accelerate an interest in comparative history, which was an influence upon his two seminal articles of the 1950s, "The Irony of Southern History" and "The Search for Southern Identity"— each, in its own way, a meditation on what it meant no longer to be fully immersed in Southern culture—and would, though only eventually, lead him to edit *The Comparative Approach to American History* (1968).[32] Lastly, Hopkins, because of its proximity to Washington, often led its faculty into advisory roles for the federal government. This did not work out for him, because his radical past led to his failing to get a security clearance for service (suggested by Samuel Eliot Morison) as a historical adviser to the Joint Chiefs of Staff. Instead he ended up advising those who sought to pressure the federal government, notably the NAACP, when it was devising a Supreme Court brief for *Brown v. Board of Education*.

All things considered, Woodward survived the world of Joe McCarthy more easily than might have been predicted for a man who had vis-

32. He seems to have been interested in comparative matters as early as 1950: see CVW to Jerome Blum, 14 December 1950, which asks for advice on Russian history, which he might use for his upcoming Fleming lectures. See CVW, "The Irony of Southern History," *Journal of Southern History* 19 (February 1953): 3–19; CVW, "The Search for Southern Identity," *Virginia Quarterly Review* 34 (Summer 1958): 321–38; CVW, ed., *The Comparative Approach to American History* (New York: Basic Books, 1968).

ited the Soviet Union in the early 1930s, helped union organizers, and
been friends with Communists who had saluted him as "brother."[33] When
Owen Lattimore, his Hopkins colleague, fell foul of the junior senator
from Wisconsin, Woodward was among his defenders and helped Lattimore keep his job.[34] No doubt this was done in part because Woodward
had a fierce commitment to freedom of speech, which went as far back
as his Gainesville membership of the American Association of University Professors—then working to defend faculty against egregious politicians and administrators—and would last to the end of his life, with
consequences for him that would prove disquietingly complicated. But it
was also done, one feels, because Woodward understood that Lattimore's
fate might have been his own, although Woodward had a greater gift for
discretion than Lattimore and, even in the 1930s, used to caution friends
about speaking too freely of his dissident opinions. ("I shall ask you to
use your discretion about communicating my Soviet enthusiasm.")[35] This
gift did not go so far as avoiding the Cold War's pariahs, not least in 1959
when he came to know Alger Hiss and spent a fascinating evening in
Manhattan when Hiss was peppered with questions about his trial, Whittaker Chambers, and pumpkins.

The 1950s is when Woodward became an organization man. The
number of his organizations is, in retrospect, dazzlingly numerous. There
is a 1963 letter in which he responded to a request that he join the board
of the AAUP by regretfully declining, because he was already committed
to "twenty-one out-of-town meetings of committees, councils, or boards
during the academic year. . . . And this after recently resigning from a
couple so as to take on the board of the ACLS [American Council of
Learned Societies], which meets five times a year."[36] Still, he usually said
yes. There were the historical organizations—the Southern Historical
Association, American Historical Association, Mississippi Valley Historical Association (which became the Organization of American Historians), in all of which he rose through the ranks to become president, and
all of which had their plethora of committees, as well as journals which

33. Robert F. Hall to "Brother Woodward," 23 July 1938; Hall was secretary of the 17th
District of the Communist Party, which was headquartered in Birmingham, Alabama.

34. For a valuable account of this affair, see Lionel S. Lewis, *The Cold War and Academic
Governance: The Lattimore Case at Johns Hopkins* (Albany: State University of New York Press, 1993).

35. CVW to Glenn W. Rainey, 11 August [1932], GWR.

36. CVW to William S. Fidler, 30 May 1963.

needed sustaining. (He stayed clear of the American Studies Association.) He also had some commitment to the Association for the Study of Negro Life and History. There were scholarly academies: the American Academy of Arts and Sciences (to which he was elected in 1958), the American Philosophical Society (1959), the American Academy of Arts and Letters (1970), and the Society of American Historians (first turned away, then accepted in 1964). There were assorted pressure groups; the AAUP, the American Civil Liberties Union, the NAACP, the A. Philip Randolph Institute, and several other civil rights organizations. There were grant-giving bodies: the Guggenheim Foundation, the American Council of Learned Societies, the National Endowment for the Humanities, the Ford Foundation, the Rockefeller Foundation. There were editorial boards in abundance and some prize-giving committees (notably the Pulitzer). All this, of course, was on top of his responsibilities to the universities that employed him, although it seems that he was selective about what he was willing to do. He never served, for example, as a department chair.

This immersion in institutions was the fate of many scholars in his time, which, for these purposes, is still our time. As the American academy grew rapidly after the Second World War, both universities and disciplines proliferated institutions and needed warm and, preferably, intelligent bodies to administer them. Universities looked kindly upon such occupations, politely and sometimes sincerely known as "service to the profession." To be sure, not everyone warmed to the idea and some declined to participate. Among Woodward's peers, the most notable recusant was Richard Hofstadter, who seldom went to conventions, joined few organizations, disliked the idea of a historical profession, and instead preferred to stay in Manhattan and write his books.[37] Arthur Schlesinger Jr., too, preferred a Democratic nominating convention to the conference hotels where historians sat in thinly attended rooms and listened to desultory papers. He once wrote in his journal: "I have always felt uncomfortable, even alienated, in academic life . . . I [have] tried . . . to define my feelings about pure academics—what is it?—the sense they give of collective unreality? collective complacency? collective pomposity? collective futility? And their jokes are so bad! . . . Why does the academic

37. His biographer speaks of "a certain autonomy from the academy": David S. Brown, *Richard Hofstadter: An Intellectual Biography* (Chicago: University of Chicago Press, 2006), 144.

environment, as distinct from the academic discipline, seem to bring out the worst in otherwise decent individuals?"[38] Woodward, for his part, was a more conscientious and civic-minded man—Schlesinger called him "a kinder, gentler, and nobler figure"—but it seems hard to resist the conclusion that there was a neediness in all this joining, in part arising from a liking for companionship, but also a desire for affirmation.[39]

After all, Woodward was an interloper and, as such, part of a trend. By 1960, the citadels of academic power were still mostly administered by Ivy League gentlemen who were not keen on Jews, blacks, and women. But there were no longer enough gentlemen to go around and it was becoming ominously clear that gentlemen, though they might be snappy dressers, were not necessarily the smartest people available.[40] So interlopers were selectively being allowed in. Of these, Jews—mostly those who had studied at the Ivy League as undergraduates (preferably) or graduates (if necessary) like John Morton Blum and Oscar Handlin—and white Southerners, even when not Ivy League, were most admissible.[41] Blacks, with the pioneering exception of John Hope Franklin who had a Harvard doctorate, and women had to wait another decade and more. This was how Yale's George W. Pierson, than whom no one was more traditionally Ivy league and patrician, appraised the situation when he hired Blum the Jew and Woodward the Arkansan, whom a Northerner might mistake for a Southern gentleman (because he had good manners), though no blueblood Charlestonian would (because he had no oil paintings of resonant ancestors to hang above his dining table). Nor, for that matter, would a black Alabamian. Albert Murray once described Wood-

38. Entry for 4 April 1981, in Arthur M. Schlesinger Jr., *Journals, 1952–2000* (2007; London: Atlantic Books, 2008), 516.

39. Entry for 20 July 1991, in Schlesinger, *Journals, 1952–2000*, 712.

40. On these matters, see William Palmer, *Engagement with the Past: The Lives and Works of the World War II Generation of Historians* (Lexington: University Press of Kentucky, 2001).

41. There had been a tradition of white Southerners at Ivy League universities, but usually, after a first degree at a Southern university, they had taken their doctorates in the North; this was the case with Woodrow Wilson (who studied first at Davidson College and Princeton, took his doctorate at Hopkins, and later taught at Princeton), Ulrich B. Phillips (University of Georgia, Columbia, Yale), and David Potter (Emory, Yale, Yale). Woodward's different experience may have had the consequence that he came of age in a Southern academy, where he felt confident of himself if not always at ease, but did not experience the alienation often suffered by outsiders who studied in the Ivy League.

ward as "the spitting image of the old Life and Casualty insurance man," which is not how you describe a Southern gentleman.[42]

Serving this world of organizations had an effect. One of the features of Woodward's career is that, after the publication of *The Strange Career of Jim Crow* in 1955, he never again published a sustained piece of historical narrative and interpretation. As Stephen Whitfield was to observe in 1987, when reviewing Woodward's *Thinking Back*, "Woodward essentially abandoned historical writing other than essays, introductions, and reviews more than three decades ago."[43] There are several ways to explain this shift, but one, certainly, is that he committed so much time to serving organizations. As he exclaimed, when turning down the AAUP in 1963, "How is a man to get on with his book?"[44] Such a busy way of life, that is, was better adapted to short-term projects, because his time was so broken up. But this was not the only reason, which his correspondence makes clear.

One is tempted to say—this will seem odd to say about a historian best known and rightly celebrated for a sustained narrative—that he was never very reconciled to what is required for the writing of long, carefully researched books: the need for focus, the long research trips, the obsessiveness, the loneliness.[45] He had, of course, to do some of this for his first book, because doctoral dissertations have to do that. And, then, while he was thinking about other projects, he was suddenly asked to write a volume for the History of the South series. He was young, he was flattered, he knew it was (what Howard Beale called) "a grand opportunity, but a whale of a job," and he agreed.[46] His careful research in widely scattered archives—obligatory because there was no adequate secondary literature to feed off—produced not only *Origins of the New South*, but *Reunion and Reaction*, essentially a more detailed explication of a shorter narrative in the former book about how the Compromise of 1877 was negotiated. In the same way, *The Strange Career of Jim Crow* grew from *Origins*. So these

42. Albert Murray, *South to a Very Old Place* (New York: McGraw-Hill, 1971), 16.

43. Stephen J. Whitfield, "Understanding Backward," *Virginia Quarterly Review* 63 (Spring 1987): 352.

44. CVW to William S. Fidler, 30 May 1963.

45. It might be objected that his edition of Mary Chesnut's involved much archival work, but he did little of this himself; instead, he presided over a small army of research assistants, marshaled by Elisabeth Muhlenfeld.

46. Howard K. Beale to CVW, 2 February 1939.

three books formed a triptych. Indeed it is arguable that, because *Origins* elaborated a standpoint articulated in *Tom Watson*, Woodward had created a tetraptych. Yet completing this artistic masterpiece posed a problem. What next? In 1955, he was forty-seven, which is still young for a historian.

It is unclear that he ever found an answer to this question. His papers show restlessness, projects begun and abandoned, contracts signed and cancelled, both before and after 1955. That in the late 1930s his first project, a biography of Eugene Debs, was put aside was not his fault, because the family would not grant him access to Debs's papers.[47] But there were other ventures. In 1941, he signed up with Little, Brown for a book to be called *Henry Grady and the Makers of the New South*, but in 1948 he cancelled the contract and his $500 advance was rolled over to a second project, as yet undetermined.[48] In April 1951, he gave the Fleming Lectures at Louisiana State University on "Southern Dissenters in Exile" and, as is usual with these lectures, was supposed to deliver a manuscript to Louisiana State University Press, but never did. In 1956, for Houghton Mifflin, he agreed to write a textbook on the history of the South, for which Clement Eaton would write the antebellum chapters, Woodward the postbellum. A contract was signed, but in 1959 Woodward backed out because he had taken on other obligations.[49] Most significantly, in 1958 he signed a contract with Little, Brown for a major book on Reconstruction, which he described as "a companion volume to my ORIGINS OF THE NEW SOUTH . . . of comparable scope, but being free of obligations to a series . . . a better book." (In the same letter, he spoke of another book, in which Little, Brown was more interested, on "the century from Emancipation to Desegregation," but ventured the opinion that, though he wished to do it, it would need to wait.)[50] So his ambition for this work on Reconstruction was not modest—he thought it might be as long as 200,000 words—and he worked on it seriously during the 1960s. His publishers stumped up a $2,500 advance, later raised to $7,500 when Norton tried to lure him away, and, with this contract in hand, he applied for and received grants, was

47. Woodward, *Thinking Back*, 43–44.

48. Stanley Salmen to CVW, 26 March 1948.

49. See, especially, William D. MacDonald to CVW, 31 December 1956; CVW to William D. MacDonald, 24 March 1959.

50. CVW to Arthur N. Thornhill Jr., 27 September 1958.

given extended periods of leave, and undertook a three-month research swing through the archives of the lower South in early 1962. The book was never done, but it seems to have been thought still possible as late as 1969, at least by others.[51] However, the venture did spill over into various lectures, essays, and reviews, some of them of importance to guiding the contemporary understanding of Reconstruction. His extant manuscripts do not make clear what happened. There is no letter in which he says, "I did not finish the book because . . ." It is possible that the interpretative backbone of the proposed book—that there was a parallel between Reconstruction and the civil rights movement, between what he called the "first Reconstruction" and "second Reconstruction"—became less tenable in the late 1960s, when, to his sharp dissatisfaction, the rise of the black power movement splintered the existing racial reform movement.

There are other explanations. Woodward had always seen himself as politically and socially engaged. Even before he settled on being a historian, he had offered himself as a cultural critic in Atlanta newspapers. His later scholarly accomplishments, which included the felicity of his style, made him attractive to editors in search of "freelance 'high journalism.'"[52] By 1939, he was reviewing books for the *New Republic,* but this scale of national visibility was then rare, and throughout the 1940s most of his reviews were for scholarly journals or literary periodicals associated with universities, such as the *Virginia Quarterly Review.* In 1951, however, he started to write often for the *Saturday Review of Literature,* in 1954 for the *New York Herald Tribune Book Review* and the *New York Times Book Review,* in 1955 for the *Nation,* in 1956 for *Commentary,* and in 1964 for the *New York Review of Books,* which became his habitual bully pulpit for the rest of his life. So this role expanded over the years and generated much correspondence with editors, as well as with readers (sometimes appreciative, sometimes indignant). Given a choice, he preferred to accept the journalistic assignment and to postpone the trip to an archive. Considering how well he performed in his bully pulpit, it is hard to quarrel with his choice, the more so since he spent so much time helping others. These assignments, of course, turned into books, just different sorts of books.

51. See Eugene Genovese to CVW, 12 May 1969, which speaks, though a little hopefully, of the project as still alive.

52. The phrase comes from Neil Jumonville, *Critical Crossings: The New York Intellectuals in Postwar America* (Berkeley: University of California Press, 1991), xv.

The Burden of Southern History (1960) was, for the most part, a collection of scholarly articles and essays, first published in the *Virginia Quarterly Review*, the *Journal of Southern History*, and the *American Scholar*. *American Counterpoint* (1971) and *The Future of the Past* (1989), by comparison, drew more on the *New York Review of Books*, though he never abandoned the scholarly essay as abruptly as he gave up the scholarly article.[53]

One other explanation needs to be offered, because it is relevant to the nature of Woodward's correspondence. Sporadically before the early 1950s and systematically thereafter, he acquired the role of literary midwife. The role is less recognized as one for a historian than, say, an editor like Maxwell Perkins or a poet like Ezra Pound, but it palpably exists. At its most modest level, it is the function of a doctoral adviser, who must help to design a dissertation and then critique its accomplishment. At Johns Hopkins and Yale, Woodward performed this function for what proved to be some very gifted historians who would rise to prominence. Since adviser and student were often separated—in those days, it was possible to get a job before a dissertation was completed—letters were a medium of criticism, though Woodward, who wrote much better than he talked, often preferred to transmit his views by letter, even if the student was on campus. But his role as midwife expanded beyond Baltimore. He became known as a shrewd critic. Historians, young and old, began to beat a path to his mailbox. Some of these manuscripts came to him in the normal manner, that is, the editor of a journal or press solicited a report from him, or he was himself serving as an editor, as he did for the *Oxford History of the United States*. But a great deal came informally, and the number of important books not written by his students, whose manuscripts passed beneath his scrutiny, is deeply impressive: almost all of Richard Hofstadter's works, from *The Age of Reform* (1955) onward, Stanley Elkins's *Slavery* (1959), James Silver's *Mississippi: The Closed Society* (1964), Eugene Genovese's *Roll Jordan, Roll* (1974), and Robert Fogel and Stanley Engerman's *Time on the Cross* (1974), to name only some. In addition, the occasional novelist and poet sought him out: Robert Penn Warren, above all, but also William Styron, who asked Woodward to read the manuscript of *The Confessions of Nat Turner* (1967).

53. CVW, *The Burden of Southern History* (Baton Rouge: Louisiana State University Press, 1960); CVW, *American Counterpoint: Slavery and Racism in the North-South Dialogue* (Boston: Little, Brown, 1971); CVW, *The Future of the Past* (New York: Oxford University Press, 1989).

These letters of criticism are among the chefs d'oeuvre of his correspondence, and anyone wishing to know how this delicate task should be done would do well to study them. Those written as anonymous reader's reports were somewhat different, because he was freer to be savage, if he was in the mood. But, in those written for friends and colleagues, usually he started with words of praise, which identified the value of a book, which was not necessarily the value discerned by the author, and he often characterized style. He then moved on to his dissents, politely but trenchantly stated: these might be interpretative or theoretical, or concern problems of evidence. He advanced to suggestions about revision, which might encompass concrete details of needed extra reading or research, a redesign of a manuscript's structure, or changes in aesthetic tone. Lastly, there might be a list of errata. He would often end with praise, because he knew that authors tend to be neurotic and need reassurance, especially when being told that not all is well with their words.

This service immensely enriched the life of the American historical mind, though it could occasion complications, discerned more by others than by Woodward himself. For he operated at several levels: as the informal reader of a manuscript, the formal writer of reader's reports for editors, and a book reviewer. Very often he did two of these things for the same manuscript, even for his own students. As late as the mid-1960s, it was not thought very improper for an adviser to write a reader's report on the work of his own former student, and Woodward never ceased to review the published works of his students.[54] Naturally, some came to think of him as the impresario of a cabal, sometimes thought to be in competition with other cabals.[55] Stephen Whitfield, perhaps the

54. For examples of CVW submitting reader's reports on his own students, see CVW to John H. Kyle (of the Johns Hopkins Press), 12 September 1958, and CVW to Henry R. Winkler (of the *American Historical Review*), 31 December 1966. As for reviewing in print those manuscripts he had read for friends, he was a little inconsistent. In 1972, he declined to review Carl Degler's *Neither Black nor White* (1971) for the *New York Review of Books*, because "I [have] had so much correspondence with him about that I would find it awkward to take issue with it in public, as I would be obliged to do should I review it": CVW to Robert B. Silvers, 22 May 1972. Yet he did review Genovese's *Roll, Jordan, Roll*, which he had also seen in manuscript and corresponded about. The distinction is, perhaps, that he thought better of Genovese's book than Degler's.

55. It was widely assumed that Woodward and David Donald were competitors; there is no evidence for this, at least up to the mid-1960s, though thereafter their connection did become more distant.

most critical of those willing to air their discontent in print, bluntly said in 1987 that Woodward's practice of benignly reviewing his own doctoral students, past and present, was "a dubious reviewing practice which, if it can be justified at all, ought to require that an interest be declared (which Woodward has not done)."[56]

By comparison to ours, Woodward's world had different ethics, was more informal, and was run by senior professors who believed they had earned the right to these prerogatives. The default presumption was that they could be trusted. (Not a popular idea of late, when there has been a decline of trust.)[57] Academic jobs for a student, for example, might be secured by Woodward picking up a telephone, calling the chair of a department, and saying the right word in the right ear, with no bother about search committees, affirmative action, and whether graduate students approved of a candidate. His correspondence is full of letters from chairmen—then, invariably, men—who would say, "We are looking for a young married man in the field of American History with a secondary field in the Far East or Western Civilization," and promptly hire whomever Woodward suggested.[58] Or someone from a Southern university in the late 1960s would ask if he knew of a presentable young Negro, who might cause no trouble, "a man who is level-headed, objective, and who, hopefully, could disregard somewhat the matter of race, as his colleagues are trying to do. . . . [someone who would] not allow himself to be 'captured' by extremists of any color."[59] Equally, a word from Woodward might secure a grant, an assignment from an editor, a book contract, or a review in a prominent place. To a remarkable degree, he exercised this patronage with discrimination, fairness, and wisdom. Still, inevitably, there were those he favored and those he did not. Naturally and rightly he favored his own students, although he was capable of calibrating his endorsements, according to his estimate of their gifts. Of those not his students and now dead—mentioning the living here would be a different matter, though the letters that follow cannot avoid them—he greatly assisted the rise of David Donald, Eric McKitrick, George Fredrickson, John Hope Franklin, and Lee Benson (for a while). He was of little help,

56. Whitfield, "Understanding Backward," 352.

57. On this, see Onora O'Neill, *A Question of Trust* (Cambridge: Cambridge University Press, 2002).

58. Flint Kellogg to CVW, 20 December 1966.

59. Robert H. Woody to CVW, 17 January 1969.

no help, or was hostile to Staughton Lynd, George Tindall, T. Harry Williams, and Herbert Aptheker.

The name of Aptheker, the Marxist scholar of African-American history and Communist Party member, raises an issue which darkened Woodward's last years at Yale.[60] The issue was a 1975 proposal by Davenport College to appoint Aptheker as a visiting scholar for a semester, during which he would teach a seminar on W. E. B. Du Bois, the editor of whose papers Aptheker then was. This was part of an ongoing program which had brought to campus many, some scholars, some not. Under the program, a college would decide whom it wished to invite, secure the person's consent, procure the sponsorship of a Yale academic department, and subsequently apply to have the formal appointment sanctioned by the Joint Board of Permanent Officers (the full professors of the Graduate School and Yale College). Along the way, it was necessary for relevant Yale departments to be consulted. Woodward was asked to chair an ad hoc committee of the Department of History, of which the other members were John Morton Blum and John Blassingame, the latter a young African-American historian who had been Woodward's doctoral student. The committee recommended that Aptheker not be appointed, because "the candidate did not measure up to the standard of scholarship we try to maintain for Yale teachers," his scholarship was "second rate," and his edition of Du Bois was so "poor" that Woodward had been obliged to resign from the edition's board of advisers. The letter concluded, "The committee's feeling was that if we could not trust him to edit Du Bois' papers—a matter of public record—we were even less able to feel confident of his teaching, of which there would be no public record."[61] What followed was cacophonous: student protests, campus meetings, petitions, controversy in the national press, and a formal investigation jointly administered by the Organization of American Historians and the American Historical Association. It took some two years to run its course, during which time Woodward had to write many letters, defending and explaining himself. The experience was—the adjective may not be too

60. Aptheker served on the National Committee of the Communist Party USA (1957–91).

61. CVW to John W. Hall, 14 October 1975. Formally, the veto came, not from the Department of History—the appointment was sponsored by Political Science and five departments were consulted—but by the Joint Board, whose meeting Woodward and others from History persuaded to a negative vote, by some margin (7 agreeing to the appointment, 25 against, 2 abstentions): see the minutes of the Board's meeting.

strong—embittering, as a 1981 letter to Eugene Genovese makes clear, and those at the time discerned. Woodward himself preferred to speak of exasperation.[62]

The "Ap-Flap," as he came to call it, seems to have had two chief contexts. The first is that Woodward, like many of his generation, was greatly troubled by the student protests of the late 1960s, mostly because he disliked anything that interfered with free speech on the campus. The experience made him alert about challenges to the university's commitment to dispassionate intellectual accomplishment. He became interested to put down markers that might signal where standards were being maintained, where weakened.[63] Earlier in 1975, he had put down a very significant marker when he chaired a Yale committee that formulated a policy on freedom of speech on the campus. The "Woodward report" was a great success, then and now, for its clarity of thought and unequivocal commitment to the value of freedom of expression, which Woodward asserted to be essential to a university's purpose.[64] The flip side of allowing everyone to speak, even if offensively, however, was that universities also had the obligation to evaluate speech and subject it to rigorous criticism. If that obligation was to be taken seriously, or so Woodward thought, Herbert Aptheker ought not to teach at Yale. For Woodward always regarded the Aptheker appointment as he might regard the ad-

62. CVW to Eugene Genovese, 6 April 1981; Peter Eggenberger to CVW, 4 March 1976, which remarks: "The tone of your last letter seems embittered to me"; and CVW to Peter Eggenberger, 15 March 1976, which denies embitterment but admits exasperation. See also CVW to Eugene Genovese, 16 April 1976: "I am misrepresented, misquoted, and lied about daily, here and elsewhere."

63. A subtheme was his concern about a "double standard," a matter he explained to Gettleman: "The fact is that our faculty is divided on this matter. It is not divided on the subject of the seminar. In fact, a number of our own department has given such a seminar before. Nor is there any division on the qualifications of Mr. Aptheker. I think there is general agreement that he is second rate at best. The division is over the issue of a double standard: first for the student-initiated college seminar instructors, and second a double standard for instructors of black students. On the latter issue my colleague John Blassingame has fought a courageous battle against the double standard for blacks or courses for them, and I have supported his struggle to the hilt, and continue to do so. . . . The History Department believes in a single standard and thinks a double standard a betrayal not only of the rules but of our students." See CVW to Marvin E. Gettleman, 15 March 1976.

64. The text is available online: http://yalecollege.yale.edu/sites/default/files/wood ward_report.pdf (accessed 29 February 2012).

mission of a student, appointment of a junior faculty member, or tenure case.[65] He made this point repeatedly at the time, that universities had to have intellectual standards, enforced by those who, by virtue of their senior position in the university, were presumed qualified to judge, and— this was the sticking point for many—confidential and so not available to be challenged. The reluctance to allow such decisions to be scrutinized was, for the most part, a practical issue. Academic life would descend into chaos if every such decision needed elaborate justification and be only provisional. Many younger people, however, felt there was an element of "father knows best" and this was but to defend an old boys network, as Blum admitted his world was.[66]

A more immediate context was Woodward's long-standing relationship to Aptheker, which had been sometimes friendly and not consistently hostile, but which had worsened significantly in the decade before 1975. Their early contacts—the first was in 1954—were friendly and business-like.[67] In the 1960s, the evidence for how far Woodward then regarded Aptheker's work as satisfactory or not is equivocal. In 1965, when discussing possible editors for an edition of Du Bois's *The Souls of Black Folk* for the John Harvard Library reprint series, he suggested Aptheker's name and observed, "I know the obvious objections, but I suspect he would do a scrupulous and creditable job." However, a few days later, he changed his mind: "On second thought I am afraid I should retract my suggestion of Aptheker for the Du bois [*sic*] book. Instead I think I will propose August Meier."[68] In 1966, Woodward commented in a session of the Socialist Scholars Conference in which Aptheker and Genovese gave papers on the "legacy of slavery and roots of black nationalism," and, on the whole, Woodward seems to have been amused and pleased to see

65. The point is made, especially, in CVW to the *Yale Daily News*, 31 January 1976, a document one younger scholar called "the single most inflammatory document that has been circulated": see Marvin E. Gettleman to CVW, 4 March 1976. Part of the difficulty in CVW's defense, as several pointed out, was that Aptheker had not applied for the position but had been invited, though for a position that required formal ratification.

66. For the critical standpoint of a younger radical, see Jesse Lemisch, "History at Yale in the Dark Ages, 1953–76," *History News Network*, 6 January 2007, online at http://hnn.us/articles/33300.html (accessed 29 February 2012). Blum, *Life with History*, 157.

67. Herbert Aptheker to CVW, 6 May 1954; CVW to Herbert Aptheker, 21 April, 16 December 1964; Herbert Aptheker to CVW, 28 April, 12 December 1964.

68. CVW to Bernard Bailyn, 14, 21 December 1965.

Genovese rough Aptheker up.[69] However, in 1967, Aptheker's *Negro Slave Revolts* was on Woodward's list of recommended—though not required—reading for his graduate students.[70] A year later, Woodward was encouraging Harvard University Press to publish Aptheker's proposed edition of the Du Bois papers.[71] In the winter of 1969–70 they had an amiable exchange about Woodward's critique of W. J. Cash, whose *The Mind of the South* Aptheker had reviewed for the *New Masses* in 1941.[72]

Then matters got more complicated, in ways that partly arose from Woodward having a finger in many pies simultaneously. In 1970 the National Endowment for the Humanities asked Woodward to evaluate Aptheker's grant application for his Du Bois edition. In reply, Woodward was skeptical and advised the NEH to consult with Harvard University Press, whose willingness to publish the edition had foundered when, after Harvard had insisted that arrangements be made to deposit the papers in a reputable archive and that a successor to Aptheker as executor be established, Aptheker had withdrawn from the venture. If these legitimate concerns could now be addressed, it might be possible to go forward; if not, not.[73] The grant was denied, but two years later Aptheker applied again and Woodward was again consulted and was again "negative."[74] There was no grant. At the same time, in the spring of 1973, Woodward was approached by the University of Massachusetts Press, which had agreed to publish Aptheker's edition, to ask if he would serve on an advisory board for the edition.[75] He agreed, after noting John Hope Franklin's concurrent willingness to serve, a consent which had laid down certain preconditions, chief of which were that the board should be able to give advice that would be heeded, and that—a continuing theme—the

69. CVW to Robert Penn Warren, 22 September 1966; CVW to Virginius Dabney, [December 1966].

70. CVW to Jack Lynch (of the Yale Co-op), 25 July 1967; see Herbert Aptheker, *American Negro Slave Revolts* (New York: Columbia University Press, 1943).

71. CVW to Ann Orlov, 10 September 1968.

72. Herbert Aptheker to CVW, 15 December 1969, 5 January 1970; CVW to Herbert Aptheker, 14 January 1970.

73. CVW to William R. Emerson, 7 August 1970.

74. William R. Emerson to CVW, 30 June 1972, 31 July 1973; CVW to William R. Emerson, 11 July 1972, 21 August 1973; William R. Emerson to Herbert Aptheker, 31 July 1973. In fact, as CVW to NEH, 26 February 1976, makes clear, CVW wrote a negative report on Aptheker's renewed application, even after the Yale affair had broken.

75. Malcolm L. Call to CVW, 12 March 1973; CVW to Malcolm L. Call, 29 March 1973.

papers needed to be deposited in an archive, so that scholars might have free access.[76] The other members of the board included Louis Harlan, Woodward's former student and the editor of the Booker T. Washington papers. Then the press was confident that the issue of access was on the way to being solved, since Du Bois's widow had agreed to sell the papers to the University of Massachusetts.[77] When the deal was sealed, Woodward was pleased, because he planned to look at the papers himself and had students eager to use them, though he was less pleased to be told that early access was unlikely, since the papers would need to be catalogued and money raised to accomplish this.[78]

In 1974, when the first volume of Du Bois's correspondence was published and Woodward judged it to be deeply inadequate, however, he resigned from the advisory board, as did Harlan.[79] At the same time, Blassingame wrote to express his own distress about the edition. His criticisms were: there was no explanation of editorial procedures, the introduction was woefully brief, a single volume was deemed sufficient to cover fifty-seven years of Du Bois's life, the editing was antiquated and Victorian, and Aptheker had failed to scour other archives to find papers that had not remained in Du Bois's possession and so passed to Aptheker.[80] Many of these criticisms Woodward immediately reiterated to Aptheker himself.[81]

This was the immediate context of Woodward's role in denying Aptheker the Yale visiting appointment. There is no evidence, at least in Woodward's correspondence, to support the accusation that this was a politically motivated decision, that it was Aptheker's Marxism and Communism that was decisive and so this was "genteel McCarthyism."[82] As Woodward often said, he had a high opinion of many Marxists (Geno-

---

76. John Hope Franklin to Malcolm L. Call, 13 March 1973.

77. Malcolm L. Call to CVW, 1 April, 3, 20 August 1973; CVW to Malcolm L. Call, 27 August 1973.

78. CVW to Malcolm L. Call, 15 August 1973.

79. Leone Stein to CVW, 19 April 1974; CVW to Leone Stein, 24 April 1974; see Herbert Aptheker, ed., *The Correspondence of W. E. B. DuBois: 1: Selections, 1877–1934* (Amherst: University of Massachusetts Press, 1973).

80. John W. Blassingame to CVW, 25 February 1974.

81. CVW to Herbert Aptheker, 27 February 1974.

82. See "If Howard Cosell Can Teach at Yale, Why Can't Herbert Aptheker?" a flyer by the Mid-Atlantic Radical Historians Organization, John Jay College of Justice.

vese, E. P. Thompson) and no desire to silence opinions contrary to his own.[83] (Others who wrote to Woodward in support were less innocent of this charge.)[84] It was just that he thought Yale should appoint good scholars only, and Aptheker was, in his opinion, not a good scholar, indeed someone who was impeding the advance of good scholarship. To complicate matters, he also thought it ought to be unnecessary for him to justify his decision, at least not elaborately, and that everyone should accept that a competent body of Yale scholars had considered Aptheker's qualifications and found them wanting. (Marvin Gettleman called this "the Yale-is-above-public-scrutiny syndrome that seems to played such an important psychological role . . . in bringing about the Aptheker affair in the first place.")[85] Here, no doubt, was a crux of the controversy. Many younger than Woodward mistrusted the authority of pipe-smoking older men in tweeds and needed to be persuaded into trust. Woodward, whose reticence and eminence could be alarming to the young, was not in the business of earning trust. Though they both came from Arkansas, he did not inhabit Bill Clinton's disorderly world, which had, a few years earlier, unfolded elsewhere on the New Haven campus, and was not someone who sat around late into the night, ate pizza, shot the breeze, talked about himself, and expected to be involved. There were barriers. As Blum later remarked, when remembering a controversial tenure decision in the late 1960s: "Some of the graduate students in history believed I should have consulted them about [Staughton] Lynd. The thought of doing so never entered my mind."[86]

Woodward's letters clarify that something shifted in his relationship to the American scene in the last three decades of his life, and it is plau-

---

83. CVW to James Green (then visiting the University of Warwick), 15 March 1976: "I hope your year has been a profitable one and that you have come to know and appreciate Hobsbawm and Thompson. If you can persuade either of them, as we have not been able to, of the advantages of teaching at Yale, I hope you will. But no second-raters, please. We believe some Marxists are more equal than others."

84. See, for example, John H. Fawcett Jr. to CVW, 1 July 1976: "I find it difficult to believe that an avowed Marxist such as Aptheker will form and profess opinions free of communist ideology. The discipline of the party will not permit him to do so. This then puts Yale University in the position of providing a forum for a propagandist rather than a teacher, and reflects unfavorably upon Yale and higher education in general."

85. Marvin E. Gettleman to CVW, 7 April 1976.

86. Blum, *Life with History*, 185.

sible to see the Aptheker affair as one symptom of this shift. In his earlier days, he had shared many concerns with those who wished to change the United States: economic improvement for ordinary people, the curbing of capitalism's excesses, and racial equality and integration chief among them. On other matters, he was less in step, because he was skeptical of the New Deal (as too moderate), an isolationist, uncommitted to Cold War liberalism, and sympathetic to populism. Nonetheless, he shared enough to feel that he belonged and was relevant, and this was especially so from the mid-1950s to the mid-1960s, in the heyday of the civil rights movement. But the world moved on to places he found less congenial. He became greatly troubled by the rise of the black power movement, disliked affirmative action, never came to grips with feminism, mistrusted what came to be called "theory," and became a strong opponent of multiculturalism and "political correctness." That is, he came to be at odds with many of the causes and preoccupations of significant portions of the American left, especially as it acted in the academy, in the late twentieth century. Some have seen this as evidence that he had become a conservative, others that he was habitually a dissident.[87] My own sense is that, if anything, he became more of a liberal, one most concerned about individual freedom, at the moment liberalism drifted out of fashion and was being harassed from both left and right.[88] (This may support the notion that he was a dissident or, at least, that he liked being out of step.) As late as 1972, he was asserting that, except for the fleeting moment of the civil rights movement, he had never been a liberal.[89] By 1988, he was the cosponsor of a manifesto, published in the *New York Times,* that reaffirmed "America's liberal tradition."[90] In part, this change arose because his old allegiance to populism, still available in the late 1950s, had become less and less available as the century aged. In part, it was his dissatisfaction with the rise of American conservatism, with which he may have shared

87. Trevor Burnard, "America the Good, America the Brave, America the Free: Reviewing the Oxford History of the United States," *Journal of American Studies* 45 (August 2011): 410; Sheldon Hackney, "C. Vann Woodward, Dissenter," *Historically Speaking* 10 (July 2009): 31–34.

88. On this fundamental commitment to individualism, see Blum, *Life with History,* 173: "By nature a pessimist, he resisted my instinctive optimism. By nature a pragmatist, I resisted his absolutism about the causes he nurtured. He believed fervently in the rights of individuals; I believed those rights had at times to yield to the needs of community."

89. CVW to Michael O'Brien, 19 May 1972 (private collection).

90. "A Reaffirmation of Principles" *New York Times* (26 October 1988): A21.

some themes, but with whose overall thrust he remained deeply unsympathetic. In 1989, for example, he received an invitation from George H. W. Bush, then president, to join the "Republican Senatorial Inner Circle"— they were after his money—and, on the document, Woodward affixed a rubber stamp, which read, "PISS OFF!"[91] Still, this was an intricate business. As he observed, in some despair in 1998, "No sooner have we placed ourselves as left-of-center than center turns out to be where right was the day before yesterday."[92] There were rifts, notably in 1991 when he sympathetically reviewed Dinesh D'Souza's *Illiberal Education: The Politics of Race and Sex on Campus*, which catalogued the sins of political correctness, and offended many, including John Hope Franklin.[93] Woodward's acceptance of an award from the National Association of Scholars, too, occasioned disquiet.

But it would wrong to read his last years as merely alienated, even though he had to endure much sadness and some loneliness, feelings occasioned by the deaths by cancer of his son, wife, and three close friends (Richard Hofstadter, David Potter, and Alexander Bickel), and, in the ordinary ways of mortality, Robert Penn Warren and Cleanth Brooks. After the death of his wife, Woodward spoke to a friend, also widowed, of their shared "private war with the world," which was "gaining on us."[94] In 1987, he added, "So declines my little world of the past. . . . the world seems to shrink with [the] years."[95] He himself had a brush with colon cancer in the early 1980s and had sundry ailments (hypertension, atrial fibrillation, cataracts, a prostate nodule, bronchitis, stasis dermatitis), which required many pills.[96] But he was tough and resilient, coped with a plethora of critics by a subtle mix of cogent reproof and wary charm, and, taken all around, had a retirement after 1977 that was marked by no little satisfaction, even moments of serenity, in the midst of the controversies that he sometimes enjoyed. Strictly speaking, he never retired, but

91. George Bush to CVW, 17 August 1989.

92. CVW to Cushing Strout, 19 January 1998.

93. See John Hope Franklin, *Mirror to America: The Autobiography of John Hope Franklin* (New York: Farrar, Straus and Giroux, 2005), 325–28.

94. Quoted in Sally Kelley to CVW, 27 July 1982: none of his letters to Kelley are preserved, at least in the Woodward papers.

95. CVW to Michael O'Brien, 8 March 1987 (private collection).

96. Lawrence S. Cohen, M.D., to Charles A. DiSabatino, M.D., 11 November 1992; Charles A. DiSabatino Jr., M.D., to CVW, 20 July 1995.

just stopped teaching in classrooms. He still wrote his reviews and essays, gave his lectures in distant places, and kept his office at Yale. His edition of Mary Chesnut's journals even won a Pulitzer prize in 1982, the one major award that had, up to then, eluded him.[97] He remained very close to his daughter-in-law, Susan Woodward. And there were his many ex-students who formed a sort of family, greatly protective and supportive.

It remains, finally, to discuss the style of his letters, which often differed from the style of his published works. The latter, though they had earlier used the occasional violent adjective and uncompromising verb, came to be notable for restraint, quiet irony, and diplomatic subtlety. His readers noticed this "elegant economy," the undercurrent of emotion controlled by form, a gift for "lucidity and conciseness and [the] apt turn."[98] William Carleton discerned in Woodward an aversion to rhetorical excess—once the bane of Southern writing, many thought, including Woodward himself—and a preference for what was "softer, more subtle."[99] This subtlety could sometimes arise from an unwillingness to be direct, a desire to participate but a disinclination to belong. He was, in his own words, "prone to keep a good deal concealed."[100] As an admiring Arkansas friend once said, with some exasperation, "You stand too far off. Come in closer, bud, and have a look if you dare."[101] Another old acquaintance from his childhood in Vanndale, who had lost touch and then reestablished it in the late 1970s, observed: "When I saw you through your books through the years, I always had the impression of a tall, aloof, irreproachable and unapproachable writer."[102] It turned out that he was very willing to be approached, but it is true that, in his prose, he preferred to be self-contained, a stranger to loose ends, irreconcilable thoughts, and vulnerability.

This is not the voice of his letters. Or, rather, ironic subtlety was only one of his voices, for he had the gift of noticing to whom he was writing, adjusting his tone accordingly, and conducting a conversation. ("Like to talk to you about it" was one of his characteristic sentences, as was "What

97. C. Vann Woodward, ed., *Mary Chesnut's Civil War* (New Haven: Yale University Press, 1981).

98. Willie Lee Rose to CVW, 11 December 1967; Haver C. Currie to CVW, 17 March 1969.

99. William G. Carleton to CVW, 5 December 1964.

100. CVW to Antonina Jones Hansell, 16 October 1937, AHL.

101. Martha England to CVW, 5 August 1958.

102. Sally Kelley to CVW, 2 April 1979.

is your opinion?") This courtesy and sensitivity could sometimes lead to his saying one thing to one person and a contradictory thing to another, though it is doubtful he did this more than most of us. Naturally enough, the better Woodward knew and trusted his correspondent, the more he abandoned indirection and would be blunt and indiscreet, so unsurprisingly his candid opinions are more reliably discerned in letters to close friends. In such letters, a good many historians, living and dead, were thereby skewered, though others praised, for Woodward saw letters as a medium of observation and criticism. So, if Woodward's critical identity was, in print, often seen through a mist of irony and indirection, in his letters that identity appears with great sharpness.

It is not clear that he wrote with an eye on posterity, or only occasionally. Now and again he would compose letters, self-consciously constructed and artful. A letter of 1958, in which he described his long night with C. K. Ogden in Bloomsbury, is probably the best example of this and is a reminder that Woodward the letter writer could also embody Woodward the gifted maker of historical narratives. But mostly he wrote with spontaneity, verve, and even colloquial freedom. He liked to be allusive, and there are echoes of Shakespeare, Thoreau, Lewis Carroll, and other authors scattered through his rapid sentences, which did not always bother with the tidy sequences of subject, verb, and object, and even have very mild profanity and exclamation marks. (In print, he was not a man for the exclamation mark.) He was not above gossiping, though usually his gossip concerned what he himself had experienced, not what others had told him about third parties. He was not a storyteller in the classic Southern sense, certainly not a teller of tales with a moral, though he was a narrator of incidents. (The 1970 letter to his daughter-in-law about his presiding over a turbulent business meeting of the American Historical Association is a case in point.) Almost above all, he had a gift for comedy, a gift which he drastically constrained in his published works. Some of this comedy was at the expense of the foolishness of others, but occasionally it was at his own expense although his self-deprecation was often a double-bluff. Mostly his comedy arose from a conviction that much in life was absurd. Hence many of his letters occasion a smile, and a few prompt laughter. I would especially single out his 1975 letter to Eric McKitrick and Stanley Elkins, in which he explained why their proposal for a multivolume history of the Federalist era, as their contribution to the *Oxford History of the United States,* was a mistake.

It is hazardous to make comparisons, not least because publication of the letters written by those in Woodward's generation of historians has scarcely commenced. (And may little do so, since this is a neglected genre.)[103] But examples from many of them appear in Woodward's own papers and it is hard to see that any but a few match the aesthetic, political, intellectual, and cultural range of Woodward's own letters. (Eugene Genovese and, somewhat unexpectedly, Eric McKitrick come to mind, however.) As for other generations of historians, at least after that elusive moment in the nineteenth century when the writing of letters ceased to be a self-conscious art, Woodward's letters seem more complex and subtle than those of Herbert Baxter Adams in the late nineteenth century or Carl Becker in the early twentieth. No doubt Henry Adams, as Woodward would have been the first to admit, is in a class of his own.[104] But, otherwise, it is doubtful that a reader can find Woodward's peer among those historians, in his time, who took the writing of letters to be a serious venture.

103. It seems to flourish more in Europe and, especially, at the University of Oxford; see, for example, Isaiah Berlin, *Flourishing: Letters 1928–1946*, ed. Henry Hardy (London: Chatto & Windus, 2004); H. R. Trevor-Roper, *Letters from Oxford: Hugh Trevor-Roper to Bernard Berenson*, ed. Richard Davenport-Hines (London: Weidenfeld & Nicolson, 2006); Gerhard A. Ritter, ed., *German Refugee Historians and Friedrich Meinecke: Letters and Documents, 1910–1977*, trans. Alex Skinner (Leiden: Brill, 2010); Johan Huizinga, *Briefwisseling*, ed. Léon Hanssen, W. E. Krul, and Anton van der Lem, 3 vols. (Veen: Tjeenk Willink, 1989–91); Benedetto Croce and Franco Venturi, *Carteggio*, ed. Silva Berti (Bologna: Il mulino, 2008); Lucien Febvre and Marc Bloch, *The Birth of Annales History: The Letters of Lucien Febvre and March Bloch to Henri Pirenne* (Brussels: Academie royale de Belgique, Commission royale d'histoire, 1991); Élie Halévy, *Correspondance (1891–1937)*, ed. Henriette Guy-Loë (Paris: De Fallois, 1996).

104. See W. Stull Holt, *Historical Scholarship in the United States, 1876–1901: As Revealed in the Correspondence of Herbert B. Adams* (Baltimore: Johns Hopkins University Press, 1938); Michael Kammen, ed., *"What Is the Good of History?" Selected Letters of Carl L. Becker, 1900–1945* (Ithaca, NY: Cornell University Press, 1973); J. C. Levenson et al., *The Letters of Henry Adams*, 6 vols. (Cambridge, MA: Harvard University Press, Belknap, 1982–88).

Editorial Note

This volume's editorial principles are few and straightforward. Whenever possible, I have provided the full text of the letters, with the exceptions that I have removed salutations and subscriptions (unless they seem unusually meaningful) and standardized the dates and places of composition. However, in the cases of letters written during the years when Woodward was at Johns Hopkins and Yale, I have omitted the place and the reader can presume it is Baltimore or New Haven, respectively, unless otherwise specified. At the end of each letter, I have noted in which archive the letter can be found and whether it is typed, a carbon, longhand, signed, or unsigned. For letters in Yale's Woodward Papers, as well as a few other collections, I have added the box and folder numbers, since they might otherwise be too difficult to locate. (So, "35/415" means box 35, folder 415.) I have silently corrected minor errors, occasioned by bad typing, but left grammatical errors, misspellings, misuse of foreign words, or whimsies which seem to be Woodward's own or, at least, eluded his copyediting. From some letters, I have removed a few paragraphs, and these are signaled by the designation "[deletion]." This was done very reluctantly, but the text became too long—Woodward wrote too many good letters—and I was forced to choose between excising whole letters, well worth retaining, or removing inessential paragraphs, almost always those in which he courteously greeted or bade farewell to his correspondent, or in which he dealt with minor administrative matters.

I have included one document that is not a letter. The memorandum that Woodward composed a few days after spending an evening in the company of Alger Hiss seemed too interesting to omit, even though formally it does not fall within the remit of this volume, except in the sense that it can be regarded as a letter to posterity.

It is very difficult to estimate the number of documents in the Woodward Papers at Yale. I took away about 20,000 photographic images of individual pages (including letters he received), of which only 294 of his own letters have made it into this volume. I doubt that I photographed as much as a third of the collection, so I would tentatively estimate that perhaps 2 percent of his letters are being made available here; in fact, the percentage is lower, since I also examined a great many other manuscripts at Yale, the Southern Historical Collection, and Emory, many of which collections furnished little that was usable. There is doubtless more material that a comprehensive search for Woodward letters might yield, but I did not issue a published call for individuals to send me letters, in part because I had more than enough to work with, in part because his habit of keeping carbons would have meant my being sent, perhaps, many thousands of pages which I had already seen.

The following abbreviations have been used.

AHL   Antonina Hansell Looker Papers, Southern Historical Collection, Wilson Library, University of North Carolina-Chapel Hill

ALS   Autograph letter signed

ALU   Autograph letter unsigned

CVW   C. Vann Woodward

CVWP   C. Vann Woodward Papers (MS 1436), Manuscripts and Archives, Yale University Library

GWR   Glenn Weddington Rainey Papers, Manuscripts, Archives, and Rare Book Library, Emory University

JHR   John Herbert Roper Papers, Southern Historical Collection, Wilson Library, University of North Carolina-Chapel Hill

LDR   Louis D. Rubin Papers, Southern Historical Collection, Wilson Library, University of North Carolina-Chapel Hill

RH   Richard Hofstadter Papers, Rare Book & Manuscript Library, Columbia University

RPW   Robert Penn Warren Papers, Beinecke Rare Book and Manuscript Library, Yale University

TCLS   Typed carbon letter signed

TCLU   Typed carbon letter unsigned

TCMU   Typed Carbon Memorandum Unsigned

TLS   Typed letter signed

TLU   Typed letter unsigned

VFD   Virginia Foster Durr Papers, Arthur and Elizabeth Schlesinger Library, Radcliffe Institute, Harvard University

The Letters of C. Vann Woodward

✧✱✧✱✧✱✧✱✧✱✧✱✧✱✧✱✧✱✧✱✧✱✧✱✧✱✧✱✧✱✱

1

Early Years, 1926–45

1. To Claude Outlaw[1]

MORRILTON, AR
FEBRUARY 20, 1926

In those days old chap we were just a pair of dreamers—or that is we were in that very sentimental age of adolescence which we are now but barely passed—nevertheless I spent then the most happy, beautiful and complete days I ever hope to spend—we did not consider the realities for we new (*sic*) nothing much of them. We had I believe the true spirit of adventure. You know we got more genuine enjoyment out of a stroll in the moonlight, or the speculation upon a new character in town, than we can now out of dozens of dances, etc. We were both dreamers by nature and found in each other a rare similarity of mind, which we enjoyed for a time, then our interests grew apart and so did we. We began to learn of the world and our natures hardened into the cast that surrounded us— Oh, I don't know, that is just my little diagnosis of the case.

CVWP, 39/473: TLS

1. A friend from CVW's Morrilton schooldays, who wrote from Piggott, AR, on 5 January 1966 to ask if CVW was the same person who had published *The Burden of Southern History;* "I immediately had a feeling that the author was none other than a cherished boyhood friend and 'fellow dreamer' whom I have not heard of in nearly forty years. . . . I know that if you are the 'Old Watson' of long ago—you will feel as I do—that Allah has been kind, and that I will hear from you." In response to CVW's reply, Outlaw observed [5 February 1966]: "Watt, I agree with you as to the long lost days of adolescence, we can look back at them now and laugh at our behavior. I can express my feelings best by quoting an excerpt from a letter I received from you on Feb. 20, 1926, I quote." There followed the above letter, which Outlaw specified as having been written from Morrilton. The "(sic)" in the text is Outlaw's.

2. To Hugh Allison Woodward[2]

ATLANTA, GA

SUNDAY EVENING [SPRING 1930]

I thought it would probably be very gratifying to you to learn that your son would not be in any immediate danger of swelling the ranks of the Bowery bread-lines next year as a climax of his very liberal education, and also to the Mater in that she may now feel perfectly free to purloin your patch pants and donate them to Uncle Billy's progeny; for you see the fact is it looks as though I will not have to call upon you or the Salvation Army either for my support.[3]

I have just finished typing an ingratiating letter to Professor Perry of the Tech English Department, accepting a position as an instructor of English at The Georgia School of Technology (best known, possibly, for my famous sketch of its geneology appearing in the Atlanta Journal).[4] I'll confess that it was a considerable surprise when I received a note last night, announcing that one of the professors that had been with them for three years has suddenly decided to leave for Harvard to complete his graduate work, leaving a position vacant. Perry said it was open to me if I were still available. So, since I was simply overburdened with availability, I pondered over his offer for a matter of probably two seconds and finally came to the decision that I would accept. Appar-

2. CVW's father, known familiarly as "Jack," was born in Franklin County, TN, in 1876; he was the son of a Methodist circuit rider, William Benjamin Woodward, who died young of tuberculosis. H. A. Woodward was educated in the public schools of his native county, but also at the Webb School in Bell Buckle, TN, one of the best private schools in the South; he later studied at the State Normal School in Winchester, TN, and graduated in 1901 from Emory College in Oxford, GA. He undertook graduate work at the University of Tennessee and the University of Chicago, before becoming a history and Latin teacher in Pine Bluff, AR, in 1903. Two years later, he became the superintendent of schools in Wynne County, before moving on (in the same capacity) to Arkadelphia and Morrilton; in 1929, he was appointed dean of Emory Junior College in Oxford, GA. He died in 1964 in Key West, FL.

3. The identity of "Uncle Billy" is unclear, but "Mater" is CVW's mother, Bessie Vann Woodward (1881–1962), who came from Vanndale, AR, and was the daughter of John Magret Vann (1845–1911) and Ida Hare (1849–1931). She married Hugh Allison Woodward in 1907. Later in life, after her children had left home, she took an extension course from Oglethorpe University and received a bachelor's degree.

4. William Gilmer Perry (1877–1951), head of the Department of English at the Georgia Institute of Technology.

ently he does not intend to fill Rainey's place, so I shall be the only man added.[5]

You really are not in a position to realize how extraordinary his offering me the position really is. I believe I have told you about some of the men with whom I was competing for the place. All of them with either more experience, or more preparation in English than I have had. If he really did know how little I had actually studied in the English department here at Emory, I am afraid all would not be so well. It's a stroke of my purest luck.

I have busied myself during the last week with an effort at landing a position as an instructor of English in Germany, as I mentioned when I saw you last. I would have been perfectly content with that, or that is the prospect of it. It would have given me my year abroad, exempt from expense, with a pretty intimate opportunity for close insight into German life. I still intend to make the European venture; probably in some other way. That way would have left me penniless and necessitated another year's teaching in America before I could continue my study. I hope to save a good deal out of the rather generous salary paid at Tech.

Please start making plans now for getting the Mater off to Atlanta for every one of the Grand Opera performances. We can't afford to let her miss a one. Aunt Mayme is expecting to entertain her.[6] Tell me at once whether or not to make the reservations.

CVWP, 60/732: TLS

3. To Glenn W. Rainey

Oxford, GA

[CIRCA. JUNE 1930]

A rather stupefying convalescence from the slight illness I was bothered with in Atlanta combined with a slight dose of ennui, which I feared even more, has kept me from writing you sooner. I have about recovered from both now, thanks to the constant application of electric

5. Glenn Weddington Rainey (1907–1989), the Georgian poet and historian, was Woodward's closest friend in the 1930s; early in 1930, he held a teaching fellowship at the Georgia Institute of Technology, in whose Department of English he was later to spend his career.

6. Mary Ann (Woodruff) Woodward, who had married Comer McDonald Woodward (1874–1960), CVW's uncle, in 1900; he was a sociologist and served as Dean of Men at Emory University (1924–42).

fans and a copy of Tristram Shandy, which, by the way, I simply insist on your reading immediately.[7] As long as my appetite and capacity for books continues at its present rate I shall be able to weather the dullest season. Reading is good for that if for nothing else, in case you are called on to defend a ravenous appetite, as I frequently am.

Howard Odum is here visiting his brother for a while.[8] I walked over the other day and had a good talk with him. He really does wean the alarming number of prize calves he claims to. I was expected to stand about admiringly while he went through the process. I am afraid I did it none too gracefully. He appeared very much interested in my plans and talked a good while about them. In spite of our unanimous opinion of his address the other night, I still can not help being impressed by the largeness of the man at closer quarters. Whatever the quality of his work may be, the man is possessed of a remarkable energy and genuine disinterestedness. He told me of the books he is working on. The Black Ulysses story it seems, is to be a trilogy, the last book of which is to come out soon. It sounds even more promising than the first, about which I am still unqualifiedly enthusiastic. It will be called "Feather in the Wind."[9] It is to treat of the present day Negro in contrast to his Grandfather, and is to be told in ghost stories. The trilogy is to be bound in one volume.

He is now at work on another trilogy on the South, the first volume of which is completed.[10] Walter Lippmann liked it very much he said.[11] Mencken wanted a couple of articles from it, but he is hesitating because he has treated the South a bit harshly and is apprehensive about intro-

---

7. Laurence Sterne, *The Life and Opinions of Tristram Shandy, Gentleman,* 9 vols. (London, 1760–67).

8. Howard Washington Odum (1884–1954) came from Bethlehem, GA, which was twenty-seven miles from CVW's parents' home in Oxford. He was the most important Southern sociologist of his generation; he founded and, for many years, headed the Institute for Research in the Social Sciences at the University of North Carolina.

9. Between 1928 and 1931, Odum published a fictional trilogy about a wandering African-American teller of folk tales, Left-Wing Gordon, of which the first two volumes were *Rainbow Round My Shoulder: The Blue Trail of Black Ulysses* (New York: Grosset & Dunlap, 1928) and *Wings on My Feet: Black Ulysses at the Wars* (Indianapolis, IN: Bobbs-Merrill, 1929); in the event the last volume was entitled *Cold Blue Moon: Black Ulysses Afar Off* (Indianapolis, IN: Bobbs-Merrill, 1931).

10. Howard W. Odum, *An American Epoch: Southern Portraiture in the National Picture* (New York: Henry Holt, 1930).

11. Walter Lippmann (1889–1974), the journalist, public intellectual, and social critic who was then writing a syndicated column called "Today and Tomorrow."

ducing the trilogy via the Mercury. It seems that he and H. L. are quite chummy, and see each other pretty often. He believes that H. L. is still our greatest critic, and has done more for the South than any other of the literati. He is rather enthusiastic and a bit surprised over the "Treatise on the Gods," said it was his crucial test and that he was satisfied with it. I suggest that you get it before emulating the adolescent Shelley.[12]

I shall be in Atlanta about next Thursday and will call you up as soon as I arrive. I shall expect you, and I hope Ernest too to return with me for a visit.[13] Please put your affairs in order. You really must not disappoint me. I am going to leave for New Orleans about the middle of July so this will be the best, and possibly the only time.

A letter from Pete recently.[14] He is rabidly engrossed in searching out the Dark Lady in the Chivers saga. He seems to have made himself quite an indispensable part of the expedition of pedants from Duke University.[15]

GWR: TLS

12. Henry Louis Mencken (1880–1956), the *Baltimore Sun* journalist and student of language who was the preeminent satirical social critic of the interwar years, with George Jean Nathan, he had founded *The American Mercury* in 1924. Mencken was famously amused by and critical of the South's intellectual mediocrity, most notably in his essay "The Sahara of the Bozarts" (1920). He had recently published an agnostic tract, *Treatise on the Gods* (New York: Alfred A. Knopf, 1930). CVW's allusion to the English Romantic poet Percy Bysshe Shelley (1792–1822), is to the pamphlet *The Necessity of Atheism* (Worthing: C. & W. Phillips, 1811), which led to Shelley's expulsion from Oxford.

13. Ernest Abner Hartsock (1903–1930), an Atlanta poet, musician, and editor, was one of CVW's closest friends. In 1929–30, he held a position as professor of poetics at Oglethorpe University, but had also worked as the organist of the Palace Theater in Atlanta, while owning and operating the Bozart Press, which published his own work. His volumes of romantic verse, inflected by his homosexuality, included *Narcissus and Iscariot* (Atlanta: Bozart Press, 1927); idem., ed., *Patterns for Pan: A Sonnet Anthology* (Atlanta: Bozart Press, 1928); and *Strange Splendor* (Atlanta: Bozart Press, 1930).

14. Edward B. Ficklen (1910–1981), an Atlanta friend known as "Pete," who came from Washington, GA; he later worked for the Works Progress Administration and participated in the interviews of former slaves.

15. This is an allusion to the ongoing scholarship on Thomas Holley Chivers (1809–1858), the Georgia poet who came from Ficklen's hometown. Then teaching at Duke University, the literary scholar Lewis Nathaniel Chase (1873–1937), an expert on Edgar Allan Poe, was helping the Brown University scholar S. Foster Damon, who was soon to publish *Thomas Holley Chivers, Friend of Poe: With Selections from His Poems: A Strange Chapter in American Literary History* (New York: Harper and Brothers, 1930). The "Dark Lady" presumably refers to Chivers's first wife and cousin, Frances E. Chivers, whose identity in 1930 was unknown, but who was referred to as

4. To Glenn W. Rainey

NEW ORLEANS, LA

22 JULY [1930]

A disappointment was in store for me here, in the last place I should
expect any degree of disappointment. It seems that the whole colony in the Vieux Carre, who made up all my acquaintances and friends,
have bodily migrated to cooler or more lucrative climates. A letter from
Price was awaiting me, saying that he was 65 miles from the railroad in
the Painted Desert and expected to be there indefinitely. There is one
chap left here, a Mexican artist, but alas, he is prosaically married to a
woman who will not let him drink—My old haunts, the Quarters Book
Shop has been taken over by a crew of homosexuals and rabid intellectuals who disgust me.

This by no means ends the list of my disappointments. For instance,
some damnable fiend, imbued with civic pride has replaced those price-
less old gas street lamps which simply *made* the quarters by night with
glaring, unwinking electric globes. I walked the streets the first day I was
here hunting the fiend with a knife. Then too, they have painted those old
pillars which supported the French market *orange* and *Green!!* Sapristi!!

I believe now that I shall return tomorrow or the next day—provided
I do not ship out on a coastwise boat, a thing I am a little tempted to do.
I observe discretely that I am becoming less the incurable romantic I was
once upon a time.

[deletion]

Saw a notice of the trial of the 6 assassins in the paper here.[16] Keep
up with it, and tell me about it when I return.

GWR: ALS

"Angeline" in his verse. She left him, after the birth of their daughter, whom she abandoned;
on this, see Charles Henry Watts, II, *Thomas Holley Chivers: His Literary Career and His Poetry* (Athens: University of Georgia Press, 1956), 113–14.

16. On 22 July 1930, six white men—Aubrey Sikes, T. F. Martin, J. G. Garvin, Tom Ber-
ryman, M. W. Harmon, and Roy S. Evans—were arraigned in the Fulton County Superior
Court for killing Dennis Hulbert, a black college student, because he was supposed to have
insulted a white woman. According to one newspaper report, "Soon after Hubert was killed
his father's home was burned and a meeting of Negroes, called to make plans for aiding the
authorities in prosecution of the slayers, was broken up with tear gas bombs which were said
to have been thrown by white men." See "Six Go on Trial In Negro's Death: Atlanta Men Are
Accused of Slaying Youth for Alleged Insult," *Washington Post* (23 July 1930): 3.

5. To Glenn W. Rainey

ATLANTA, GA

OCTOBER 1, 1930

[deletion]

An incident occurred yesterday which you only have an ear for. An accident two blocks from here happened, in which a Negro was seriously hurt. A large crowd gathered about the man. An ambulance arrived, a way was cleared for the stretcher bearers who no sooner found that the man was black than they folded up the stretcher, got back into the machine and drove off. The Negro lay there until a colored ambulance arrived. The whole meaning of the incident, however, was more in the faces of the crowd. Their reaction stirred me considerably. I simply had to tell someone about it.

[deletion]

GWR: TLS

6. To Glenn W. Rainey

ATLANTA, GA

JANUARY 24 [1931]

[deletion]

A letter from Rick today assures me that the trouble of the world and me is due purely and simply to Romanticism and Rousseau. He promises to pray over my condition with his own saint, Irving Babbitt, who, he adds, is the greatest American, and will be remembered along with Aristotle. The dear fellow has gone stark Humanist—raving, and probably dangerous.[17] He is leaving the field of Fine Arts (what a loss) and is devoting his hours to meditations on the inner check, looking under his bed every night for the shades of Rousseau. Furthermore he is taken to reading papers on Browning to Ladies Sewing Circles—he even enclosed

17. Irving Babbitt (1865–1933) taught Romance languages at Harvard and was, with Paul Elmer More, the founder of the "New Humanism." Babbitt's *Rousseau and Romanticism* (Boston: Houghton Mifflin, 1919) had contended that unhealthy principles of unbridled egotism and overimaginative creativity had, since Rousseau, corrupted Western culture, which needed restoration by the application of those principles of discipline and moderation, best expounded in classical literature. The movement had excited particular attention in 1930, with the publication of Norman Foerster, ed., *Humanism and America: Essays on the Outlook of Modern Civilization* (New York: Farrar and Rinehart, 1930), which included essays by Babbitt, More, and sundry others, including T. S. Eliot.

a clipping from the paper to prove it.[18] May God help him! Better had he taken the cloth!

I have about decided that I shall accept the Tech place if it is offered to me for the next year, tentatively, in my own mind at least. I don't know what to think of myself for not stepping out next year upon some determined course of study or activity. But so it is. I am no less provoked with myself than you are about me. Maybe I shall see the light before it is too late. I am going to go somewhere for study this summer. Probably New York or abroad. But now that I am planning to be here next year, you must redouble your determination to come to Tech. Write Perry as soon as you can. It is possible that there will be another vacancy besides Jack's, but there are several applicants already.[19] I hope we can make it together.

I went out to see the Hartsocks as soon as they returned from Florida. Mrs. Hartsock looks much improved, while Mr. Hartsock seems to be doing some business.[20] He told me that he could settle Ernest's bill with Neff right now if he wanted to. He does not seem to want to. If he does not adopt a different tone with Neff I am afraid he is going to have trouble with him. The sale of the books seems to be keeping up strongly. I talked with them about disposing of the letters, MS., etc., and they said they were willing to keep it at Emory. I am going to take it out there next week. I attended a meeting of the Writer's Club recently, at which What's his name, the Oglethorp man had considerable to say. I find it difficult to look on him with out a turn of the stomach. Otherwise I suppose he is quite reputable. The anthology of Ga. verse he has put out seems to [be] a creditable work.[21] Whatever reasons he might have of his own, he is doing quite well by Ernest. He is having a bronze bust made of him, instead of simply the mask. I am glad of that, and I know you are. Glenn, I

18. The English poet Robert Browning (1812–1889) was very popular with the American middle class, which sponsored many a "Browning Society."

19. Andrew J. Walker, a friend of CVW who was to spend his career in the Department of English at Georgia Tech; he was later the coauthor of Edwin H. Folk and Andrew J. Walker, *A Handbook for Public Speakers* (Atlanta: Department of English, Georgia Institute of Technology, 1940).

20. The poet's father was also called Ernest Abner Hartsock (1867–1935); he had once owned a tea store in Atlanta and in 1930 was a real estate agent; his wife, whom he had married in 1889, was Alta Sanner (b. 1870).

21. Thornwell Jacobs, ed., *The Oglethorpe Book of Georgia Verse* (Atlanta, GA: Oglethorpe University Press, 1930). In 1913 Jacobs (1877–1956) had revived Oglethorpe University, which had been founded in 1835 in Midway, GA, but expired in 1872 after a relocation to Atlanta. Jacobs was the college's president for three decades.

have been thinking of attempting that biographical sketch of him. What you think. Should I wait? And am I the one to do it. I know there are others much better qualified to do it, among them being yourself. I would hate to make a mess of it. I shan't do that, either.

[deletion]

   GWR: TLS

7. To Glenn W. Rainey

The reading of your letter demonstrated to me that I am not yet incapable of feeling a sense of guilt at neglecting my correspondence. It was good of you to write me about my grandmother's death. You knew something of how I longed for her release from it all. When I got the message, and indeed until I reached home, I was calmly contented that it happened when it did, that is before the summer months, which were worse on her. But as soon as I entered the house I felt strangely guilty for my attitude. Mamma's distress, while perfectly natural, came as a surprise to me, and added another shade of guiltiness. My sympathy for her was frankly greater than my grief, which is more than I had anticipated. Then, since the barbaric custom of sitting up with the body had to be conformed with, I insisted on doing it myself rather than having some outsider. I have never overcome an animal awe for the dead which worked on me dreadfully that night. Another vestigial emotion in me is my inability of associating, without considerable effort, the personality that I knew in life with the dead body. That had also been my experience in Ernest's death. It is perhaps the thing that horrified me most about it. Your escape of the physical horror of the thing probably explains your personal feeling about it. I am afraid that for me there will always be the pictures that I associate with the death.

   I talked with Mrs. Hartsock yesterday. Musser was here last week but I failed to see him. Mrs. Hartsock said that he had completed a biography of Ernest which he was planning to publish soon.[22] She read the manuscript and seem to be satisfied with it, although there were some

22. Benjamin Francis Musser, *Ernest Hartsock: An Appreciation* (Landover, MD: Dreamland Press, 1931). Musser (1889–1951) was a Roman Catholic poet, several of whose volumes of verse had been published by Hartsock's Bozart Press.

things which she seemed to feel doubtful about. It is to be largely an appreciation and critical evaluation, with a minimum of biographical material. I wish, of course that I had been able to see the manuscript. Mrs. Hartsock says that he is to return during the latter part of March, and if the book is not published by that time I hope I will be permitted to read the manuscript. I suppose you would agree with me that Musser is as well qualified to do the work as anybody, that is in view of his poetic ability and appreciation of Ernest's work. But I know that you will also share my apprehensions in another direction. I read two letters of condolence which he wrote Mrs. Hartsock, and they seem to me to be on a normal and genuine tone. If the biography is of the same quality we have nothing to fear. (Parenthetically, I might add that he visited your friend, Mr. Jackson, while in the city.) He also told Mrs. Hartsock that he hoped to go through the unpublished manuscript sometime with a view of making up a posthumous volume. I really hope he will attempt this, but I do not believe there will be nearly enough to make up a volume.

Your idea of my coming up there next year is certainly tempting enough. It would be great to be with you, and I rather believe I should like the place. But, Glenn, I don't believe I shall make the step. I told you, I believe that I had applied for the Rosenwald scholarship which is headed locally by Dr. Alexander.[23] I talked to him pretty frankly about my lack of direction and my hesitency of obligating myself, too frankly I am afraid. They might give it to me however. He talked like he would. Even then I don't know whether I should accept it. As the Germans so picturesquely put it, *Ich habe kein Sitzfleisch.* I have asked Dr. Perry to recommend me for reappointment for next year.[24] Perhaps another year here would not be bad for me. The work seems to take less and less time, which leaves me leisure for a rather prodigious amount of reading that I am doing. If I do return, I shall probably spend the summer in New York or Germany studying. That's rather vague, but it's the best I can do it present.

23. The Julius Rosenwald Fund gave fellowships to promote "the development of higher education through grants that discover potential leaders." Will Winton Alexander (1884–1956), a Missourian, was a Methodist minister, director of the Commission of Interracial Cooperation in Atlanta, and a member of Rosenwald Fund's fellowship committee; he was later head of the Farm Security Administration.

24. Literally, this German saying means, "I have no flesh on my bones when sitting." In effect, this translates as "I have no patience," or "I am not steady enough to stick with something."

I believe you are doing exactly the right thing in remaining there for another year.[25] You guessed correctly last Christmas that I thought you were making a mistake by coming back to Tech. Your largest opportunity lies there I am sure. I was more surprised that you had not joined the Socialist party before, than that you were thinking of it. Even as a purely political move I do not think you are making a mistake, though there is some question about that. At least you will be able to say in the words of Will Rogers, when he lost his famous campaign of '28, "as for me I had rather be right."[26]

GWR: TLS

8. To Glenn W. Rainey

ATLANTA, GA
MAY 11, 1931

[deletion]

I seem to recall several ideas about which I wrote you at white heat, that have had time to cool. Here is one which you mustn't allow to cool. You know, I see, of the scholarship-Columbia plan. I must explain some of my decisions; at first I was not at all inclined to accept the offer. Not in the direction I was aiming. Offered no attractive future; more interested in disinterested subjects, e.g., philosophy, language, literature, etc.; a bit repulsed at the whole business; rather in love with the easily gleaned satisfactions to be had at Tech. Then my friend Ferguson of N.Y. arrived— told you of him; author and general literary go-getter—persuaded me that I ought to pile out of bed and get down to business.[27] I am persuaded that he is right, though I don't know just how far right he is. He said take the scholarship as a sign from the gods and work at it only as I would a job that paid me $750.00. Do it in half time. On the side accomplish more

25. "There" is Evanston, IL, where Rainey was undertaking graduate study at Northwestern University. He was enrolled in 1929–31, and again in 1932–33.

26. William "Will" Penn Adair Rogers (1879–1935), the Oklahoma humorist and social critic, had run mockingly for president in 1928 upon the campaign pledge that, if elected, he would resign.

27. Charles W. Ferguson (1901–1987), a Texan and Methodist minister who had studied at the Union Theological Seminary and the New School for Social Research; he was to become president of Round Table Press, a New York publishing house, in 1932 and was subsequently a senior editor of *Reader's Digest*.

personal ends. Now about these personal ends—which is the pivot upon which my decision turned. He knows of my interest in the Negro. He says that he sees a need, i.e., a market, for a book on the subject. Can give you only a general idea of it because I have only a general idea myself. The book is also to be general; a graphic and rather panoramic picture of the Negro in America since the Civil War from all the angles—economic, religious, esthetic, social, etc. Something, perhaps in the style of Siegfrieds book on America.[28] Breathtaking, isn't it? Even amusing, perhaps? Well, I want your idea whatever it is, and as soon as you can give it to me. The considerations involved are multitudinous, legion. For that reason a long conversation between us would be essential to a real understanding on your part. But you can give me your impression for whatever it is worth. I might sum it up by saying that the task would involve, would absolutely necessitate, a complete reorganization of my way of living—not only its forms but its tempo and intensity. You of all people should know what a languid and indolent life the student's and teacher's is, except, of course, when the two are coupled as in your present position. No more indolent than other professions of course, but we know of these two—the only two we are accustomed to. Now Ferguson is an unbelievable fanatic on the religion of work of the heartbreaking type, which he succeeds in making a game. Wrote his first book at noon hours of five months. He approached me in somewhat the manner of a Billy Sunday gone intellectual—rather by storm.[29] I believe he made a convert. I hit "the sawdust trail" but the vicissitudes of the "straight and narrow path" are still before me. I repeat the creed to myself: only way anything is done; get at it at once; takes all kinds of guts; all a matter of sheer work; face it now or never; others have, you can; and so on through the entire recitation, which, like other creeds, is true for the believer.

Naturally I met with discouragement from Dr. Woodward, as Ferguson predicted. I would from all academicians probably. It's exactly the thing the academicians are organized to discourage, for reasons that are obvious to you. Not that this work would not make pretences at authenticity, even careful documentation; but that would not be the primary aim. Rather would it be attractiveness and wide appeal to people of my own interests, such as you. Something that would be bought and read

28. André Siegfried, *America Comes of Age: A French Analysis* (New York: Harcourt Brace, 1927).
29. Billy Sunday (1862–1935), the popular evangelist.

and commented upon—in other words, as offensive as the odor is to your environs, a book that would *sell*. It would require two or three of my best years, and concentrated almost exclusively. It would involve the development of an attractive and salable prose style as a medium. It would necessitate, well, innumerable sacrifices . . . Well what is your opinion? I am particularly anxious to get it. If you know anybody there with whom you can profitably discuss the idea please do so, but otherwise please keep it quiet; even your family, you know. I know it's not your nature to do so but it happens to be mine.

[deletion]

GWR: TLS

9. To Boulware Martin[30]

OXFORD, GA

JULY 19 [1931]

What I could have written you and what I should have written you during the past several months is now uppermost in my mind— not what I shall write you. All that I have written to nobody because nobody has replaced you as my chiefest inspirer and trouble-bearer. Very likely nobody will.[31]

But now after that declaration I must know about you. I left you in Horatio, you remember, weaving yourself a bright mourning veil of your philosophy of gallantry.[32] Are you still there? and how have you made out these long months? I have wanted to write you and say that I was thinking of you, for I have thought of you very, very often. I am heartily ashamed that I did not. Now tell me what you have done, thought, and read. What are your plans for next year and all about that? Are you in New Orleans

30. Ellen Boulware Martin (later Ohls) (1901–1984), usually called "Bola," had taught freshman English to CVW at Henderson-Brown College, to which she came in 1925, after having taught high school in El Dorado, AR; in later years, she became the college's alumni secretary.

31. Light is cast on Martin's feelings about CVW (less so about his for her), in a letter she wrote to him in 1950, after he had revisited Arkadelphia. (The main letter is undated, but has a postscript dated 18 April 1950.) The letter speaks of their parting in New Orleans as "a little like dying," of her continued feelings for CVW, and ends with, "I've always loved you . . . and . . . am very proud of you and not a bit surprised."

32. Horatio, AR, in Sevier County, was where Martin had been born, though her family later moved to Arkadelphia.

again this summer.[33] Be sure and tell me that, for I am likely to run down for a visit. I could want nothing better than a good, long talk with you in Jackson Square under the banana trees.

I too have said my farewell to academia—my aufwiedersehen, let us say more accurately. I was getting too comfortable and fat (in my head) at Tech. I am so miserably constituted that I cant endure even moderate amounts of comfort and pleasure, though I can spend immoderate lengths of time anticipating them. At any rate, I resigned and accepted a skinny scholarship on which I am going to Columbia for next year. I did it not without considerable moral perturbation you may be sure. The scholarship, you see, was granted for the study of social sciences. So again, after a brief sojourn, I say farewell to my classics. Damn such vacillation, you say. And I damn it too, vociferously. But damn the capitalists, they wont pay you to study classics. I guess that's pretty weak but it's about my only alibi. And why did I select Columbia? I didn't. I selected New York. I have sold myself to the metropolis and my birthright for a pot of message, as I was accused of (not very originally). I become quite upset over the sordid bartering at times, but I soon start rationalizing and rock my conscience to sleep. Anyway, I would like to have your opinion about it. It is always interesting.

I finally put to rout the devil dog of romantic adventure that hounds my steps every summer. I am spending the time at Oxford. I love the place more and more, and will probably never appreciate it properly until I spend a year in New York suspended between the 'L' and the subway. I cant appreciate anything properly without contrasts, however. Witness *your* teaching and some later teaching I recall, particularly my own.

I am reading a lot of books but nothing good for my soul. Please give me your prescription on the basis of my own diagnosis above.

Affectionately (the one I use when writing to a maiden aunt, but cant think of another) yours,

CVWP, 35/415: TLS

---

33. She was studying for an M.A. at Tulane University; her thesis came to be on "The Personalities and Literary Relationship of Byron and Shelley: A Study of the Letters" (1932). She subsequently took graduate courses at the University of Chicago, the University of Oklahoma, and Columbia University, but without completing a doctorate.

10. To Glenn W. Rainey

NEW YORK, NY
SEPTEMBER 17 [1931]

So far I can not call Manhattan my own, though I am already finding her to my liking, bawdy wench that she is. I dare say I have already developed enough civic pride to dispute successfully with you the respective merits of slaughter houses and penthouses. Anyway it seems to be the concensus of New York opinion that Chicago is a "hick town."

My few friends here have been extraordinarily decent to me. Ferguson had me out to his apartment. Sonya is having a party to which she is inviting Langston Hughes and other Harlem celebrities.[34] Williams, the Harvard chap you did not like, is here on his way to France and is coming out to-night.[35] Consequently I do not feel as completely alone as I had feared I would. It will be some time before the glamour of the city will wear off for me, and Broadway become as dull as Peachtree. Until then I shall have small trouble in amusing myself.

You must try the boat trip up from Savannah sometime. And you must pick your time better than I did. All the placid sobriety and sombre melancholy of the waves which I so anticipated were, alas, not to be enjoyed on that boat. It seems that all the stenographers and shopgirls in lower Manhattan were vacationing and that each and every one of them was in rut. Owing to this unfortunate circumstance I was compelled to make myself as inconspicuous as a stowaway.

[deletion]

GWR: TLS

11. To Glenn W. Rainey

NEW YORK, NY
OCTOBER 20, 1931

Before me lies my Nemesis, a ponderous volume of Constitutional law by one Evans.[36] My soul lies somewhere smashed between its leaves.

---

34. Langston Hughes (1902–1967), the African-American poet and man of letters, who was a leading figure in the Harlem Renaissance.

35. CVW had known Edward Brown Williams (who came from Arkadelphia) at Henderson-Brown; he would later work for the National Recovery Administration and become a corporate lawyer in Washington, DC.

36. Lawrence B. Evans, *Cases on American Constitutional Law* (Chicago: Callaghan, 1898), and many subsequent editions.

I wish [I] could reply to your letter (which I only received today) with some of the jubilance with which it was written, but I must first unburden myself of a few of my woes. You know that I left for New York with but the vaguest notions of what I was going to do. I shall cut the rest of the tale to its essentials. I signed up for a course in Sociology. I found the professor under whom I would inevitably be thrown a hopelessly dodering sentimentalist.[37] He read us Kipling's If the first day and recommended that we ponder these chastening lines.[38] I chucked the department and signed up for a course that would be as inoffensive and as profitable as possible, but which did not at all impress my official advisor with my academic zeal. I became heartily disgusted with myself and the school and set out to see all the shows on Broadway. In the midst of this performance Charles Pipkin, visiting professor of Political Science, and a former neighbor of mine in Arkansas showed up.[39] My quandary was so complete that I let myself be persuaded to sign up for what is known here as Public Law, more nearly political theory. So here I am. I have slipped into a defeatist attitude about it that I must rid myself of before I do anything at all. You see I feel that it is a year spent in plodding in the wrong direction, with the dim hope that when I come to the end I shall find the right direction and start over again. You can understand that this isn't at all a pleasant way to spend a year.

I have about decided that unless I hit upon a field that really challenges my interest, something that I can be happy in studying that I shall turn to something else besides teaching—anything. Anything would be better than becoming something that I despise when I see it in another person.

I perceive on reading that that I appear to have lost all claims to a sense of humor. Please forget these confessions and do not pass them on

37. This is William C. Casey (1891–1978), a Midwesterner who had only just arrived from the University of Chicago and taught two introductory courses, "Recent Trends in Sociological Interpretation" and "Introduction to Sociology." He went on to publish little, but was very popular with undergraduates less averse than CVW was to Kipling.

38. Rudyard Kipling's poem "If" (1895), which begins, "If you can keep your head when all about you / Are losing theirs and blaming it on you," and ends, "you'll be a Man, my son!"

39. Charles Wooten Pipkin (1899–1941) was professor of political science at Louisiana State University and a former Rhodes Scholar; in 1935, while Dean of the Graduate School, he was instrumental in founding the *Southern Review* and became its editor in chief, with Robert Penn Warren and Cleanth Brooks as managing editors. His parents had lived across the street from CVW's family in Arkadelphia, and, like CVW, he had attended Henderson-Brown, though earlier, having graduated in 1918.

to anyone else. I would have to blush to face anyone else but you who knew them.

'I'he year will not be totally wasted. Even the academic part of it, for that matter. I have met some interesting people already. Langston Hughes for one. My friends have been cordial. My quarters are infinitely better than I had hoped for. I am sharing a rather large apartment with Pipkin who is pleasant company even if he is one of these human dynamos. He is teaching the first semester and writing two books the second.

All my confessions are forthcoming in this one letter. The second: I have applied for a Rhodes Scholarship. I must have said some unpleasant things about people who do that in my time, but I shall not deny that I would be delighted with the chance of three years at Oxford. Understand, however, that I do not entertain illusions about my chances for an appointment. Mine are the slimmest of chances but I could not resist the temptation to apply. Never have I conceived of myself as the type of rah rah Übermensch they seem to admire. I am trying to create the fiction that I am an intellectual giant in embryo that only requires three years of Oxford atmosphere to hatch me out. But I have never given the prospect of an appointment a serious thought, depend upon it.
[deletion]

GWR: TLS

12. To Glenn W. Rainey

OXFORD, GA
DECEMBER 1, 1931

This letter is consciously and maliciously calculated to make you miserable with envy. At this moment I am happily sunk into an armchair before an open fire in my own room smoking my own pipe. If you remember, it is a room you can stand up in as suddenly as you will without fear of butting your head into the ceiling. Outside the sky looks exactly like that of Egdon heath in the opening scene of The Return of the Native.[40] I

40. "A Saturday afternoon in November was approaching the time of twilight, and the vast tract of unenclosed wild known as Egdon heath embrowned itself moment by moment. Overhead the hollow stretch of whitish cloud shutting out the sky was as a tent which had the whole heath for its floor." Thomas Hardy, The Return of the Native (1878; London: Macmillan, 1952), 3.

have spent a good part on the day cutting wood and kicking about in piles of dead leaves, talking to Miss Lynn and smiling benignly at little nigger boys, and admiring my flag stone accomplishment in front of the house and realizing how beautiful dead trees are—that is, trees that have lost their leaves.[41] I find it as impossible to imagine myself riding in a subway at the rush hour, dining in an auto-mat, or butting through a Broadway crowd as Augustus B. Longstreet, the first inhabitant of this house, would have found it in 1837.[42] And Oxford is about as far removed from the era of automats and tabloids as it was in the time of that estimable worthy. It was not until quite recently that I was faced with fundamentalism's alternative—tabloids. Between the two I lose no time in flying to Bishop Candler's bosom![43]

I left New York by bus last Wednesday night arriving in Atlanta Friday morning—physically miserably and spiritually at peace with the world. I did not have to be here till the 5th but I was afraid that if I stayed there any longer I would receive notice that I had been eliminated and my excuse to come home would vanish. The first two days of my visit were as

41. Verlinda Harris Branham (familiarly known as "Miss Lynn") (1866–1958) boarded students at Emory College and was something of a local institution; she was the daughter of William Richardson Branham (1813–1894), a Methodist minister, and Elizabeth Flournoy Branham (1819–1904). Her brother, also called William Richardson Branham (1850–1934) and also a Methodist minister in Oxford, was married to Aldeline Lake Singleton Branham (1861–1947). All three lived in the so-called Branham House at 1223 Wesley Street; it was a Greek Revival house built in 1849, purchased by the Branham family in 1855, and adjacent to the Woodwards' house.

42. Augustus Baldwin Longstreet (1790–1870), the antebellum Georgian humorist, Methodist minister, and college president. He is best known for what was first anonymously published as A Native Georgian, *Georgia Scenes, Characters, Incidents, &c., in the First Half Century of the Republic* (Augusta, GA: S. R. Sentinel Office, 1835). He was president of Emory College—which is why CVW's family occupied his former home, since Hugh Allison Woodward was, though with a different title, de facto Longstreet's successor—and subsequently held the same position at the University of Mississippi and South Carolina College. However, Longstreet was president of Emory (1839–48), so CVW's date of 1837 is an error; the college did not begin to admit students until 1838, and the house had been built by Emory's first president, Ignatius A. Few.

43. Warren Akin Candler (1857–1941), from 1898 a bishop of the Methodist Episcopal Church, South. He was chancellor of Emory University (1914–22) and instrumental in persuading his brother, Asa Griggs Candler (1851–1929), founder of the Coca-Cola Company, to give $1 million, plus land, to Emory and facilitate the removal of its main campus to Atlanta.

hectic as a subway ride—Ida had five bouncing Wesleyan freshmen home with her that had lost all inhibitions.[44] They are gone now, and I go about listening to the stillness. My friend Pipkin was in Atlanta for a conference yesterday and came down to spend a night. But now I have the place to myself and family.

I had a few minutes in Atlanta yesterday. Went by Ed's, whose beer is improving and whose baby's [cries] are noisier.[45] He told me you had your place at Tech sewed up. I plan to go by and see the Doctor on my own behalf. Ed tells me there is to be another vacancy. I am not taking the possibility of the Rhodes appointment into account, but it seems negligible anyway. There is still some chance, of course. Your people were out at the time, but I shall call on them when I go back to Atlanta.

I got a fragmentary account of your plans for Christmas thru Ed and Ruby. Please let me know as soon as you can. The apartment is still at your disposal. There are three beds—one double and two single besides my own. We could manage it some way. I am looking forward to it.

I did not bring any but your last letter home, of course, and hence can not compare the versions of the sonnet. But I do like "Earth to earth" better than "ashes to Ashes" which I believe was the previous version. The last line seems changed and better too. I think the imagery of the whole sonnet is as superb as the *snow* poem you did for the annual. [deletion]

GWR: ALS

13. To Glenn W. Rainey

[NEW YORK, NY]
TUESDAY [CA. APRIL 1932]

I was just pondering the tempestuous waywardness of your career in its contrasts with my own, which is the way of wisdom. So, I decided I would write you words of condolence and commiseration.

---

44. CVW's only sibling, Ida Elizabeth Woodward (later Barron) (1912–1987), who was then a student at Wesleyan College. She was a musician (piano, cello) and subsequently led an all-female jazz band called "Four Girls of Note"; she ended up living in Key West, FL.

45. Edwin Henry Folk Jr. (b. ca. 1902), originally from Edgefield, SC, taught in the English Department at Georgia Tech (1924–59); his wife was called Ruby (b. ca. 1907) and, in 1931, they had a one-year-old baby, also called Edwin Henry.

The last several hours I have sat by a wide open window and watched the first thunder and lightening storm of the season and let my soul thaw out. This afternoon I finished my thesis, pronounced it the work of a thwarted genius, went down to the corner speakeasy and drank beer and listened to the Philharmonic orchestra play Strauss over the radio. The bartender and I have such good taste. At present I am possessed of a benevolent mood which is greater than myself, and with you I would share it.

Parenthetically, if you have not read Thomas Wolfe's latest addition to the slender shelf of American classics, get the April number of Scribners and do so at once.[46] Having just read it I am ready to proclaim the arrival of America's age of Helenic splendor and Elizabethan glory. (For the sake of my critical reputation, please make allowances for the Beer and the Strauss and the thwarted genius complex, when you quote me on this)

I might take this occasion to remark upon the amazing parallels in our recent past. I too have made my mark upon the boards. My premier in New York took place last month in a play which the Harlem Experimental Theatre staged. It played four nights, two in the New School (which you saw) and two in Harlem. Since I knew the author, and in a moment of weakness and inebriation had told her she had no living rival outside of William Shakespeare, I was obliged to take a part—the only white one. The play was called "Underground" and it was a plagarization and a dramatization of Uncle Tom's Cabin, minus the blocks of ice and the bloodhounds and Little Eva.[47] I was Simon Legree turned wrong-side out to prove with flesh and blood, a goatee and a broad "a" that after all slave owners were not all bad but slavery was a degrading institution and the emancipated people should forgive the people of the South and that democracy is the best of all possible forms of government provided the Negro is not disfranchised and he must be given the vote or something terrible is likely to happen. I accomplished the entire interpretation with a few well chosen gestures, a subtle inflection of my "a's,"

46. Thomas Wolfe, "A Portrait of Bascom Hawke," *Scribner's Magazine* 91 (April 1932): 193–98, 239–56.

47. *Underground*, a play about the Underground Railroad, was written by Regina M. Anderson (1901–1993), who worked professionally as a librarian in the New York public library system (during the 1920s at the 135th Street branch); she was a notable contributor to the Harlem Renaissance. The Harlem Experimental Theater evolved out of the Krigwa Players, which W. E. B. Du Bois had helped to found in 1924.

and some intricate pantomime while twirling my cane and mixing a mint julip—there was also a big black cigar.

Secondly, I have just finished a students revolution which put Nicholas Murray Butler in his place, brought him to his knees, and extracted a recantation which accomplished the entire demands of the strike.[48] In this performance I had the minor role of first soap-box speaker, who was used as a decoy to draw all the eggs before the main speakers were introduced. I was congratulated by all subsequent speakers for my effectiveness.

As I intimated, the Tom Heflin piece turned out to be remarkably good.[49] Having started it as an academic joke, I took the first two chapters to the person under whom I am doing it, and after reading them he practically offered me his place, which I declined with depreciatory gestures. He really did say he thought I could get a fellowship out of it, though he hasn't read the last eight chapters yet. I had a good deal of fun with it. Now, having read your entire thesis (for a reward of a mere fifty dollars) I think it only fair to expect you to do as well by me. It will run to a mere 200 pages or so, and I shall thrust it upon you next year.

The Mater visited me all of last week. The idea was to see me once more before she trusted me to the graces of the U.S.S.R. I think I told you about it. I shall sail from N.Y. without going home first, provided I can borrow the money. My plan is to spend the first month in Russia and the rest of the time, as long as my money lasts, in Germany. If I had the slightest hopes of tearing you away from your family for the summer I would begin a propaganda barrage that would put Stalin to shame.

That is about all for present. That is except Pipkin's symposium on the South, which I mentioned to you last Christmas. Macmillan is really going to publish it, probably next winter or spring. Pipkin invited me to do a chapter on something about what my generation thinks about the

48. A student called Reed Harris, editor of the Columbia student newspaper, had published what the university authorities considered to be slanderous remarks about standards at Columbia's dining halls and, for this, had been expelled. There had followed a general strike by students, in protest at a violation of free speech, and there had been orations in front of the Low Library and a little violence; the upshot was Harris's reinstatement by Nicholas Murray Butler (1862–1947), president of Columbia University (1902–45).

49. CVW had written his Columbia master's thesis on James Thomas Heflin (1869–1951), then U.S. senator from Alabama; see CVW, "J. Thomas Heflin, the Nativist" (M.A. thesis, Columbia University, 1932).

future of the South. Which I intend to do with considerable eclat. I shall wave the red flag and expect to point to you, in a pinch, as the rest of "my generation."[50]

[deletion]

GWR: TLS

14. To Glenn W. Rainey

VIENNA

AUGUST 11 [1932]

I have only been here some 5 days, just long enough to get myself thoroughly scrubbed, deloused, deodorized, laundried, and a deep and abiding thirst thoroughly quenched. You must know that my contact with Russian life was no polite matter of brushing elbows with the proletariat! One doesn't accumulate bed-bugs that way.

There is much I could say about what I saw, but it is useless to begin here. I can only urge you and the rest of the blessed to adopt the attitude of the three philosophic monkeys toward any thing about Russia good or evil—until I come bringing the word and the light. In regard to the rumor of counter-revolution that was circulating some weeks ago (at least in Berlin) I might give you the opinion of Louis Fisher that Russia is the most stable government this side of the Atlantic to-day.[51] Had a long talk with Fisher in Moscow, by the way. We had an excellent interpreter for our group which contributed wonderfully to the success of the trip. If I had not acquired some very capitalistic debts which I must pay off next year, I would have remained in Russia. I was offered an attractive place in Moscow teaching English. Might go back next year. No place in the world could be as interesting.

Got your letter here. Also one from Dr. Perry. He says I must be back Sept. 19 when classes begin, and that he would like to have me a little earlier. I sail from Bremen on the Columbus Sept. 4, landing Sept. 11.[52]

---

50. CVW to Glenn W. Rainey, 28 January 1932, has: "[Pipkin] is editing a sort of "I'll take my Stand" book for McMillan and I am trying to persuade him to let me do a chapter on the Negro." But Macmillan published no such book.

51. Louis Fischer (1896–1970), Moscow correspondent of the *Nation;* he was widely regarded, then and subsequently, as an apologist for the Soviet regime.

52. The *Columbus* belonged to the Norddeutscher Lloyd line and carried 1,650 passengers (400 first class, 600 second, and 650 third).

I'm tempted to stay in Vienna the rest of the time. Arrived here with a journalist I met in Russia. We were so dazzled with the bourgeoise splendor that we dove into the flesh pots to the extent of an elaborate suite of rooms. They look as if they might have just been vacated by the Hapsburgs. We pay about 6 shillings per night or about 45¢ a piece.

But I am going to Berlin for the rest of the time. It must be the most interesting place west of Moscow just now. And I want to improve my German.

I had never realized the tenseness of political feeling that Europe is capable of until recently. You can't walk across a café without stumbling over somebody's sword, now, anywhere in Europe.

Your Antaen affection reminds me of the neo-Confederate agrarians in Nashville whom I dubbed the typewriter agrarians.[53] Your cult might well be known as flower-pot earthiness. Cf. Pete on my "begoniaism."[54]

For God's sake Glenn, you can't be serious about the Roosevelt person![55] I hope what you said in your letter was a badly manipulated jest.

Write me in Berlin—Am Express.

Not being Jehovah or G.B.S. I shall ask you to use your discretion about communicating my Soviet enthusiasm.[56]

GWR: ALS

53. The reference to Anteus, the mythological Greek giant, is obscure. Less so is the allusion to the so-called Southern Agrarians, the authors of Twelve Southerners, *I'll Take My Stand: The South and the Agrarian Tradition* (New York: Harper, 1930); these included Robert Penn Warren, John Crowe Ransom, Allen Tate, and Donald Davidson.

54. The allusion to "begoniaism" may be to a passage from Henry Adams, whom CVW admired. In *The Education of Henry Adams: An Autobiography* (Boston and New York: Houghton Mifflin, 1918), 292, Adams remembered being called for his journalism "a begonia" by Timothy Howe, U.S. senator from Wisconsin, and playfully described the qualities of the begonia: "The begonia is, or then was, a plant of such senatorial qualities as to make the simile, in intention, most flattering. Far from charming in its refinement, the begonia was remarkable for curious and showy foliage; it was conspicuous; it seemed to have no useful purpose; and it insisted on standing always in the most prominent positions. Adams would have greatly liked to be a begonia in Washington, for this was rather his ideal of the successful statesman."

55. Franklin D. Roosevelt (1882–1945), then running for president.

56. George Bernard Shaw (1856–1950), the Irish playwright and essayist.

15. To Glenn W. Rainey

[OXFORD, GA]

TUESDAY [JULY 1933]

Page ten and Tom is still in his angel infancy![57] I feel rather like I expect Bishop Sterne did when he got to page 578 and found that Tristram was just a-borning. The trouble is that I have a severe attack of
Faulknerian galloping-hooves. . . . The, poor, poor old South I write and
snatch a blotter to save MSS from briny ruin of a heart wrung sob. Gallop a Gallop—I thought I'd never get Tom's old man through the war
and tear him away from the old homestead. The fact of the matter is that
nobody should write anything about the South right here in the middle
of it all. He should get a room on the Loop or overlooking the elevated on
Third Avenue where the mere mention of whip-poor-wills would make
him snigger and give him the critical jitters. Why goddam it, here I sit in
the very middle of a Mammy song and try to be hard-boiled. From where
I sit I can see "through magnolia blossoms" old man Kitchens across the
road sewing oats—I mean literally sewing them—not setting them out
with a tin contraption—but sewing them with sweeping, Biblical motions
exactly as in the parables.[58] Next door (or as near 'next-door' as there is)
Miss Lynn is having a family reunion of the house of Branham, where
hundreds of the tribe will gorge themselves in downright ante-bellum
fashion, and talk about their ancestors till "the moon rises slowly over the
honey-suckle vine and the magnolia leaves glitter with *polished metalic luster,*
and the *mocking bird hushes in the mimosa . . .*" Goddam it, I say, how can you
help sounding like Thomas Nelson Page and Al Jolson?[59] It all makes me
suspect the redoubtable Bill Faulkner of being bemused on tobacco juice
and dipping his pen in the garbage can.

How now, good pint pot—I bubbled over, a habit I've fallen into.
Your word, lush.

Dear God, what an angelic writer your man Proust is. I don't know

57. CVW was beginning to write on Tom Watson as part of his proposed study of Southern demagogues.

58. The U.S. census of 1930 identifies a John C. Kitchens, aged sixty-five, who shared a
residence with his wife, Sallie J. Kitchens, and grandson Billie.

59. Thomas Nelson Page (1853–1922), the Virginia novelist, was known for his sentimental
celebrations of the Lost Cause, and Al Jolson (1886–1950), the Jewish popular singer, for his
blackface performance of songs like "Swanee."

why I ever put the Swann down.[60] I have returned to it. I find him perfectly maddening—every sentence a *tour de force*—with effort apparently, but always successful effort. He never slips up, not one time. Infallible as the Hound of Heaven and as godlike.[61]

[deletion]

GWR: TLS

16. To Glenn W. Rainey

Oxford, GA

Monday, September [1933]

[deletion]

I have about decided that it is got to be a whole book on Tom. Remember the book I showed you, saying it had fewer words than my MSS? Upon counting I found it actually had only about half as many. Forthwith realized that I had given birth to twins—while under the impression that I was only menstruating—and decided my maternal propensities were gargantuan. And in two months, mind you; what's the period for the rabbit?

Wrote to Farrar asking his judgment on a biography, but have not heard from [him] yet.[62] I think I'll go ahead with one anyway. Ferguson said he thought one book on Tom had a better chance than one on several demagogues. Started rewriting MSS (before discovering my prodigious maternity), but have quit now, waiting to do more research. I like to talk to you about it.

Another thing: I am afraid my loins are teeming (I don't seem to be able to dispel the Freudian muse) with a litter of magazine essays. Simply tumescent, in fact. (To out-Reade Reade.)

Letter from J. D. Wade, who said he might come by here on his way to Vanderbilt.[63] Have invited him, needless to say. (More Southern Hos-

---

60. Marcel Proust, *À la recherche du temps perdu* (1913–1927); it was translated into English by C. K. Scott Moncrieff between 1922 and 1931.

61. "The Hound of the Heaven," the most celebrated poem of Francis Joseph Thompson (1859–1907), the English writer; it begins, "I fled Him, down the nights and down the days; / I fled Him, down the arches of the years."

62. John Chipman Farrar (1896–1974), who had founded the publishing house Farrar and Rinehart in 1929.

63. John Donald Wade (1892–1963) of Marshallville, GA, one of the Southern Agrarians (if diffidently). In 1933, he was known for his biographies, *Augustus Baldwin Longstreet: A Study of*

pitality) He gave me his blessings on my Watson effort, so I gather he is no longer on the market.[64] He added that he knew some things that I "surely" ought to know before publishing. I suspect he intends to shake a bloody-but-unbowed head and admonish—Beware of Brewton.[65] But he will probably be a help. Like to have him read the MSS.
[deletion]

GWR: TLS

17. To Georgia Doremus Watson[66]

DURHAM, NC

OCTOBER 3, 1933

After two days I still find it a bit difficult to believe in the entire reality of our eight hour "chat" (it actually was eight hours by the clock; can you believe it?) I can't rid myself of the mood of self-accusation such as I feel after being swept off my feet by a highly improbable novel—'Am I losing my taste for reality,' I ask myself—

And yet it was so palpably real at that. I will never forget the passionate dispassion with which you told that story—fragmentary as it necessarily was. But so movingly, so understandingly, so sympathetically unfolded. It is bound to remain for me a challenge to my best abilities, and a new bench mark of emotional integrity—inimitable as it is.

---

the Development of Culture in the South (New York: Macmillan, 1924), and John Wesley (New York: Coward-McCann, 1930). Between 1928 and 1934, he taught in the English Department at Vanderbilt University, but then went to the University of Georgia, where he spent the rest of his career; he founded and was the first editor of the Georgia Review.

64. Wade had published an essay on Watson: see John Donald Wade, "Jefferson: New Style," The American Mercury 18 (September–December 1929): 293–300.

65. William Wade Brewton (1891–1972?), who had published on Watson, thought he had exclusive access to Watson's personal papers, and was vigilantly hostile towards others who also attempted to write about the Georgia populist. See The True Tom Watson (Atlanta: Sage, 1922) and The Life of Thomas E. Watson (Atlanta: The Author, 1926).

66. Georgia Doremus Watson (1906–1998), the granddaughter of Tom Watson; in 1938 she was to marry Avery O. Craven (1885–1980), a historian of the antebellum South and Civil War who spent most of his career at the University of Chicago. In the preface to his book, CVW would, by mistake, call her Georgia Durham Watson, which was the name of Tom Watson's wife; see CVW, Tom Watson: Agrarian Rebel (New York: Macmillan, 1938), ix.

And how can I ever thank you for your spontaneous, almost intuitive understanding of myself and my purpose. Not that I am so obscure—but that you made explanation so unnecessary. Nor is it possible to tell you how much I appreciate your generous act of confidence, which I did so little to earn. But most of all I am grateful for discovering inadvertently— may I say?—a kindred spirit.

I find that my work here will keep me longer than I expected—so that I shall probably not get off to Chapel Hill till Thursday. You must know how earnestly I hope you have succeeded in winning your cousin for me. I can hardly wait to inquire for her letter at Chapel Hill.

You may be sure that I expect to see you on my way back home. I already have questions. But even if they were all answered, I would want to see you. I shall write as soon as I know when I am going to return.

JHR: ALS

18. To Glenn W. Rainey

CHAPEL HILL, NC

FRIDAY [EARLY OCTOBER, 1933]

Arrived here today after four days at Duke. I suppose [I] had told you about my good fortune with Georgia Watson. Frankly, it was the greatest surprise I have had in all the chase for Watsoniana, and will remain the most pleasant experience connected with the job. She is an ally, and I am now entirely relieved from the (unconsciously) depressing sense of betraying innocent and unsuspecting kinsmen of the Sage—no matter what I write. I'm most happy over it. She is the only one of the tribe that could have risen to it. But she is a remarkable person, unless my enthusiasm has run away with me. I talked quite as frankly with her as I could with you about her grandfather—more so perhaps, since she laughed at your objection to making 'Top' a "man of meeker stuff." She *sees* the thing, intimately and analytically & dispassionately. Wants to do a novel of her family. I'm just afraid she hasn't got it in her, though hope she has. It would make as powerful stuff as the "Angel," if she could—drunken, raw, & full of roil and passion. If you think I sound a bit ecstatic, wait till you hear the story. It's pretty awful (in the real sense of the word). It struck home to me like nothing else the shallowness of my formulae, clichés, & catchwords. Also the sheer inadequacy of biography vs fiction.

She got permission for me from her cousin at Washington to use Watson material.[67] (Cousin inherits "Top's meeker stuff" she tells me—hence her previous refusals to writers & it has been attempted before. Hamilton surprised I got consent—& I am first to [get] at it.)[68] There are 5 large packing boxes full of letters, etc, and two full of scrap books. Untouched except by rats & age. But God how rich! Also Georgia has Roosevelt & Debs letters she has promised me.[69]

Odum says "important hell, it ought to be worth two books." But he doesn't think I can do it, I could tell. Bit chagrinned I thought. He was in [a] hurry, being brain trustee & captain of (research) industry. Vance is doing my original idea—"Spell-binders of South"—but was pleasant & helpful.[70] Going to hit Odum for money later.

More stuff at Duke than I thought. Duke was a case of loathe at first sight for me—Middle Gothic in celophane; gigantic, turretted, battlemented entrances with pneumatic hinged swinging doors in place of iron portcullisses—innumerable chimneys—all dummies—there being a central heating plant; concrete gargoyles, great ivy vines, clamped on with tin. Cloistered picture show. Replica of Westminster, with elevator in tower. Leaded windows in library that let in no light. Attended opening meeting of Graduate club—Herr Doctor Katzenjammer of German Dept., just back from Vaterland lectured dithyrambically on *Der Führer und der Neue Geist*—*Hitler saving Western civilization from barbarism*—Professors applauded & Woodward muttered & finally puked on the floor. Goddam, how I loathe that place—

Chapel Hill is lovely & has all but restored my customary serenity & faith in capitalism. I love the place and want to live here. It is an Oxford

67. The cousin was Georgia Watson Lee Brown (1906–1935), a granddaughter of Tom Watson and wife of Walter Brown; she was to die young of tuberculosis.

68. Joseph Gregoire de Roulhac Hamilton (1878–1961), Kenan Professor of History and Government at the University of North Carolina and founder of its Southern Historical Collection.

69. The Thomas E. Watson Papers, now in the Southern Historical Collection at the University of North Carolina, contain correspondence with both Theodore Roosevelt and Eugene Victor Debs (1855–1926), the union leader and socialist, about whom CVW would later fleetingly plan to write a biography.

70. Rupert Bayless Vance (1899–1975) was born in Plummerville, AR, and (like CVW) attended Henderson-Brown. After Howard Odum, Vance was the South's most important regional sociologist, whose most significant early work was *Human Geography of the South: A Study in Regional Resources and Human Adequacy* (Chapel Hill: University of North Carolina Press, 1932).

planted on more fertile soil than Methodism, & unraped by Coca Cola or Chesterfield.[71] Did you walk around the town much? I didn't dream there was anything like it left in existence. I'm a little sick I didn't get to come here to school instead of Emory. I would have been a more pleasant person, I dare say.

I shall probably stay here till my money runs out. It will likely take me three weeks or more to go through the Watson boxes. Then if I have any money left I'll sit here and invite my soul.

Going over to Durham to see Green Pastures Tuesday—[72] [deletion]

    GWR: ALS

19. To Glenn W. Rainey

OXFORD, GA

APRIL 1 [1934]

I am not sulking in my tent like a dipsomaniac Pete—by the way I heard from him lately, enclosing two poems, with a civil tongue in his mouth, or cheek, I do not know which—It is simply that you remain persistently away from home every time I come by or call up. Is it a woman? Three times recently, and no luck. I'm damned if I make appointments—

Do you remember my wondering how I could ever have put Proust down after having started him? Well, I've found out why. It's because he's dull, damned dull, and I care not who says he's not because if he does he's a liar and a two faced one like the man who loves the organ-throated stops of Milton's P. Lost, or worse. Something that is charming and wise and exciting is the Letters of D. H. Lawrence which I am reading.[73]

The mana still falls from on high and I lie on my back in the grass with my mouth open and one eye on a restive Sinai. It only takes the mornings now and I put in the afternoons contemplating the mechanism of a typewriter and occasionally hitting a key—gingerly, tentatively to see

71. As noted above, Emory University had received land and money from the founder of the Coca-Cola Company. Duke University had likewise been endowed by James Buchanan Duke (1856–1925) of the American Tobacco Company, one of whose brands, for a while, was Chesterfield cigarettes.

72. Marc Connelly's play The Green Pastures (1930), which had an all-black cast and was a dramatization of the Old Testament; it became a film in 1936.

73. Aldous Huxley, ed., The Letters of D. H. Lawrence (New York: Viking Press, 1932).

if they work. But I am getting back in the traces—if only to realize that I'm a pedigreed wheel-horse with a double load. The trouble now, of course, is that I have too much stuff and that I clogg up the works with it, with it and citations—ten to a page. Dear God! I am as thoroughly intimidated as any Ph.D. alive. What did it, I wonder? Then too I haven't the courage to burn up the first MSS nor the strength to resist looking at it, nor the will to refrain from using old smooth sentences, nor—well I *do* have a lot of notes, like poor Jimmy Hinton when he died. Mrs. H. sent them to Harvard, where they may now be consulted *ad lib.* Rainey, promise me, as a friend you won't send my notes to Harvard! cast them to the winds, throw them to the dogs, give them a pauper's grave, but don't send them to Harvard!

How about buying me three seats to Barrets of Wimpole St. at an afternoon performance at not more than 1.50 apiece if they are that cheap?[74] Thanks. You can buy them when you get yours, *together* by all means. For you must go. I saw it in N.Y. and it has its good points.

GWR: ALS

20. To Boulware Martin

Oxford, GA
May 19, 1934

[deletion]

Well, we are leaving Oxford. That, I believe, is the most momentous news I have, and likely you won't be impressed at all, because you don't know Oxford. I am really sick over it. I have spent the whole year here and have grown passionately fond of the place. I have exactly eighteen more days here and I go about sensually prolonging the pleasure of them. Chiefly, it's the house and the place I hate leaving. I told you, didn't I, that it was built by Gus Baldwin Longstreet (do you know J. D. Wade's biography of him. Must. Wade's fine) in the early '40s. But I shall become maudlin. I don't know yet where I'll go when the family leaves here. I am seriously thinking of going to New Orleans for the summer. Is there

---

74. A film about the courtship of Elizabeth Barrett and Robert Browning, *The Barretts of Wimpole Street* (Metro-Goldwyn-Mayer, 1934) featured Norma Shearer, Fredric March, and Charles Laughton, and was directed by Sidney Franklin; it was adapted from Rudof Besier's 1930 play.

a chance of your being there? That would help me decide. Please let me know soon if you are. I would like so very much to see you.

I have spent some time now hammering away intermittently at a typewriter with no very tangible results. But I have enjoyed myself thoroughly nevertheless. That's what I suppose I shall do this summer, I don't know how enjoyably, though, nor with what further results. Trying to get the plutocrats to endow me for a year. Might. And may I expect to hear from you very soon?

[deletion]

> CVWP, 35/415: TLS

21. To Antonina Jones Hansell[75]

CHAPEL HILL, NC

WEDNESDAY [13 JUNE 1934]

Your letter. Depressing. What's the matter with the 4th? Thou dost protest too much. Why psychologically? Anyway, it looks like the 4th will be too early for me. But it doesn't matter, that is any time you say I shall come. Maybe week after 4th? Have that understood before you take the job.

Rockefeller finally came through—most generously. I'm now an honest man. Can you believe it? Addressed the Kawanis club. Me? Like going to Paris to live on the Right Bank. I won't do it again though.

There is no evading me, you must understand. The coast is a better idea. Is there someplace near Baltimore? You suggest one. I would like that. And plan for more than a weekend too. A whole week or more at the very least.

Love to you,

Comer Vann Woodward

Of Arts, a bachelor

By Columbia

75. Antonina Jones Hansell (1898–1987) had become CVW's lover in 1933. Nina, as she was usually known, came from Atlanta and had been married to John Elwood Macdonald, by whom she had a son called Ross; they were divorced in 1933. She had worked as a psychiatric aide in Atlanta and Philadelphia and, in 1936, would move to New York City, where she studied psychoanalysis with Alfred Adler, Bernard Glueck, and others; later she undertook psychiatric work, mostly with children. She would marry Reginald Earle Looker in 1947.

(Gym of the Ocean)
Called Master
Though
Really
Unwed.

    AHL: TLS

22. To Glenn W. Rainey

[Oxford, GA]

[Undated (summer 1934)]

Look. Go to see Viva Villa.[76] I stake all my painfully won reputation on that recommendation. If you don't like—the worse for my opinion of your judgment.

I am quitting On-Our-Way Roosevelt's job.[77] Howard On-Our-Way Odum informs me that John You-Can-Be-Had Rockefeller consents to make a kept man, and suggests that I come over to Chapel Hill for nuptuals before he (On-Our-Way) gets off to New York via California, which will be the 9th, so I'll go about 6th, but don't think I'll stay, if I can persuade them (like I did FERA) that work must be done in Oxford.

    On our way,

    GWR: TLU

23. To Antonina Jones Hansell

Oxford, GA

September 2, 1934

[deletion]

Just one request. Forget about the "Norah" analogy.[78] It doesn't mean anything. I have even forgotten what she is like. She can't be like you—no one could. Like you (I imagine) I have at times wondered vaguely when we would drift away from each other, lose interest, forget, find other attachments.

I see now that this will not happen. I can not imagine it happening. I

---

76. *Viva Villa!* (Metro-Goldwyn-Mayer, 1934), a biography of Pancho Villa; it starred Wallace Beery, Fay Wray, and Leo Carrillo, and was directed by Jack Conway.

77. CVW had had a summer job with the Federal Emergency Relief Administration.

78. Perhaps Nora Barnacle (1884–1951), James Joyce's wife, but probably someone CVW had known.

know I shall always want to see you when I can, and will go a long way to do so. I even believe that should I become very much interested in some one else, I should still have the same affection and interest for you. You would argue this point, I know. I have given up trying to understand this current predilection of monogamy which precludes 'all but one.' Now you are saying 'some one else.' Wrong again.

I leave Tuesday for Chapel Hill. Write me there—say whether there is any chance of seeing you.

Augusta was charming. Write you about it.

AHL: ALS

24. To Glenn W. Rainey

[Chapel Hill, NC]
September 24, 1934

[deletion]

History department here seems to be cracking up like the English department did several years ago. People all on point of leaving. It's possible I might not stay after all, but don't say anything about it. Craven, Chicago, is coming through next week, and I shall talk to him.

I followed the strike pretty closely, making some trips. I learned little, except that the only way to learn anything about American labor is through first-hand observation. Don West, now traveling for the C. P. under the name of Weaver (warrants for his arrest in three Southern states) and I helped him organize some protest of terrorism, etc. Communism was pretty much eclipsed in the strike; much weaker than in '29.[79]

---

79. In September 1934, there was a strike of textile workers at the Burlington (NC) Mills, in part organized by representatives from the Communist Party, prominent among whom was the north Georgian Don West (1906–1992), who was to have a long career as a party organizer. After much violence between the National Guard and "flying squadrons" of militant strikers, including the explosion of a dynamite bomb in the mill yard of the E. M. Holt Plaid Mill, and after the intervention of the National Recovery Administration, the strike was settled, with all the strikers rehired. CVW had known West earlier, since the latter had been involved in the defense of Angelo Herdon in Atlanta, and would further assist him when, in January 1935, he joined a committee of University of North Carolina academics, who went to investigate the prosecution of eight workers for the bombing. On this, see James J. Lorence, *A Hard Journey: The Life of Don West* (Urbana: University of Illinois Press, 2007), 53–63, and Charles H. Martin, *The Angelo Herndon Case and Southern Justice* (Baton Rouge: Louisiana State University Press, 1976), 110–13.

I don't understand it. Still it is stronger than you might suspect. Heard Thomas in Durham.[80] He helped crystalize sentiment against NRA, but employed pretty sissy tactics. Several workers who were bayoneted appeared in Chapel Hill with West and ruffled the still waters of academic complacency slightly. Graham (President) went bail for State socialist organizer—all of which matters not at all.[81] You saw clearly enough, I suppose, that every method of fascism was used in the South. What happened in Georgia?
[deletion]

> GWR: TLS

25. To Glenn W. Rainey

CHAPEL HILL, NC

OCTOBER 27 [1934]

[deletion]

For the clippings much thanks. The one about the suit was the first wind I got of my seeming victory, other than a vague hint.[82] I suppose I should feel elated at my vindication. But it seems that lawyers do for my zeal for justice what professors do for my ardor for learning: desiccate it. I shall receive the money like I shall receive a degree—wages earned. And the getting of the one, I dare say, is as problematic as the getting of the other. Which is to say, Very!

But as for degrees and their worth, my good man, you have ever been a bit frivolous and profane. I would admonish you that becoming a Ph.D. is in on the order of becoming an A.T.O.—you will know something then that no one else in the world knows but a Ph.D.[83] Does that not give thee pause? Let us dwell on this thought. As an example, only this evening a part of the ritual of Ph.D. was disclosed to me. I read a three hour paper to a seminar group on the taxation system of the states between Confeder-

---

80. Norman M. Thomas (1884–1968), leader of the American Socialist Party.

81. Frank Porter Graham (1886–1972), president of the University of North Carolina (1932–49), U.S. senator (1949–51), and a leading Southern liberal.

82. For budgetary reasons, in 1933 Georgia Tech had fired thirty professors, including CVW, while changing the method of paying salaries from a monthly schedule to nine payments per annum. This had the effect of denying remuneration for work already performed by those who had been let go. There had been a court case, as a result of which CVW and others had received compensation.

83. "A.T.O." is Alpha Tau Omega, a student fraternity.

ation and Constitution—and my mind is now a plum-pudding of esoterica of the order. But I must not lift the curtain too far before profane eyes.

Oh, God! As soon as *The Daily Worker* adopts the slogan that "the Ph.D. is a dirty capitalist trick for taking the intellectual's mind off the class struggle," I shall raise the red standard and bare my bosom to Führer Hudson's storm troops.[84] Then I shall grip the bars till my knuckles whiten handsomely and intone, "And why aren't you here too, Waldo?"[85] If I were in a position to support your family I would wish that they had sent you up with poor Mr. Allyng. The Scottsboro boys are worn a bit thin, and that would have made a show—or I don't know my Barnum & Bailey.[86] "Tech Non-fraternity Fraternity Storms Prison": "Communism Rears its Ugly Head in Tech Y.M.C.A.": "Britton Debating Club Spurns Food in Hunger Strike": "100 Machine Shop Students Perish in Black Pit: Want Rainey" "Co-ops go Co-mmunist" "Perry Perishes at Own Hand!" God what a story! "Pink-Tornado Strikes for Higher Wages and Higher Grades." "Regents Rage."

Writing has about come to an impasse. Courses take up all my time. Might drop them after this quarter and get the job done, or well along. Not complete—so I can get grant renewed. Met Craven of Chicago and fairly pleased with him. History, I find, is a collection of facts. Should have looked into that before going so far. Nothing but contempt for facts. Opinion all that matters. Proper attitude.

Voluminous letter from Pete that warmed the cockles of my heart. Banish Pete, and banish all the world.[87] I want to see a fervent reunion between you two.

Have you read taking on Taine on Eng. Lit.? Best thing at all. Try it.

84. Possibly Hosea Hudson (1898–1988), an African-American prominent in the Communist Party USA.

85. An allusion to an incident in 1846, when Henry David Thoreau had gone to jail for refusing to pay his local poll tax, in protest of the Mexican War. Puzzled at the gesture, Ralph Waldo Emerson had visited his friend and is said to have asked, "Henry, what are you doing in there?" to which Thoreau replied, "Waldo, the question is what are you doing out there?" However, the story is unreliably documented and is probably apocryphal.

86. In 1931, eight black teenagers were convicted in Scottsboro, AL, for the rape of two white women on a freight train; there followed a long and controversial series of appeals and retrials, which went on for many years and focused the issue of judicial discrimination against African-Americans.

87. An allusion to Falstaff's injunction to Prince Hal: "Banish not him thy Harry's company: banish plump Jack, and banish all the world." Shakespeare, *Henry IV, Part I*, act 2, scene 4.

You can get it now in 2 vols—nice—for $2—Millers.[88] See this week's *Sat. Rev. of Literature* for fascinating psychoanalytical study of Faulkner's *Sanctuary*.[89] For the rest—God spare you Lecky's *Hist. of Eng. in 18th Cent*—8 vols: I have 7 ⁶/₇ volumes to go and must be about it.[90]

[deletion]

GWR: ALS

26. To Glenn W. Rainey

CHAPEL HILL, NC

FEBRUARY 4, 1934 [1935]

You were right, of course, in assigning the reason for my stolid silence. But it was an easy guess and you deserve no credit for it. For weeks after my return I sank deeper & deeper in a muck of doldrums, till I was in up to my ears and no longer able to grin comfortably, much less laugh at myself. It was impossible to write anybody. The mere thought of myself wrung tears of compassion from my soul—not a very wholesome mood, you see. I still don't trust my sense of humor, if indeed, I have any left, and the well of words is quite dry to the bottom, as this letter will more than prove.

There is at least one bit of news concerning the Work-not-in-Progress. Seeking partly some solace, partly an excuse to postpone work, partly an excuse to chuck the whole works, I took the MSS—as it was when you saw it, plus a chapter—to J. G. de Roulhac Hamilton (all of it) to read. Hamilton (Reconstruction, Letters of Jefferson, biography of H. Ford, article in Am. Mercury, etc.) is a Menckenian Tory, with Southern Gentleman pretensions, only teaching one quarter a year, giving rest of his time to Southern Collection. He read it and to my mild amazement liked it, suggesting only a few changes to make it acceptable as a dissertation—and they relatively unimportant ones, such as cutting down percentage of "sons of bitches, bastards, and goddams.["] But this does

88. There were many English editions of Hippolyte Taine's *History of English Literature* (1863), in the translation of Henri Van Laun, but usually in three volumes; I can find no evidence of one published by a publisher called Miller, but CVW may mean a bookshop called Millers.

89. Lawrence S. Kubie, "William Faulkner's *Sanctuary*," *Saturday Review of Literature* 11 (20 October 1934): 111–12.

90. Likewise there are many editions of W. E. H. Lecky's *History of England in the Eighteenth Century* (1878–90).

not mean much, after all. He affects a contempt for academic stuffiness that makes him unique here and anywhere else, so far as I know. It would be impossible to find another of his rating who would take that attitude. Furthermore, he is unable to take over the direction of the work because he is leaving teaching after this year to give all his time to collecting. Who will take it I do not yet know. It is not yet known whether Craven will be here or not.

[deletion]

    GWR: ALS

27. To Glenn W. Rainey

Chapel Hill, NC

March 3, 1935

Thanks for your frivolous and non-committal letter. Happily it was supplemented shortly after by a sheaf of MSS from Pete, who still lays claim to the title of omniscience. There was no letter among the MSS, but there was a four page article (in his most unhappy *Time* style) all about the red scare in Georgia, written I know not why. The rest was two documents (there is no other word) that might have come out of *transition* in its palmiest days, handling such subjects as blasphemy, incest, and all varieties of neuroses.[91] Before Christmas he sent me one right creditable poem, but this stuff is diseased. Do you ever see him at all?

The clipping pretty much explains itself. The Burlington workers referred to were framed on a charge of dynamiting a mill thirty miles from here. Pretty raw sort of thing, with not even a half-hearted regard for the formalities of legal decorum. I helped organize a mass meeting to raise funds, appeal, propaganda, etc. Paul Green, Couch *et al* on the committee.[92] This gives you the prevailing undergraduate opinion. Strange situation here—or is it true elsewhere? The radical and advanced liberal opinion is mainly among the faculty (a very few, two Socialists among

---

91. Published in Paris (1927–38), *transition* specialized in experimental modern literature, including that written by expressionists, surrealists, and Dadaists; it also published excerpts from James Joyce's *Finnegan's Wake*.

92. Paul Green (1894–1981), the North Carolina playwright, then best known for *In Abraham's Bosom* (1926), which won a Pulitzer prize, and for directing the Carolina Playmakers at the University of North Carolina; William Terry Couch (1901–1989), then director of the University of North Carolina Press.

them) and the graduate students in the English department. You know perfectly well that in our undergraduate days it was in the student body, if anywhere, that the radical opinion lay. So soon are we superannuated?

There is a bare possibility I might be home in a couple of weeks. Not very probable, however. Chances are I'll stay here during holidays and work. Plans for next year are not settled. Odum is half-way committed to get me something, whether a renewal of the Rockefeller grant, I don't know. None of the other stipendaries here are in hopes of a renewal. It is still unknown whether Craven is going to accept the position here. My plans are rather contingent upon his decision.
[deletion]

GWR: ALS

28. To Antonina Jones Hansell

CHAPEL HILL, NC

APRIL 7, 1935

Please try to avoid that gone-but-not-forgotten tone unless you really feel that way about me. I find that, if any thing, you become more instead of less important to me, and I protest against becoming a memory, however roseate.

I wish I had written you when I had the impulse to, right after I got your letter. There seemed to be pages of things that urgently demanded saying to you. Most of it flattering, as I recall. I had just gotten back from Atlanta, where I spent the holidays, and naturally I had been thinking much of you. I remember passing through 16th St. once, by accident and becoming so preoccupied as to draw comment. Well, just after reading your letter I was moved to tell you what I thought then. I am sure it must have been eloquent, for that was the way I felt. It was also just after I finished *Of Time and the River*.[93] I was oratorical about everything for a few weeks. I see this is a letter about the letter I might have written you. Oh, but it would have been a fine letter! You would have then known how I felt about you, what all the nights meant, and you would have had a fine opinion of yourself (like you should have, instead of what doctors tell you) and of me.—But now it's no use. I feel cross and dull and I am only writing to earn a reply.

93. Thomas Wolfe, *Of Time and the River, a Legend of Man's Hunger in His Youth* (New York: Charles Scribner's Sons, 1935).

But you must read this book of Wolfe's, darling. Not since Melville has there been any thing like him, no such power and magnificent abundance of language, richness and passion of feeling, and torrential floods of experience. I feel actually grateful to the man as if for some imponderable debt. Like I do toward you sometimes.

Of course I am perverse and rebellious, but only because I prefer to be perverse and rebellious rather than complacent and smug in the face of the sort of thing I am compelled, or compel myself, to put up with. Thanks for the "1, 2, 3" admonition. I do that alright, but for recreation I am rebellious, and it takes a great deal of recreation for me. God, how I wish I could see you. For one thing, when I got around to it, I would make you respect a first class rebellion when you saw one.

Yes, I am glad you turned down the husbands you didn't want, and I hope you get the husband you do want. That is, I hope that as a philanthropist. But, Nina, it will be utterly ridiculous for me to go about respecting any of your hypothetical marriage vows. Don't you see that it will? Yes, I suppose I love you, too. At least it seems that way at times. Are you ever coming South?

[deletion]

AHL: ALS

29. To Glenn W. Rainey

[CHAPEL HILL, NC]

APRIL 29, 1935

Your letter to Malone apparently—doubtlessly—turned the trick.[94] He wrote asking for a thousand words on Tom for which he promised $20, rejected or accepted (the words not the money). The situation was that John Wade, haunted with visitations of Confederate Brewton's wrath, backed down after the article he wrote was already in Malone's hands, and refused to allow his name to be connected in any way with the business. (Sad picture of typewriter-Confederate confronted by the genuine article in the flesh.) Malone said he wrote me this "in confidence." It appears that Malone then wrote an article himself. Says he will use mine if it is better than the one he has. Vance tells me the invitation should

94. Dumas Malone (1892–1986), later known for being Thomas Jefferson's most indefatigable biographer, had since 1929 been an editor (and from 1931 editor in chief) of the *Dictionary of American Biography*.

impress the local Sanhedrin mightily, so I shall be careful to pour rumor in the porches of their ears. Now that you have made a scholar out of me I am half disposed to retract a certain percentage of the maledictions I have launched against your name. Go, but prithee sin no more.

The matter of my stipend for next year is still unsettled, and consequently so are my plans. I have about concluded that, since in all seriousness I can say that I have not gleaned a single sickly idea from any professor here, I would be no more likely to fare any better with the professors who taught these professors. Then with the year's start I have, I might hope to educate a few of them in another year. One hoards petty triumphs, you know. Just recently, one of my brighter young masters, after absorbing a paper of mine (I was careful to clear up obscure points in a conference) broke forth and in a lyrical article of protest, demanding a militant teacher's union which could employ the strike as freely as labor. You will understand the pardonable pride I take in him.
[deletion]

GWR: TLS

30. To Glenn W. Rainey

CHAPEL HILL, NC
SEPTEMBER 11, 1935

If you had been clever, here's what you would have said about your Russian atrocity book: "This book, no doubt, contains the truth about Soviet methods. It is the truth about an orchard spraying from the viewpoint of the woolly aphid and the coddling moth." I wish I had said that. But I didn't.

GWR: TLS[95]

31. To Antonina Jones Hansell

CHAPEL HILL, NC
SEPTEMBER 25, 1935

I have waited much longer than I intended, or thought I had, to write you. Knowing the penalty, I am amazed at my own remissness. Your last letter places me under really heavy obligations to you. It did me that much good. First your protestations of affection (I always need them,

95. The signature is typed and the date comes from the postmark.

remember, plenty of them) and then the revelation that you were still yourself in spite of all your efforts to the contrary. I'm sure, darling, that I would never have been interested in the person you evidently strive to become. Not the slightest. My only fear is that you will. And your apologies for visiting accumulated repressions, discouragements, temper tantrums on me merely amuse me. Delight me, in fact. It is only when you lift your eyes in Christ-like patience and mute martyrdom that I become seriously alarmed, my sweet. Please don't get Christ-like on me again. More temper tantrums, a thousand times rather.

Quite as single as ever, dear, but rather more than twenty-three. Fewer hairs on my head; more on my chest, but no wife. You see, Nina, it is easier by far to find one with whom one can sleep, than it is to find one with whom one can laugh. You might—melancholy reflection—prove the last as well as the first I find. My mistrust of romantic love might in final analysis turn out to be an incapacity for it. I'm pretty sure I am not romantically in love with you, yet I am also pretty sure I could live with you a long time as happily as I have in the past. Don't you think so? I'd like to tell you about one I met in Macon this summer, sometime.[96] She was married to one man and in love with another, though. You would have liked her.

I too have some traffic with the rich bastards. Sort of kept man, my critics say. Big shirt & collar tycoon built a model house for four undergraduates—one from each class—and one graduate. I am the latter. His son & two nephews are three of the former. The place is so god damned nice I am thoroughly uncomfortable, & quite glum. It is profitable to me, though, and I stay. Interior court, fountains, etc, etc. And me a revolutionist. Ugh! I shall indoctrinate the young tycoons with subversive ideas if I get the time.

I find it next to inconceivable that you are going to stay on up there without visiting South another year. I fairly yearn to see you. And I am haunted by the fear that the next time I see you you'll be married. That will simply prove awkward. You'll see! Yes, I know quite well it has been a year. More than that. Yes, I do remember the cove—

AHL: ALS

96. CVW had worked during the summer of 1935 for the Works Progress Administration in surveying rural poverty around Macon, GA.

32. To Glenn W. Rainey

I am feverishly trying to gather up odds and ends of normal existence once more—suspended for weeks by prospect of preliminary orals—and so far I have gotten to your letter.

The orals came yesterday. Rather formidable, as I expected. I performed adequately, of course, but not brilliantly. There is simply nothing in the idea of examinations that challenges my temperament. I seldom rise to them more than sufficiently. A new man in the department, Beale, whom I count a friend, and under whose direction I will do the thesis, was generously enthusiastic. He has a ponderous book on the history of freedom of teaching coming out this summer, which I can count on you not attempting.[97]

I am indulging myself the dubious pleasure of some extravagant forgetting. No niggardly date here and a dictator there, but whole dynasties at a time—Poof, there go the Hapsburgs, poof the Hohenzollerns. (I made the mistake of forgetting the Hanoverians before the orals.) A continent or two, an ocean of diplomacy, and a library of books. Alcohol proves an excellent solvent for the unused impedimenta of information after examinations.

[deletion]

GWR: ALS

33. To Antonina Jones Hansell

I read your letter with an amount of feeling that would have overwhelmed you and even surprised me. A large part of the feeling was a complex sort of gratitude, I believe. You would probably understand it better than I do. I am becoming accustomed to the weakness of relying on you to tell me what I feel. I know that you are the wisest woman I shall ever know. I received your analysis of the "cold reality" of our relationship as from an oracle. But all the same, darling, "cold reality" is hardly

---

97. Howard Kennedy Beale (1899–1959), who was later to move to the University of Wisconsin; see his *Are American Teachers Free? An Analysis of Restraints Upon the Freedom of Teaching in American Schools* (New York: Charles Scribner's Sons, 1936).

an accurate designation for my feeling for you and for our relationship. I don't know what it was I said about you that you were so determined "not to take with any seriousness"—but, without wasting protestations, I believe I can rely on your understanding something of the depth of my feelings for you.

[deletion]

AHL: ALS

34. To Glenn W. Rainey

CHAPEL HILL, NC

JULY 2, 1936

I got here in the middle of the Carolina monsoons. Took the Seaboard, going out of the way in order to get an air-conditioned train, and before I got out of Georgia moisture began forming on the *inside* of the windows—which according to the new physics meant that it was cooler outside than inside. The weather is fine, the house quiet, and really quite perfect (except for a puppy that pukes on the floor and barks all night). There is really not an available excuse for putting off work. Not that I want to, either. I am really pretty keen over it, and am warming over my enthusiasm—after a year in the cooler—much more successfully than I had hoped. This thing, by God, has really got to be good. There is no earthly excuse for its not being. I am discovering new possibilities. I am rusty on ideas and words have to be dragged out—but, God, what could I expect after two years of lectures and examinations? It's a wonder I have an idea left in my head. For a long time I thought I hadn't, but now it's better.

I guess you will about have to read Granville Hicks' *John Reed*. It's calculated to re-kindle a few fires in you, and I expect that's what you need. Santayana's novel will light no blazes but you might read it.[98]

The war in Arkansas has got me upset—it looks like my planter uncles and cousins—with which Cross County is overrun—are out to barbecue all the nigger croppers along with the foreign devils from Memphis.[99] I

98. Granville Hicks, *John Reed: The Making of a Revolutionary* (New York: Macmillan, 1936); George Santayana, *The Last Puritan, a Memoir in the Form of a Novel* (1935; New York: Charles Scribner's Sons, 1936).

99. This refers to the brutal repression occasioned by the activities of the Southern Tenant Farmers Union, whose leaders were H. L. (Harry Leland) Mitchell (1906–1989) and Henry

came pretty near going out there with a committee from Chapel Hill. I think you and I and the rest of us are not raising enough hell, and I think if we don't start it pretty soon we are going to suffer a severe deflation in self esteem. I really feel that pretty strongly.

[deletion]

   GWR: ALS

35. To Glenn W. Rainey

I only got your letter yesterday, having just returned from a week on the Chesapeake as brown as a ripe tomato and feeling vulgarly healthy and in robust spirits. I am genuinely delighted, if a bit incredulous, at your lusty appetite for cramming. It might well be some undiscovered kind of neurosis. I am well acquainted with the gnawing ache at the base of one's skull, but only as a symptom of incipient madness—as while reading Constitutional law. The patient who finds perverted pleasure in such a symptom is likely suffering from a manic depressive ordering on a rarefied masochism. See a psychiatrist. But for God's sake don't let him cure you till you pass your exams. I got back on the job today. Did a little while gone, but hope to strike a steady pace from now on and make tall strides this summer.

I am getting a good deal of pleasure out of Ralph Barton Perry's *William James.*[100] As an educator (sic) I have about decided what education should be: besides teaching people what to hate and what cherish it should equip them with proper heroes and proper villains. Rather an old fashioned idea. Carlyle and that sort of thing.[101] But you don't have to believe heroes make history to realize that if you don't give them he-

---

Clay East (b. 1900). It was founded in Tyronza, AR, which is in Poinsett County, immediately to the north of Cross County, where CVW was born. The union was racially integrated, involved women, was partly inspired by socialists, and used the techniques of evangelical religion, in order to protest the evictions of sharecroppers, organize strikes, lobby for federal legislation, and form cooperatives.

   100. Ralph Barton Perry, *The Thought and Character of William James, as Revealed in Unpublished Correspondence and Notes, Together with His Published Writings*, 2 vols. (Boston: Little, Brown, 1936).

   101. Thomas Carlyle, *On Heroes, Hero-Worship, and the Heroic in History* (London: J. Fraser, 1841).

roes Hollywood and Hearst damn well will.[102] And heroes whether from Hollywood or Harvard are damned important furniture in a freshman's mind. Ummmm.

Judging from the first 118 pages of Margaret Mitchell's new novel, it's all about how a tart little bitch gets all the men in North Ga. in rut by exposing two inches more of breast than is conventional & other feminine wiles.[103] I was seized with a violent muscular contraction in the esophagus once. Maybe I didn't give her a chance, but one doesn't have to drink all the sea to call it salt—despite your belief. She was probably getting ready to do something worth while when I quit. It was doubtless a tough job, and all, but somehow I got tired. It's awful long. I get more and more tired of novels anyway and have for some time.

Thanks for the Pseudosomething. I liked Allen's article. Of course I remember him. Is he still in that godawful hole?[104] I know Phillips kin here. I promise to subscribe. You might be asked about the Webb's 2 vols on Soviet Communism.[105] Better look it over. Worth doing.
[deletion]

GWR: TLS

36. To Antonina Jones Hansell

CHAPEL HILL, NC
JULY 15, 1936

[deletion]

Adventures on a day coach—Paul Spurlin sat down opposite me on the train from Baltimore to Washington—first time I had seen him since the time your telegram was handed me two years ago saying we could meet in Philadelphia—I opened the message in his presence and

102. William Randolph Hearst (1863–1951), the newspaper magnate.

103. Margaret Mitchell, *Gone with the Wind* (New York: Macmillan, 1936).

104. John Daniel Allen's review of Allen Tate and Herbert Agar, eds., *Who Owns America? A New Declaration of Independence* (Boston: Houghton Mifflin, 1936), in *Pseudopodia* (1936), a periodical (in 1937 renamed the *North Georgia Review*) edited by Lillian Smith. Glenn Rainey sometimes wrote for it; two of his poems are reprinted in Helen White and Redding S. Sugg, *From the Mountain* (Memphis, TN: Memphis State University Press, 1972), 256. Allen (b. 1898) was from South Carolina and taught journalism at Mercer University in Macon, GA (presumably the "godawful hole").

105. Sidney Webb and Beatrice Webb, *Soviet Communism: A New Civilization?* (New York: Charles Scribner's Sons, 1936).

had to do some of my most brilliant lying to explain my elation.[106] My angel of judgment. At Richmond a gentleman sat down opposite me and opened a copy of James' *Pragmatism*.[107] I quickly closed my book. Two volumes of metaphysics on one day coach—and the thermometer at 105°! At Petersburg I extricated a plump but tenacious sand tick from my temple. Poor fellow, says I, he slept between us like somebody's sword—(or did he sleep?) Tenderly I deposited him in the brass cuspidor. How could I bruise me own blood?

We missed the most delicious part of the James book by not reading the last three chapters. Do it sometime. On the train I ran across a certain passage and instinctively looked up to read it to you. James relates to his wife an experience that befell him in the Adirondack mountains. I quote: "The intense significance of some sort, of the whole scene, if one could only *tell* the significance; the intense inhuman remoteness of its inner life, and yet the intensive *appeal* of it; its everlasting freshness and its immemorial antiquity and decay . . . and you, and my relation to you part and parcel of it all, and beaten up with it, so that memory and sensation all whirled inexplicably together. . . . It was one of the happiest lonesome nights of my existence, and I understand now what a poet is . . ."[108] That was what I wanted to say to you that night on the sand. Yet I dared not analyze it for fear of disintegrating the whole spell. James felt it transcendentally as a mystic. I felt it immediately, physically, yet somehow mystically, too. What sprang spontaneously to my mind was the Greeks—not Greek poetry—but Greek men and women, so near me I could touch them, and understood then what the pagan was.

I harbor an elusive feeling of guilt that in my greediness I hogged the pig's share of our experience together. Forgive me, darling, I was so mortally hungry for every thing you could give me. And you lavished such rich gifts upon me, and so generously, that I turned Midas. Approbation,

106. Paul M. Spurlin (1902–1994), a scholar of eighteenth-century French literature from Fayetteville, GA. He graduated from Emory in 1925 and completed a doctorate at Johns Hopkins in 1936; he later taught at Louisiana State University, the University of Alabama, and the University of Michigan.

107. William James, *Pragmatism, a New Name for Some Old Ways of Thinking* (New York: Longmans, Green, 1907).

108. Perry, *William James*, 2:676; CVW has tellingly, after "decay," omitted the phrase "its utter Americanism, and every sort of patriotic suggestiveness."

sympathy, admiration, approval, affection, praise, courage, vindication, love—all in such a bewildering golden flood that I could think of nothing but to hold out greedy upturned palms and cry for more. And Midas-like I hoard it every bit. You would be amazed at the accuracy with which I remember everything you said.

Reluctantly, for the sake of society, I begin to discount my treasures. To realize what self-flattery it is, what vanity, to believe you the wisest of women. Bitterly I admit that my oracle has clay feet. It turns out that Gretchen—not Ed—suggested the line that Nina said "only a man could have written." Oh! fallible woman! Then, soberly, I reread my manuscript. "Lean prose"! Indeed! My God, how dumb Nina is! "Lean prose!" Blobs of fat connected by unsightly tendons.

I enclose a card from your intended. My services are at your command. I'll put in a word about your housekeeping. Truly, a marriage of convenience—'A close trim man like a belt well buckled.'[109]

We were unfair to your friend Margaret Mitchell. Scarlett was really a stooge set up to protect the author from her fear of sentimentality—as Benet intimates.[110] The latter half of the book is a deep well of dull, immemorial heart-ache. I love her for feeling it.

AHL: ALS

37. To Antonina Jones Hansell

Your letter of a month or so ago, before the more recent note, deserved better of me. It was a letter that so strongly tempted me against my better biographer's experience, that I have kept it and shall keep it—future biographers please note (also snooping spouses). But I thought I would wait till I saw the beauty I wrote you about before I wrote. Perhaps, then, I reflected, I wouldn't be in such a fine frenzy. I was right—but the reasons are complex, and you must hear me to the end, I entreat you. Once more I shall try your patience and beg advice.

109. A line from the Stephen Vincent Benét's poem "King David"; the phrase describes Uriah the Hittite.

110. Stephen Vincent Benét, "Georgia Marches Through: *Gone With the Wind*," *Saturday Review of Literature* 14 (4 July 1936): 5.

I thought you would nod approval at my bold resolutions to inhibit the crawfish reflex. I was quite in earnest about it. But, oh dear, I have already proved apostate to my new professions of your faith. It all came of applying the principle too consistently. I beg your indulgence for erring on that side instead of the opposite, as an apostle of weaker faith would. Nonsense aside I feel like I have made rather a mess of the business, and am sinful and penitent both. Tell me what you think.

I saw her this week—as much the beauty and as freshly young and enthusiastic as ever.[111] It's what's happened between then and the time I met her that's the trouble. It was this way. I went to a picnic, innocent of any intention save stuffing myself and swilling beer and being agreeable. But somehow the crowd began dispersing and I was left alone with an agreeable young lady of charm and parts. And that's the way it happened. (It would amuse you, and you will doubtless find it incredible, that it is the first time I have ever been unfaithful to you since we met—not especially because of any resolution on my part, mostly, doubtless, the way things happened.) After that, there was no good reason I could see for sternly banishing her from my side—especially since she would like to go to the mountains for a few days and could borrow a car and camping trailer. And that's the way it happened. She is nearly my age, rather pretty, mature, traveled, taste, intelligence—we had a class together at Columbia, but didn't know it—experienced, never married, never in love. She does not love me and does not expect me to love her. Yes, I asked her. She was rather afraid I would, before that. Simple, ingenious, independent.

Well, somehow I feel like an apostate. Backslider. There is no puzzle about this girl such as the one I wrote you about presented. Simple and understandable, also not so perturbing, and, well, 'upsetting.' Has my cowardice merely became more subtle in tricking me? I tried to fool myself by saying this affair could make no difference in the more exalted feelings toward the other girl, so I asked her over from Greensboro. For a while I thought it *didn't* make any difference. She was so pretty, and I so vain & pleased with myself. But of course it *did* make a difference. (I wish

111. This is Glenn Boyd MacLeod (1910–1982), who was born in Chapel Hill, NC, the daughter of David Vincent MacLeod (1876–1961) and Glenn Anna Causey MacLeod (1880–1959). She grew up in Greensboro, NC, graduated from the University of North Carolina in 1930, and took a master's degree at Columbia University in 1932 (where, as he notes, she shared some classes with CVW). They married on 21 December 1937 in Chapel Hill.

you had met her.) However, she is not possessive, either, and inclined to independence also. So I let things rest like that. An unwonted rôle for me, I assure you, but there I am. Now what do you think of the matter?

Please write me soon and give me a better address. Done anything about the proposal? I think of you often and always shall. You are a permanent part of my "frame of reference."

Sorry about the job. You have another? Writing moves along.

AHL: ALS

38. To Antonina Jones Hansell

CHAPEL HILL, NC
SEPTEMBER 17, 1936

[deletion]

Evidently you hadn't received my last letter of lamentations when you wrote. I sent it to Mary Watson. Please get it at once and write me at once. The situation is still a situation, though more complications now. It will work out some way. I like the girl here, and she adjures me to fear nought—that she wouldn't marry me even if she had triplets, or words to that effect. She's not, so far. The other girl got your invitation after she got home, and *says* she wrote you thanks. Just as well.

You were perfectly right about her. Your letter was another gem and I have salted it away with your other oracular utterances. Some day I'll edit them in a book of proverbs—'Out of the Horse's Mouth' or something. I'm deeply grateful to you for remaining that fond of me. I suppose I am depending heavily on your continuing to do so. I have no intention whatever of ever giving you up no matter what happens to you or to me. Do you understand that?

I have no idea of marrying soon, as a matter of fact. But, like Mrs. Patrick Campbell (you may quote) 'I long for the deep, deep peace of the double bed after the hurley-burley of the chaise longue.' [112]
[deletion]

AHL: ALS

---

112. Beatrice Stella Campbell, née Tanner (1865–1940), the English actress; in full, the quotation is, "Marriage is the result of the longing for the deep, deep peace of the double bed after the hurly-burly of the chaise longue."

39. To Antonina Jones Hansell

ATLANTA, GA

[LATE DECEMBER, 1936][113]

[deletion]

I didn't mean to be reticent about my 'love life,' dear. It was only that it has become so elemental that it probably would not interest you professionally. The girl I wrote you about first I have not seen since last summer. She wrote me that she was in love with me and had better not see me again. That made me feel like a wretch and a louse. I wanted to ask you what to do, but decided not to be so damned infantile and dependent. I wrote her sort of remorsefully that she was probably right, and mentioned the girl in Chapel Hill. Then she decided she had better see me again anyway, and I agreed, but she has not yet done so. The affair has about made me decide I am a low fellow, lacking in all but grosser feelings, capable of no more exalted emotions than an anthropoid—except where you are concerned. I still feel the same toward you I always have, and see no reason why I shall not continue to. The girl in Chapel Hill, so far as I can tell, is about as elemental—or is it complex?—in her feelings as I am. Neither of us is cynical about the matter, and neither expects very much. Both recognize it as lacking something. She is not possessive. I miss in her a great many things I find in you. You provided me a difficult standard, dear, but now I have it, it will have to be met.

I shall call your hotel with baited breath just on the bare possibility you will have changed your plans. If you have, leave word. I shall not send you a present, if you wish, though I wanted to. I still expect the picture though. Write me in Chapel Hill.

AHL: ALS

40. To Antonina Jones Hansell

CHAPEL HILL, NC

MAY 6, 1937

T hank you for the letter. I have the guilty feeling that that was what I wanted you to say. I mean about the girl. I try not to make too much of an Oracle of you, but I am afraid that I do. You know how much I depend on your opinions. Now, that makes you feel pretty responsible,

113. The letter is dated by Hansell, not CVW, as "[pm 29 Dec 1936]," which probably indicates when she received it.

doesn't it. Seriously, I want to talk with you about this problem. I am not trying to dodge it, and I am not putting the responsibility on someone else. I mean to make up my mind staring facts straight in the face and without impulsiveness. But you could help a great deal, if I could only talk with you. I made the problem much too easy in my letter. I am the unsocial and irresponsible one. Not she. She has been as unselfish as she could possibly be, and she loves me a great deal I am sure. I am the selfish and proud spirited one, and I am under great obligation to her, emotionally and in other ways. I am not fool enough to think that the obligation can be paid and my selfishness dissolved by marrying her. She knows that too and recognizes it honestly. I know that I would be doing her as well as myself a great injustice by marrying her for such reasons as that. But the great question is how much my reluctance to give into more powerful feelings is honest, and how much is rationalization of irresponsibility, selfishness, pride, and stiff-necked independence. Honestly, Nina, I don't know, and I am profoundly troubled by it. Is this just a repetition of the pattern I am destined to repeat again and again? If it is I want to smash it. It is not fair to other people. The only two ways that have occurred to me to destroy the pattern are to give in completely or to withdraw completely. Neither of those can be entirely voluntary.

The written exams were finished other day, and there is only one more hurdle toward the last of the month.[114] I haven't a sign of a job for next year. I have enough money to see me through the summer. I intend to spend the whole summer here writing and doing research. Let me hear from you soon.

AHL: TLS

41. To Glenn W. Rainey

CHAPEL HILL, NC
MAY 7, 1897 [1937]

[deletion]

I finished my writtens a couple of days ago. Formidable enough, but I feel all right about them. Three weeks more before final orals. Then I hope the cursed ordeal will be over. Really the year hasn't gone so badly for me. I have had to take no courses since Christmas. The dissertation

114. His doctoral examinations at the University of North Carolina.

took longer than I expected since it ran to about six hundred pages. I would not have been able to do it without the research and writing I had done before I came here. It is in pretty poor shape as it stands—that is, for anything except a dissertation. Because Beale was the director of the work I was allowed much more latitude than otherwise. I had considerable fun with it in spite of certain restraints and having to work under pressure. My faith in the story is fundamentally unshaken. That is I still think it is worth the telling. Couch says it will have to come down to 350 pages before publishing becomes a financial possibility. If he does it, that is, and so far as I can see he is my best bet. The boiling down process will be difficult.

[deletion]

    GWR: TLS

42. To Glenn W. Rainey

GAINESVILLE, FL

SEPTEMBER 11, 1937

I'm still a bit shaky on me pins, and not altogether sure it's true. I got the letter when I went in to interview my boss and just had time to open it and catch the word "contract" when he came in.[115] Then I had to sit there an hour and a half pretending that I was listening to what the ass was saying about this course Man and the Other World or something. I didn't hear a thing he said for an hour and a half and then when I did get a chance to read it before I was out of the hall I guess the guy thought I was nuts. I mean of course the letter was from Macmillan accepting Tom. I feel a little circumspect about it still because I'm not sure it's not all a hoax. The terms are that generous. They must be cockeyed. You know I had given up hope after what Odum told me a couple of weeks ago. He even advised me to write for the manuscript so that I could send it on to Prentice Hall or start cutting it down for Couch. That was why it was such a shock. I guess I acted like a madman. I met dozens of people without knowing what they said or remembering their names or anything. Of course I couldn't very well blurt out that Macmillan was going to publish Tom, so all I could do was go out on the campus and yell and walk half the night and drink beer—the only thing obtainable. I quote:

---

115. The letter from Macmillan, offering to publish *Tom Watson: Agrarian Rebel*; Harold S. Latham to CVW, 7 September 1937.

"I may tell you now, flatly and at the very outset of this letter, that we are very much pleased indeed with the biography, or, rather, with your work, for it is more than a biography, and shall be glad if we may publish it for you." Zoweee! I remarked after that one, and all the deans looked out the window. But the amazing thing is their generosity about the length of the MS. You know I had written, after Odum's report, suggesting that I cut it down to 350 or 400 pages since I "realized that in its present length it is completely impracticable as a publishing venture." Well look what he says about that: "We should certainly not like to have you do anything in the way of size reduction about the wisdom of which you were at all in doubt. It would be a pity it seems to us to omit the bibliography altogether—perhaps it could be somewhat shortened; we should not object to the omission of some of the footnotes. We do not know what part of the text you are thinking of omitting. We like the book about as it stands, and we hope you do not contemplate changing it too much. With this caution on our part that you do nothing in the way of condensation which you do not wish to do, we are ready to leave the matter entirely in your hands."

Drunken as I was at the moment I could not help grinning at such prize phrases as "and 15% after the first 7500." These babies must be cockeyed as boiled owls if they think they are going to make any money on this venture, but you may be sure I am resigned to letting them learn by their mistakes. "I hope very much this offer may be acceptable, and if it is I will send you a contract embodying the terms. (! And is it Acceptable!) We all look forward with much pleasure not only to the publication of this book, but we hope to others which you may do following it." The Deans looked out the window again. Secretaries phoned doctors.

Well now, my fine publicity agent, at last I am disposed to allow you to exercise your talents to the limit. Aye, get a sound-truck and charge it to Macmillan and give em hell with all horns.

Your advice in Chapel Hill about careful rechecking of details was a good point and shall surely be observed. I am determined not to let them rush me on this business. I still think some cutting would help and a lot of polishing. I intend to be about it right away as soon as I get through blowing.

On the strength of this news I rented a five room apartment just so I could walk up and down in it and think what a fine fellow am I.

GWR: TLS

43. To Antonina Jones Hansell

GAINESVILLE, FL
OCTOBER 16, 1937

[deletion]

I got this job at Florida right at the last of the summer after fighting several attempts to exile me in Arkansas, or at some "university" in the Great Dismal Swamp. It is beautiful here and I like many features of the work. At least it opens the gates of expression that have been locked so long. I have found a few interesting friends too. It's a job I'm lucky to get.

I am glad you broke that engagement. I thought you would. About my problem there is nothing conclusive to say. I am glad I did promise you to wait till after a separation, but I doubt if it adds to my clearness of perception. The way I feel now, I think I will probably marry her. I shall see her next month when I am in Chapel Hill for a convention. I believe I see her better now in relation to other affairs. She stands out clearly as different from them—how much I don't know. In the year I knew her she became associated in some way with almost every recess of my private self—and as you know I am prone to keep a good deal concealed. Moreover I emotionally reject the idea of her becoming disassociated. What bothers me, I think, is that I miss that intuitive immediate conviction which is so characteristic in intellectual matters with me. It is paradoxical that I should be so plodding and hesitant about such a purely emotional decision, and intuitive and fervent about intellectual convictions. I want the same experience in both. I am not committed yet, and I can't tell what will be the outcome. I am interested in finding out what your conceptions of three perfect mates for me turn out to be.

[deletion]

AHL: ALS

44. To Antonina Jones Hansell

GAINESVILLE, FL
NOVEMBER 7, 1937

[deletion]

E very letter of yours is another confirmation of my deep conviction that you have been elected by fate to serve as my special Oracle. You would doubtless find my eager scanning of those sage utterances rather touching—just as I am sometimes transfixed with a pang of guilt when I catch the hungry, eager eye of some freshman pinned upon me. No, really, Nina, I do treasure your counsel on some matters above all others. And I do so for a very adequate reason—because you know one part of me better than anyone, and not only that, but I know too that you are genuinely and unselfishly concerned for my well being. Does not the simple statement of those facts tell you how deeply grateful I am to you?

About the girl, I feel pretty much as I did when I wrote you last. I am perhaps no nearer to a definite decision, but now I feel inclined to leave the matter up to impulse.[116] Reason and rationalization have done about all there is to do in their particular sphere of influence—which, after all, is not all-inclusive. That means, you will say, that I have already decided. Perhaps I have. I don't know. On your advice I have become [illegible] to the dichotomy between intellectual convictions and emotional convictions. I suppose I was drawing a false analogy. It did have me puzzled however. What I feel to be her genuine love for me has done more than anything to deepen my feeling for her. If you will recall your Robert Briffault, you will understand the basis of this experience.[117]

One of my classes has become familiar with a certain authority referred to as "my friend, the elderly Jewish lady." So much respect do her opinions command, that I am afraid I have foisted upon her several opinions of which she is guiltless. That however, is merely an ancient pedagogical device, for which I make no apology—no more than did my worthy predecessors the Hebrew prophets when—confronted by an exasperating skepticism on the faces of men—they added a "Thus sayeth the Lord!"

[deletion]

AHL: ALS

45. To Glenn W. Rainey

GAINESVILLE, FL

JANUARY 10, 1937 [1938]

[deletion]

The Miami trip was perfect. Weather splendid, and we enjoyed it all. Drove back through central Florida to Gainesville, then to Charleston and on up. The proof reading took more time than I expected. The

---

116. He married six weeks later.

117. Robert Stephen Briffault (1876–1948), an English novelist and anthropologist, who wrote extensively on sexuality and marriage.

morning I finished it I put it on the floor and went out on the beach for several hours. Returning I missed the proof. A long & frantic search finally unearthed it along with the MS & two batches of page proof at the bottom of the Hotel ash can along with sundry cigarette butts, beer bottles, etc. The maid explained it looked like trash to her. I started to remonstrate but Glenn reminded me that one does not descend to caviling with one's critics. Better luck with subsequent critics maybe.
[deletion]

A surprise today from Beale. He said Allan Nevins looked him up at Philadelphia to discuss me. It turns out that Nevins, of all people, was the reader for Macmillan.[118] Beale is inclined to be effusive in such matters, but anyway he said Nevins was enthusiastic about the book—especially about my alleged "maturity," and is thinking about getting me to do a biography for his series on Oscar Underwood—God save the mark![119] I don't know what I would say to such a proposal, but that can wait till he makes it. But the surprising thing was that his recommendation should have sold the book—for if there was any one contemporary biographer that I had in mind in a measure 'answering' it was Nevins. And I was so fully expecting criticism from him & his school that I am a little dashed at being taken into his fold, and just a little resentful. Maybe I wasn't outspoken enough. He said some harsh things about Tom in a superficial way in his *Cleveland,* you know.[120]
[deletion]

GWR: ALS

118. Allan Nevins (1890–1971), formerly a journalist and, after 1931, DeWitt Clinton Professor of American History at Columbia University; he wrote very widely, was skeptical of a narrow professional historiography, and saw history as a narrative art. In 1949, he founded *American Heritage* magazine. CVW's later guardedly cool assessment of Nevins can be seen in the former's review of Ray Allen Billington, ed., *Allan Nevins on History* (New York: Scribner, 1975); CVW, "Allan Nevins: Defender of the Faith," *Reviews in American History* 4 (March 1976): 25–26.

119. Oscar W. Underwood (1862–1929), U.S. senator from Kentucky (1915–27), Democratic minority leader in the Senate (1920–23), and an unsuccessful contender for his party's presidential nomination in 1924.

120. "[Watson was] a voluble hothead who made political demagogy and the editorship of a Populist weekly pay well": Allan Nevins, *Grover Cleveland: A Study in Courage* (New York: Dodd, Mead, 1933), 594.

46. To Antonina Jones Hansell

GAINESVILLE, FL

JANUARY 12, 1938

[deletion]

Glenn returned to her job in Chapel Hill on the fourth and I to mine at Gainesville the same day. She feels obligated to finish up some work for which she is responsible and help train her successor. She will not join me here till March. I think that is just as well. I am terribly busy now finishing up proof-reading, (she is doing the Index) and I shall have to get another apartment. Then perhaps she realizes that I need even more gradual introduction to this annoying institution than I have enjoyed already. Never, never in the world could I have gone about it in the approved fashion—down the flower-strewn aisle after the tom toms of the journalists had announced & advertised the intended fornications up and down the land. She knows that, feels that way herself, and that is fortunate.

And what do I now think about my momentous step? As a matter of fact I have had no revelations, and expected none. It is still a hazardous experiment, and what will come of it I would not venture to guess. I rather suspect I shall always view the institution with a fishy & suspicious eye. If our venture goes awry, however, it will be my fault. Not hers. She is quite unselfish. I beg your blessing.

[deletion]

    AHL: ALS

47. To Andrew J. Walker

GAINESVILLE, FL

JANUARY 30, 1938

[deletion]

With your accustomed perspicacity you struck just the right note of warning in wishing me as much happiness as is "compatible with my temperament." Aye. I have taken precautions. Glenn has been converted to my radical pessimism, and shows real aptness as an apostle. We plighted our troth with the solemn vow that, with apologies to the story books, we will hereafter live together forever and ever in complete and unmitigated misery. Not to put our vow to too severe a test all at once, we parted company immediately after the honeymoon and therefore are grandly miserable—but not, it is true, together. We also grimly and bravely predicted to one another from time to time that as like as not she will have triplets every nine months and I shall wind up a Dean of Men ere my prime. With such precautions I think we shall manage to bear up under the slaps and stings of such plagues of happiness as fall our lot. Even then we shall have The Sorrows of Werther and Rousseau to console us.[121]

As a matter of fact I have scarcely had time to miss my bride since I returned—what with periodic inundations of proof and that sort of thing. Glenn was supposed to do the index, but she had to go and catch the flu, and left the index on my hands. I just finished it yesterday. And that, I hope, is the last of the Tom Watson job—aside, of course, from investing and managing the thousands upon thousands that the royalties will bring in. [deletion]

GWR: TLS

48. To Glenn W. Rainey

GAINESVILLE, FL
MARCH 9, 1937 [1938]

[deletion]

Macmillan sent me one advance copy of Tom last week. Without telling me anything of their plan they changed the jacket and binding entirely since making the dummy. I am tremendously pleased with those changes. The jacket is now much more attractive, done in yellow, gray, and black with a racy arrangement of the title and the picture of Tom. The binding is light gray with the title stamped in red and black, which I like much better than the green binding of the dummy. To tell the truth I was a bit determined about being pleased with that dummy, in somewhat the manner a parent is pleased with his offspring. But I have no reservations to make about the final product. It seems to me a handsome job and I could suggest no change that would improve its appearance. I fancy that I have myself prepared for the worst from the reviewers—even to be ignored. I don't care so much now that it is out. I already know the faults of the book. If you run across any clippings you think might inter-

---

121. Johann Wolfgang von Goethe, *Die Leiden Des Jungen Werthers* (Leipzig: Weygandschen Buchhandlung, 1774), the classic account of lovelorn youth.

est me please send them along. So far as I know the publishing date is still March 22.

Concerning the observations of your last letter on Tom and the Negro, I should say unequivocally yes and no, right and wrong. I would certainly agree with you about the appeal to the Negro in 1880 and 1882. However, I think I am justified in distinguishing the Watson of '90 from the Watson of '82. In the 'nineties Tom was, at least temporarily, deeply swayed by the radicalism of the national agrarian movement. He read widely, and was influenced by, labor literature, and sought to make allies of both labor and Western farmers—both of whom he was anxious to please on the race question. I don't see how you can read his article in the *Arena* and not be impressed by this.[122] It was precisely when he went reactionary on the race question in 1906 that Western Progressives and labor denounced him and he gave them up as allies. And it was because of this issue that Southern agrarianism, unlike Western agrarianism (under La Follette, Norris, etc.) became isolated and went reactionary.[123] I wish you would look up my article in the February issue of the Journal of Southern History and tell me what you think.[124] I should send you a reprint but I did not get any. You are probably right that I paint too glowing a picture of Tom's position on the Negro, but I don't think I am as far wrong as you say. I would like to know what Du Bois would say to the article and if I can get some reprints I shall send him one.[125]

[deletion]

GWR: TLS

122. Thomas E. Watson, "The Negro Question in the South," *Arena* 6 (October 1892): 540–50.

123. Robert Marion La Follette (1855–1925), Wisconsin progressive and governor who ran for president as an independent Progressive in 1924; George William Norris (1861–1944), U.S. senator from Nebraska (1913–43, until 1936 as a Republican and then as an independent Progressive), opponent of American entry into the First World War and a chief sponsor of the Tennessee Valley Authority.

124. CVW, "Tom Watson and the Negro in Agrarian Politics," *Journal of Southern History* 4 (February 1938): 14–33.

125. William Edward Burghardt Du Bois (1868–1963), the preeminent early twentieth-century black intellectual, who in 1938 was teaching at Atlanta University.

49. To W. E. B. Du Bois

GAINESVILLE, FL
APRIL 3, 1938

I am sending you a copy of an article of mine, "Tom Watson and the Negro in Agrarian Politics." It is written in a spirit that I hope you will approve, whether you can agree with my conclusions or not.

I have followed your work with interest and profit for a number of years. I should like especially to acknowledge my indebtedness for the insight which your admirable book, *Black Reconstruction,* provided me.[126] I visit Atlanta now and then, and I should like sometime to talk over a plan of research that I have in mind if I may come out to see you.

CVWP, 85/2: TLS

50. To Antonina Jones Hansell

GAINESVILLE, FL
APRIL 11, 1938

T hanks for writing me—no sooner, it's true, than you should have. But thanks just the same. I need to hear from you for you [to] remain in my mind, a permanent feature of my "frame of reference" and you will continue to you may be sure.

I think Glenn and I have done remarkably well in adjustments. The two months of separation soon after the marriage were a marvelously fortunate accident—more or less accident, that is. I did my adjustments, burned out my rebellion, and accepted the situation in her absence,—an extremely fortunate thing for both of us. She understands that, and, it is possible, planned it. I don't know. I think now that our future is brighter than I dared hope before our marriage.

Of course I am pleased over the reception of my book. I am not surprised that it is not understood. I did not expect it to be. The fact that it has been treated respectfully is at least encouraging. I am wondering if you received the copy I sent you some 2 or 3 weeks ago. Please let me know at once, for I had it insured. I want you to read it sometime and write me your reactions. I prize your opinion much.

[deletion]

AHL: ALS

126. W. E. B. Du Bois, *Black Reconstruction in America: An Essay Toward a History of the Part Which Black Folk Played in the Attempt to Reconstruct Democracy in America: 1860–1880* (New York: Harcourt, Brace, 1935).

51. To Glenn W. Rainey

GAINESVILLE, FL

APRIL 24, 1938

Judging from testimonials received my ability to please is exceeded only by Lydia E. Pinkham.[127] In the same mail last week, for instance I received notice that *Tom* was made an alternate choice for April by the Communist Book Union (book of the month club) and an effusive letter of congratulations from the Publicity Chairman of the Ga. Division of the United Daughters of the Confederacy. Match that combination if you can! After all you have only your Major Generals. Besides, my two most flattering reviews have come from the reactionary N.Y. *Herald-Tribune*, one in Lewis Gannett's daily column, and one in last Sunday's (April 17) book review section by Henry Commager.[128] I hope you will look up Commager's review. It is by all odds the best I have had, and, as I told you before, I value his opinion more than that of any of the reviewers. So far I have received three unfavorable reviews—and all three were from Massachusetts. Up the Rebels! Praise from such a source would have been dishonor!

Yesterday I went through the Macon ordeal. They took the event with apalling seriousness. Twenty score of elderly matrons, all aged 61 and spouses. Pretty awful. Elderly ladies always like me. I was congratulated for loyalty to the Confederacy. If only my Communist Book Union public does not hear of this. Miss Aken was swell and I saw John D. Allen. [deletion]

GWR: ALS

52. To Glenn W. Rainey

GAINESVILLE, FL

AUGUST 20, 1938

[deletion]

I don't believe I have any news of much moment. I have had some letters I would like to show you. A really fine one from John Donald Wade that I much appreciate. He confessed to "writhing" at one or two shots,

---

127. Lydia Estes Pinkham (1819–1883), whose "vegetable compound" was one of the most popular patent medicines of the nineteenth century and later; as was typical, its advertising contained many enthusiastic endorsements.

128. Lewis Gannett (1891–1966), literary critic and writer on sundry topics (John Steinbeck, Jack London, the First World War); Henry Steele Commager (1902–1998), a liberal and historian who taught at Columbia University (1936–56) and whose main publications by 1938

but soared above his prejudices to say some awfully kind things. Also Matthew Josephson wrote a most cordial letter, and we have struck up a correspondence.[129] And did you see Rupert Vance's article in the last *Southern Review?* It was quite good; "Rebels and Agrarians, All."[130] If my fame is not spread to the 4 corners it will not be the fault of the C.P. Rob Hall, secretary of the Miss. Ala., Ga. district of the party, and editor of the red magazine, *The New South* (sic!) at Birmingham, ran a couple of articles on the book. He turns out to be a former classmate at Columbia and a rather intelligent sort.[131] We have been corresponding a good deal. The other day he sent me a large four page broadside with headline in bold capitals: "IF TOM WATSON WERE ALIVE TODAY HOW WOULD HE VOTE ON SEPTEMBER 14?" With quotations from me to prove beyond doubt he would plump for the New Deal & Camp. It is signed "Georgia State Committee, Communist Party." They are scattering them over the state—much to the glee, I dare say, of Mr. George. The New Masses also ran a review—not especially enlightened. Of course the reds seize on Tom as an addition to their renovated hagiography—along with T. Jefferson, A. Lincoln, et al. to prove themselves more "American" than the American Legion. Did you [see] Maury Maverick's statement after his defeat comparing himself with Tom?[132] I think I'll write him.
[deletion]

GWR: TLS

---

were Henry Steele Commager, *Theodore Parker* (Boston: Little, Brown, 1936), and Samuel Eliot Morison and Henry Steele Commager, *The Growth of the American Republic* (New York: Oxford University Press, 1930), which had many subsequent editions.

129. Matthew Josephson (1899–1978), who wrote widely for left-wing journals in the 1930s and was then best known for *The Robber Barons: The Great American Capitalists, 1861–1901* (New York: Harcourt, Brace, 1934).

130. Rupert B. Vance, "Rebels and Agrarians All: Studies in One Party Politics," *Southern Review* 4 (Summer 1938): 26–44.

131. Robert F. Hall (1906–1993), who was born in Pascagoula, MS, but grew up in Alabama; he studied at Columbia University under Irwin Edman, the philosopher, and Rexwell Guy Tugwell, the economist; Hall joined the Communist Party in the mid–1930s and remained in it until 1956; early on, he was editor of the party's *Student Review* and, from the early 1940s, an assistant editor of the *Daily Worker.*

132. Maury Maverick (1895–1954) was a U.S. representative from Texas from 1935 to 1939; he had been a strong supporter of the New Deal, but was defeated in the Texas Democratic primary in 1938.

53. To Glenn W. Rainey

GAINESVILLE, FL
OCTOBER 2, 1938

[deletion]

Tom Wolfe's death caused me something nearer personal grief that anything since Ernest's death.[133] It was strange, since I had never even seen the fellow, but I realize now that I harbored a warmth of affection for him that I would for a personal friend. There is nothing so abundantly vital as he was left in the South. Did you notice that he died in Johns Hopkins hospital, where he described old Gant's horrible death, and recall that in describing it he said that he could vividly imagine himself dying there?[134]

I find a long four page letter from Maury Maverick waiting for me here. He said TOM fortified him for his defeat and that he now turned to it instead of the Bible for consolation. Said he went about making speeches on it, and other gratifying things. Also enclosed a nine page article he had written at the request of Sat. Rev. of Lit. under their suggested subject of "How to Read." His article contained a half page on that subject, roughly, and 8½ pages on Tom and H. Long.[135] He could not imagine, he wrote, obviously puzzled, why they didn't publish it! It is as harum-skarum as his "Maverick American"—which you should read.[136] Also in his letter he said some interesting things about how he was defeated. The article contained a rather surprising tribute to Huey. Anyway I'm for M. Maverick, and right hearty, too. (By the way, please read Jonathan Danial's article "Bread is Democracy" in the last Va. Quarterly Rev. and tell me what you think in detail.[137] Especially interesting for mention of Atlanta as fascist city, and for what seems to me profound observations on the hinterland.)

What should turn up this week but a letter from our favorite comic-

---

133. Thomas Wolfe (b. 1900) died in the Johns Hopkins Hospital, Baltimore, on September 15, 1938.

134. Oliver Gant, the alcoholic father of Eugene Gant, the protagonist of Thomas Wolfe, *Look Homeward, Angel* (New York: Charles Scribner's Sons, 1929).

135. Huey Pierce Long Jr. (1893–1935), the assassinated former governor of and U.S. senator from Louisiana.

136. Maury Maverick, *A Maverick American* (New York: Covici, Fiede, 1937).

137. Jonathan Daniels, "Democracy Is Bread," *Virginia Quarterly Review* 14 (August 1938): 481–90.

strip character Col. T. R.—Ben Turpin Spingarn—spectacles aglitter, still, with zeal for saving the recently emancipated race.[138] For a second time he proposes to return to alien corn and fight the good fight on enemy soil. It's really a pretty insidious strategy—as he intimates—pledging me to secrecy profound. It takes the innocent-appearing form of a two-weeks seminar on comparative criticism at Atlanta University. He would like to know (but ever so cautiously) if any of the Ga. Tech English faculty would be interested in sitting in on the seminar. It will be in January or February. I ran the risk of using the U.S. mails to inform him of your address!

I'll still stick to my "neo-Metternich era" to describe future prospects for Europe.[139] The present seems engaged in furnishing forth events to elaborate the analogy. We all but have the neo Quadruple Alliance now framed, a new concert of powers for the purpose of suppression. Except that it might turn out that Napoleon sits at the Hofburg of Vienna instead of Metternich. Tovarich Litvinov's phrase has the situation pat.[140] The atmosphere over Europe is as thick with "lies and hypocrisy" as with bombing planes. And historian James Truslow Adams publishes a book this week to the effect that "the English gentleman is the sort of man with whom you would like to go tiger hunting"—that is, I take it, if you didn't mind coming back inside the tiger, like everybody that tried it has, from the Manchurians to the Czechs.[141] By the way, if you feel like you rather need to lie down and laugh now, by all means try "With Malice toward Some."[142]

I pretty much missed a trick while I was away. A letter came the day after I left from the New Republic asking me to do them an article on the Agrarians, and then the day after I answered it three weeks later a letter from them said it was now too late. Please let me hear from you soon.

GWR: TLS

138. It is unclear who this is, but various members of the New York Jewish family the Spingarns were prominent in the NAACP.

139. Prince Klemens Wenzel von Metternich (1773–1859) was chancellor of the Austrian Empire for many decades after 1815 and a leader of European reactionary conservatism.

140. Maxim Maximovich Litvinov (1876–1951) was, in 1938, the People's Commissar for Foreign Affairs of the Soviet Union.

141. James Truslow Adams, *Building the British Empire* (New York: Charles Scribner's Sons, 1938), xiii.

142. Margaret Halsey, *With Malice Toward Some* (New York: Simon and Schuster, 1938), a satirical look at English society and its ways.

54. To Glenn W. Rainey

GAINESVILLE, FL

MARCH 26, 1939

[deletion]

The Debs venture has been laid aside for at least three years, perhaps longer. I had done considerable correspondence on the idea and had some fairly attractive promises of material. I finally became convinced that there was really nothing left of his private papers in the hands of the family. The rest of the material was of questionable value. At least I could not know its value till I had gone and examined it—in Milwaukee, New York, etc. The prospect seemed much too vague and unsettled to stake a year's leave of absence on the hope that I would find sufficient material. I therefore withdrew my application for fellowships from Rosenwald and Social Science Research Council with the idea of spending the summer assuring myself of sources.

Then came an invitation from Prof. Ramsdell of the Univ. of Texas asking me to agree to write volume nine, "The Origins of the New South" for the series, "The History of the South, 1607–1940" that he and Stephenson of LSU are editing.[143] The series is heavily subsidized by a foundation and promises to be something really good. There are ten volumes planned, 125,000 words each, with a stipend of $1,250 to the author of each volume. Rupert Vance is doing the last volume, "The Present South." The dates of my period are 1880–1913. Ben Kendrick had signed a contract to write volume nine, but backed out of it a couple of months after signing.[144] Then he, Odum and Vance urged me on the editors. Other authors in the series are, some of them, Avery Craven, Coulter (Reconstruction), Ramsdell, Abernathy of Va., Philip Davidson, Sydnor, (Duke).[145]

143. The History of the South series, funded by the Littlefield Fund for Southern History at the University of Texas and published by Louisiana State University Press, was first edited by Charles W. Ramsdell (1877–1942) of the University of Texas and Wendell Holmes Stephenson (1899–1970) of Louisiana State University.

144. Benjamin Burks Kendrick (1884–1946), who taught at the Women's College of the University of North Carolina, Greensboro, and who had published Benjamin Burks Kendrick and Alex Mathews Arnett, *The South Looks at Its Past* (Chapel Hill: University of North Carolina Press, 1935).

145. Ellis Merton Coulter (1890–1981), who taught at the University of Georgia and was among the most conservative of Southern historians; Thomas Perkins Abernethy (1890–1975) of the University of Virginia and a historian of the early American republic; Philip David-

It looked like too good an opportunity to sacrifice, especially since the Debs idea was still quite tentative and might prove impossible on further investigation. I really felt little hesitation about accepting the Ramsdell offer. I have already signed the contract which gives me three years in which to complete the job. After all I don't see how I could hope for a better chance of having my say on the period. From many viewpoints the period I drew is exceptional. The other periods have all been pretty frequently worked over, except Vance's, and that is too recent for history. Whereas there are scores of books and monographs on such periods as the Confederacy or Reconstruction, the New South period has hardly been opened to research. It seems to me then that there is a chance to lay down the main lines of interpretation and to do something fairly definitive rather than merely summarizing or condensing. Naturally, there is the other side of the coin. The fact that there has been so little published on the period means that the pick-and-shovel work is much vaster than that demanded by any other volume. That was the reason they gave me three years, and the others only two. The prospect is honestly pretty staggering, if I do the job with the thoroughness I should. There will be twelve states to work in the first place. It will be impossible to do the research here, of course. I plan to take at least one year off if I can get a grant from some foundation, and then work only half time another year if I can swing that. Glenn might go back to work. I need to make my headquarters near a good library and do considerable travel. This job is many times larger than the Watson book, and in some ways perhaps more important, if somewhat more academic. I think it is the plan to put out each volume on its own and to do an attractive piece of book-making on each volume. Still there is little likelihood of popular sales to any extent. For me I figure it is more important professionally than anything else I could write just now, and I know damned well that it is from teaching and not writing that I am going to have to make my living.

The New Republic has paid me generously for an article called "South Winds of Doctrine," but they have had it over a month and I don't know when if ever they are going to publish it.[146] I would like to

_____

son (1902–2000) of Agnes Scott College and later of Vanderbilt University, a historian of the American Revolution; Charles S. Sydnor (1898–1954), a historian of the antebellum South who taught at the University of Mississippi and (after 1936) Duke University.

   146. They never did.

know what you think of it if it ever appears. I also wrote an article for Pipkin which I think was too hot for him. Bruce Bliven and family were down on the east coast last month and Glenn and I had a pleasant stay with them.[147] I have also done some reviewing for him.[148]

[deletion]

> GWR: TLS

55. To Glenn W. Rainey

GAINESVILLE, FL

APRIL 23, 1939

[deletion]

Here are some of the lack-luster profundities that I would be dishing out on foreign affairs if I were taking your place as luncheon club pundit:—The ideological gulf between opposite camps in Europe is largely a fiction of columnists' invention. We fell for it in 1917. Why again? Wilson at least waited till the Kerensky revolution to advance the nonsense about saving "Democracy."[149] What excuse for such a fiction is there now? What kind of Democracy is that in Poland, Greece, Romania, Russia, etc., etc. And what kind of an alliance for the preservation of Democracy is there between England and France, that will sell out the Spanish Democracy and calmly desert Czechoslovakia, the last democracy in central Europe—and then bristle up in a frenzy of "Democratic" zeal for the preservation of the Polish dictatorship? And what was our experience in our recent experiment in following British orders in "Democratic" foreign policy in Spain? Well, aside from assisting Fascism into power in that country, we also generously ushered Germany into the North Atlantic and North Africa to create a new problem for the U.S. Navy; That may be good "Democratic" policy, but it damn sure is not good U.S. policy. And now describe if you can how "Democracy" is involved in the conflict between Italian and French policy. What is it in God's name but a disgusting squabble over the African loot of the last

147. Bruce Bliven (1889–1977) was editor in chief of the *New Republic* (1930–53).

148. CVW, review of Hugh Russell Fraser, *Democracy in the Making*, in *New Republic* 97 (4 January 1939): 265, and, soon to appear, CVW, review of Stanley F. Horn, *Invisible Empire: The Story of the Ku Klux Klan, 1866–1871*, in *New Republic* 99 (26 July 1939): 341–42.

149. Alexander Fyodorovich Kerensky (1881–1970), prime minister of Russia in the summer and autumn of 1917, after the February Revolution.

World War? And where is the moral issue involved? Who can take seriously the sanctity of the solemn "mandates" by which Britain gobbled up
whatever it was she wanted . . . Mr. Walter Hines Page Kennedy to the
contrary notwithstanding.[150] And if the Axis powers must be stopped to
preserve the balance of power in Europe, then why don't the opposing
powers stop them? They have all the advantages in men, resources, training, strategy, territory, and everything else they need. Moreover, it seems
somewhat oblique as a way of staying out of war to announce to the
world that if there is one we are going to intervene in it. There is nothing
divinely preordained about our intervention. If we intervene it will be
because of public opinion in the U.S., or at least an effective minority of
public opinion, *wants* us to intervene. I say it's time to begin talking down
that desire, and to quit talking about the "inevitability" of intervention. If
such a policy seems callous and "immoral" to the Reds or Mr. Kennedy
or Mr. Chamberlain or Miss Thompson, I say to hell with them.[151]

Now those are the things I think need to be said right now. I am not
even sure how much of it I believe myself. I am sure of my feelings against
the opposing policy, and of the need to counteract its rising tide just now.
From what you write I judge you would put this all down as isolationist
obscurantism, but maybe you agree with me more than I think.

I get a gratifying patontheback from Mary & Charles Beard in their
recent AMERICA IN MIDPASSAGE—a history of the period 1929–1939.[152]
Summer plans are to teach here first half and go to Chapel Hill the second half. Can't you come down to see us after your exams? Why not?

[handwritten postscript] I am glad you have set aside the summer
for the dissertation. I hope you will keep it set aside and go through with
the business. Have you seen the new *Journal of Politics* being published

150. Walter Hines Page (1855–1918), originally a North Carolina journalist, was American ambassador to Britain from 1913 to 1918 and very pro-British; Joseph Patrick Kennedy
(1888–1969) of Massachusetts was ambassador from 1938 to 1940 and rather anti-British.

151. Neville Chamberlain (1869–1940), who was prime minister of the United Kingdom
from May 1937 to May 1940. "Miss Thompson" is probably Dorothy Thompson (1893–1961),
the syndicated columnist.

152. Charles A. Beard and Mary Beard, *America in Midpassage* (New York: Macmillan,
1939), 917, has: "When the geography of ideas was taken into account, it was perhaps just to
say that the most fertile and penetrating historical writing of the midpassage was produced
by Southern investigators, such as F. L. Owsley, B. B. Kendrick, A. M. Arnett, D. D. Wallace,
Rupert Vance, and C. Vann Woodward, to make a selection." On the same page, CVW's *Tom
Watson* is singled out.

here. My friend Manning Dauer is Managing Editor and is doing a grand job.[153] Are you going to the Southern Asso. next Nov. at Knoxville?[154] I am supposed to read paper, but will back down if you don't go. Dauer will drive up & you can go with us.

GWR: TLS

56. To Charles W. Ramsdell

CHAPEL HILL, NC
AUGUST 30, 1939

I am sending you with this letter a tentative outline for the volume I am doing on the Origins of the New South. I wish to emphasize the word tentative. I am perfectly sure that I will decide on numerous changes in organization and content as the work progresses.

I am aware of certain gaps and deficiencies that perhaps you can help remedy. For one thing, I know very little about the Southwest during this period and consequently there is a gap in that regard. I would like to tell you my theory regarding social, cultural and intellectual history. You will notice that there are no separate chapters on such subjects as Education, Literature and Race Relations. My hope is that I shall find a way to integrate such subjects within the body and framework of the story as it progresses from beginning to end. I hope in that way to give such history more meaning than it would have in an isolated treatment. It might be, however, that I will find it necessary to resort to the topical treatment in some cases. I already feel that the chapter called "The New South Romanticism" is somewhat overcrowded.

I will appreciate whatever suggestions you and Professor Stephenson may have to offer. Mr. Vance and I have compared notes this summer and believe we have adjusted the division of our periods suitably. I have not corresponded with Professor Coulter, however, and would like very much to see his plan and to know if there are any possible conflicts.[155]

It is now my plan to make application for grants or fellowships that will enable me to be free from teaching during the academic year, 1940–

153. Manning Julian Dauer (1909–1987) taught political science at the University of Florida, where he and CVW became friends. Dauer later became an expert on Florida politics; among his works, however, the best known is *The Adams Federalists* (Baltimore, MD: Johns Hopkins Press, 1953).

154. That is, the Southern Political Science Association, which first met in Atlanta in 1929.

155. Coulter was writing the volume on Reconstruction in the same series.

1941. If this is possible I expect to spend the year at work on this volume. I rather expect to make application to three places: Rosenwald, Guggenheim, and the Hayes Foundation which is at the disposal of Mr. Garrison.[156] I understand the Guggenheim application will have to be in by early fall. I mention this matter because I should like to ask your help in supporting my various applications. May I use your name in this connection? I would also appreciate any suggestions you may make regarding the various foundations.

[deletion]

    CVWP, 70/102: TCLU

57. To Glenn W. Rainey

CHARLOTTESVILLE, VA

DECEMBER 10, 1939

[deletion]

I am at the stage of the Work in Progress where the future seems endless work and no progress. It really begins to look like somebody had set me bailing out the ocean with a sieve. And I was taken in by the prank. I am in need of a good deal of encouragement and stimulus, and there is no one here I can talk to about my work with any satisfaction. I have made my bows and scrapes to the foundation for next year. Something might possibly come from that direction, though I doubt it.

    Thanks for loyally reading my pronouncements. There is something else I would much like to have you see and write me about. It is an article by Donald Davidson, "The Class Approach to Southern Problems" in the current number of the *Southern Review*.[157] It is an answer to the article of mine on Nixon's book.[158] Davidson's article is about three times the

156. Curtis Wiswell Garrison (b. 1901), librarian and bibliographer, who ran the Hayes Memorial Library in Fremont, Ohio, which housed the presidential papers of Rutherford B. Hayes (1822–1893).

157. Donald Davidson, "The Class Approach to Southern Problems," *Southern Review* 5 (Autumn 1939): 261–72. Donald Grady Davidson (1893–1968), the poet and social critic, was, perhaps, the most conservative, aesthetically and politically, of the Southern Agrarians; by 1939, he had published *The Tall Men* (Boston: Houghton Mifflin, 1927); *Lee in the Mountains, and Other Poems, Including The Tall Men* (Boston: Houghton Mifflin, 1938); and *The Attack on Leviathan: Regionalism and Nationalism in the United States* (Chapel Hill: University of North Carolina Press, 1938).

158. CVW, "Hillbilly Realism," *Southern Review* 4 (Spring 1939): 676–81. Herman Clarence Nixon (1886–1967), a political scientist from Alabama, had been one of the contributors to *I'll*

length of mine—a broadside of formidable proportions, though not as scathing as he is capable of. We have had rather an interesting exchange of letters since his article appeared. He is an agile dialectician and a brilliant writer—to be so dead wrong—and so right about some matters. He admitted that it was a hard article to write and a distasteful job, since he is fond of Nixon. Anyway I would like to know your reactions to his article. Again, there is no one here to talk to.

In regard to your thesis I might mention a thesis written at Chapel Hill last year by Vernon Wharton, on the social history of the Negro in Mississippi from 1865 to 1890 that everyone said was especially good.[159] I understand it is to be published and I know he came to revolutionary conclusions regarding Reconstruction in Mississippi. You might keep an eye out for it.

Teaching American history for the first time is considerably more of a task than I intended for it to be. The sections are large (70 in one, 80 in the other) and classes have to be conducted on the straight lecture method. What time I have for research I use to fair advantage—which means reading one book after another—stack after stack of them, alternated by running through one periodical after another. I mark passages for copying, note them on the slip, and Glenn follows up by typing the notes. It looks like an endless job.

[deletion]

GWR: ALS

58. To Antonina Jones Hansell

CHARLOTTESVILLE, VA

OCTOBER 15, 1939

I am eager to know more about your novel. Nina, dear, you don't need to know a thing more than you know to write that book. Everybody writes about his family anyways, however he disguises the fact. As for the

---

Take My Stand but drifted more to the left than most of the others, as his participation in the Southern Conference for Human Welfare indicated; he had recently published Forty Acres and Steel Mules (Chapel Hill: University of North Carolina Press, 1938), of which "Hillbilly Realism" was a review.

159. Eventually published as Vernon Lane Wharton, The Negro in Mississippi, 1865–1890 (Chapel Hill: University of North Carolina Press, 1947).

history and sociology and implications—I believe novelists are the most cockeyed theorists in the world. Forget about Implications and stick to emotions—in which field I have long held you deeply versed and wise. Ellen Glasgow got her Social Implication together pretty well, but her novels are old fashioned of course.[160] She deals with much the same period you would treat.

I have no especial news about my marriage. In this case perhaps no news is the best news. The experience has been singularly lacking in soul-disturbing problems, complexes, maladjustments, or even an infidelity. I must be an exceptionally simple fellow—truth to tell—that is, compared with the majority of my masculine acquaintances. Take the one in Chapel Hill whom I had selected for you: he was married last Christmas and is already seeking a divorce. His second mishap, poor fellow. This time I feel pretty certain it was the woman's fault. You would have been just the one for him. There were five other divorces among my friends in Chapel Hill in one year, two of them swap-outs. I see nothing of the sort on our horizon. It has not been a very exciting or stimulating arrangement—and perhaps it should not be. Glenn fell into the feminine and submissive role naturally, and it seems to suit her. I had once fancied that such a fine fierce fellow as myself demanded a mate equally independent and bent on her own high destiny, which would cross mine only tangentially, and perhaps a bit casually. Maybe so. Maybe not. I guess one always wonders about such matters and never really knows.
[deletion]

AHL: TLS

59. To Glenn W. Rainey

CHARLOTTESVILLE, VA

OCTOBER 27, 1939

If it is any comfort to you, I have felt keenly my negligence in writing you. Especially in such a crucial time you should have been instructed in the correct view and proper information. It is encouraging, however, to find that you have not done so badly for yourself. Your words about Russia are almost verbatim those of my friend Manning Dauer. I share the notion myself, though I am not "valiantly defending her." That is, I

160. Ellen Anderson Gholson Glasgow (1873–1945), the Virginia novelist.

don't feel any enthusiasm for anything that is taking place on any of the three or four sides of the struggle abroad, except for the "phony" aspect complained of by Mr. Ford.[161] The phonier the better, says I. My disgust with Franklin D. has been whetted by his last two inspirations—I mean the Anglican Prayer together with posed portraits and the sermonizing of Ambassador Grew.[162] What can the man be up to?

I am delighted to hear that Nina McDonald looked you up and that you liked her. I hope you were able to cheer her up a bit. I heard from her a few weeks ago for the first time in a year, and she complains of a long siege of illness that struck her pretty low.

[deletion]

And how do I like Virginia? I haven't made up my mind yet. I know first of all I am completely seduced by the beauty of the place. It doesn't seem to pall on one. Only tonight when I walked through the lawn I completely yielded to its loveliness. As for the rest, I confess I am sometimes reminded of the stuffiness of Emory; though when I am, I lift up mine eyes to Monticello and reflect that these colonnades were not constructed on the proceeds of coca cola stock. Once again I am back to architecture, which surely cannot make a university, though it can do a damn lot to help. The primness and formality and smug traditionalism are pretty difficult to stomach. However, if traditionalism is your chief reliance, it would be hard to find better traditions. The people, a few of them, have been kind after their fashion. I find Lee, the editor of the Virginia Quarterly, an engaging fellow, though a bit back on his information.[163] No soulmates in sight on the faculty, certainly not on the history faculty. I have met few others.

[deletion]

GWR: TLS

161. Henry Ford (1863–1947), the automobile manufacturer, was a vocal opponent of the New Deal and a supporter of the America First Committee, an anti-interventionist and isolationist group.

162. Joseph Clark Grew (1880–1965), the American ambassador to Japan since 1932, gave a speech to the America-Japan Society in mid-October 1939; he advised the Japanese to change their foreign policy or else they would occasion American military and economic hostility.

163. Lawrence Lee (1903–1978) was a poet and editor of the *Virginia Quarterly Review* (1938–42); see *Monticello and Other Poems* (New York: Charles Scribner's Sons, 1937).

60. To Donald Davidson

CHARLOTTESVILLE, VA
NOVEMBER 15, 1939

This is not the first time I have had an impulse to write to you. It is merely the first time I have been unable to get the better of the impulse. Then, too, I felt that your article in the Southern Review (excellent, I thought) might have originated in an impulse to write me a letter of—shall I say, remonstrance. My little review was too frail a craft to call forth, or for that matter, to withstand, such a broadside.[164] I'll have to report "*spurlos versunkt,*" I'm afraid.[165]

I do want to thank you for your friendliness of tone and your generous compliments. If my remarks seemed unfriendly they were not so intended. No, you gentlemen won my heart long ago—It's only my head that remains hard—and maybe dense. This division may account for the "confusion" you find in my ideas. I was delighted to learn that you liked my book on Tom. But when I try to express what I fancied were the same notions in abstract language you'll have none of them. Maybe the moral is I should stick to my last and let who will do the theorizing. I'll be content to earn your "A" on my history.

I quite deserved the reprimand for that wicked quotation and I apologize. But that remark was made by a fellow Arkansan, and it has festered under my skin a long time. It had to come out! Also, I agree with you about the "great magnolia stink," but call on Mr. Nixon to share the blame.[166] Now, will you reciprocate by withdrawing the Marxian stink? That ought to be a fair swap.

Aside from these small matters I do think that you emphasized properly one real and important point of dispute—not merely between us—

164. CVW, "America on the Way," *Virginia Quarterly Review* 15 (Autumn 1939): 632–36; this was a review of the Beards' *America at Midpassage*, plus Howard W. Odum, *American Social Problems: An Introduction to the Study of the People and Their Dilemmas* (New York: Henry Holt, 1939) and *These Are Our Lives: As Told by the People and Written by Members of the Federal Writers' Project of the Works Progress Administration in North Carolina, Tennessee, and Georgia* (Chapel Hill: University of North Carolina Press, 1939).

165. "Spurlos versankt" means "sunk without trace" in German.

166. "Magnolia stink" is Davidson's phrase: "Nowhere in *I'll Take My Stand* or in later discussions have any of the 'agarians' envisioned 'a charming agarian past of the golden age.' That great magnolia stink is of hoary antiquity. Its sentimental history runs at least as far back as *Uncle Tom's Cabin*": Davidson, "Class Approach," 264.

but between schools of thought in the South. It took no labor on my part to "dissociate" Mr. Nixon from you on that point. There is a real difference. Also, that may be a corner of the old flag you spot sticking out of Ben Kendrick's pocket. If it is, that doesn't diminish my affections for Dr. Ben one bit. But I took it for an old bandana—the same honest rag that Mr. Owsley spotted on Mr. Nixon, but appears to have mistaken for a Rooshun hammer and sickle! (Please remonstrate with Mr. Owsley about that.)[167]

I too would like to see these differences honestly aired, without any name-calling and debaters' tricks. I too claim to be Jeffersonian, and maybe our differences are not so great as we think. My notion that the democratic classes in the South should combine in politics with the same classes in other sections seems to me thoroughly Jeffersonian. What else did Jefferson preach in organizing to overthrow the Federalists North and South? Maybe I am too much preoccupied with my Populists, as you say, but they still seem to me to follow the Jeffersonian tradition.

This may be my only means of answering the questions you raised. However, back last January the New Republic sent me your *Attack on Leviathan* asking me to make it the basis of an article. I hesitated, knowing your feelings about the journal, and preferring to keep the sport intramural. I wrote something, however, reflecting that otherwise the book—which I respect highly—might fall into the hands of some vicious ignoramus. I later received proof on the article, but it has never appeared and maybe never will. For one thing I devoted about a third of it to what I considered a conscientious attempt at setting forth your thesis, another page to my agreements with you—with a crack at the New Republic on my own part—and the rest to argument. Consequently it may never see light; and [p]erhaps that is all to the good.

I believe all this might have gone better over the glasses, and I hope some day we may talk it over.

CVWP, 14/153: TCLU

167. Frank Lawrence Owsley (1890–1956), a Southern historian from Alabama and among the most conservative and anti-Communist of the Southern Agrarians; he was then teaching at Vanderbilt University.

61. To Hunter D. Farish[168]

CHARLOTTESVILLE, VA

FEBRUARY 5, 1940

A friend of mine who has read my tentative outline for a study of the New South period has made a suggestion that strikes me as a good one. He points out that if I am going to make the hillbilly and the cracker understandable, I must not neglect his religion. The hillbilly's religion, like his politics, has left few memorials and documents. Can you make any suggestions about sources for such sects as the Holy Rollers, Foot Washers, Holiness people, Jehovah's Witnesses, and sundry other "come to Jesus" movements in the South? I must confess that I am stumped completely, yet it is something interesting that I don't want to neglect. It occurred to me that you might have run across something of that sort. [deletion]

CVWP, 17/201: TCLU

62. To Manning J. Dauer

CHARLOTTESVILLE, VA

MARCH 22, 1940

Your excellent dissertation in answer to my own reached me just as I was leaving with Glenn for a trip to Greensboro. After our return exams were on me and I have been pretty busy since then. Incidentally, we bought a second-hand Ford again, a '38 model this time, that appears to be in excellent condition and shines with a most splendiferous shininess.

By all means send me "The Political Economy of John Adams," and tell me what you are writing it for—I mean, a book chapter or a long essay for a learned journal.

I sent your criticisms of Owsley's article and his review of Shugg's book to Shugg, with whom I have been in correspondence.[169] I have been

---

168. Hunter Dickinson Farish (1897–1945), director of the Department of Research at Colonial Williamsburg; he was an expert on Southern religion. See, especially, *The Circuit Rider Dismounts: A Social History of Southern Methodism, 1865–1900* (Richmond, VA: Dietz Press, 1938).

169. The article was Frank L. Owsley and Harriet C. Owsley, "The Economic Basis of Society in the Late Ante-Bellum South," *Journal of Southern History* 6 (February 1940): 24–45, and Owsley's review of Roger W. Shugg, *Origins of Class Struggle in Louisiana: A Social History of White Farmers and Laborers During Slavery and After, 1840–1875* (Baton Rouge: Louisiana State University Press, 1939), in *Journal of Southern History* 6 (February 1940): 116–17. Roger Wallace

in hopes that I would hear from him and could give you his reactions, but he has not yet written. I am innocent on the score of the De Bow census of 1850.[170] Accepting your information about it, however, I certainly agree with you about your criticism. One matter, however, which neither you nor Bill took up was Owsley's figures to establish that land ownership was strikingly increasing among non-slaveholding farmers between 1850 and 1860.[171] That seems to me perhaps the most important of his points and I am at a loss as to how to answer it. Do you accept it or what do you have to say about it?

As for my effusions on the non-rational in history: back of them is my puzzlement in grappling with the race question in the period I am working on. The further I go the larger this enigma looms. It is interwoven with every editorial, every production factor, every speech and letter that I run across. In my interpretation of the race factor in Populism, I was able to relegate it satisfactorily in my own mind to a conventional economic interpretation. It may be that race factors will fall into that pattern for the earlier and later periods if I get deeper enough under the surface. Just now, however, they seem elusive, tortuous, and emphatically non-rational. Sex phobias crop up continually and in the most unexpected places, whole classes sway under race prejudices in flagrant contradiction to their economic interest. Maybe it would be possible to cram all these riots, hysteria, and phobias into a neat rational economic pattern, but at present the cramming would seem to do violence to plain fact.

CVWP, 15/165: TCLU

Shugg (1905–1993), then in the Department of History at Princeton, later worked for Alfred A. Knopf and, in 1954, became director of the University of Chicago Press.

170. James Dunwoody Brownson De Bow (1820–1867), the antebellum Southern economist and editor of *De Bow's Review*, was in charge of the 1850 U.S. census.

171. "Bill" is William Graves Carleton (1901–1982), a lifelong friend of CVW; he taught history and political science at the University of Florida from 1926 to 1962, when he decided to become a freelance author and lecturer. He came from Evansville, IN, and received his M.A. from Indiana University in 1934, after having earned a J.D. from the College of Law in Gainesville in 1931. He wrote eclectically, but was mostly interested in foreign policy; his main works include *The Revolution in American Foreign Policy, 1945–1954* (Garden City, NY: Doubleday, 1954) and *Technology and Humanism: Some Exploratory Essays for Our Time* (Nashville: Vanderbilt University Press, 1970). He was a popular and charismatic speaker both on and off campus, and known as "Wild Bill" to his students.

63. To Roger W. Shugg

WASHINGTON, DC

AUGUST 11, 1940

I have read and re-read your fine letter and shall read it again in the future. It leaves me indebted to you for many things. You undoubtedly know how important it is to keep one's faith in the importance of what he is doing from slipping, and how difficult it is during such times as these. Your good words would offer sturdy props to anybody's faith and I am especially grateful for them.

You put your hand unerringly on my major problem of organization—that of form versus content. Some of the multiplicity of subjects you mention can I justify myself in omitting. Yet you are quite justified in replying that the framework of my outline is not at present stout enough to support all of these additions. I am determined on one rule. That is that my final object is construction, not merely gathering material. I want something that resembles an architectural unity when I finish, yet I cannot justify a blueprint that does not provide enough roofage to house the things for which the structure is being built. It might be that I will have to end by taking on a few unsightly wings and lean-toes labeled "fertilizer and roads" or "migration, diet and mortality." This would certainly not improve the appearance of the structure, but there is something to be said for getting all the people under the roof. Still I do not believe that I have exhausted all the possibilities of integration that might avoid the necessity for unintegrated outhouses. I have already realized the necessity of considerable shifts of emphasis in the outline you criticized. The dominant unifying theme, however, still seems to me to be the struggle between populistic and Bourbon or agrarian and capitalist forces. I hope I am not stretching this theme too far. Many of your suggestions were quite fresh and revealing to me. That, for example, on the economic parallel to the South's demand for political laissez-faire, together with the sources suggested. Your suggestions about religious sects and social implications reveal one of the many weaknesses in my blueprint. I am aghast, too, at the problem of treating such things as the prohibition crusade which, if treated in the proportion to which it engrossed the interest of millions of southerners, would loom up largely in the book. These reflections and your letter indicating what an intelligent and informed critic will reasonably expect of my book are somewhat staggering. Remember me in your prayers!

I was much interested in your comments on Dauer's criticism of Owsley. I showed them to both Dauer and Beale who were in a mood for issuing pronunciamentos for your vindication. The three of us have looked forward weekly to your long postponed arrival in Washington. Beale has left for Vermont, but Dauer and I are still holding out hopes. I am leaving on August 25 for Claremont, California, to take the Scripps job. May I hope to see you before then? I have arranged for a semester's leave from the job beginning February 1st, after which I shall return East, making my headquarters for the most part in Washington. I hope we can at least get together during that time.

It was awfully kind of you to tell me of the use of Tom Watson in the Dabney course.[172] Naturally it made me feel very good. And thank you again for your splendid letter.

CVWP, 50/589: TCLU

64. To William G. Carleton

[CLAREMONT, CA]
OCTOBER 15, 1940

Your letter from the homeland was as welcome as ever one could be to immigrants to a strange and far country. It almost made me forgive your unforgivable passing us by at Washington this summer. That was a bitter disappointment to us both and we will expect a very long visit indeed in compensation next summer. I hope our meeting will be possible before you are an unfrocked scholar and have taken the cloth of a dean. My frivolous prediction about the fate of both you and Dauer would seem to have overtaken you in the very prime of your years. I shall not abandon you to deandom until after earnest prayers with you.

I feel impelled to unburden myself of this place, and that before I am sure just what my impressions are. There must be a sort of puritanism of poverty to which I am addicted and you will discount much for that. Take my classroom, for instance. It opens out into a balcony overlooking a palm-shaded patio in the center of which a fountain rises in the midst of a blue pool. A window looks out on peaks of the Sierra Madre mountains.

172. Virginius Dabney (1901–1995), editor of the *Richmond Times-Dispatch* (1936–1969) and author of *Liberalism in the South* (Chapel Hill: University of North Carolina Press, 1932), had been asked to teach a course on the New South at Princeton when Thomas Jefferson Wertenbaker (1879–1966), the colonial historian, went on leave.

The students sit around a long polished mahogany table in handsomely upholstered chairs. Woodward at one end squirms like a roundhead at high mass. The president showed signs of wanting to assign me to an office, that of my late predecessor Stephenson, kept as a sort of memorial to the gentleman.[173] It represents, roughly, a sixteenth century Spanish refectory, baroque fireplace, a mantelpiece at the end, mahogany tables, red leather chairs. I rebelled and was assigned more modest quarters with my colleagues on the third floor, quarters that would do justice to the waiting room of an expensive dentist. For all my squirming, I am first to admit that the place is as beautiful as a place could well be, and mostly in good taste. After a few days I was relieved to notice that the girls were not beautiful and that every face was a small replica of the general run of faces I have faced across any desk in Georgia, Florida or Virginia. You know my sensitiveness to snobbery, yet I have still to find any of it among the students. Either I have been lucky in my classes, or the level of intelligence and preparation is distinctly higher here than any I have run across. They are also more docile than any, but that might be because they are women, I don't know. I have one girl working on Veblen who has as keen an interest and good a background as any student I have ever had.[174] The change in the size of classes amounts almost to a change in one's profession—one has fourteen, the other eight. These are considered normal size. Then I direct a couple of individual reading courses and a couple of senior theses. I am also on the third-year Humanities staff. All the comprehensive courses of Florida along such lines are grouped as Humanities here and run through three years of required work. Sciences are minimized. Treatment is chronological, the third year being 18th century to the present. Reading is all in sources, none in text, thus Fielding, Voltaire, Rousseau, Kant, Herder, Adam Smith, Goethe, Jefferson, etc., knowledge of French taken for granted. I have yet to make up my mind about the course. There are only thirty odd students in the whole junior class.

The director of the Humanities staff, with whom I work closely, is a German exile for ten years professor of social philosophy at Heidelberg,

173. Ernest J. Jaqua (1882–1972), the first president of Scripps College (1927–1942); Nathaniel Wright Stephenson (1867–1935), historian and author of various works on Lincoln, the Confederacy, the Mexican War, and Nelson Aldrich; see Ward Ritchie, *In Memoriam Nathaniel Wright Stephenson* (Claremont, CA: Scripps College, 1935).

174. Thorstein B. Veblen (1857–1929), the economist and social critic, best known for *The Theory of the Leisure Class: An Economic Study in the Evolution of Institutions* (New York: Macmillan, 1899).

a scholar in the finest humanist tradition, with a learning that makes me feel undergraduate; and he is the most congenial company and the best mind I have found on the campus.[175] He is south German and utterly un-Prussian, tough from years of battles with his hoodlum compatriots, and seasoned with a stoicism and invaluable sense of humor which is the reason he has not gone mad long ago. His name is Bergstraesser. There is another German, an attractive and angelic youngster named Caspari, who instead of Bergstraesser's toughness is afflicted by what Bergstraesser calls his damned gentleman's education of a doctor's degree at Oxford.[176]

These men are under constant suspicion by local flagwavers, snoopers and war mongers, and as a result I see myself plunged into factions almost at once. Manning's puritan friend is the chief witch-hunter, a bigot and a man of impervious stupidity. How I will be able to get along with him at all is difficult to see. It's plain that the witch-hunting will increase in intensity in the next months. Can the madness be as consuming in the East as it is here? There is nothing especially remarkable about the rest of the faculty. They all seem eager to be friendly and I like most of them. The President seems to be a man to be depended on and is keeping his senses in the midst of the local hysteria so far. The political situation of my German friends is that they are not only spied upon by the patriots but watched by the Nazi consul, and have given up hope of ever returning to Germany. Bergstraesser has heard rumors that he is receiving at night a messenger from the Mexican border, that he is correspond-

175. Arnold Bergsträsser (1896–1964), was a cultural historian and sociologist who had studied at Heidelberg with Max Weber, later taught at the University of Chicago, and returned to Germany in 1954 to assume a chair at Freiburg, where there is now an institute named for him. He wrote widely on humanist culture, nationalism, the state, and Goethe.

176. Fritz Wilhelm Eduard Carl Caspari (1914–2010), partly educated at Heidelberg and St. John's College, Oxford (1933–36), where he studied economics and modern history, but only as an undergraduate. (So he did not have an Oxford D.Phil.) As a Rhodes scholar Caspari was a contemporary of the Arkansas novelist Charles Pendleton Lee (1913–1978), a connection that led both to teach (1936–37) at Southwestern College in Memphis, TN, after which Caspari returned to Hamburg to begin a doctorate; he became an émigré in 1939, not because he was Jewish but because he disapproved of Nazism. After Pearl Harbor he was twice briefly interned by the American authorities as an enemy alien. In 1943, he went to work at the Newberry Library, then in 1946 to the University of Chicago, where he taught German language and history. In 1954, he returned to West Germany and joined the Foreign Service, in which he was to hold several high offices; he received an honorary knighthood from Elizabeth II in 1972.

ing secretly by radio with Nazi agents, that he is a Nazi fifth-columnist, and was thrown out of Germany as a communist—and the man can still laugh!

Thanks many times for sending the syllabus.[177] I had been eager to see it ever since Manning told me that you had taken time off to do a finished job. Unfortunately you forgot to mark the chapters in the Table of Contents that you wanted me to read, as you said you would do. I want to read it more carefully, but my general impressions I can mention. It seems to me the sort of thing I wanted all the time I was at Florida. I guess that given the assignment of mass production education, wholesale methods, a staff of spotty caliber, that your job represents the best that any man could do and better than any man I know would have the imagination and energy to do. Of course you will recall my often-expressed despair at the possibility of doing the job at all under the circumstances. Your chapters on party history seem to me the best in print. They will be stolen unless you copyright them I predict, and I wish you would make them the core of a political science textbook that ought to make you rich. I watched especially for over-simplification and the fallacy of abstract generalization. I think they have been neatly and plainly avoided by your introduction 'Word of Caution' and summary. But then you will turn around and defeat your purpose by turning out reams of those slot-machine exam questions which are nothing but high-pressure drill and mechanical dogmatism slipshod guess work, of course that is not your fault. It is the stretch-out and assembly belt. I wonder, too, about the embarrassment of the lecturer who in effect has to repeat the textbook that is before the students, and the discussion leader who has to do it again. But I realize the toughness of your problem and I am amazed at the deftness with which you handled it. Will you do something for me? Please ask Minna Dunn to mail me a copy of the Humanities syllabus and send me a bill for it, or at least for the postage.

I am already looking forward to getting back to research the first of February. A brief look around at the libraries leads me to the belief that I will simply have to do the work in the East. Avery Craven has agreed to come out here for the second semester to take over my courses while I am away, only he wants to teach the Old South instead of continuing my

177. The American Institutions (C-1) curriculum at the University of Florida, of which Carleton was the chief designer: see William G. Carleton, *Free Lancing Through the Century: A Memoir* (Gainesville, FL: Carleton House, 1988), 98–100.

course in modern history. I don't think the administration will approve of that idea.

It's late and these are only a few of the hundreds of things I have thought of writing you during the past month. I will try to get a few more of them on paper if you will write me again.

CVWP, 11/114: TCLU

65. To Rupert B. Vance

CLAREMONT, CA

NOVEMBER 16, 1940

It was downright tough luck, my missing you in Morrilton by a few hours. If we could only have counted on your coming that day, but your mother was not sure about your arrival and we had a couple thousand miles ahead of us. The trip across Arkansas was my first return since I left there thirteen years ago. We bumped over an unpaved road from Memphis, through those desolate bottoms through Earle, and across the St. Francis and on into Cross County to Wynne to look up places I had not seen since I was aged 10, and then out to Vanndale on a sentimental journey. I suppose you know the experience of the view through the wrong end of the telescope that such impressions leave. Then on across the God forsaken stretch through back roads from Wynne to Morrilton. It was rather like reading one's own biography. You mention John Gould Fletch[178]—have you run across a little novel by one C. P. Lee, called "The Unwilling Journey"?[179] It is our Arkansas biographies to age 15, and I recommend it. He grew up in the cotton country in the backwoods on the Arkansas River out of Pine Bluff. It is a quiet and unpretentious but accurate and fairly penetrating book for a youngster. No Sturm und Drang of the Wolfian romantics, no Poe-esque horror of the Faulkners—the boy remembers that he is writing about Arkansas. He has another one coming out shortly.[180]

---

178. John Gould Fletcher (1886–1950), the Arkansas poet and author; he came from a wealthy Little Rock family, attended Harvard, and then spent several decades in London, where he was (for a while) a friend and ally of Ezra Pound. He contributed an essay on education to *I'll Take My Stand*, but quickly fell out with most of the Agrarians. He returned to live in Arkansas in 1931 and later wrote his state's history; his *Selected Poems* (New York: Farrar & Rinehart, 1938) won the Pulitzer Prize.

179. C. P. Lee, *The Unwilling Journey* (New York: Macmillan, 1940).

180. C. P. Lee, *High Noon* (New York: Macmillan, 1943).

I was surprised that I had not written you about the Scripps business. I had a long correspondence with Odum about it and thought that I had corresponded with you also. It turns out to be a beautiful place and an especially good school. My first experience at teaching in a small college, and I begin to realize why people don't write books who teach. It is another thing entirely from the University life, and it doesn't seem to go much with scholarly work of the research sort. I am to get a semester's leave of absence beginning the first of February when I am to go back to work on the book, traveling through Texas and Louisiana for some research, and on up through Georgia and North Carolina on to Washington where I expect to make my headquarters from about March 1st to September 1st. My hope is to wind up the necessary Eastern materials during those months. That will leave the dirty business of writing for later, and it doesn't seem likely that I will do any of it while teaching.

What about taking time to write me a little about your own doings and feelings? I mean something more than the annual note done between classes. I need some word of cheer from the home country and nobody could give it better than yourself.

CVWP, 57/684: TCLU

66. To Esmond Wright[181]

[CLAREMONT, CA]
DECEMBER 1, 1940

[deletion]

What you write concerning the sacred cows of American research and scholarship is just the sort of thing we should have thrashed out over many a glass of beer. I am the loser there and curse myself again for missing the opportunity. I must add, however, that in Professor Abernethy you happened upon a rather extreme example of the "research for research's sake" school, but again I must admit that he is by no means unique. Some of the young American scholars are going to have to stage a deliberate revolt from this academic Philistinism or our scholarship will lapse into an untimely dotage.

181. Esmond Wright (1915–2003) was a British scholar of American history; he held a Commonwealth Fellowship at the University of Virginia (1938–40), where he met CVW; Wright was later Professor of Modern History at the University of Glasgow (1957–67) and Conservative M.P. for Pollock, Glasgow (1967–70).

Your remarks on the wartime political situation in England interest me profoundly and confirm certain suspicions that have been growing in me upon the English propaganda. Everything we get here from England puts great stress upon the prominence of labor in the new government, and one is always running across references to "the leveling effect of the crisis" and "the groundswell of democracy," the revolutionary camaraderie between estranged classes. We are given to understand that a great silent revolution has taken place with the usual British decorum and that the bomb cellar has become a melting pot for class snobbery. Listening to the English platform propagandists, one gets the impression, subtly conveyed, that Mayfair has embraced a shirt-sleeve frontier democracy that puts to shame the American brand. One is already regarded as something of a Nazi if he professes any skepticism at democratic England. So you see it was refreshing to get your views on the subject. It must be conceded that British propaganda has been very effective, and I have seen remarkable changes worked on public opinion since last summer even. On the matter of the class-ridden society, if you have the opportunity, I wish you would read a chapter in Thomas Wolfe's new novel *You Can't Go Home Again,* called "The Universe of Daisy Purvis." Tell me if that attitude [bottom of page missing] and if it is as purposely ineradicable as [bottom of page missing] Coventry type of bombing which has been adopted since your last letter was written. Accounts of it here sound pretty distressing. They sound as if the effect is something more tangible than psychological.

I don't know what type of American political news I can give you that you do not have. I feel somewhat reassured over the New Deal victory for a third term, though it is hard to fathom the real significance of it. Undoubtedly, it seems to me that without the international crisis Roosevelt would not have run, and if he had run, would have been defeated. Whether another candidate would have been successful on a New Deal platform or not is extremely doubtful. The tide of reaction was deep running and strong. Among the upper crust and the wavering intellectuals I find that the intellectual temper is strongly conducive to an American brand of fascism. It seems to me that the New Deal has spent its force for domestic reform and will be largely preoccupied with foreign issues and war preparation, if not actual military adventures. A way out for economic embarrassments will be sought probably in high pressure militarism. While American industry, complete geared as it is to England's war economy, will be more and more dependent on military economy both abroad and at home. This relationship returns us to the situation of the American economy in 1914–1917. Under the exigencies of these compulsions, it seems to me, the Johnson Act and the Neutrality Act are headed for limbo and our last defenses against involvement in the chaos will be broken down.

[deletion]

CVWP, 60/736: TCLU

67. To Howard K. Beale

CLAREMONT, CA

DECEMBER [15?], 1940

Your good and generous soul never prompted you to do a more charitable and appreciated thing than to write me such a long letter. We both greedily read all of the detailed calendar of events and people and tea parties that only your diary-like mind could possibly chronicle. If you had deliberately set out to draft a document to inspire homesickness, however, you could hardly have done better. All the people and places and the issues and the fights are familiar and sound like home, though I know that I would probably get as bored and angry and resentful with them as I could when I was at home. In spite of that both of us recognize that Chapel Hill is "home" and probably always will be, and that consequently there is no place like it for better or worse.

Thank you especially for telling me about the Charleston meeting.[182] I always enjoy them and particularly regretted missing this one and can't help hoping that I was missed. Were Tom Govan and Gerald Johnson there?[183] I want to remind you urgently that you neglected to send me the letter from Owsley that you promised to send, the one that you said re-

182. The sixth annual meeting of the Southern Historical Association, 7–9 November 1940; it was based at the Francis Marion Hotel and was attended by 279 people; the presidential address was given by Frank Owsley: see "The Fundamental Cause of the Civil War: Egocentric Sectionalism," *Journal of Southern History* 7 (February 1941): 3–18.

183. Thomas Payne Govan (1907–1979) was then professor of history at the University of the South; he had done a doctoral thesis at Vanderbilt University on "Banking and the Credit System in Georgia, 1810–1860" and would later write a biography of Nicholas Biddle; Gerald W. Johnson (1890–1980) had taught journalism in Chapel Hill in the early 1920s, and in 1926, at the invitation of H. L. Mencken, joined the editorial staff of the *Baltimore Evening Sun*, where he remained for the rest of his career; he was a leading Southern liberal.

vealed that "these people are going to get me." I am especially interested
in seeing what he said. Thank you also for sending me the instructions
you wrote to the panel on Southern Demagogues. I want to beg you to
write me one of your most informing chronicles on your session and also
on the convention as a whole—whom you saw and what they said. If
Louis Hacker calls a meeting of the group on the Beard book and I am
asked about, you might say that I am still to be counted upon.[184] I want
to talk to you about that problem when I see you. President Jaqua intends
to be there during one of his fortnightly transcontinental flights. By the
way, he is looking for a medievalist and possibly a man in English history,
also a professor of French literature, not to mention a musician and lecturer on music. If you have any friends in mind whom I know and whom
you would like to push, please tell me and I will approach Jaqua about
them. Also a friend of mine from here, young Fritz Caspari, instructor
in German and history, will be at the convention. You would enjoy him I
think. I resent bitterly not being able to take the trip myself, but it is out of
the question. I intend to go to San Francisco to attend the Pacific Coast
branch meeting. I have been to a couple of informal sessions of the local
guild of historians from the Los Angeles-Southern California region and
must admit that I have not been particularly impressed and found few
congenial spirits. Do you know any American historians in this vicinity?

A few trips to Huntington Library have been made with indifferent
results. Louis Wright, formerly of Chapel Hill and a research director of
Huntington, was very kind but we were unable to unearth a great deal of
material of my interest.[185] There is one large collection of Virginia manuscript, mostly ante-bellum, but that is all. The Southern newspapers in
southern California are a negligible quantity so that I will have to do all
of that work, which is the great bulk of my work, in the East and South.
That is also true for the periodicals, except for the scholarly journals of
course. I am fighting a haunting suspicion that I have disastrously length-
ened my supply lines in pushing this campaign to the West Coast. Much

184. Howard Beale, Merle Curti, Eric F. Goldman, and others were planning a sort of
Festschrift to honor the contribution and influence of Charles A. Beard (1874–1948), one of
the preeminent progressive historians and an important influence on CVW. Louis M. Hacker
(1899–1987) had been mentored by Beard at Columbia University and later (1935–51) taught at
the same university. This volume was to appear only after Beard's death: see Howard K. Beale,
ed., *Charles A. Beard: An Appraisal* (Lexington: University of Kentucky Press, 1954).

185. Louis B. Wright (1899–1984), who was a colonial American historian.

will depend on what I can get done during my semester's leave beginning in February.

I am enjoying the outrageous good fortune of an additional two weeks' vacation from teaching. Last Friday, December 6, the "flu" epidemic reached such proportions that the administration suspended classes in both Scripps and Pomona until December 2. I am now paying through the nose for a gleeful celebration of the flu epidemic. I am practically down with a minor touch of it or a heavy cold myself, dripping from eyes and nose. It doesn't put one in a happy mood to write letters or do anything else and please take account of that when reading this. Glenn and I have become better acquainted and better acclimated since I last wrote you. We find a number of congenial, if quite casual acquaintances and friends, especially among the younger group—in fact almost entirely among the younger people. I have cultivated and enjoyed my relations with some of the older ones, however, though probably not as much as I should have. The Scripps faculty is at the moment in a transitional period, a matter more for rejoicing than not. Its original faculty, grouped around a number of old wheelhorses with important names that they had earned sometime before, like Nathaniel Wright Stephenson, Hartley Burr Alexander, and a couple of others not so prominent.[186] The named have died, a third is leaving next year, a fourth is retiring and a fifth is to retire soon. I hope this turn-over will bring in some young and congenial men. Jaqua, however, has a weakness for titles, foreign accents and beards, and might come back from one of his perennial flights East with a staff of exiled dignitaries in stuffed shirts. A depressing circumstance is that the California patriots are howling for the blood of my two German friends and all indications are that there is a good chance of satisfying them.

Glenn and I have had some minor adventures in traveling about southern California. We have explored the coast on several trips and made one exploration down into Mexico to the little town of Ensinada, which litters the banks of a beautiful jewel of a bay with a degree of poverty that reminds me of backwoods Arkansas.[187] Also some trips into the

186. Hartley Burr Alexander (1873–1939), who wrote miscellaneously (poetry, studies of mythology and Native Americans, and on iconography) but was, by training, a philosopher and metaphysician.

187. Ensenada is in Baja California, about sixty-two miles south of the U.S. border.

mountains at our back door, which are occasionally snow-covered even now. We are looking forward to seeing San Francisco region and the trip up there.

I read your letter to the Tar Heel on Muste's speech and found it quite moving and altogether up to your standard.[188] I suppose that preceding letters or speeches did something toward implementing these well stated ideals with a practical program of action in meeting the crisis, though in discussing your ideas with you I don't remember your outlining your practical proposals beyond suggesting that we must get along with the new order with some pragmatic compromise or other. I am still with you on a non-interventionist platform, though the alternative that I see to intervention is not lovely and certainly not as noble as the ideal that you have outlined. The alternative I see is a sternly imposed autarchy necessitating a revolutionized economy strictly controlled by the corporate state method, with the unwelcome but apparently inevitable necessity of protective imperialism toward the South even beyond Panama and toward the north to include Canada. This is presuming that we abandon Britain's cause and face the Hitler imposed new order abroad frankly. Now, as grim as this alternative is, I would prefer it to what I fear will happen. I don't think, in the first place, that there is any probability of America's abandoning Britain's cause without more frantic efforts to save her, which as you say, will lead to intervention. Moreover, I think this would have been quite as inevitable under Wilkie as under Roosevelt, whom, by the way, I supported not because of his foreign policy but because of his domestic policy in the past and faint hopes for the future.[189] It seems to me that not only our present false prosperity boom is completely geared to Britain's war economy, but that the hopes of our economic powers-that-be for the future of American economy are all geared to the hopeless dream of saving not only Britain but a vanished world economy of free trade. I believe that we will be driven to fight for that lost world and I believe, like you, that the fight is lost before it is begun.
[deletion]

CVWP, 7/66: TCLU

188. Abraham Johannes ("A. J.") Muste (1885–1967), trade unionist and Christian pacifist.
189. Wendell Lewis Willkie (1892–1944), the unsuccessful Republican candidate for the U.S. presidency in 1940.

68. To Wendell Holmes Stephenson

I send you with this letter the review of Cash's book.[190] I enjoyed review-ing it very much. Thank you for letting me have it.

I have been turning over in my head several ideas concerning my book in the series and would very much like to have your reflections upon them. The first concerns the matter of the date limits and the title—1880–1913. The more I think of them the more embarrassment they cause me. It is not that I particularly object to the limits set by these dates, but that their prominence in the title inevitably lends them much more significance than I would attach to them. In other words, I feel that they obligate me to make some case for beginning a period at 1880 and for ending one at 1913. I simply do not want to assume that task if I can help it. It would falsify my own interpretation of the period to magnify either of those dates into any prominence at all. I understand that in dividing up the work among the authors some such arbitrary dates must be set, but I wonder if there is not some way of playing down their prominence. Just as one suggestion, could they not be relegated to an inconspicuous subtitle? Perhaps the subtitle to each volume might run "A History of the South from——to——." Then the regular title, *Origins of the New South, The South During Reconstruction*, might appear on the spine or cover. I hope these suggestions don't sound presumptious. While the problem of dates might not bother other authors, they have given me some trouble.

The other matter that I had in mind concerns a book of essays cel-ebrating Charles A. Beard and edited by Louis Hacker. I agreed some time ago to contribute to the volume and now the Editor wants to pin me down to a definite subject and the promise of a manuscript. The only thing I can get ready for him would be from the work I am doing now. The title that I proposed to Mr. Hacker was "The Sequel to Reconstruction." In it I would handle much the same subject that I would treat in my first chapter of *The Origins of the New South*. Most of the essay would probably be "lifted" from the book. Now I know that this sort of thing is done, but I would like to have your frank opinion on the idea before I go ahead with it.

As you predicted, I am feeling much better about the work on the

---

190. CVW, review of W. J. Cash, *The Mind of the South* (New York: Alfred A. Knopf, 1941), in *Journal of Southern History* 7 (August 1941): 400–401.

book than I was when I talked with you in Baton Rouge. I am much pleased by the remarkable amount of fresh and unexploited material I am turning up. Aside from that I am constantly realizing that the real opportunity of this book lies in the fact that it is the first time anybody has attempted to correlate and make some sense of the scattered state and local history of the period in the South. There are plenty of headaches ahead of me, but at least I am out of the stage of despair I was in when we talked last.
[deletion]

    CVWP, 70/102: TCLU

69. To Fritz Caspari

WASHINGTON, DC

MAY 30, 1941

My many thanks for your full chronicle of the crisis in Pomona Valley. It was the first inkling I have had that things had developed so far in this direction. We have had a couple of letters since that added details, but none so complete as your story. Naturally I got no wind of it from my talk with Jaqua. May I beg enlightenment on subsequent developments as soon as possible? You see, Jaqua has written me that he is expecting to be in Washington June 10 and 11, and wants to see me. Before that time I want to get a much clearer picture of the situation than I have now. For one thing, I have been offered a government job at over a thousand dollar increase above my Scripps salary. It would involve writing, editing, and some travel, but would keep me in Washington mainly. I have no desire to give up teaching, and the additional money doesn't constitute a serious temptation, not nearly so much as the Library of Congress does. However, if I am faced with returning to a college that is ridden with dissension and intrigue and plots and political feuds, I would seriously think about taking this offer. I should like very much to have your frank prophecy on the situation next year in the light of my problem. I surely do not expect Scripps to metamorphasize miraculously into a harmonious Garden of Eden. I can put up with the normal amount of scrapping and back-biting but I do not want to take lodging in a madhouse if I have any alternative. I would also like to have Arnold's advice on the matter if you will be good enough to ask him.
[deletion]

    CVWP, 10/103: TCLU

70. To Manning J. Dauer and William G. Carleton

CLAREMONT, CA

SEPTEMBER 29, 1941

Many thanks for your letters—Manning's greetings from the home-land and Bill's cryptic notes from abroad. Please, if you love us, don't let these be the last. I seize the opportunity of a glow of optimism to write before it passes into my customary gloom. I am always optimistic at academic opening and go down from that the nine following months to bottom in June. This year I seem to have started off at a new high. This seems to be due to a number of things. Some of my more difficult colleagues have passed off the scene and the new ones seem to be a great improvement. The truce in the local civil war is lasting for the duration of a peace conference at least, with Dr. Jaqua concealing the Mr. Hyde in him. I always believe the best about new colleagues before I know the worst, but these seem especially starry-eyed and fortunately not all female. I have attracted, or somebody has run out seven or eight Pomona students, among them five or six males, four of exceptional quality, one extraordinary. Both classes are quite large for the school and start off ex-cellently. I count on having more fun out of the history of American po-litical ideas course than any I have ever taught. An encouraging sign is the fact that they swallowed Calvin's *Institutes* and Mather's *Magnalia* without losing their cookies, only one casualty from the rolls.[191] They take to Par-rington like Nazis to de Gobineau.[192] I also have a couple of theses and two tutees along with added work in 3rd year Humanities. This is added work due to a diminished faculty the result of Jaqua's last firing squadron. However it is all enjoyable and I still hope for some time for writing. I have also been given a new office which somewhat gilds the last lily. One window opens on San Gorgonio and the other on San Antonio; below in the courtyard the fountain rises ten feet and plops in a pool,—most ridiculous. Also in a burst of welcome the President suggested my moving up my predecessor's library, or the remaining parts of it, into my office.

191. John Calvin's *Institutes of the Christian Religion*, a foundational text of Reformed theol-ogy, was first published in Latin (1536) and in French (1541); Cotton Mather's *Magnalia Christi Americana* (1702) was, among other things, a history of New England Puritanism.

192. Vernon L. Parrington, *Main Currents in American Thought: An Interpretation of American Literature from the Beginnings to 1920*, 3 vols. (New York: Harcourt, Brace, 1927–30); Joseph-Arthur, comte de Gobineau (1816–1882), a racial theorist known for his *Essai sur l'inégalité des races hu-maines* (1853–55).

Since old Stephenson scattered his shot so widely and collected on each subject, the collection proves a pretty widespread one. There is a library of Washingtoniana Manning would enjoy, and there are works of Lincoln, Franklin, Jefferson Davis, etc, several hundred volumes. This added to my new acquisitions which include beside the Jefferson and Webster a good set of Calhoun, etc., makes a handsome working library.[193]

We had three good days at the Hayes Memorial in Fremont, lunch with Craven in Chicago, a pleasant trip across 'til we got to the Black Hills when nature seemed to run amok with a snow storm in the Big Horns, rain at the Grand Tetons, a sand storm in Salt Lake City, with some fog and sleet thrown in—not enough to spoil the trip, however, which was mainly a success.

As for Bill's municipal report on Los Angeles, I returned to that city this week to refresh my impressions and if necessary revise my judgment. I beg to report no revision necessary. For me it remains the debris apron of the last watershed of western civilization. Of course, I know some people like debris *de gustibus,* as the jook organ for example.

CVWP, 15/165: TCLU

71. To Glenn W. Rainey

CLAREMONT, CA
OCTOBER 28, 1941

[deletion]

I have been pleasantly surprised at my feelings about this place and my work since [my] return. As you know I rather dreaded coming back. The main thing, I expect, has been my teaching which I feel much happier about than I did last year. I am really having a lot of fun, especially with the History of Am. Political Ideas. I have entirely abandoned lecturing, which always bored me, and is useless in small classes anyway. Also thrown out textbooks, assigned readings in sources, along with Parrington & first-rate writers, which are analyzed and discussed in class. This along with reports & papers. I avoid doing their thinking for them as much as possible. About half of them are men, attracted from Pomona—*not,* I must honestly confess, entirely by my own charms. One of them works all night in an orange grove and sends two children to school. I have

193. The set would presumably be Richard K. Crallé, ed., *The Works of John C. Calhoun,* 6 vols. (New York: D. Appleton, 1854–57).

overcome the uneasy feeling of being governess to pampered darlings by discovering that they are not really that, that they work harder than any students I have had, and are considerably above the average in brains as classes go. In tutorial work I am having them read classics I did not get (some of them) in graduate school: Machiavelli, Hobbes, Harrington, Sidney, Locke, Montesquieu, Paine, A. Smith, Rousseau, Jefferson, Mill, Marx, etc., partly because I wanted to do some of them for the first time myself.

I still find some time for the book, all classes coming on Mon, Wed, & Fri. I am as yet in the exasperating stage of note filing. The Faculty-President feud, resolved last spring in an awkward compromise of check & balance plus a faculty spy, is not ended, and the compromise has yet to prove workable.

[deletion]

  GWR: TLS

72. To Howard K. Beale

CLAREMONT, CA
JANUARY 28, 1942

[deletion]

Perhaps I do not see enough of my fellow Californians to have a fair sample of opinion, but so far I have been surprised that the attitude toward the Japs in California has not taken as nasty a turn as I had rather anticipated. There is probably much undercover brutality and injustice, but it does not appear in the newspapers. Japanese trucksters and shopkeepers continue in business. There are plans for evacuating them from certain important areas. Racial feeling could easily take a turn for the worse and probably will later on.

[deletion]

  CVWP, 7/67: TCLU

73. To Will W. Alexander

CLAREMONT, CA
FEBRUARY [22?], 1942

I remember a story that you told me about Ulrich Phillips' coming into your office back in 1917 with the announcement that he felt like putting southern history aside for the more pressing job at hand in the war.[194] I have recalled the story often lately and it is with the same motive that I am writing you now.

I don't know what government work you are now doing, but my guess is it would be something that I would be interested in. Is it possible also that I could be of some use in your work? I would, of course, like more than anything to work with you, but I would appreciate any suggestion you might have regarding a Defense job elsewhere. You know my field of interest and my training. I know you will understand when I say that I feel strongly impelled to get into some useful branch of war work. Perhaps I could be most usefully placed in connection with some southern problem. Will you be good enough to let me have your advice?

CVWP, 92/13: TCLU

74. To Glenn W. Rainey

CLAREMONT, CA
JUNE 27, 1942

It seems pretty unlikely that I shall see you this summer. After prolonged agonies of indecision we have decided to settle here for the summer. Washington seemed out of the question for a number of reasons—partly because much of the manuscript collection, and an undetermined amount of the other material has been removed from Washington to parts unknown. Chapel Hill was full of Air Corps with no living quarters available. Driving through was out of the question and train travel uncertain.

About the least consolation you might offer is a letter—a prompt one, at that. This much I demand, not request! You might throw in what speeches, clippings, broadsides, excursions, and alarums you have handy. News from the home country has been so fragmentary that for all I know you may be in Iceland or Burma by this time. If not I want to know your draft classification and your speculations about the probabilities of your being called in. Like everyone in III-A I have debated much about what steps to take—whether a commission, whether army or navy, or whether to wait. I have waited, taking no steps yet. I would much appreciate your advice. So far I have heard of no one with a bona fide dependent being called in out here. I hear there is much of it in the East—in Florida and

194. Ulrich Bonnell Phillips (1877–1934), a Georgian and, in his day, the leading historian of American slavery; between 1911 and 1930 he taught at the University of Michigan, before moving to Yale.

Carolina at least. My guess is that if $4\frac{1}{2}$ million more are inducted this year as planned, a heavy toll will be taken from our group within six months or so anyway. I don't see how that is to be avoided. Do you? What is your plan? Since you gave up your Reserve Officer commission, I would suppose you are in much the same status as I. Also what effect does Dot's employment have on your case?[195]

If I were in agreement with most of the opinion I get here concerning the length of the war, I would not give a serious thought to my own future in military service. But I still say it's no short war—East or West. And as soon as the Russo-Jap show begins it's likely to look longer than ever. Incidentally that phase of the war seems to me long over-due in getting started. What do you think about both matters?

For me the year has been about as painful and distressing as any I've been through—so far as life in a college is concerned. Two phases were particularly bitter: the fight in behalf of my German colleagues and other with the President. The Germans under constant suspicion, investigation, and petty persecution, were locked up Dec. 8—one of them snatched out of a committee meeting I was attending. Then there was the fight to get them out—lasting three months. Meanwhile the French exiles began concerted smear campaigns. Once the Germans were released from the clink, the Legionaires joined the fight, sending a letter containing clippings charging the Germans with being Nazi spies to all parents of the student body. Then a long fight with the Legion. Complicating all this was a continuation of the feud between faculty and President that split the faculty and community along much the same lines: the anti-Germans being up with the President. Students meanwhile rending the air with petitions—and serving as intermediaries between professors who did not speak to each other. Parents protesting and counter-protesting. Mass meetings, demonstrations, breast-beatings, resignations, faculty meetings at the top of one's voice, spying, counter-spying. You would never believe how much hell can be packed into such a small space. One fortunate outcome is that the President was kicked out—just before he was able to kick me out, incidentally—having given me full notice that he intended to do so in a nasty interview.

Well, you can perhaps understand why I got exactly nothing what-

195. Rainey's wife, Dorothy Quattlebaum (b. 1907) of Columbia, SC, who taught in the Atlanta public schools for many years; they were married on 3 February 1940.

ever done on the book during the year. I am now struggling to get back
into the job, trying to remember what it was all about, what this note
meant, and what that book was, and why I was ever remotely excited
about the project anyway.

[deletion]

GWR: ALS

75. To Glenn W. Rainey

CLAREMONT, CA

OCTOBER 19, 1942

Many, if belated, thanks for your letter of last summer, written at
my urgent demand. My need was urgent and the letter met the
need quite well. Last year was low ebb for me—an all time low, I believe,
though I have gone through such fits of depression before. Never so pro-
tracted nor so low as that one, however. I might analyze at length, but I
will spare you the amateur psychiatrics. A few obvious factors—the war,
the treatment of my German friends, the policy toward the Japs, and—
worst of all—our own tea-pot tempest, the revolution that overthrew the
college president. The combination just about finished me off. The spell
lasted throughout the summer. The last week before school we drove up
into the High Sierras and camped out in the open by a lovely lake for a
week—then back by way of Stanford for a conference and home. I came
back rested, but still, as I had all summer, dreading facing a class, hating
teaching, and everything about it. Then—poof—the whole stupid fog
lifted overnight, magically, and for no reason I have been able to discover
. . . Teaching from the start became the true delight it can be on rare
occasion—and kept on being. Lecturing became no effort at all. And in
spite of a sizeable increase in duties, being chairman of two combination
staff courses, I suddenly found more time on my hands than ever. I began
to work on the book and have written as much since school started while
teaching as I did all summer long with nothing to do but write. Moreover
it's better writing at that. As a matter of fact I only wrote one chapter
last summer—a long one and the hardest, that is, the first. This second
one looks to my impartial eye like a damned fine job, after some pruning.
Would you like to see it? Would you have time to critique it?

What have you been reading? Oh, I remember you never took up the
habit. The happier & wiser fellow, of course. Osmosis is adequate among

the more sensitive plants, of course. I still have to root for nourishment or starve. Among recent rootings: H. Laski, *The American Presidency* not bad, but less original than I had expected. Somebody Kohn, *World Order in His-torical Perspective*—recommended, but not required. Jacques Barzun, *Darwin, Marx, Weber*—highly diverting and unreliable. Davis & Lindley, *How War Came*—a good deal that was not in the papers, but uncritical, Rilke, *Collected Poems*, translated—you would like him. Eudora Welty, *Curtain of Green*—what appears to be the best short story writing being done in the South now. *Compulsory*. I have not been able to get hold of Wm Faulkner's latest—which I understand is one of his best—*Go Down, Moses,* he calls it.[196] The more I think of it, the more I am convinced that Faulkner is *tops* of contemporaries—a high sense of tragedy and humor as rich as W. Shakespeare and more so than M. Twain's.

Has my mother told you we are in a family way? Highly uncharac-teristic. Admitted! and a double betrayal because my impulse toward pro-creation coincided almost exactly with the lowest ebb my opinion of the race has ever reached. Which isn't very high. Hence a treasonous con-spiracy to contribute to the perpetuation of the verminous breed. Serve me right if it's a monster or resembles its progenitor. In contributing to my remorse, I admit that my more philosophical qualms are outweighed by the somewhat belated realization that in all probability the creature will be expected to live here in the house, with me! That consideration has only been borne upon me in concrete fashion by furtive observation of my neighbor Tom Glenn & Earnest Strathman whom I believe to be, or have been, men of kidney—now dwelling amid savage yells and name-less obscenities in puddles of infant urine. There for a spermatazoon goes C. V. W.! All these matters require pondering and some philosophy not yet disclosed to my earnest searchings. May it be revealed to me before March!

I forgot to mention among evidences of my progressive literacy, read-ing Van Doren's *Franklin.*[197] Among all consolations of the spirit that I

196. Harold J. Laski, *The American Presidency: An Interpretation* (New York: Harper & Broth-ers, 1940); Hans Kohn, *World Order in Historical Perspective* (Cambridge, MA: Harvard University Press, 1942); Jacques Barzun, *Darwin, Marx, Wagner: Critique of a Heritage* (Boston: Little, Brown, 1941); Forrest Davis and Ernest Kidder Lindley, *How War Came: An American White Paper: From the Fall of France to Pearl Harbor* (New York: Simon and Schuster, 1942); Eudora Welty, *A Curtain of Green, and Other Stories* (New York: Harcourt Brace, 1941); William Faulkner, *Go Down, Moses, and Other Stories* (New York: Random House, 1942).

197. Carl Van Doren, *Benjamin Franklin* (New York: Viking Press, 1938).

have sought of late it has brought richest reward. Main virtue of Van Doren is that he quotes liberally from Franklin—but also has a genuine flair & feeling for his subject. But the fine picture of the sagacious old satyr living serenely, and wittily and contentedly midst his howling illegitimates and mistresses and would-be mistresses and madmen and traitors and marplots and war mongers and cutthroats and revolutionaries (being one himself at the age of 70) and toppling empires sweetened in some measure a whole summer—otherwise diverted with contemplations of homicide.

Speaking of homicide, are you any nearer to taking it up as a profession? Perhaps we all are. Hearing that a goodly number of ex-colleagues at Chapel Hill have commissions at Camp Lee at Petersburgh, Va., with the unsanguine job of writing textbook, I investigated and have wrung some evidence of interest from the major in charge. He writes, no opening now, but I will hear from him in the near future. I don't know what, if anything, will come of it. After spending last year yearning for a soft post as sapper & miner for a Solomon Island missile squadron—quite frankly as an easy escape from local turmoil and my own state of mind— I now feel no inclination toward heroism whatsoever and would contemplate with bliss serving out the duration as a school master in a young ladies' seminary doing my daily stint of writing about the antics of our grandfathers.

By the way I received what I seriously esteem as the most genuine tribute *Tom* ever got in a recent letter from a Mrs. Hamlett of Zephyrhills, Fla. I quote: "My husband and I edited the Kourier [KKK organ] for several years and were pretty close to most of the people in the Klan— but never so close that we would violate any loyalties by telling what we know. I, personally, was never in it emotionally (nor even mentally) but my aunt was head of the woman's organization in Georgia and my husband had such illusions about it that he had a nervous breakdown when he lost faith in it." She concludes with a tribute to my fairness and scholarship & offers to send inside material on the Klan. There, I felt was a real triumph. I know you will be pleased to hear that *Tom* sold 51 copies in its 4th year of publication.
[deletion]

GWR: ALS

76. To Glenn W. Rainey

CLAREMONT, CA

OCTOBER 27, 1942

I have just had your thrice welcome letter. This precipitant reply will doubtless horrify you and dry up every generous impulse. But I am so eager to have you read a chapter that I send it flying on the first faltering show of interest. You are first reader. Not that such admonition is needful in your case, but you need not be too tender with my feelings. The chapter I send came as an unforeseen necessity. It had no place in my projected outline, and I did not take notes with a view to writing it. It simply became necessary. For that very reason I feel rather confident in it—as defended by a sort of "inevitability." In all writing I have pushed back my assigned starting point three years to 1877, as the only one that makes any sense. As it stands this chapter will have to be cut at least a fifth, probably a fourth. Extending plans on the same scale would add up to a volume almost twice the length contracted for. I am just starting the third chapter which will be on the Independent Movements (c. 1877–1884), probably including treatment of Convict Lease, certainly the Debt Repudiation problem (resulting in internal splits of the Party in only 3 states—resolved *within* the Dem. Party in *all* other of the 12 states after more or less tough fights). I am amazed at the complexity of this chapter—and have resolved to diagram and chart to bring some order out of chaos. It will be a hell of a tough job—though not as tough as Chapter I, which I have not yet had Glenn type, and is really in bad condition. What do you think of making the chapter I send you Chapter I? Then follow with the chapter on the Redeemers, and next on the Independents? The chapter I send might be called "The Forked Road to Reunion." In a left-handed way it is a refutation of Paul Buck's (Harvard Prof) *Road to Reunion* (Pulitzer Prize, 1938—a natural for that sort of thing, since it is conservative, optimistic, mild, and sees the Silver Lining behind the merest suggestion of a cloud.)[198] This chapter should have relentless criticism since it is a new interpretation and lays me open to all sorts of attack. This is a 2nd carbon, so you may write all over it—please!!

Odd that you should have turned to Freud—odd *any* time for *you*—but especially since I had the same impulse at the same time. Took out a book by Horney, *The Neurotic Personality of Our Time*—this in my low-

---

198. Paul H. Buck, *The Road to Reunion, 1865–1900* (Boston: Little, Brown, 1937).

est moments.[199] On opening it I immediately perceived that it was written entirely about Woodward. Absorbed, I continued—getting lower & lower. Then I suddenly said the hell with it! What am I doing but making the colossal *non sequitur* (not to say grotesque *egotismes*) of seeking the explanation of world chaos in my own storm-blasted personality? And *furthermore* is not that *non sequitur* in part or perhaps largely (when multiplied a thousand fold) responsible for world chaos? Can the world, and events and affairs really have any order that is not imposed upon them by ordered and confident minds? This implies more heroism than I am guilty of. But I do think the Freudians & their ilk stand accused of muddled thinking. Do they not, when confronted with a victim of social, political, & economic chaos, make the fatal mistake of seeking all the cures and causes *within* the victim's personality—ignoring the storm that did their client in? Well, all this calls for more pondering than I have given it. [deletion]

P.S. If you think by sending Chapter II I have gone with the Zephyr & become a Confederate patriot, wait till you see Chap I on the Redeemers! [deletion]

GWR: ALS

77. To Glenn W. Rainey

CLAREMONT, CA
DECEMBER 4, 1942

Many thanks for your heartening letter. I asked for criticism, but fortunately you understood that my first need was a few bravoes at this time. Not that I don't need the criticism—in the long run—much more. Yours I thought excellent, and with a few exceptions, I agree with all. Particularly the point about the East-West axis. I realized that and had used the expression "New York-Philadelphia axis" in lectures before, but somehow, I failed to see the importance of having it in when I wrote the chapter. Undoubtedly it belongs. And your analysis of the Northeast's game of playing both ends against the middle clarified my ill-formulated thought most helpfully.

You will be interested to know that Howard Beale (who has been in Frisco the last two months working with the Friends to locate Japanese &

---

199. Karen Horney, *The Neurotic Personality of Our Time* (New York: W. W. Norton, 1937).

Am. evacuated students in interior colleges) visited me last week and his independent criticism almost exactly paralleled yours. He made a special point of the need for more help to the gentle reader—transitions, summary, etc. Of course that is an old fight between Beale and me—we had a long and loud tussle over *Tom* on the same score, with me yielding ground only when I had to. Of course you and I have had the same fight. You remember my theory that the reader should do some of the work, appreciates the flattery, and in the end, enjoys more what is not spoonfed. I do not believe in intentional obscurity however, and if that is what I achieve I should be made to realize it. Please give me hell for it, if you are convinced I need it.

I believe the revelations I make on the Compromise of 1877 are of more significance than you think. I hope for more light after further research. 1878 I regard as a temporary relapse. The pact of '77 lasted till '96—which really was only another temporary lapse. As for my rather elaborate analogy between the Compromise of '77 and the Constitutional Convention of 1787, I readily grant you that there are some dizzy transitions here. But I'm afraid I am too much in love with it to give it up. It does involve a number of tenuous assumptions: (1) the validity of Beard's thesis of the Civ. War as the Second Am. Revolution (2) Morison & Commagers thesis of the Fed. Const. of '87 as the Thermidore of the First Am. Revolution—i.e., what Robespierre's execution and the establishment of the Directorat was to the French Revolution; the conservative reaction to extremism that comes in every revolution: Cromwell, Stalin, etc.[200] So Hayes threw overboard the abolitionist element of the Rad. Rep. party & joined forces between conservatives, North & South. Well, I don't insist on this, and will not press it, but it seems to me one of those suggestive analogies that one can afford to send up as a flare in the darkness, but should not attempt to employ as a searchlight. As the latter it would only serve to draw fire from the enemy.

I was always a drunken metaphorist—but always penitent, and always ready to reform. Thanks for the temperance lectures. I'll try my best to reconcile my cathedral with my clipper—or at least get the latter dry docked—God, here I go!

200. Charles A. Beard and Mary Beard, *The Rise of American Civilization*, 2 vols. (New York: Macmillan, 1927).

Now, to put further strain on your good nature—last Thursday I shipped you two more chapters. These, you will see, are in much worse shape. They were written in anguish last summer, at my low ebb, squeezed out of an opened vein in my right arm on pressure at the rate of one page a day. Sheer torture. I want to know what to do with them. I say "them." They were written as one chapter—supposedly the first. They are not blessed with introduction or conclusion—or for that matter transition. I turned out the first part mechanically: Ala., Ark., Tenn., etc., on through, more or less. May be that will work, with some few added transitions and explanations.

Specific questions I would like you to consider are these:

(1) Which of the three chapters you have read should come first?
(2) The others in what order?
(3) Can I afford to boil the two you now have down to one?
(4) The question of cutting down generally—you see I am now writing a fourth chapter. Yet I planned only two to take me this far along.
(5) Most important—which of what you have read should I attempt to whip into shape for a 20 minute paper before the Pacific Branch of the A.H.A. at the Christmas meeting. Don't you think the first one you saw involves too many complex ideas to be developed in 20 minutes?

How would you like this title for Chapter 4 which is on the Independent movements, readjustment & repudiation, etc "Solid South,"— "Procrustean Bedfellows"? Very bad, you think? I am growing a bit fond of it I confess.[201]

Now, another favor! Please let me hear from you before Dec. 20—especially in re the question of the 20 minute paper.

To all inquiries about when we are expecting delivery I blandly reply perhaps in two years, perhaps longer. After all, Glenn is only with child. I'm the one with book. Labor in the latter case is coterminous with gestation—the entire period. Hence priorities on attention & concern for delivery. The other is due in March.
[Deletion]

GWR: ALS

---

201. This survived as the title for chapter four of *Origins of the New South*.

78. To Bess Woodward

CLAREMONT, CA
FEBRUARY 18, 1943

U nto you a grandson is born customary number of ears legs etc. according to nurse.[202] Havent seen it myself. No star appeared, alert signal sounded however. Glenn doing well, slowly recovering myself born 8 pm letter follows

CVWP, 60/732: TELEGRAM

79. To Glenn W. Rainey

CLAREMONT, CA
APRIL 4, 1943

T here have, as you know, been Developments which I hope you will take into account in explaining my silence. Development I, my only begotten son, Peter Vincent, in whom I am not at all hours of the night well pleased, should at least be mentioned in this connection. A serious, humorless, and uncompromising savage as ever interrupted the meditations of civilized man and made him yearn for the comparative privacy of the sailor's fo'c'sle. In spite of daily and nightly lung exertions that would have debilitated the veriest demagogue, this Peter Vincent continues to increase in wisdom and stature and in disfavor with God and man at the rate of an ounce and a quarter a day until he now weighs nine pounds five ounces and tears any passion to tatters at no provocation whatsoever. In all these afflictions I beg no sympathy—only understanding.

Development II—I expect to be in uniform by June. Since Christmas I have been stalling off the local board with deferments requested by local college presidents. Chiefly those of the Pomona president, for whom I am teaching 200 army meteorology cadets American history—a knowledge of which, it seems, is necessary in the accurate prediction of meteors.[203] Unfortunately the local draft board, my eloquent demonstrations to the contrary notwithstanding, has of late not always been able to appreciate the true worth of American history in this matter of meteors. So obtuse have these gentlemen proved, in fact, that they propose to classify me as 1-A next week. I shall, as an exercise in pedagogical patience,

202. Peter Vincent Woodward (1943–1969), CVW's only child.
203. Elijah Wilson Lyon (1905–1989) had become president of Pomona College in 1941 and would serve for twenty-eight years.

appear before them once more and demonstrate in words of one syllable the subtle connection between historiography and meteorology. Previous failures, however, have led me to expect no sudden improvement in their wits. As a matter of fact, premonitions of their denseness in this respect had led me about a month ago to make application for a commission in the navy. It is now a matter of doubt whether I can devise to continue my instruction of the Board and the Meteorologists until my commission comes through—if indeed it does—which depends somewhat upon whether the priesthood of the Naval Sanhedrin discover my heretic views concerning virgin birth and divine inspiration of their patron saint, Captain Mahan—and all his works, which I have never read.[204]

Development III—Work in Progress. Not as gratifying in extent and quality as could be wished. I enclose the only chapter completed since the last batch I sent you. Along with it is one of the numerous work-sheets and drafts that I had to use in organizing the chapter. I hope it will be the toughest and most complex chapter I shall have to write. You above all should appreciate some of the complexities and perplexities of the job. It ran into much too many pages, and will have to be cut down considerably. Any suggestions for cutting will be appreciated. Also please give attention to dubious interpretations and let me have the full weight of your deliberations and dissent.

As for the last two chapters—you were completely right. They were both on one subject. They were written as one chapter, then cut arbitrarily in equal halves, merely because together they were too long. I don't know what I shall do with it or them. Perhaps in the silent watches of the South Seas, along with meditations upon the mysteries of the Four Freedoms, some revelation will come to me as to the Ancient Mariner, and I shall heave the whole MS overboard.

I am now half way through another chapter and hope, with luck, to have time to complete it and another one before turning my attention to ballistics and navigation and Capt. Mahan.

Altogether this has been the happiest year I have had as a pedagogue. For the first time the job has seemed both easy and pleasant. We are closing early. All classes will be over at Scripps next week. My contract for teaching the meteorites will continue till the end of April, but it is

204. The most notable being Alfred Thayer Mahan, *The Influence of Sea Power Upon History, 1660–1783* (Boston: Little, Brown, 1890).

little trouble and takes little time. Moreover, it has been doubly welcome in appreciably increasing the income about the time we went down to Bethlehem.

[deletion]

[handwritten]Have you seen Carroll Kilpatrick's article in the March *Harper's?*[205] If not, do. Write him, Nat'l Press Bldg., Washington.

GWR: TLS

80. To Glenn W. Rainey

CLAREMONT, CA
APRIL 25, 1943

The conspiracy to miscast me has another whimsicality. First pedagogue in a ladies' seminary, next *pater familias,* and now the military. Notice arrived Wednesday from Los Angeles that my commission had come—Lieutenant (jg), to which is added some honorific degree described as A-V (S). The "S" I am told means Specialist, and I am uninformed about the other two letters.[206] They appear nowhere in this particular combination in the Manual of Academic Heraldry. Content with a modest Ph.D., I hesitate to accept this distinction. Especially since I have a growing suspicion that the "A" might refer to Aviation—which sounds a bit hazardous. In combination with "Specialist" it poses questions of hazards to the life and limb of my fellow citizens more than to that of the enemy. Perhaps I am too modest about my qualifications. At any rate I am persuaded to give my consent—you will doubtless hear of me next as Lieut. jg Woodward, Ph.D, A-V (S), Squadron Leader of Falstaff's Falcons, vigilantly patrolling the coast line of Bolivia.

Before I assume these dread duties I should like your blessing and your opinion on the "Procrustean Bedfellows." If I am granted the respite of three weeks I hope for I intend to complete a couple more chapters. I have put my muse on notice, however, that I could not love her quite so much, loved I not honor more. Incidentally, my duties at Scripps end this week and next week I complete my contract with Pomona for the instruction of meteorites on the influence of weather on the history of

205. Carroll Kilpatrick, "Will the South Secede?," *Harper's Magazine* 186 (March 1943): 415–21.

206. A-V (S) meant "Aviation Officer of the Volunteer Reserve Appointed for Special Service."

the U.S. So the commission comes in good time. Glenn will stay put till she is sure that I shall be assigned to the Bolivian post with the Falcons, then join me later. Peter waxes as a mighty pisser and yeller and soiler of pants.

And so, *allons*, I gird my loins, and in the spirit of that mighty warrior, the Knight of Sack, and with that Latin zest for battle that so well characterizes the average Genoese, I take up the sword![207] In the silent watches of the South Seas amid meditations on the mysteries of the Four Freedoms I shall think of you.

[deletion]

GWR: ALS

81. To Glenn W. Rainey

ARLINGTON, VA

MAY 7, 1944

[deletion]

Many thanks for doing your bit to make me safe and dull enough for the Office of Naval Intelligence. My New Deal friends suspect me of having got in under an assumed name or of having sold out. They look at me ruefully over their G.I. shoulder stripes. As a matter of fact the job has turned out to be pretty interesting. As you know I was sent here under temporary orders. The first job was quite out of aviation, in which I was classified and trained. That took a couple of months, after which I expected to be sent to some naval air station or back to school for further training. We lived temporarily with my friend Ed Williams, Glenn commuting from North Carolina in a series of agonizing trips with Peter. We did not know how long I would be here and anyway it seemed impossible to find a house or an apartment, and on temporary orders I was not entitled to have my things moved from California. Ed joined the Marines and we moved to another house temporarily vacated by a colonel I knew. By that time, although I was expecting new orders any day, we decided we must find a place of our own. Weeks of systematic search finally located a really quite satisfactory house with plenty of yard and trees in Arlington only about 12 minutes by bus from the Navy Department. I think we were pretty lucky for the place is going to be cool I believe.

207. "The Knight of Sack" is Falstaff.

Everything regarding my orders remained in uncertainty until March 1, when I finally got permanent orders for duty here. That does not mean "permanent" in the dictionary sense, but at least it eased the uncertainty under which we had been living all that time to some degree. It looks like now I shall be here for some time, perhaps through the summer. The present work is quite interesting. My commanding officer is a reasonable and quite intelligent and well informed man. My associate officers are, for the most part, a congenial lot, some of them excellent company. As a point of vantage for keeping up with current military goings on it could scarcely be improved upon.

It looks like I am going to have trouble with William W. Brewton, who is threatening to bring suit against Macmillan on account of my book. Until he does I will ask you not to mention the matter, but I want to tell you about it anyway. He claims that he has a bona fida contract with the Watson heirs that gives him exclusive proprietary rights to all the material in the Watson Collection and has produced a document signed by one O. S. Brown, now dead, who was the father-in-law and guardian of Georgia Lee Brown, granddaughter of Tom and cousin of Georgia Watson. Writes Brewton: "All the material in Woodward's book which I had published is an infringement whether he got it out of my book or not. He could not get it out of my book without a license from me or by violating the scope of the license he had; but furthermore, he could not use any source of an original nature found among the Watson Papers, if I had already published the same matter from that same source. . . . I copyrighted the matter when I published it in my book. Thereafter, not even the Watsons could publish or print it. . . . My exclusive license embraced the whole cache. It embraced the whole cache. It embraced transcripts, photographs, copyrighted books, and everything." I have written to Georgia about this but have not heard from her. I knew nothing about this contract, of course, and neither did she that I know of. Georgia Brown and Walter Brown both knew I was using the collection and he showed me some material not in the collection. They did not mention the contract and had no objection so far as I know to my using it. She is now dead.

Brewton also claims that I involved him in "a work of defamation" against Watson, the people of Georgia, the South and God by listing him in my bibliography and citing him five times in footnotes. Besides that it seems that I am charged with piracy every time I mention any event, summarize any speech, give a date, enumerate an election result, tell a story or state a fact that he has touched upon in his book. I did not "necessarily" steal the date of Watson's birth though I "might" have, but everything between that and Watson's death I clearly stole from him. Especially his "organization" and "arrangement" of facts. Also chapter headings: my first chapter "The Heritage" clearly stolen from his chapter "Great Mother, Great Son." Wherever there is a difference it is a "colorable alteration." This goes on and on.

President Brett of Macmillan has sent me the whole correspondence—about a hundred pages of it.[208] The first letter was 14 pages legal-sized paper, single-spaced. It is simply incredible. It seems he has been trying to sell Macmillan his books for twenty years, his Watson first. But that company has criminally conspired against him and the south to defame the latter and persecute him. He first suggested $1000 to salve his feelings, then $2500, and next $5000. His latest offer mentions that he intends to sue Scribners (publishers of the Dictionary of American Biography—it seems that the editor Dumas Malone was "also a renegade and apostate son of Georgia who sold out") for my sketch in the DAB. Then he is going to sue me. But if Scribners and Macmillans will get together in a friendly way and write him a check for $10000 he will forget the whole matter. Or better let Macmillan pay him for his, I quote, "200,000 word novel of the South today to be called DIANA OF THE EPHESIANS. It is the story of the clash between fundamentalism and modernism in the South today. Many exciting developments and much plot." Or let Macmillan pay him advance royalties on his new and definitive life of Watson.

As for his ability to prove his charges, Brett should have no doubt. For was he not the man who proved, among other things that "The very darling of all scientists from the beginning of learning to now, towit that the shortest distance between two points is a straight line, is utterly, absolutely, categorically false, never was true, never will be, never can be. These may all sounds strange to you; yet I may tell you, with full unction, that they are not as strange as was your conduct in throwing them out of your window."

But Macmillan is worried. He Brewton promised to bring the whole Frank case into court. He quotes from a pamphlet he has written entitled

208. George P. Brett Jr. (1893–1984) was president of the American division of Macmillan (1931–58).

"Jews, Prejudice Against" (quoted from the index of my book) which he says he may be forced to print. He has got a New York lawyer interested in the case on the basis of splitting fees. He goes into pages of tirade against Macmillan Company textbooks and threatens to take the crusade into all states of the South. He also told Brett that the present Governor of Georgia has offered him a place on the State Board of Education on the state textbook commission, and suggests what he can do if he accepts.[209] I suspect this latter is untrue, and I wonder if you have any means of finding out whether it is true. If so the Governor should be warned. I hope you will let me know if you find out anything about the matter.

He repeatedly says he only read my book last year and that the law permits him to bring suit within two years of the time he discovers his grievance. Georgia Craven told me three years ago that he had approached her attempting to get her to file suit against me for libel. This may be one way of stopping him. But it looks like a long and nasty affair now. You will remember that he succeeded in extracting money out of Knopf Co. for an article of John Donald Wade's in the *Mercury*. I hope Macmillan will not do this too, and I don't think they will. Brett says one crackpot cost them $50,000 in lawyers fees, however. Legally I am liable for the company's expenses in such a suit. Pleasant thought this is. Well, I've written too much already.
[deletion]

    GWR: TLS

82. To Harold S. Latham[210]

ARLINGTON, VA

OCTOBER 6, 1945

Thank you for your letter of September 28 concerning the book on the Battle for Leyte Gulf.

I wish it were possible for me to comply with your request that I send you a chapter. The fact is that I am writing against time in an effort to complete the book and get it off my hands before I get out of uniform. I

---

209. Ellis Gibbs Arnall (1907–1992), a progressive Democrat of sorts, who served as governor of Georgia (1943–47).

210. Harold S. Latham (1887–1969), a vice president of Macmillan; he is best known for having been Margaret Mitchell's editor.

hope to accumulate enough "points" for release from the Navy by Christmas. I do not feel that I can take the time to put a chapter in final shape. Then, too, I would have to carry it to New York, since it could not go through the mail, and I might also get into trouble over security regulations for releasing it before it has passed the reviewing board.

If it would help any, I might give you my conception of the treatment of material and organization of the story. It is almost entirely an action story, extremely violent action at a very fast pace. The narrative, I think, should be kept as devoid of plush as a *Fletcher* class destroyer. The battle was much too critical, dramatic, and in one phase tragic, to permit any kind of "publicity" writing. The loss of the *Princeton*, for example, and the tragedy of the *Birmingham*, or that of our escort carriers off Samar, or the suicidal attack of three destroyers against the battle line of the Imperial Fleet—any one of them is as dramatic a story as there is in naval history. The writing should be kept clear of "navalese" and unnecessary technical jargon. If that is done, any layman can easily follow and understand this complex battle. It is complex in the sense that, unlike other actions— Coral Sea, Midway, Guadalcanal, Philippine Sea it was not confined to a single type of combat, whether carrier aircraft or surface action. It involves all possible type of naval combat and craft: submarine action, a battleship night battle by the Seventh Fleet (in which most of the damage was done by PT boats and destroyers); Halsey's carrier aircraft action; and the most unequal engagement of the war, the daytime surface action between the unarmored escort carriers and the main battleship force of the Japanese Fleet.[211] It also includes the first organized Kamikaze attacks by enemy planes.

The story falls naturally into five parts:

1. Sortie of the Japanese Fleet.

This was the long awaited event for which a large part of the U.S. Fleet was constructed. The development of the enemy plan for a three-point convergence on our transport fleet in Leyte Gulf, the plan to draw off our fast battleships to the north. Submarine and aircraft attacks on the approaching enemy fleet during October 23 and 24. Loss of the *Princeton*. Halsey leaves San Bernardino Strait unguarded to steam

211. William Frederick Halsey Jr. (1882–1959) was vice admiral and commander of the South Pacific Force and South Pacific Area after October 1942; during the battle of Leyte Gulf, he commanded the Third Fleet.

north against enemy carriers. A divided command of two fleets with their only superior in Washington.

2. The Battle of Surigao Strait.

The largest torpedo action of the war. PT boats attack in the southern end of the Strait. Destroyers torpedo action, the right and left flank cruisers. Finally the old battleships, relics of Pearl Harbor. Some Japanese break through into Leyte Gulf. The Japanese disaster.

3. The Battle off Samar.

Main Japanese battleship force, having slipped through San Bernardino Strait during the night, catches our Jeep Carriers by surprise. Gunnery action. Sacrifice torpedo attack by destroyers. Air action. Kinkaid appeals to Halsey for battleships. Enemy turns back, breaks off engagement. Kamikaze attacks.

4. The Battle off Cape Engano.

The Japanese carrier striking force caught without planes aboard. Third Fleet aircraft sink four enemy carriers, damage two battleships. Cruisers finish off cripples. Was Halsey's decision justified?

5. The Mop-up.

Aircraft from the Third and Seventh Fleet carriers pursue and strike retreating Japanese forces. Destroyers join in. Cripples and stragglers finished off. The Japanese plan *might* have succeeded. The enemy fleet reduced to mere nuisance value.

I respect your judgment in the matter of sales. However, while I suspect the public is fed up with the war correspondent series on BLEEDING BATAAN and TERRIBLE TARAWA, etc., I should think they might by the first of the year have developed some appetite for the real thing in a now-it-can-be-told (if, indeed, it can!) manner. They have had a partial sample in BATTLE REPORT—which, incidentally has sold 50,000 and is coming out shortly with 25,000 more, and a second volume is to appear soon.[212] My book is being done under the same authorization, but I hope to go further in the way of revelations. I do not pretend to know the mind of the reading public. Maybe Macmillan of London could not have sold an authoritative book on the Battle of Jutland in 1919.

While I feel reasonably sure of finding a publisher, I would like to

212. Walter Karig and Welbourn Kelley, *Battle Report: Pearl Harbor to Coral Sea* (New York: Farrar & Rinehart, 1944); Walter Karig, Earl Burton, and Stephen L. Freeland, *Battle Report: The Atlantic War* (New York: Farrar & Rinehart, 1946); eventually there would be six volumes.

have Macmillan do the job. However, I should not like for you to undertake it with any reluctance, especially if you are not prepared to take
advantage of the superb collection of photographs that I hope to make
available. These pictures are exceptionally good and include some of
the most remarkable shots of the war. Very few have been published.
To my mind they would constitute one of the most valuable parts of the
book. There would also be a few diagrams and detail maps. It now looks
like the book will run to about 65,000 words, perhaps more.

CVWP, 68/80: TLS

2

Johns Hopkins, 1946–62

83. To the Board of Governors

of the Johns Hopkins Club

December 18, 1947

I understand that a ruling of the Board of Governors made several years ago now stands in the way of admitting a Negro graduate student of the university to membership in the Johns Hopkins Club.

As a member of the club I should like to ask the gentlemen of the present board to reconsider this old ruling. It seems to me that changed conditions call for new rules. In the first place the university has demonstrated its willingness to accept Negro students on an equal basis. This would seem to call for a new policy of the Hopkins Club to bring it into harmony with university conditions.

It is my hope that the change can be made in the club as it was in the university, where it was accomplished quietly and effectively and without adverse criticism. The cheerful acceptance of the new university policy reflects credit on the good sense of the students, the faculty, and the administration. It is my belief that a corresponding change in club rule would be accepted in the same spirit. The issue will inevitably have to be faced in the club, and if it could be settled by the board at an early meeting the problem would be disposed of with a minimum of difficulty.

In addition, I feel that a rule which discriminates between students on the basis of race is not consistent with the liberal tradition of the Johns Hopkins campus.[1]

CVWP, 28/327: TLS

84. To William B. Hesseltine[2]

DECEMBER 8, 1948

[deletion]

First, how do you react to these general notions. That the sessions be (1) *shorter* and (2) *better*.[3] As for the first, never more than two papers per session, even one for some if it's good enough. Never three. That flat rule ought to take some of the torture and boredom out of the meeting—as well as some load off our shoulders. As for quality, I can't see why we should not shoot for top-flight stuff. Not necessarily *names*, but stuff of quality, breadth and wide interest. No dreary dishes of spade-work, but interpretive essays, synthesis, revisionist challenger if any. Something to keep them awake. A fight if possible.

Second, import a few live Yankees who are unabashed by their ignoble origins. Break up the tradition of parochialism.

Third, would a round-table session on research topics in progress at the graduate schools (North and South) on Southern history be acceptable? The boys play their hand awfully close to their chests on research subjects. Would they loosen up?

Fourth, a session on the South in the New Deal. V. O. Key, Political Scientist at Hopkins is finishing a revolutionary study of southern politics during the period, and we might mix him up with Arthur Schlesinger, Jr.[4]

1. The board replied (15 January 1948) that it "does not disapprove of admitting Negroes as members as a matter of principle but feels that it must consider the wishes of the membership at large," and would appoint a committee to discuss the matter.

2. William B. Hesseltine (1902–1963), a Virginian, had taught at the University of Wisconsin since 1931; he was a Civil War historian.

3. CVW was chair of the Program Committee for the fifteenth annual meeting of the Southern Historical Association: it was held in Williamsburg, VA, 10–12 November 1949.

4. V. O. [Valdimer Orlando] Key (1908–1963), the political scientist, was about to publish *Southern Politics in State and Nation* (New York: Alfred A. Knopf, 1949); Arthur Meier Schlesinger Jr. (1917–2007), the American historian and political liberal, was then an associate professor of history at Harvard and had, a few years earlier, published *The Age of Jackson* (Boston: Little, Brown, 1945).

Fifth, a session on some phase of race—as controversial as possible.

Finally, what about sending me a list of subjects and people to do them, anything good that comes to mind.

[deletion]

CVWP, 51/603: TLS

85. To Lester J. Cappon[5]

JANUARY 31, 1949

Assuming your earlier letter on tentative program was green light I spoke to Franklin retraction embarrassing to association should think stop would not association instead of college have responsibility and blame[6]

CVWP, 51/604: TELEGRAM

86. To J. Merton England[7]

FEBRUARY 2, 1949

A second reading confirms my first impression that Kirwan's dissertation is a hell of a good job.[8] I would, without much hesitation, call it the most satisfactory political history of any Southern state during the

5. Lester J. Cappon (1901–1981), who came from Wisconsin, was the archivist for Colonial Williamsburg and director of the Institute of Early American History and Culture; he was president of the Southern Historical Association in 1949 and so presided over the Williamsburg meeting; he is perhaps best known for Lester J. Cappon, ed., *The Adams-Jefferson Letters: The Complete Correspondence Between Thomas Jefferson and Abigail and John Adams* (Chapel Hill: University of North Carolina Press, 1959).

6. John Hope Franklin (1915–2009) received his Harvard doctorate in 1941; in 1949, he was teaching at Howard University. He had recently published what would remain the standard textbook on black history for many years: *From Slavery to Freedom: A History of American Negroes* (New York: Alfred A. Knopf, 1947). In the autumn of 1948, when Franklin was at the Library of Congress, CVW had visited his study room and suggested that Franklin read a paper to the SHA (and so become the first African-American to do so), "*if* the next annual meeting was not held in one of the more racist towns in the South." On this, see John Hope Franklin, *Mirror to America: The Autobiography of John Hope Franklin* (New York: Farrar, Straus and Giroux, 2005), 140.

7. J. Merton England (1915–2007) was director of the University of Kentucky Press and an American historian.

8. Albert Dennis Kirwan (1904–1971), whose 1947 doctorate at Duke University would be published as Albert D. Kirwan, *Revolt of the Rednecks: Mississippi Politics, 1876–1925* (Lexington: University of Kentucky Press, 1951); he was later president of the University of Kentucky.

post-Reconstruction period. It is more realistic than Miss Halsell on Mississippi, and to my mind is on par with Wharton's job on the Negro.[9] That last is intended as praise. It pins down the man's name, date, price, and how he earned his beer & skittles. Only one who has plugged through dozens of conventional state histories can appreciate what I mean. In my opinion the thing deserves publication, and with some patience and imagination I believe it can be whipped into publishable shape. So much for the orchids—now for the brickbats. I shall emphasize the latter only because I hope that is what you are primarily interested in. His virtues speak for themselves.

> Brickbat #1.   The thing smells of the stacks and has "PhD" stamped on it in bold letters. Much of what I have to say by way of suggestion has to do with efforts to efface this very onus. If I did not think it could be done I would frankly recommend that he chop it up into articles or publish it by offset. But I think it *is* possible.

> BB #2.   It is burdened with excessive elaboration of example and illustration. This is the inevitable temptation of the dissertation writer, and it is perfectly natural to yield to it. In effect the candidate is saying to his examining committee: "OK, you asked for research, industry, exhaustiveness, thoroughness—I'll give you a bellyfull." So, instead of being content with a couple of beautiful illustrations that prove his point to the hilt, he stacks up [a] dozen illustrations (many not so good) and lays them on the counter. This no doubt delights the profs (though not invariably) but it bores the innocent reader. Take for example his chapter on McLaurinism.[10] This is chock full of rich stuff. That letter from Cousin Joe to the Gov. is a perfect howler. It is right out of Falstaff's dialogue: "Hal, rob me the exchequer!" With a bit of buildup that alone would clinch the point. But no, he buries it in a flood of such let-

9. Halsell's contribution lay in articles: see Willie D. Halsell, "Republican Factionalism in Mississippi, 1882–1884," *Journal of Southern History* 7 (February 1941): 84–101; idem., "James R. Chalmers and 'Mahoneism' in Mississippi," *Journal of Southern History* 10 (February 1944): 37–58; idem., "The Bourbon Period in Mississippi Politics, 1875–1890," *Journal of Southern History* 11 (November 1945): 519–37.

10. Anselm Joseph McLaurin (1848–1909) was a U.S. senator from Mississippi (1894–95, 1901–9) and governor (1896–1900); he was sympathetic to the economic plight of white farmers and, in the 1890s, though he defeated the Populist candidate for governor, advocated free silver and opposed protectionism.

ters nowhere near so good. I could illustrate this tendency at length—only to be guilty of the offense I am charging.

#3. It stands in need of cutting. This follows in part from the above, though is worth separate consideration. I estimate the book would gain by the deletion of 75 to 100 pages. Nor do I believe that this much cutting would sacrifice a single one of the numerous virtues of the work. In the main, I believe the cutting should be done along the lines suggested in #2, but I think the author will find other opportunities if he sets his mind to the job. It is a matter of shifting the gears of selectivity—from the low-gear of academic, professional standards to the high-gear intelligent reader standards. I grant that the reader-appeal of this type of study will be largely limited to historians, professional and amateur, and to academic-minded people (though not entirely, to be sure, and that is a considerable public itself), but even so, a different standard from the Ph.D. committee.

#4. It is over-documented. I am sure the author realizes this already, but a few suggestions might be worth while. For example, the four footnotes on page 73 might be consolidated to one. Footnote #11 could be eliminated, since the idea is not original with the source cited, and the author is under no real obligation to the source for a matter of common knowledge. Also strike out footnote #12, consolidating with #9. Also, one reference to Kendrick's article in the chapter is sufficient to acknowledge the debt. Similarly, I recall a reference to my book on Watson, though the text does not reveal that the author owes me anything since the idea or information was common property. I would suggest striking out all "courtesy" footnotes, all padding that might have pleased a committee once, but is no longer required. Cut down citations to the minimum of source of quotation and ideas which the author really borrowed. The only standard should be honesty and good sense.

#5. It could stand some more scrupulous checking for consistency and accuracy. As I told you, I would not undertake a reading of this sort, since I do not have the time for it. On the whole the work impresses me as careful and scholarly. But I have yet to see a manuscript that was entirely free of bugs. For example, on p. 4 the author says Lamar was chosen in 1876 to succeed B. K. Bruce in the Senate. On p. 88 he speaks of Lamar and Bruce as colleagues in the Senate. On p. 199 he says J. Z. George succeeded Bruce in the Senate in the early 1880s.[11] Something's SNAFU here. I don't mean to say this is typical, but if a cursory reading picked this up, there are probably more to keep it company.

#6. It makes no concessions to the non-professional, non-specialized reader. Once more, OK in a dissertation, but not in a book—not if he hopes to have a larger reading public than a committee on dissertations, or a few fellow-historians like myself. The only hint of the hell & monkeybusiness of 1875 and what preceded the reader is given is, on the opening page, the statement: "When Governor Adelbert Ames resigned in 1876 . . ." Now I ask you, who the hell but a handful of specialists know who Adelbert was and why.[12]

#7. It is lacking in vivid biographical sketches and portraiture. This follows from #6. To my taste, and it probably is largely a matter of taste, biography is the essence of political history. And in the personal type of political history Kirwan writes, it is doubly important. There was never a more colorful crowd of rogues & asses & clowns & showmen than is assembled in these pages. And yet, but for a suggestion here and there (Vardaman and other exceptions) who would guess it but those who already knew it?[13] He introduces most of his main personages with scarcely a personal note. Bearded, bald, knockneed—it's all one. Surely he can spare us a sentence or so for a convincing picture of Private Allen in action—or Lamar, George, Walthall.[14] There are some marvelous contrasts, and they are not irrelevant, but essential to the point of his story.

11. Lucius Quintus Cincinnatus Lamar (1825–1993) served as U.S. senator from Mississippi from 1877 to 1885, Blanche Kelso Bruce (1841–1998) from 1875 to 1881, James Zachariah George (1826–1897) from 1881 to 1897. Technically, George (a Democrat) succeeded Bruce (a Republican) in the "Class 1" seat, while Lamar, a Democrat, succeeded James Lusk Alcorn (1816–1894), a Republican, in the "Class 2" seat.

12. Adelbert Ames (1835–1933), Republican governor of Mississippi (1874–76), resigned to evade his impeachment trial by a newly Democratic state legislature.

13. James Kimble Vardaman (1861–1930), the leading Mississippi political demagogue of the early twentieth century, was governor (1904–8) and U.S. senator (1913–19).

14. John Mills Allen (1846–1917) of Tupelo was a U.S. representative (1885–1901). Known as "Private Allen" for having served at that rank in the Confederate army, he was fond of telling funny stories when giving speeches; for a few samples, see Arthur Palmer Hudson, ed., *Humor of the Old Deep South* (New York: Macmillan, 1936), 198–205. Edward Cary Walthall (1831–1898) was a Confederate general and U.S. senator (1885–94, 1895–98).

And I don't mean a lot of phoney Claude Bowers gossip-column stuff.[15] I mean that when a main character is a preposterous clown or a moral monster the writer owes it to his subject and reader to let us in on the fact with a tersely sketched picture. Now, I don't mean that he is completely lacking in this respect, for there is a lot of color in his stuff. I only call for more where needed and ask him not to miss a punch. I wonder if Kirwan knows Robert Penn Warren's novels. If not, I suggest he take a gander at his "At Heaven's High Gate," or "All the King's Men" for an example of the master of the craft of portraiture.[16] For God's sake, I'm not asking him to be a novelist, but there is something to learn from them. Or try some Faulkner. He, incidentally, knows Mississippi.

#8. It is too inhibited on the score of generalization. This follows, again, from the dissertation complex. Who could help being inhibited in the face of an examination on his dissertation. So he doesn't stick his neck out. Well, I suggest he throw off some of those inhibitions and call the shots as he sees them. He need not necessarily call them the sons of bitches they were, but he could suggest the fact more strongly. And, apart from the personalities, he might throw his weight around a bit more with interpretation.

#9. It stands in need of more orientation with and reference to the broader regional and national scene. I am especially aware of the broader significance for the whole South of what he has to say. His Mississippi "Bourbons" (I don't like the word and neither does he. I refuse to use it myself), Independents, Populists, disfranchisers, Mclaurins, Vardamans, Bilboes, etc., have their counterparts in almost every Southern state.[17] Kirwan knows that, of course, but I think he ought to let the reader in on the thing. It wouldn't take much space, and no amount of research. Simply point up the facts with a few references to contemporary goings on in Alabama, Tennessee, Loui-

15. Claude G. Bowers (1878–1958) was a journalist who wrote popular history; see, especially, *Jefferson and Hamilton: The Struggle for Democracy in America* (Boston: Houghton Mifflin, 1925), and *The Tragic Era: The Revolution After Lincoln* (Boston: Houghton Mifflin, 1929).

16. Robert Penn Warren, *At Heaven's Gate* (New York: Harcourt, Brace, 1943); idem., *All the King's Men* (New York: Harcourt, Brace, 1946).

17. Theodore G. Bilbo (1877–1947) was Vardaman's successor as the Mississippi demagogue par excellence; he served as governor (1916–20) and U.S. senator (1935–47).

siana, South Carolina, etc. The same could be said for orientation with national developments, though the need here is less than is the case with the regional picture. I emphasize this point because I believe the book is more than a history of Mississippi. If it were only that I would not recommend publication, and I don't think you would be considering publication seriously. I believe the author can make the reader aware of the broader implications of his study by the simple devices I have suggested.

#10. Its present title is impossible. Here I am not telling you anything that both you and Kirwan don't already know. The choice of title is a publisher's art and should be an author's prerogative. God knows: THE ONE-PARTY SYSTEM, POLITICS IN THE DEEP SOUTH, THE FAULKNERIAN POLITY, SNAFU ALONG THE LEVEE, HILLBILLIE AND BLACK BELT, DELTA DIRT, in short almost anything but the present one. But seriously, I think you are perfectly justified, assuming the alterations suggested in #9, in giving the book a wider label and in making broader demands for attention.

Well, I have pontificated at a hell of a clip—as if I know all about the publisher's business and the author's subject. I must admit I don't. All I have tried to do is to call the shots as I see them. Looking back over what I have written, I realize that some of the comments have been hard punches. However, with as intelligent a man as Kirwan, I don't think I will give offense. So if this will be of any help to him you need not withhold my name nor anything I have said. I feel sure he will understand my good intentions in the business.

P.S. It goes without saying that you could publish the job with a minimum of alteration pretty much as stands. I simply had in mind that the publisher has other obligation than those to scholarship—namely a budget to balance. Also there is always the temptation to mess with a good thing to make it better, along with regrets at seeing a good work ignored for want of readability.

P.S. #2. Aghast at the stupid remark Kirwan attributes to me on page 113 (and footnote 27) I asked a librarian to check. I have not checked myself, and he may have some justification. But please have him check again. In the statement before the House Sub-Committee I was generalizing about the disfranchisement by poll tax in the South as a whole. That is when I said it was a movement mainly backed by "commercial and industrial interests." I knew the Mississippi movement was agrarian, but I could not lecture the (pretty short-tempered) congressmen on exceptions to the rule. South Carolina was another exception, and in part other states, but I think not Alabama, Louisiana, Virginia, North Carolina, etc. I did not apply the statement to a particular state and certainly not [the carbon breaks off here]

    CVWP, 55/660: TCLU

87. To John Hope Franklin

FEBRUARY 4, 1949

O ur plans for the Williamsburg meeting next November are taking shape, and I want to know if you will be able to read us a paper on the Martial Spirit of the Old South. I particularly hope you will agree to do this for it is important to the shape and character of the program planned. The invitation is not, be assured, something I put over on my own. I was determined to press the matter, but it did not prove necessary. Two other members of the committee suggested your name independently and the others fell in quite heartily. There was no disagreement within the committee. The invitation is therefore unanimous and cordial.

If you accept, will you give me a tentative title as soon as possible. I rather hope it will be the one above, but of course you must decide. The title for the session would be The Old South and there would be two papers only—in conformity with a decision not to drag things out past endurance. There would be no "discussion leader," aside from the chairman who would invite comment from the floor. I am at a loss for a man to pair with you in the session. Preferably a paper on some other cultural phase of the Old South—religion, economics, etc. Can you offer any suggestion? We need a white Southerner to balance a good many Yanks on the program. The emphasis of the program is to be upon interpretation, reappraisal, and synthesis, rather than reports on spade work. Also do you know anyone who could give a critical reappraisal of historical literature on slavery to pair with Vernon Wharton on the literature on the Negro as freedman?

    CVWP, 51/604: TLS

88. To John Hope Franklin

FEBRUARY 23, 1949

I am delighted at your acceptance.

As for the question you raise, this is the most illumination I can give. There will be no "discusser." That means you won't have to submit a formal paper to anybody. Hence nobody will be running down your citations and picking you up on some silly "point." Hence what you say is to a large degree off the record. I am opposed to "discussers" because I think they inhibit speakers and obstruct intelligent exchange of ideas and good conversation—and if these affairs don't result in that then what good are they? Discussion, if any, will be from the floor. So I think you are free to make such sensible observations as are tedious or sometimes impossible to "document" and therefore often get omitted from "scholarly" productions.

As you see, all this leans to the broader, more interpretative sort of paper. But it is all up to you and I will be happy with any decision you make, I am sure. The program-making policy is to seek out people who are interested in interpretation, synthesis, revision. But obviously not all good scholars are ready at one time to hand out conclusions and interpretations. You are the judge.

Our good Yankee friends down the coast are in a buzz-buzz over the intricacies of Southern race ritual. If I didn't think you had a sense of humor I would never have let you in for this. Our friends amuse me no end, and I am giving them no help. Just watching with detached irony. My only suggestion so far is that they set up a table tagged "untouchables," another "Brahmins," etc. We'll see what happens. If I could catch J. G. de R. H. with the right number of old fashions under his belt I would simplify the whole business by suggesting he invite you to the speakers' table.[18] He would probably do it.

P.S. Have you thought about sleeping arrangements for Williamsburg? Cappon is thinking of seeking some local family for you or if you have a car, commuting to Hampton Institute.[19] I said you would probably bring a pup tent and "K" rations.

CVWP, 51/604: TLS

18. Joseph Gregoire de Roulhac Hamilton.

19. The Hampton Institute was the closest black college to Williamsburg. In the event, Franklin stayed with Douglass and Virginia Adair, in their house close to William and Mary: see Franklin, *Mirror to America*, 141.

89. To John Simon Guggenheim Memorial Foundation
[NOVEMBER 1949]

CONFIDENTIAL REPORT ON CANDIDATE FOR FELLOWSHIP

NAME OF CANDIDATE: DR. JOHN HOPE FRANKLIN

REPORT REQUESTED OF: DR. C. VANN WOODWARD, HISTORY DEPARTMENT

For a long time American historians have been hopefully awaiting the emergence of a Negro historian for whom it was not necessary to make any apologies or allowances on account of his race. There have been some vigorous Negro scholars who have written important historical works, but their primary interest has usually been the promotion of a cause—the cause of their race. This is understandable and laudable in its way, but it has set the Negro scholar apart, sometimes distorted his work, and prevented wholehearted acceptance among the craft of professional historians.

In Mr. Franklin I believe we have a Negro historian of the type we have been hoping to see. It is true that his published work so far has been primarily in the history of the Negro, but it is freer of race-consciousness and propaganda than preceding works of the kind. I am pleased to see that he is turning in his future research to non-racial subjects such as the two mentioned in Plans for Work.

As Chairman of the Program Committee of a recent meeting of the Southern Historical Association at Williamsburg, I was mainly responsible for inviting Mr. Franklin to present a paper. He did this in a first-rate style and was cordially accepted. It was the first time in the life of the association that a Negro historian took part in one of the programs. The success of the experiment was in large part due to Franklin's good judgment.

As for the book he plans on "Southern Travelers in the North, 1800–1860," it seems to me to be well-conceived.[20] There is certainly a place for such a study. All the emphasis so far, as he points out, has been upon the views of Northerners on the South. His researches should turn up some interesting contributions not only to Southern intellectual history but to national history as well. He has demonstrated by his previous publications that he is capable of handling the job. I believe that my opinion

---

20. This took a long time to appear: see John Hope Franklin, *A Southern Odyssey: Travelers in the Antebellum North* (Baton Rouge: Louisiana State University Press, 1976).

would find wide support among Southern historians in the North as well
as in the South.[21]

CVWP, 22/263: TLS

90. To Angus Cameron[22]

JULY [16?], 1950

This is on the revision problems. I wish we could talk about them
instead of write. If the Baltimore trip you were considering materializes please postpone reply until then. If you cannot come down maybe
we can hammer out our differences this way.

One problem is background for the general reader. I am building my
interpretation of 1876–1877 on Beard's concept of the Second American Revolution plus Howard K. Beale's interpretation of the election
of 1866 in his THE CRITICAL YEAR.[23] I wish you had read the latter. It
treats the high point of "radicalism" in the revolutionary process, showing how the Lincoln-Johnson moderate plan of restoration of the South
was defeated by the Radicals combined with business interests who saw
in the immediate return of Southern representatives to Congress the ruin
of tariff, bank, credit, money, subsidy, tax arrangements enacted during
South's absence. To offer those reasons for defeating Lincoln-Johnson
Restoration plan would not be politic for it would offend Western agrarians and push them into an alliance with Johnson and the South against
the Eastern business and radical combination. Instead Eastern leaders
put forward the idealistic war aims for defeating Johnson: equality, justice,
freedom, loyalty, 14th Amendment, Civil Rights, etc., and played down
economic issues on which the wartime allies, East & West were divided.
Victory enabled them to keep the South out until the economic system
was consolidated and better entrenched, keep the West in line behind an
economic program of dubious advantage to that region, instal governments in the Southern states that not only realized to some extent the
idealistic war aims of equality, justice for the Negro, but at the same time

21. Franklin did receive a Guggenheim fellowship: see Franklin, *Mirror to America*, 145.

22. Angus Cameron (1908–2002), editor in chief at Little, Brown from 1938 until driven
out by McCarthyite accusations; he was working with CVW on the latter's *Reunion and Reaction:
The Compromise of 1877 and the End of Reconstruction* (Boston: Little, Brown, 1951).

23. Howard K. Beale, *The Critical Year: A Study of Andrew Johnson and Reconstruction* (New
York: Harcourt, Brace, 1930).

sent representatives to Washington who voted solidly with business representatives on the *economic* war aims—the new system of privilege, which
Johnson said was as offensive to democracy as the old system of planter
privilege. Thus in 1866 the idealistic and the pragmatic aims of the revolution were working hand-in-hand.

On that foundation I picture the final stage of the revolutionary
process—Thermidor. (I have consciously refrained from using the word
in my book for fear it was a bit fancy and perhaps a bit strained. Do you
think I should use it?) Now my intention is to fill in rapidly the background of the earlier stages of the revolution in my first chapter, perhaps
right at the start, the second page or so, maybe for three or four pages,
trying to make it plain why I am doing it and what bearing it has on my
subject. In that I should work in a picture of the ante-bellum Whigs, their
meaning, etc.

A second general problem. You are bothered about the way I use the
word "carpetbagger." First, it seems unavoidable to use the word. I think
it would be selfconscious and pretentious to stop and write out "Northern men who came South during or immediately after the war and took
a prominent part in Southern political and/or economic affairs"—
everytime I meant "carpetbagger." Of course the word is also an epithet with a derogatory meaning. This was partly the result of Southern
propaganda, partly because some of them amply earned the reputation
they got. But the Republicans themselves used the expression—even the
carpetbaggers themselves. It was always necessary to make the distinction, and that was too handy a word. I propose to explain that I am using
it to designate "Northern men who came South etc." without stopping
to decide in each case whether that particular man deserved or did not
deserve the derogative connotations. Some did, some did not. Some were
"sincere," some "adventurers." But I have yet to find one who was not
used—consciously or unconsciously—to further the pragmatic and economic aims of the revolution. However zealous they proved in defending
Negro rights and equality in the South (and they rarely had any political
plums to spare the Negroes) the men they sent to Washington voted right
down the line with Blaine & Conkling & Butler and the rest for the New
Economic Order. Witness the specimens figuring in my narrative.[24] Sena-

24. The first two of these were prominent Republican national politicians: Maine's James
Gillespie Blaine (1830–1893), Speaker of the House of Representatives (1869–75), senator
(1876–81), and secretary of state (1881, 1889–92); New York's Roscoe Conkling (1829–1888),

tors West, Dorsey, Clayton, Spencer, Conover—carpetbaggers all, and all in bed with Scott and Huntington.[25]

But so were the Redeemers, you will say. But because I demonstrate that the men of "Thermidor" were scamps, it does not follow that the Men of the "Terror" were saints. It is quite possible that the scamps were numerous in both camps. And also it is possible for both of them to conceive of themselves as promoting righteous ends, if sometimes making regrettable concessions to the expedient. You jump on me hard for letting the Hayesites and Redeemers strike a heroic pose once. I admit that I gave the wrong impression there by failing to make clear that I did not take the pose at face value. But as I see it I must let them strike the pose—healing the tragic breach, reconciling estranged sections, solving the national crisis, peaceable solution to ugly situation, preventing violence and civil war. Then side-by-side with that show what they were saying in their private correspondence. But the devil must have his due. There is an element of the valid in their pose, and they can not be expected to put forward less creditable motives when the more attractive are lying around. You did not expect the Republicans to do that in 1866 & all that. It was the only way such people (maybe I should just say "people") could rationalize such shenanigans as the Scott Deal.[26] Without such motives this story would seem to me less credible.

---

congressman (1859–63, 1865–67) and senator (1867–81). The third is less clear, since CVW might mean one of two possible Butlers: Matthew Calbraith Butler (1836–1909), a Confederate general, Democrat, and senator from South Carolina (1877–95); or Benjamin Franklin Butler (1818–1893), Union general, congressman (1867–75, 1877–79, as a Republican), and governor of Massachusetts (1883–84, as a Democrat).

25. The first five names are all Northerners and ex-Union soldiers who moved to the South after the war and became prominent Republican national politicians. That is, Joseph Rodman West (1822–1898), Union general and senator from Louisiana (1871–77); Stephen Wallace Dorsey (1842–1916), senator from Arkansas (1873–79); Powell Clayton (1833–1914), governor of Arkansas (1868–71) and senator from Arkansas (1871–77); George Eliphaz Spencer (1836–1893), senator from Alabama (1868–79); Simon Barclay Conover (1840–1908), senator from Florida (1873–79). The two last names are railway magnates: Thomas Alexander Scott (1823–1881), president of the Pennsylvania Railroad in 1874 while still president of the Texas and Pacific; Collis Potter Huntington (1821–1900), a chief builder of the transcontinental railroad and, at various times, in charge of the Central Pacific, the Chesapeake and Ohio, and the Southern Pacific railroads.

26. This was Scott's proposal that Southern Democrats would consent to the election of Rutherford B. Hayes to the presidency, in exchange for various subsidies that might offer economic assistance to the South, including money for Scott's own Texas and Pacific Railroad.

I hope I am not being youthfully cynical, because I am too old for that. I am sure much idealism went into the making of Reconstruction. I am equally convinced that this idealism was employed as a mask to advance the Whig economic program, and that as soon as the economic program was entrenched the mask was discarded—along with the idealism. And often the idealists and pragmatists (Thad Stevens) were one and the same, with sometimes one set of motives and sometimes the other taking the upper hand.[27] I suppose I tend to discount idealistic and humanitarian motives in proportion to the distance of subject from object. In those terms the distance from Boston to New Orleans is comparable with the distance from Washington to Soeul or Moscow to Saigon.

But before I go all out in calling names it seems to me I am obliged to have in mind some sound and practicable course of action to offer as an alternative to the one I am denouncing. And I confess I don't have one handy. A few suggestions, perhaps, but not all the answers. Suppose the Southerners had joined the extreme Tildenites in maintaining a filibuster and causing an interregnum. Suppose Hayes had attempted to maintain the carpetbaggers in office for another term in Louisiana—or Grant had seized power illegally and restored them in all the Southern states. Who was "right" in Louisiana? Well, I don't know. But it wasn't the Redeemers and it wasn't the carpetbaggers.

It still seems possible to me to use the "Compromise" thesis in order to give the story a broader historical framework in American history. Your idea of the historian following the stream, where it came from where it is going. But being more guarded and tentative, and pointing out carefully certain departures from the older type of compromises. They had been struck to maintain a sectional balance of power without breaking the peace. The Compromise of 1877, on the other hand, while it also dealt with the sectional balance of power, in effect made the South a satelite of the dominant region, promised a share of the material blessings of the New Order, and at the same time by special dispensation exempted the South from complying with the idealistic tenets of the Revolutionary ideology. The New South leaders, for their part, agreed to withdraw their support from the internal enemies of the New Order in the North (Democratic reformers and Western agrarians and labor) in exchange for a share of the material rewards.

27. Thaddeus Stevens (1792–1868), congressman from Pennsylvania (1839–53 as a Whig, 1859–68 as a Republican), one of the leading Radicals during Reconstruction.

Please let me remind you that you promised to send me a copy of your report on my manuscript. I hope you will send along the unflattering parts too. I am not very thin-skinned. I wish it were possible for us to argue these debatable points by the hour.

I must finish up my revision by the first week in August and I very much hope we can thresh out our differences before that time. I have no further inspiration on the title problem. Is there any word yet on the scheduling of publication? I am returning the contract under separate cover with a letter.

CVWP, 71/109: TCLU

91. To Thomas P. Govan

NOVEMBER 30, 1951

The members you suggest, Wiley, Wall, Dierke, and Charlie Smith, seem first-rate to me.[28] Could you round up a Texan to complete the list? As for the Knoxville situation, Professor J. W. Hoffman is chairman of Local Arrangements Committee.[29] I asked him if possible to make dining and meeting arrangements that would permit unembarrassed attendance of Negro members. He took the request without blinking and I assume but do not know for sure that the arrangements will be made accordingly. I hope you will be able to take advantage of this but as you know colored talent is scarce and we would not want to make a choice purely on the basis of colored. The proposed theme for the program sounds as if it might give a unity and interest to such as we want. Naturally the theme could be strained to the point of appearing forced, but I trust your judgment to prevent that happening.

Since I am not only an admirer but an envyer of Warren's historical talents, I would consider a paper by him as the triumph of the occasion. By all means do everything you can to enlist his interest. Of course we

28. Govan was chair of the program committee for the eighteenth annual meeting of the Southern Historical Association, held in Knoxville, TN, to which CVW would give his presidential address. Three of the four named here would serve on the committee: Bell Irvin Wiley (1906–1980), a Civil War historian, then at Louisiana State University (1946–59); Bennett H. Wall (1914–2003) of the University of Kentucky and a historian of business, who would later serve for thirty-three years as secretary-treasurer of the SHA; and Harold Alfred Bierck Jr. (b. 1916), a Latin American historian at the University of North Carolina. Charles E. Smith, a European historian at Louisiana State University, would not serve, but Dayton Phillips, a medieval historian at Vanderbilt University, would.

29. A historian at the University of Tennessee.

would take anything he suggested, but if you can get him on the theme of the bane of Southern history which he has in mind in all his novels and his projected novel, it would be wonderful. As for Faulkner you might work on it if you have an inside track but he is, of course, awfully eccentric. I would certainly be happy to take a chance, and there are certain indications that he might be interested.[30] As soon as you get me another name I will get out the letters of appointment for your committee, but if the ones you have mentioned are agreeable, by all means go ahead now.

[deletion]

CVWP, 51/605: TCLU

92. To Colonel Thomas G. Dobyns[31]

JANUARY 14, 1952

Thank you for your letter of January 9. While I am sure I would have enjoyed working with you and your staff I am, as a matter of fact, relieved to know that my services will not be needed. The pressure of other interests would have made this additional work a great burden.

On the other hand, I am greatly concerned by the implications of your letter. I can only infer from what you say that the Intelligence people have made an unfavorable report on my application.[32] This is naturally disturbing. I feel so confident of my own record and my loyalty that I am not seriously worried about myself. But I confess that I am deeply troubled that the government, because of its regulations, is forced to deprive itself of the help of qualified specialists in our universities. I have seen this happen before, but this instance brings it home to me sharply.

There has been no personal inconvenience in this matter and I am sure it is not your fault that I have not been able to join you. If regulations permit you to give me any insight upon the questions I raise, I should greatly appreciate hearing from you.

CVWP, 54/640: TCLU

30. Neither Warren nor Faulkner spoke at the Knoxville meeting.

31. Dobyns helped to organize the Historical Section of the Joint Chiefs of Staff, a body which CVW had been tentatively invited to join.

32. CVW was denied a security clearance for his past involvement in radical organizations; on this, see CVW to Thomas A. Krueger, 19 July 1963, printed below.

93. To James W. Silver[33]

APRIL 13, 1953

The point of the paper was this: Southern history has been written with too much preoccupation over the mid-nineteenth century sectional conflict, its antecedents and consequences.[34] The framework needs to be expanded beyond national boundaries and northern comparison to embrace comparisons with regions and countries more analogous to the South in climate, economy, racial composition, and history. Fruitful sources of such analogies can be sought in other English-speaking regions around the world or in other agrarian raw-material economies with comparable problems.

As for publishing the paper, what you mistook for a paper were some ideas that might be used for a paper if I ever got around to writing it, which at the moment seems unlikely.
[deletion]

CVWP, 50/590: TCLU

94. To Daniel J. Boorstin[35]

MAY 17, 1953

I want to tell you with how much excitement and admiration I read your book, and how I regret that I had not read it when I saw you in Lexington.[36] For it suggested a hundred things to talk about that I would never get around to writing you about. Some themes you tackle have not been handled, to my mind, with more illumination and insight since Tocqueville. I do not know how readily you would acknowledge the debt, but it seems to me that you come nearer than anyone I think of to applying the Frenchman's critique to twentieth century America. And I think it is done with much originality and brilliance.

33. James W. Silver (1907–1988), professor of history at the University of Mississippi; he came to Oxford first in 1936, after getting his doctorate at Vanderbilt University.

34. CVW had recently given a paper in Jackson, MS: see Silver to CVW, 8 April 1953.

35. Daniel J. Boorstin (1914–2004), an American historian notable among the "consensus historians" of the 1950s. Born in Atlanta, he grew up in Oklahoma, attended Harvard, was a Rhodes Scholar, and took his doctorate at Yale; before becoming Librarian of Congress, he spent most of his career at the University of Chicago.

36. Daniel J. Boorstin, *The Genius of American Politics* (Chicago: University of Chicago Press, 1953). The Mississippi Valley Historical Association had held its annual meeting in Lexington, KY, on 7–9 May 1953.

There are things I would like to argue—and probably come to agree—with you. You would, I know, scorn any basis of complacency for your views. And yet I think they will be perverted to the uses of the complacent regardless of your intentions.

Also I wonder if a closer scrutiny of the inner sanctum of American faith would not turn up at least two graven images that we might call Mass and Speed. They are not peculiarly national idols, but idols of the time that have a large American cult.

The point of the continuity and imminence of the American past is impressively supported and I think soundly conceived. I learned a lot from it. But I would like to argue your extension of the point to the South. I would like to write an essay sometime about the broken continuity of the South's past, and started to once. If I do I will try it out on you. I was surprised to learn that we grew up as close together as Oklahoma and Arkansas. I don't know whether you ever shook off the Southern heritage. I set out deliberately to do so in several attempts, but I never really did. I will have to work it out some day in order to live with it.
[deletion]

   CVWP, 8/86: TCLU

95. To Charles Grier Sellers[37]

MAY 22, 1953

My delay in writing you is no indication of lack of interest in the copy of your letter to Bob Lively dated April 6.[38] Quite the contrary. I am more than grateful for being permitted to listen in on this conversation and I would very much like to hear more of it.

You seem to be grappling with a problem—or a set of problems—that I have been playing with independently myself for some time. I came

37. Charles Grier Sellers Jr. (b. 1923), a North Carolinian who had a doctorate from the University of North Carolina, was then teaching American history at Princeton and would later move to the University of California-Berkeley. His early scholarship concerned James K. Polk, but in the 1950s he worked on the liberal manifesto that would eventually be published as Charles Grier Sellers Jr., ed., *The Southerner as American* (Chapel Hill: University of North Carolina Press, 1960).

38. Robert A. Lively (1922–1973), who taught American history at the University of Wisconsin, was then the coeditor with Sellers of the proposed symposium, though he did not appear in the final book. He was best known for *Fiction Fights the Civil War: An Unfinished Chapter in the Literary History of the American People* (Chapel Hill: University of North Carolina Press, 1957).

at it through individual instances. First I thought a study of G. W. Cable would be the way.[39] His spiritual schism was obvious and he was conscious of it—of the clash between conscience and heritage, conviction and loyalty, Massachusetts and Louisiana, mother and father, etc. Then I got absorbed in ante-bellum antecedents and forgot Cable. They are complicated and their assorted motivations complex, but they have enough in common to support comparisons. Limiting the group to those whose internal conflict drove them into exile I believe that I isolated those that illustrate the spiritual schism most poignantly and dramaticly. They would include Birney and the Grimke sisters together with a more obscure group of Southerners in Lane Seminary who joined the shock troops of abolitionism. These I would call the "Men of the Thirties." Then there is the second group in the Fifties: Helper, Conway, Mattie Griffith, Hedrick, Goodloe, John Fee, etc. Well, I gave some lectures on the theme at LSU and expect to make a small book on the subject before long.[40] In the process I hope to shape up the background to some of the questions you people are asking yourselves, or at least contribute the perspective of a century or so. But no more than that.

It has been twenty-three years since the Nashville group published their manifesto. I was old enough to have been on the periphery of that event. I remember going to Nashville with Bill Couch, who gave battle to the agrarians in mortal debate and sustained minor but honorable wounds from the encounter.[41] Many of us could not accept the Nash-

39. George Washington Cable (1844–1925), the New Orleans novelist and racial liberal.

40. In April 1951, CVW gave the Walter Lynwood Fleming Lectures at Louisiana State University on "Southern Dissenters in Exile." The figures he mentions were all Southerners who ended up in the North or abroad. These were: James Gillespie Birney (1792–1857) of Kentucky, the abolitionist; Angelina Emily Grimké Weld (1805–1879) and her older sister Sarah Moore Grimké (1792–1873) of South Carolina, who were abolitionists and proponents of women's rights; Moncure Daniel Conway (1832–1907) of Virginia, the abolitionist, transcendentalist, and Unitarian minister; Mattie Griffith Browne (1825?–1906) of Kentucky, abolitionist and advocate of female suffrage; Benjamin Sherwood Hedrick (1827–1886) of North Carolina, chemist and antislavery leader; and Daniel Reaves Goodloe (1814–1902) of North Carolina and John Gregg Fee (1816–1901) of Kentucky, both abolitionists.

41. This was a session, held at Vanderbilt University, at the second annual meeting of the Southern Historical Association in Nashville on the afternoon of Friday, November 19, 1936. Donald Davidson read a paper on "The Agrarian South: An Interpretation" and Couch, in rebuttal, on "The Agrarian Romance"; there were commentaries by Percy L. Rainwater and John Donald Wade. Couch's paper was subsequently published: William T. Couch, "The Agrarian Romance," *South Atlantic Quarterly* 36 (October 1937): 419–30.

ville doctrine, even when we admired their boldness and daring. But we did nothing really about our opposition. Some went to New York, carefully curbed that tell-tale Youall, that ill-timed Sir, and tried to be more American than the Yanks. I tried it several ways—the rage for Harlem, for the New Republic, for Marx. I don't regret any of the experiments, but they were all inconclusive. Nothing really was gained by denying my southernness for I never got away from it.

I am not happy about Bob's contention that "The South has vanished." Maybe I don't understand what he means. But I would suspect the Vermonter who announced that "New England has vanished" or the Iowan who declared the "Midwest has vanished." I guess I am not ready to embrace an indiscriminate nationalism, any more than I am prepared to embrace an aggressive sectionalism. I would very much like to find some definition of a Southerner with which I could identify myself. And maybe your group is working toward such a definition. I would like to keep in touch with the course of your thinking and make any contribution of which I am capable. Do let me hear from you.

CVWP, 50/581: TCLU

96. To Henry F. May[42]

DECEMBER 15, 1953

I was most appreciative of your letter and of the penetrating questions you raise.[43] I think the answer to the first one—does defeat necessarily induce a sense of human limitations and irony—is clearly "no." There have been too many instances of defeat to generalize about. Among the ranks of the defeated I have been most interested in Germany, Japan, and the South. I couldn't even generalize on the basis of those three. My play on the point in the paper you read came in the search for a basis from which to criticize the American legend. I think it might offer such a basis

---

42. Henry F. May (1915–2012), the American intellectual historian who had taught (like CVW) at Scripps College (1947–49) and then went to the University of California-Berkeley, where he spent the rest of his career; he is, perhaps, best known for *The End of American Innocence: A Study of the First Years of Our Own Time, 1912–1917* (New York: Alfred A. Knopf, 1959).

43. In connection with CVW's 1952 presidential address to the Southern Historical Association; CVW, "The Irony of Southern History," *Journal of Southern History* 19 (February 1953): 3–19.

if properly used, along with the numerous other deviations of Southern experience from the American norm—if anything so abnormal as the American experience can be described as "norm."

The second point you raise interests me greatly and has for some time. I would gladly swap reflections on it with you from time to time. I mean whether the ironic view and acceptance of human limitations—to an extent incompatable with the Jeffersonian idea—necessarily results in a paralyzing despair. Whether irony implies cynicism. I suspect we would agree that evolution and the idea of progress are no longer acceptable substitutes for Jeffersonian optimism, since we no longer believe in either. And yet it seems to me that the American legend still rests on some such facile assumption of human salvation. I don't want to try to destroy American confidence. But there are risks to confidence and security in suddenly discovering that the supporting legs of the platform on which one has been standing are missing.

I am unable to reconcile my naturalistic approach with Niebuhr's neo-fundamentalism. But I find in his thought a more cogent critique of the American legend than almost anywhere else.[44] The possible exception is Robert Penn Warren. Most explicitly in his recent Brother to Dragons, in poetic and concrete form. But also in World Enough and Time, in Night Rider, in All the Kings Men, in Heaven's High Gate. And in his early (and immature) study of John Brown.[45] I would be interested in your reaction to the Dragons. I know a few critics think him meretricious. But to me he looks at the realities of the problem that interests us with greater integrity and more steadily than any other writer—even Faulkner, who sometimes grapples with the same theme.
[deletion]

CVWP, 68/81: TCLU

44. Reinhold Niebuhr (1892–1971), the Lutheran theologian and social critic, whom CVW would come to know when both were at the University of Oxford; CVW refers here to Niebuhr's *The Irony of American History* (New York: Scribner's, 1952).

45. Robert Penn Warren, *Brother to Dragons: A Tale in Verse and Voices* (New York: Random House, 1953); idem., *World Enough and Time: A Romantic Novel* (New York: Random House, 1950); idem., *Night Rider* (Boston: Houghton Mifflin, 1939); idem., *John Brown: The Making of a Martyr* (New York: Payson & Clarke, 1929).

97. To Eric L. McKitrick[46]

MAY 19, 1954

Mr. David Riesman let me read your paper "A Meaning for Turner's Frontier."[47] I want to tell you how much I enjoyed it and how stimulating I found it. It is rare at any time and rarer still in the frontier history field to find a scholar with a new idea and a fresh pair of eyes. I think you have both. I very much hope you will pursue this notion and that your paper will be published in some form.

If I may offer a few reflections, not very deeply pondered, I would raise the question whether there were really enough Marse Chans to go around in the South.[48] He is a valid symbol all right, but he is not quite the counterpart nor the contemporary of George F. Babbitt.[49] Growing up in those parts in the 1920s I was familiar with both types. But [I] found George F. in the saddle more often than Marse C.

I do not want to whittle down the sharpness of your dramatic contrast. It deserves to be stated in that fashion, but I think that when you round out your study of the Southern frontier some of the sharpness will disappear from your contrast. Of course Fletcher Green will not agree with you but you might profit from his criticism.[50] Also, another look at

46. Eric L. McKitrick (1919–2002), then a graduate student at Columbia University and working on what would become *Andrew Johnson and Reconstruction* (Chicago: University of Chicago Press, 1960); he was to spend his career at Columbia.

47. David Riesman (1909–2002), the American sociologist, best known for *The Lonely Crowd: A Study of the Changing American Character*, collaborators Reuel Denney and Nathan Glazer (New Haven: Yale University Press, 1950). McKitrick's paper was published in two parts as: Stanley Elkins and Eric L. McKitrick, "A Meaning for Turner's Frontier: Part I: Democracy in the Old Northwest," *Political Science Quarterly* 69 (September 1954): 321–53, and idem., "A Meaning for Turner's Frontier: Part II: The Southwest Frontier and New England," *Political Science Quarterly* 69 (December 1954): 565–602.

48. "Marse Chan" is a short story that first appeared in *Century* magazine in 1886, then in Thomas Nelson Page, *In Ole Virginia or Marse Chan, and Other Stories* (New York: Charles Scribner, 1887). In the story, a postbellum Northern visitor to a Virginia plantation is told, in black dialect by a freedman, of the tragic death during the war of the former slave's master (Tom Channing or "Marse Chan"), his chivalrous conduct and love for the plantation, his slaves, and childhood sweetheart.

49. The philistine protagonist of Sinclair Lewis, *Babbitt* (New York: Harcourt, Brace, 1922).

50. Fletcher M. Green (1895–1978), a historian of the antebellum South at the University of North Carolina (1936–60).

the Southern Whigs might be taken in view of Charles Sellers' article in the last AHR.[51]

CVWP, 75/10: TCLU

98. To Howard Jay Graham[52]

JUNE 16, 1954

I am sending you separately a couple of reprints of "The Irony of Southern History," and assure you that I consider myself the gainer in this swap. I was much impressed with the earlier form of your study on the Fourteenth Amendment and will read this and your review of Crosskey's with pleasure, I am sure.[53]

Naturally I am also delighted with the Supreme Court's decision of May 17.[54] I confess I am also greatly confused as to how to advise my Southern friends who, beyond the need of exhortation, are now calling for advice on practical expedients and urgent legislation. I have to confess to them that I am stronger on principles than on practice. And I am baffled by some of the technical problems they raise. I wish very much I could talk to you about such problems, and if you are in the East this summer I hope you will let me know.

I suppose you received from the NAACP a request for permission to reprint your contribution as did I. I have heard nothing more of the idea since then and wonder what came of it.

[deletion]

CVWP, 21/256: TCLU

51. Charles Grier Sellers Jr., "Who Were the Southern Whigs?," *American Historical Review* 59 (January 1954): 335–46.

52. Howard Jay Graham, a bibliographer at the Los Angeles County Law Library and recently the author of *The Early Antislavery Backgrounds of the Fourteenth Amendment* (Madison: Law School of the University of Wisconsin, 1950).

53. Howard Jay Graham, "Crosskey's Constitution: An Archaeological Blueprint," *Vanderbilt Law Review* 7 (1953–54): 340–65, a review of William Winslow Crosskey, *Politics and the Constitution in the History of the United States* (Chicago: University of Chicago Press, 1953).

54. *Brown v. Board of Education of Topeka*, 347 U.S. 483 (1954), which declared the racial segregation of public schools to be unconstitutional. CVW had prepared a monograph on the history of segregation for the NAACP's Legal Defense and Educational Fund; on this, see CVW, *Thinking Back: The Perils of Writing History* (Baton Rouge: Louisiana State University Press, 1986), 88–89.

99. To Rupert B. Vance

JUNE 21, 1954

Over a year ago I agreed to deliver a series of three lectures at the U. of Virginia and also to permit their publication in book form.[55] What with one thing and another I am just getting around to the job. It remains to be seen whether I can do it. Since they are scheduled for the last three days in September (I take off October 1 for England) I have only three months.[56]

I would give anything for a chance to talk over some ideas with you. Will you be up this way anytime soon? Failing that I beg your reaction to an extremely vague notion I am trying to give birth to. Very generally, the idea is to mark off the end of an era of Southern history that opened with the end of Reconstruction. Not as dramatically as previous Southern eras ended: in 1861, or 1865, or 1877, and certainly not as sharply nor as definitely. But nevertheless the crumbling of an old regime, which like all the other old regimes seemed the final settlement, the permanent, the unalterable order. This was the New South, considerably older in years than the Old South ever attained, and therefore quite the longest of the several old regimes that have come and gone. Or I might want to call it the Era of the Compromise, because I want to identify the racial, political, economic, and social arrangements of the period as originating with the events of 1877 and to say that they are what have crumbled in the last five, ten, twelve (how many would you say?) years. Obviously the date 1913 did not mark the end of anything but Taft's administration. But when can I claim the demise of the New South? Or can I claim it at all? The Second New Deal? The Second World War? The Segregated Schools Decision of May 17?

Could I make out a case for the crumbling of the Compromise in three areas (lectures): Racial, Political, Economic? I. The New Emanci-

---

55. These were the James W. Richards Lectures in History (1954), which would be published as CVW, *The Strange Career of Jim Crow* (New York: Oxford University Press, 1955), a book on the history of segregation, not the subjects discussed in this letter. Since only a few months interceded between this letter and the lectures, given in October, it would seem that CVW improvised his topic somewhat rapidly.

56. CVW had been elected as the Harold Vyvyan Harmsworth Professor of American History at the University of Oxford. The chair had been created in 1922 by Harold Sidney Harmsworth, first Viscount Rothermere (1868–1940), the newspaper proprietor, in memoriam to a son who had died in the First World War.

pation II. Shift in the Demagogue Belt (NO!) III. Break in Colonial Status. But the most obvious and striking change, crumbling—as in 1865 and 1877—was in the racial area. And as the case of the First Emancipation, the Negro was the fortuitous beneficiary, a by-product of a falling out of white men, a product of (again) ill winds that blow somebody good: war, crisis, nationalism. As in the Second Emancipation: total war, manpower shortage, foreign propaganda—and the very Conformity against which we preach. Perhaps one of the few redeeming features of Conformity, but more the product of that than of the preachments of the new abolitionists. Not much flattering unction to lay to the souls of suffering liberals of these days in that Second Emancipation. Perhaps not so much as the abolitionists were due in the first instance? Would you say? Lecture II: end of the white primary, poll tax, decline of the demagogue, rise of Negro voting, etc. Lecture III: End of colonial status or merely a new phase of it? Not qualified to say or know. Perhaps I should anyways stick to the shift in racial status as the touchstone of change.

Now I am not proposing to turn sociologist and explain these changes. I merely want to chronicle them to mark off the end of an era and then return to my last. My contribution should be to set off these changes against their historical background. I would in other words attempt to indicate by historical essays how far we have come and by what general routes, starting with 1877 and sticking mainly to the early period.

How I wish your book were available.[57] Should I attempt this without that? Should I attempt it at all? Have I got a worthwhile point to make? I am far from convinced myself, very far. Preceding books in the series are by Brinton and Nevins.[58] Hard to live up to and I will chuck the whole thing, despite embarrassment, if I am not convinced.

Also I am not committed to this notion, for there is still time if I do it in the next week or so to shift to something else. But if I do, what shall I read on recent developments? Any and all suggestions appreciated and implored.

57. Vance was supposed to be writing the volume that would chronologically follow CVW's *Origins of the New South* in the History of the South series, but never did; the project was inherited by George B. Tindall (1921–2006), a South Carolinian who taught for most of his career at the University of North Carolina-Chapel Hill (1958–90).

58. Nevins seems never to have given the Richard lectures, but Crane Brinton (1898–1968), a European intellectual historian at Harvard, did in 1952 and these were published as *The Temper of Western Europe* (Cambridge, MA: Harvard University Press, 1953).

Enjoyed enormously having David Riesman as colleague at Hopkins last term. What do you think of his stuff? He talks better than he writes.

Laski-Holmes correspondence makes awfull amusing reading.[59] What an entertaining liar Laski is and old Holmes must have known it but he was amused anyway and read them avidly.

[deletion]

CVWP, 57/684: TCLU

100. To Clinton Rossiter[60]

AUGUST 2, 1954

[deletion]

Let me say in general how much I enjoyed the book and how much I was impressed with the astuteness and penetration of your treatment. One thing that fascinated, and at the same time exasperated me was the strong sympathy I have felt for the abstract treatment of Conservative doctrine as you described it, and then the almost uniform disappointment and sometimes revulsion I felt toward the individual exponents of the Right. One preconception I found ably confirmed in your treatment was the intellectual bankruptcy of the American Right. It is most astonishing to find repeatedly such liberals as the junior Schlesinger and such complicated liberals as Niebuhr turning aside from their own doctrines to give aid and assistance to conservatism, and to beg the conservatives to state their own case with a minimum of intelligence. I realize I am not telling you anything you do not know.

One suggestion that you have doubtless considered and rejected for your own reasons is the usefulness for your methodology of the sociological approach to the history of ideas. I have in mind especially the work of Karl Mannheim and our colleague David Riesman.[61] As an exam-

59. Mark De Wolfe Howe, ed., *Holmes-Laski Letters: The Correspondence of Mr. Justice Holmes and Harold J. Laski, 1916–1935* (Cambridge, MA: Harvard University Press, 1953). Oliver Wendell Holmes (1841–1935), legal philosopher, author, and associate justice of the U.S. Supreme Court (1902–32); Harold Joseph Laski (1893–1950), a British political theorist who was at Harvard (1917–20), where he first met Holmes: he spent the rest of his career at the London School of Economics.

60. Clinton Rossiter (1917–1970), a historian who taught at Cornell University (1946–70); he wrote widely on American political history and was then completing his *Conservatism in America* (New York: Alfred A. Knopf, 1955).

61. Karl Mannheim (1893–1947), the Hungarian founder of the study of the sociology of knowledge and author of, especially, *Ideology and Utopia: An Introduction to the Sociology of Knowledge*

ple, the motivation of what Riesman calls the tradition-directed people. That perception is, I think, of especial value in understanding Southern conservatism.

I find no exception to take to your treatment of Calhoun, Fitzhugh, Southern agrarians, and the Negro.[62] I was particularly interested in your treatment of the conservative approach to the race question. It coincides with an interest of my own of a development of a little study of the history of segregation. An aspect that has been overlooked in your history is the restraining influence of the conservative tradition in the South and the eventual and tragic capitulation of the conservatives to extreme racism toward the end of the century.

[deletion]

    CVWP, 46/538: TCLU

101. To the Editor of the *New Statesman and Nation*[63]

QUEEN'S COLLEGE, OXFORD

NOVEMBER 14, 1954

I hope you will allow me to correct what I am sure was an unintentional error in your issue of October 30. In his article on "The Oppenheimer Story" Mr. R. H. S. Crossman remarked in passing that "Lattimore was a private citizen teaching at Johns Hopkins when he was smeared and hounded out of his professorship."[64]

(1929; New York: Harcourt, Brace, 1936). Mannheim had also published in 1926 a book on conservatism, but it was not translated into English until 1986.

    62. John C. Calhoun (1782–1850), the South Carolinian politician and political theorist, and George Fitzhugh (1806–1881), the proslavery thinker.

    63. This letter was not published, doubtless because a very similar letter from George Boas (1891–1980), a philosopher at John Hopkins, was: see George Boas, "Owen Lattimore," *New Statesman and Nation* 48 (11 December 1954): 788.

    64. Richard H. S. Crossman (1907–1974), a Labour Party politician, journalist, and diarist. The referent here is the case of Owen Lattimore (1900–1989), the diplomatic adviser and scholar of modern Chinese culture and foreign relations, who came under attack from Joseph R. McCarthy (1908–1957), a Republican U.S. senator from Wisconsin (1947–57) who was notorious for his damaging anti-Communist witch hunts. McCarthy had urged Johns Hopkins to dismiss Lattimore, who twice had been questioned by congressional committees: in 1950 by the so-called Tydings Committee, investigating the loyalty of State Department officials; and in 1952 by the Senate Internal Security Subcommittee, which charged him with having been "a conscious articulate instrument of Soviet policy" and a perjurer. The Department of Justice twice unsuccessfully attempted to indict Lattimore for perjury, but did succeed in withdrawing his passport.

The fact is that during the four years that he has been under almost continual attack there has been no change in the status of my colleague Owen Lattimore at The Johns Hopkins University. When he was finally brought under formal indictment the university granted him leave of absence with full pay until his case was settled. He needed both the time and the pay in order to defend himself. His defense was greatly assisted by the large fund raised by his Hopkins colleagues under the leadership of Professor George Boas. Both my colleagues and the university have been under heavy attack for the stand they have taken.

Those who are fighting to defend academic freedom in America welcome your help and criticism, but they deserve your recognition for their contribution to a common cause.

CVWP, 37/444: TCLU

102. To Boyd C. Shafer[65]

QUEEN'S COLLEGE, OXFORD

NOVEMBER 16, 1954

I am sorry I have not been able to write you earlier about the Harmsworth Professorship election matter.[66] I thought it best to take my time and learn all I could about it first. I have also consciously tried to clear my mind of preconceptions and look at the facts in a detached and objective way. I believe I appreciate as fully as anyone the concern expressed over the implications of the *Reporter* article last summer with regard to the elec-

---

65. Boyd C. Shafer (1907–1992), executive director of the American Historical Association and editor of the *American Historical Review* (1953–63).

66. The "matter" was a controversy over how the Harmsworth Professor was elected. As CVW explains, the American ambassador to the Court of Saint James's was a voting member of the Harmsworth electoral board. Late in his tenure, Ambassador Walter S. Gifford had said that Oxford's suggestion of Arthur Schlesinger Jr. was unacceptable to him, because Schlesinger was too liberal. In 1953, when Oxford renewed the nomination, the new Eisenhower-appointed ambassador, Winthrop W. Aldrich (1885–1974), was said to have "exploded and refused to sign the minutes of the Electors' meeting until the historian's name was removed." (Aldrich was a conservative Republican, formerly head of the Chase National Bank.) Oxford then ventured the name of Merle Curti, but Aldrich objected to electing a pacifist. Ironically, CVW was the compromise candidate, because "less controversial." It would seem Aldrich knew little about CVW's ideological history. On this, see Robin W. Winks, *'To Stimulate Some Action: The Harmsworth Professorship, 1920–2000: An Inaugural Address Delivered Before the University of Oxford on 18 May 2000* (Oxford: Oxford University Press, 2001), 12–14.

tion of the occupant of the chair for next year.[67] As a consequence I have looked into the matter as thoroughly as I could.

The University Statutes create an Electoral Board made up of seven members, four of whom are Oxford dons. One of them is elected by the Hebdomadal Council, one by the Faculty of Modern History, and two by the Governing Body of Queen's College. The other three members are the U.S. Ambassador, chairman, the Chancellor of Oxford University, and Viscount Rothermere and successive holders of the Viscountcy. Regarding the Ambassador the statues have this, and nothing more, to say: One of the members [s]hall be "The Ambassador from the United States of America to the Court of St. James at the time of the election, or a deputy appointed by him to act from time to time, who shall have a casting vote in the election." Since by general statute four members have to agree in order for there to be an election, there can be no tied vote. Hence the power of "a casting vote" is of no real significance. The statue describes the other electors and then adds: "The American Ambassador, after consultation with such of the leading Universities of the United States [as] he may select, will submit recommendations to the Electoral Board."

Statuta Universitatis Oxoniensis (Oxford, 1953), IV, 11, H, 17.

For its part, the University has not interpreted the statute's instructions to the Ambassador to "submit recommendations" as an exclusive power of recommendation. The electors have not made the presumption of exclusive power in practice. And the Ambassador denies that he is given exclusive power and refuses to have that interpretation put upon the statute. There is no mention of any veto power in the statue. So far as is apparent from the record, the Ambassador has one vote in seven, with four required to elect.

The practice for some time has been for the Ambassador to ask S. E. Morison to suggest names, and then to pass on these together with others that came in informally.[68] At a meeting of the electors in November, 1953 (after my election) it was decided that in the future the American Historical Association should be asked to submit recommendations through the Ambassador. You received no formal notice of this action, I understand,

---

67. "Getting Even with George III," *The Reporter* 11 (20 July 1954): 2.

68. Samuel Eliot Morison (1887–1976), the Harvard historian, had been the first holder of the chair (1922–25).

and only received a telephone request for names from the State Department. You then appointed a panel of members who apparently suggested individually a number of names to the Ambassador. My information is that the name of Merle Curti was not among those so submitted.[69] It was suggested to the Oxford electors by Max Beloff.[70] They in turn took it up and agreed informally that Curti would make an appropriate appointment in view of the new arrangement with the A.H.A., of which he was the new president.[71]

As for what happened in the discussion at the meeting of the electors last May there is conflicting testimony about what was said and the significance of what was said. My handbook on historical method contains no handy rule for solving this one. I am convinced that there was dissatisfaction on the part of some of the electors over what they thought the Ambassador said and the interpretation they put on his remarks. Others present disagree about what he said and how it should be interpreted. I was not present. As for stories of an ambassador's "veto" or improper intervention in previous elections, I have been able to find no confirmation in Oxford.

About the future of the chair a few things at least are clear. One is that the Electoral Board as constituted by statu[t]e has four members, a majority, who are Oxford dons elected by University governing bodies and responsible to them. My brief acquaintance with Oxford people discourages any fears for the integrity of our common academic traditions at their hands. I cannot believe they would condone, or wink at, or in any way tolerate practices we would consider improper.

I think it would be entirely proper for you to write to Sir Douglas Veale, Registrar of the University, requesting him to clarify what is expected of the American Historical Association with regard to submission of names for the chair in the future.[72] This might serve to clear up any

69. Merle Curti (1897–1997), the leading American intellectual historian of his generation, who taught for many years at the University of Wisconsin; his most important book was *The Growth of American Thought* (New York: Harper & Brothers, 1943).

70. Max Beloff (later Baron Beloff) (1913–1999), a fellow of Nuffield College, Oxford (1947–57), later Gladstone Professor of Government and Public Administration (1957–74).

71. In the event, Curti never became Harmsworth Professor.

72. Sir Douglas Veale (1891–1973) had been registrar since 1930 and was a fellow of Corpus Christi College; he worked in the Clarendon Building, familiarly referred to as the Hotel de Veale.

uncertainty left by the published letter of Lord Halifax to Ambassador Aldrich: "That the Ambassador's duty under the University Statutes of submitting recommendations to the electors is discharged by his obtaining a list of suitable names from the American Historical Association."[73]
[deletion]

CVWP, 40/482: TCLU

103. To George B. Tindall

QUEEN'S COLLEGE, OXFORD

MARCH 8, 1955

I would have profited by a talk with you before jumping into the Jim Crow lectures. Best thing now is to send you my set of galley proof. Page proof is in but the book won't be out till toward the end of May. No—I remember now—my set of galley is not complete. I will instead write the Oxford press in NY to send you a set of proof. I welcome and beg a full exchange of ideas on the whole subject, because we have some apparent differences to iron out.

Curious thing is that your book and Wharton's are responsible mainly for inspiring a different interpretation of segregation from the one you tentatively outline.[74] In fact my main emphasis is upon the relative recency of the Jim Crow system, and I find in you and Wharton persuasive evidence of that emphasis. It is true that pro-slavery propaganda developed that popular conviction of the Negro's innate inferiority, but it did not follow that the inferior had to be segregated. In fact slavery was in many ways incompatible with segregation and prompted intimacy of association, an intimacy that outlasted slavery and even reconstruction. The new factors of urbanization, competition, slums, crime, etc. that made for estrangement and in part gave rise to segregation did not exist under slavery.

It seems to me that we have to break up analytically Southern doctrine and thought about the Negro. The tenets of biological and intellectual inferiority have existed longer than the doctrine of segregation. The former may g[i]ve aid and comfort to the latter, but they have not

73. Edward Frederick Lindley Wood, first earl of Halifax (1881–1959), Conservative politician and Cabinet minister, was chancellor of the University of Oxford (1933–59).

74. George B. Tindall, *South Carolina Negroes, 1877–1900* (Columbia: University of South Carolina Press, 1952).

always been combined with the latter. Some proslavery thought of course defended slavery as the school of an undeveloped race, preparing it for civilization and advancement. This conception implied room for growth and development.

I try to point out three indigenously Southern philosophies of race relations that offered alternatives to extreme racism and segregation: that of the Conservative Redeemers, that of the radical Populists, and that of the liberals, or liberal, for Cable is virtually alone. And the first two were the only ones given a practical tryout. Of course the very proto-type of your conservative patrician, the paternalist of the old school is Hampton, by no means a unique example.[75] These gentry, as you point out, did not believe that subordinates had to be ostracized, nor inferiors segregated—though they believed both in subordination and inferiority of the race. Nor did they go the whole way in racism when some Negroes were more capable of holding office than some whites. The Populists rejected extreme racism also and even offered the Negro a limited sort of equalitarianism—that of a common grievance and a common op-pressor. It was when the Conservatives forfeited their moral authority on race relations by unleashing Negrophobia against the Populists, and the Populists in turn became disillusioned with their Negro allies and blamed them for their defeat, that these two restraining influences upon extreme racism were relaxed. And toward the end of the century other restraints—that of Northern liberals, the courts, etc. were simultaneously relaxed. And on top of that came the Yankee plunge into imperialism and the consequent need for a new racial doctrine in the North. Only then it seems to me was the way open for the real development of harsh segregation and systematic Jim Crowism.

It seems to me that the rationale of segregation, at least among the articulate and semi-articulate, was not proslavery thought, but the flour-ishing schools of contemporary sociology—particularly those of Sumner, Giddings, and MacDougall—along with the racist and imperialistic phi-losophies springing up in the North, South, West, and Europe.[76] How

75. Wade Hampton III (1818–1902), a Confederate general who was later governor of (1877–79), and U.S. senator from (1879–91), South Carolina.

76. William Graham Sumner (1840–1910), a Social Darwinist sociologist at Yale and best known for *Folkways: A Study of the Sociological Importance of Usages, Manners, Customs, Mores, and Morals* (Boston: Ginn, 1906); Franklin Henry Giddings (1855–1931), a sociologist at Columbia University (where one of his doctoral students was Howard Odum), notable for *The Principles of*

eagerly the South snatched at the wonderful notion of Sumner's in-scrutable, impervious, imponderable, unchangeable, age-sanctioned Folk-ways. Stateways can't change folkways. I was brought up on it—bottle & breast.[77] And so was my generation. And to make the folkways rationale stick, of course, they had to be lent the sanction of antiquity. They had to have a past lost in misty dawn of race relations—at least as old as slav-ery. Very old, very, and practically impossible to alter—however desirable alteration might be admitted to be. Meanwhile our fathers were busily employed in using stateways to alter folkways in the opposite direction by the Jim Crow laws.

Well, I only try to suggest my thesis. I hope you get the proof, promptly from Oxford and let me have your reflections. I can't believe that we are as far apart on this matter as might first seem. There are matters of defi-nition and concept to agree upon.

We leave March 28 for Rome and an absence of about four weeks. Hope I can hear from you before departure.

CVWP, 53/632: TCLU

104. To Dewey W. Grantham[78]

QUEEN'S COLLEGE, OXFORD

MAY 4, 1955

I have your letter of March 26, but I have not spent all the intervening weeks pondering the questions you raise. The letter must have arrived after I left Oxford on March 28 for travels on the continent as far as Rome from which we did not return until April 25.

It is good to learn that you have kept the Southerner As American alive and in fact breathed much new life into the idea. As you know I was taken by the notion from the start and only recently remarked in a letter to George Tindall that I hoped it had not been dropped.

Sociology: An Analysis of the Phenomena of Association and of Social Organization (New York: Macmil-lan, 1896); William McDougall (1871–1938), an English psychologist and proponent of eugenics who taught at Harvard (1920–27).

77. Howard Odum was very influenced by these Sumnerian ideas.

78. Dewey W. Grantham Jr. (1921–2004), originally from Georgia, studied at the Uni-versity of North Carolina and joined the faculty of Vanderbilt University in 1952; he was a historian of Southern progressivism; his first book was *Hoke Smith and the Politics of the New South* (Baton Rouge: Louisiana State University Press, 1958).

The assignment you have framed for me is indeed a tough one and I suspect that you are expecting too much from me. My guess would be that each one of the Nine Young Men (or eight young and one graying) is hoping that one of the other eight has what he lacks—the assurance or faith or inspiration that will somehow fuse eight unwritten essays into an exciting book unified by a brilliant conception. Well, at any rate, that is not something I have got up my sleeve. I would have to enter this venture like I have always entered literary ventures, with the blind faith that something needed saying and that if I sweated and labored enough the muse would eventually grace my efforts with an idea. And I suspect I would not be the only one in this predicament, though I may be wrong. Anyway, I am signing up and here's my hand on it. And doing it without any notion of what needs to be said or how it should be said, but only the feeling that something should be said at about this time. This is not an act of faith in myself as much as it is proof of faith in my eight collaborators who will save me from my mistakes and help me find out what I think. For I welcome the venture not as a means of self expression but as a means of clarifying my own thinking. The only condition I attach is that nobody respects anybody's vanity and that criticism flow free and unconfined. I can't imagine any one of my collaborators, as I know them, taking exception to that rule.

I read Charlie's prospectus with admiration and profit and felt assured thereby that we are not starting from scratch. Thanks, I realize, to a lot of thinking and planning on the part of the rest of you to which I have not been able to make much contribution. In general I am for it and believe it has enough pegs to hang the contributions on and a lot of sound thinking already done.

What I would like to do first is to enter a caveat not against what has been said, but against a tendency that might be implicit in the title and subject to which we are committed, if we are fully committed to anything. I mean the tacit or unconscious use of "American" in a normative sense and conversely the use of "Southern" or "Southerner" in a pejorative sense. Without much prior reflection I have, I confess, an initial resistance to those possible tendencies. This comes mainly from a growing aversion to the trend of pietistic or moralistic nationalism in the States. It is one reason I resist the swing to "American Studies" as an academic or graduate discipline, even though some fine scholars, like Henry Nash

Smith, are associated with it.[79] I even wince when I hear Negro rights defended by our moralistic nationalists, and I think John Hope would understand why. To my mind, the Southerner's not for burning, only cauterizing, maybe, or purging by the flame. I'm quite ready to apply the blowtorch in spots. But I'm not ready for a general conflagration. As a court of inquisition we can retain the rack and foreswear the bonfire. Too much we cherish might go up in smoke. For one thing, call it the South or not, something in that latitude has been responsible for the finest flowering of letters in our time. I cherish all this, am proud of it, and go around boasting about it. Cornered by one of our pietistic brethren I am not above using it to stop his braying for a moment while I think of something to say. For another thing, during this year abroad I have had reason to be embarrassed oftener for being an American than for being a Southerner, though there have been embarrassments on both scores. I have not brought myself to say it outright yet, but to myself I have said it more than once, that that sort of thing just isn't done in the South—not even to Negroes. I mean the sort of thing that embarrass me for being an American, and I don't have to be more specific to you. Well, here's something that's not for burning. Not by me, anyway. And in a time when the American brand of nationalism has become associated with so much that we find revolting and alien to our deeper values I think we have got to be especially cautious about any normative use of the word "American."

So much for my strawmen. Of course I am not attributing these tendencies I fear to any one of my collaborators. I am simply trying to open up my mind to you with the hope that we can all understand each other. I take it we would all prefer no book at all to one we felt apologetic about, or even to one we were not proud of. I think we have a marvelous title, an excellent set of contributors, and a highly timely moment in which to say something that needs saying. What more could we ask? Probably most of it is up to each man and his typewriter. But maybe something could be derived from a seminar type of periodic foregathering, perhaps at the annual conventions, Southern and national. Perhaps a bit of preparation could get a couple of papers circulated in advance of each meeting and

79. Henry Nash Smith (1906–1986), the literary critic and historian, best known for *Virgin Land: The American West as Symbol and Myth* (Cambridge, MA: Harvard University Press, 1950), which won the Bancroft Prize in 1951.

then the nine of us could give an hour or so to discussion of each. Why
not start with the two papers to be presented at the next AHA meeting?
We could have a private session perhaps at dinner after the papers had
been read and then lay plans for the future.

I am staying on here through the summer, arriving back in Baltimore
about the first of September. So far the year has been rich fun and rare
delight and I look forward as keenly to the next four months as I did to
the first eight. Do let me hear from you.

CVWP, 22/257: TCLS

105. To Merle Curti[80]

QUEEN'S COLLEGE, OXFORD

JUNE 3, 1955

[deletion]

On the personal side, while not going as all out as Ray Billington
seems to have of the Oxford way and charm, I do feel that it has
benefitted me a lot in ways too numerous to list.[81] For one thing it is the
perfect way and place to establish acquaintance and friendship among
these people. Your foreign acquaintance is of course much wider than
mine. My first English contacts began winter before last when I lectured
for a month at Univ. College London. But this year at Oxford has greatly
widened the circle. Almost everybody comes here during the course of
a year, or to Cambridge. And in as tightly integrated society as this a
residence in Oxford opens all the doors you have time to enter. But you
know that from your previous visits here. Perhaps you know as many of
them as you care to, but my curiosity about them is boundless and I find
much to learn from them. I am not put off by their odd ways as Merrill
Jensen probably was.[82] In many ways coming to England seemed like
coming home. True I had to put up with some stuffy relatives[,] revive
some ancient family quarrels, and endure domestic presumptions. But

80. Belatedly, Curti had been offered the Harmsworth chair and was trying to decide on
whether to accept.

81. Ray Allen Billington (1903–1981), William Smith Mason Professor at Northwestern
University, was CVW's immediate predecessor as Harmsworth Professor; he was a scholar of
the American frontier.

82. Merrill M. Jensen (1905–1980), an American political historian of the late eighteenth
century; he taught at the University of Wisconsin and had been Harmsworth Professor (1949–50).

as has been said of home before I believe there is still no place quite like it. These are all personal reactions which may not apply in all cases. But another important benefit I have derived would seem to have universal appeal. That is the blessing of leisure and freedom. I admit that social duties have been heavy, but for me they have been mainly a pleasure. And it would be easy to avoid much of that sort of thing that I have not sought to avoid because I enjoyed it. One can write his own ticket here as in no other place I know. Lecture duties can be discharged by one lecture a week the first term (8), two a week the second (14), and as it works out five lectures the last term. There are no other duties, formally speaking. Of course there are invitations to speak from all over, but I have confined those to academic occasions and not too many of them. Ray did a good deal more. But again it's your own choice. Queen's is not the most brilliant college. But it is a good one, pleasant company, quiet, and comfortable, with not an undistinguished past of more than six centuries. Food and wine are excellent. Among the very best in Oxford, and I have sampled pretty widely.

It would be only fair to mention some negative aspects. There is not very much interest in lectures here generally, and especially lectures on American history. The History Schools syllabus is a tightly organized and narrow one, mainly English history, with only one "special subject" devoted to American history in the whole works: "Slavery and Secession, 1850–1862." But there is an interest and movement to change the subject and broaden the place of American history and by the time you came you would be most helpful in giving guidance on these lines. But if one expected large audiences and student enthusiasm he might be disappointed. Knowing that, I have been perfectly contented to see students come and go as they pleased. They do anyway. Professors have little contact with them. Tutors much. And tutors are the only ones who count. Professors are fifth wheels. So much the better for one's freedom.

In brief that's the picture I have of Oxford. I hope you would like it as much as I have. And I do hope you are able to accept. Mind you, you are very much wanted for your own sake here. That is evident in the two attempts that have been made to get you to come. I think your coming would lend needed prestige to the chair, and I hope you would enjoy the experience.

[deletion]

CVWP, 13/151: TCLU

106. To Eric L. McKitrick and Stanley M. Elkins[83]

QUEEN'S COLLEGE, OXFORD

JUNE 10, 1955

Thank you for sending me your "Slavery in the United States."[84] I opened it with an eagerness inspired by your work on the frontier and with both hopes and doubts that you could repeat your success so quickly in another field. But you did not let me down. I feel strongly that here you have provided at last a way out of the blind alleys down which the Herskovits and Apthekers and Cravens and Schlesingers and Randalls have led us—which are not awfully different from those where the Garrisons and Calhouns left us long ago—and through which we have all been wandering so long.[85] Your concluding pages demonstrate that a post-war (The War) generation has at last come to maturity after a couple of generations that didn't. And the whole thing suggests that your elders have got to master a new vocabulary to keep up with the craft.

I offer some random observations for what they may be worth. My criticism is handicapped by a gap in the copy of the manuscript I received, pages 32–45 being missing. And I judge it was about there that you came to real grips with the themes introduced in your first chapter. What I had missed up to that point, page 32, may of course well be supplied in the next fourteen pages. So I will go light on that first chapter, hoping that you can send me the missing pages later.

83. McKitrick has been noted above; his close friend and later collaborator, Stanley M. Elkins (b. 1925), also a Hofstadter student, was then working on what would become *Slavery: A Problem in American Institutional and Intellectual Life* (Chicago: University of Chicago Press, 1959).

84. This is presumably an early version of what would be later published in two parts: Stanley Elkins and Eric McKitrick, "Institutions and the Law of Slavery: The Dynamics of Unopposed Capitalism," *American Quarterly* 9 (Spring 1957): 3–21; Stanley Elkins and Eric McKitrick, "Institutions and the Law of Slavery: Slavery in Capitalist and Non-Capitalist Cultures," *American Quarterly* 9 (Summer 1957): 159–79.

85. Schlesinger and Calhoun have been mentioned above. The others are: James G. Randall (1881–1953), mostly a historian of the Civil War and Abraham Lincoln, for many years at the University of Illinois; Melville J. Herskovits (1895–1963), an anthropologist who was trained by Franz Boas (1858–1942) at Columbia University and later taught at Northwestern University (where he founded the study of African culture), and who is best known for *The Myth of the Negro Past* (New York: Harper & Brothers, 1941); Herbert Aptheker (1915–2003), the Marxist scholar of African-American history, author of *American Negro Slave Revolts* (New York: Columbia University Press, 1943), and later the editor of the papers of W. E. B. Du Bois; William Lloyd Garrison (1805–1879), the abolitionist.

You probably need no caveat about the use of law as historical evidence. But since I am strictly in the glass house on this subject I might throw a few pebbles. My recent venture on the subject of segregation invites showers of stones which I will no doubt receive. The convenience and availability of law is the irresistible temptation. My fear is that they are rather poor evidence for dating a practice, that they lag behind actual practice sometimes and anticipate it at others, and that they are not a very reliable indicators of what practice was actually followed. Still one has to use them. I only counsel caution and reservations. In the missing pages you probably pointed out that the debt of the Carolinas and Virginia to Barbados was great, that the West Indies (British) deserve credit for originating the codes. I am sure you are aware of the origins of the divergence between Latin and Anglo-American law in the contrast between English and Spanish law and the break that cut English law off from that of the ancient world and its humanitarian heritage, though I don't recall your mentioning this. Your statement on p. 24 that "their price would undoubtedly have dropped by half" is not supported by adequate evidence and I think is too strong a statement.

I wonder why you do not make more use of Gilberto Freyre's work.[86] Its implications as worked out by Tannenbaum for the comparison of Latin with Anglo American slavery have greatly impressed me.[87] I do think there are some inconclusive points. What is needed is some studies of the Brazilian freedman such as Kardiner, Ovesey, Klineberg, and others have made of the Children of Bondage in the U.S.[88] They probably

86. Gilberto de Mello Freyre (1900–1987), the Brazilian author and politician who wrote extensively on slavery, notably in *The Masters and the Slaves (Casa-Grande & Senzala): A Study in the Development of Brazilian Civilization*, trans. Samuel Putnam (New York: Alfred A. Knopf, 1946).

87. Frank Tannenbaum, *Slave and Citizen: The Negro in the Americas* (New York: Alfred A. Knopf, 1947).

88. These are all psychoanalysts and social psychologists who studied the black personality and/or the effect of cultural environment on personal traits: Abram Kardiner (1891–1981), who studied with Freud and wrote *The Individual and His Society: The Psychodynamics of Primitive Social Organization* (New York: Columbia University Press, 1939); Lionel Ovesey (1915–1995), a clinical professor of psychiatry at Columbia University and the coauthor of Abram Kardiner and Lionel Ovesey, *The Mark of Oppression: A Psychosocial Study of the American Negro* (New York: W. W. Norton, 1951); Otto Klineberg (1899–1992), a Canadian who taught at Columbia University and whose works were influential in justifying the social psychology that underpinned the *Brown* decision of 1954: see Otto Klineberg, ed., *Characteristics of the American Negro* (New York: Harper & Brothers, 1944), and idem., *Race and Psychology* (Paris: UNESCO, 1951).

don't exist. Minor point: I seem to recall someone saying that the U.S. actually got the term "Sambo" from Latin America. At least the term is said to be common there. I believe it denotes a shade of color—the blackest. Whether it carries any of the connotations of the U.S. stereotype I don't know. But is the evidence clear that none of that stereotype exists in L. America? It has been a long time since I read Freyre, but as I recall it there was a hint of its existence. I believe he was rather enamored of the analogy between Brazilian and American plantation life and may be suspect. But your statement that "The literature of Latin American slave system contains no sambo" bothers me. The fact is I am not at all well acquainted with the literature of Latin American slavery. Why not ask Freyre to read your work?

Would it not be well to qualify somewhat the statement that there were no institutional restraints on American slavery at all? Certainly nothing to compare with the Iberian crown and church. But the piety of the 19th century South was as proverbial as that of the North. Your Virginia planter had no Jesuit priesthood spying on his cabins and no confessional, but he had a conscience and a formidable public opinion to contend with, and he often took his creed his church and his Bible seriously.

You have opened up a ghastly treasure of insight in the Nazi torture camps and have exploited the possibilities with great astuteness. It is therefore worth while, it seems to me, in guarding against a natural impulse to discredit the validity and legitimacy of the comparison. Because you are going to [be] made to shoulder the invidious and morally explosive implications of your analogy. The results could be ironic. For here you have done more than anyone probably to rescue this dispute from the clutches of the abstract moralists and put it into a concrete psychological framework. And yet you go tossing about moral dynamite with what seems reckless abandon. Because of course the Belsen records are not just so much scientific data. Belsen is the modern symbol of sin, sin of a more loathsome and revolting type than Concord ever dreamed of in its theology. We Southerners are likely to respond in much the manner our ancestors did to the anathema from Concord. I know you don't mean it quite that way, but here you place Thomas Jefferson being welcomed to Monticello by his slaves in the role of the S.S. sergeant of Belsen fawned upon by his trembling victims. This just won't quite do. Can't you suggest that the analogy is not complete. That the moral depravity, the bestial sadism, the planned and plotted diabolism, the genocide ovens were not standard equipment of the Southern plantation. Couldn't you go even further and suggest that the wonder is that with as much unlimited opportunity for brutalized tyranny as slavery offered, it did not produce at least one SS lieutenant per plantation? Perhaps you would not appease my Southern bias to the extent of a passing comparison of the often neurotic personality of the abolitionist with the sometimes moral wholeness and integrity of the planter.

Have you taken sufficient account of the exceptional case under slavery? And were there not perhaps more opportunities for the development of moral personality and individuality under slavery than you suggest? I do not recall your citing the big diary of the Natchez Barber published by the LSU Press a couple of years or so ago.[89] He doesn't fit into your categories. And the editor of the diary told me he knew of several such documents yet unpublished.

You would be interested in the record of James G. Birney's stages of progress through internal reform in the South toward Abolitionism. I am sure you know of it, but his letters are worth attention.[90]

I should think the point about F. T. Carlton's thesis worth more than a footnote.[91] Have you seen the paper David Donald read along the same lines at the AHA meeting of 1951?[92] I don't know whether he ever published it. In general, by the way, my inclination would be to pull more of the footnotes into the text and cut down on the rest of them.

One gap in evidence is that to match the testimony of survivors of the Nazi concentration camps. To complement this for your thesis you

89. William Ransom Hogan and Edwin Adams Davis, eds., *William Johnson's Natchez: The Ante-Bellum Diary of a Free Negro* (Baton Rouge: Louisiana State University Press, 1951).

90. Dwight Dumond, ed., *Letters of James Gillespie Birney, 1831–1857*, 2 vols. (New York: D. Appleton-Century, 1938).

91. This allusion is unclear, unless it is to Frank Tracy Carlton, *The History and Problems of Organized Labor* (Boston: D. C. Heath, 1920).

92. CVW chaired a joint session of the Southern Historical Association and American Historical Association at the latter's convention in New York, 28–30 December 1951, at which Donald gave the paper "Toward a Reconsideration of Abolitionists"; it was later published in *Lincoln Reconsidered: Essays on the Civil War Era* (New York: Alfred A. Knopf, 1956), 19–36. David Herbert Donald (1920–2009), who grew up in Goodman, MS, did his doctorate with James G. Randall at the University of Illinois before teaching at Columbia, Johns Hopkins, and Harvard. For the most part, he was a biographer; by 1955, he had published *Lincoln's Herndon* (New York: Alfred A. Knopf, 1946).

need comparable testimony of Negro slaves. There's the rub. I have usually been disappointed in what I have read in the way of slave memoirs. They were often propaganda vehicles sometimes ghosted and carry little conviction. But I don't know the literature well and I should think something of the sort could be turned up that was useful.

The year's residence in Oxford has probably sharpened my appreciation of your comparison of the British and American antislavery movements. I have nothing but praise for the way this is handled and the perceptions derived therefrom. The contrast is full of profound and neglected meaning and can be projected instructively through the succeeding century. One winces at the implications for the coming of American socialism in a comparable period after the British experiment. Again, the total commitment. Which of this M & E team is the Englishman in the woodpile? In connection with your treatment of the intellectual elite in the British anti-slavery movement I wish you could see a paper Mr. Ammon of Cambridge read the other night in Oxford on "The English Intellectual Aristocracy in the 19th Century." It is to be published as part of a Festschrift for G. M. Trevelyan and he read from the proofs. I would suppose it was forthcoming soon.[93] His point was the astonishing degree to which these people were intermarried and related, the tightness of the integration. He thought that the foundation was the antislavery movement.

In all this I have presumed a good deal. Please attribute any sharpness to my genuine interest in your work and my good wishes for its success.

I am staying on through August. The Hofstadters have just arrived.[94]

CVWP, 75/10: TCLU

107. To Virginia Foster Durr[95]

DECEMBER 9, 1955

It was so good to hear from you again. I wish it could be oftener and that we could see you and Cliff as well as hear from you.

93. Noel Annan, "The Intellectual Aristocracy," in *Studies in Social History: A Tribute to G. M. Trevelyan*, ed. J. H. Plumb (London: Longmans, Green, 1955), 241–87.

94. Richard Hofstadter (1916–1970), an American historian at Columbia University, one of CVW's closest friends, and the doctoral adviser of both Elkins and McKitrick; Hofstadter had married Beatrice Kevitt, his second wife, in 1946.

95. Virginia Foster Durr (1903–1999), a civil rights activist born in Birmingham, AL; she briefly attended Wellesley College in the early 1920s and married Clifford Judkins Durr (1899–

I did clip William Faulkner's speech which was printed in full in the Memphis *Commercial Appeal* and sent it to a man at Princeton with the request that he read it, but I have not got it back yet.[96] I will be glad to send it if and when it does return. In the meantime, however, plans are definitely made to publish the speech along with two others delivered at the same session. One of them by a Negro is better than Faulkner's. Copies can be had for a small sum as soon as they are published by writing Professor Bennett Wall, Journal of Southern History, University of Kentucky, Lexington, Kentucky.

You are probably right that I was a little optimistic in the Jim Crow book. It was written in the immediate afterglow of the Supreme Court decision on schools. After a year's reaction to the decision I would not be so hopeful as I was then. But I am still surprised that nothing worse has happened.

I have followed Cliff's case as much as possible in the press but have not seen Ellen Barth's book yet.[97] It came out while we were away. I had the family with me last year at Oxford and only returned last September. It was a great year for us all.

[deletion]

CVWP, 16/183: TCLU

1975), a lawyer who later became a New Dealer and worked for the Reconstruction Finance Corporation (1933–41) and the Federal Communications Commission (1941–48). While living in Virginia, she became active in many causes, but especially the campaign to repeal the poll tax. After a brief excursion to Colorado, the Durrs returned in 1951 to live in Montgomery, AL (his birthplace), where they became active in supporting the African-American cause during the Montgomery Bus Boycott; later the Durrs were hospitable to both the Freedom Riders and members of the Student Non-Violent Coordinating Committee (SNCC). CVW and Virginia Durr had first met in 1940, when both had lobbied for a poll tax repeal act, sponsored by Claude Pepper. They would later become more personally connected when CVW's graduate student Sheldon Hackney married Durr's daughter Lucy.

96. At the twenty-first annual meeting of the Southern Historical Association, held in Birmingham, AL, 9–12 November 1955, William Faulkner participated in a session—held on the Thursday evening in the Continental Ballroom of the Peabody Hotel—on "The Segregation Decisions." The other speakers were Cecil Sims, a Nashville lawyer, and Benjamin E. Mays, the president of Morehouse College.

97. Alan Barth, *Government by Investigation* (New York: Viking Press, 1955); Barth's first name, Alan (not Ellen, as CVW has it), is given correctly in Durr's letter of 5 December 1955; Barth was a journalist for the *Washington Post* and this was a critical study of various investigative congressional committees, one of which, the Senate Internal Security Subcommittee—known as the McCarran Committee for its chairman, Pat McCarran of Nevada—had subpoenaed Clifford Durr in 1954.

108. To Harry J. Carman[98]

FEBRUARY 19, 1956

R emarkable how close together we came working independently.[99] My ranking is as follows:

1. Hofstadter and Metzger, A History of Academic Freedom in the U.S.
2. Hofstadter, The Age of Reform
3. Bridenbaugh, Cities in Revolt
4. Higham, Strangers in the Land
5. Hidy and Hidy, Pioneering in Big Business[100]

We should have time to swap letters before the deadline, but I foresee no trouble getting an agreement. I will give you briefly my general views on the leading candidates. In my opinion both No. 1 and No. 2 are fine books. I am somewhat more critical of No. 2 than of No. 1, possibly because I know more about the subject matter. It undoubtedly contains brilliant insights and fresh generalizations along with some lapses in judgment and emphasis (as what bold and original book does not?). On the other hand No. 1 seems to me impeccable in scholarship, learned, and beautifully written. Both authors hold up their end well. No. 3 seems to me richer in information than in ideas. I would be reluctant to see it take priority over either No. 1 or No. 2, though I am willing to discuss that. Since you put it ahead of my No. 1, it looks like our best chance of agreement for the top place is No. 2 on my list.[101] I could go along with that without a troubled conscience. Maybe there is a rule against joint authorship prizes anyway. I will be much interested in your views. If there is need for it, we can talk it over by phone.

CVWP, 45/527: TCLU

98. Harry J. Carman (1884–1964) was a political scientist and American historian at Columbia University; he had been dean of Columbia College (1943–50).

99. Carman and CVW were the two-member panel, commissioned to recommend to the main Pulitzer board who should receive the 1956 Pulitzer prize in History.

100. Richard Hofstadter and Walter P. Metzger, *The Development of Academic Freedom in the United States* (New York: Columbia University Press, 1955); Richard Hofstadter, *The Age of Reform: From Bryan to F.D.R.* (New York: Alfred A. Knopf, 1955); Carl Bridenbaugh, *Cities in Revolt: Urban Life in America, 1743–1776* (New York: Alfred A. Knopf, 1955); John Higham, *Strangers in the Land: Patterns of American Nativism, 1860–1925* (New Brunswick, NJ: Rutgers University Press, 1955); R. W. Hidy and M. E. Hidy, *History of Standard Oil Company: Pioneering in Big Business, 1882–1911* (New York: Harper, 1955).

101. Hofstadter's *Age of Reform* did win the prize.

109. To George Washington Williams[102]

[deletion]

Unfortunately I did not see the article in the Sun to which you refer, and I am unable to tell you whether it reported my remarks accurately.

If the article suggested that I advocated amalgamation of the races, it was certainly misleading and inaccurate. There was once a great deal of amalgamation, much more than occurs now. I think you would agree that most of it took place when the subordinate race was most completely subject to the will of the dominant race, and that the amount of amalgamation was in proportion to the extent of domination. If we would minimize amalgamation (I doubt that it can be stopped completely) it would seem that we should do what we can to minimize domination. I doubt that there is very much danger of voluntary amalgamation through intermarriage—at least on the part of white women or men. It takes the consent of both races if there is voluntary amalgamation.

I have had nothing to say on the subject of deportation as a solution of the race problem. That, frankly, seems to me too impracticable to consider.

CVWP, 60/722: TCLU

110. To David Riesman

[deletion]

This is really about another matter entirely. I agreed to join a group of Southern historians in getting out a volume of essays under the title, "The Southerner as American." My collaborators, who are several years younger than myself, seem pretty generally disposed to wash up the regional heritage and bury the by-gone South. They are not an unsophisticated group, but I think unconsciously they are swayed by their impatience and disgust with the current reaction below the Potomac against the desegregation drive.

My inclination is to contribute a sort of "Yes, but . . ." essay as the tail-piece.[103] Conceding all the erosions that have washed away regional

---

102. George Washington Williams, a white Baltimore lawyer and a member of the Baltimore Association for States Rights.

103. This was not published in the Sellers symposium, but as CVW, "The Search for Southern Identity," *Virginia Quarterly Review* 34 (Summer 1958): 321–38.

distinctiveness and all the deposed myths and legends that have been disposed of, I want to point up a residue of distinctiveness that derives from the separate historical experience of the region.

One method would be to take various works that have attempted to define national character and show in what degree the South fails to conform because of its divergent history. One example would be Dave Potter's thesis of abundance as against the South's acquaintance with poverty.[104] Other examples would be Niebuhr's "innocence," Schlesinger's habit of success and victory, Boorstin's historical continuity, Thornton Wilder's "abstraction."[105] Probably Brogan, Mead, and Santayana would yield their examples of regional exceptions to national norms.[106] Perhaps you would have other suggestions (you always do!). But particularly what to do about the Riesman thesis? Does difference in the population curve of the South, fertility, etc., constitute the basis for a meaningful exception to your thesis? As you say in the L.C., ". . . no nation is all of a piece, either in its population characteristics or its economy—different groups and different regions reflect different stages of development, and social character reflects these differences."[107] Could I impose upon you for a few helpful leads along this line?

I recently met for the first time, after corresponding with them for some years, your two excellent colleagues McKitrick and Elkins. What a refreshing pair of anarchists!

CVWP, 47/550: TCLU

104. David M. Potter, *People of Plenty: Economic Abundance and the American Character* (Chicago: University of Chicago Press, 1954).

105. Niebuhr's work has been noted above; Arthur M. Schlesinger, "What Then Is the American, This New Man?" *American Historical Review* 48 (January 1943): 225–44; Boorstin, *Genius of American Politics;* Wilder's Charles Eliot Norton lecture at Harvard in 1952, later published as Thornton Wilder, "Toward an American Language," *Atlantic Monthly* 190 (July 1952): 29–37.

106. The reference to Denis W. Brogan, "The Illusion of American Omnipotence," *Harper's Magazine* 205 (December 1952): 21–28, is clear, though those to Margaret Mead (1901–1978), the anthropologist, and George Santayana (1863–1952), the philosopher, are not. It is probable, however, that CVW had in mind their reflections on national character: see Margaret Mead, *And Keep Your Powder Dry: An Anthropologist Looks at America* (New York: William Morrow, 1942), and George Santayana, *Character and Opinion in the United States* (New York: Charles Scribner's Sons, 1920).

107. This sentence does not occur in the first edition, but in the 1953 abridged and revised version: see David Riesman, *The Lonely Crowd: A Study of the Changing American Character,* collaborators Reuel Denney and Nathan Glazer (Garden City, NY: Doubleday, 1953), 24.

111. To John F. Kennedy[108]

FEBRUARY 25, 1957

In reply to your letter of February 11, requesting my nominations of five senators to be portrayed in the Reception Room, I have the following suggestions to make:

1. Senator George W. Norris, for his leadership in the field of social legislation.
2. Senator Henry Clay, for his adroit statesmanship in times of crisis.
3. Senator Daniel Webster, for his contribution to the art of compromise.
4. Senator Robert M. La Follette, for his independence of spirit and qualities of leadership.
5. Senator John C. Calhoun, for his contributions in constitutional theory.

CVWP, 30/354: TCLU

112. To Robert A. Lively

SEPTEMBER 4, 1957

First let me say I find your plans for White Reconstruction most excit-ing and promising.[109] It is just the kind of thing the book needs. I am sure you don't intend to turn the conventional picture *completely* upside down for the hell of it, though it would be fun to try. I remain to be con-vinced of the contribution of Reconstruction to the spiritual reunion or concerning its benefits as an ersatz Marshall plan. But I have an open mind and an eager interest. I promise criticism if I have it.

Second, I think the essays of Sellers and Tindall are the best things in the book so far, really worth while.[110] I have only minor suggestions if any on the margins. I remember none worth repeating. Both have something fresh to say, don't waste time with what is known, and press home their points without pretense or ambiguity.

As for Dewey Grantham's study, I frankly think it is up to you to pre-sume upon friendship and advise him to jack up the title and run a new essay under it.[111] It is all right as narrative history, but it is not new and

---

108. John F. Kennedy (1917–1963), then the junior U.S. senator from Massachusetts.

109. As mentioned above, Lively ended up not contributing.

110. Charles Grier Sellers Jr., "The Travail of Slavery," in *Southerner as American*, 40–71; George B. Tindall, "The Central Theme Revisited," in *Southerner as American*, 104–29.

111. Dewey W. Grantham Jr., "An American Politics for the South," in *Southerner as American*, 148–79.

I don't think it is appropriate to the theme. I think he should be urged to abandon narrative for analysis and undertake a job of political science that only a historian of his ability can do, and I am sure he can do it. I suggest he grapple with the impact of war, depression, boom, and of White Primary, desegregation struggle, the new Civil Rights Act, the Negro voter, the resurgent Republicanism, Southern racism and reaction and what the whole mess means in terms of his title. It is a highly timely subject and a wonderful opportunity. I hope you can persuade him to undertake it in good spirit.

On Tom Govan's essay I have two points.[112] (1) This is too important a revision to be blunted by overstatement and I am afraid there is some. For example I think the importance of slavery as a differentiating factor between the sections is quite unduly diminished by the statement that the Old South was "a part of the United States in which slavery continued for some sixty years after it had been give up in other areas."[113] This suggests that the essential difference was only a matter of sixty years. But of course he knows that differences in kind and quantity were far more important than differences in time and duration. After the opening of the 18th century slavery was never anything like as important in the North as in the South. And the number of Negroes in the North was never comparable with the number in the South after 1700. To say that slavery merely lingered in the South a bit longer is to distort the real differences. (2) Govan's attack on the economic foundations of the "two civilizations" thesis is most important and his blows at economic determinism as the key to political sectionalization are most telling. But does he not trade in an old model of economic determinism for an even older one? Isn't he saying that the historians merely misread the dialectic in finding that economic differences produced political sectionalism, and then saying that a true reading would show that economic similarities produced, or should have produced, national unity and in any case made cultural differences of the South "inconsequential"?[114] But he is still holding that the key to the whole question is economics. Were there not some "conse-

---

112. Thomas P. Govan, "Americans Below the Potomac," in *Southerner as American*, 19–39.

113. This sentence remained in the published text.

114. Again, this adjective survived: "Viewed against this background, the cultural distinctions which separated one group of Americans from another during the antebellum periods seem minor and inconsequential, and no more important than the cultural distinctions between the inhabitants of the different counties of the small and unified kingdom of England" (32).

quential" differences and were they not essentially psychological instead of economic?

John Franklin's essay bothers me most. I think it contains implications that I could not accept. (1) The second paragraph on page 18 lists several reasons why "the South went to war in 1861" such as "a long tradition of lawlessness," "an obsession for preparedness," "goose-step militarism."[115] I think it should surely be acknowledged in passing that the North also went to war and that it bore a large share of war guilt. It is impossible for me to reconcile the Southern soldier as David Donald describes him and as I understand him with anything resembling "goose-step militarism." As Donald says, this was the very quality the Confederate army lacked. See his description of Jackson's men and Lee's men on the march, and their general lack of discipline, their incorrigible individualism, and unruly democracy—good fighters but poor soldiers, bellicose but unmartial.[116] Also, if there were "an obsession for preparedness" it certainly did not result in preparedness, for the South was as unprepared as the North, or more so. (2) Franklin writes: "As this view gains acceptance it may be possible for white Southerners to make some comparisons, albeit invidious, about this period of their history and the history of other peoples of similar experience and fears."[117] In context this broadly suggests or invites an analogy between the South and Hitler's Germany. Is such an analogy intended? If so, is it justified? A couple of years ago two young scholars sent me a manuscript drawing an elaborate analogy between Southern slavery and Hitler's concentration camp at Belsen, comparing the psychology and attitudes of prisoners with those of slaves. There was a vivid picture of Jefferson's fawning slaves and the S.S.'s fawning prisoners. I hope I convinced those scholars that there are limits to comparative history. (3) Having suggested the comparison, Franklin writes "they [white Southerners] may be inclined to turn from it." The final pronoun bothers me. I cannot, for one thing, find an antecedent to the pronoun. Nor am I sure what "turn from it" means. The next sentence offers a clue, but still

115. This paragraph was softened down and, in the published text, read: "Other recent research in Southern history has shown that Southerners answered Lincoln's attempted relief of Sumter with gunfire because, among other things, of their long tradition of individualism carried to the point of lawlessness, and because of their continuing fascination with the military show" (16).

116. CVW is referring to Donald's contribution to the symposium: David Donald, "The Southerner as a Fighting Man," in *Southerner as American*, 72–88.

117. This sentence disappeared.

leaves much to be clarified. "Perhaps," he says, "they would be inclined to spend less time glorifying such a past and more time trying to overcome it."[118] (4) Now the phrase "such a past" takes in a good deal of territory, and many periods and aspects of Southern history have been mentioned or referred to in the foregoing essay. Does he mean all periods, aspects, and persons having to do with slave ownership? That goes back before the Mayflower and takes in a lot of territory. It includes persons and ideas and values that I am sure he and I cherish deeply. Is it the proper function of the historian to "overcome" the past? Does this not give him a moralistic role? Rather like the pacifist historians who "turned away" from war? Can the historian ever properly reject the past? Reject myths and illusions about the past surely. But not the past, not even war, feudalism, slavery, or imperialism. But apart from the question of the historian's function, there is an important question of values involved here. There are values in the South's past that we neither want to turn away from nor overcome, including some of the most admirable figures in our history, many of whom were slave holders. A few of them even fought for the C.S.A. and the U.S.A. I think John means the South should reject flattering illusions about slavery and race, but his statements are capable of a wider interpretation. (5) I never quite understand what he means by the South's "cult of history."[119] I think the South's creative writers have a special sensitivity to the past and its continuity in the present and that this accounts for much of the special excellence of Southern letters today. Perhaps some of this sensitivity is shared by the popular mind. I don't know. But to call it a "cult" means to disparage what I consider a virtue. (6) A matter of personal taste: I simply think Bassett a rather dull fellow and am loath to see him held up as a turning point of anything in particular.[120]

As for David Donald's essay, it seems to me admirable in its own way but rather tangential to the central theme. I think it would be an asset to

118. This, too, was removed from the final text.

119. This, however, remained: "Having failed to establish a separate nation and having gone down to defeat on the field of battle, Southerners in the period after the Civil War turned their attention to their own past with a concentration so great that the cult of history became a permanent and important ingredient of the southern culture" (8). The word "cult" is used elsewhere, too: "the cult of the Lost Cause" and "the cult of history" (9, 17).

120. Franklin did not change his suggestion that John Spencer Bassett (1867–1928) helped to transform the writing of Southern history. Bassett, a North Carolinian and Johns Hopkins Ph.D., taught successively at Trinity College, Durham, and Smith College, and wrote widely on American history.

the volume, but I am sure he is capable of an essay more relevant if you can persuade him to do it.

The essay I am thinking about now for my contribution has not jelled yet. It too would be an essay rather than an article. I should like to examine what has been eroded or interpreted away from the Southern tradition by historians, anthropologists, psychologists, etc., as well as by time and industry and the Supreme Court. Concede that all this erosion leaves very little of what the older generation thought of as a distinctive Southern tradition. Then examine what is left that has not changed and that is salvagable or worth saving. What is left that is not simply "American." I think the answer is its history, the collective experience, full as it is and as these essays demonstrate of thorny paradoxes, contradictions, inner conflicts, inner divisions, and divided loyalties and impulses which the straightforward "American" does not share and finds it hard to imagine. I hope this will work out and that you will be as candid in your criticism as I have tried to be in mine.

[deletion]

CVWP, 71/111: TCLU

113. To Lyndon Baines Johnson[121]

NOVEMBER 5, 1957

I appreciate very much your cordial letter about my article.[122] I only hope that the magnificent work that you accomplished last summer has not been destroyed by the events in Arkansas.[123] I confess that those events make me less hopeful for the future of the Democratic party as well as for a solution to the integration problem.

CVWP, 28/325: TCLU

121. Lyndon Baines Johnson (1908–1973), then the senior U.S. senator from Texas and majority leader.

122. CVW had sent Johnson an autographed copy of CVW, "The Great Civil Rights Debate: The Ghost of Thaddeus Stevens in the Senate Chamber," *Commentary* 24 (October 1957): 283–91, in which Johnson's role as Senate majority leader in passing the Civil Rights Act of 1957 was praised. In reply, in a letter of 30 October 1957, Johnson said, "I do not know whether I am entitled to the accolade of 'a genius of a Henry Clay' but I do feel that the results of the debate were constructive." He added: "The fact that this was recognized by a man of your standing and scholarly attainments is heartwarming and I will always be grateful to you."

123. The Little Rock school desegregation crisis, which had come to a head in September 1957.

114. To the Editor of *Commentary*[124]

DECEMBER 8, 1957

No friend of civil rights who has followed Senator Morse's record of thirteen years in the Senate can doubt his sincerity or fail to admire his courage.[125] Nor can anyone read the full twelve pages of his speech in the Congressional Record from which he and I quote without being convinced that he is a consistent champion of Negro rights. And certainly, as he says, he is no "over-nighter in the advocacy of reforms for America's racial problem."

I did not quote Senator Morse to accuse him of inconsistency. On the contrary, I said his claim to consistency in the Civil Rights debate was stronger than that of liberal weeklies, labor unions, and civil rights groups who were more willing to compromise. One of the most valuable and attractive qualities of his liberalism has been his devotion to procedural as well as substantive safeguards for civil rights. In last summer's debate he stood up courageously in defense of safeguards for legislative processes that were under attack by his own liberal colleagues. There will be great need for Morse's principles and for his devotion and courage in debates that are to come.

My purpose in quoting Senator Morse was to illustrate both the hopes that urge on the demand for immediate desegregation and the misgivings that plague those hopes. Neither of us approves of "carpetbagging and strong-armed tactics," and both of us prefer methods that are "orderly, constitutionally lawful." Yet we thoroughly agree that the movement for racial justice must not be disbanded by the threat of disorder, frustrated by constitutional pettifoggery, nor intimidated by mobs and demagogues.

Senator Morse read into my article a despair and defeatism that is not there. I agree with him and with Professor Handlin that now is the time for firmness and resolution.[126] It is perfectly clear that nothing but defeat can result from compromise with blackmailers and that the sort of "moderation" that amounts to a confession of weakness and an invitation to aggression must be abandoned.

124. Elliot E. Cohen (1899–1959), who was the first editor of *Commentary*, a magazine founded in 1945 by the American Jewish Committee.

125. Wayne Lyman Morse (1900–1974), U.S. senator from Oregon (1945–69).

126. Oscar Handlin (1915–2011), most notable as a historian of American immigration, came from Brooklyn and was the child of Jewish migrants from Russia; after 1939, he taught at Harvard. His most influential work, which won a Pulitzer prize, was *The Uprooted: The Epic Story of the Great Migrations That Made the American People* (Boston: Little Brown, 1952).

It is not defeatism and despair, however, to face our difficulties realistically. In the ten states of the old Confederacy apart from Texas there are more than thirteen hundred school districts. In the three and a half years since May, 1954, only fifteen of the thirteen hundred have been desegregated, and those on a token basis involving usually a handful of Negro children in three states. The question is how this process can be speeded up and how compliance can be given more than token substance.

The answer is not an army jeep full of frightened children under armed escort or school corridors patrolled by troops. If that becomes the image of desegregation in the popular mind or the model of procedure, the cause is surely lost. The American people will abandon it as they abandoned the first experiment in reconstruction. That can happen.

Firmness and resolution and willingness to use force to uphold the Constitution are necessary, *but they are not enough.* The active cooperation of a sufficient number of responsible Southern white people is absolutely necessary to make this movement succeed in any meaningful and lasting way. These people must be encouraged and protected. The real defeatist among the civil rights forces is the man who denies that there are any such southerners and holds that desegregation will have to be imposed by superior force from outside.

CVWP, 13/137: TCLU

115. To Stanley M. Elkins

JANUARY 26, 1958

I am sorry to have held you up this long, but I got around to the manuscript as quickly as I could.[127] Of course I have had my say on an earlier version already and will try not to repeat earlier criticism save only where I feel you have not adequately met my strictures.

One overall observation before turning to particulars (and this applies to much of what I have seen of yours and Eric's work), that they tend to be a series of disconnected essays rather than an integrated whole. In the present case this is not a book on American slavery and anti-slavery. It contains brilliant contributions to particulars on both subjects. There is almost a willful indifference to the relevance of one to the other. I thought there were possibilities for connecting the study of the treatment of the

---

127. The manuscript of what would become Elkins, *Slavery.*

slave personality and anti-slavery, but you throw this away or overplay it. I do not ask a reorganization on this score for dissertation purposes, but I believe you might think of it for future revision.

PART I. This part I have not seen before. It seems to me that it definitely belongs in the study and is a skillful and penetrating essay so far as it goes. I am worried on a few scores. One is that you brush off a lot of historians very hastily. A second is that to the unsympathetic reader and in one or two cases even to me, you come near being patronizing or condescending. Remember you are taking on the whole field, and it will cost you nothing to be as respectful as you can. One specific request in view of the vulnerability of your own historical method, please in your reference to Stampp, delete the crack about "the very time consuming character of doing it this way—of pouring over the sources."[128] I need not elaborate on what a critic could do with that phrase in attacking your treatment.

PART II. I think the marginal comments of Dick and myself take care of most of the criticisms of this section.[129] I would like to caution you about what I suspect of the Handlin treatment of the origins of slavery in Virginia.[130] I do not question the facts so much as the implications. It seems to me that further investigation will reveal that the slave purchasers in the first half of the 17th century were damn well aware of what it was they were buying from the very date of purchase, and that they in all probability acted accordingly. This is a speculation. I have done no investigation to back it up. Since you make so much of a point of chronology, can you well afford to ignore the history of slave law in the British West Indies and in the northern colonies? Another point, by your use of quotations, it seems to me you rather beg the question involved in the slave-breeding charge as I am afraid Stampp does too. A technical point: too many original sources are quoted from secondary sources. Also in your long treatment of slavery in Spanish and Portuguese America I recall not one Spanish or Portuguese work, primary or secondary, cited in the original. I do not say go and learn Spanish and Portuguese. I do say:

128. A reference to Kenneth M. Stampp, *The Peculiar Institution: Slavery in the Ante-Bellum South* (New York: Alfred A. Knopf, 1956). Stampp (1912–2009) was a historian, not only of slavery, but of the Civil War and Reconstruction; for most of his career, he taught at the University of California-Berkeley (1946–83).

129. Richard Hofstadter.

130. Oscar Handlin and Mary Handlin, "Origins of the Southern Labor System," *William and Mary Quarterly* 7 (April 1950): 199–222.

"let us pray." I would repeat what I said before: I think your treatment of anti-institutionalism is a major contribution, though at the same time it seems to me that it is much more relevant to the section on anti-slavery and the intellectual, and it seems rather a pity that the force of it should be expended so early in the manuscript.

PART III. Here I am afraid that I go along with many of Dick's strictures on the use of the concentration camp analogy. I would stick to my original concession, that it is a useful and meaningful device, but I confess I am disappointed that you are able to make no more concessions to my criticisms than you evidently do. I doubt that you can bring off the analogy in as short a space as Dick suggests, but I do think that you should drastically cut it down. There is, as he says, a failure in proportion in your dwelling for a score or more pages upon the obscenities and horrors of the camp. Your denials that you are identifying the plantation with the camp do not take care of the situation. You can afford to keep in mind the attitude of the hostile critic without compromising your own scholarship. He will be tempted to say that the old abolitionists were confused in their comparisons to the puritanical evangelist's picture of hell, and that the image was a fairly amiable one compared with what Hitler cooked up and you employ here.

I think you should work on some of the implications of your analogy. You are convinced about the infantilization of the slave personality, but the continuity of this personality generation after generation long after the induction process ceased contains a strong implication that slavery was one prolonged concentration camp, constantly renewing and repeating the shock tactics, and thus perpetuating the psychological type. The trauma of induction was not hereditary. You come close to reversing the fallacy that Phillips makes in treating the plantation as a school for savages, since he implies that schooling requires many generations.[131] Again you say that "both systems cut off all prior connections . . . disrupted all prior standards of their recruits," but, unlike the Nazi victims, the prior standards of the slave were most often those of slavery. Your point about the "alternative roles" open to a few exceptional nazi victims is blunted by the fact that "alternative roles" of many kinds were actually open to the general run of slaves. Whatever the law said, they did have the roles of

131. Ulrich Bonnell Phillips, *American Negro Slavery: A Survey of the Supply, Employment and Control of Negro Labor as Determined by the Plantation Regime* (New York: D. Appleton, 1918).

husband, father, patriarch, preacher, etc. The house servants and many of the field hands also had important "underground functions." Many were also committed to truck gardening, handcrafts, and religious activities.

Your reduction of the whole equation to a purely psychological one is rendered questionable for one thing by your own admission that certain African tribes gave more trouble as slaves than others. Then there is the question of the failure of efforts to reduce the Indians to slavery. You may be able to handle this question but I do think you must acknowledge it somewhere.

PART IV. I have already expressed my admiration for this part, and another reading confirms my impression. I do think that the earlier section on anti-institutionalism could more effectively have been used as an introduction to this part. Also I advise you to avoid where possible the documentation from anthologies. One point I wish you would think through in connection with your whole treatment—that is, that you write of the abolitionists and their problem as the problem of reformer and reformed. You draw your comparisons from other reform movements. I query the validity of this assumption. Actually you query it in your own treatment and in your criticism of the abolitionists. Reform was alien to the abolitionist and death to their movement. Actually they were revolutionists of the root-and-branch puritan school.

I am prepared to go along with you provided you can make reasonable concessions to my criticisms. Do take Dick's admonitions to heart. Remember that you are challenging or flaunting an imposing list of conventions, conventions of size, scope, subject, documentation, method. On top of this you are challenging an imposing list of reputable historians. I am not saying do not do this. I am saying, make what concessions you can and prepare for the consequences.

P.S. I must see a full documentation of Part I.

CVWP, 75/10: TCLU

116. To Howard H. Quint[132]

MAY 13, 1958

I have read your proof and written the Foreword. Took me a whole Sunday on the piece. Polished up it is not bad, I think. But it won't do and I am not going to send it. To be acceptable a foreword must first of all

132. Howard H. Quint (1917–1981) had received his doctorate from Johns Hopkins in 1947 and was, in early 1958, teaching at the University of South Carolina. He was about to publish

be an endorsement, and to be good it should be an enthusiastic endorsement. My Foreword is neither. Instead it is a subtle kind of an argument. A foreword is no place to argue with an author. That's for a review or an article. So I am not going to send it. I probably would be a source of embarrassment for you. I think it would for me. I doubt that I would welcome such a foreword from a friend, and I would not want to have to tell him that I would prefer not to use it after I had asked him to write it. That is another reason I am not sending it.

As for the argument I have with you, it is involved and somewhat academic. It is not that I disagree with you about the childish and irresponsible and often vicious conduct of many South Carolinians. You have done well to expose and condemn that and do it firmly by quoting their own words. It is not that. Part of our difference is summed up in an essay of mine the *American Scholar* will print next fall, and I will send you a copy.[133] It was originally delivered as a paper at a shindig Allan Nevins put on at Gettysburg last November.[134] The Charleston *News & Courier* picked it up from the N.Y *Times* and ran an editorial Nov. 25 attacking me for prostituting history for purpose of propaganda. After prodding the *News & Courier* finally printed a brief reply of mine.[135] In brief I contended that the "Third War Aim" of equality was a commitment of the Civil War on which the Union defaulted. It fought the war on borrowed moral capital and then repudiated the debt—just about totally. The Supreme Court under wrote the repudiation eloquently and repeatedly until four years ago next week. The Union loyally embraced the repudiation as the "law of the land." Then conscience suddenly and very recently caught up with commitment and the Court executed an about face.

This is why, without qualification, I find it hard to accept the stark contrast between S. Carolina and "a liberal, equalitarian, democratic

---

Profile in Black and White: A Frank Portrait of South Carolina (Washington: Public Affairs Press, 1958), for which he had asked CVW to write a foreword. The book, when published, created a controversy, which led to Quint's resignation from the university.

133. CVW, "Equality: America's Deferred Commitment," *American Scholar* 27 (Autumn 1958): 459–72.

134. To mark its 125th anniversary, Gettysburg College held a conference (organized by Nevins) on the Civil War, 17–19 November 1957.

135. CVW to the editor of the *Charleston News and Courier* [Thomas R. Waring], 16 December 1967.

America outside the South." I estimate there are approximately as many hypocrites per capita on one side of the line as on the other. Your second conclusion equating Southern extremists with Nazis also gives me trouble. If you want to end the discussion with a stinging insult that is the way—and there is much justice in it. But I want to continue arguing, continue to be listened to, even reluctantly and with little effect until I am drowned out. The third conclusion in which you are "obliged to question not only the sincerity but also the intelligence" of segregationists I find hard to accept. The hell of it to me is the indubitable sincerity of most of them.

That's the way it is. You may well misunderstand me, my friend, I hope not. But that is a risk I must take. And may good fortune attend your every enterprise—especially this one on which we could not join forces.

CVWP, 45/533: TCLU

117. To Howard H. Quint

MAY 20, 1958

[deletion]

I still feel, however, that there is a need for keeping in business the kind of Southerner I happen to be. Hutchinson (I believe that was his name) in the last editorial he wrote for the *Christian Century* called me the Hinton Helper of the current impending crisis.[136] The number that carried the editorial also carried the notice of his death, otherwise I would have written in protest. I certainly do not want to be the Hinton Helper of the new crisis. I can still talk to Negro audiences and white audiences in Georgia, as I did this year, and make them listen to what I have to say. And I can talk to integrated audiences in Virginia, too. I do not know how many Southerners there are left who can do that. If I endorsed your approach to the problem I am sure I would no longer be one of them.

[deletion]

CVWP, 45/533: TCLU

136. Paul Hutchinson (1890–1956) had been editor of the *Christian Century* since 1923. The allusion is to Hinton Rowan Helper (1829–1909), a North Carolinian who, because he thought slavery damaged poorer whites and Southern economic development, was opposed to the survival of the institution. The publication of Helper's *The Impending Crisis of the South: How to Meet It* (New York: Burdick Brothers, 1857) occasioned a great controversy and was thought by some, then and now, to have hardened North/South animosity and hastened the coming of secession and war.

118. To Herbert G. Nicholas[137]

JUNE 10, 1958

I must post you upon recent developments in U.S. academic customs and practices. In most such matters, as you know, there is still a slight tendency to defer to Old World precedent, particularly in ceremonial and ritual matters. But at Johns Hopkins University under the Milton Eisenhower regime there is a gratifying effort to keep abreast of the march of time.[138] This is aptly illustrated by the efficiency with [which] Hopkins conferred a degree upon the Prime Minister and another upon the President of the U.S. this morning.[139] None of your Old World dawdling about the matter. No wasting of invaluable statesmanship upon receiving lines, chit chat with professors, greeting of local dignitaries, attending garden parties and wanton munching of strawberries and sipping of champagne. No, Sir. Not a moment. In his native land the PM would doubtless have submitted to such time-consuming nonsense. But as you well know, there is not as much time over here as you have over there and we have to be more sparing with the use of it. Hopkins solution is simple. At 10 A.M. on the dot we start academic procession and the degree mill that awards 615 earned degrees to candidates in 55 minutes. At 10:40 A.M. the President and the PM leave the White House, having put in a hard morning at negotiating treaties, swapping H-bomb secrets, etc., pop into two helicopters with their parties—the copters already warmed up and waiting on the White House lawn—and off they are whisked to Baltimore, their roar drowning out the names of the last dozen or so Ph.D. candidates as the 'copters land precisely in the middle of an adjacent playing field at precisely 10:55. Whereupon the Marine band strikes up a suitable tune, your humble acquaintance seizes the mace and off we go with Brother Milton and a bevy of deans to greet President, PM, Ambassador Caccia, and a dozen assorted peers and brass as they de-'copt if you will permit the neologism.[140] PM exhibited dawdling tendencies

---

137. Herbert George Nicholas (1911–1998) was then a fellow of Nuffield College, Oxford, and Nuffield Reader in the Comparative Study of Institutions (1956–69); he was later the first Rhodes Professor of American History and Institutions (1969–78).

138. Milton S. Eisenhower (1899–1985), the brother of the U.S. president, was president of Johns Hopkins (1956–67 and [ad interim] 1971–72).

139. Maurice Harold Macmillan (later 1st Earl of Stockton) (1894–1986), a Conservative, was prime minister of the United Kingdom (1957–63).

140. Harold Anthony Caccia (later Baron Caccia) (1905–1990), British ambassador to the United States (1956–61).

to extent of remarking upon strange sight of my Oxford gown (broken out specially for occasion) midst savage regalia, but whipped into line of procession with Ike as partner; with no more nonsense we hotfooted it back to the stage, stashed the mace and got underway with God Save the Queen with everybody singing My Country Tis of Thee followed by Star Spangled banner but only one stanza of each to save time. Next the two degrees—my copy of the TV script by which we operated allotted them 6 ½ minutes apiece including citations (in good American and none of your Sanskrit or heathen Latin). Then Bro. Milton introduces Bro. Ike, and Bro. Ike introduces Bro. Mac, and Bro. Mac takes off on the main address of the occasion which contained perhaps two grains of sense among the chaff but graciously spoken. Meanwhile some seventeen TV cameras representing every known hookup, network, setup, & outfit. Which of course accounts for the necessity for split-second timing to accommodate TV time and all those valuable breakfast food and hair tonic and toothpaste programs that were given up for President and PM. As Bro. Milton remarked to me in his sage way, "Best publicity break Hopkins ever got." He was troubled by the reflection that any subsequent show would be anticlimax. I said I would suggest B & K, only Oxford had already done that and only K was available anyway.[141] He failed to see the humor of this proposal. Managed to slip the PM and some of his party a whiskey in the robing room, then back to the waiting copters and off to the White House lawn and back to work at the Summit Conference protocol and treaties and all that. One hour and thirty-five minutes, portal to portal!

[deletion]

CVWP, 38/464: TCLU

141. That is, Nikita Sergeyevich Khrushchev (1894–1971), first secretary of the Communist Party of the Soviet Union (1953–64), and Nikolai Alexandrovich Bulganin (1895–1975), premier of the Soviet Union (1955–58). The latter had been forced from office in March 1958. The two had traveled abroad together—to Britain, Yugoslavia, and India—and had been notably successful in charming their hosts and the press. They visited the University of Oxford in April 1956.

119. To Alan Keen[142]

JUNE 12, 1958

I write in response to your letter in the *Times Literary Supplement* of May 2 inviting contributions to your study of the nocturnal habits of the late C. K. Ogden which you propose to call *Oft in the Stilly Night*.[143] My own particular Gordon-Square night's entertainment may have been in no wise unusual or noteworthy in the life of Mr. Ogden. I am frank to admit, however, that it was quite unusual in the life of a man of my somewhat more regular habits and hours.

It was one evening late in January of 1954. I had dined as the guest of a member of the Atheneum Club, but for some reason—I believe it was a Sunday night—the Atheneum was not serving dinner and its members were accommodated by previous arrangement at the United Services Club across the way.

It was an unusually cold night, I recall, and the few who remained for drinks after dinner were huddled closely around the one tiny grate that burned in the vast hall. Under the circumstances one could hardly keep from overhearing neighboring conversations. For some time I had been

142. Gordon Alan Keen, a former advertising and radio scriptwriter who became a London dealer in antiquarian books and manuscripts; he was involved in the disposition of C. K. Ogden's estate and specialized in selling older British books to American universities.

143. Charles Kay ("C. K.") Ogden (1889–1957), psychologist, who as an undergraduate at Magdalene College, Cambridge, founded in 1912 the *Cambridge Magazine*, which became successful beyond the university. After the war, partly in collaboration with the literary critic I. A. Richards, he became interested in linguistics and aesthetics. He went on to invent and promote "Basic English," which he described as: "an auxiliary international language comprising 850 words arranged in a system in which everything may be said for all the purposes of everyday existence. Its distinctive features are the selection of words so that they cover the field, the restriction of the vocabulary, and the elimination of verbs except for the sixteen verb-forms which deal with the fundamental operations ('put,' 'take,' 'get,' etc.) and their replacement by the names of operations and directions ('go in,' 'put in,' etc.)." Ogden himself either wrote or sponsored some two hundred printed titles on the subject and his movement was briefly successful in the 1930s and 1940s, both in Britain and elsewhere, and won a notable convert in Winston Churchill in 1943. Ogden was almost as famous for his personal eccentricities, well captured in this letter of CVW's. Chief among these was his remorseless bibliophilia. After his death, his library of one hundred thousand books was acquired by the University of California-Los Angeles. At various times, these had been distributed among many London homes: two in Gordon Square (44 and 45), 1 Montague Street (also in Bloomsbury), Frith Street (Soho), Dartmouth Street (Westminster), Cadogan Square (Kensington), and other houses in Buxton, Derbyshire.

conscious of a spirited exchange among four gentlemen to my left when the most animated member of the group suddenly turned and without any preliminaries asked for my views on the question of whether animals have souls. Before I had finished fumbling for an answer to that one, he had fired several more. He and his three companions were, it turned out, a committee for the abolition of cat traps and were at the moment in consultation with a Member of Parliament, one of their number, about a bill on the subject. I was assured that the cat trap evil was growing and that London cats were having rather a bad time of it.

It is barely possible that we had been introduced before dinner, though I am strongly of the impression that we had not. If we had been, I had certainly not caught his name and he did not know mine. When the group broke up for the evening I was therefore quite unprepared for his invitation to drop me off on his way home. When I protested he assured me before he learned my address that it was not out of his way in the slightest. Once in the cab, however, he gave the driver a Gordon Square address, explaining vaguely that he would only stop briefly. Arriving there, he urged that I come in for just a moment to sample his champagne. While I was protesting the lateness of the hour—it was close to midnight—he dismissed the cab and there I was, still wondering who my companion could be.

As soon as we stepped inside my wonderment increased. We paused a few moments on the first floor, long enough for him to start two of the dozens of music boxes that crowded the floor chiming simultaneously. The only help he offered by way of explanation for the oversupply of music boxes was that one of the larger ones the size of a spinnet had belonged to a maharajah. When I expressed admiration he regretted that this one was out of order and suggested that we go upstairs, leaving the two boxes tinkling away below and starting a couple more on the way up.

Out of the corner of my eye as we mounted the stair I caught from letters hung in frames on the wall several signatures that set me to wondering even more. On the second floor there were more music boxes, scores of clocks, and stacks upon stacks upon stacks of books—piled upon the floor, on the music boxes, the clocks, the tables, the chairs, everywhere. And over everything layers of dust, the number of layers depending apparently upon the recency with which the article had been disturbed.

Still talking incessantly, my host guided me through the maze, stopping occasionally to clear the way, and arriving finally before an undersized, unlighted electric heater. Clearing the books off a couple of chairs and turning on the heater, he remarked cheerfully: "Now, we will be as warm as toast in no time at all." I agreed dubiously through chattering teeth. As a matter of fact I had arrived only recently from America and was not clothed to withstand the rigors of English indoor climate. The heater made no perceptible difference in the temperature of the room. Our breath continued to frost in the air as we talked and I was unable to master an occasional shiver and a chattering of teeth.

The talk was of rare books. I was quickly beyond my depth, for my competence in American history was quite unwarrantedly assumed to extend to rare Elizabethan imprints and manuscripts. One treasure after another was laid before me to admire. The problem of authenticating one of his possessions, a manuscript attributed to Sir Francis Bacon, brought forth perhaps a dozen contemporaneous volumes for purposes of reference. A quick dart in one direction or another and a plunge into a pile of books produced the desired work every time. His repeated success at this was uncanny. It was hard to say which was the more astonishing, the fact that he actually possessed such books or his ability to find them in all the confusion of stacks and piles.

It is impossible to recall just when I began to suspect the identity of my host but it could not have been long before I was sure who he was. This enabled me to change the subject safely and relieve him of the increasing strain of maintaining the pretense of my expertise in Elizabethan calligraphy and orthography.

A question or so about his friends of the Bloomsbury Circle started a grateful flow of anecdotes about Virginia Woolfe, Lytton Strachey, and his next-door neighbors, the John Maynard Keyneses. I remember particularly several stories illustrating Virginia Woolfe's painful sensitivity to criticism and others about the eccentricities of Lord Keynes' ballerina wife.[144] I could have listed with pleasure a long time, but it was obviously getting late.

One thing more difficult to ignore than anything else in the Ogden

144. All members of the so-called Bloomsbury Group: (Adeline) Virginia Woolf, née Stephen (1882–1941), the novelist and publisher; (Giles) Lytton Strachey (1880–1932), the biographer and literary critic; John Maynard Keynes (later Baron Keynes) (1883–1946), the economist; Lydia Vasilievna Lopokova (1892–1981), the ballerina, who married Keynes in 1925 after she had divorced her first husband, Randolfo Barocchi. The Keyneses lived at 46 Gordon Square.

establishment was the passage of time. Not all of the scores of clocks were running, and not all of those that were running were of the chiming sort, but there were enough of the latter to set up a din not only on the hours but on the quarter and half hours as well. Since no two clocks seem to have kept the same time there was much reiteration of the chiming and striking. During the musical uproar that signalized 2:00 A.M. I made the first of my several unsuccessful efforts to take my departure.

This only served to remind Mr. Ogden that he promised me champagne. While he was searching for a corkscrew I abandoned all polite pretense of comfort and went to get my overcoat. Our breath was still frosting everywhere save immediately before the small burner. While I was about it I took a turn about my neck with my muffler. Mr. Ogden returned talking, and without commenting upon or even apparently noticing my change in attire, presented me with a distinctly dusty champagne glass. There was no opportunity to blow out the dust for he promptly filled the glass.

If it is the object of the perfect host to make his guest oblivious of time, it would seem that Mr. Ogden deliberately set himself fantastic obstacles. There were not only the clocks but there were his chosen hours of entertainment—hours when time drags heaviest and entertainers have to resort to their more sensational tricks. The next gambit was good for stretching my contracting span of attention over another hour and a quarter. This was evidently one of his prize possessions—a small portrait of William Shakespeare alleged to have been painted from life. The entertainment was the story of the hunt for evidence of its authenticity and his masterly marshalling of the evidence. Whether it added up pro or con I have forgotten, but it was a fascinating story.

Several half-hearted gestures of leave taking had been brushed off or drowned out by new anecdotes or simply ignored. But my next exhibit of determination about departure, shortly after the 3:45 burst of clock chimes, seemed to goad Mr. Ogden into desperate expedients of entertainment. He was determined to keep this American Caliban charmed if he had to resort to handsprings and funny faces. The devices to which he felt compelled to resort must have hurt his pride. I recall for one a music box in the form of an oriental maiden who held a cobra in her hand and executed a mechanical belly-dance in time with the mechanical music. He reached deeper into cabinets for fabulous curios, ransacked files for rare autographs, pulled out letters from famous contemporaries and read long passages, exhibited fantastic editions. He even tried unsuccessfully to start up the maharajah's music box, remarking ruefully, "it was guaranteed to charm a snake."

It was certainly not that I was bored or even very sleepy. The fact was that I was slightly dazed by the display of treasure and learning and more than half hypnotized by the fantastic man himself. More than that, I was bemused by the puzzle of why he should drive himself to such extremes to entertain a complete stranger until dawn, a stranger with absolutely no claim upon him and one without the capacity to appreciate many of his treasures and much of his erudition.

As if to offer some sort of answer to my unasked question, he made much of his interest in Jeremy Bentham—on whom he was, of course, an authority—and of the coincidence that I had a connection with Queen's College, Oxford, at which Bentham was a student, and was lecturing currently at University College, London, where the good Jeremy's bones, fully clothed and ensconced in a chair, may be viewed by the curious in the library.[145] But the fact was that Mr. Ogden only discovered this very tenuous Bentham connection of mine long after he was committed to his all-out program of entertainment. There was in fact no explanation save Mr. Ogden's whim and his apparent compulsion to go to any limit to keep a guest entertained once whim had dictated his choice.

There was no question of his success in my case. I was enormously entertained, flattered, amused, astonished—as much so as he could have wished. Unacquainted with his habits, however, I mistakenly thought I was imposing upon him and consequently kept up an intermittent effort to say goodnight and take my leave. These efforts, on the other hand, he construed as evidence of some shortcoming in the entertainment provided and consequently redoubled his efforts, or resorted to more obvious devices.

The game continued until shortly before 5:00 A.M., when, hat in hand, I finally gained the front door and my host's reluctant consent to depart. Then suddenly his eyes lighted up, as I had seen them do so often over the past five or six hours. "Of course, I shall walk you to your place! Wait till I get my coat!" He would listen to no objection I raised. It was not

145. Jeremy Bentham (1748–1832), the legal philosopher and utilitarian. In 1953, before his death, University College, London, purchased Ogden's manuscripts and incunabula, including a large collection concerning Bentham.

too far, too cold, too late, or for that matter too early. It was in fact just right, his favorite time for a walk. "Besides, I must see my plumber," he added for good measure. "Anyways there are no cabs and you might get lost."

Off we went through deserted streets, morning wind blowing our words back in our teeth. There had been snow and the cold was intense. My address was well beyond Russell Square. Mr. Ogden appeared in no wise discouraged by the distance nor the worse for his evening's efforts. His manner suggested that he was just starting the day, that this was his favorite stroll, and that by extraordinary good fortune he had fallen in with a congenial acquaintance. My efforts to rise to his level of spirits were by no means adequate.

The entertainment was not over. The performer was not only taking a curtain call but throwing in a generous encore as well. There were stories about famous occupants of houses we passed, about his cat named St. Thomas, new anecdotes about Jeremy Bentham, tales about interesting chimpanzees he had known. One had the feeling that the performer would continue his encores indefinitely unless the audience discreetly withdrew. There was a long pause at my doorstep while Mr. Ogden finished one story and told another. By this time I was numb with cold and groggy with drowsiness. I could not bring myself to ask him in. As we parted he slipped a little book in my hand. It was a paper-back edition of one of his own works. On the title page he had written: "C. K. Ogden, January 31—February 1, 1954." The entertainment had indeed run from one month into the next.

CVWP, 29/342: TCLU

120. To Henry Nash Smith

SEPTEMBER 5, 1958

[deletion]

Curious the strong reaction I get to the guilt theme. David Donald an able and sophisticated historian doubts the South has ever been troubled by guilt over slavery or segregation either, save a few intellectuals and pietists.[146] But I go along with you and only wish my depth psychology were deeper and I more secure in its use (and if you have anything that would improve my grasp pray pass it on. I mean any citation.)

146. I am unsure Donald had expressed this view in print by 1958, but he latterly argued it in David Donald, "The Proslavery Argument Reconsidered," *Journal of Southern History* 37 (February 1971): 3–18.

Guilt projection can have fascinating variations, and the Negro himself is only one favorite target. A broader and more legitimate one is the USA and its wickedness. You were calling for Ameses.[117] My native state is teeming with them, eloquent ones, inspired ones, and all from the Faubus state. There is for example my one-time classmate Oren Harris, incorruptible nemesis of Sherm Adams, relentless exposer of the moral pretense and emptiness of the Ike Team and its preposterous pose of moral superiority over Truman.[148] Wonderful medieval morality play character names: culprit Goldfine, lawyer Robb, secretary Paperman.[149] And there is Senator McClellan, Torquemada of corrupt, sin-sodden, venal labor racketeers and gangsters Hoffa & Co. and all their bought-off, intimidated politicos, and their hoods and thugs and thieves and the respectable connections and high sounding offices.[150] And then most conscience-stricken, guilt-bitten, and pathetic (because I identify with him most readily) Senator Fulbright lashing away by the hour with cold and brilliant fury and inspired indignation at the moral bankruptcy of the USA, its sodden apathy, its two-ton chrome-spangled parlor sofas on wheels and late Roman obesity and laxity . . . It's really worth looking up.[151] Rarely since Jeremiah has inspired eschatology reached such peaks. Maybe not so much projection as transfer of guilt.

[deletion]

CVWP, 50/596: TCLU

147. The referent here is unclear, but is probably to Nathaniel Ames (1708–1764), the physician and almanac maker whose dizzy prediction in 1758 of future American greatness had been quoted in Smith, *Virgin Land*, 139–40.

148. Oren Harris (1903–1997) was a U.S. representative from Arkansas (1941–66) whose congressional subcommittee had claimed that Llewelyn Sherman Adams (1899–1986), President Eisenhower's chief of staff (1953–58), had accepted, as a bribe, a vicuña overcoat and oriental rug from Bernard Goldfine, a Massachusetts textile manufacturer, then under investigation by the Federal Trade Commission. In the ensuing furor, Adams was forced to resign.

149. Roger Robb (1907–1985) was a Washington lawyer who acted as Goldfine's attorney during the congressional hearings over the Adams affair: he had become prominent as the prosecutor at the Atomic Energy Commission hearings in 1954 on the loyalty of J. Robert Oppenheimer; Mildred Paperman (1912–1995), Goldfine's secretary and bookkeeper who was later briefly jailed for contempt of court in connection with Goldfine's many tax problems.

150. John L. McClellan (1896–1977), U.S. senator from Arkansas (1943–77) whose "Committee on Improper Activities in the Labor or Management Fields" investigated labor racketeering, including that by Jimmy Hoffa (1913–[perhaps] 1975), president of the Central Conference of Teamsters from 1953 to 1964, when he was convicted of jury tampering, fraud, and conspiracy.

151. J. William Fulbright (1905–1995), U.S. senator from Arkansas (1945–75), notable for his liberalism in cultural politics and foreign policy, but also for his discreet conservatism on race.

121. To Arthur H. Thornhill Jr.[152]

SEPTEMBER 27, 1958

[deletion]

I welcomed the opportunity we had to talk over my writing plans and exchange ideas on the subject while you were in Baltimore. It was helpful to
me, and I share your hope that it will lead to renewed ties with Little, Brown.

As I told you, I have for some time felt the need for a more definite
commitment than I have ever acknowledged to the task of writing a serious general book on Reconstruction. I have known for some time that I
wanted to tackle this job, and have from time to time done some research.
Lacking a firm commitment, however, I have been too often distracted by
quicker and easier opportunities. What I need is a contract.

The book I want to do could be thought of as a companion volume
to my ORIGINS OF THE NEW SOUTH, covering the period immediately
preceding the one treated there. It would be of comparable scope, but
being free of obligations to a series, I think I could make it a better book.
I should not feel obliged, as I was in the earlier book, to cover all aspects
of the period. The book should consequently have more focus, more individuality, and I hope more importance and wider interest. It would not
be so narrowly regional, for a large part of the story is the relations *between*
regions, the impact of North on South, the gradual absorption of the
impact, the blunting of Northern purpose, and the eventual frustration
of the revolution.

Several things have combined to sharpen my interest in the idea.
Three dissertations have just been completed on the period under my
direction. Two of them will be published before long and will compel
some striking revision of ideas that have dominated interpretation of the
period for more than a generation. Three more are under way. Things
are happening in this area. It will soon be time for a new synthesis. Apart
from that there is the thundering relevance of this subject for what I have
called the Second Reconstruction, the one that is currently approaching
one of its several crises. This one will be with us for some time to come,
and it cannot but heighten interest in the First Reconstruction. I need
not labor the point, but it should be obvious more than any other period
in our history, Reconstruction is one of unresolved and live issues. Compared with it the Progressive Era and the New Deal are wrapped in the

152. Arthur H. Thornhill Jr. (b. 1924), an editor at Little, Brown and later its president.

sanctity of the accepted, or at least the accomplished, with both parties to each dispute accepting the outcome without serious thought of challenge. As for progress toward acceptance of Reconstruction, I refer you [to the] latest bulletins from Virginia and Arkansas, and future ones from South Carolina and Georgia, or Alabama and Mississippi. My guess is that we will probably celebrate the centennial anniversary of the First Reconstruction long before its principles and aims are achieved by the Second.

As for the book you are admittedly more interested in—the one covering the century from Emancipation to Desegregation—you may well be right that it could be the more significant and popular one. I hope I can get around to that one later on. It would certainly seem worth doing. Yet to be solved however, are the questions of the text with Eaton for HM Co., and the question if I do that whether the book for LB & Co. would suffer from repetition and HM would have a legitimate complaint.[153] And if so whether I should do the one or the other. Eaton left for Europe a year ago, while the restriction imposed by Macmillan was unsolved (still remains unsolved) and I have not been in touch with him since his recent return. In the meantime the question has been shelved and its reopening depends somewhat on my initiative. I am rather puzzled what to do.

At any rate I should like a contract for the Reconstruction book first, though only if you are convinced it is a book you would like to publish. I am reluctant at this stage to propose limits for delivery and length of manuscript. It could hardly be completed before the fall of '62, depending on how much leave I can wrangle from Johns Hopkins, how much help from foundations, etc. It would not likely be less than 150,000 words, and probably run closer to 200,000. As for the amount of advance royalty, I should not like to take any before 1960, but I would propose $2500 as an amount I could draw upon if I needed it after 1959. You are of course a better judge of the prospects of such a book than I. But considering the sales of ORIGINS OF THE NEW SOUTH, a heavier and more academic book than the one I propose, I should think the prospects are good. The market will be glutted with Civil War books, but the more relevant subject of Reconstruction goes begging.
[deletion]

CVWP, 71/108: TCLU

153. CVW was supposed to be writing, jointly with Clement Eaton (1898–1980) of the University of Kentucky, a history of the South for Houghton Mifflin; it was never done.

122. To Richard Hofstadter

[deletion]

The Ford people sent me your manuscript on the "Extreme Right Wing" and I read it yesterday.[154] I think it is a really fine thing, written with a new confidence and assurance that comes out in deft use of understatement. I like many things about it, particularly the undercurrent of compassion, the almost affectionate appreciation of the cranks, avoidance of the stiff-necked disdain, achievement of an earthy touch. If you are specializing in cranks, after all, there is no more fruitful field of research than among the highbrows. And I don't think it will do to be too high handed about the cranks. The dividing line is a narrow one and one could easily mistake a saint or so for a mere crank. Personally I would rue the day the last crank disappeared from American politics. The passing of Jenner almost causes me a pang, unfelt in the passing of McCarthy.[155] What seems to be coming about currently with the defeat of Bowles, Benton, Dilworth, Finletter is a sort of homogenization of politicos at the level of the pro who is in it strictly for the gravy:[156] No Stevensons and no McCarthys.[157] But I'm wandering. On the negative side I can't help feeling you are missing a few nuances. Lumping together the Antimasons, Know Nothings, APA, KKK and McC. with the Pops seems to

154. This would seem to be an early version of what would become "The Paranoid Style in American Politics," first given as the Herbert Spencer Lecture at Oxford in November 1963 and published, in full, in Richard Hofstadter, *The Paranoid Style in American Politics and Other Essays* (New York: Alfred A. Knopf, 1965), 3–40.

155. William Ezra Jenner (1908–1985), a Republican U.S. senator from Indiana (1947–59) and a strong supporter of Joseph McCarthy.

156. All these are politicians who failed in bids to secure Democratic nominations in 1958: Chester Bliss Bowles (1901–1986), a Connecticut liberal for the U.S. Senate; William Burnett Benton (1900–1973), U.S. senator from Connecticut (1949–53), in the same race; Richardson K. Dilworth (1898–1974), the Democratic mayor of Philadelphia (1956–62) who considered a run for governor in 1958 but was forced to abandon the venture after criticism of his suggestion that the People's Republic of China be accorded diplomatic recognition by the United States; and Thomas Knight Finletter (1893–1980), Secretary of the Air Force (1950–53), who failed to secure the Democratic U.S. senatorial nomination in New York.

157. Adlai Ewing Stevenson II (1900–1965), liberal Democrat and governor of Illinois (1949–53) who ran unsuccessfully for president in 1952 and 1956. CVW had supported him on both occasions; see CVW to Walter Johnson, 3 October 1952, and K. Slingbuff to CVW and "Volunteers for Stevenson working in the 12th ward" [November 1956].

me to obscure some distinctions. The Populists (and I do think you confuse things by using caps and lower case too indiscriminately) particularly
differ from the others too much to be used as the prototype. Admittedly
there is no better example of the Populist crank become reactionary than
Tom Watson. But the Pop crank is the Pop frustrated, where the rest of
the gang start out cranks at the beginning. Also what you are accounting
party traits might often be class and region traits, more midwestern than
southern. The Pops underwent the sort of frustration that produced Pav-
lov's neurotic dogs. But I hope we can talk about all that later.
[deletion]

    CVWP, 26/302: TCLU

123. To Richard Hofstadter

FEBRUARY 16, 1959

Good talk with Dave Riesman the other day in Cambridge. I feel sure
he would not like to be repeated, but then I am sure you would be
interested in his reactions to the place and will keep it to yourself. It was
pretty clear he missed Chicago. People were politer at Harvard, but more
withdrawn, no "colleagueship," no intellectual polemics, only personalities, provincial smugness, stuffy social life, no real community, several different communities with no contact, chilled at faculty attitude toward
students, who are neglected and pretty lost. Other hand, found student
response gratifying, students more diversified, more "naïve," more rewarding. Much missed intellectual stimulus of Chicago colleagues. In
general, he would seem to confirm your decision—though we did not
mention that. Please don't quote me.

    In the USA the great rush continues among all & sundry to get as
near to the middle of the road as possible. Congestion in dead center is
terrific, frightening! You have to listen closely to tell the NAM from the
ADA, the NAACP from the White Citizens Councils.[158] As one slight
straw in a hushed wind, within one week I found myself quoted with
approval in the Richmond Times Dispatch and the New Republic on
segregation of all things. In desperation I am simultaneously editing a

---

158. That is, the National Association of Manufacturers, the Americans for Democratic
Action, the National Association for the Advancement of Colored People, and various Southern pro-segregation organizations.

pro-slavery book for the Harvard Press and promoting the Mau Mau in Ga.[159] Walk the streets in search of cranks. Advise you to suppress that anti-crank monograph and write a pro-crank piece. By the way what have you done with that Fund for the Republic essay, anyway?

Thanks for advice on the Stanford Center. I will write Turner when I summon the nerve, though I don't know him.[160]

I know how you chafe there at getting nothing much done for I did the same thing.[161] It did make me realize, however, how much of my work was compulsive. Regards to Frank Thistlewaite and Brock.[162] We are having Laslett down from Princeton.[163] I find him most amusing. Only problem is getting a word in edgewise. Love to Bede and the family. We are in fair shape but parents on both sides are crumbling and expenses mounting.

CVWP, 26/302: TCLU

124. Alger Hiss Memorandum[164]

This is dictated on May 3, 1959, as a record of a conversation that took place on the evening of May 1, 1959, between about 9:15 p.m. and 1:15 a.m. I had met Alger Hiss for the first time at the home of

159. George Fitzhugh, *Cannibals All! or, Slaves Without Masters,* ed. CVW (Cambridge, MA: Harvard University Press, Belknap, 1960). The Mau Mau were an anticolonial resistance movement (1952–60) in Kenya; presumably "Ga." means Georgia.

160. Possibly Victor Turner (1920–1983), an anthropologist originally from Glasgow, Scotland; he left the University of Manchester in 1961 to become a fellow of the Center for Advanced Behavioral Sciences at Stanford University.

161. Hofstadter was spending the academic year, 1958–59, as Pitt Professor of American History and Institutions at the University of Cambridge.

162. Frank Thistlethwaite (1915–2003) was a fellow of Saint John's College, Cambridge, and a scholar of transatlantic economic history; he helped to found the study of American history at Cambridge. His contemporary William Ranulf Brock (b. 1916), a fellow of Selwyn College, Cambridge, from 1947 had been among the few research students of G. M. Trevelyan and began his scholarly career as a historian of early nineteenth-century Britain, but in 1952 the Cambridge Faculty of History asked if he would convert his lectureship into one dedicated to American history, a subject he followed thereafter. He met CVW in 1955, when the latter was at Oxford, and was a Commonwealth Fund Fellow (1952–53, 1958) when he visited the University of California-Berkeley, Yale, and (in 1958) Johns Hopkins. His most important early book in American history was *An American Crisis: Congress and Reconstruction: 1865–1867* (London: Macmillan, 1963).

163. (Thomas) Peter Ruffell Laslett (1915–2001), fellow of Trinity College, Cambridge (1953–2001), a social historian of early modern England and editor of the works of John Locke.

164. Alger Hiss (1904–1996), a State Department official (1936–47) and president of the Carnegie Endowment for International Peace (1947–49). In 1948, before the House Committee

George Boas, near Baltimore, on April 12, and dined with him there and afterwards took him to the train. We agreed to meet for dinner when I came up to New York on May 1 to attend a meeting of the Social Science Research Council the next day. Hiss wrote confirming the engagement but saying that he had learned that he was committed to visit some people that evening who he was sure would welcome me as well. He named the people, only one of whom he knew personally. This was Waldo Frank who had asked him to spend the evening with some people who would like to know him.[165]

Hiss and I had dinner together and then at nine o'clock we took a taxi to 444 West 20th Street, the home of Dr. George S. Klein, a psychiatrist, and his wife.[166] There we found Frank and his wife and a Mr. and Mrs. Gibson.[167] Gibson is the author of the current Broadway play, *Two for the Seesaw*, and his wife is a psychologist who had made a special study of the Hiss trial. It was apparent almost from the moment we arrived

---

on Un-American Activities, Hiss was accused by Whittaker Chambers (1901–1961), an editor at *Time*, of having been a Communist in the 1930s. This was denied by Hiss who, when Chambers repeated the charge later, sued for slander. In the trial, inconsistencies in Hiss's testimony and evidence from Chambers which suggested Hiss had been a Soviet spy, led to a charge of perjury, of which Hiss (after two trials, the first having reached no verdict) was found guilty on 21 January 1950. He was sentenced to five years in prison, of which he served three years and eight months. These events were pivotal in the anti-Communist *alarums* of the late 1940s and 1950s.

165. Waldo D. Frank (1889–1967), a literary and cultural critic long associated with the *New Republic*, perhaps best known for his novel *The Death and Birth of David Markand: An American Story* (New York: Charles Scribner's Sons, 1934).

166. George Stuart Klein (1917–1971), psychologist, was a professor at New York University as well as a consultant to the Menninger Foundation; he was very interested in the nature of perception, including the effects upon cognition of various drugs, including LSD and mescaline. His wife, Bessie Boris Klein (1917–1993), was a painter.

167. These are: 1) Jean Klempner Frank, Waldo Frank's third wife, whom he had married in 1943; she had been his secretary. 2) William Gibson (1914–2008), playwright and novelist, best known for his play about Helen Keller, *The Miracle Worker* (1959). 3) Margaret Brenman-Gibson (d. 2004), whom Gibson had married in 1940. She had received her doctorate in psychology at the University of Kansas and worked at the Menninger Clinic in Topeka; she was later a collaborator of Erik Erikson, from whom she learned the practice of psychobiography, and came eventually to teach at Harvard. Her most notable work, in this genre, was *Clifford Odets, American Playwright: The Years from 1906 to 1940* (New York: Atheneum, 1981). She discusses the Hiss-Chambers affair in "The Creation of Plays: With a Specimen Analysis," *Psychoanalytic Review* 64 (1977): 237–88.

that Mrs. Gibson expected to use this opportunity to question Hiss about his trial. It was also apparent that Hiss had not expected this turn of events and was a bit taken aback and apologized to me and to the other guests. Without preliminaries Mrs. Gibson opened her remarks with this question:

> *Mrs. Gibson:* To break the ice may I ask why it was that Chambers picked you?
>
> *Hiss:* Frankly, I do not know. I have of course often wondered and I do not know why. [After some hesitation][168] I do have a theory.
>
> *Mrs. Gibson:* Please tell us your theory.
>
> *Hiss:* You must understand, Mrs. Gibson, that this was no case of the sort that Sherlock Holmes investigated, with the ordinary sort of motives and clues. So far as I know there are no motives or clues of the usual sort. You will remember that in his book Chambers tells of his brother's suicide and of a suicide pact with his brother which he did not fulfill. I believe that the guilt of this episode preyed upon him. He spoke of wanting to join his brother, and I believe that his frequent references to going underground had some symbolic reference to this impulse. His motives for embracing communism were, I believe from the evidence of his book, of a personal and psychological nature.
>
> *Mrs. Gibson:* I hope that you do not mind my probing into the past and that this is not painful for you.
>
> *Hiss:* I must admit that I avoid talking about it rather deliberately. I had to live in the past a good deal when I wrote my book, but I have a life to live and I do not want to become self-centered or past-centered.[169] And this episode has quickly slipped into the past. A professor friend of mine told me recently of having referred to Chambers and Hiss before a class only to discover that not a single member of the class knew anything of the case.
>
> *Mrs. Gibson:* Was there any evidence of homosexuality involving Chambers?
>
> *Hiss:* Very definitely yes. In fact my lawyers had witnesses who were fully prepared to testify to Chambers's advances to them which they repulsed. But the lawyers decided not to introduce this evidence for fear of the jury reaction and public relations.
>
> *Mrs. Gibson:* I hope you will permit me to be frank. There were many rumors during the trial and since then that you were shielding some-

168. The interpolations in square brackets in this memorandum are CVW's.
169. Alger Hiss, *In the Court of Public Opinion* (New York: Alfred A. Knopf, 1957).

one dear to you from terrible exposure and embarrassment, and that this might have strongly influenced your testimony and defense. One of the rumors was that you were protecting your stepson Timmy from exposure in his relations with Chambers.[170]

Hiss: About Timmy, this is the only thing about which I shall not speak with complete frankness. There are some things that do not belong to one. I will say, however, that I believe Timmy completely in his saying that Chambers never made any advances to him and that there was no such relation between them.[171] In fact there was nothing regarding him about which I had reason to be ashamed.

Mrs. Gibson: Did Chambers have any homosexual impulses toward you?

Hiss: Chambers never made any homosexual advances to me. His attitude toward me, however, and his relations were strange and I did not understand them. There were many evidences of his identifying himself with me. He imitated me in some ways and went to the extent of becoming Episcopalian, which is my religious faith. One remarkable episode was a visit which a law school classmate of mine, McLean, a conservative Republican corporation lawyer, paid Chambers at his Maryland farm.[172] This was before the trial took place, and I should add that McLean abhors the very idea of Sigmund Freud and any fanciful psychological theories. But he told me that during his visit Chambers excitedly told him that he had a slipcover that belonged to Alger Hiss and he wanted to show it to him, that he ran upstairs and came down bearing a scrap of slipcover that he showed McLean with adolescent eagerness and assured him that it belonged to me.

Mrs. Gibson: How would you describe his attachment to you?

Hiss: My guess is that he had some obscure sort of love attachment. He was embarrassingly eager to learn everything about me, and he came to hate my wife.

Mrs. Gibson: But his attitude toward you was one of love of some sort?

Hiss: Yes, something of the sort.

170. In 1929, Hiss had married Priscilla Fansler Hobson (1903–1987), previously married to Thayer Hobson, by whom she had had a son called Timothy (b. 1926), who was gay and was discharged from the Navy because of his sexual orientation: on this, see Ed Gold, "At Alger Hiss Conference, Gay Debate Gets Red Hot," *The Villager*, 11–17 April 2007, an account of a conference at New York University, at which Hobson spoke about his homosexuality; it is online at http://www.thevillager.com/villager_206/atalgerhissconference.htm [accessed 28 October 2011].

171. There had been rumors that Chambers had sexually abused Hobson in the 1930s.

172. Edward Cochrane McLean (1903–1972), who had been Hiss's classmate at Harvard Law School and was one of Hiss's lawyers at both perjury trials.

Mrs. Gibson: Then how would he come to wish to injure and ruin you?

Hiss: That is something I have never understood. There are a number of possibilities. It may have been because of his feeling of rejection and exclusion, though I would never intentionally hurt anyone and I allowed this connection to go on much longer than I wished in order to avoid hurting him. Perhaps the psychoanalyst could find some evidence of a transfer of guilt to me, guilt of his own in connection with his brother. But since you have read his book and testimony you will know that this is an extremely complicated man.

Woodward: Chambers is still living. Is there any possibility of his ever renouncing his testimony?

Hiss: I do not think so. I think it even possible that he believes it himself by now.

Woodward: Were you ever tempted to confront him?

Hiss: As a matter of fact during my recent visit to Maryland I planned to go out to his farm and walk in on him and simply say something of this sort: you once professed a great regard for me.[173] Why did you do it? Not that I expected much to come of that, but it would have been some satisfaction I think. My lawyers, however, very strongly advised against it. For one thing they thought it was dangerous. The man might murder me and it would provide him with a very convenient motive for doing so. In the second place my lawyers thought that the public would construe my visit as evidence of a deep attachment, and so I was dissuaded from carrying out the plan.

Dr. Klein: What about the strong support that Mrs. Chambers gave her husband's testimony?[174]

Hiss: Mrs. Chambers wore the pants in that family. She had lived through miserable years of degrading poverty and had only recently enjoyed some prosperity while her husband was employed by TIME magazine.[175] It was she who had the ambition and the insistence on improving their lot. Any suspicion of Chambers perjury would have been a terrible menace to their security. I do not find it hard to understand her support of his testimony.

Mrs. Gibson: You keep using the pronoun "they" in speaking of the people who organized this attack upon you. How many do you think were involved?

173. Chambers had a farm near Westminster, the seat of Carroll County, Maryland, to the northwest of Baltimore.

174. Esther Shemitz Chambers (1900–1986), an artist and illustrator, whom Chambers had married in 1931.

175. As a young woman, she had worked as a typist, an advertising saleswoman, and secretary; the Chamberses had had very little money until he started working for *Time* in 1939.

Hiss: Not very many really.

Mrs. Gibson: Do you think that any of the prominent politicians were involved in a conspiratorial way or knew the truth of the matter? In other words, would they have any real conviction of your guilt?

Hiss: I do not think it necessary to think of their attitude in that way. As you know lawyers are accustomed as a matter of course to make the best case they can for their client. [He told several stories to illustrate the point.] With politicians the matter of conviction presents no problem at all.

Dr. Klein: Then what was their motive?

Hiss: One only has to recall the charged political situation of 1948 and 1949. The air was full of accusations of subversion and disloyalty in the democratic party, and these along with the charges of graft were the main reliance of the republican assault on their opponents.

Mrs. Gibson: Why would they single you out?

Hiss: That puzzles me. It seems that given the range of possibilities they could have picked a much more likely victim because there were some Democrats around the place who had a known background of radicalism.

Mr. Frank: Of course in those days we all knew a lot of radicals and had communist friends. I was never a communist myself, but I knew many of them in those days.

Hiss: Perhaps so in New York, but I grew up in Baltimore and the Eastern Shore of Maryland. I went directly from Johns Hopkins to the Harvard Law School and from there to Washington as the secretary to Mr. Justice Holmes. I did have some radical friends in New York but I had very little association with them. As a matter of fact I am much more radical now than I was in those days.

Woodward: Could you explain how the prosecution handled your taking the initiative in unearthing the controversial typewriter?

Hiss: They simply said I knew it would be unearthed soon enough anyways. As a matter of fact the colored man who discovered it for me told me that "dem F.B.I.'s is all around that house" and had been for some time. They were evidently waiting for me to find it.

Mrs. Gibson: Is it your theory that the documents were forged?

Hiss: Oh yes. I made much close investigation and I am satisfied that it is a simple matter to make typewriter forgeries though the machine has to be constructed by an expert. There is testimony on the part of Chambers that he had connections with communists who were alleged to be operating on Nazi ships, agents who were adept at such forgeries.

Mrs. Gibson: How many people do you think knew about this forgery?

Hiss: In all probability not more than three people.

Mrs. Gibson: Who would they be?

Hiss: Chambers, of course, though he probably has effaced the memory of it from his curious mind. The other two are first the man who made the machine and one other.

Mrs. Gibson: Who was that?

Hiss: I have a theory here and a good deal of evidence to support it though nothing conclusive. My theory is that it's a New York journalist named Isaac Don Levine.[176]

Mrs. Gibson: What was his connection with this case?

Hiss: He was known to have visited Chambers and was also known to have been associated with several cases involving forged or suspicious documents. The most recent of these involves a Mrs. _____ who belongs to the uppercrust society in which the Roosevelts moved.[177] She had psychopathic traits and is at present in a hospital.[178] One of her obsessions was that she acted as an intermediary between Franklin Roosevelt and Earl Browder, and she is alleged to have turned over a large number of letters on White House stationery, typewritten and signed "Franklin," addressed to her and "Dear Earl." Levine used these documents in the preparation of a book exposing this relationship.[179] He received a royalty advance from a New York publisher who had a contract to publish it. The publisher had the documents checked by an expert who passed on them as authentic. Still unsatisfied, the publisher showed them to Mrs. Roosevelt. She in turn returned them to the publisher saying that she had had the Hyde Park Library searched for evidence of this correspondence and had found absolutely none. She pronounced the documents fraudulent and assured the publisher that if they were published she would bring suit. The publisher then gave up the venture but has so far refused to permit me or my lawyers to examine the documents.

176. Isaac Don Levine (1892–1981), originally from Mozyr, Russia, came to the United States in 1911; he took a special interest in Soviet affairs, both before and when he worked as a columnist for the Hearst newspapers in the late 1920s and 1930s; he was the editor of *Plain Talk*, an anti-Communist magazine (1946–50).

177. This is Josephine Adams; on this, see Harvey Klehr, "The Strange Case of Roosevelt's 'Secret Agent,'" in *The Communist Experience in America: A Political and Social History* (New Brunswick, NJ: Transaction Publishers, 2010), 233–43.

178. The Norristown Sanitarium in Pennsylvania.

179. *I Was Roosevelt's Secret Emissary* was to be published by David McKay in 1957; Earl Russell Browder (1891–1973) was general secretary of the Communist Party USA.

Woodward: Do you believe anybody else would have knowledge of this forgery?

Hiss: I do not think so. In fact I think it highly unlikely. Certainly I do not think that any of the politicians engaged in the questioning have knowledge of it.

Woodward: What about the F.B.I. and could one suppose that someone there had guilty knowledge of it?

Hiss: I very much doubt it, and I do not believe the F.B.I. ever suborned a witness in this case.

Woodward: I am surprised to hear you say that.

Hiss: You should not be. As a rule these are only hardworking men, not often very bright, but on the other hand conscientious and sometimes well trained. They are required to have some law training. They are simply given a job to do and they do it with all the thoroughness for which they are famous.

Mrs. Gibson: But do you not think they tampered with the witnesses?

Hiss: It was not necessary. On his own testimony Chambers spent three months eight hours a day going over evidence and documents with the F.B.I. And as for other witnesses I would not say that the F.B.I. planted ideas or interpretations, but people as a rule are eager to cooperate, they want to please, especially such a powerful agency as the F.B.I. They want to say what they know they are expected to say or desired to say. Being exposed to plausible ideas they adopt them as their own. There was the case of one of the colored maids [I cannot recall her name], who testified to things she could not have known and should have known were false.[180] Yet she is a simple and honest woman and I believe it altogether likely that she was thoroughly convinced that what she testified was the truth. As you will recall there was a high degree of public excitement and press coverage of this story and an atmosphere of suspicion was widely prevalent. I will give you an illustration of F.B.I. attitudes. This story was told me by a very good friend of mine who was questioned by an agent. As usual he was asked if he knew of anything against me. The agent was not interested in anything *for* me. My friend gave him a story of an impeccable reputation and an abiding faith in my integrity, but seeing the man's reaction—there is just one suspicion that I think I should pass on to you. I suspect that Hiss had an ambition to be a federal judge and that this was his secret motive in his politics. My friend said that the agent was enormously pleased to have discovered some motive in an otherwise inexplicable career.

180. Claudia Catlett.

Mrs. Gibson: Could you tell us about the articles by Nathaniel Weil, who said that he saw you as a member of a communist study group with whom he frequently met in Washington and that you were definitely a communist?[181]

Hiss: Weil's story is very interesting. You will recall that he published a book entitled I believe *Treason* just before my trial took place.[182] It was a lengthy affair in which he exploited to the fullest his alleged knowledge of subversion in the government. It was a sensational book in which he mentioned many names. It is interesting, however, that he made no reference to me in the book. The articles that you mention came out after the trial when his memory was somehow stimulated to recall the episodes that he recounts. Of course I was never a communist nor a member of this group.

Mr. Gibson: What did you think about Remington?[183]

Hiss: Well of course I met Remington when he came to prison, but I must admit that I did not like the man nor did he like me, and our relations were very cool. When he arrived at prison I welcomed him and shook hands with him, but he was distinctly chilly and I withdrew. He was an unhappy man and lived a life of withdrawal in the prison and made no friends. He was given work in the hospital which increased his unpopularity because anyone in that job is under constant pressure to steal things, especially dope, for the prisoners. The man who murdered Remington was in my opinion a psychopath who by all means should have been under confinement. Remington caught him stealing cigarettes in his cell. There was a fight and the man killed him with a stone in a sock.

Mrs. Gibson: What were your relations with the other prisoners?

Hiss: The Sicilians of whom there were several sent up mainly for counterfeiting were mentally the healthiest inmates of the prison. They had absolutely no sense of guilt. They had merely been captured by the enemy. Theirs was the morale of prisoners of war.

181. Nathaniel Weyl (1910–2005), an economist who was a graduate of Columbia University and the London School of Economics and who worked for several federal agencies during the 1930s and early 1940s, before serving in the army; after the war he became a journalist. He had joined the Communist Party in December or January 1932/1933 but left in 1939 in protest of the German-Soviet non-aggression pact. He testified before the Senate in 1952 and 1953.

182. Nathaniel Weyl, *Treason: The Story of Disloyalty and Betrayal in American History* (Washington, DC: Public Affairs Press, 1950).

183. William Walter Remington (1917–1954), an economist who worked for various federal government agencies in the 1930s and 1940s (including the Tennessee Valley Authority and the Council of Economic Advisers). Like Hiss, he was accused of spying, he sued for libel, and after several trials he was found guilty of perjury and incarcerated in 1953; however, he was beaten to death in prison a year later.

Mrs. Gibson: Did you get along with them all right?

Hiss: Certainly. They believed me. But they never ceased to wonder at my motives in politics. 'Al,' one of them said, 'you seem like a right guy, but what I can't figure out is how with all them opportunities you had in Washington you never took any graft.'

Woodward: Have you heard from any of them since you were released?

Hiss: Oh I made some very good friends there and have kept in constant touch with many of them. They write me about their troubles and I try to give them advice.

Mrs. Gibson: Could you go back for a moment to some of those famous symbols, such as the rug that Chambers gave you?

Hiss: Oh yes I still have the thing as a matter of fact. And why did I take it? Well, the fellow was not paying his rent and I jolly well was glad to get something out of him, and it was a good rug.

Mrs. Gibson: And what about the car?

Hiss: Why I gave him the car? A dealer had told me it was only good for junk and that I could not get more than $25 for it.

Woodward: That is in 1934, wasn't it? I remember that I bought a Ford for myself in June, 1934, and paid $30 for it, used it all summer on an FERA government job and then turned it over to a junk dealer for perhaps a couple of dollars when it had run its last.

Hiss: Chambers had a wife and child and very much needed the car. He had taken over the vacant apartment on which my lease had not expired and I threw in the car because he needed it. I had a sort of affection for the machine for it had done good service for several years.

Mrs. Gibson: When was it that you were secretary to Justice Holmes?

Hiss: That was in 1929 just after I had finished Harvard Law School. Holmes said that that was the way he wanted it because a man knew more law then than he ever would know again and he wanted the full benefit of my wisdom. Of course he really made no use of what I offered. [He went on to tell many stories about Holmes, especially Holmes's reminiscences about the James brothers and his easy reference to them as William and Henry.] Holmes was a peculiar man to live with and had some very odd notions. One of them was that he did not allow a typewriter to come in his house.

Woodward: If only you had followed the example of your master, Mr. Hiss.

Hiss: You know I have often thought how fortunate it was that this case came at the time it did. Had it been ten years earlier, before I had in any way established myself, I could never have recovered. As it was my own son was only six or seven and too young to be deeply affected by it, and my stepson was old enough to withstand the effect.

Dr. Klein: I am surprised that a more vulnerable person was not the victim. You can be sure that we were glad that you were not Jewish.

Hiss: Yes, I do not understand quite why one of my sort happened to be the one.

Woodward: It seems to me you made an ideal target, Episcopalian, old family, Ivy League, Harvard Law, Justice Holmes, New York foundation, in fact if you will pardon it, an elite symbol.

Hiss: Perhaps they might have been shooting at all of those things.

Dr. Klein: What do you hope for in the way of an eventual clearing up of the case or a vindication? What are the chances for a retrial?

Hiss: There are absolutely no chances for a retrial. I could go into the law—but I am convinced of that as an impossible solution. But my lawyers are constantly at work on the case. They have very limited funds but are resolutely following up every lead and there are new ones all the time. I have by no means given up and still hope that the forgery can be tracked down and the people responsible discovered.

Mrs. Gibson: But what then, what legal action is possible?

Hiss: Only one thing and I admit this seems rather a forlorn hope. I mean a presidential commission, one of the sort that was appointed to investigate the Mooney-Billings conviction.[184] Of course I cannot hope for that under the present administration, and it would seem very difficult in any case.

CVWP, 75/17: TCMU

125. To Richard Hofstadter

MAY 22, 1959

A thousand thanks for your reflections on my essay on the Populists and the Radical Right.[185] It helped wonderfully to clarify my own thinking and suggest new lines of approach. And I was much gratified to discover

---

184. Tom Mooney (1882–1942) and Warren Billings (1893–1972), both socialists and trade unionists, were convicted of a bombing that killed ten and wounded forty people in San Francisco in 1916. Mooney was sentenced to death, Billings to life imprisonment. It rapidly became clear to many that they had been framed, and campaigns to exonerate them continued for many years. These campaigns led to Mooney's sentence being commuted and, eventually, to both being released in 1939; in 1961, Billings was officially pardoned. However, although Woodrow Wilson took an interest in the case and Franklin Roosevelt was asked to intervene, there was never a "presidential commission."

185. CVW, "The Populist Heritage and the Intellectual," *American Scholar* 28 (Winter 1959): 55–72.

what a wide area of agreement we have in common, much wider than I had assumed. This in all matters but the one you singled out, and there it may be that we are even farther apart than I had assumed. But of that later.

Both you and John Higham, who also read it, hit on the fallacy of my distinction between the Populists and the "pseudo-Populists."[186] I am going to abandon that term and the reference to Adorno's term, "pseudo-Conservatives."[187] It suggests that I think there is as much difference between the Populists and the "pseudo-Populists" as there is between the conservatives and the "pseudo-Conservatives." That would be quite misleading and I had no such intention. Out with it. But while abandoning the term, I still want to maintain a distinction and define a difference. Perhaps the term "quasi-Populists" might serve the purpose. But I would like to limit it to the popular agrarian movements from the Greenbackers through the Silverites.

But that leaves the question unsettled about the terminology for tendencies common to popular movements as early as Jackson (and earlier) and as late as McCarthyism (and the future), what you call in your letter "the larger traditions of populism," or "the general character of American democratic sentiment and ideology." The thing is, I wonder about the usefulness of retaining either "Populism" or "populism" as the designation for what we are talking about. Especially when as you put it "the Populists of the 90's were actually an optimal variation of populism." And particularly if "status politics"—largely absent from Populism—is an essential ingredient of "populism." Isn't what we are talking about the ancient fallacies of the democratic dogma, its tendency to glorify the mass, to bow before the majority, to minimize the importance of liberty, to give short shrift to minorities, to undervalue excellence, to override dissent, to sacrifice everything (including reality) for the sake of unanimity. What you aptly called "the utopian diffusion of social decision." The mystique of "consensus." Tocqueville may have overlooked a few of these fallacies, but not very many. The findings of Riesman and other modern sociologists would suggest that these faults are more common in twentieth century democracy than they were in nineteenth century setting. They may be right. I still have an open mind. But if they are, there

186. John Higham (1920–2003), the American intellectual and social historian, then teaching at Columbia but about to move to Rutgers.

187. Theodor W. Adorno (1903–1969), the German sociologist and leading member of the Frankfurt School.

would seem to be even less reason for returning to the nineteenth century for our classic prototype.

Now as for our "real difference" on the relative proneness of populists and conservatives to hysteria and irrationality, and more specifically to conspiratorial ideology. You have an initial advantage here, for I have to concede on the outset that the unlettered, the inexperienced, the unsophisticated, and the disinherited are more likely to fall for the oversimplifications of conspiratorial ideology than are the educated, the competent, the privileged. And I would assume, as you do, that the Populists as well as the populists embrace a larger proportion of the former group than the latter. On the face of it, almost by definition, you have the upper hand. But like you I appeal to research that has not yet been done, history that has not yet been written. We are both guessing, only you bet that when the work is done you will be right, and I am betting the results will not be nearly so conclusive. Meanwhile I believe I can produce more than two swallows to make my summer. Before we could argue this closely we would have to agree on the essentials of "conspiratorial ideology." Begging that for the moment, take the classic "scare" episodes in U.S. history. You would have to grant that the Jacobin Scare had the greater appeal by far for the Federalists, the conservatives, the ins, and that the Jeffersonian outs were the victims, fighting for minority rights, freedom of speech, freedom of press, etc. Witness also the appeal of Know Nothingism for Whigs. Nor do I think you could fairly fasten the German Scare-Red Scare, 1917–1920 (which merged into each other) (More closely than did the German-Scare-Red Scare, 1941–195?) on the populist mentality. Fighting Quaker Palmer and his Dollar-a-Year patriots were no populists.[188] The Populist and populist forces in that fracus were more properly represented by Gene Debs and Tom Watson, both of whom felt the heavy hand of Palmer. Watson narrowly escaped prison and Debs didn't, and both had their publications excluded from the mails and were hounded mercilessly by federal police and super-patriots. So were the Texas-Oklahoma Greencorn Rebels, anti-war agrarians. And Bryan's anti-war sentiment had long since taken him out of Wilson's cabinet.[189] And in the McCarthy movement I believe a close study would

188. Alexander Mitchell Palmer (1872–1936), who, as attorney general under Woodrow Wilson, mounted a series of raids on radicals during 1920, raids which led to many imprisonments and deportations; there had been two attempts by anarchists to assassinate him in 1919.

189. William Jennings Bryan (1860–1925) resigned as U.S. secretary of state in June 1915.

reveal a considerable element of college-bred, established-wealth, old-family, industrialist support. What the negative response of the South meant I am not sure, but at least it raises doubts about the proneness of the populist-minded in that area to the new conspiracy appeal.

To look at a conspiracy ideology of a different sort, take the Great Slave Power Conspiracy. This was the particular pet of the abolitionist and anti-slavery movement. If Dave Donald is right about the origins of abolitionist leadership, here was no populist outfit, nor were they unlettered. In fact the slave power conspiracy seemed to have a special appeal for the intellectual elite. And after abolitionism became respectable during the Civil War, the conspiracy ideology became a built-in feature of Republican credo—the really important feature of the Rum-Romanism-Rebellion image of the Dirty Democrat.

Enough of this. I am raising my voice and pounding the table.

I have a new novel for Bede's collection, yours too. Carl Marzani, THE SURVIVOR (Cameron Associates, the leftish Angus Cameron, my old Little, Brown editor).[190] Anyway, Tom Watson & Woodward are leading characters. Astonishing. All the fascination of a hall of distortion mirrors. [deletion]

CVWP, 26/302: TCLU

126. To Wilma Dykeman Stokely[191]

DECEMBER 1, 1959

[deletion]

I am happy to write you the little I can about my relations with Dr. Will. They were entirely personal. I came to Atlanta in 1928 to enter Emory, finished there in 1930, and taught at Georgia Tech in 1930–1931, was away a year and then came back in 1932–1933. It was during those years that I knew Dr. Will. He was a friend of my uncle, Comer M. Woodward, then Dean at Emory. I forget when I knew him but probably as an

190. Carl Marzani, *The Survivor: A Novel* (New York: Cameron Associates, 1958); the novel, which concerns a loyalty hearing for a State Department employee suspected of Communist leanings, features a retired Southern senator who had been a friend of Tom Watson and who recommends Woodward's scholarship on the New South.

191. Wilma Dykeman Stokely (1920–2006), a North Carolinian novelist and journalist, then writing a biography of Will Alexander with James Stokely, her husband; it would be published as Wilma Dykeman and James Stokely, *Seeds of Southern Change: The Life of Will Alexander* (Chicago: University of Chicago Press, 1962).

undergraduate first. Then later, in my years at Georgia Tech, I saw him more often. It was usually at his office in the Inter-racial Commission place that we talked. The remarkable thing was his generosity with time, and his patience. After all I was very much a stripling in my teens or early twenties in those years. As a teacher I see a good deal of boys of that age and of course give them a good deal of time. But that is my duty and it is more or less expected. In the case of Dr. Will there was no obligation on his part, and certainly no duty to give me as much time as he did. I realize now that I imposed upon him terribly. I would come and talk at really considerable length and he never seemed to be in a hurry and always seemed ready to hear what I had to say. I remember particularly my dealings with him during a ruckus over a forgotten cause of the early 1930's. It must have been in 1932 that the case of Angelo Herndon arose in Atlanta. You will recall that he was indicted for a capital offense under an old Reconstruction law for inciting to insurrection. His identifications were Communist and this came out pretty early in the game. I got involved as a committee of local citizens to defend him because the committee could not get a Mrs. Walter Millis to take the chairmanship when they wanted her.[192] I was prevailed upon to become temporary chairman. Eventually she took over the job. There was a mass meeting called for support of the action, and once the mass meeting had been assembled under respectable auspices, the expected happened. The gentlemen from Union Square popped up and gave them a hot harangue on the party line. Whereupon Mrs. Millis resigned her chairmanship and the mass meeting broke up in a turmoil and I found myself in a mess.

Dr. Will had talked to me about the action several times and advised me in a kindly way but never pressed his advice. I had been impatient with his reluctance to come out and take a strong stand, and had told him so, and then in private correspondence with the lawyer for the defense who was only a name to me in New York. I expressed some of this impatience with the position Dr. Will had taken. Whereupon the lawyer, who was of course, one of the party, published my letter and it came to Dr. Will's attention. One of life's darkest moments was the little note I got from him to the effect that the cut of a friend was the unkindest of all. Of

192. Mary Raoul Millis (1870–1962) had joined the Socialist Party in 1909 and remained active in it, as its Georgia state secretary (1915–19), state representative for the campaign committee (1932), and educational director of the Atlanta local (1933).

course he quickly forgave me and he was simply letting me learn about life. I learned a good deal in that particular episode, you can be sure.

There is little else to add except that I am pretty sure he had a hand in convincing Dr. Odum that I ought to have his support for a fellowship that I was seeking and that with that support I went to Chapel Hill for graduate study. I cherish the memory of the man with great affection and a sense of strong personal obligation. He was one of the best.

[deletion]

CVWP, 52/620: TCLU

127. To Francis Brown[193]

JANUARY 4, 1960

I quite agree with you that the quality of the year's crop of biographies is not at all distinguished. But when you recall that in very recent years Senator Kennedy's trivial collection of essays and Walworth's two-volume turkey on Woodrow Wilson were recipients of the prize, it is some comfort to know that we can do better than that.[194] In fact, I think there are several better than either. I haven't read them all yet by any means, but would assume that Chambers, *Stonewall Jackson,* Leech, *McKinley,* and Miller's *Hamilton* ought to be taken with some seriousness in addition to Morison's *Jones.*[195] If you run across others that you think belong on the serious list, I hope you will let me know. It is a pleasure to have such a hardened skeptic as a fellow-juror.[196]

CVWP, 45/527: TCLU

193. Francis Brown (1904–1995) was editor of the *New York Times Book Review* (1949–71); he and CVW served as the jury for the 1960 Pulitzer Prize in Biography or Autobiography.

194. John F. Kennedy, *Profiles in Courage* (New York: Harper, 1956); Arthur Walworth, *Woodrow Wilson,* 2 vols. (New York: Longman's Green, 1958).

195. Lenoir Chambers, *Stonewall Jackson* (New York: William Morrow, 1959); Margaret Leech, *In the Days of McKinley* (New York: Harper, 1959); John Chester Miller, *Alexander Hamilton: Portrait in Paradox* (New York: Harper, 1959); Samuel Eliot Morison, *John Paul Jones: A Sailor's Biography* (Boston: Little, Brown, 1959).

196. Brown and CVW recommended that the prize go to Leech, but the Pulitzer board ruled that this belonged to the History category and gave her that award, with Morison getting the biography prize. The board thus overruled two juries, since it thereby negated the History jury's recommendation of May, *American Innocence;* on this, see John Hohenberg, *The Pulitzer Prizes: A History of the Awards in Books, Drama, Music, and Journalism, Based on the Private Files over Six Decades* (New York: Columbia University Press, 1974), 277.

128. To Antonina Jones Hansell Looker

JANUARY 17, 1960

Your letter would have had the instantaneous and gallant response your slightest wish normally evokes, only times were not normal. The day your letter came the roof fell in. Late that afternoon the wife of my friend and colleague, Sidney Painter, the famous medievalist, called to tell me she had just found him dead in his study.[197] There were a hundred duties and arrangements in the days following, during which a trip to New York had to be worked in, a visiting Englishman turned up on schedule and had to be entertained, and then three days ago I was felled by a flu bug in my digestive viscera that strongly but temporarily implanted the death-wish in me. I'm better thanks but still weaving.

My weakened condition doubtless also accounts for my inability to rise to the occasion even now and act up, verbally at least, to that bright image of the young author of twenty years ago that you claim to cherish. Twenty-*two* years, by God, to be brutally honest. I can but envy you your happy illusion that "time remains a dot" and "essentials never change." Dot or blot, with me it marches on relentlessly and this week I am older by three years than last. The happier reminders, the ones I prefer to recount, are that my only begotten son towers over me an inch and a quarter and outweighs me at the time you knew me (not now, alas) by twenty pounds, and goes off to Yale next fall.

Yes, I do get next term off, though not *from*, but *to*, work. Headquarters remain in Baltimore with family, operations headquarters in the Library of Congress, mainly to put 35 miles between me and interruptions daily, and occasional forays into remoter archives. I have also arranged for two more years of leave in the next four. It's Time's winged chariot hurrying near—that you apparently never hear—but at my back I always hear.

Another of your time-blind hallucinations, charming though it be, is that I am as keen on belles-lettres as that dimly remembered youth, up to the last minute and all that. Matter of fact I haven't had time to read anything since Wordsworth. I'm strictly a square on modern verse and can't abide the beats either in prose or verse. I do well to try to keep up with some of the Southern mods but have almost given that up since

197. Sidney Painter (1902–1960) had taught at Johns Hopkins since 1931; his wife was Nivea Forbes Painter.

Flannery O'conner petered out.[198] Literary friends assure me I'm dated for admitting I liked Red Warren's Cave, but defiantly I propose to dedicate my next book to him anyhow. It's high time I was dated anyway.

But I am interested in Look's work and want to do anything I can.[199] It is true that my time is not as free as when I wrote him last May, but why not get him to send me parts in which my alleged historical competence would have some relevance. It cannot be very much, nor can my contribution be of much worth, but for what it's worth I am glad to do what I can. Obviously Hillhouse is a literary powerhouse with two dynamos going at once.[200] What energy! Best wishes for the *Ghosts*.

My best to your mother. I remember her well and fondly.

AHL: TLS

129. To Donald R. Ellegood[201]

FEBRUARY 20, 1960

[deletion]

I am not completely wedded to the title I chose—one of those suggested by Dan Boorstin, incidentally.[202] But after trying several this was the best I could do. Second choice was "The Southern Experience." It has the merit of greater brevity, but Jack Kyle spoiled it by asking "experience in farming?"[203] It might be used with a subtitle, but I would like to avoid subtitles if possible. I realize too that "Burden" has two quite different meanings (if not more), but the ambiguity is deliberate. I will be interested in your reaction and those you might try it on. If we can do better I am willing.

198. Flannery O'Connor (1925–1964), the Southern novelist and short-story writer. CVW perhaps spoke of petering out, since she had not published a book for five years: see *A Good Man is Hard to Find, and Other Stories* (New York: Harcourt, Brace, 1955). However, she did publish a novel later in 1960: *The Violent Bear It Away* (New York: Farrar, Straus & Cudahy, 1960).

199. Her second husband, Reginald Earle Looker (d. 1976), who was working on a Civil War novel entitled *Yesterday's Tomorrow*, in which the South wins the battle of Gettysburg: see Reginald Earle Looker to CVW, 22 April 1959.

200. Hill House was Antonina Looker's home in Lakemont, GA, as it had been her mother's before her.

201. Donald R. Ellegood (1924–2003), director of Louisiana State University Press (1954–63).

202. That is, *The Burden of Southern History*.

203. John H. Kyle, an editor at the Johns Hopkins University Press and author of *The Building of TVA: An Illustrated History* (Baton Rouge: Louisiana State University Press, 1958).

I am sure you will take a personal interest in the production, and I hope you will be able to do something attractive and distinguished in the way of design and typography.

P.S. What are the chances of a cheap "Student Edition" of the History of the South with a good royalty payment to the abused & neglected & downtrodden authors?

CVWP, 68/81: TCLU

130. To Glenn MacLeod Woodward

MAY 7, 1960

I was pleased to find both your letter and Mater's on returning from Cambridge. In fact all seemed in order. Peter not only met me at the airport but had fed Robbie and watered the lawn—without, as yet, producing a blade of grass alas no grass. Mrs. R says gravely bide my time and I do and shall.

What a remarkable coincidence that this critical illness of Mrs. Z's beloved brother should have befallen him the instant Ida was out of ear-shot! A scurvy trick. How long will she be gone? And is a substitute available. It was not my idea to send you into domestic service. See what you can do. When do you expect Mrs. Z back?

Harvard rolled out the crimson carpet with a big do at the Harvard Club in Boston with all manner of brass on hand & hundreds of the illuminati eating steak in honor of the occasion. Pusey was absent in Virginia inaugurating Fred Cole at W & L and his second in command McGeorge Bundy substituted.[204] Something of a legend Bundy already and rather tends to live up to billing. I was placed by him at dinner and found him entertaining. Bill Bentenck-Smith & wife were on hand and sent regards.[205] Many deplored your absence—including devoted spouse. Drinks afterward with Bundy & beauteous wife and Howard Jones &

204. Nathan Marsh Pusey (1907–2001) was president of Harvard University (1953–71); Fred Carrington Cole (1912–1986), a Southern historian who had formerly been dean of the College of Arts and Sciences at Tulane University, was president of Washington and Lee College (1959–67); McGeorge Bundy (1919–1996) was then dean of the Faculty of Arts and Sciences at Harvard, and later a national security adviser in the Kennedy and Johnson administrations, and president of the Ford Foundation (1966–79).

205. William Bentinck-Smith (1914–1993) was personal assistant to the Harvard president, as well as a historian of the university; his wife was called Phebe.

Bessie and Henry Nash Smith—goodly company all.[206] This completes my appointment of two years on the board, but Tommy Wilson urged that I accept reappointment and I said I would think about it.[207] Hotel in Boston last night over-run with Afro-American bachannalians who woke me up four times until I put the police on them. Old city lovely with springtide. Boston Common opposite Little, Brown & Co. a deep canyon preparatory to making an underground parking lot!

The choosing of brothers-in-law is rather as hopeless as the choosing of parents. I gave up long ago and composed my soul to accept in good part what the gods might send. This time they seem bent on sending a mortal man. Very mortal from all accounts and my own observation. Compose yourself, my dear, but don't feel obliged to feed his mortal face every time it opens.

I shall write Henry Pelling at once to stand by for a call from Ida on May 28.[208] I am sure he will oblige. There will not be time for a reply from him and a word to Ida. I suggest that you write Ida to call him at Queen's on arrival. Mater's letter said Ida had decided to come directly back to Key West from New York instead of staying over and for me not to meet her. This is a shame. You must size up the situation and advise me what to do, and having decided to write Ida I will—or will not—as you decide meet her in New York.

You will be cheered to learn that I have rooted up all the maple shoots I could find on the bank. Thousands. I probably missed many small ones that are so nearly like the new leafed ivy. The two-year old shoots would have been beyond your strength to pull up. It was all I could do with two hands sometimes. Tomorrow I shall pluck the pansies as directed. Seems to me I was to pluck something else, but damned if I can recall what. Tulips? Flowers are still lovely, aezalia and tulips and others as well.

---

206. Bundy's wife was Mary Buckminster Lothrop, whom he had married in 1950. Howard Mumford Jones (1892–1980) taught American literature at Harvard and formerly had been on the faculty at the University of North Carolina; Jones's second wife, whom he married in 1927, was Bessie Judith Zaban Jones, a Georgian of Hungarian parentage, who was a historian of science.

207. Thomas J. Wilson (1902–1969) was director of Harvard University Press (1947–67) and previously had been director of the University of North Carolina Press; CVW had been on the board of the John Harvard Library, a Belknap Press series of scholarly editions of significant American texts.

208. Henry M. Pelling (1920–1997), a British historian of labor and trades unions, was then a fellow of Queen's College, Oxford.

Elizabeth Ahlgren's address is 2714 Lombardy Place, Memphis 11.[209] Do send a note. The day you left Ed Williams called up with Dick Huie and put pressure on for me to come over.[210] I drove over Wednesday night and had dinner with them and Margaret. Richard the same minus perhaps 30 pounds. Ed not quite so bitter perhaps. Both showing me the startling mirror of time. Dick had in tow one Joe Somebody, a rather nice Arkansan withal of some 50 summers, a planter from Grady, Ark. (unknown perhaps even to Mater), a place of 300 souls according to Joe. Dick is managing Joe's campaign to defeat Faubus for reelection as Governor, and both insist in & out of their cups that the number of the Faubus is up and that the next Gov of Ark is Joe for sure.[211] I gave them my blessing.

You must know that the place is somehow not the same in your absence and that both son and spouse have remarked as much. My love please to Mater and Dad.

I have about decided that a dehumidifier is essential even if we later on decide on an air conditioner to boot. Thing is the latter only affects moisture in operation and mildew forms worst when house is closed up and there is no circulation. We will try this solution anyway.

[Handwritten] Why not let me get your return tickets through the Metropolitan [illegible] people? It might be simpler. If so, let me have the date as soon as you can.

CVWP, 60/731: TCLS

131. To Glenn MacLeod Woodward

MAY 15, 1960

[deletion]

Your letter Saturday was most welcome but seemed to me slow in coming. With all that time on your hands, how about more frequent letters? No time on *my* hands. I told you the separation would be educa-

---

209. Elizabeth Alley Ahlgren (1909–1992), who married Frank R. Ahlgren (1903–1995) in 1932; he was editor of the Memphis *Commercial Appeal* (1936–68).

210. This is Edward Brown Williams, noted above; the other is Cyrus Richard Huie (1908–1984), a friend and classmate of CVW's at Henderson-Brown and later a lawyer in Arkadelphia.

211. Joe C. Hardin was president of the Arkansas Farm Bureau (1948–55); he ran second (with 16.35 percent of the vote) in the 1960 Democratic gubernatorial primary in Arkansas to the incumbent governor, Orval E. Faubus (1910–1994), who got 58.75 percent.

tional & theraputic. I find my job and yours too much for me to handle successfully. Of course it is yours that gets neglected. I also got an instructive insight on your budgetary & financial problems. It's the unforeseen that knocks the holes—a $50 advance to Yale (admission official now—with Peter insistent that he had to fill out the space asking for "Guardian") plus heavy fees for Peter's advance placement examinations—several of them, which he is taking this week. He placed 25th in the state-wide physics scholarship examination taken by over a thousand. Gilman got 9 of the first 11 places, 17 of the first 59.[212] Of the latter Poly got 2.[213] Only one Gilman winner accepted state scholarship—to Hopkins. He takes all these things in his stride and assumes as a matter of course that he will do well in them—and does. Much ado and abuzz these days over matters academic and social. He is spending the afternoon at the Gilman gym constructing the Arc de Triumph etc. With my consent he threw a party with 13 guests (male) in the spring house Thursday night. I attended strictly to my own business.

Much of the latter on hand. Last week to give you an idea I finished and got off revision and retype of the Chicago paper to the AHR, considerably expanded.[214] Good with brilliant spots but not really super as it might have been. Still, not bad. No sooner in the mail than there arrived galley proof of the new book for LSU Press with demand for immediate return to keep a production schedule which they have promised to send me but never have. That kept me at it hard and up a good part of one night to complete and got it in the air mail Friday. I have a pretty good feeling about it, though with the normal amount of apprehensions I always have about a new book until it has actually run the critical gamut. It undoubtedly has some of the best things I have done. But the question is whether they hang together and add up to a book with sufficient unity. Sometimes I think it has, but it's a wavering conviction and not a sure thing. There are some arbitrary inclusions and I am far from secure about the title and the Preface. I have still page proof and index to do.

212. The Gilman School, a private preparatory school in Roland Park, Baltimore; it was founded in 1897 as the Country School for Boys.

213. The Baltimore Polytechnic Institute, a public high school founded in 1883.

214. On 28 December 1959, at the American Historical Association meeting in Chicago, there had been a session on historical interpretation; it was chaired by Allan Nevins and there were papers by Isaiah Berlin, H. Stuart Hughes, and CVW. CVW's paper was published as "The Age of Interpretation," *American Historical Review* 66 (October 1961): 1–19.

You might be drafted for the latter job. But just to keep me out of mischief I had to read ten doctoral examination finals and sit on three orals. Gilchrist busted to my disappointment, but seemed to expect the blow and face up to it.[215] Wyatt-Brown may also.[216] McPherson absolutely excellent, a remarkable mind, precise beyond my comprehension.[217] Still to prove distinction however. Then on top of that Nina's husband's novel manuscript—with which he has threatened me for a year—and he expects me to read & criticize. An impossibly fantastic conception, the first 200 pages of it, embarrasingly gauche and stuffily sexy, a Civil War novel unravelling the secrets of the slave mind etc etc., over 500 pages of the stuff. What on earth! Bad enough to read it, but far worse to write him about it and not hurt Nina. I have never met him.

Other developments on the professional front include a letter from Larry Fuchs wanting to know if Brandeis could interest me in the Harry Truman Chair of history at their place at unspecified but "unusual salary."[218] Apologetic "no consideration" on that one. Also a long telephone conversation with Vice President of Univ. of Pittsburgh offering me a visiting Mellon Professorship next year at $20,000 plus a furnished apartment for free. Of course I said it was impossible. But then he brought up the question of a permanent professorship, saying he had been informed about my previous rejection of their offer. Hoped a new look might con-

215. David Trowbridge Gilchrist (1924–2011), who had done his B.A. at Princeton and M.A. at Harvard, was later director of publications at the Eleutherian Mills-Hagley Library and Museum in Wilmington, DE.

216. Bertram Wyatt-Brown (1932–2012), who would become a leading intellectual and cultural historian, would publish his dissertation as *Lewis Tappan and the Evangelical War Against Slavery* (Cleveland: Press of Case Western Reserve University, 1969); he would teach at Case Western University until he went to the University of Florida (1983–2004). He is, perhaps, best known for *Southern Honor: Ethics and Behavior in the Old South* (New York: Oxford University Press, 1982).

217. James M. McPherson (b. 1936); his dissertation was published as *The Struggle for Equality: Abolitionists and the Negro in the Civil War and Reconstruction* (Princeton, NJ: Princeton University Press, 1964). He later taught at Princeton, where he became a historian of the Civil War; see, especially, *Battle Cry of Freedom: The Civil War Era* (New York: Oxford University Press, 1988).

218. Lawrence H. Fuchs (b. 1927), a political scientist at Brandeis University (1952–2002); he was then in the Department of Politics, but in 1970 would found Brandeis's American Studies program.

vince me. Has now signed up Murdock of Yale and others.[219] Would not take a no by phone and asked if he might write & I said he might.

Also a letter from Lilly Endowment, Inc., saying my application would go before their board at its June meeting and could I run out to Indianapolis to "discuss my plan in somewhat more detail" before the board meets and would I suggest two or three dates. I suppose this means they propose to recommend the approval to the board, so I must get out there. I suppose also it will have to be before you return. However, they ask me only for lunch and I assume—yet to investigate—that I can get out for lunch and back that evening by air in one day. Keep your fingers & toes crossed. This is crucial for I have about despaired of the big eastern foundations. They have been asking around. Oscar Handlin told me at Harvard he had been interviewed about me. Also Shafer.

Other chores include a lunch at the Century Club tomorrow in New York with a committee of the Am. Ac. of Learned Societies on the DAB supplement, with possible talk with Harcourt Brace. And on Thursday lunch in Philadelphia with the "Meeting Committee" of the Am. Philosophical Society with Mr. Moe in the chair.[220] I would plead off but for him and my obligations to him and the fact this is my first appointment.

And where, you might legitimately inquire, has my leave for research gone to—to say nothing of solemnly accepted assignment of fertilizing bushes, shrubs, trees, plants, etc.??? So. Also Harcourt, Brace is breathing down my neck about the textbook revision, which I will have to get to soon.[221]

Your flowers are still in their glory. Tulips, a few, still good. Iris luxuriant and not yet fully blooming will probably. The reluctant Liburnam (?) has a full frock of glorious yellow "grapebunches," and all the white-blossom shrubs whose names I never remember are out in full. Not a blade of grass. Mrs. R. still promises it will come or money back. Ivy looks healthy and so does the periwinkle.

About how you should return and when, I better leave it up to your

219. George Peter Murdock (1897–1985), an anthropologist who in 1960 moved from Yale to Pittsburgh, where he held the Andrew Mellon Chair of Anthropology.

220. Henry Allen Moe (1894–1975), president of the American Philosophical Society (1959–70).

221. John M. Blum et al., *The National Experience: A History of the United States* (New York: Harcourt, Brace & World, 1963); CVW was to write chapters 16–21, dealing with the end of Reconstruction to the death of McKinley.

judgment. I will hold off till your next letter about the date for the tickets, whether you come on June 1 or 3, with or without Mater. Would a compromise on June 2 be possible, with you all spending the night in Miami to catch up on the adventures of Ida, and then catch the Eastern flight direct to Baltimore next day with Mater? How would that work? We have had one letter from Ida, including the bull fight and her anti-Spanish preference for the bull. Post me on any checks you write. June 2 by Eastern seems to me best & Ida could take Dad and drive back to Key West same day. But you will know best. Anything you say.[222]

Peter requires your immediate advice on his list of friends to receive invitations to his Gilman commencement. He received ten copies to send out and can get more as required. I told him that was strictly your problem. What about it? Dudley and Lorraine Williams phoned but would not come by when they learned you were away.[223]

Fight off the sand flies & midges and get a good tan before you come back. Hire a sitter and a nurse if you can. Obviously Mrs. Z is off for the duration. A hug for the folks.

The place was Lillianized Wednesday & still sparkles. Ella on duty Friday. Pete & I haven't time to dirty it up. Parties at Swanson, Clapps, Mandelbaums, Smiths, & Berthels.[224] Milton assures me Ford money is in sight but none for library next year. Did you get the Snow novel I sent. Reviewed in last Sunday *Times*.[225]

Woodruff appointment gas bill & mtge check[226]

CVWP, 60/731: TCLS

222. This sentence is written in hand in the margin.

223. F. Dudley Williams (1912–2004), a physicist, was an old friend of CVW's; he had grown up in Covington, GA, attended Emory College in Oxford, and did his doctorate at the University of North Carolina. He went on to teach at various universities, including the University of Florida (which he left in 1941), and later at Kansas State University in Manhattan (1964–82). He worked on the Manhattan Project in Los Alamos during the Second World War.

224. Identifying Maurice H. Mandelbaum (1908–1987), the Andrew W. Mellon Professor of Philosophy at Johns Hopkins, is straightforward. The identity of the others, probably all Johns Hopkins faculty, is conjectural, but one may guess at: 1) Carl P. Swanson (1911–1996), a biologist and dean of undergraduate studies (1960–62), and 2) John H. Berthel (1914–1992), the university librarian (1954–74), and his wife, Elizabeth Edwards Berthel.

225. C. P. Snow, *The Affair* (New York: Scribner, 1960).

226. This sentence is also in hand and in the margin.

132. To David Riesman

JUNE 7, 1960

I am more than happy to uphold your hand in defending protest and dissent from the charge of irrationality. For that, I am afraid, is what the psychological interpretation of history often comes to of late. It tends to postulate a norm—the status quo, the consensus, the establishment, the American Way, as the case may be—and to regard any serious deviation as abnormal, if not irrational. And this without substantive reference to the causes and environment of protest and dissent: poverty, hunger, insecurity, alienation, unemployment, frustration, all in the midst of potential abundance and fulfillment.

Of course anxiety can be irrational and can produce neurotic personalities and movements and political upheavals—provided there is no discoverable substantive cause for anxiety. But the historian's first concern, it seem to me, should be those very substantive, concrete, and relevant circumstances. Anxiety can be perfectly rational and highly creative in criticism, social protest, and political dissent. To my mind, the Populists had ample and rational grounds for anxiety and plenty of healthy reasons for protest. For my part, old Veblen's polysyllabic growling and grumbling and muttering are divine wrath, not paranoid obsession, and I cherish him for it. And fashion to the contrary, that goes also for old Parrington and Beard and many of our currently despised elders and betters.

What a contribution for the generation that grew up in the Great Depression to make! The conclusion that protest and radicalism and dissent are somehow the manifestations of neurotic personality. And this arrived at in the fifties and sixties, when moderation and quiescence had become catatonic, and when conservatism and conformity were the plain marks of irrationality! I have for some time been tempted to try my hand at an essay on "Complacency and Anxiety in American History." Could you reach in that magician's hat of yours and pull out a bibliography for me? Your suggestions are invariably fruitful.

I am putting that essay you cited in a book, and if page proof comes in next week as expected I will send you the citation. The book will be called *The Burden of Southern History.*
[deletion]

CVWP, 47/550: TCLU

133. To Robert Penn Warren

SEPTEMBER 4, 1960

I think there are some fine things in your Life piece.[227] Among them I liked particularly your point on the Civil War as the origins of Pragmatism. Maybe it won't bear any more weight than you put on it, but it supports all you do put on it. Holmes made some eloquent and quotable statements on his war experience, as you know, but I always felt that they tended to get a little rhetorical and unlike [what] the man really was. Maybe it is as well not to use them.

Also the two pairs of Reb-Yank antitheses: "Revelation" & "Deduction" and "The Great Alibi" & "The Treasury of Virtue" I thought quite happy. I wonder that you don't make something of Kentucky, Lincoln-Warren country between revelation-happy Yank and deduction-bitten Reb, Alsace-Lorraine of pragmatism between the crusaders. There is a suggestive essay on Lincoln the politician in David Donald, *Lincoln Reconsidered*.[228] I know the quotation you want to use from the Preface of Melville's Battle Pieces, which is fine.[229] There are some possibilities in speeches he puts in the mouth of Confederate Vet "Ungar" in the interminable poem *Clarel*.

The part on the inner tension of Grant and Lee and Lincoln are magnificent for understatement and effectiveness. I like these and other parts of the statement so much that I feel carping and impertinent in some of the criticisms I have put in the margins. They take care of what little I have to suggest except a few points.

I think the puzzle "inevitability" is indeed one of the ways in which the Civil War has stirred the American imagination. Of course that is one for the metaphysician and not the historian. It was no more or less "inevitable" than any other war. But the main thing, it seems to [me], is not the answer to the question, but why the question clings to the Civil War. Why not any other of our wars? It seems to me that is your problem,

---

227. Robert Penn Warren, "A Mark Deep on a Nation's Soul," *Life* 50 (17 March 1961): 82–83; this was subsequently published as *The Legacy of the Civil War: Meditations on the Centennial* (New York: Alfred A. Knopf, 1961).

228. David Herbert Donald, "A. Lincoln, Politician," in *Lincoln Reconsidered: Essays on the Civil War Era* (New York: Alfred A. Knopf, 1956), 57–81.

229. "Let us pray that the terrible historic tragedy of our time may not have been enacted without instructing our whole beloved country through pity and terror": quoted in Warren, *Legacy of the Civil War*, 107.

not speculation about whether it really was—which I felt a bit abstract and inconclusive.

"The Civil War was the secret school for 1917–18 and for 1941–45." OK, but can you really leave it at that?[230]

"Lincoln had a very logical mind." This troubles me when I think of the unkind things you have said about logic. For that kind of logic he was something like the antithesis.[231]

Right about immigrants participating imaginatively. Another type that joins Civil War Round Tables by the thousands. Maybe some figures on their proliferation? It's a cult. And the meaning of the reinactment of all the battles, 1961–1965. Anything like it ever happen before?

Many thanks for the new volume of poems and kind inscription. I have read it with much pleasure. I send off my son Peter to Yale next week. Maybe that will bring me up your way before very long and I will take you up on the invitation. All the best—

RPW, 82/1609: TLS

134. To George W. Pierson[232]

NOVEMBER 7, 1960

What a letter. What an invitation. What a temptation. Before I read it I did not see how I could accept. After reading it I do not see how I can refuse. My impulse is to say yes and be done with it. But that would be too easy and too unfair and I cannot do it that way. I only wish I could.

What I now have to do is to listen to the other side—beginning at tea this afternoon with an old friend who always gave me the impression of being able to see through me down to the gizzard. And then there will be sessions, casual for the most part, and without any "pressure," even sympathetic. It is not so much what they are going to say that I dread as what they are going to refrain scrupulously from saying—about friendship and loyalty and a common cause long sustained against odds and about what I have said to some of them about defections in the past. I only wish there

---

230. This remained in the book, but with the added sentence, "Neither the Kaiser nor the Führer had read the right history book of the United States" (46).

231. This became "Lincoln had a very clear mind" (105).

232. George Wilson Pierson (1904–1993), Larned Professor of History and chair of the Department of History at Yale.

was one real son of a bitch among them, somebody I hated and could blame. Unfortunately I can't think of a one. I would rather face the Holy Inquisition for my sins or take a doctor's orals.

How long is it going to take to run this gauntlet without cutting corners I cannot say as yet. The president is trussed up in a plaster cast in bed with a slipped disk and a pending operation.[233] This could mean I will be spared that much of the ordeal, or it may mean being obliged to wait until he is able to see me. Being flat on his back, he has the greater claim on my sense of fairness.

You may be sure, at any rate, that I will not prolong this business longer than I feel I have to. It would be intolerable on both sides to do so. Whatever the outcome, please assure your colleagues how fully sensible I am of their good will and faith and the great honor they have done me. I cherish especially the letters of Ed Morgan and John Blum and will write them later on.[234] I may have some questions for you after I have had time to think a bit. But I should expect to arrive at a conclusion within three weeks at most, and sooner if possible. For the warmth and personal appeal of your letter I shall not attempt to thank you enough, but you may be confident that this counts a great deal with me.

CVWP, 86/12: TCLU

135. To David M. Potter[235]

NOVEMBER 13, 1960

I used to repeat, and believe, the old saw that I never knew what I thought until I read what I had written. Later I learned better. I learned to wait until Potter had read it and told me—not what I had written, necessarily, but what I would have written if I had understood what I thought when I was writing it. If I were so fortunate, as I have often been, as to get the word before publishing my efforts, it was then a simple matter of revising the manuscript to incorporate my "thoughts." In the instance at

---

233. Milton S. Eisenhower.

234. Edmund Sears Morgan (b. 1916), historian of colonial America, had been at Yale since 1955; John Morton Blum (1921–2011), historian of modern American politics, since 1957.

235. David M. Potter (1910–1971), originally from Georgia, studied with Ulrich Phillips at Yale and remained there (1942–61) before moving to Stanford; he was to die of cancer, not long after the suicide of his wife. He was a historian of the origins of the Civil War, but also wrote on the concept of nationality.

hand, several of the essays in the *Burden* had already benefitted from this process, as you no doubt noted in rereading them. Even so, on reviewing them as a collection you come up with additional revelations and convince me the process is endless. The verb *to potter* has thus acquired a new definition in my vocabulary. Once again, many thanks.

In my present quandary about Yale I cannot help feeling deprived of the counsel that would be of most value to me. I hope I appreciate the constraints you are under, and I only fear I did not respect them enough at our talks at Skytop. Those talks were nevertheless of much help to me. I shall not press you further. There are some questions, however, that I can't very well ask George (though they are no secret from him), and which I should ask some non-Yale historian. If you do not feel like writing about them, maybe you might show them to Ed or John or both, or neither, according to your judgment. And maybe the answer to these questions is simply that neither you nor Ed nor John is a product of Yale College.

The questions are partly prompted by George's history of the College.[236] Maybe I misread him and maybe the qualities he attributes to the College are historic only and not present-day characteristics at all. But I am not quite sure. I have in mind such things as a passage on p. 5 about the nineties, where he says the College "preferred discipline to free thinking, organization to originality, athlete to scholar, customs to books." Of course my instinctive order of preferences is almost the reverse. Probably George's and modern Yale's is too. But later on, p. 19, "Yale was patriotic and Yale conformed—two qualities which were so marked and would prove so enduring that a word about each is in order. Yale conformed. There was no doubt about it. . . . The joiner and the man of faith were beautifully at home." Just *how* enduring is the question, I suppose. I am not unpatriotic nor am I a beatnik, but neither am I a joiner or a man of faith or a conformist. And neither are any of you. Red Warren says forget it and come on. But I can't help wondering. I have promised not to wonder long, but I shall give another week to it.

Thanks again for the review and your marvelous gift of telling me what I think.

CVWP, 86/12: TCLU

---

236. George Wilson Pierson, *Yale College, an Educational History, 1871–1921* (New Haven: Yale University Press, 1952); he later published *Yale: The University College, 1921–1937* (New Haven: Yale University Press, 1955).

136. To Arthur M. Schlesinger Jr.

MARCH 1, 1961

My wife was disturbed the other night by gleeful chortles, frequent yips, and occasional cries of Give em Hell, Arthur! They were coming from me, reading your textbook chapters.[237]

I only hope, Arthur, that you are not really as confirmed a partisan as your admiring reader. But I confess there are times when I wonder. Never mind. Those chapters are bracing stuff and set a new pace and standard for textbook writing. I am quite frankly delighted with them.

In a period so contemporary or recent there is bound to be some difference of opinion. For example, I could never take Peter Viereck seriously and was surprised to find that you apparently did.[238] And I think Paul Goodman is overrated.[239] And there are some novelists we could argue about. I hope you will check the implications of the statement about withholding Salk vaccine. It was new to me.[240]

I go daily to my appointed task the more serene in the knowledge that you are where you are—and the more sober in the knowledge that but for a handful of votes a Russell Kirk or a God-knows-who would be sitting there instead.[241]

CVWP, 49/577: TCLU

237. Schlesinger was writing chapters 28–33, from the New Deal to the present, in Blum, *National Experience*.

238. Peter R. E. Viereck (1916–2006), an American poet and conservative social critic, best known for *Conservatism Revisited: The Revolt Against Ideology, 1815–1949* (New York: Charles Scribner, 1949). Schlesinger speaks of Viereck, along with Clinton Rossiter, as humane conservatives whose philosophy "endorsed the purposes, if not always the methods, of New and Fair Deals." See Blum, *National Experience*, 806.

239. Paul Goodman (1911–1972), anarchist and sociologist, a founder of the gestalt therapy technique; his most famous book then was *Growing Up Absurd: Problems of Youth in the Organized Society* (New York: Random House, 1956).

240. This seems to have been removed from Schlesinger's text.

241. Russell Kirk (1918–1994) was an American conservative historian and social critic, most influential for *The Conservative Mind: From Burke to Eliot*, rev. ed. (Chicago: Henry Regnery, 1953). "Sitting there" means the White House; Schlesinger was a speechwriter for and special assistant to President Kennedy for Latin American affairs.

137. To David Riesman

DECEMBER 26, 1961

I was disappointed that we were unable to snag you even momentarily in flight to or from Tokyo, for I very much coveted a first hand account of your adventures and impressions and an opportunity to exchange my rusty eight-year-old view of Japan for your own brand new version. The selections from your diary were some compensation. I was much amused, for they recalled my own experiences. The stiff-set time for the interview, the tea, the conference: the hierarchy of functionaries, the incredible wives, the pathetic students, the language and custom confusion. Yes, I would guess that Matsumoto was fully capable of rigging the press conference with reporters deficient in English.[242] Though the possible alternative is the impossibility of finding enough of them *proficient* in English!

We must find time to talk about Japan. But what is most on my mind at the moment is your admirable piece on the Berlin Crisis in the *American Scholar.*[243] I liked especially your point about our influence on the Russians, and more depressingly the snowballing paranoia and the reciprocal responses in kind. How to break out of the vicious circle! And how to stop or slow down the futile acceleration of the race within it! You will already have noted the stepped up pace of right-wing reactionism during your absence abroad. What you may not have appreciated is the extent to which the dominant opinion and the administration have yielded to right-wing mythology of world trends – the paranoiac simplification of East vs. West, and the frightful blindness to the complex realities and pluralism of the real world. The horrid thing is the needlessness of this nightmare vision, the ignored alternatives.

Glenn and I leave on January 6 for research trip through Miss., Ala., La., and Tex to last till mid-March or later and wind up with a rest in Mexico. I will be working on the 1860's & 1870's in the archives but outside them hoping to make sense of the reactionary wave of the present

---

242. Shigeharu Matsumoto (1899–1989), a Japanese scholar of American culture who founded the International House of Japan, a Rockefeller-funded center in Tokyo whose purpose was to promote cultural understanding between Japan and other nations; in this capacity, it hosted many visiting Americans. Riesman gave lectures on "Aspects of American Culture" at the Center in 1962.

243. David Riesman, "Dealing with the Russians over Berlin," *American Scholar* 31 (Winter 1961–62): 1–27.

and especially their effect on universities and freedoms. I find I validly confuse the 1860's and 1960's in my thinking. Suggestions and leads solicited for both investigations.

[deletion]

    CVWP, 47/550: TCLU

138. To Richard Hofstadter

I saw Carl first and he quickly and painlessly eliminated himself—a matter of some relief.[244] Lunch with Merrill next day seemed to go splendidly. He has seven more chapters to write on his big Revolution book, which he might be able to do next summer. He is willing to postpone his book on the Constitution.[245] Will give us a definite answer before the end of January. Breakfast with him and Hollinshead next morning revealed no hitch.[246] Long dealings with the Oxford press smoothed the way. The big Oxford bibliography he did is all to the good, and he has a short draft of a Colonial history he once thought of doing for the Chicago Press. Only problem is he is beginning a three-year stint as head of the department. He has some hope of worming out of it early. I believe he will sign up and am convinced it would be a good thing.

The best suggestion I have for volume 4 at this point is Dick Current.[247] What do you think? For volume 5 I should think Sam Hayes might be considered.[248] He had a promising paper at Washington.[249] But there is not much published work to go on. Probably Higham is safer. One or

244. Carl Bridenbaugh (1903–1992), then at the University of California-Berkeley, had been asked to write the colonial volume for the *Oxford History of the United States,* which CVW and Hofstadter were beginning to edit. The conversations, detailed in this letter, were held at the annual meeting of the American Historical Association in Washington, DC.

245. Merrill Jensen, *The Founding of a Nation: A History of the American Revolution, 1763–1776* (New York: Oxford University Press, 1968); idem., *The Making of the American Constitution* (Princeton, NJ: Van Nostrand, 1964).

246. Byron S. Hollinshead Jr. (1901–1987), executive editor of the Education Division at Oxford University Press in New York, with whom CVW and Hofstadter were working on the series.

247. Richard Nelson Current (b. 1912), then at the University of Wisconsin; his coauthored J. G. Randall and Richard N. Current, *Lincoln the President: Last Full Measure* (New York: Dodd, Mead, 1955), had won the Bancroft Prize in 1956.

248. Samuel P. Hays (b. 1921) of the University of Pittsburgh; he was a scholar of the progressive movement whose monograph *Conservation and the Gospel of Efficiency: The Progressive Conservation Movement, 1890–1920* (Cambridge, MA: Harvard University Press, 1959) had been

the other seems to me the alternative to Ken.[250] I would be willing to wait if Ken were considering Volume 4, but 5 seems to me another matter. I doubt if he would bring as much new and original to it as either Hayes or Higham. I have not heard from Bailyn.[251] All I hope for is some further degree of involvement. Jensen bridled slightly at my mention of Bailyn, but I think it only an elder-junior situation that is natural and he seemed to fall in with the notion. Perhaps I should not have mentioned Bud, but felt it called for.

[deletion]

CVWP, 41/487: TCLU

139. To Louis Ruchames[252]

JACKSON, MS

FEBRUARY 1, 1962

I was disappointed to learn that you thought me capable of praising the southern police and sheriffs who so often serve as agents or act as members of the White Citizens Council.[253] I would be pained that any reader of the REPORTER should so misread me, more especially one who claims some familiarity with my writing. I am perhaps more conscious of the injustice of the charge because of the scores of interviews I have had during the last month in Alabama and Mississippi with the victims of legalized racism. These people have been mercilessly harassed, some of them driven from their professions, ostracised, insulted, and a few physically abused or beaten. Some of these people are my friends, friends of

very influential, as had his general survey *The Response to Industrialism, 1885–1914* (Chicago: University of Chicago Press, 1957).

249. In a session entitled "New Approaches to Recent American Political History," Hays gave a paper on "From Reconstruction to the Armistice, 1918," in which he suggested historians should pay more attention to the social processes inherent in industrialism.

250. Kenneth Stampp.

251. Bernard Bailyn (b. 1922) of Harvard University, a historian of colonial and revolutionary America.

252. Director of the Hillel at three Massachusetts colleges (Amherst, Smith, and the University of Massachusetts-Amherst); he had published Louis Ruchames, *Race, Jobs and Politics: The Story of FEPC* (New York: Columbia University Press, 1953).

253. CVW had written a review of Milton R. Konvitz, *A Century of Civil Rights* (New York: Columbia University Press, 1961); see CVW, "The Second Reconstruction," *The Reporter* 25 (12 October 1961): 56–68.

long standing for whom I have respect and affection. I also have great admiration for their courage, even heroism, displayed under circumstances of danger to themselves and their families. A federal judge in Alabama told me two weeks ago that after his racial decisions his telephone rang all night and his neighbors insulted him. A distinguished lawyer in the same city, connected with some of the most distinguished families in the state, has for years been subjected to intolerable abuse because he takes the cases of Negroes and civil rights defenders. I can tell you many such stories which you perhaps have not heard, stories of people who command more of my respect and admiration than any champion of civil liberties, however fearless, maintaining a residence in New England. I do not have a copy of my review at hand, but it seems to me I was talking about federal judges and it was they I certainly had in mind. Again I am sorry you misunderstood me.

As for your second complaint about my comment on sectional stereotypes frustrating the First Reconstruction, I did not say that these were the only things that frustrated Reconstruction, nor did I mean to suggest this. There are certainly many other things. In fact I wrote a whole book on the frustration of Reconstruction without mentioning sectional stereotypes. I would readily agree with all the suggestions you have for additional explanations. I have offered them myself, together with many others, but the part that sectional stereotypes played seems to me an historical truism and I am surprised to find you dismissing them. These stereotypes were the result of a generation of sectional controversy plus four years of bitter war. There is no understanding Reconstruction and its unhappy history without the presence of these stereotypes. At least I think Reconstruction would have a different history without them. I very much hope that these remarks clarify my position.

CVWP, 48/564: TCLU

140. To David Riesman

AUSTIN, TX
MARCH 11, 1962

I don't know whether you know how close [to] home you came in the journal of your Georgia trip. You know I took my A.B. at Emory and my first teaching job was at Georgia Tech. I thought your apercus were uncannily accurate. Arriving at Emory a raw Arkansas country youth,

I remember to this day the depressing effect the place had on me, particularly the cloying politeness and vacuous gentility of the place. I remember joining a fraternity in order to get a job and then never going back. And I remember that everybody seemed to be running for some elective office, being more than anything else careful not to offend anybody. Georgia Tech was a crude and unpolished place, but the contrast was welcome even then.

[deletion]

   CVWP, 47/551: TCLU

141. To David Riesman

MARCH 21, 1962

I really have little but admiration to offer for your "Postscript" to the "New American Right."[254] It is written subtly and with great perception. It is the first successful attempt to set forth the transition from the Eisenhower-McCarthy era to the Kennedy-Birch era. It breaks out of the pretense of polarity and contrast that so many intellectuals have fallen for and confronts us with the real similarities, differences, and subtle shifts of emphasis. It spotlights some unsuspected alliances, that of the Catholic and Protestant fundamentalists, for example. And it explains better than anything I have seen the bemused apathy of the liberals and intellectuals under the new order.

I must have missed Margaret Mead's attack (could you tell me where to find it?), but I agree with you that you were right in emphasizing domestic sociology and politics in your account of McCarthy phenomena.[255] And even admitting the intensification of the Cold War and the increasing provocations from outside, I think you are still right in turning to the same domestic scene for the key to your "Postscript" on the 1960's.

There is nothing about your statement that "the South does not today reflect the wisdom" of its historical experience to which I can take excep-

254. David Riesman, "The Intellectuals and the Discontented Classes: Some Further Reflections," in *The Radical Right: The New American Right Expanded and Updated,* ed. Daniel Bell (Garden City, NY: Doubleday, 1963), 137–59.

255. Margaret Mead, "The New Isolationism," *American Scholar* 24 (Summer 1955): 378–82, had questioned whether Riesman's stress on the social and cultural sources of the American right's anxiety did not underestimate how far, during a Cold War and nuclear age, it was rational to be anxious.

tion. The South is the most protectionist minded and perhaps the most nationalistic and anti-Communist region at the present time. I quite agree. Of course I was holding up the South's unique historical experience in America as something it *might*, and I hope someday will profit from. I can still hope. It did resist McCarthyism (perhaps for the "wrong" reasons), but it shows little resistance to General Walker and company.[256] I was impressed in Montgomery where there is little industrialization and urban expansion, with the helplessness or apathy of the old elite in the face of mobbism.

There was one feature of the original edition of these essays, though I recall no instance of it in yours, that did trouble me at the time. This was the repeated attacks on Populist doctrine, leaders, and regions. Those by Dick Hofstadter were restrained and sophisticated (though in some degree, as I told him, misguided). But in others, those by Viereck, Shils, Parsons, and Ferkiss, they were often grossly misinformed and biased. I published a mild protest in the Am. Scholar of 1958, "The Populist Heritage and the Intellectual."[257] But Western historians have been provoked to elaborate and strongly worded refutations. There are now three books in preparation, two near completion, along this line. What I have seen of them leads me to believe that they will leave little standing of the thesis that Populism was proto-fascism, racism, etc. But that thesis is so essential to the class and regional analysis of McCarthyism in many of the essays that I doubt it can be successfully muted or retracted without extensive revision.

I am sure you mean to polish up this draft of your own essay. I have

256. Major General Edwin Anderson Walker (1909–1993) was in command of the 24th Infantry Division in Germany (1959–61), where he distributed anti-communist propaganda to his troops and was said to have advised which conservative Republicans the soldiers should vote for. He was relieved of his command by Robert McNamara, the secretary of defense, but resigned before being reassigned to Hawaii. In 1962 he ran last in the Democratic primary for governor of Texas. It is claimed that, early in 1963, Lee Harvey Oswald attempted to kill him.

257. These authors are all cited in this essay, reprinted in CVW, *The Burden of Southern History* (Baton Rouge: Louisiana State University Press, 1960), 141–66. The relevant texts are: Peter Viereck, *The Unadjusted Man* (Boston: Beacon Press, 1956); Edward A. Shils, *The Torment of Secrecy: The Background and Consequences of American Security Policies* (Glencoe, IL: Free Press, 1956); idem., "The Intellectuals and the Powers: Some Perspectives for Comparative Analysis," *Comparative Studies in History and Society* 1 (October 1956): 5–22; Talcott Parsons, "Social Strains in America," in *The New American Right*, ed. Daniel Bell (New York: Criterion Books, 1955), 117–40; Victor C. Ferkiss, "Ezra Pound and American Fascism," *Journal of Politics* 17 (May 1955): 173–97.

only a couple of suggestions. On p. 3 "the bulging middle of our middle-class society" evokes the wrong image. And the last sentence of the long paragraph on p. 4 gets too complicated. But on the whole it is brilliant and thanks for letting me see it.

We got home in surprisingly good shape and with a new respect for the Woodward toughness and seaworthiness after two and a half months of living out of suitcases in motels.

CVWP, 47/551: TCLU

142. To John Higham

APRIL 10, 1962

Keep talking. Nice to have the silence broken once in a while. I knew I was misbehaving, or behaving out of character, but I thought it would be worth it to provoke a discussion, get a rise, break the silence.[258] Of course it should have been done by a true blue Yank, but no true blues seemed about to volunteer. All shooting the other way—to a man so far. Maybe Ken Stampp, or Ray Billington, or Filler, or someone else will do his duty like a man in the learned journals.[259] But I will be rather surprised if they do, and if they don't this monstrosity will of course be awarded the Nobel Prize with palms and become an immortal classic like everybody says except you and me and then we will pick up the pieces of historical criticism and lurch on to canonize the next immortal who takes the "right" point of view.

No, it wasn't Dumond who got my back up.[260] It was the chorus of hosannas from my contemporaries and juniors who ought to know better—and in fact do. Then why did they acclaim it in cold print "definitive," "superb," "incomparable," and all that?[261] You suggest, rightly I think, that it was because they were "saluting an old guy" who presumably clung to the right point of view. Or what in my opinion is even

258. CVW, "The Antislavery Myth," *American Scholar* 31 (Spring 1962): 312–28.

259. Louis Filler (1911–1998) taught at Antioch College in Ohio and was a historian of progressive reform, with a special interest in the antislavery movement; see, notably, Louis Filler, *The Crusade Against Slavery, 1830–1860* (New York: Harper, 1960).

260. Dwight Lowell Dumond (1895–1976), who taught at the University of Michigan (1930–65), was a historian of abolitionism.

261. "It" was Dwight Lowell Dumond, *Antislavery: The Crusade for Freedom in America* (Ann Arbor: University of Michigan Press, 1961).

worse, because of "current events and the current mood." But what kind
of canon of historical criticism is this and where does it lead us? Now
is the time for all good men to praise abolitionists. Quite. In fact I say
so myself in the most forceful words at my command. But this does not
mean uncritical praise. And it does not mean that every writer who treats
them in favorable terms deserves all the superlatives in the critical vocabulary. In fact, they can be writing very bad history, as Dumond was,
according to your own admission. Yet he is praised, and so is somebody
named Leder (I think) who wrote on the Abolitionist "Brahmins."[262] If
so, what are we to tell our students about standards? I have a couple
who are red hot abolitionists and who are writing about abolitionists. Is
Dumond their model? Any more than Phillips or Coulter are models for
those writing on slavery?

Your comparison with Coulter is just and accurate. And when John
Franklin undertook his critique, I egged him on and applauded his work
and insisted on my students reading him and still do.[263] And I agree with
you that "the sectional myths are equally alive in both sections." I would
make a distinction between the professional and the popular attitudes
here, and perhaps I slurred over the distinction in my review. But I did
so with the provocation that the Yank professionals were so uncritically
reflecting popular myths in both their writing and in their criticism, even
more than the Southern professionals do in theirs. (And we may wait to
see if I am confounded if Dumond's book falls into the hands of some red
hot Confederate!) I admit that Dumond does not reflect modern critical
standards, but if he is so "very unrepresentative of current professional
opinion," why is current professional opinion so unanimous in his praise?

On what you call the "broader picture" I doubt that there is any important difference of opinion between us, though we have never explored
each other's views and I may be wrong. On the semantics of "myth" we
may be miles apart. That is too complex a subject for now. But I hold
we cannot and do not escape using the term and that you are mistaken
in saying we must accept the vulgar pejorative as correct. If there is a
slavery myth, an Aryan myth, a Zionist myth which we do not share and

262. Lawrence Lader, *The Bold Brahmins: New England's War Against Slavery, 1831–1863* (New
York: Dutton, 1961).

263. John Hope Franklin, "Whither Reconstruction Historiography?" *Journal of Negro
Education* 17 (Autumn 1948): 446–61, a critique of E. Merton Coulter, *The South During Reconstruction, 1865–1877* (Baton Rouge: Louisiana State University Press, 1947).

may deplore, there is also a Christian myth, an equality myth, a frontier myth, and antislavery myth which we do share and may cherish. But our favorable or unfavorable attitudes do not determine which are myths and which are not. And whatever our attitude may be, as quote myself, our history if it is serious history should be the critique and not the embodiment of myth. But I did not mean to preach.

[deletion]

    CVWP, 63/4: TCLU

143. To David Riesman

APRIL 11, 1962

I can only quote Virginia Foster Durr on where mobs come from in Montgomery, though perhaps you have already talked to her about her experience. You remember that she mingled with the mobs who attacked the Freedom Riders, and she was struck by the number of people she recognized, the gaiety with which they egged on the hoodlums. She did not say she actually knew anyone who took part in the violence, but seemed to think that such people had an appalling amount of middle class support.

Yes, of course I recall the essay that you and Lynd did on Veblen.[264] I have never met Staughton Lynd but I am interested in knowing him, particularly since I learned that he prefers to stay at Spellman College in Atlanta rather than accept an offer from Yale.[265] I did meet a colleague of yours recently who interested me a great deal, Erik Erikson.[266] We must

264. David Riesman and Staughton Lynd, "The Relevance of Thorstein Veblen," *American Scholar* 29 (Autumn 1960): 543–51.

265. Staughton Craig Lynd (b. 1929), the historian and social activist, then teaching at a black college in Atlanta and active in the Student Nonviolent Coordinating Committee; he was later to have a temporary appointment at Yale. As a graduate student at the University of Chicago, Lynd had helped Riesman prepare what would become David Riesman, *Thorstein Veblen, a Critical Interpretation* (New York: Charles Scribner, 1953); they collaborated on the introduction to the 1960 paperback edition. Lynd had recently completed his doctorate at Columbia on "The Revolution and the Common Man: Farm Tenants and Artisans in New York Politics, 1777–1788" (1962).

266. Erik H. Erikson (1902–1994), the German developmental psychologist and psychoanalyst—he had studied with Anna Freud—who emigrated from Austria (via Denmark) to the United States in 1933; he is notable for having coined the term and concept of the "identity crisis." He had historical interests, especially in psychobiography, and had been controversial for his *Young Man Luther: A Study in Psychoanalysis and History* (New York: W. W. Norton, 1958).

have talked an hour, and he said that he had talked to me more than to any historian at Harvard. Why don't people at Harvard talk?

CVWP, 47/551: TCLU

144. To Richard Hofstadter

MAY 11, 1962

I have finished the seven chapters of "Anti-Intellectualism" you brought me, and I feel even more confident of their quality and admiring of their brilliance than when I talked to you last after I had read the first four chapters.[267] As I told you then, I think they include some of the best things you have written, and I would now say some of the most masterful and penetrating pages of intellectual history in our historical literature. I will not undertake to praise everything I admired, for that would run to too many words. But I admired particularly the control, the confident understatement, the judicious restraint with which you state your case; the (almost invariable) understanding, charity, and humor with which you deal with the adversary; and the deftness and skill with which you anticipate and turn aside criticism—particularly in your superb Chapter II. This is great stuff, and no mistaking it.

Down to the final pages of Chapter IV I followed you with scarcely a quiver of the blue pencil. I will return to such few quivers as there were later. But first let me take up the only important quarrel I have with the part I have read.

You have established the anti-intellectual tendency of the fundamentalist thoroughly. But in the last couple of pages several things happen that are uncharacteristic of the manuscript as a whole. You identify the fundamentalist with the far right and all its poisonous prejudices. You then refer to "the one-hundred percent mentality"—and here I am not clear whether you are talking about the fundamentalist, the far right, or both, or whether you have shifted categories. Anyway, you say it is not only anti-intellectual but then you let go with both barrels: millennial, apocalyptic, puritanical, cynical, nationalist, quasi-fascist, anti-foreign, anti-Semitic, anti-statist, anti-Communist, anti-liberal. Now I think you could make a case that the present-day fundamentalists, or some of them, are guilty of some of these charges, though I think you have

267. The manuscript of what would become Richard Hofstadter, *Anti-Intellectualism in American Life* (New York: Alfred A. Knopf, 1962).

been much more circumspect and cautious in charging this and other classes with anti-intellectualism. But that is not quite the point. For suddenly we are not talking about present-day fundamentalists, or some of them, but fundamentalists throughout our history—"an ancient and thoroughly indigenous refrain," the Amens of "a million sectaries out of the past . . ."

Dick, you just can't do this. No amount of Adorno, Stouffer, Hartley, etc. will sustain it.[268] If you mean by fundamentalists those addicted to "literal scanning of Scripture" you take in a hell of the proportion of the population from the seventeenth down through the nineteenth centuries—including a hell of a lot of intellectuals, even some leading ones way down into the nineteenth century. I see several dangers here. One of them is anachronism, for a lot of people would be accused of opposing things that did not really exist in their time. Of course anti-foreign sentiment is probably as old as human nature or older, but what about bringing this charge against people who—whether they welcomed it or not, at least tolerated, permitted, begrudged, acquiesced in the greatest peaceful migration-invasion of foreign people in history, maybe thirty million in one century. From time to time outbursts of anti-foreignism occurred and were politically exploited, but I doubt that fundamentalism was the essential element. Quite apart from the anachronism involved, what about lumping together the charges of anti-Communism and anti-liberalism when liberals are anti-Communist and vice versa? As for anti-Semitism, you recall our old argument about that. I have just read a dissertation on Simon Baruch, whose twenty-five years in South Carolina illustrate something of what I mean.[269] At least I think you ought to make a distinction between twentieth-century fundamentalists and earlier fundamentalists. The man who clings to fundamentalism today is bound to be something of an odd ball and his oddness undoubtedly manifests itself in other ways, including many of the unpleasant traits you attribute to him. But being a fundamentalist before the twentieth century was, I should guess, "normal" for the vast majority of Catholics and Jews as

268. Samuel A. Stouffer (1900–1960), the American sociologist who helped to pioneer survey research, best known for *The American Soldier*, 2 vols. (Princeton: Princeton University Press, 1949). "Hartley" is presumably Eugene L. Hartley, author of *Problems in Prejudice* (New York: King's Crown Press, 1946).

269. Simon Baruch (1840–1921) was a German Jewish immigrant to South Carolina; he worked as a surgeon under Robert E. Lee during the Civil War.

well as Protestants. If a lot of them turned out to have some poisonous prejudices, I doubt it was because they were fundamentalists.

Then remember Henry Adams on U. S. Grant: "The type was pre-intellectual, archaic, and would have seemed so even to the cave-dwellers."[270] Could it be that this is a category that should be taken into account? Not really anti- so much as pre-intellectual?

Is it worth identifying a couple of sub-categories? You have considered the question I am sure. But just as there is an anti-clerical tradition that does not necessarily involve anti-intellectualism, isn't there a type of anti-academic who combines contempt for the professoriat with respect for intellect? Undoubtedly most anti-academic bias is anti-intellectual, but isn't it worth while making a distinction with perhaps a historical note on anti-professoriat stereotype, its origins and development?

Then for the few quibbles and queries.

Chapter I. How many Harvard professors does it take to make a "swarm?" p. 22 I rejoice in the safeguards and qualifications announced here.

Chapter II. p. 5. "For the intellectual . . . the whole world of values is attached to ideas." Does this not tend to confute your denial of the stereotyped intellectual as a bloodless, passionless, abstraction?

p. 17 of Chapter II was missing from my copy.

Chapter III. Was abject poverty and cultural privation on the western frontier more conducive to anti-intellectualism than abject poverty and cultural privation in the slums of the East?

Chapter V. Would Clement Eaton or Charles Sydnor be worth citing for light on the decline of the gentleman?

Chapter VI. Cite published version of Hoogenboom's book.[271] The link between anti-intellectualism and anti-woman's suffrage is not so clearly established as the tie between anti-intellectualism and anti-civil service reform.

Chapter VII. p. 3. Don't you mean in the first line to say ["]leaders of the Progressive movement" rather than leaders of the Progressive era? The latter would seem to me to take in too much territory.

270. *The Education of Henry Adams: An Autobiography* (Boston and New York: Houghton Mifflin, 1918), 265.

271. Ari Arthur Hoogenboom, *Outlawing the Spoils: A History of the Civil Service Reform Movement, 1865–1883* (Urbana: University of Illinois Press, 1961).

I am interested in the political chapters that reveal a fairly regular and frequent ebb and flow of prestige and status of the intellectual in the politics of the twentieth century. Would some comment or speculation on this phenomenon be in order and a comparison with the relative absence of ebb and flow in the nineteenth century, which seems to be a period of fairly steady decline?

Thanks for your note on my letter to Hollinshead. I agree that we will round up authors some how and sometime. Despair not.

The dreaded throes of uprooting and departure draw upon us and we wonder if we will survive.

CVWP, 26/302: TCLU

145. To John Hope Franklin

AUGUST 15, 1962

I received your manuscript and got around to it as soon as I could.[272] Congratulations on the speed of dispatch with which you have tu[r]ned out this book and also for the impressiveness of the performance. It strikes me as a forceful and spirited presentation of the subject nearest your heart. There is a place for such a book and there could not be a more appropriate time for it than 1963.

I will concentrate on criticism rather than praise for I know that it is criticism you want. Mine is going to be demanding and possibly severe.

There are two ways of dealing with my criticism: there is a simple way which I hope you will be able to use, and there is a more difficult way which I hope you can avoid. The simple way—and it seems to me a perfectly legitimate one—would be to change your title in some way so as to indicate that you are commemorating the centennial of emancipation with a history of Negro rights as your main theme. Simply the addition of a subtitle might serve the purpose. If you could do this much of my criticism could be avoided.

The present title commits you to a history of civil rights in America. I think it lets you in for a criticism that your book is not balanced, well

272. Franklin had been asked by the U.S. Commission on Civil Rights to prepare a report on civil rights since 1863; after a tortuous process, it was eventually published as U.S. Commission on Civil Rights, *Freedom to the Free: Century of Emancipation, 1863–1963: A Report to the President by the United States Commission on Civil Rights* (Washington, DC: U.S. Government Printing Office, 1963).

proportioned or adequate in its coverage. If I were reviewing it I would
have to say this.

I am not speaking primarily of the emphasis on the Negro though I
do believe that other ethnic minorities are given disproportionately small
space. I do not think you write with the same conviction and involvement
about other groups. Were I an Indian, a Mexican or a Jew, I would feel
slighted. I realize that the Negro is the most numerous of the ethnic minorities and has suffered the worst infringement of rights. But this was a
hard century on the Indian, for example, and I do not believe you give
the subject enough attention. There is more space given, for example, to
the East St. Louis riot of 1917 than to the whole matter of Indian rights.

What I am mainly concerned about, however, is the lack of attention
to a whole category of civil rights not associated with ethnic groups: there
are the civil rights that were associated with Jefferson, Holmes, Hughes,
Al Smith, Zachariah Chafee, and with the American Civil Liberties
Union.[273] The ACLU, by the way, deserves not only a mention but a
full account in any history of American civil liberties. And so I think do
Roger Baldwin and Chafee.[274] I am thinking of the defense of freedom of
speech, press, association, assembly; the defense against censorship, wiretapping, labor oppression. The worst beating in recent years has been
taken by radicals and left-wing spokesmen. I am thinking of the Smith
Act of 1940 and the McCarran Act of 1950 and the Communist Control
Act of 1954.[275] I think that civil rights never have been placed in graver

273. Thomas Jefferson and Oliver Wendell Holmes are self-evident. "Hughes" is less so,
but is presumably Charles Evans Hughes (1862–1948), at various times governor of New York
(1907–10), secretary of state (1921–25), and chief justice of the U.S. Supreme Court (1930–41);
in this last role, he was allied with Holmes in using the Bill of Rights to protect personal liberties. Alfred E. Smith (1873–1944) was governor of New York (1919–21, 1923–27) and the unsuccessful Democratic candidate for president in 1928, an election he lost in part because of his
Roman Catholicism. Zechariah Chafee Jr. (1885–1957), a Harvard lawyer, wrote widely on civil
liberty, especially in *Freedom of Speech* (New York: Harcourt, Brace and Howe, 1920).

274. Roger Nash Baldwin (1884–1981), who was imprisoned during the First World War as
a conscientious objector, was the chief mover in the foundation of the American Civil Liberties
Union in 1920.

275. These are: 1) The Alien Registration Act—called the Smith Act for its sponsor, Congressman Howard W. Smith of Virginia—which criminalized those who advocated the overthrow of the U.S. government and required all noncitizen adult residents to register with the
federal government; 2) the Internal Security Act—known as the McCarran Act, after its sponsor, Senator Pat McCarran of Nevada—required Communist organizations to register with

jeopardy in this country than during the McCarthy rampage; yet this is not mentioned. The Senator was careful to avoid racial discrimination but he was still one of the worst enemies of civil liberties we have had.

There is also a neglect of the attack on civil liberties during and after the first World War. Apart from the rights of Negroes, I am thinking of the Attorney General Palmer raids and of the whole range of episodes summed up by Robert K. Murray in his *Red Scare* and also by Peterson & Fite in *Opponents of War*.[276]

Under your present title, it seems to me, you would be obliged to cover the subjects I have mentioned more adequately than you do. I hope you can avoid this by the simple method I suggest. The alternative would involve some extensive revision.

Please do not hesitate to call me if you think a talk would help. [deletion]

CVWP, 19/222: TCLU

146. To David M. Potter

AUGUST 21, 1962

Thanks much for the reprint of "The Historian's Use of Nationalism."[277] It prompted me to read the essay a second time and it strengthened my impression that you have scored a breakthrough in a historiographical impasse that we have been milling about in for a century. I judge it first by the way it clarified my own thinking. I have been saying for some time that the most distinctive marks of Southernism are post bellum—the experiences of defeat, reconstruction, guilt, poverty, etc.—and then shrugging off as "paradoxical" the fact that the peak of

the U.S. attorney general and established a Subversive Activities Control Board to investigate dissidents, who might be denied entry to the United States or the right to citizenship, or have their citizenship stripped; 3) the Communist Control Act, which banned the Communist Party of the United States and made membership in it, or supporting it, a crime.

276. Robert K. Murray, *Red Scare: A Study in National Hysteria, 1919–1920* (Minneapolis: University of Minnesota Press, 1955); H. C. Peterson and Gilbert C. Fite, *Opponents of War, 1917–1918* (Madison: University of Wisconsin Press, 1957).

277. David M. Potter, "The Historian's Use of Nationalism and Vice Versa," *American Historical Review* 67 (July 1962): 924–50; this was an abridged version of an essay later published in Alexander V. Riasanovsky and Barnes Riznik, eds., *Generalizations in Historical Writing* (Philadelphia: University of Pennsylvania Press, 1963), 114–66.

distinctiveness followed instead of preceded the peak of separateness. In doing so, of course, I was unconsciously accepting the fallacy of requiring a culture-conflict explanation of the Civil War. You have cleared this up beautifully and many other things as well. The bonus, perhaps even an equal contribution, is the superb revelation of how the historian arrived at the impasse in the first place by following the grooves of nationalist assumptions about what constitutes and justifies national identity. We now see how the controversy took the shape it did, why historians stretched and strained the evidence to exaggerated contrasts and peculiarities, to manufacture sharp antitheses and stark polarities, what blinded them to racism in the North and commercialism in the South, what converted valid regional distinctions into gross caricatures and blew up diversities into irrepressible conflicts. What your insight does is to force a reappraisal of a large part of the historical literature on the subject. Some scholars have turned out whole shelves of books with considerable less effect. We will be coping with your troubling reflections for some time to come. One very minor quibble on your statement that "no southerner could possibly support [the Union] for any other than national reasons." Did not some believe sectional interests, even slavery, would fare better in the Union than out?

Yes, I got a wry grin out of Mrs. Brodie's efforts to make decent citizens out of both of us.[278] Obviously you would not have made the list had she seen the AHA essay, nor I had she seen my strictures on Dumond. The curse of our origins will out. There is no cure. Your piece, by the way, will thenceforth serve as my stock illustration of the historical insights derivable from said curse. I frankly find it impossible to imagine this contribution originating along Boston-Detroit latitudes. The ironical thing is those latitudes will agree and consider it another reason for resisting your thesis. I will be interested in any regional pattern you discover in correspondence provoked by the essay. The reaction to my Dumond essay was strictly according to the M & D Line: pro below, con above. No exceptions.

CVWP, 44/520: TCLU

278. Fawn M. Brodie, "Who Won the Civil War Anyway? Some Recent Interpretations Are Protested by a Historian," *New York Times Book Review* (5 August 1962): 1, 22.

❖✳❖✳❖✳❖✳❖✳❖✳❖✳❖✳❖✳❖✳❖✳❖✳❖✳❖✳❖✳❖✳❖✳❖

3

Yale, 1962–77

147. To James W. Silver

DECEMBER 28, 1962

You undoubtedly know that Meredith is having serious trouble in some of his courses. Maybe you also know that he was in New Haven last week, persuaded by his lawyer, Miss Motley, to come here for special tutoring and rest.[1] I did not see him for I had been called to Key West by the death of my mother. But friends of mine here found him an apartment and took care of him. From them I get some disturbing reports that I feel I should pass on to you. They tell me that he was in a despondent and distressing emotional condition, that he was unable to study, very depressed and melancholy, that he resented being persuaded to come here, that he thought he should not have left Mississippi, and that he gave up after four days and started driving back home. It was after he left here on Saturday the 22nd, and while he was on the way home, that news came that his father's house had been fired into. They have not heard from him since. I gather that he did not believe he would be able to pass his courses—algebra and French, I think. But he said that if he did not pass he was determined to "get himself killed," meaning that he intended to provoke violence against himself deliberately in Mississippi. I do not know how seriously to take this, but my friends were con-

1. James H. Meredith (b. 1933), who on 1 October 1962 had become the first African-American to be enrolled at the University of Mississippi. Because of the extraordinary pressure and harassment which he endured during his first semester and which resulted in poor grades, his lawyer Constance Baker Motley (1921–2005) suggested that he spend part of the Christmas break in New Haven, where she had been born.

vinced he meant it. If his condition is as disturbed as they say it is it would seem entirely possible that he would be capable of doing something of this sort. I do not pretend to be able to advise you what to do or to say that it is your responsibility to do anything. I can only trust you to use this report according to your best wisdom. You probably know more about his real condition than my friends do up here anyway.

CVWP, 50/590: TCLU

148. To David Entin[2]

FEBRUARY 25, 1963

Y ou will undoubtedly find a better account of the Herndon case in the press of the time than I can reliably remember after some 30 years. Briefly, my memory is that I joined with a group that included Ben Davis, the Negro leader who later became a Communist, to form a defense committee for Herndon.[3] The committee persuaded me to be temporary chairman. I was then a young instructor at Georgia Tech and it was clearly the hope that a person of more prominence and standing could be found to take the permanent chairmanship. Eventually Mrs. Walter Millis, mother of the prominent New York journalist and head of the Socialist Party was elected chairman. She took the job with the understanding that the communists would let her manage the affairs without interference. At the big mass meeting in the city auditorium, attended by several hundred, things went well for awhile. A good deal of money was pledged and enthusiasm was high. Then a Communist from New York took the stage and handed down the party line in an offensive speech, whereupon Mrs. Millis got up and resigned her chairmanship. I made an effort to keep things in order, but the meeting broke up in loud and disorderly debate and charges of betrayal. I lost interest in the efforts thereafter and learned my first lesson about collaboration with the communists. It is true that I was fired from my job at Georgia Tech, but I was one of some 30

2. A graduate student at the University of North Carolina; he was writing a master's thesis on Angelo Herndon.

3. Benjamin J. "Ben" Davis (1903–1964), originally from Georgia, graduated from Harvard Law School in 1930 and then practiced in Atlanta; he became a Communist as a result of his involvement as Herndon's attorney. Davis later moved to Harlem, where he was elected to the city council (1944–49); in 1950, he was prosecuted under the terms of the Smith Act and imprisoned.

and the reason a cut in the budget rather than my participation in this affair.

[deletion]

CVWP, 17/185: TCLU

149. To William P. Fidler[4]

MAY 30, 1963

I feel a lot more obligation and attachment to the A.A.U.P. than I do to many of the professional associations on whose committees, councils, and boards I am currently serving. But when I got your letter notifying me of my nomination to the A.A.U.P. council I began to count up the number of such obligations I now have. The result was rather sobering, not to say shocking. All told I find that I am already obligated to attend twenty-one out-of-town meetings of committees, councils, or boards during the academic year—all of them professional in one way or another. And this after recently resigning from a couple so as to take on the board of the ACLS, which meets five times a year! How is a man to get on with his book?

Now if you tell me that in spite of all this I should agree to run for the AAUP, I guess I will do it. But if you can let me off this time without serious embarrassment to you or the nominating committee, I would appreciate it. And maybe I can come up again after I get rid of some of the current burdens. Do let me hear from you on this.

CVWP, 2/13: TCLU

150. To Thomas A. Krueger[5]

JULY 19, 1963

Somewhere I have a file of correspondence that dates back to the period in which you are interested. A search for it last winter was unsuccessful. If I succeed in finding it in the future I will be happy to let

4. William Perry Fidler (b. 1906), a scholar of nineteenth-century Southern literature who taught at the University of Alabama, was general secretary of the American Association of University Professors (1958–67).

5. Thomas A. Krueger (1936–1986), who later taught at the University of Illinois (1966–86), was then working on the doctoral dissertation at the University of Minnesota that would become *And Promises to Keep: The Southern Conference for Human Welfare, 1938–1948* (Nashville, TN: Vanderbilt University Press, 1967).

you have anything I find in it. I doubt that there will be very much. My memory of my connection with the Southern Conference is quite dim.[6] It was so dim, in fact, that I was surprised when a security officer of the Joint Chiefs of Staff who was desperately trying to get security clearance for me turned up proof that I had accepted a minor office in the organization. The slip of memory might have gotten me in trouble, and the evidence certainly prevented my security clearance. I then remember that I had accepted this appointment at the request of Frank Graham. I would have done anything Frank Graham asked me to do. I had complete faith in him and in his integrity and have never had reason to lose that faith. I have very different feelings about Paul Crouch and the reliability of his testimony, which I am perfectly sure victimized some innocent people.[7] This is not to say that I am sure that no Communists infiltrated the Southern Conference. I should think it probable that some did.

I would gladly tell you, if I could remember, whether I ever resigned formally from the Conference. The fact is, I have no memory of doing so, though I may have. All I can advise is that you trust your judgment in the use of the documents and not my memory. I will say that I do not regret my association with the Conference and am glad I had the experience. I promise to write later if I turn up anything that might interest you.

CVWP, 29/345: TCLU

151. To James W. Silver

SEPTEMBER 25, 1963

All three shipments of your manuscript arrived together on Monday and I have had time to read the ninety-five pages pretty thoroughly

6. The Southern Conference for Human Welfare (1938–48), which was based in Birmingham, AL, was a radical group dedicated to social reform, civil rights, and repealing the poll tax; its desire to desegregate seating at its conferences occasioned especial turmoil. Its first meeting was in Birmingham on 20 November 1938 in the Municipal Auditorium, where the delegates included Hugo Black, Aubrey Williams, Mary McLeod Bethune, the Alabama governor Bibb Graves, and Virginia Durr; a quarter of those attending were black. The sense that the organization was a Communist front led many moderates and liberals, fairly rapidly, to abandon it.

7. Paul Crouch (1903–1955), a former Communist and one of the founders of SCHW, who testified before both the U.S. Senate's Internal Security Subcommittee and the House's Committee on Un-American Activities, where he portrayed the organization as having been infiltrated and manipulated by Communists.

but without checking or re-reading.[8] I note that you are trying to meet a deadline of October 1 and consequently I am going ahead to write you. With the deadline that near I doubt that you would have time to make much use of my suggestions. I know that you want me to be frank and that is what I intend to be.

This is a terrible and an impressive indictment of Mississippi society, its politics, its press, its pulpit, its bar, its schools, its bench, and pretty much the whole works. The evidence you marshal persuades me the indictment is deserved, and I hope you will make it. Coming with the authority that you carry it is bound to make an impression even in Mississippi, though as you probably realize it will get more attention elsewhere. I do not have to tell you the need for accuracy and soundness and I will waste no time on that. I am not concerned here about your presidential address. There you can use no more than about twenty pages out of what must be five or six times that much in the present draft. I am sure you will do an admirable piece of work there.

What I am concerned about is the use of this material in the pamphlet you intend to distribute in Mississippi. On that score let me urge you not to rush into print and not to publish this draft without extensive revision, reorganization and re-writing. I do not think it will do as it stands. My criticisms will have to be impressionistic rather than detailed, but I will let you have them for what they are worth.

In the first place, I do not think you make effective use of historical analogy. I got the impression from the first section that you were going to do considerable with this, comparing the 1850's with the 1950's. Actually you forget about the analogy after the opening. I think you could use this comparison effectively with more skill and organization, or simply as an introductory gambit of a few paragraphs. Certainly the ordeal of the past

8. The manuscript of what would become James W. Silver, *Mississippi: The Closed Society* (New York: Harcourt, Brace & World, 1964); it was first given as a presidential address on 7 November 1963 to the Southern Historical Association in Asheville, NC, and published as an article; see James W. Silver, "Mississippi: The Closed Society," *Journal of Southern History* 30 (February 1964): 3–34. Not unexpectedly, the publication of this book would occasion a bitter controversy in Mississippi, and one of the state's White Citizens Councils campaigned to have Silver fired from his position at the University of Mississippi. In 1965, he went on leave and taught temporarily at Notre Dame University; he did not return to Mississippi, instead permanently going to the University of South Florida-Tampa in 1969.

decade cries out for a comparison with historic crises of the past. You are the man to do this and this is an admirable occasion to do it.

The meat of your manuscript and the part that will get attention is the treatment of the last decade and of course the last few years. This part is full of admirable things and impressive treatments of little known facts. I think it could be improved by better organization and more logical sequence. There are some abrupt jumps from present to past and some rough treatment of chronology. I believe you ought to give attention to transition from one subject to another. I sometimes miss a sense of narrative sequence, a feeling that you have a clear sense of the development of events and their relation.

There are a number of unclear and sometime ominous passages, for example page 20: "The day cannot be far off when great moral and physical courage can be recognized as having very little to do with color."[9] That might mean a number of things and you can count on your enemies to make it the worst. On the same page: "In such psychopathic writing Mississippi always represents the South and the South is a solid and unfaltering unit."[10] Ditto above. Page 35: "It may be agreed that, statistically, Mississippi has contributed nothing since World War II to the defense or even the running expenses of the national government."[11] This is calculated to bring down on your head every Korean Gold Star Mother and every indignant taxpayer in Mississippi. Page 52: "The society of Mississippi has been almost absolute for too long, the orthodoxy too completely accepted for any internal readjustment of significance to take place."—an impossible sentence.[12] I think that the dignity and seriousness of your indictment are jeopardized by a number of faults. Page 74: the State Legislature may be "a snarling pack of jackals" but is this the place for that? Mr. Simmons is undoubtedly "a redheaded bigot" but please blue-pencil.[13]

9. This sentence was removed.

10. This became, "In such neurotic writing, Mississippi invariably represents the South, and the South is always regarded as a solid unit" (29).

11. This became, "It may be argued that, financially, Mississippi has contributed nothing since World War II to the defense or even the running expenses of the national government" (75–76).

12. It was removed.

13. Both of these phrases were removed. William James Simmons (1916–2007) was executive director of the statewide organization of the Citizens Council from 1954 to 1967.

At random, page 79, I question JFK as George Washington at the Whisky Rebellion.[14] Page 71, U. S. Grant's decision not to destroy the University is clever, but can you use it somewhat less personally? Page 89: "The ousting of a few professors from time to time does have a salutary effect on faculty conduct"—how's that again, Chum? Page 93: "traumatism" is an unknown word to me.[15]

You have used several statements in quotes without identifying the author. Often it seems to me that identification is called for.

I hope you will not find all this discouraging. You know I have great respect for your courage and great sympathy with what you are trying to do. My only concern is that you do it well.

CVWP, 50/590: TCLU

152. To Glenn W. Rainey

DECEMBER 4, 1963

[deletion]

As for my news. A smaller family and shorter chronicles. Peter preceded me here by two years and is now strapping senior of six-two temporarily fascinated by metaphysics & girls and rather at a loss about the Next Step. Applying for everything in the hope that Something Will Turn Up. I hope so too. But not grandchildren just yet. Engaging youngster of fearful innocence and premature sophistication. Only consolation is recollection of fearful innocence of his sire at twenty-one, thirty-one, etc. When did we lose our innocence? Or did we? Glenn is in fair shape, weathering the ailments common to her sex and the afflictions attendant on having a crazy academic for a husband. I marvel how she endures both.

Or how either of us endured the uprooting and transplanting of last year I sometimes wonder. For a time I doubted I would. For one thing the Ice Cap slipped and overlapped New Haven for several months. It was all strange and confusing and obsessed and suddenly everybody seemed younger than I was and I did not approve of the new collegiate architecture going up or the old coming down and the furnace broke down and thieves broke in and stole my typewriter. But this year it's better and

14. This remained: "Kennedy performed his constitutional obligation in the same spirit George Washington had exhibited in the Whiskey Rebellion" (121).

15. These three passages/words were excised.

I rather like it and besides I would have regretted it if I hadn't just like I knew I would if I did, like most hard decisions and the human condition. But it is an exciting place and powerful and marvelous human beings all about young and old but terribly demanding and I obviously won't live as long as I would had I stayed put but what the hell.

My mother died last December in Key West where she and Dad have lived with Ida for about ten years. Dad lives on with very little memory left. I go down now and then. Ida was married, widowed, and remarried and endures incorrigibly hopeful and loyal.

It is good news about The Bloody Seventh. And don't be disdainful of university presses. It probably is their meat. They might do well by you. I had two books published by university presses and don't regret it.

I will try to send a very short piece on the presidential succession of no consequence but rather hopeful and done right after the horror. Of all places I am to be in Dallas tomorrow and with mixed feelings you may imagine.

The years do pass my friend and I see you too seldom. How about repaying just one of those score of one-way visits?

GWR: TLS

153. To Richard B. Sewall[16]

DECEMBER 19, 1963

About the women?[17] You must list me among the embarrassed *cons*. I say embarrassed because the con position appears so stuffy, so unprogressive. Also it does less than justice to my genuine feelings about the opposite sex whose company I assure you I cherish. In fact, the social life of New Haven offers a great range of opportunity for heterosexual association in which I revel, but one evening a fortnight I would gladly absent myself from felicity and put up with monastic company. Also, it occurs to me that if we would elect a woman she would feel obliged to attend and I cannot help wondering how I would feel as the single male fellow of a female fellowship.

Of course, if my colleagues prevail in this pro-woman movement, I will compete with the rest for as much of the new fellow's attention as I can get.

CVWP, 61/720: TCLU

---

16. Richard B. Sewall (1908–2003) was a professor of English at Yale, master of Ezra Stiles College, and an expert on Emily Dickinson.

17. It was proposed to admit them as fellows of Stiles College.

154. To S. Douglass Cater[18]

SEPTEMBER 10, 1964

Do you think there is a place for a committee of intellectuals for Johnson, or professors for Johnson, or historians for Johnson?

I am of two minds on the subject. If you go out to get the most distinguished names (and why not?), then you are likely to wind up with a delegation from the Ivy League. This simply sets up another target for the Goldwater "gun club."[19] On the other hand, if you try to get names from all quarters and states, you wind up with names that nobody ever heard of.

Some of us at Yale are interested in this and would like to have your ideas.

P.S. When is Lyndon going to give them hell?

CVWP, 10/103: TCLU

155. To Staughton C. Lynd

APRIL 19, 1965

I very much appreciate your letter about radicalism in SNCC. It confirms some impressions I had, corrects a few, and clarifies others. I want to learn all I can about the movement. I need to know more. Admitting my ignorance, I should like to invite your comment on a few tentative suggestions and observations.

One of the most attractive things about SNCC is its openness and pragmatism, a movement without a program or an ideology. This is at the same time a source of strength and a point of vulnerability. For the very absence of program and ideology creates a vacuum that will, it seems to me, inevitably be filled by people who *do* have a program and an ideology. The permissiveness of SNCC, the open invitation to "anyone who can do the work" begs for that, I am afraid.

I hope that I am aware of the dangers of comparing one period with another and identifying the problem of one generation with the next. I realize that Russia is not what she was in the 1930's and that Communists are neither as numerous nor as aggressive. I assume that alarmists have exaggerated the Communist infiltration of SNCC, but I am also

18. S. Douglass Cater (1923–1995), born in Montgomery, AL, was special assistant to Lyndon Johnson (1964–68), with a brief on health, education and welfare. As an author, he was best known for *The Fourth Branch of Government* (Boston: Houghton Mifflin, 1959).

19. Barry M. Goldwater (1909–1998), U.S. senator from Arizona (1953–1965, 1969–1987), the Republican candidate for president in 1964.

persuaded that they are present and active in it. As you know, the press has been full of the subject lately, and we may expect more. I realize that whatever SNCC, does, admits, or excludes, it will be accused by its enemies of being Communist dominated. And I understand that other issues in addition to this are dividing SNCC from SCLC and NAACP and other parts of the movement.

Nevertheless, I think SNCC is treating the Communist infiltration issue too lightly. I think this issue can destroy the movement and that it is likely to do so if it is not met properly. SNCCers are rightly impatient with the "lessons" of the older generation. But my generation had more experience with the Communists than the present generation. We learned the hard way. I hope the present generation will not have to learn it all over again the same way. You say that SNCCers have no ideology. But they do have a built-in commitment to non-violence, call it ideology or not. I know that you personally have such a commitment. I do not think it consistent or compatible with Communism. And I doubt the sincerity of any Communist who professes non-violence. I believe there is an element in SNCC that would deliberately provoke violence, and I do not think these tactics are consistent with the non-violence commitment.

Perhaps it is impossible to keep Communists out. But the leaders could make a firm disavowal of Communism and Communists tactics and you would do a service to the movement by so persuading them.

Many thanks for the copy of your paper on Jefferson. I will write you as soon as I have a chance to read it.

CVWP, 33/397: TCLU

156. To Roger W. Shugg

SEPTEMBER 13, 1965

I have reread Johnson's book as you requested.[20] Actually, I can scarcely claim that I read it at all when it came out. I remember dismissing it then impatiently as a piece of academic Tomism and the feeling that I "knew all that stuff anyway." My reappraisal amounts to an admission that I was wrong and the hunch that you are right in considering this for reprinting. This is a piece of American anthropology that is worth preserving. The type of life that gave a rise to it is disappearing so fast, and Negro iden-

20. The University of Chicago Press was considering a paperback edition of Charles S. Johnson, *Shadow of the Plantation* (Chicago: University of Chicago Press, 1934).

tification with that kind of life has become so unfashionable that a memory of it is likely to be lost. Reading about those people in Macon County now is like reading about people as remote as New Guinea. I hope you will republish it and by all means preserve the photographs if you can.[21]

CVWP, 54/650: TCLU

157. To Martin Luther King Jr.

FEBRUARY 7, 1966

I am concerned to know what progress has been made on the American Foundation on Nonviolence whose Board of Directors I joined last year.

Ever since our meeting in New York I have felt I owed you an explanation for my departure before the end of the meeting. This was because of an emergency and not because of any lack of interest in the meeting or indifference to its outcome. I am very much interested and would like to keep informed.

CVWP, 30/360: TCLU

158. To Eugene D. Genovese[22]

APRIL 1, 1966

Thanks for your letter and the copy of your paper.[23] I read it with pleasure and the satisfaction that you were doing so well that I was trying to suggest needed doing in my brief introduction to *Life and Labor*.[24] Regional identification partly, but mainly lack of authority in the field inhibited me. If I had any argument with you it would be that you might afford a bit more generosity to him on the point of relativism—not merely of background and origins, but more significantly period. I mean the

21. The press decided against republication, but the book appeared elsewhere, though two decades later: Charles S. Johnson, *Shadow of the Plantation*, introduction by Joseph S. Hines (New Brunswick, NJ: Transaction Publishers, 1996).

22. Eugene D. Genovese (1930–2012), the leading historian of slavery and the antebellum South in his generation, was then teaching at Rutgers University.

23. A paper delivered to the American Historical Association on 30 December 1966; CVW was on the program committee. This was subsequently published as Eugene D. Genovese, "Race and Class in Southern History: An Appraisal of the Work of Ulrich Bonnell Phillips," *Agricultural History* 41 (October 1967): 345–58.

24. CVW, "Introduction," in Ulrich B. Phillips, *Life and Labor in the Old South* (1929; Boston: Little, Brown, 1963), iii–vi.

twenties, 1918–1929. In that context think of his peers of the profession, any of them save Du Bois. (Who was both more and less than his peer.) (More of prophet and poet and less of a historian.) And try to think of any other Dunning student making the limited transition he did. It would be a mistake to exaggerate this or be "enthusiastic," but I do think the shift from biological to cultural was more critical than you do, more than "merely one of emphasis." Still a racist, yes, but it seems fair to project his rate of change beyond his years and credit him with the possibility of further change in view of it. The concession would seem to fit with your strictures of our friends who live in a world of absolute good and evil.

I was not sure what you were saying—well, more sure of that than what was implied—in your reference to Fanon.[25] His book seemed to me so charged with hysteria as to place much of it beyond the limits of rationality.

These are minor things and passed on in the spirit of candor we both profess. I am delighted that you are prepared to undertake the program assignment and will proceed accordingly. If prior publication would embarrass you I should think Wentworth would adjust publication dates accordingly.[26] But my guess is you will find much more to say. The paper should be about 45 minutes.

Our session with Bill Styron was all I hoped and I am sure he felt the same.[27] Let me know when you return for another session with Marse Ulrich so that we can have another good visit.

CVWP, 21/240: TCLU

159. To Robert Penn Warren

APRIL 8, 1966

The few suggestions I have are trivial and minor and are scratched in on the margins along with the spontaneous applause I could not seem to repress.[28] I did try to read it with detachment and critically—the

---

25. Frantz Fanon (1925–1961), the Martinican critic of colonialism and author, notably, of *The Wretched of the Earth* (New York: Grove Press, 1963). There is no reference to Fanon in Genovese's "Race and Class," but there is in his "Foreword: Ulrich Bonnell Phillips & His Critics," in Ulrich Bonnell Phillips, *American Negro Slavery* (1918; Baton Rouge: Louisiana State University Press, 1966), xx–xxi.

26. Richard L. Wentworth, director of the Louisiana State University Press (1963–70).

27. William Clark Styron Jr. (1925–2006), the novelist.

28. CVW is responding to "Introduction: Faulkner Past and Present," in *Faulkner: A Collection of Critical Essays*, ed. Robert Penn Warren (Englewood Cliffs, NJ: Prentice-Hall, 1966), 1–22.

first part especially. But that was the part where detachment came hardest because it was voicing so many unformulated emotions and obligations and resentments of my own. Especially the part about the initial impact of Faulkner on the Southerner before there was any criticism. I began reading him in college (1929) avidly without knowing what the hell he was saying but without ever a doubt that he was saying it to me and that it changed everything. And then on through the Depression and cryptoStalinist years when defending Faulkner and the New Republic was like the Catholic with the Holy Eucharist and the quantum theory on his hands (and no milk-and-water symbolism about it). I think you have zeroed-in on placing WF in history as well as placing the Faulkner exegesis in historical context. But more than that this sketches out a whole theory of the historical relativism of literary criticism and provides a terribly deflating and sardonic commentary on the whole tribe of critics—or at least a large delegation of them. (I would like to see the theory applied to the corpus of criticism on fiction dealing with race relations in the last decade or so!) Connecting up WF and his special relation to World War I and the South to the latter is subtle and profound and I hate to disturb its symmetry and perfection of it by a pedantic quibble over calling the war "*the* communal effort that made the US" by inserting a "one of the" or an "among the." And forget it anyway and forget Cuba libre and all that. Grimm and Hightower as you say *are* projections of WF and his non-experience and the Civil War. And the autumnal stasis of the post–World War South is very right I think. So too the counterpoint of history-as-action and history-as-ritual. And the newness of WF vs the new and chic of the headlines and leftism. Just as well he carried it off in the thirties. I doubt if even he could have carried it off in the sixties. Maybe we will never have any more literature about Miss. except propaganda. Well the only thing I see wrong with this introduction is it is going to overshadow anything that follows. See you both Wednesday.

CVWP, 59/703: TCLS

160. To David H. Donald

JULY 11, 1966

Don't believe for a moment that I am taken in by your pose of being a butterfly type, a "frivolous historian," flitting from clover patch to poppybed just to sip the honey. Nonsense. I know you better than that.

I am, however, somewhat reassured about what you say with regard to your attitudes on the quantification fad. It was not so much what your students were doing that gave me pause, but more your little monograph on Reconstruction.[29] I was asked to review the book by the AHR and took the precaution to read it before accepting. My rule now is not to review books of friends unless I can say something gratifying. Having satisfied myself on this with a reading, I agreed to review it, whereupon my students assaulted me with questions and criticisms that forced me to confess some reservations. It was then too late to chicken out and so I did review it, duly expressing a few reservations.[30] I hope you will agree with them, but in case you don't, I will promptly write the editor saying that you were right and I was wrong.

As for my own students with this inclination, I find that the pedagogical situation is not too bad. My theory is that there should be a tension between teacher and student. The usual one puts the teacher in the role of innovator and the student in the role of resistance. In my case the roles are reversed, but the tension remains, and I believe remains a productive one. No doubt, however, they consider me a cynic and a block to progress. Like you, I don't expect anything very ennobling to come out of this trend but in some cases I do expect contributions of some significance. I am of the opinion that the True Believers will not sweep the profession into submission. The experience with Benson last summer confirmed my impression that he is the most amiable madman of my acquaintance.[31] His present project would seem to be designed to establish the slave power conspiracy dated 1836 by means of the Guttman scalagram. But this is a subject for conversation rather than letters in hot weather.
[deletion]

CVWP, 16/176: TCLU

29. David Donald, *The Politics of Reconstruction: 1863–1867* (Baton Rouge: Louisiana State University Press, 1965).

30. CVW, review of Donald, *Politics of Reconstruction*, in *American Historical Review* 72 (July 1966): 315–17.

31. Lee Benson (b. 1922) came from Brooklyn and, like Eugene Genovese, was a member of the Communist Party until expelled from it, in Benson's case in 1949. He did his B.A. at Brooklyn College, M.A. at Columbia, and doctorate at Cornell, and came to prominence with *The Concept of Jacksonian Democracy: New York as a Test Case* (Princeton, NJ: Princeton University Press, 1961). During the late 1950s and 1960s, he became convinced that historical writing could be made scientific by the use of statistics and quantitative data; he was among the founders of the Social Science History Association in 1973. CVW supported several grant applications of Benson and had an extensive correspondence with him, without ever being convinced of the cogency of Benson's project.

161. To Linda Moses[32]

AUGUST 10, 1966

Thank you for your letter of August 3 and the clippings. I have read these things and everything I could on the subject. I have followed the change in SNCC with growing concern and doubt as to what I should do.

If I sponsor the SNCC Faculty Fund, I shall be sponsoring a split in the civil rights movement, a split not only between organizations and leaders, but between races within the movement. You force me to choose between Stokely Carmichael on the one hand and A. Philip Randolph and Martin King on the other.[33] By taking one side I oppose the other. I cannot consistently support both. If I let you use my name in this drive, I should have to resign a board of Randolph's and one of King's on which I now serve. I cannot do that. I respect both men and their work too much and would not do anything to embarrass or discredit their leadership. If you compel me to choose, I will have to choose their way instead of Carmichael's. I would prefer not to have to turn my back on any part of the movement, but you leave me no choice.

I hope SNCC will return to a course I can support, but I will have to wait until it does.

CVWP, 52/623: TCLU

162. To Robert Penn Warren

SEPTEMBER 22, 1966

Enclosed is my contribution to a doctrinal brawl between a couple of Marxists before a multitude of assembled comrades at something called a Socialist Scholars Conference.[34] Couldn't resist the opportunity

32. Linda Moses (1937–2006) worked in the New York office of SNCC.

33. Stokely Carmichael (later Kwame Ture) (1941–98) was a Trinidadian who came to Harlem in 1952; he was one of the Freedom Riders and was imprisoned in Mississippi in 1961. He later worked as an SNCC organizer in Lowndes County, MS, and became chairman of SNCC in 1966; he was among the first to articulate the idea of "black power" and later was associated with the Black Panthers. Asa Philip Randolph (1889–1979), a socialist in his youth, was the founder of the Brotherhood of Sleeping Car Porters and one of the leading civil rights leaders in the generation before Martin Luther King Jr.

34. CVW, "Comment on Eugene D. Genovese, 'The Legacy of Slavery and the Roots of Black Nationalism,'" *Studies on the Left* 6 (November–December 1966): 35–42; the same issue contained Genovese's paper, as well as the commentaries of Aptheker and Frank Kofsky (University of Pittsburgh); the session had been chaired by Nathan Hare (Howard University). The Socialist Scholars Conference had been founded in 1965.

to have a little fun. Comrade Aptheker was apoplectic and Genovese had the better of the battle. Your piece in the NY Review on Black Power etc inspired me to send this along.[35] Looks like the Second Reconstruction is about over, 1954–1966. The reaction is on us and strong, northern liberals in full retreat and nothing in sight to turn them back. Colored ranks in confusion or knifing each other. Rustin & Randolph battling for Powell, McKissick & Carmichael screaming incoherently, King & cohorts all but silenced in the general melee, all the blacks exchanging charges of betrayal, Congress wiping its hands of the whole cause, LBJ backtracking, backlash lashing, Kluxers kluxing, G. Wallace booming.[36] May blow over, but I think not with the election coming up and the turn of temper the whole country over. All the classic '77 signals are up. Well, it had for to come some time, and it looks like the twelve-year cycle is par for the course as in '65–'77. Same thing only different.

The new book of poems has just arrived and we thank you and are prouder of our poem than ever.[37] I am surprised at how few of them I had missed. A couple of things I hoped you would include are missing but so many fine ones are there. I gather a whole new collection is shaping up in France.

Much local stir over musical chairs in the State Dept and the Law School take over. Wrote Gene Rostow that Mother Yale had a castration complex, having de-Balled and un-Manned the Department in one fell blow.[38] It won't mean any change in policy I'm afraid.

[deletion]

    RPW, 82/1610: TLS

35. Robert Penn Warren, "The Negro Movement in Upheaval," *New York Review of Books* 7 (18 August 1966): 22–25.

36. Apart from George C. Wallace Jr. (1919–1998), the governor of Alabama, these are leaders of the civil rights movement: Bayard Rustin (1912–1987) had been active in the movement since the 1930s but was latterly an important figure in the Southern Christian Leadership Conference; Adam Clayton Powell Jr., (1908–1972), U.S. representative (1944–67, 1969–71) from the congressional district that included Harlem; Floyd Bixler McKissick (1922–1991), who led the Congress of Racial Equality.

37. Robert Penn Warren, *Selected Poems, New and Old, 1923–1966* (New York: Random House, 1966).

38. Eugene V. Rostow (1913–2002), dean of the Yale Law School (1955–65); in 1966, he was undersecretary for political affairs in the U. S. State Department. George W. Ball (1909–1994) had been undersecretary of state for economic and agricultural affairs in the same department, but resigned because of his opposition to the Vietnam War. Thomas C. Mann (1912–1999), also a State

163. To Glenn W. Rainey

OCTOBER 4, 1966

Is it really as bad as it looks? Or is that possible? Or is it some nightmare about the ghost of Tom Watson? Or can half a century roll back and Georgians suddenly revert to the Leo Frank days of howling mobs led by grinning goons? Or does history really go backward? I feel like Rip van W. in reverse. Where have I been, anyway? Maybe Weltner and Arnold were dreams and Tom the only reality.

Hell of it is that it does not look like a local phenomenon. West Coast, East Coast, Midwest. All closing in fast. And my colored friends at each other's throats or screaming incoherently or retreating to fantasy. Looks much like 1877 from where I sit. Chaos and old night. Can you cheer me up?

GWR: TLS

164. To David H. Donald

NOVEMBER 24, 1966

To take your problems in chronological order, I take up the Schouler Lectures first.[39] On the darker side, if you reject Martin King you have to go down several notches in the scale. If you want a Mississippi activist, I would take Aaron Henry rather than Charles Evers.[40] If you take either, whether you care or not, you are siding with a faction in Negro and national politics. In fact both men are on the conservative side against the CDGM, which was the largest Head Start outfit in the country and has recently been decapitated by an embarrassed Shriver under orders.[41] Much anguish over this with Shriver as the General Howard of

---

Department official, resigned in June 1966, not because of Vietnam but because he had supported Johnson's invasion of the Dominican Republic, an event which had prompted great criticism.

39. The James Schouler Lectures in History and Political Science, given annually at Johns Hopkins.

40. Aaron Henry (1922–1997), who was prominent in the Mississippi branch of the NAACP and its president in 1959, went on to found the Mississippi Freedom Democratic Party. James Charles Evers (b. 1922) replaced his brother Medgar as leader of the NAACP in Mississippi, when the latter was assassinated in 1963; he was later mayor of Fayette, MS.

41. The Child Development Group of Mississippi; Sargent Shriver (1915–2011) was director of the Office of Economic Opportunity, the federal agency charged with administering the "War on Poverty."

Johnson II.[42] A possible alternative is John Wheeler of Durham, President of the Southern Regional Council, President of the big wealthy Mechanics & Farmers Bank of Durham.[43] He personally financed much of the civil rights movement in North Carolina. Elegant, suave, very upper class, excellent speaker, presence.

From the intellectual community, on second thought I don't think Bill Styron would do though you would not find a better writer. But he does not fit the role of pundit or prophet. For two birds (one black) with one stone, there is Ralph Ellison.[44] He clings rather tenuously to a Southern identity from Riverside Drive, but admittedly lacks much claim on being a Southerner. Brought up in Oklahoma and went to Tuskegee, but not residence since. Robert Lowell's wife Elizabeth Hardwick has a steeltrap mind, but her Southern origins are pretty dim.[45] I never met Walker Percy but admire his work.[46] Afraid he might go into a "fugue." Better find out. The Fugitives have all fugited. What's left? I have a tender regard for Eudora Welty but she seems to have retreated into silence.[47] A new Southern novelist is hatched in every Sunday Times, but no more O'Connors—blessed be her precious name. Red Warren would not come back for this in the spring. So, I have run out of names without settling on one I am sure about. Sorry.

Now, about the SHA in Atlanta. David, that's a calendar year off! Summit conferences are scheduled on shorter notice. What gives? Feeling like I do now about that outfit, I would not want to attend, much less speak. And all this to-do about being billed as the elephant in a one-ring circus! and the alternative of competing with the sessions on prohibition in Arkansas is worse. Can't you just put me on as chairman of anything

42. General Oliver Otis Howard (1830–1909), head of the Freedman's Bureau during Reconstruction.

43. John Hervey Wheeler (1908–1978), president of the Southern Regional Council (1964–69).

44. Ralph Ellison (1914–1994), the novelist, best known for *Invisible Man* (New York: Random House, 1952).

45. Elizabeth Hardwick (1916–2007), the literary critic, short story writer, and novelist, was born in Lexington, KY, but later lived in New York, where she was among the founders of the *New York Review of Books;* she was married to Robert Lowell (1917–1977), the poet, from 1949 to 1972.

46. Walker Percy (1916–1990), the Southern writer whose first novel won a National Book Award: *The Moviegoer* (New York: Alfred A. Knopf, 1961).

47. Welty had not published a novel since 1954, although she did have a volume of short stories published in 1965.

that needs a chairman and let it go at that? It would be a favor I would never forget. Give the spotlight to the bright youngsters. I have half a dozen candidates. Think about this, really.

CVWP, 16/176: TCLU

165. To Johnny Lee Heatly[48]

NOVEMBER 26, 1966

I am ashamed at the way I have postponed a reply to your letter after all the trouble you took to prepare that elaborate questionnaire. The fact is I have a complex about questionnaires and can never bring myself to fill one out. Perhaps I can give you the information you want less formally.

Most of the information you ask about me can be found in *Who's Who*. About my parents, my father was a public school superintendent in various towns in Arkansas while I was growing up, and later president of a junior college in Georgia. My mother was born in my birthplace, Vanndale, named for my grandfather. He saw four years service in the Confederate Army and was mustered out of the age of nineteen. He was a general merchant and factotum of the village. My grandmother was named Ida Hare. The Vanns and Hares moved to Arkansas from the Albemarle Sound region of North Carolina in the 1850's, where the two families had been planters and slaveholders back to the middle of the previous century. The largest holding I know of was that of my great-great-grandfather, who held forty-odd slaves toward the end of the eighteenth century. He was a member of the state legislature for a couple of terms and a county magistrate. My grandmother's mother came from Virginia and her name was Turbevil. There is a village Turbevil south of Petersburg named for the family. My father's parents, from Tennessee, where he grew up, died in his infancy and I know little about them save that my Grandfather Woodward was a preacher, and that his people came from Virginia. His wife's name was Lockhart, and she or her parents came from Scotland. I doubt that any of my grandparents had any college education. As for more immediate influences, I think my writing reflects

---

48. Johnny Lee Heatly (1943–2006) was a graduate student at Hardin-Simmons University in Abilene, TX; he had written (24 October 1966) to inform CVW "that in my graduate study I have chosen you as an outstanding historian of which I would like to obtain more personal information."

the impact of the Great Depression (in Tom Watson), the Second World War (in the Battle for Leyte Gulf), my long residence in the South, and the movement for racial justice and Negro rights. I never had any great teacher or any very good education. I owe much to Howard K. Beale, but more as friend than teacher. As for my critics I try to understand them, and as for my students I try to keep up with what they are writing. This keeps me pretty busy.

CVWP, 23/267: TCLU

166. To Linda Vollmar[49]

DECEMBER 6, 1966

If you discover that I have a philosophy of history I hope you will let me know what it is. I have never been able to define one and am reluctant to admit I have one.

What I have is hardly a philosophy, but more a complex of intellectual problems arising, first, from being a southerner at one and the same time being out of line with the dominant southern attitudes and yet deeply attached to the South and, second, being an American with comparable ambivilance about that experience as well and, third, being a human being with comparable ditto and, fourth, trying to say something sensible about the history of my region and country without disloyalty to my region or my country or myself or rather to the better nature of all three.

What results is more of a compromise between two contradictions than it is a philosophy.

Does this help any?

[deletion]

CVWP, 57/682: TCLU

167. To Virginius Dabney

UNDATED [DECEMBER 1966]

I can readily see how Miss Widener['s] account of my "identifying with Mr. Aptheker" might have bugged you.[50] It did me too, but I decided

49. A senior history major at Macalester College in Saint Paul, Minnesota; she was taking a course with Boyd Shafer on philosophies of history and wrote to ask about CVW's; see Linda Vollmar to CVW, 30 November 1966.

50. Alice Widener (1905–1985) was a conservative journalist with her own magazine, *U.S.A.* (1952–84); she had recently published a hostile account of CVW's encounter with Geno-

not to do anything about it. A slight case of quoting out of context. If you are interested, this is the story.

I was offered the irresistible opportunity of mediating between two embattled Marxists before their comrades. Genovese mounted a formidable and devastating attack on Aptheker's book AMERICAN NEGRO SLAVE REVOLTS, which is a picture of revolutionary and heroic resistance (250 "revolts" or plots) by demonstrating that American slaves were uniquely submissive and accommodating, and followed with the non sequitur that their only hope today was black nationalism. Aptheker replied with an explosion of outraged indignation calculated to put a young whippersnapper in his place. I remarked with amusement that [t]his was "a generational confrontation such as I am accustomed to face more and more as a teacher and scholar" a conflict "as common in the Ivy League as in the Black Ghetto and left wing politics." I then said that on the generational side, "I naturally identify with Mr. Aptheker, since we are of the same generation." Then went on to agree entirely with Genovese about slavery and Aptheker's errors and to disagree entirely with his conclusion that black nationalism was the wave of the future. The comrades were clearly divided, with the grayheads cheering Aptheker and the youngsters cheering Genovese. I had a lot of fun, and if the price is being pictured as a Bolshevik by Barron's Weekly, I guess some pleasures are worth their cost.[51]

Incidentally, at the Southern Historical Association meeting in Richmond a year ago last November Genovese read a paper that was the first sympathetic treatment of the ante-bellum South in non-Confederate circles for twenty-odd years.[52] Your reporter sat through it and devoted his entire article to Genovese's views on Vietnam.[53] I was amused. If you want a story for your readers, have a reporter at the NY Hilton at 9:30 A.M. on December 30, the AHA convention, where Genovese will give

---

vese and Aptheker; see Alice Widener, "In the East and West Ballrooms: A Special Report on the Second Annual Conference of Socialist Scholars," U.S.A. (September 16, 1966).

51. Widener's article was picked up by Barron's Weekly and subsequently inserted into the Congressional Record (October 18, 1966): 26267–70, and (October 21, 1966): 27425–28.

52. Genovese read a paper on "The Economic and Social History of Negro Slavery: Possibilities for Hemispheric Interpretations" in a session entitled "Prospects for Research and Interpretation in Southern Economic History"; a second paper was given by Gerald D. Nash on post-1880 economic history, and the commentators were Harold D. Woodman and Thomas B. Brewer.

53. That is, the reporter for the Richmond Times-Dispatch, of which Dabney was editor.

an eloquent defense of the scholarship of Ulrich B. Phillips on slavery, the first kind word, apart from a few of my own, in a long time. Also see his introduction to a new edition of Phillips' AMERICAN NEGRO SLAVERY, the LSU Press.

If you do have a look at my Harper's article I would be curious about your views.[54] What I am saying is that when the Second Reconstruction, largely concerned with the South, threatened to become a Third, largely concerned with the North, it ground to a halt.

CVWP, 14/160: TCLU

168. To Alfred A. Knopf[55]

JANUARY 8, 1967

First time I was ever called "too calm, cool, and collected."[56] Maybe I was leaning over backward. I didn't feel that way when I wrote the piece. But I admit my targets of indignation at the time did not include some I have since added. Another critic who commands my highest respect thinks I was too light on the Negro leadership for their own share in bringing on the reaction.

I admit also that I am pretty sick over the rally of respected Negro leaders who have taken up the crusade for the "ineffable Powell."[57] I am going to see King and Rustin next Wednesday and will take the liberty of quoting you among others I have heard from on this score. I think they are driving nails in their coffin. King so far has kept quiet and may have some restraining influence, but Randolph and the rest are too far committed to retract. The damage is already done. I was dumbfounded to hear John Franklin the other night make private apology for the stand taken by the Negro establishment on Powell. He admitted that he would not go on public record that way, but nothing would surprise me now. It is evident that we whites have lost contact with the Negro mood. I now think I was too optimistic in my article—another way of admitting I was too calm, cool, and collected.

54. CVW, "What Happened to the Civil Rights Movement?" *Harper's Magazine* 234 (January 1967): 29–37.

55. Alfred A. Knopf (1892–1984) founded his publishing firm in 1915.

56. Knopf had written on 3 January 1967 [the letter is misdated 1966] to express disappointment at CVW's "What Happened to the Civil Rights Movement?" Knopf was also continuing his always-frustrated campaign to secure CVW as a Knopf author, a failure that seems to have occasioned some resentment on Knopf's part.

57. This phrase is used in Knopf's letter, in reference to Adam Clayton Powell.

Like all your parties, back over the years to the first I attended with HLM in Baltimore, the last one was a memorable occasion.[58] Thank you again for your hospitality, your good will, and your unflagging interest.

CVWP, 30/364: TCLU

169. To the Editor of the *New York Times*[59]

JANUARY 13, 1967

The move to make Adam Clayton Powell the symbol of Negro grievances and rights has grave implications. Votes in the House of Representatives have inadvertently contributed to this end. Now the legitimate national leaders of Negro rights organizations, divided over other issues, would seem on the point of uniting over Powell. They appear to be prepared to take all the prestige, moral authority, and resources of good will so painfully accumulated over the years and lay them on the line over this issue.

The probable result will be to enhance the national popularity of Powell among Negroes at the cost of the authority and effectiveness of established leaders. It would be a sad and ironic outcome if men of the stature and reputation of Martin Luther King and A. Philip Randolph were replaced as national spokesmen of the movement they have done so much to build by a man of the stature and reputation of Congressman Powell.

The enemies of the First Reconstruction, a hundred years ago, were able to discredit the Negroes and their cause by identifying both with a few corrupt leaders. It would be doubly ironic if the enemies of the Second Reconstruction were assisted in the same strategy by Negro leaders of irreproachable integrity.

CVWP, 38/460: TCLU

170. To Ed Hamlett[60]

APRIL 11, 1967

I only got your letter yesterday though it was postmarked March 27. Otherwise I would have responded more promptly. Especially so in view of the dedication of the *New Southern Student*. I am much honored

---

58. H. L. Mencken, whom Knopf had published.

59. This letter was published as "Powell as Symbol," *New York Times* (18 January 1967): 34.

60. Ed Hamlett (b. 1939), from Kentucky, was the SNCC director of the White Southern Students Project (1964–66), which was part of the Mississippi Freedom Summer; he was on the national council of the Students for a Democratic Society (1965–66) and in 1967 began working

not only by that but by the numerous references to my work in the several essays.

No I am not embarrassed by being coupled with Stokely Carmichael in the dedication. I am, of course, amused and somewhat baffled by my company there. As you know I have made no secret about my reservations concerning his doctrine. If you are in any doubt please see that last issue of STUDIES ON THE LEFT for a sample of my views.[61]

The main source of my gratification is that I have been able somehow to bridge the gap between my generation and your own or at least that some members of your generation can find meaning for them in what I have had to say. What some of your writers make of what I have written strikes a sympathetic chord. I do admit to some misgivings about the reading that others have made. This applies especially to your use of the phrase "Southern Nationalism." The word nationalism in any context is troublesome and ambiguous. I find it so in the slogan "Black Nationalism," but even more so in Southern Nationalism. In the latter case one is haunted by a lot of unfortunate historical connections with historical precedents of a devious nature. I hope you will rethink your statements under this heading and that you will challenge your Negro friends in their use of the same troublesome word.

It is my feeling that Southerners, black as well as white, should work toward a conception of regional identity that is meaningful to both and yet free from either racial exclusiveness and separatism. If I can ever be of any help in that effort I would be much gratified.

You ask about any movement for non-violence in the white South. The Southern advocates for abolition were non-violent in doctrine as were Northerners, but only Southern Quakers made a doctrinal issue of non-violence. [deletion]

I read in the paper yesterday morning about Carmichael and the rumble at Fisk. I hope you will send me anything you write on the subject.

You are free to quote any of the early part of the letter you like.

CVWP, 24/275: TCLU

---

with the Southern Students Organizing Committee, which sponsored a monthly magazine, the *New Southern Student*.

61. That is, his commentary on Genovese at the Socialist Scholars Conference.

171. To William Styron

APRIL 11, 1967

If you are going to be living it up with the Romans till May I guess I better write you now instead of waiting for a talk after your return. I took Nat along to Grenada and read him on the beach under the palms with the trade winds fanning my brow and all that.[62] Must have been some sort of acid test. Because if the Confessions can evoke absolute skin-prickling horror under these special circumstances, I guess they will have that effect just about anywhere, any time. In short I think you have just about gone and done it, Bill, up to the very hilt. (But where in hell did you soak up (or bone up) all that Old Testament learning? Beats my sainted Grandma. And it is just that Hebraic syntax that does it. Nothing else would I am convinced.) Kept thinking of the obvious comparison, Babo in Benito Cereno.[63] Only other major attempt to get at a slave rebellion in our literature. But Melville never attempted to get behind the black mask and maybe that was what he was up to—the white man faced with the impenetrable black enigma. Skin-prickling enough, all right. Not bad as a mystery. But as far as I know, you are the first to do it from behind the black mask (who else?). And so it stands alone. And I think very high. But more, much more, about a hundred other things when we eventually get together over the drinks.

On the history side I caught you out on just one booboo and that a minor one that only a specialist would catch. On page 104 you speak of "the demand of ten million Englishmen for a pipeful of bright Virginia leaf." A slight anachronism. The big monograph on The Bright Tobacco Industry by my friend Nannie Tilley has it down cold that bright tobacco was developed, really invented, by Stephen, slave of Eli Slade of Caswell County, N.C., in 1839, and did not really get going in the market until the 1850's.[64] Piddling point, but probably worth a correction.

Other points are slight matters of judgment. P. 177, "God is dead" echoes a modern slogan, but that doesn't really matter. P. 412 where you say "Moore felt young Dred was too lacking" etc., don't you really

---

62. The manuscript of William Styron, *The Confessions of Nat Turner* (New York: Random House, 1967).

63. Herman Melville's novella, first serialized in *Putnam's Monthly* in 1855, later included in Herman Melville, *The Piazza Tales* (New York: Dix & Edwards, 1856), 109–270.

64. Nannie M. Tilley, *The Bright-Tobacco Industry, 1860–1929* (Chapel Hill: University of North Carolina Press, 1948).

mean Francis instead of Moore? P. 457, the repetition of the story of the drunken overseer's blow on Nelson's head may be necessary, but I raise the question. P. 459, another repetition, this about the dismal Swamp for Negroes who had gone on a hunting trip—same question. P. 468, "a translucent concealing godless, infuriating veil"—I paused over "godless." P. 482, I stand in awe of your command over dialect, but in "I gots to kill dem white folks" the word "gots" gave me a bit of trouble.

The only point about the plausibility of your reconstruction of Nat's strategy of rebellion—given the convincing picture of his intelligence, shrewdness, and realism—that gave me trouble was what he really proposed to do after seizing Jerusalem. Apparently he had ruled out the Dismal Swamp as a stand for resistance and defense. There was some talk about "blue water," etc. Maybe your point is that he really wasn't much interested in what came after, or that he was realist enough to know without admitting that there was no solution, that he was prepared in advance to face the militia and shoot it out to the last man and settle for that. Maybe you have to leave it that way. In my own mind there was the comparison with John Brown, less intelligent and less a realist than Nat, who firmly believed that he could establish a "maroon" situation in the mountains for a long term hold out and eventual triumph. I doubt if Nat ever deluded himself that much. But I wonder.

Stan Elkins spent last night with us and I had him gasping with admiration over quoted passages. On the beach at Grenada I ran into, of all people (Dr. Livingstone I presume), David Davis, the Problem of Slavery in Western Culture man, and I treated him to the same foretaste and same results.[65] Also Dick Hofstadter & wife who were with us on the trip. You already have a public in the history trade.

What shall I do with the manuscript? Hang on till you get back? When will that be and how soon can we see you? Give our love to Rose and the Warrens if you see them.[66]

CVWP, 52/626: TCLU

---

65. David Brion Davis (b. 1927), then teaching at Cornell University; he came to Yale in 1970. The book in question is *The Problem of Slavery in Western Culture* (Ithaca, NY: Cornell University Press, 1966).

66. Rose Burgunder Styron (b. 1928), the novelist's wife.

172. To Wallace Notestein[67]

JUNE 4, 1967

I do not wonder that you find yourself "almost unbelieving" that I should associate myself with any such views as you attribute to Professor Kessen.[68] I certainly have not endorsed any such policies and was not aware that he had.

No more than you do I believe that we can "just pull out" of Vietnam and "leave tens of thousands of our supporters to be killed off." I do not believe in any simple or drastic solution. I do not know of any solution that I can at present endorse without reservations.

I do believe that the present policy is misguided and wrong. The statement that Kessen and I circulated to full professors at Yale did not propose any policy.[69] It said that a new policy was very much needed. Our purpose was to encourage the Berkeley professors' effort to engage some of the best minds of our country in meeting to seek out a suitable alternative to the present Vietnam policy, one that the rest of us can urge upon our government. I do not know what policy they would recommend. It may well prove impossible for them to agree upon an alternative policy. But my sense of the desperate need for change and experiment persuades me that the effort is worth while, even if it turns out to be futile.

More than a hundred Yale professors have signed to indicate their support of this effort. I find it hard to believe that any of them want to "help out enemies" or might suspect us of such intentions. I am most relieved to find that you also express discontent with present foreign policy. For by doing so you acknowledge that dissent does not necessarily mean disloyalty. If it does come to that and dissent and disloyalty are equated, then we are in a worse plight than I had believed.

Do let us reason together on this matter.

CVWP, 37/445: TCLU

67. Wallace Notestein (1878–1969), Sterling Professor of English History at Yale (1928–47) and a scholar of Elizabethan England.

68. William Kessen (1925–1999), a psychologist and pediatrician who had been at Yale since 1952; he would later develop an interest in treating Chinese children and would visit the People's Republic.

69. Members of the Yale faculty, including CVW, had sent to Lyndon Johnson a letter calling for an unconditional halt to the bombing of North Vietnam.

173. To David M. Potter

JUNE 23, 1967

I used to say that I did not know what I thought until I had read what I had written; now I say I don't know what I have written until David Potter tells me what I meant. You have been doing this a long time, and I continue to benefit from the exercise—from your latest effort most of all.[70] I was amused in reading it to find how often ideas you attributed to me I really got from you—an essay here, a suggestion there over the years.

If I have any complaint it is the embarrassment of being overrated. You are generous to a fault and compassionate beyond reasonable call of duty. Your criticisms are all justified, and more would have been. And your grasp of my dilemmas and the contradictions of my own commitments and impulses is more comprehensive than my own. I think I have been aware of all of them more or less, but never with the clarity you contribute. For this, and for your many generous and kind words, much thanks.

[deletion]

CVWP, 44/521: TCLU

174. To Richard Hofstadter

AUGUST 9, 1967
LITTLE COMPTON, RI

To tell you the truth, I rather dreaded reading you on Beard.[71] I knew you would have to be crushingly critical of his history and I could not bear to see you be crushing about the man. There was just too much I cherished in the old codger, too much I loved him for. And I was afraid that these values would get battered in the critical process—and that I would have to tell you I didn't like it.

But I should have known better. You spared me any such embarrassment. You left me nothing to complain about on that score. You are as protective of those values as I could have wished. And without pulling your punches in the critical assessment. That to me is the most gratifying

70. David M. Potter, "C. Vann Woodward," in *Pastmasters: Some Essays on American Historians*, ed. Marcus Cunliffe and Robin Winks (New York: Harper & Row, 1969), 375–407.

71. Part III of what would appear as Richard Hofstadter, *The Progressive Historians: Turner, Beard, Parrington* (New York: Alfred A. Knopf, 1968).

achievement of the whole treatment and I congratulate you. You make it possible to admire the man without endorsing his history. Those final pages about the "ruin" are as grand as anything you have written.

The critical assessments are far more than a synthesis of the monographic stuff and full of fresh apercus. The whole picture rounds out to a satisfying and authoritative judgment that should stand for a long time. There are some marvelous things like the passage in Chap. VII about Beard's "scourging of the Fathers" for being reactionaries and conservatives and then turning them over and scourging them for being revolutionaries and radicals. You really get at the root of his ambiguities and the mystery of his motivation.

I got over my nit-picking impulses after the first few pages, but might as well pass on the trivialities I jotted down. P. 3, I suppose Beard was a more legitimate member of the "possessing classes" than Veblen, but the contrast seems to suggest that T. V. was one of the dispossessed. P. 5, chronological question: Beard would have been nineteen in '93, so why "a few years before"? P. 6, if Beard graduated in '98, there would seem to be two or three years unaccounted for. P. 15, no dictionary at hand, but can an aquiline nose look like an eagle. Anyway he did. After that I seem to find no nits to pick or got too absorbed in the story to pick em. But I see I queried, as a purist, "bred out of the native grain," P. 34 of IX. And in VIII "rounders" left me uninformed, but doubtless in a negligible minority.

In VII, p. 40, on absence of Bill of Rights in the Articles of Confederation, might it not be as well to concede en passant that the weakness of the government under them suggests less need for one.

In VIII, p. 23, "but which I believe fatal to any sound understanding of the U.S. in the Jacksonian era" seems a trifle magisterial.

On Beard's generosity to young scholars, I remember the pride with which I found myself mentioned in about 1939 in his America in Mid-Passage, and a note he wrote me.

I wondered a little about the comparative attention given the Origins of Jeffersonian Democracy which always seemed to me his most durable contribution—granting the limitations you point out. But I mean in comparison with the space given to An Economic Interpretation.[72]

72. Charles A. Beard, *Economic Origins of Jeffersonian Democracy* (New York: Macmillan, 1915); idem., *An Economic Interpretation of the Constitution of the United States* (New York: Macmillan, 1913).

I know you do not shoulder the obligations of a biographer, but I wondered about Mary's part in the collaboration and the extent of her contribution. Also you do not mention his brief spell on the Johns Hopkins faculty and his break with President Bowman about 1941 or so.[73]

Nothing you have not considered and weighed, I'm sure. Anyway, if the part on Beard is a fair sample, the new opus bids fair to be one of your best. Which is saying a hell of a lot. Shall I return the copy I have?

P.S. To your gracefully aging bride.

Dear Bede:

The place turns out lovely to look at, view etc. But unsatisfying as to bathing utility. Water temperature OK, but full of (blood-red) sea weed and only piddling surf. Great disappointment so far. Local prohibition on use of those boards you have, of which I bought a couple, and now can't use. Very frustrating. Anyway it would be great to have a visit from you. Romance complicates schedule. We leave the 16th for New Haven, the 18th for St. Paul. The Piersons insisted on attending wedding and on our doing the Expo with them on the way back. Back here the 24th. Honeymooners arrive 27th and we vacate to them till Sept. 1 and are here alone till the 18th. Hope against hope to draw you down. Telephone 635–8976. Doing sights of Newport should be some inducement.

Lovingly,

Rabbi C. Vann Finkelstein

RH, BOX 9: TLS

175. To Frederick Burkhardt[74]

OCTOBER 9, 1967

While I am very fond of my cousin Richard Vann, I strongly suspect that Mr. Nadel is a nitwit.[75] At any rate I am so impatient with the sort of talk that goes on about history among these philosophers that

73. Isaiah Bowman (1878–1950), who was president of Johns Hopkins (1935–48); he and Beard disagreed over American entry into the war.

74. Frederick H. Burkhardt (1912–2007), president of the American Council of Learned Societies (1959–74). He had written to invite CVW to be the ACLS's representative at a conference on "History and Social Science," to be held at Wesleyan University, 4–7 April 1968.

75. Richard T. Vann (b. 1931) taught at Wesleyan University, where he was one of the founders and editors of *History and Theory;* George H. Nadel (b. 1923) was an editor of the same journal and an associate of the Warburg Institute in London.

I would feel very much out of place at their conference on history and social sciences. Would you be good enough under these circumstances to excuse me?

My colleague Jack H. Hexter has a lower tolerance than I for this sort of thing and he might be interested in doing it.[76]

CVWP, 2/15: TCLU

176. To Richard Hofstadter

FEBRUARY 19, 1968

[deletion]

It was a difficult thing to do, and I think you have done it superbly well.[77] Fair yet firm and unevasive about real differences. It makes more sense than anything I have read on the subject. The decision to avoid discussion of your own work was wise, and you carry that off grandly. You are generous to a fault with Hartz and Boorstin, but you unerringly point out their shortcomings without rubbing it in.[78]

I cannot guess the nature of your anxieties about the chapter. There are two areas where I would suggest more thought.

One of them is what might be a superficial incongruity about the emphasis on consensus—given your careful dissociation from popular and political uses of the term—in a time when things appear to be on the point of coming apart at the seams. I mean something more than threatened race war and support for foreign policy disintegrating. A vocal element of the population just does not want to be governed, by anybody. There is a disposition to defy authority in all departments—parental, academic, professional, ecclesiastical, the works. Some healthy, some sick. It might be hard to turn up in the West a proletariat more alienated than our black one. Domestic conflict seems to be the disorder of the day. Some might ask where is the "comity" between races. You know all this better than any one, but I think you might acknowledge it somewhere.

76. Jack H. Hexter (1910–1996), a Tudor-Stuart historian who taught at Yale (1964–78).

77. This letter continues CVW's critique of the manuscript of Hofstadter, *Progressive Historians*.

78. Both Louis Hartz, *The Liberal Tradition in America* (New York: Harcourt, Brace, and World, 1955), and, among his other works, Daniel J. Boorstin, *The Genius of American Politics* (Chicago: University of Chicago Press, 1953), were associated with the so-called consensus school, with which Hofstadter himself was often linked.

The last five pages make some of the most fascinating reading in the chapter. But perhaps it is more of a conclusion to the book than to the chapter. It takes off on some highly important themes like commitment and detachment, but their strict relevance to subject of the chapter is not as clear as it might be. You might do some fiddling with that part with this question in mind.

I have read most of the Parrington chapters with delight and will talk to you about them later. I believe I am seeing you next Saturday anyway.

RH, BOX 9: TLS

177. To Kingman Brewster Jr.[79]

FEBRUARY 19, 1968

One brief glance backward into the errors of our past before we plunge into the reforms that will give race the desired prominence in the Yale curriculum.

In that bygone era it was taught that race was the least useful of explanatory variables in accounting for human worth, variety, and behavior and that skin pigmentation and hair texture were superficial bodily trivialities. Some went so far as to hold that the whole concept of race was a "myth," that there was no scientific basis for distinctions based on the concept, that race was a dangerous generalization of demagogues and an obsession of white supremacy fanatics. Not everyone in the academic community believed all these propositions or acted on them. But they represented the received opinion, the conventional wisdom—up through the term before last.

Now, with new light, we know better. We know that race is of prime importance—enough importance to become the vital organizing principle of a curriculum. Skin pigmentation and hair texture are back with us in full force. "Integration" is the bad word, the slogan of demagogues, not "race." To be equal we must be separate. Peaceful coexistence is the best we can hope for, if we can hope for that. Such would seem to be the received opinion, the conventional wisdom—at least for the next semester.

Onward and upward with the arts.

CVWP, 62/749: TCLS

79. Kingman Brewster Jr. (1919–1988), president of Yale (1963–77).

178. To Ralph Ellison

I have persuaded Red Warren and Bill Styron to join me as participants in a session on "The Uses of History in Fiction," at the annual convention of the Southern Historical Association in New Orleans on Wednesday, November 6, 1968. I hope very much I can persuade you to be a fourth member of the panel. The plan would be for a fifteen minute statement from each participant, then I as chairman would raise questions agreed upon in advance, then open for questions from the floor. The purposes would be the standard ones: the advancement of learning and the glory of God. The rewards and inducement: satisfaction derived from those worthy objectives. In other words, there is no fee and no expense account. Fringe benefits would be the companionship of all concerned. I strongly hope you will be able to make this commitment and let me send in your name with the others for publication in the program.

CVWP, 17/194: TCLU

179. To Tilden G. Edelstein[80]

I was fascinated by your account of the game of academic Russian roulette that you are playing in your role of white-faced end-man for the Rutger's Negro minstrel [show]. The absurdity and ridiculousness of the situation escalates daily. Hardly a day passes but that I get a call asking for a Negro historian who is black. My standard advice now is, resort to the burnt cork solution. I really think that a bit of rough and tough ridicule is in order. Imagine if you can a protest movement of white students demanding a white professor to teach white history, and similarly, a demonstration demanding white dorms for white students. How ridiculous do you think we can get?
[deletion]

CVWP, 17/189: TCLU

---

80. Tilden G. Edelstein (b. 1931), a graduate student of CVW's at John Hopkins, whose dissertation was published as *Strange Enthusiasm: A Life of Thomas Wentworth Higginson* (New Haven: Yale University Press, 1968); in 1968, he was teaching at Rutgers University.

180. To Wilma Dykeman Stokely

JUNE 3, 1968

I fully share your outrage at the racist campaign against Bill Styron's novel. The thing is so well organized that one branch of the movement is going to fight his movie. Another group is publishing shortly, by the Beacon Press, a whole book of essays attacking the novel.[81] Fortunately, the book of essays has been placed in the hands of Gene Genovese by *The New York Review of Books* and he will deal with it properly.[82]

In my opinion, our Black Nationalists, or some of them at least, are taking a decidedly Fascistic, racist and anti-intellectual line. I see no excuse for condoning, much less encouraging, this trend, and I am shocked to find the kids in SSOC lending themselves to this movement.[83]
[deletion]

CVWP, 52/620: TCLU

181. To Peter V. Woodward

SEPTEMBER 27, 1968

I did sign the application and sent it on to the American Express. I have no fear that you will plunge us into bankruptcy, but I do find that I forward a good many bills from various gas companies whose credit cards you are evidently using in rotation. The credit card neurosis is one symptom of the American Jonesmanship syndrome and I do hope you will not get hooked on that.

Your question about the populism of George Wallace interests me. I recently got a call from Gil Harrison, ed. of the New Republic asking me to do a piece on that and another from the CBS on the same thing.[84] I turned them both down. The reason is I have too much respect for the Populist heritage to encourage this popular identification. That was just the issue between me and Dick Hofstadter, Dan Bell, et al, and the reason I attacked their position in an essay I reprinted in the *Burden*. They sought to identify all the retrograde, reactionary, and fascistic tendencies of American politics

81. John Henrik Clarke, ed., *William Styron's Nat Turner: Ten Black Writers Respond* (Boston: Beacon Press, 1968).

82. Eugene D. Genovese, "The Nat Turner Case," *New York Review of Books* 11 (12 September 1968): 34–38, reprinted as "William Styron Before the People's Court," in *In Red and Black: Marxian Explorations in Southern and Afro-American History* (New York: Pantheon Books, 1971), 200–17.

83. The Southern Students Organizing Committee.

84. Gilbert A. Harrison (1915–2008), editor of the *New Republic* (1953–74).

with the Populists. My position is that the Populists had rational grievances, basically though not exclusively economic, and that they responded rationally—in so far as that term is applicable to political behavior, and granting that all politics and mass action have irrational components. The Joe Mc-Carthyites and the Wallaceites have grievances too, but they are psychic, "status" problems and their responses are not "rational" in the usual sense. They are not concerned about economic problems in their politics even when they have such problems. So I think it is a distortion of history and a disservice to a valid tradition of protest to foster this identification.

On the presidential electoral problem when no majority of electoral votes is produced by the Electoral College, the law is still that of the Twelfth Amendment (1804): ". . . if no person have such majority, then from the persons having the highest numbers not exceeding three on the list of those voted for as President, the House of Representatives shall choose immediately, by ballot, the President." Theoretically you are right that the lowest man could be elected. This opens some ominous possibilities, of course. I pointed out some of them in a review of a book in the New Republic last summer.[85] I hope the 1968 crisis will at least scare the country into an amendment that will drastically change the electoral system.

I cannot share your hopes for "a Kennedy take over of a demolished Democratic party."[86] A demolished party is not much good for any purpose, and yet that is precisely what some Democrats are promoting. Parties have been demolished before and I cannot view the act as very constructive. I was glad to read this morning of George Ball's resignation as UN ambassador and his reasons for it: that Nixon would be a disaster to foreign policy. I confess I am shocked to find you saying that "stability would be better insured by a clear-cut Nixon victory." I fear the influence of your unstable mentor in this.[87] I found some hope for Princeton in Professor Levy's reply to him.[88]

85. CVW published two reviews in the *New Republic* in 1967: of Styron's *Nat Turner* (7 October, 25–28) and of Joseph L. Morrison, *W. J. Cash: Southern Prophet—A Biography and a Reader* (New York: Alfred A. Knopf, 1967) (9 December, 28–30).

86. Since Robert F. Kennedy (1925–1968) had been shot on 5 June and died the next day, this refers to his younger brother, Edward M. Kennedy (1932–2009), the senior U.S. senator from Massachusetts.

87. Harry H. Eckstein (1924–1999), a political scientist who migrated from Germany to the United States in 1936, attended Harvard, and taught at Princeton (1959–80).

88. This is probably Marion J. Levy Jr. (1918–2002), a sociologist and student of modernization theory; he had been at Princeton since 1947.

Robin Winks tells me that one Richard Simeon here has just submitted a dissertation to La Palombara on Canadian federalism with case studies of Quebec, New Brunswick, British Columbia, Saskatchewan, and Ontario with specific reference to pensions and budgets.[89]

I hope that Sue has received a little package that we mailed her yesterday.[90] Give her our fondest love and tell her that in my experience women usually do better than men on exams but they tend to want to postpone them more and sometimes have to be dragged in by the heels screaming and weeping. Then they calm down and do well. Tell her that postponement is the worst thing—only aggravates the neurosis. Tell her to get you to say something that will set her laughing for three days running before the exams. Much better therapy than weeping. Tell her that I have a distinct premonition that she will wow them.

No, young man, I am not yet "too old and too wise" to take ideas seriously—especially my own—not *that* old! But I do fancy I am maturing a bit.

May we hope to see you soon? Give us a ring about it.

CVWP, 60/734: TCLU

182. To Charles A. Barker[91]

OCTOBER 8, 1968

Your comments on Genovese's review of Lynd make me regret that we did not have time to explore our differences.[92] Gene was hard but I think not unfair in charging him with mushy-mindedness, obscu-

---

89. Peter Woodward was planning to write a dissertation on Canadian federalism and Quebec; see Richard Edward Barrington Simeon, "Federalism and Policy-Making: Federal-Provincial Negotiation in Canada" (Ph.D. diss., Yale University, 1968). Joseph LaPalombara was an expert on Italian politics.

90. Susan Lampland (b. 1944), a political scientist who was Peter Woodward's contemporary as a graduate student at Princeton and his wife; she would later become an expert on the Balkans and, after various appointments in the United States and Britain, become a professor at the Graduate Center of the City University of New York.

91. A friend from CVW's Baltimore days, Charles A. Barker (1904–1993) was at Johns Hopkins (1945–72); his most important book was *Henry George* (New York: Oxford University Press, 1955).

92. Genovese was reviewing Staughton Lynd, *Intellectual Origins of American Radicalism* (New York: Pantheon Books, 1968); see Genovese, "Abolitionist," *New York Review of Books* 11 (26 September 1968): 69–74; it was reprinted as "Staughton Lynd as Historian and Ideologue," in *In Red and Black*, 354–67.

rantism and anti-intellectualism. I also agree that he plays havoc with almost every historical subject he touches. That bit about "defending the institutions of the heart against the paralyzing analyses of the head" seems to me altogether too typical.[93] I hope we can talk more about this later.

CVWP, 7/60: TCLU

183. To Gerald W. Johnson

MARCH 2, 1969

Your astute perception of the causes of the Civil War marks a turning point in American historiography. I shall endeavor to spread the word.[94] Maybe it will help stop the boredom and the gabble that is leading straight toward another civil war among Civil War historians.

Of course the last Civil War didn't stop the boredom and gabble among historians. It only egged it on.

And I wonder if the cease fire among the populace was more than a temporary truce. Only this time it is more truly civil war, because there are no sectional lines.

But in order to appreciate fully how intolerable the boredom over Negro rights can get, you really have to be a card-carrying member of the academic community. I know it looks bad enough from the outside, but inside it's much worse. Twenty-four hours a day—gabble, gabble, yak-yak. Integration, separatism, autonomy, black history, black studies, black math, black magic, black deans, black co-eds. Back in the Good Old Days the firing line was in the Black Belt where it belonged, the latitude of Selma and Montgomery. Now the firing line is along the Cambridge-Berkeley axis and the targets are not the Bull Con-

93. The text reads "the intuitions of the heart" (24).

94. Johnson had written in response to CVW, "White Racism and Black Emancipation," *New York Review of Books* 12 (27 February 1969): 5–11. In his letter, Johnson had observed: "Your discussion of the six books confirms me in my heretical opinion that the Civil War was neither a moral crusade nor an economic conspiracy, but the revolt of a nation (north and south) against intolerable boredom," because the "yakking had gone on for 30 years without producing a single new idea, yet it was next to impossible to get in a word on any other subject, and quite impossible to get any other subject considered on its merits without reference to this": Gerald W. Johnson to CVW, 20 February 1969.

nors and the Jim Clarks, but the Kingman Brewsters and the Clark Kerrs.[95]

In my opinion the prime movers are nearing the point of talking themselves out of the white sympathizers they have left. There will always be a few white Negroes left, but even in academe their ranks are thinning already.

[deletion]

CVWP, 27/323: TCLU

184. To Kingman Brewster Jr.

MARCH 4, 1969

May I put in a word of unsolicited advice about the proposal to establish a black student center on the campus?

My advice is that whatever response you make should be on a temporary basis. The demand as I understand it comes largely from the freshmen and sophomores rather than from the upperclassmen. Insecurity among freshm[e]n is not an unusual phenomenon, and among black ones it is to be expected.

In my opinion this whole movement of black separatism is a reaction against the shock of white competition. Segregation has protected them from competition for generations. Southerners were not wholly hypocritical in saying that the Negroes preferred Jim Crow. Separatism is a militant stance but a defensive reaction—in effect a regression to the old way of dealing with competition.

I hope that before long the separatist impulse will fade out as confidence grows. But if a black student center is established I am afraid it will be very hard to get rid of it after the temporary need has disappeared. It could then become the source of endless trouble.

CVWP, 62/749: TCLU

95. Theophilus Eugene "Bull" Connor (1897–1973), the Commissioner of Public Safety for Birmingham, Alabama (1936–52, 1956–63); Clark Kerr (1911–2003) was president of the University of California-Berkeley from 1958 until his dismissal in 1967, a firing in part prompted by the state's new governor, Ronald Reagan, who thought Kerr was too liberal in dealing with student protests.

185. To Martin Duberman[96]

APRIL 9, 1969

I read your *Evergreen* reflections on the historian's career choice with special admiration for its candor.[97] I see we share a memory of distaste for graduate training, mine to the point of revulsion. I seem to have been more fortunate in my motivation for the dissertation work—which was the only reward that made toleration of the "training" acceptable, acceptable only as a means of financing the writing. And somehow I never shared your expectations of history for "problem-solving." And so never suffered the experience of disillusionment. On the other hand, somewhat illogically, I cannot endorse your permissive exemption of the problem-solvers from exposure to history and your willingness to turn them all over to the social scientists for ad hoc action. In fact I am appalled at the memorylessness—mindlessness with which action—now problem solvers among the undergraduates plunge into their tasks. They are evidently quite happy to accept your exemption from History 1 as well as 2, 3, and 4. The decline in history-course registrations at Harvard over the last couple of years has been on the order of 40 per cent, and the decline at Yale has been only slightly less. I wonder about Princeton. I am glad to see that you do not join Lynd in tailoring history to position papers, that is the only alternative abdication? You seem to come near saying that.

CVWP, 16/179: TCLU

186. To Eugene D. Genovese

JUNE 21, 1969

Count on my cooperation if the occasion arises to cooperate with your subversive apparatus next fall at Rochester.

I enclose a clipping about mischief afoot in those quarters which Howard Lamar picked up on the highway on his way to California.[98] I read it as a sympathetic editorial and hope I am right.

96. Martin B. Duberman (b. 1930), historian and playwright, then teaching at Princeton; he was known for his biographies of Charles Francis Adams and James Russell Lowell, as well as his editing of *The Antislavery Vanguard: New Essays on the Abolitionists* (Princeton, NJ: Princeton University Press, 1965).

97. Martin Duberman, "On Becoming a Historian," *Evergreen Review* 13 (April 1969): 57–59, 85–90.

98. Howard R. Lamar (b. 1923), a historian of the American West and ad interim president of Yale (1992–93).

I suppose there's an element of offhand justice in your statement that "I cannot abide any suggestion of separatism." Nevertheless it is rather like saying I cannot abide the facts of life. What I really find hard to abide is the deluge of nationalistic moonshine, the phony mystique, the fascistic violence in too much of the arrogance and the increasingly bloody terrorism that increasingly accompanies so much of this separatism. Did you see Roy Wilkins's letter in the Arts Section of the TIMES last Sunday?[99] Whatever you think of him I thought he was if anything too mild about this tom-tom series of Black Heritage broadcasts.[100] Now published in 16 mm. films and a series of textbooks, this will become the daily curriculum for millions of kids.

I hope the honeymooning goes well. Our love to Betsy.[101]

CVWP, 21/240: TCLU

187. To Monroe F. Swilley III[102]

JUNE 23, 1969

Your questions about Ernest Hartsock take me back some forty years to my college days. Those times are so dim in my memory that I really do not trust it to furnish any useful material for your purposes. I certainly would not undertake to recall any statements on politics or social problems that he made. My impression was that he was not primarily interested in politics or social problems. My relation was one of boyish admiration for a poet slightly my senior. I can say that I was with him at his death at the Emory Hospital. It was the first death I ever witnessed and it was a profound shock. Since I was the only one with him at the time I don't think the doctors expected him to die. We had talked a little casually during the evening, but he had long been unconscious and I

99. Roy Wilkins, "Not the Real Black Experience," *New York Times* (15 June 1969): D19.

100. WCBS was running a series on the "Black Heritage." Wilkins felt the series distorted the record, in particular by overplaying Marcus Garvey's "Back to Africa" movement (which was given four episodes), underplaying the contribution of the NAACP, and generally favoring the role of radicalism over strategies of moderate protest.

101. Elizabeth Fox-Genovese (1941–2007), a historian of modern France who would later become a scholar of the American South and feminism; she was then working on what would be published as *The Origins of Physiocracy: Economic Revolution and Social Order in Eighteenth-Century France* (Ithaca, NY: Cornell University Press, 1976).

102. A graduate student at Georgia State College in Atlanta; he had recently published Monroe F. Swilley III, "Ernest Hartsock and His *Bozart* Magazine," *Georgia Historical Quarterly* 53 (March 1969): 57–67.

thought sleeping peacefully when he suddenly stopped breathing. For the rest, I think you had best stick to the written record and whatever you find in his papers.

CVWP, 49/575: TCLU

188. To Maurice H. Mandelbaum

JULY 25, 1969

I really need a philosophical talk with you, but I think you are in California and I will have to write instead.[103]

I am working on my speech to the AHA.[104] My general thesis is that the history trade in the US enjoyed an unusually felicitous couple of decades following World War II but that it is now headed for trouble. To break out of the bind it was left in by Beard and the relativists and the social scientists at the end of the war the profession combatively struck some mighty poses. It laid claim imperiously to autonomy. Neither art nor science it was sui generis. Same time others claimed it was both, yet subject to the discipline and criticism of neither—really. Best of both worlds. Arbiter between the Two Cultures, reconcilers of art & science, the only discipline that used both, "half-scientific, half-artistic" (Stuart Hughes), a fabulous centaur creature among the squares, men and horses, a sort of Pegasus centaur, sailing over the barriers of logic and criticism and landing invariably on its feet.[105] Wildly exaggerated, of course, but a recognizable caricature. And the latter-day revival of such romantic concepts as intuition, inside, empathy, Collingwood idealism, imagination combined with off-hand casual employment of the gadgets of psychology, sociology, and quantitative analysis lend plausibility to the caricature.[106] Pretty high ground to take, considering the low ground we were reduced to in 1945.

Am I right that some of these postures, historical autonomy at least, found defenders among philosophers and logicians? Louis O. Mink,

103. Mandelbaum, CVW's former colleague at Johns Hopkins, had long been interested in the philosophy of history and was then working on *History, Man, and Reason: A Study in Nineteenth Century Thought* (Baltimore, MD: Johns Hopkins University Press, 1971).

104. His presidential address, published as CVW, "The Future of the Past," *American Historical Review* 75 (February 1970): 711–26.

105. H. Stuart Hughes, *History as Art and as Science: Twin Vistas on the Past* (New York: Harper & Row, 1964), 3.

106. "Collingwood idealism" refers to the neo-Hegelian philosopher Robin G. Collingwood (1889–1943), who taught at Oxford and is best known for the posthumously published *The Idea of History* (Oxford: Clarendon Press, 1946).

William H. Dray?[107] Any others? What to read? That they undertook a
defense against the Hempelian critique.[108] Perhaps against the Mandelbaum critique? I am as poorly read in the field as most of my historian
colleagues. But didn't the centaurs get some aid and comfort from these
quarters? Any from theologians? Niebuhr? There were some few indul-
gent social scientists.

Who is Hayden V. White and what do you think of him?[109] Am I to
take his "Burden of History" (History & Theory, 1966, No. 2, pp. 111–134)
seriously? A hatchet man, but some of his blows seem to me to strike
home. I find some corroboration of his view that history is falling in status
among the sciences and the arts, particularly creative letters. If he is even
half right then history really is in trouble. Are there any other critiques
along this line? Has his criticism been answered? My intention is to strike
a blow at complacency and smugness in the profession—always a safe
target—but am I aiming in the right direction? The moment I am stalled.
Could you give me an early reply?

[deletion]

CVWP, 35/414: TCLU

189. To Norman Pollack[110]

SEPTEMBER 16, 1969

Your suggestions about the constitutional amendments came in good
time for the meeting of the Council on the 13th.[111] I believe you will
be gratified to discover that a number of blows were struck for populism.

---

107. Louis O. Mink (1921–1983), who taught at Wesleyan University and had published a
book on Collingwood; William Herbert Dray (b. 1921), a Canadian philosopher, also with an
interest in Collingwood, and perhaps best known for his *Philosophy of History* (Englewood Cliffs,
NJ: Prentice-Hall, 1964).

108. Carl Gustav Hempel (1905–1997), a German émigré and logical empiricist, notable for
"The Function of General Laws in History," *Journal of Philosophy* 39 (15 January 1942): 35–48.

109. Hayden White (b. 1928) was to become one of the most influential philosophers of
history in the late twentieth century, through his essays, first collected as *Tropics of Discourse: Essays in Cultural Criticism* (Baltimore, MD: Johns Hopkins University Press, 1978), and his general
study, *Metahistory: The Historical Imagination in Nineteenth-Century Europe* (Baltimore, MD: Johns
Hopkins University Press, 1973).

110. Norman Pollack (b. 1933) was then teaching at Michigan State University; his 1961
Harvard dissertation had been published as *The Populist Response to Industrial America: Midwestern
Populist Thought* (Cambridge, MA: Harvard University Press, 1962).

111. The Executive Council of the American Historical Association.

While we did not get at the objective in your manner all the time, the consistent thrust of change was in the direction of membership power. This was largely done through enhancing the effectiveness of petitions. Another way was in cutting down *ex officio* voting power on the Council. For example, ex-Presidents were granted voting rights for only one year instead of three—with my hearty approval as the first victim of this franchisement.

I was of course gratified by your reactions to "Clio with Soul." You might appreciate a recent comment of Dave Potter on the title. The only trouble with it, he remarked, was that those who knew what "Clio" meant did not know what "Soul" meant, and those who knew what "Soul" meant did not know what "Clio" meant. This incident was borne out by the Chairman Merrill Jensen, who introduced me by saying I would speak on "Clio With A Soul."

I am compelled to beg your patience with my reading of your manuscript. The fact is I am delayed by grave illness in the family.[112] You may be sure I will get to it as soon as I can.

CVWP, 44/518: TCLU

190. To Virginia Foster Durr

OCTOBER 16, 1969

It was like you to write so promptly, so lovingly, and so understandingly. We both appreciated your letter, and also Sheldon and Lucy coming to the service at Yale. Princetonians turned out in incredible numbers. I am amazed at what depth of feeling these two young people stirred at home and abroad in such a brief time.

The ordeal was mercifully short but all the more poignant and bitter. The most haunting and unbearable part was watching those two living up their last two months together in the knowledge that it was the last of it all.

Susan has gone to Montreal to close their apartment and store their things—notes, books, manuscripts, everything—a rough assignment. Then back for a visit with us, and a visit with their beloved Professor Harry and family in Switzerland. Then back to Princeton and later to Jugoslavia for her research. We will carry through with earlier plans and take her to Greece with us in late spring. She has been perfect throughout. Glenn is bearing up and we are both slowly convalescing.

VFD, 1/257: ALS

112. The cancer of his son, Peter. The article discussed in the preceding paragraph was CVW, "Clio with Soul," *Journal of American History* 56 (June 1969): 5–20; it was CVW's presidential address to the Organization of American Historians.

191. To Bell Irvin Wiley

NOVEMBER 12, 1969

My paper on Cash should be appearing soon in *The New York Review of Books*.[113] I hope you will watch for it and write me your reactions. It was something I have long wanted to write and thoroughly enjoyed doing it.

David's performance was indeed a bit stranger than usual, though quite in character.[114] I decided after hesitation to react mildly. I'm sorry he was hissed. He is not a well man and I am concerned about his state of mind.

[deletion]

CVWP, 59/719: TCLU

192. To Gerald W. Johnson

DECEMBER 2, 1969

Many thanks for your thoughtful ruminations on my piece about W. J. Cash.

You are probably right that my strictures concerning his neglect of the Negro's "mind" were too severe and ill-considered. Someday I would like to argue the point with you a bit, however. I am always a little suspicious of the claims that cultural nationalists invariably put forward that their "mind" (spirit, culture, style, folkways, etc.) are too mysterious and unique to be penetrated by any outsider. The pretensions of this sort advanced by the Black nationalists go as far in this respect as such as any of their predecessors, including our Confederate forebears, our Jewish, Scottish, Welsh and Flemish contemporaries. American Afro-

---

113. CVW, "W. J. Cash Reconsidered," *New York Review of Books* 13 (4 December 1969): 28–34; it was subsequently revised as "The Elusive Mind of the South," in *American Counterpoint: Slavery and Racism in the North-South Dialogue* (Boston: Little, Brown, 1971), 261–83.

114. Woodward had given a paper on Cash at the thirty-fifth annual meeting of the Southern Historical Association in Washington, DC; the session had been chaired by Clement Eaton and the commentators were David Donald, Joseph L. Morrison, and Eugene Genovese. (Genovese was absent and his paper was read by Richard Maxwell Brown, chair of the program committee.) According to Brown's report on the meeting, "Woodward's long paper evoked a sharp divergence of opinion. David Donald of Johns Hopkins University praised Cash, incisively denied Woodward's conclusions, and maintained that 'In basic matters the South is, and always has been, unchanging": see Richard Maxwell Brown, "The Thirty-Fifth Annual Meeting," *Journal of Southern History* 36 (February 1970): 64.

Saxons are further removed from African origins than a great majority of American whites are removed from European origins and have been subjected in the past to a more intensive process of acculturation. It was longer and more intensive than the Africans have had in any other new world experience, since virtually all of our population derives from Seventeenth and Eighteenth Century origins. As you see, I am reluctant to encourage the White Americans to abandon all efforts to penetrate the Black Sphinx.

[deletion]

CVWP, 27/323: TCLU

193. To Susan L. Woodward

JANUARY 1, 1970

There it is, the 70's already. We saw them in sober & quiet, having got back from Washington only the night before after the whirling had stopped but the giddiness continued. Still some giddiness, but with it a good deal of quiet satisfaction and—I might as well admit it—some elation and secret twinges of euphoria about the academic politics.

But to start with—Barbados. It was great hearing your voice coming in sweet and clear from Oslo there on the gay tropical terrace overhanging the roaring Atlantic beach. Just great, only I couldn't tell at the end whether you were still on the line and said good-bye. And also, although the Oslo operator had called the day before to ask if I would accept charges, I could never get a bill. To make up, call us collect here sometime before long when you get lonesome. The island was as lovely as I remember it from the brief visit before, and the weather as perfect but for a few suddenly-over rainsqualls. Trade winds constant, moon full, beach incredibly exotic with cliffs, rock, sand, palms, surf—nature imitating Winslow Homer or doing its damndest—flower & fauna positively psychedelic with outrageous color and impudent birds competing for one's breakfast every morning.[115] Natives considerably more genial than Jamaica, more like Grenada. The Hofstadters blew in a couple of days after we landed bringing Sally and the Zinbergs with their two little girls, and two days before Christmas the Bickels with their two, Chessie &

115. Winslow Homer (1836–1910), the American painter; CVW may be referring to the fact that Homer visited the Bahamas in the 1880s and 1890s.

Claudia absolutely bug-eyed with the wonder of it all.[116] Watching them was like playing den mother for a Brownie moon landing. Anyhow (to borrow your favourite oath) it was all as many light years as it was possible for us to put between this Christmas and last. And it was just as well. Just as well, too, that we were not together this time. Next Christmas, maybe. I simply couldn't have taken it at home. Even so, there were paroxysms of blinding anguish. I hope Oslo served you better. And maybe we had both best wait and hope for time to do what no amount of space seems capable of doing. "Time present and time past/Are both present perhaps in time future . . ."[117]

Anyhow (more Susanian stoicism) we took off from Barbados soaked with Badjun sun and Badjun rum on Christmas evening into a madly gaudy tropical sunset and landed at Kennedy Airport five hours later in a madly blinding blizzard combining snow, sleet, rain, and wind of gale velocity. It was a problem first of finding the road and second of staying on it, combined with constantly frosted-over windshields, one-lane driving, and dizzily skidding traffic. Kennedy closed down a couple of hours after we landed, and with more than an hour of additional snow we would not have made the drive home. As it was we pulled in—even negotiating the driveway after a second try—at 1:30 AM dead. Next morning plowing out of snow and as deep in the stack of accumulated mail. Planes grounded, I left Glenn to follow and took the train that afternoon for Washington.

Arrived in a political hurricane and quickly established self in eye thereof which was not all that calm at the moment. New complications and storms of rumor. But my intelligence forces had been at work in my absence and piled up some solid data from inside by phone. The preparations paid off and I had pretty well second-guessed the Rads on every turn. Besides, I was immediately in touch with the two main faction leaders, seeing them separately, both furious at each other, but

116. Sarah Hofstadter (b. 1952) was Richard and Beatrice Hofstadter's daughter. Alexander Mordecai Bickel (1924–1974), a migrant from Romania, was one of CVW's closest friends and Chancellor Kent Professor of Law at the Yale Law School; his wife was Josephine Ann Napolino and his daughters Francesca Ann and Claudia Rose. Norman E. Zinberg (1922–1989), a psychoanalyst at the Harvard Medical School, and Dorothy Shore Zinberg had two daughters (Sarah and Annie); they were friends of the Hofstadters.

117. The opening lines of "Burnt Norton," the first section of T. S. Eliot, *Four Quartets* (New York: Harcourt, Brace, 1943).

fortunately not at me. Besides I had a lot going for me. It's a good Council, with all but one in attendance and meeting next morning, 9 to 5 PM, immensely helpful. Also marvelously efficient local arrangements committee that had taken care of security and press and electronic stuff and a mountain of paperwork. Also Paul Ward and staff worked around the clock through Christmas preparing for every possible contingency.[118] That night the preparatory Radical Caucus met and my agents turned in a complete report before midnight. As expected, they split and could not agree on their own constitution, which I had directed Ward to print up and distribute at AHA expense and place on agenda. That was their first embarrassment. Second was our discovery that 27 of the 207 names on the Lynd nominating petition were phoney.[119] I called in Lynd, Waskow, and Zinn and promised them I would swing the Council to waive the disqualification and try to carry the meeting for validating his nomination if they would be a bit cooperative.[120] Lynd read my promise to the caucus and replied to jeers by saying that he knew me for an honorable man who would do what he promised. For which I was grateful. Some last minute agreements tidied things over. Lynd pale and tense but reasonable.

At business meeting next night (about 2200, or ten times previous record) my main trouble was my professional parliamentarian that your political scientists sold me. Spent most of my time explaining to him sotovoce what was going on. Laurence Stone seen stalking out of meeting swearing he was damned if he, an Englishman, would sit and hear a demented Greek butcher parliamentary law.[121] Demeter by name.[122] Radicals screamed & ranted a good bit but observed most of amenities. No

118. Paul Langdon Ward (1911–2005) was the executive secretary of the American Historical Association (1965–74).

119. Staughton Lynd was nominated by the Radical Caucus to be president of the AHA.

120. Howard Zinn (1922–2010), who taught for most of his career at Boston University; he had been active in the civil rights movement, mostly in SNCC, and had taught at Spelman College in Atlanta. His more important early works were *The Southern Mystique* (New York: Alfred A. Knopf, 1964) and *SNCC, the New Abolitionists* (Boston: Beacon Press, 1964).

121. Lawrence Stone (1919–1999), an Oxford social historian of early modern England who taught at Princeton after 1963.

122. George Constantine Demeter (1896–1983), a Massachusetts lawyer and politician, the author of *Manual: How to Master the Rules of Parliamentary Law and Procedure. Based on the Standard Rules of Procedure as Now Nearly Universally Recognized and Practiced Throughout the Land* (Boston: Mosher Press, 1948), later often revised.

obscenities (over mikes at least), no profanity (ditto), and only one breach
of decorum when Waskow called George Pierson a liar. And he apologized and audience applauded when I called him to terms. That night we
got Bob Palmer elected (800 plus to 400 plus) and more amazingly got
our whole constitutional amendment program adopted but yielded to a
recess until the following night after (instead of in place of my presidential address) for the Radical show.[123]

Next night before Paul Ward introduced me to speak four dashiked
blacks suddenly swarmed on podium to grab the mike. I took firm grip
on large gavel and asked leading dashiki what the hell he wanted and
he showed me a two-sentence announcement of a meeting and I told
Ward to let him read it and they retired marching to hidden tom-toms.
Then award of prizes. Then my immortal words of wisdom received in
surprising respect & gratifying acclaim. Then I grabbed gavel again and
called to order recessed session. Radicals had given prior assurance not to
move reconsideration of amendments and to abide by p. law. Only a few
infractions of agreements, a hell of an uproar. Forgot to say in first session
Gene Genovese was the sensation with searing denunciation of Lynd &
Co. as totalitarian barbarians. This time I kept Greek oracle grounded
and guessed at law. Second night Stuart Hughes was the star with denunciation of the Zinn resolutions against Sin & Running Dog Capitalist
Establishmentarian pigs.[124] After hours of debate latter defeated by 2 to 1
vote. Whereupon in deafening uproar I put motion to adjourn, declared
the Ayes had it, and practically broke the gavel & deadened the mike.
That at ten of one. All's well with establishmentarian pigs.

Cable from Alex Bickel: Barbados casts 1000 votes [letter breaks off
here]

Afterward grudging thanks from Lynd, Waskow, & Zinn, and Gene
grabbed me around the neck and kissed my cheek.[125]

CVWP, 60/735: TCLS

123. Robert R. Palmer (1909–2002), a Princeton historian of France and late eighteenth-
century revolution; most noted for *The Age of the Democratic Revolution: A Political History of Europe
and America, 1760–1800*, 2 vols. (Princeton, NJ: Princeton University Press, 1959–64).

124. H. Stuart Hughes (1916–1999), an intellectual historian of modern Europe who was
then teaching at Harvard.

125. This last sentence is written in longhand in the left margin.

194. To Lucinda Woodward[126]

MARCH 20, 1970

That's evidently what you must be. The evidence is overwhelming. Second cousin, I would say. Isn't that the way it works out? If your father and my father were first cousins, doesn't that make us second cousins? Do check up on it. Seems to be a generation missing somewhere, though. That is, assuming you are a college student and not a rather decrepit graduate student. I must be of your father's generation. But how did he get to be my father's first cousin? Mystifying. I have no means of checking up. My Uncle Comer died in 1960 and my father Hugh five years later. I did not know about you at all.

I heard much about your grandfather, whom I believed was called "Uncle Wesley."[127] I think I even met him once. And it is perfectly clear how your father came by his name. I remember the Bishop quite well, the old tyrant.[128] He was incredible. He used to make "visitations" (no less) to Oxford while my father was head of Emory Junior College there. He was clearly of the impression that he was God's vice regent. Talked that way all the time—to everybody. I thought he was too, at the time, and it gave me a rather poor impression of the Almighty at a tender age. I hope your father didn't "take after him" as we used to say.

I never used my first name, in order, I suppose to avoid confusion with my Uncle Comer, but I was deeply devoted to him. You would have been too. A dear man, and everybody loved him.

We must get acquainted. The Woodwards seem to be diminishing. My hopes for perpetuating the name ended tragically last fall with the death of my son from cancer. We are still much shaken by the loss and feel cut off from the next generation. No other children. Are you a hippie with granny glasses or a square with horn-rimmed? Revolutionist or jock, it doesn't matter. The cousinship is the thing, and you must still have something of the southerner in you or you wouldn't ever have bothered to write. Do send us your picture.

CVWP, 60/73: TCLU

126. Lucinda Woodward, a student at Sacramento State College; her letter to CVW, 11 March 1970, explained that her father, Warren Candler Woodward, was a cousin of CVW's uncle, Comer.

127. Her letter had mentioned that her paternal grandfather, Samuel Wesley Woodward, had left Winchester, TN, and moved to Clovis, NM.

128. Warren Akin Candler.

195. To Tom Kahn[129]

MAY 12, 1970

I wish I could respond more fully to your letter about the Yale experience of last weekend, but I am leaving immediately for Europe. The
best I can do is make a few informal observations here.

There is no simple or single explanation for the triumph of non-
violence at the Yale weekend.[130] I think there would have been violence
without the combined efforts of three cooperating forces: (1) Yale University, (2) the city police chief and administration, and (3) the radical Blacks,
including the Panthers. To consider those in the order named:

(1) Kingman Brewster deserves high marks for preventing a polarization of the University and splits between students and faculty, as
well as between the administration and students. On the student
strategy his open endorsement of the demand for a fair trial and
his profession of sympathy for motivation of the student strike were
first in importance. The faculty responded by in effect co-opting the
strike, but making attendance optional. The students responded by
a solid and effective majority against violence and for protest. The
hundreds of student marshalls, some of them Black and some of
them radicals, most of them moderate, were instrumental in heading off confrontations with police.

(2) The Police Chief Ahearn is to my knowledge unique as a type
in that office—young, intelligent, realistic and tough.[131] Both police and national guards were under his control. Result: no busted
heads, very few arrests, restricted but effective use of tear gas.

(3) The Panther leaders very firmly renounced violence and publicly
and repeatedly urged adherence to non-violent methods. They

129. A coordinator for the Academic Committee of Correspondence in New York and
also involved with the League for Industrial Democracy, whose 1970 conference, according
to Kahn, CVW had been going to attend. One purpose of the committee was "to establish a
network of communications for faculty members concerned with both academic reform and
the preservation of academic freedom and civil liberties on the campus. . . . [and] to circulate
among our members first-hand reports on campus events and developments by professors on
those campuses." See Tom Kahn to CVW, 7 May 1970.

130. There had been a trial of several Black Panthers, charged with murdering an alleged
police informant, and for two days there were demonstrations, attended by thousands, on New
Haven Green.

131. James F. Ahern (1932–1986) was the New Haven police chief (1968–70); he later
served on the President's Commission on Campus Unrest and, still later, became expensively
embroiled in a lawsuit which charged the New Haven police with illegally wiretapping political
activists, as well as criminals.

made it plain they were not disavowing violence for the future, but that this was no time for it. Other black leaders in the city helped out with the same strategy of non-violence.

Our good fortune is to be explained by this combination and not otherwise. Which of the three deserves most credit I am unable to say.

It is only realistic to add the blessing of luck. Had the Kent State news or the full implications of the Cambodian invasion broken at the wrong time, we would have had it too.

If this answers your purpose, you are welcome to distribute as you indicate.

CVWP, 1/1: TCLU

196. To Susan L. Woodward

SEPTEMBER 3, 1970

L anded at JFK virtually on schedule, rented a car with the Palmers, and so to bed by 1 AM New Haven time or 11 AM Tashkent time by which we went to bed two nights before—with consequent disorientation of the human clock.[132] Though what with the drag of fatigue and nimbutal I managed to clock a big sleep of ten hours and wake up in the pink in a crisp, sparkling, premature autumn morning feeling simply great. Poor Glenn abstained from pills and tossed all night. It seems we missed the hottest August in fifteen years as a bonus.

But to fill you in on events between that and our tearful parting in Budapest. The Russians put us up in the Rossia, their counter-weapon hotel, a monster accommodating 7000 just off Red Square. The mad turnips of St. Basils soared out our window with the towers of the Kremlin in view. Some 350 US delegates (mostly unknown to me) and over 3000 foreign delegates—in other words, about half the size of an average AHA convention and madder by 40-odd foreign tongues simultaneously shouted on all sides. Simultaneous translations in Russian, French, and English at sessions. Opening show at the new glass Palace of Soviet Congresses within the Kremlin walls with address by Joukov on "Lenin & History" followed by caviar buffet for 4000 followed by the Bolshoi Ballet doing

132. CVW had attended the thirteenth congress of the International Committee of Historical Sciences in Moscow, 16–23 August 1970; the group meets once every five years. He was accompanied by his wife, Glenn. The "Palmers" are Robert R. Palmer and his wife, Esther.

Gisel.[133] After 30 minutes of Lenin & History I punched Glenn and we self consciously & painfully withdrew to lobby where we were shortly joined by most of the US delegates I knew including the Handlins, Freidels, and Pipes of Harvard (The Russians assumed it was calculated of course, which it was not of course).[134] But the caviar and vodka was plentiful and the Bolshoi Ballet was super (Last time we saw Giesel was in Copenhagen in '65, also a Bolshoi troup and the Royal family sat on the front row.) After we rapped with the Handlins & Pipes till dawn in a doubtless bugged hotel room.

My paper came up next day, stupidly stuck in a session on Class Struggle and Nationalism in Underdeveloped Countries with which it had nothing whatsoever to do. Endless wrangling between East Germans & West Germans over African Colonial history with long sermons on Lenin from Russians & satellites. I dozed and after two hours of the endless afternoon session simply got up and walked off the platform and out through the audience and left. One Pole and one Russian commented on my paper (the Russian after I withdrew) and rather favorably to my surprise & slight embarrassment. I only returned to one more session during the five day congress—equally boring. The Russian US specialists did make special effort to establish CONTACT. And one or two of them were interesting and ingratiating. One of them took us to the Bolshoi to see a spectacular Sparticus performance, tickets for which otherwise unobtainable. A group of younger Russian US historians made formal overtures for the establishment of a biennial Russo-American Seminar meeting alternately in Russia & the USA and something may come of that, though they warned us that if the Soviet government appointed the wrong man to take charge they would pass the word to call it all off.

Incidental events included a reception at the US Embassy where I had a good talk with Ambassador Beam, a very nervous gent who incidentally wanted to get his gangling son into Yale but took a hopeful view of the next few months and thought the Muscovites would be on their best behavior till the Middle East Crisis was under control.[135] Then there

---

133. Subsequently published as E. M. Joukov, *Lénine et l'histoire* (Moscow: Naouka, 1970).

134. Handlin's wife was Mary Flug Handlin (1913–1976), also a historian; Freidel's (his second) was Madeleine Bicskey, whom he had married in 1956. Richard Edgar Pipes (b. 1923), a Russian historian born in Poland, taught at Harvard (1950–96) and was director of its Russian Research Center (1968–73).

135. Jacob Dyneley Beam (1908–1993), the American ambassador to the USSR (1969–73).

was a press conference where I established an undeserved reputation for command of the Russian tongue as follows: the audience was strictly iron curtain correspondents and all but Bob and me among those interviewed were ditto. After each satellite had made a speech about the results of the Congress establishing that Lenin was the source of all sound doctrine in history, I made a little speech pointing out a remarkable orthodoxy among Soviet historians and that for one I suspected that "Lenin was not the only source of truth." The translator who had perfect command of English stuck on the last word and hesitated and then asked me to repeat said word and I promptly shouted "Pravda" and actually got a slight laugh. There was also an uneventful radio interview.

But mainly Glenn and I stuck to sight seeing, mainly in Moscow. The Russians characteristically signaled out a privileged class among the delegates for red-carpet treatment and since I was a beneficiary I had no serious objection. We put in a splendid day doing Leningrad and another doing ancient Vladimir and Suzdal, which I had missed on my 1932 trip. Great mass of 11th to 14th century churches, convents, monasteries, monuments, ikons, well preserved or restored—about 220 kilometers from Moscow—rural, mysterious, charming, heart and soul of Muscovite culture. Wouldn't have missed it for anything. Hope pictures turn out well. Ruskies have evidently struck a new gold mine and lavished the works on their ancient monuments. Every turnip top glitters with blinding gilt, even the statues at Peterhof and every curlicue of baroque in the Hermitage. Barbaric splendor in gold leaf.

The big thing of course was the post-Congress five days in central Asia—roughly the distance of the Rockies from New Haven and a six hour 3 time-zone flight. Many floored by the 105° degree heat, but I had expected worse and also worse accommodations and was pleasantly surprised. You know what a sucker I am for ruins and I was not prepared for the scale and splendor and magnificence of those in Samarkand and Bokhara. Late Roman in scale—baths of Caracalla for example, and all plastered with brilliant colored ceramics. The *frison historique* was Tamerlane's tomb. Staggering. Also son Ulbeg's astronomical observatory and 100 meter sextant. And mosques the scale of Sophia. Nothing of Alexander the Great's conquest in evidence but Russians are discovering things. Tashkent earthquake of '66 wiped out monuments, but modern buildings impressive. International incident at takeoff: After an hour in packed plane with 100 degree heat with NO AIR every stitch drenched and tempers frayed. Finally engines start & stewardess passed candy. American long-hair grabs handful and flung it in her face. Russians (justifiably indignant) Captain orders offender off plane. Another hour of sweat puddles, stench, and suffocation in tense atmosphere, then off.

Bede Hofstadter phoned day after return that she thought Dick was dying and for us to come at once.[136] We spent yesterday at the hospital in New York.[137] He could talk at intervals, but he can't last long. Doctors are still fighting and it may be days, weeks. I will let you know, for I know you will want to write Bede. That malady has a way of singling out the dearest and the best, as we know. Manning arrives this afternoon for a visit. Fitzroy McLean book not in print.[138] No letter yet. We miss you darling.

CVWP, 60/735: TCLS

197. To Alexander M. Bickel

OCTOBER 30, 1970

Many thanks for your reassuring letter from the Center and your recent note of distress from New Orleans about the news of Dick's death. His terrible illness has haunted the whole fall and the end has been inevitable for some time. We go to Columbia tomorrow for the memorial service and I am obligated to do the dread honor. Bede will come next week to spend a week with us.

Dennis Wrong is Dennis Right in his forthcoming piece, a commentary on the *New York Review of Books*.[139] Poor Bob Silvers. Such a nice man, such excellent taste in literature, and such deplorable ideas about politics. I blush for him.

An easy blusher, I blush also for you. The company you keep—you on the same page of the Times in company with Charles Reich and Arthur Waskow.[140] Shame, oh shame! As for Charlie, I am reminded that

136. He had leukemia and would die on 24 October 1970.

137. Mount Sinai Hospital.

138. In view of Susan Woodward's interests in the Balkans, this is possibly Toni Schneiders, Tošo Dabac, and Dimitar Čulić, *Yugoslavia* (New York: Viking Press, 1969), a book of photographs, with an introduction by the British novelist Fitzroy Maclean, who had been sent by Churchill on a mission to Yugoslavia in 1943; however, it is puzzling why it should be designated as "not in print."

139. Dennis Wrong, "The Case of the *New York Review*," *Commentary* 50 (November 1970): 49–63.

140. Alexander M. Bickel, "The Courts: Need for Change," *New York Times* (22 October 1970): 47; Charles A. Reich, "The Rebirth of a Future: II," *New York Times* (22 October 1970): 47;

my mother insisted in cooking oatmeal all night for breakfast. The result reminds me strongly of the condition of Charlie's mind. Somebody told me the other day he had been strongly urged to read Charlie's effusions. He could not remember who it was had mentioned it, except that he was extremely impressed with the man. I asked him if he could possibly be Dick Sewell. "The very man," he replied.

[deletion]

> CVWP, 8/76: TCLU

198. To William Styron Sr.[141]

NOVEMBER 17, 1970

You are right that Dr. R. T. Vann was the president of Meredith College and that he was a great-uncle of mine.[142] I remember him well. He had lost both arms in a sorghum mill in his youth, but he was an expert shot with a rifle, could kill a squirrel at 100 feet, and was known to embrace and kiss women without any arms. I always thought of him as a great man.

[deletion]

> CVWP, 52/626: TCLU

199. To Eugene D. Genovese

DECEMBER 3, 1970

[deletion]

Some observations on your two slavery essays, both of which I enjoyed enormously and praise highly.[143] First, about the *New York Review*

Arthur I. Waskow, "The Jewish Contradiction," *New York Times* (21 October 1970): 47. Charles A. Reich (b. 1928), professor of law at Yale, had recently published *The Greening of America: How the Youth Revolution Is Trying to Make America Livable* (New York: Random House, 1970).

141. The father of the novelist.

142. Richard Tilman Vann (1851–1941) was president of a woman's college in Raleigh, NC (1900–15). The college changed its name during Vann's tenure; it had started as Baptist Female University in 1891, became Baptist University for Women in 1904, and Meredith College in 1909. It was named for Thomas Meredith, a founder of the Baptist State Convention of North Carolina and editor of the *Biblical Recorder*.

143. Eugene D. Genovese, "American Slaves and Their History," *New York Review of Books* 15 (3 December 1970): 34–43. The other essay is less clear; Eugene D. Genovese, "The Influ-

piece. If you are shooting birds, especially small birds, like Lemisch, number 8 standard bird shot will do. Save your buckshot for bigger game. I was not sure how much you were backtracking on the Black nationalists. I wondered if the prominence of the drivers in post-emancipation settings was not simply due to the fact that he knew more about seed and planting and prices and markets than anybody else available. Your use of the Louisiana Diaries as evidence was expert but I am sure you will have more to back up your point.

I also liked the piece on slave religious history and found myself in agreement, but one of your research assignments is to be a witness to a real primitive black church service, preferably in the black belt. Don't trust video tape or TV, and I doubt if it is transportable to the ghetto. You have to see it in the flesh and you might have the help of O Marster. It can be arranged. Second, I don't think you can duck analysis of the spirituals as evidence, as thorny as that subject is. Also, in spite of thorniness, I think you have to explore the psycho-analytical approach to De Lawd, as father image. Ditto on "the linguistic side," especially speech as verbal gesticulation.

I agree that Willie's piece on Brown was quite something.[144]

I will be writing you after Christmas in response to the letter signed by you and Engerman on the comparison of slavery systems.[145]

CVWP, 21/240: TCLU

---

ence of the Black Power Movement on Historical Scholarship: Reflections of a White Historian," *Daedalus* 99 (Spring 1970): 473–94, does contains remarks on the importance of studying slave religion, but can scarcely be described as a "piece on slave religious history."

144. Willie Lee (Nichols) Rose (b. 1927) had been CVW's graduate student at Hopkins; after a period at the University of Virginia, she taught at Johns Hopkins. See Willie Lee Rose, "Killing for Freedom," *New York Review of Books* 15 (3 December 1970): 12–19, a review of various books on John Brown, Frederick Douglass, and black abolitionists; this was later reprinted in her *Slavery and Freedom*, expanded ed., ed. William W. Freehling (New York: Oxford University Press, 1982), 148–60.

145. A conference was proposed in 1972 on "International Comparison of Systems of Slavery": see Eugene D. Genovese and Stanley Engerman to CVW, 2 December 1970. The letter asked for suggestions about topics and scholars, including graduate students, active in the inquiry.

200. To Robert F. Berkhofer Jr.[146]

DECEMBER 9, 1970

Many thanks for the copy of your review of the Comparative Approach, which I have read with much interest and profit.[147] With many of your criticisms I am in agreement and with some of them I think you are actually too light-handed. Had I undertaken the same exercise myself from your particular point of view I would have probably been less generous. You know perhaps that similar collections of essays were published for all the social science disciplines with authors of comparable standing. I wonder how many of these books received comparable attention in the learned journals of anthropologists, economists, etc., and how sternly the ten page "think pieces" of these authors were held to the standards of social science. Doubtless they should have been, but you will see that what I am suggesting is that you may have given this book more attention than it deserved. This may have been my fault in dignifying a collection of popular essays with too pretentious a title.

My worst failing, however, entirely escapes your attention, mainly because you were one of its victims. That is, my failure to make myself understood. It is clearly illustrated in your impression that "for Woodward, comparison is not to establish similarities but uniqueness." My whole intention was the opposite, to make some breach in the cult of uniqueness. I do, I find, point out in the opening section that "emphasis on uniqueness and distinctness are the result of a national 'insecurity of identity'" and in the final pages report "the conservative uses of the doctrine of American exceptionalism[.]" I refer to the Great Depression as undermining "the myth of American uniqueness," and refer in the same paragraph to "the legend of American exceptionalism," and in the next applaud the erosion of "the foundations of the old faith," that is, the faith in uniqueness. I do make concessions of propitiatory sort to the strong cult of uniqueness in our guild. I admit that the American myths of invincibility, success and innocence are "not wholly without foundation in history," but all along I have an underlying attack on the Yankee myth

---

146. Robert F. Berkhofer Jr. (b. 1931), a historian of American Indians with an interest in the philosophy of history, then at the University of Wisconsin.

147. Berkhofer, review of CVW, ed., *The Comparative Approach to American History* (New York: Basic Books, 1968), in *Journal of Social History* 3 (Winter 1969–70): 163–71.

of uniqueness and much of what I have written about Southern history is—and in fact I regard that history as—a means of undermining these myths. But obviously I was unable to make myself understood. As an experienced teacher you will know that lessons taught are not necessarily lessons learned.

I am, however, venturing on a project in comparative history in which I will welcome your advice. This is a study of emancipations and reconstructions. I am impressed with the light that comparative history has brought to the understanding of slavery and think it might also contribute to the understanding of emancipations. Do such writers as David Davis, Gene Genovese and Stanley Elkins qualify as comparative historians according to your tests? I have, of course, read your book and learned much from it.[148] I do not share your optimism about history qualifying as a science and establishing laws. Perhaps I should avoid the word 'comparison,' though I am reluctant to abandon it to the social sciences along with the other good words which have been defined out of common usage. My hope is simply to put thinking about the American experience into a context of hemispheric experience and rescue it from the parochialism and moralism that has characterized the field. I would hope to be not only descriptive but analytical in some measure. Is such an enterprise doomed to failure for not finding "truly comparable units of analysis"? Am I bound to some Karl Deutsch ruse of a game?[149] Could I evade the rules by avoiding the preempted term "comparison"? Would I be too frivolous if I undertook, as I said in one of my essays, to "illuminate a discussion after the manner of an imagined and disciplined use of simile, metaphor and analogy"?

You obviously keep up with the literature on this subject much better than I do and I will eagerly follow any of the suggestions you make about models and methods.

CVWP, 6/52: TCLU

148. Robert F. Berkhofer, *A Behavioral Approach to Historical Analysis* (New York: Free Press, 1969).

149. Karl W. Deutsch (1912–1992), a Czech political scientist who taught at Harvard; he was an influential theorist of nationalism, notably in *Nationalism and Social Communication: An Enquiry into the Foundations of Nationality* (Cambridge, MA: M.I.T. Press, 1953).

201. To Herbert Aptheker

JANUARY 26, 1971

I was delighted to learn that you had completed the first volume of the DuBois correspondence and that it is to be published this year.[150] At the same time, I am worried to hear that the project is limited to four volumes and that the first volume will go all the way down to 1934. I cannot believe that this will give you adequate coverage. The Booker Washington papers are probably going to run to ten volumes, and talk of a new edition of the Douglass papers in terms of the same scope. Is there any chance of expanding the project?

I am thinking of course about the needs of other scholars that will not be fully met by such a limited publication. May I ask if the original manuscripts down to 1934 may now be made accessible to qualified research students in some good and accessible library? Have any plans been made to find such a library? May I open the question with the Yale Library. The presence here of the James Weldon Johnson papers is an argument in itself for the addition of the DuBois papers. You must be aware of the great need and demand among historians for free access to this material and I am sure you will want to find an appropriate solution.

Needless to say, you are at liberty to use the youthful letter of mine you found in the DuBois papers in such a way as you please.[151] To answer another question, I did not talk to DuBois after that letter. I had, however, talked to him much earlier, I think it was in 1931 or 1932, when I was a graduate student at Columbia. My impressions are really not worth much since they were characteristic of a much over-awed and nervous young man.

My very best wishes for your work. I am extremely interested in the progress and plans and I hope you will keep me informed.

CVWP, 85/2: TCLU

202. To Herbert Aptheker

FEBRUARY 16, 1971

Many thanks for your letter setting me right on my misconceptions of your publications on Du Bois. It is a genuine relief to learn that you were not regarding the two volumes of letters for Lippincott as an

---

150. Herbert Aptheker, ed., *The Correspondence of W. E. B. DuBois: 1—Selections, 1877–1934* (Amherst: University of Massachusetts Press, 1973).

151. Reprinted above.

adequate publication of the Du Bois correspondence. You would readily agree that, as useful as these are, they would not be what the scholarly community requires. I note that you have provided in your contract with Lippincott that you retain the right to contract for the publication of a full and complete edition of the correspondence elsewhere. This plus your legal custody of the Du Bois papers surely provides you with ample protection for any competitive edition.

There are many instances, and you can think of them, where editors of private papers have proceeded with their editions over long periods of years while the manuscripts they are editing are made fully available to qualified scholars. I wonder if you could not reach some agreement with a library that would benefit both you and the other members of the scholarly community who need to use the papers for other purposes. I know this must be an embarrassment to you to have a constant request for use of the Du Bois papers and that you must regret having to reject legitimate use by others. Could we correspond about this matter, or meet and discuss it? I might be of some help in finding a solution.

P.S. I must look up the grave of Du Bois' grandfather.

CVWP, 85/2: TCLU

203. To Robert B. Butler[152]

APRIL 26, 1971

[deletion]

As for your other questions: (1) I do not define history, (2) I am interested in Southern history because it is obviously the most interesting subject available, (3) I will leave to my critics the estimate of my contributions, (4) As to my purposes in writing books, they might be defined as to amuse, instruct, and turn an honest buck.

[deletion]

CVWP, 6/56: TCLU

204. To Robert Penn Warren

JULY 22, 1971

I tossed off *Homage to TD* in one self-indulgent gulp only to realize, with a scorched throat and whirling head, that it was made for sippin and not

---

152. A student at Lakeland College in Plymouth, WI.

gulping and that I would have to do it again slowly for the real flavor.[153] But I did get the impact that way even if I missed much of the finer points and the benefits of aging and concentration.

It took me back to the thirties and a youthful visit to Terre Haute to see about the possibilities of doing biography of Gene Debs. Talking to a lot of old people with that in mind, I didn't find out anything about Dreiser but remember having him in mind and wondering about him and trying to relate him to that forsaken town. (Debs' brother didn't like my southern accent and wasn't about to let me into the papers.) What a story! And Debs might have been too in a different way.

And I need not add how much Glenn and I were moved by the dedication and the inscription.

RPW, 82/1611: TLS

205. To Michael O'Brien[154]

MAY 19, 1972

It was most kind of you to send me a copy of your paper on my work. You may be sure that I have read it with much interest. Once more I have the good fortune to find a critic who is not only fair minded and generous but perceptive. The least I can do is to give you a candid response.

You show a great deal of understanding and, I think, sympathy for my problems. It would have been easier to use hindsight to expose ambiguities and inconsistencies. Those you have pointed out with restraint are in the main accurately identified and placed in context. Of course I have been aware of some of them myself, and tried to acknowledge and sometimes correct them. My last book contained several such exercises. But you have sharpened my awareness of certain problems and pointed out others I have neglected or that escaped me. For all this I am most grateful.

The "Liberal" label has given me most trouble. The only time I felt comfortable with it was during the Civil Rights Movement of the

153. Robert Penn Warren, *Homage to Theodore Dreiser, August 27, 1871–December 28, 1945, on the Centennial of His Birth* (New York: Random House, 1971).

154. Michael O'Brien (b. 1948), an English historian of American intellectual culture. Just before becoming a research student at the University of Cambridge, he had written an essay on CVW's work; it was published as "C. Vann Woodward and the Burden of Southern Liberalism," *American Historical Review* 78 (June 1973): 589–604.

1960's—simply to distinguish one from those who were in the opposition. The only "Liberal" in the period about which I wrote most with whom I felt any identification was George W. Cable—and for the same reason. I need not underline for you my aversion to the Grady, Page, Mims school, which as you say celebrated the arrival of the Southern bourgeoisie.[155] And for all my strictures on the Conservatives, I suppose I would have found them rather more congenial—especially on the "lessons." With the Liberals of the 1940's and 50's, save on the race issue, I never felt much closeness, especially on the consensus question and on the Cold War. Liberals of that period were too conservative for me. One of my problems you failed to see was my close friendship with Hofstadter and Potter, with whom I understated my differences on some matters. But Potter was quoting me correctly in once calling myself "a liberal, even more, a Southern white liberal." But you must understand the context. I had been called in to a Socialist Scholars Conference to mediate between two embattled Marxists, Aptheker and Genovese. Thoroughly enjoying the opportunity, I pointed it up by giving myself that unfortunate description. If I were compelled to accept some label from the past I would better have called myself a Populist—and opened myself to all *those* problems. So far as my history writing is concerned, I think I am more at home with Marxism. I believe my interpretation of the post Civil War South fits rather well with Genovese's reading of the Old Regime—though we have our differences on the class-race question. You might conclude that I am claiming to be a Liberal Conservative Populist Marxist! Actually I am trying to shun all labels. But critics will use them, and I suppose they have to.

Should you indeed pursue the matter of publication, if your interest in [the] subject has not been completely exhausted, I suggest you have a look at two items. One is my *American Counterpoint* published last year by Little, Brown & Company. Its subtitle, by the way, is "Slavery and Racism in the North-South Dialogue." It contains several things you have not

155. All these were publicists for the New South creed and believers in the South's industrial modernization: Henry W. Grady (1850–1889), editor of the *Atlanta Constitution;* Walter Hines Page (1855–1918), a North Carolina journalist, notable for *The Rebuilding of Old Commonwealths, Being Essays Toward the Training of the Forgotten Man in the Southern States* (New York: Doubleday, Page, 1902); and Edwin Mims (1872–1959), an English professor at Vanderbilt University and the author of *The Advancing South: Stories of Progress and Reaction* (Garden City, NY: Doubleday, Page, 1926).

seen and indicates some of my discomforts and responses to criticism. A second item you may find of interest is an essay by Sheldon Hackney of Princeton assessing *Origins of the New South* after twenty years. It appeared recently in the May issue of the *Journal of Southern History*.[156] The latter journal will have had all it can use of this subject. I really don't know about the AHR.[157] You might think of the Journal of American History, the American Quarterly or the British Journal of American Studies. In case you do pursue the matter further I hope you will let me know, especially if the new items I mention alter your view in any way.

Again, let me say what pleasure and profit I took in your essay. The question occurred to me as I read it that your name might furnish a clue to your interest in the history of the South. No?

Private Collection: TLS

206. To Wallace T. MacCaffrey[158]

SEPTEMBER 18, 1972

I am happy to write as you requested about the qualifications of Professor David Donald for an appointment in your department.

When I resigned from Johns Hopkins in 1961, I recommended the appointment of David Donald, then at Princeton, to take the place that I was giving up in the Hopkins History Department. I told my colleagues that I thought he was the best man in his field, that it might not always be easy to live with him, but that I thought that the effort would be well worth making. I believe that his performance and usefulness to the Hopkins department have more than justified my recommendation.

In the last ten years, Donald has reached a high level of productivity and maintained high standards in what he has published. I have not always agreed with what he has written, but I think well of his Sumner biography, and I appreciate the boldness of his experiment in quantify-

---

156. Sheldon Hackney, "*Origins of the New South* in Retrospect," *Journal of Southern History* 38 (May 1972): 191–216.

157. It had been suggested to O'Brien by a friend, Jonathan Steinberg, that the essay be sent to the *American Historical Review*. Like CVW, O'Brien was dubious of the idea, but agreed to Steinberg submitting it.

158. Wallace T. MacCaffrey (b. 1920), a historian of Elizabethan England and chair of the Harvard Department of History.

ing Congressional voting during Reconstruction, even if I do not find his methods always acceptable.[159]

From the talks with students we have had in common both at Princeton and at Hopkins, I am convinced that Donald is a superior and inspiring teacher both at undergraduate and at graduate levels.

It is not possible for me to comment about his future work. I have talked with him about some of his plans, but not recently, and I am not at all sure what his major project is at present. Past performance, however, persuades me that he is still at the crest of his powers and that he has years of productivity ahead of him.

You asked for possible alternative appointments to consider, but I am at a loss to think of any who would offer serious competition. I think that your department would do well to appoint Mr. Donald.

CVWP, 25/285: TCLU

207. To Paul J. Vanderwood[160]

JANUARY 22, 1973

It is true that I did join a temporary board of advisors on David Wolper's film series on American history.[161] However, I have recently resigned from the board. I have actually a great deal of respect for the one sample of his historic films I have seen, namely the one on Appomatox. I withdrew because I did not like the idea of association with future films over which I would have no control.

To answer some of your questions, of course film productions have to take liberties with facts. It is a kind of historical fiction. I recognize the necessity of this license, but I am uneasy as an historian about offering any fictionalized history to students. Historians normally distort history enough without assistance from the movies. I have never tried such experiments as the one you describe at San Diego State called "History Through Film." I frankly shudder at the thought. Of course, such films as you mention could be offered as "documents," as "products of the

---

159. David Donald, *Charles Sumner and the Coming of the Civil War* (New York: Alfred A. Knopf, 1960); idem., *Charles Sumner and the Rights of Man* (New York: Alfred A. Knopf, 1970).

160. Paul J. Vanderwood (1922–2011), who taught Mexican history at San Diego State University and had an interest in media and history.

161. David Lloyd Wolper (1928–2010), the leading producer of historical documentaries for American television.

time and culture," but not to my taste, as "Historical representations of the event under study." I suppose that this means that I reject not only the future but the present.

CVWP, 57/681: TCLU

208. To Robert W. Fogel[162]

FEBRUARY 6, 1973

I read the latest batch of manuscript, especially chapters five and six, with a continued sense of the intellectual excitement attending an important breakthrough in American history. I don't know how much I can eventually accept or prove, but I can feel confident that what you are doing is important.

I think most of your troubles will come from within your own tribe of econometricians. In their criticisms I cannot participate. The following observations are of a different character.

First is the matter of your title, *Time on the Cross.* In spirit and rhetoric, this is a thoroughly neo-Abolitionist phrase. It seems to me wholly out of character with the thesis. The first sentence in your prologue identifies the "time" as the time of slavery, yet your thesis is that the ills of slavery have been greatly exaggerated, and that the ordeal that followed slavery was even worse. Are you being deliberately paradoxical, or are you being propitiatory? If the latter, it is unworthy of you; if the former, it is confusing.

My impression is that Olmstead's observations on slavery underwent some significant revision between the time of their appearance in the New York *Times,* and their publication in the final edition in 1860.[163]

I am disturbed by your dismissal of all historiography between Helper and econometricians and think you might temper that with some exceptions.

I like this version of your prologue better than any previous one.

162. Robert W. Fogel (b. 1926), the American economic historian, then at the University of Chicago; CVW was reading the manuscript of what would become Robert William Fogel and Stanley L. Engerman, *Time on the Cross: The Economics of American Negro Slavery* (Boston: Little Brown, 1974).

163. CVW seems to mean Frederick Law Olmsted, *A Journey in the Back Country* (New York: Mason Brothers, 1860), although he had earlier published *A Journey in the Seaboard Slave States: With Remarks on Their Economy* (New York: Dix & Edwards, 1856).

I am sometimes reminded of George Fitzhugh in some of your flights of analogy: In Chapter 6, pp. 43–47, you lightly compare "athletes, movie stars and minors" with chattel slaves as "human capital property right in line," and on p. 47, the analogy to the use of parental force today.

I am troubled by your tossing off the penalties of slave status as "non-pecuniary disadvantages" and assessing them as greater than 50% of the wages of free labor. My brain reels also as you fix "non-pecuniary disadvantages" of gang labor as $75 and accounting the "non-pecuniary loss of $90,000,000 offset by $60,000,000 of pecuniary return."

Is it accurate to describe slave income as "pecuniary" when that word refers to money?

In your Epilogue, you say that "all but a few black historians" brought "the crude racist premise" to the rights of Southern history down to World War II. I hesitate to remind you that I published a book in 1938 on Southern history, and that I disclaim the "crude racist premise" in that particular work.

You say that Abolitionists "did as much as any other group, perhaps more, to fasten the spikes that have kept blacks in their agony." I think you ought to have a look at a book by a former student of mine, Jim McPherson, *The Struggle for Equality*, which is a defense of the Abolitionists against that charge.

Here's wishing you luck in your struggles against your fellow econometricians. I look forward to the next installment of the manuscript.

CVWP, 18/216: TCLU

209. To Lee Benson

MARCH 16, 1973

M any thanks for sending me your latest manifesto.[164] I read it with the interest I always have in your pronouncements.

I was troubled by your indictment of historians "as a group" as having "contributed little to the advancement of social thought." What troubles me is the large number of worthy historians that are put beyond the Pale by this criterion. I can think, for example, of Perry Miller, *Mind of*

---

164. Lee Benson, "Group Cohesion and Social and Ideological Conflict," *American Behavioral Scientist* 16 (May–June 1973): 741–67.

New England, Sam Morison's *Columbus,* Braudel's work on the Mediterranean and my old colleague Brad Lane's life work on the history of Venice.[165] Must I now dismiss these worthies as frivolous fellows, failing to "contribute to the advancement of social thought?"

Permit me one admonition. You know, Lee, you are writing at the top of your voice. I estimate that the average page in this essay contains 17.38 italicized words. You even add italics to quoted passages. How can I tell what is important if everything turns out to be important?

Power to you.

CVWP, 8/73: TCLU

210. To Eugene D. Genovese

APRIL 2, 1973

I enclose for what they're worth my jottings on Book I at Guadeloupe.[166] I think they are legible. They are certainly candid. Some of them may be a trifle rum-soaked. I hope they're worth looking over.

I confess I turned to the manuscript with misgivings because of your firm prediction that I was not going to like it. I cannot imagine at this juncture just what you had in mind. The fact is that so far I like it better than anything you have done. You seem to be writing with greater assurance and authority, with more balance and ease than you have before. What you write seems less abstract, less thesis-ridden, more soaked in concrete evidence. The only thing that I quibble about is toward the end of Book I. I suddenly encountered a kind of preachy note there quite uncharacteristic of the rest of the manuscript. Maybe this was what you had in mind when you said I wasn't going to like it. I only hope it does not increase in the parts to come.

---

165. Perry Miller, *The New England Mind: The Seventeenth Century* (New York: Macmillan, 1939); idem., *The New England Mind: From Colony to Province* (Cambridge, MA: Harvard University Press, 1953); Samuel Eliot Morison, *Admiral of the Ocean Sea: A Life of Christopher Columbus* (Boston: Little, Brown, 1942); Fernand Braudel, *La Méditerranée et le monde Méditerranéen à l'époque de Philippe II* (Paris: Colin, 1949); Frederic C. Lane, *Venice and History: The Collected Papers of Frederic C. Lane* (Baltimore: Johns Hopkins Press, 1966); idem., *Venice, a Maritime Republic* (Baltimore: Johns Hopkins University Press, 1973).

166. CVW was reading the manuscript of Eugene D. Genovese, *Roll, Jordan, Roll: The World the Slaves Made* (New York: Pantheon Books, 1974).

I have received the second shipment and have already started reading it. More notes will follow when I have the time; less rum-soaked and tropic-softened.[167]

[deletion]

GUADELOUPE

Introduction to Book One

On paternalism Philip Mason, *Patterns of Dominance* may interest you. I can't agree with him in making paternalism a post-slavery phase. But he is worth arguing with. On this he has changed his view from the essay *Prospero's Magic*.[168]

Your distinction between "a direct relationship" of individuals and a relationship between races is most important. Still, as you admit, there was a lot of overlapping. The extent of that is the argument between us.

Note apparent contradiction of p. 14 (reproduction of slave population *before* closing of slave trade) on p 15 ("reproduction of slave population occurred *after* the closing of the slave trade")[.]

You probably do it later, but I felt the need of explicit comparison of "introduction" of slavery with and slavery without paternalism.

On p. 18 point (6) I would have preferred "race paternalism" to "class paternalism." But that introduces an essentially post-bellum (post-slavery) issue concerning the new order that you may not want to handle here.

Book One: Part I

On overseers, pp. 30–32, how much stock do you take in Fogel & Engerman's estimates of the percentage of planters who employed white overseers. (I wonder how to get the data.)

You handle the "impish paradox" of the overseer's lot with subtlety. What a tightrope he walked! What a hell of a life he led.

The transition from overseers to beginning of the law seems abrupt to the point of non-sequitur.

167. The ensuing text is in longhand.

168. Philip Mason, *Patterns of Dominance* (London: Oxford University Press, 1970); idem., *Prospero's Magic: Some Thoughts on Class and Race* (London: Oxford University Press, 1962).

On the administration of law in slave cases you *must* see a Harvard dissertation by [169]

A few articles from it have been published, one on Texas, one on Alabama, and others. I believe you cite one.[170]

I was surprised to find no reference to James Hugo Johnston, *Race Relations in Virginia, 1776–1860*[.][171]

I was impressed by your delineation of the dual law system of the slave South, but not always sure I understood it. I felt the need of a few concrete examples. I thought it needlessly abstract. I think you could handle my objection with a little thought.

Your "paradox" of 1831–61 as reaction-and-progress seems to me to hold up. A phrase might be added absolving the liberals of consciousness of paradox. *If* you are implying that the Virginia debates represented any serious effort of abolition, I think you are wrong.

You know, you might make concessions to Bill Freehling's picture of Jefferson's *long-range* statesmanship of confinement and constriction of slavery without damage to your main thesis of the dominant paradox.[172] Jefferson himself does not belong in the paradox[.]

So far (p. 100) this is an admirable book about the masters and their problems, not about slaves and theirs. An observation, not criticism. Still, the title led me to expect something else. Later perhaps.

A bit troubled (p. 122) over the analogy between A. Jackson's expectations and discipline of his slaves and his demands of his Indian fighting troops. Discipline of a sort, yes. Slavish civility—decidedly not! And the degree of discipline sustained in the Jacksonian ranks would have

169. There is a space here, presumably because CVW could not remember the name. But it is Arnold Edmund Keir Nash, "Negro Rights and Judicial Behavior in the Old South" (Ph.D. diss., Harvard University, 1968).

170. The eventual text cited two articles, but not the dissertation: A. E. Keir Nash, "Fairness and Formalism in the Trials of Blacks in the State Supreme Courts of the Old South," *Virginia Law Review* 56 (February 1970): 64–100; idem., "The Texas Supreme Court and the Trial Rights of Blacks, 1845–1860," *Journal of American History* 58 (December 1971): 622–42; see Genovese, *Roll, Jordan, Roll*, 684, n.6.

171. James Hugo Johnston, *Race Relations in Virginia and Miscegenation in the South, 1776–1860* (Amherst: University of Massachusetts Press, 1970).

172. The standpoint of William W. Freehling, "The Founding Fathers and Slavery," *American Historical Review* 77 (February 1972): 81–93.

appalled the modern drill sergeant as much as that in the Confederate ranks[.]

I am struck by your neglect so far of the class conflict between blacks (not merely slaves) and nonslaveholding whites. White planters drew significant lines between classes of whites, the blacks, so far as I can see, perceived only two classes of whites. All non slaveholders for them seem to have been po' whites. And they were the hated and feared patrollers[.]

The common elements in the harshest and the most flattering portraits of the slave masters are skillfully blended. You make a telling point in citing both and showing what they have in common.

About the quotations from *Children of Pride* (excellent all) remember that the editor is a jealous and litiginous man. *En garde!* He can be very difficult, as the Y U P can tell you.[173]

[illegible word] grave repercussions.

Your paragraphs of summation on master attitudes toward slave defections (p 156) is superb. And in the whole section its marshaling of evidence is masterful.

Book One, Part 2

p. 200—Still no penetration of the Black mask? No. There has been. But by inference. By their own acts of defection and "unfaithfulness." So far, however, it's a book about the masters—of which I have little but admiration. With such riches, why should I complain?

But I see very shortly that I complained too soon.

p. 238. The fourth rum punch. Low sun through the bougainvillea and acacia. Soft slush of surf on the beach, rustle of palm leaves overhead—"de kindness, suh," and that "possessive pronoun that worked both ways." And into the rum punch splashes one salt tear. Holy Mary, Mother of God! "Furl that banner / furl it slowly / for it is holy." Maybe, Gene, you are the only one who could get by with this. Who else would dare? One more rum punch and I will be prepared for whatever comeuppance you will deal out to ole massa. After all, he in de cole, cole ground[.]

CVW, 21/241: TCLU/ALU

173. Robert Manson Myers, ed., *The Children of Pride: A True Story of Georgia and the Civil War* (New Haven: Yale University Press, 1972).

211. To Marcus Cunliffe[174]

APRIL 16, 1973

I had hoped to talk to you about this matter, but evidently you are not coming over before next fall, and I do not expect to be over there before then. A letter will have to do. Though if you are disposed (as I hope you will be) to explore the question further, Byron Hollinshead, Jr., Vice-President of the U.S. Oxford University Press, will be flying over April 23 for five days and hopes you will get in touch with him at Ely House, the London headquarters of Oxford Press, while he is there.

But I am getting ahead of myself. The situation is this: Bill Freehling had agreed to do Volume 5 in the Oxford History of the United States, the period 1848–1865, but now wants to be relieved of the assignment.[175] I am disposed to accommodate him. (After Dick's death, I took over the task of editing the series without a collaborator.) I want to know if you would be interested in taking over Volume 5 of the Oxford History.

You will immediately ask why I do not turn to an American specialist in the period. The reasons are numerous, but there is always something wrong. For one thing, American specialists generally either begin or end their period of specialization with 1860. There are no more Nevinses. Dave Potter is gone, and the generalists dislike military history. Then, too, I confess I find American specialists in this field suspect. They tend to feel justified in writing a new book only by adding a "new interpretation" or "new data"—which oftener than not turn out to be tedious, pedantic, or unimportant. What is needed for this task are skill in synthesis, the gift of blending narrative with analysis, detachment, balance, and above all, writing ability. So I turn to you. Besides the Civil War is, of all American history, an English subject. English historians are not frightened by the specialists. All Americans would be first off or intimidated by the knowledge that Potter's posthumous work on the coming of the Civil War is going to be published. But you would properly consider that sheer good fortune.

174. Marcus Cunliffe (1922–1990), a British scholar of American studies whom CVW had first met when the latter was Harmsworth Professor and Cunliffe was at the University of Manchester. In the 1970s he was Professor of American Studies at the University of Sussex; in 1980 he moved to George Washington University.

175. William W. Freehling (b. 1935), then teaching at Johns Hopkins, was best known for *Prelude to Civil War: The Nullification Controversy in South Carolina, 1816–1836* (New York: Harper & Row, 1966).

Still, I am quite aware that it is a large undertaking, perhaps the largest of your career. I know you would not undertake it lightly. The volumes are intended to run as long as 600 pages. We had set 1976 as the publication date. A few of the volumes are well along and will appear by that time, but several will come along later. Starting late, you would need more time, but I should feel compelled to get the volume published by 1980.

Your fellow authors in the Oxford History would be John Alden, down to 1750; Robert Middlekauf, 1750–1789; Eric McKitrick and Stanley Elkins (two non-specialists for your company), 1789–1812; Charles Sellers, 1812–1848; Morton Keller, 1865–1900; William Harbaugh, 1900–1929; William Leuchtenburg, 1929–1945; Ernest May, 1945–1970. I may have some of these dates slightly askew, but in any case, there will be overlapping. In addition, there will be a volume of economic history by Stuart Bruchey and one on foreign relations by Norman Graebner.[176]

It is our intention to make this a distinguished history, outstanding for its appeal to the intelligent laymen as well as to the academic reader. Our long-term market will be largely college and university users. The Oxford University Press is strongly backing the venture. You will, I think, find the contract offered by the press unusually attractive, and its representative ready to talk about advance royalties. I will not go into these subjects here. Byron Hollinshead can answer all your questions along those lines. I only hope you will see him while he is there.

Is it still your plan to teach in the U.S. next fall? Would it not be the ideal time to start on Volume 5 of the Oxford History? It would be great to work with you on this book. It would have the additional merit of bringing us together more and bringing you over more often. I do hope very much you will find the idea both attractive and feasible.

CVWP, 13/147: TCLU

212. To Sheldon Hackney

JUNE 26, 1973

I did not feel so much like an artifact as a man reading his obituary—an obituary by a rather ill-informed writer.[177] The fellow sent me his paper last year. It never occurred to me that he would persuade anybody to publish it, or I would have set him right on a few points. As it was, I

---

176. In the event, none of these, apart from Middlekauf, published volumes in the series.
177. Michael O'Brien.

merely cautioned him about the simplifications of the "liberal" tag and pointed out that it was no secret that I was instead a conservative, Populist Marxist. I assume the fellow meant well by the whole matter.

I would be more interested in your assessment of my exchange with another critic in the JAH of recent issue.[178] Unfortunately, the editor invited my reply but tucked it away in the back.

[deletion]

> CVWP, 24/272: TCLU

213. To Bertram Wyatt-Brown

AUGUST 2, 1973

Your remarks about our difference over the theme of continuity in Southern history recall an exchange I had with my old and great friend Bill Carleton, who is writing a book in which continuity is the overriding theme and the folk mind a basic concern. The two of you have much in common and I wish you could know each other. It was partly in response to correspondence with Carleton that I made concessions to the theme of continuity and to Cash in *American Counterpoint,* pages 275–276. In that, I say Cash's "insistence on the durability of the folk mind, the cultural heritage and anthropological constants in Southern history is healthily corrective." I admire your essay (was it ever published?) on the folk mind for the same reason.[179] I think that history is impossible without the geological, the biological and the anthropological constants. On the other hand, I do not think of these constants as essentially history. History is the record of change in time. Admittedly, anthropology changes, but more at the pace of evolution than at the pace of history. I suspect the Russian peasant's mind was much the same under feudal serfdom, under capitalism and under communism. But in the meantime, history was undergoing some important changes. My generalizations on continuity are, of course, highly relative and the references are obviously to the rest of the United States.

[deletion]

> CVWP, 61/738: TCLU

---

178. Allan Peskin, "Was There a Compromise of 1877?," *Journal of American History* 60 (June 1973): 63–75.

179. Presumably Bertram Wyatt-Brown, "The Antimission Movement in the Jacksonian South: A Study in Regional Folk Culture," *Journal of Southern History* 36 (November 1970): 501–29.

214. To William R. Emerson

AUGUST 21, 1973

This is in reference to the application of Dr. Herbert Aptheker, Log #10097.

I had assumed when I agreed to serve on Mr. Aptheker's Board of Editorial Advisors that the "papers" of W. E. B. Du Bois certainly included his correspondence. I now learn from his letter to you of August 2 that the term "papers" does not apply to correspondence. Under these conditions, I am unable to support his application. I realize that he is publishing a couple of volumes of the Du Bois correspondence separately, but the first one, already in print, covers more than sixty years of his life and cannot be a serious contribution to scholarship.

I am writing Mr. Aptheker urging him to reconsider his plans. Until he does, my attitude toward his application is quite negative. My recommendation to your committee would be to defer the matter.

CVWP, 85/2: TCLU

215. To Herbert Aptheker

AUGUST 21, 1973

I have just learned that your project for ten volumes of "Unpublished papers and manuscripts of W. E. B. Du Bois" will include none of the Du Bois correspondence. This comes as a surprise to me. I had assumed when I agreed to serve on your Advisory Board that the correspondence would be the main material included.

I realize that you are publishing separately a couple of volumes of "selected correspondence" but since the first volume includes all the correspondence down to 1934, I assume that this is for popular consumption only. By 1934, Du Bois was older than Booker Washington when the latter died and must have had quite as important a correspondence. Louis Harlan says that eighty per cent of his volumes will be given over to correspondence. I feel sure you would agree that Du Bois is no less a figure than Washington in our history and that his letters deserve an equally serious edition.

I hope you will reconsider your plans and persuade your publisher to support your decision. I could not in all conscience remain on your Board in support of the present plan. Do let me hear from you.

CVWP, 85/2: TCLU

216. To Walter Johnson[180]

SEPTEMBER 6, 1973

I found your letter on my return from a vacation in the Canadian Rock-ies where I have been almost as far removed from the news as you have in the Fiji Islands.[181] But, of course, I did listen fairly faithfully to the Sen-ate Committee hearings and absorbed much of the flood of comment that the hearings have precipitated. You know the kind of people I talk to, and I cannot for a moment pretend that their reactions, nor mine, are typical of anything. For what they are worth, though, here are a few impressions.

I think it is fair to say that the interest of the informed public is by no means confined to the question of Nixon's personal responsibility for the Watergate affair. There is a pretty wide understanding that the affair is significant for several constitutional and moral crises that it symbolizes. Nobody is blind to the extent of the crisis—the fact that it involves virtu-ally every branch of the executive department.

I had dinner last night with Alex Bickel and Gil Harrison. We agreed that the next three years were fairly unthinkable without some resolution of the charges against the Administration. I differed from them in not ruling out impeachment. Alex thinks that Agnew is bound to be indicted and that this will open the way for what he calls the "Compromise of 1973."[182] Since the indictment would call into action for the first time the Twenty fifth Amendment and make it mandatory for the President to nominate a Vice President who would have to have the approval of a majority of both houses, Alex thinks that this would necessitate a grand compromise that would resolve differences between the Congress and the President as well as between the Judiciary and the President. I am scepti-cal of this outcome but Gil agrees and thinks that the overall effect would be a cancellation of the "mandate" Nixon claims and a substitution of a moderate democratic type administration. Gil is despondent about the mood of the country. He thinks that the dominant mood is an apathetic feeling that it might have been worse and that this is the best we could do

180. Walter Johnson (1915–1985), a historian of postwar America who had taught at the University of Chicago (1943–66), then at the University of Hawaii (1966–82).

181. Johnson was on sabbatical from Hawaii and teaching for a semester at the University of the South Pacific on Suva, Fiji.

182. Spiro T. Agnew (1918–1996), Richard Nixon's vice president.

anyway considering the system we've got. For the immediate future the critical issue lies between the Executive and the Judiciary. In case Sirica's decision is upheld by Bazelon and the Supreme Court, Nixon could, of course, resolve it by firing Cox, but he doesn't have the nerve and that would be an issue to precipitate impeachment.[183] I look for a showdown on this part of the crisis by mid-October. Barring the "Compromise of 1973," which seems to me unlikely, that still leaves Richard Milhouse to "turn and twist in the wind" for some months to come.
[deletion]

CVWP, 28/326: TCLU

217. To James M. McPherson

OCTOBER 5, 1973

This is in response to your request of an opinion about Gene Geno- vese as a possible appointment at Princeton. I got to know him be- fore he became so visible in the profession, though after he had become a controversial public figure. In spite of occasional brief misunderstand- ings, we have developed a personal friendship that I value very much. The relationship continues and should be taken into account in weighing my opinion of him. From the start I have found his writings stimulating and valuable. Partly because of their own merits, but also because of a long felt need that the American community of historians would profit by admission in full standing of a Marxist of intellectual reputability. We have had Marxian historians before, but none quite up to scratch intellectually. Gene seems to fill the bill, and that was one reason for my cordiality. I found other reasons as I got to know him better. One was a growing faith in his personal integrity and his intellectual integrity. I

183. John Joseph Sirica (1904–1992) was the chief judge for the U.S. District Court for the District of Columbia and presided over the trial of the Watergate burglars, during which he ordered that the tapes, made by Nixon in the Oval Office, be made available. David L. Bazelon (1909–1993), chief judge of the U.S. Court of Appeals for the District of Columbia Circuit (1962–78), was to preside over *Nixon v. Sirica*, the case in which Nixon attempted (but failed) to deny Sirica's order by claiming executive privilege. Archibald Cox Jr. (1912–2004) of the Harvard Law School was appointed special prosecutor to investigate the Watergate scandal in May 1973; when Nixon, in order to evade Sirica's order, offered a compromise, by which Senator John Stennis of Mississippi would, after listening to the tapes, publish summaries of their contents, Cox refused the offer and was fired by Nixon on 20 October 1973.

think he is capable of mistakes of judgment and of passionate impatience that sometimes gives offense in personal relations, but I do not think him capable of anything low or mean or deliberately unfair. Some of the mistakes of the sort have cost him dearly. But his scrupulous fairness to opponents and his generosity of spirit to those with whom he is in complete disagreement have set a standard that few conservatives or liberals have matched. He amused me recently in a long letter of criticism to one of my students, an Alabama conservative of aristocratic heritage, by lecturing the young man roundly (and rightly) on his manners.[184] Alabama has something to learn in this respect from Sicilian sources.

I have a growing respect for Gene's breadth of learning. His special field of scholarship has been rather narrow, but he brings to bear upon it an impressive command of historical and humane literature. As I told you, I have recently read his latest work, some 1,500 pages of it, entitled "Roll, Jordan, Roll." Each chapter begins with a quotation from the Scripture—and they were not lifted from Bartlett! This work revises upward my estimate and admiration for Gene's scholarship. It has more of the enthusiasm for understanding and appreciating than the zeal for proving and disproving that often characterized earlier work. If there are occasional polemics, they are low voltage and tempered by weighing different points of view. It is a major work of prime importance, comparable in significance with any work in the field.

It seems to me likely that Gene's stature as historian will grow. Already I think he stands on a par with David Davis and has surpassed Carl Degler, two of his contemporaries.[185] Confidentially, I much regretted that we here were forced to choose between Davis and Genovese, since we could not afford both. Davis clearly filled our teaching needs in intellectual history better, but I would much like to have both as colleagues. I think he would be an asset and an ornament to your department.

CVWP, 36/423: TCLU

184. J. Mills Thornton III (b. 1943) of Montgomery, AL; his Yale doctoral dissertation, undertaken with CVW, was to be published as *Politics and Power in a Slave Society: Alabama, 1800–1860* (Baton Rouge: Louisiana State University Press, 1978).

185. Carl N. Degler (b. 1921), who taught at Stanford; best known then for *Out of Our Past: The Forces That Shaped Modern America* (New York: Harper, 1959) and *Neither Black nor White: Slavery and Race Relations in Brazil and the United States* (New York: Macmillan, 1971).

218. To James Morton Smith[186]

NOVEMBER 5, 1973

It was most kind of you to invite me to participate in celebrating the Bicentennial by writing one of the volumes. I am afraid that your letter catches me in a non-celebratory mood. I am, in fact, beginning to wonder what there is to celebrate and whether the U.S. was not a mistake. In that mood, needless to say, I am not very useful to your purposes and must ask to be excused from the assignment.

CVWP, 1/2: TCLU

219. To Herbert Aptheker

FEBRUARY 27, 1974

You may be sure that it was with great reluctance that I withdrew from the Board of Advisors for the Du Bois project. I certainly owe you and your publisher an explanation.

The main difficulty I have is with a decision already made and largely implemented before I agreed to join the board. I refer to the decision to devote one short volume to the correspondence of Du Bois through 1937. This covers the first 69 years of the man's very active life. I cannot but compare this scale with that of Booker T. Washington papers while remembering how much more articulate Du Bois was by comparison. I had assumed before this volume had appeared that it would be a popular and preliminary edition and that the two volumes contemplated would be fuller and more thorough. I only later discovered that it was to be included in the ten volumes and would represent all of the correspondence to be obtained for the first seven decades of Du Bois' life.

In the second place, the first volume raised doubts about the editorial procedures and principles of selection. The "Introduction" gave no clear idea of the principle of selection or what the editor meant by "representative letters" and the grounds for omission of some correspondence and the enclosure of other correspondence.

The first volume left me in considerable doubt about the thorough-

186. To mark the bicentennial of the Declaration of Independence, James Morton Smith (b. 1919), a scholar of the late eighteenth century, was editing *The States and the Nation Series*, to be published by W. W. Norton and sponsored by the American Association for State and Local History.

ness of the search for Du Bois' correspondence. We are told that Du Bois saved literally everything, but there are reasons to doubt that all the important correspondence was in the editor's hands. For one thing, we find that Du Bois neglected to save a copy of a letter he wrote to President Wilson.

Among collections known to contain Du Bois' letters that were apparently not searched for [in] this edition are those papers of

R. R. Moton at Tuskegee
George W. Cook at Howard
Ray Stannard Baker at the Library of Congress
Arthur B. Spingarn at the Library of Congress
William S. Braithwaite at Cornell and Syracuse
Charles W. Chestnut at Fisk[187]

Apparently there was no attempt to use the letters of Du Bois at the American Academy of Arts and Sciences. Mr. Herman Kahn of the Yale Library tells me that no use was made of a large collection of Du Bois' letters in the Manuscript Division.[188] My fear is that the editor placed too much reliance on the personal collection kept by Du Bois himself and that much of importance has been overlooked.

My hope is that the ten volumes contemplated by the Massachusetts Press could be devoted to a full edition of the Du Bois correspondence on the scale of the Booker Washington papers.

Please let me know if I can be of further help.

CVWP, 85/2: TCLU

187. With the exception of Baker, all these are notable African-Americans, almost all with connections to the NAACP. Robert Russa Moton (1867–1940) succeeded Booker T. Washington as president of the Tuskegee Institute (1915–35); George William Cook (1855–1931), born a slave, served in many capacities at Howard University, including those of dean of the School of Commerce and Finance and acting president; Ray Stannard Baker (1870–1946), a progressive muckraking journalist; Arthur Barnett Spingarn (1878–1971) was involved with the NAACP from 1911 and served as its president (1940–66); William Stanley Braithwaite (1878–1962) was a poet; Charles Waddell Chesnutt (1858–1932), the novelist, best known for *The Conjure Woman* (Cambridge, MA: Riverside Press, 1899).

188. Herman Kahn (1907–1975), who had been director of the FDR Library at Hyde Park (1948–61), was (after a fleeting retirement) an associate librarian for Manuscripts and Archives in the Yale University Library.

220. To Elizabeth Fox-Genovese

What a bore. It seems I left my pajamas in your study. They are blue. Awfully sorry.

Now for the promised admonitions. Both you and Gene are self-destructively inclined. You are smoking too damned much, both of you, overworking, and not getting enough sleep. Four hours a night is the quick path to the grave. Now that you have both established yourselves as Übermenschen, super-front-page scholars, super-Marxists, and super-conference holders, why don't you let up a bit. Live longer and enjoy a ripe old age as much as I do.

CVWP, 19/221: TCLU

221. To David Riesman

[deletion]

I appreciate your comment on that commencement address I gave at Florida. I have long since come to agree with you about the effect of the student intervention in the war crisis. In other words, I think I was wrong at that time in my tribute to their effect. In all probability, the extremists prolonged the war and neutralized the more important opposition of the working-class people. What a can of paradoxical worms that whole tragedy has been. My thanks also for the correction about my date of your essay.

You mentioned reading the report on freedom of speech at Yale. I hope you have seen the news of the institutional showdown on that issue last week. Within three days the University held without disruption speeches by a leader of the PLO and a debate in which William Shockley participated.[189] There is still vocal opposition to free speech at the University, but predominant opinion in the student body and the firmly consolidated support of the administration and the corporation is supporting

---

189. William Bradford Shockley Jr. (1910–1989), a Nobel Prize winner in physics (for inventing the transistor); later in his career, he became interested in eugenics, expressed concern about the purported declining intelligence of black Americans, and urged a response by policy makers to the problem. In 1974, he tried to participate in a Yale debate with William Rusher, publisher of the *National Review*, but was shouted down by students and unable to speak; twelve students were subsequently disciplined.

the cause. I think a real victory has been won and that this may change the tide.

My experience at South Carolina since February could best be discussed rather than written about. I think I have learned a great many things while here: at least one of them was a renewed appreciation of my native culture. I don't mean that I have abandoned all of my reservations, but I see the problem in a comparative light after a dozen years of residence in New England.

I see our old friend Red Warren is to be awarded the Thoreau-Emerson prize by the Academy in May.[190] That will take some hard swallowing for Red, in view of his opinion of those two worthies. I do hope to be able to attend the occasion, and, if so, I will hope to see you and Evey. In the meantime, our fondest regards.

CVWP, 47/551: TCLU

222. To Thomas L. Haskell[191]

JULY 10, 1975

[deletion]

It looks as if you are asking me to referee this bout.[192] I am reluctant to assume that role, but if I should, I would probably have to call a foul on page 15 when you quote the student as comparing Fogel with Richard Nixon. Though it is a glancing blow, I am very much afraid it landed below the belt. On page 3 it is not a foul but what seems to be a fault when you say that the Rochester Conference consigned the book to the "outermost ring of the scholars hell: obscurity." On second thought, wouldn't you say that what they were doing was consigning it to publicity—at any rate, something other than obscurity?

From my sideline point of view that is all to the good. From the start of this business, which goes back years before publication, my strategy has been governed by an old maxim of politics: when one's opponents

190. The American Academy of Arts and Sciences gives the Emerson-Thoreau Medal in recognition of "distinguished achievement in the broad field of literature."

191. Thomas L. Haskell (b. 1939), an American intellectual historian who taught at Rice University.

192. Haskell had written a review of various recent books on slavery; it would be published as "The True & Tragical History of 'Time on the Cross,'" *New York Review of Books* 22 (2 October 1975): 33–39.

fall out and start beating each other over the head, wisdom dictates a benign neutrality.

I hope it is not too shocking, but I do consider both sides of this controversy as a part of the opposition. That is because, from my point of view, both sides of the quantification battle are extremist quantifiers. I take a certain amount of quantification in stride, but the extremists seem to be a menace to our kind of history—the best kind. The consequence is I have welcomed this rather bloody imbroglio. What it means is that the econometricians embattled against each other have done more to point the limits, abuses, and outrages of doctrinaire quantification than we "conventional" critics could have done in years and years of preaching and criticizing. From the sidelines then I say, to paraphrase Judge Longstreet, "Go it, Fogel—go it, Such; go it, Engerman—go it, Davis."[193]

I think it would be a mistake to absolve all the econometric critics of Fogel and Engerman from bias and passion or, for that matter, from egregious error. For example, Such's paper on slave breeding and stud farms makes as many outrageous misuses of statistics as Fogel and Engerman on the same and similar subjects. And incidentally he seems to me as full of passionate conviction as ever an abolitionist professed. Also, there is my good friend Herb Gutman who is nursing a grievance at being scooped.[194] It was Herb, and not Bob and Stan, who originated the defense of the integrity of the black family under slavery, claiming that the nuclear family emerged from slavery in powerful form, and incidentally, that its destruction is due to the disintegration of urban capitalism.

So you see I take some satisfaction in seeing the predictions of my own review of TOTC come true, especially the one about the most

---

193. Augustus Baldwin Longstreet (1790–1870), the Georgian author and humorist, whose presidential house at Emory College had been one of CVW's early residences; the allusion here is presumably to a character in Longstreet's *Master William Mitten: Or, A Youth of Brilliant Talents, Who Was Ruined by Bad Luck* (1864), who remarks, "I'll go it, mis'ess, like a streak o' lightnin'." "Such" is Richard Sutch, then associate professor of economics at the University of California-Berkeley and one of the contributors to Paul A. David et al., *Reckoning with Slavery: A Critical Study in the Quantitative History of American Negro Slavery* (New York: Oxford University Press, 1976), which was a critique of *Time on the Cross;* "Davis" is David Brion Davis, who had been involved in the *Time on the Cross* controversy.

194. Herbert G. Gutman (1928–1985), an American social and cultural historian who taught at the University of Rochester; he would later publish *The Black Family in Slavery and Freedom, 1750–1925* (New York: Pantheon Books, 1976).

damaging criticism of the cliometricians coming from within their own tribe.[195]

[deletion]

CVWP, 23/267: TCLU

223. To Stanley M. Elkins and Eric McKitrick[196]

AUGUST 18, 1975

[deletion]

I know that it's your problem and that this is free and unsolicited counsel. But I cannot resist putting in an oar—sharing profound reflectings— shedding the sweet light of reason, etc.

So—Once upon a time in the Golden Age of the Gentleman Scholar, having come into his patrimony and reached a mature age, retired from sight and squared away to do the Great Subject. And within a surprisingly few decades the public's patience was rewarded by the appearance, volume by volume, of the Masterpiece. Thus, to our enormous good fortune, we were endowed with Ferdinand and Isabella, Rise of the Dutch Republic, Conquest of Mexico (not to mention Peru), The French in America, Jefferson and Madison.[197] A Golden Age, indeed, and but for a belated Prescott named S. Morison, we were not likely to see their likes again.[198]

---

195. CVW, "The Jolly Institution," *New York Review of Books* 21 (2 May 1974): 3–6.

196. The context of this letter is that Elkins and McKitrick had contracted to write the volume in the *Oxford History of the United States* that dealt with the period 1789–1815, but wished to expand beyond a single volume. Over thirty years later, the Oxford volume was eventually to be published: see Gordon S. Wood, *Empire of Liberty: A History of the Early Republic, 1789–1815* (New York: Oxford University Press, 2009). Elkins and McKitrick's own venture turned into Stanley Elkins and Eric McKitrick, *The Age of Federalism* (New York: Oxford University Press, 1993), but in one long volume.

197. William H. Prescott, *History of the Reign of Ferdinand and Isabella, the Catholic*, 3 vols. (Boston: American Stationers' Company, 1838); John Lothrop Motley, *The Rise of the Dutch Republic: A History*, 3 vols. (New York: Harper and Brothers, 1856); William H. Prescott, *History of the Conquest of Mexico: With a Preliminary View of the Ancient Mexican Civilization and the Life of the Conqueror, Hernando Cortes*, 3 vols. (New York: Harper and Brothers, 1843); idem., *History of the Conquest of Peru, with a Preliminary View of the Civilization of the Incas*, 2 vols. (New York: Harper and Brothers, 1847); Henry Adams, *History of the United States of America*, 9 vols. (New York: Charles Scribner's Sons, 1889–91).

198. CVW perhaps has in mind Samuel Eliot Morison, *History of United States Naval Operations in World War II*, 15 vols. (Boston: Little, Brown, 1947–62).

So—when Dick told me of your bold proposal, the mind reeled. An anachronism! a blessed anachronism! I said. An improbable throwback—three, four generations of time defied—the candle and the quill. Could such things be, and overcome us like a summer's cloud without our special wonder? Of course the regular way, the beaten path that all others now follow is (1) the dissertation (2) revised for publication in the Series (3) the exploratory monographs, and only after due recognition and appropriate acclaim for leadership in The Field, (4) the ripened fruit of reflection—"The Subject, 18XX to 18XX."

Still—it was worth a gamble. It might work. An odd pair from birth— a birthing that required heroic surgery to separate them at the start and any amount of whipping into shape. Not dissertations, properly speaking, at all—but precocious manifestos. And now, having earned the right to some authority in Slavery and/or Reconstruction, they kick over the traces again and propose to square away at the Eighteenth Century in which they have no authority whatever. Defiance—defiance! What would it all come to?

Nevertheless—we would see. Face the problems when they came. And they would come. All this enormous investment of time and energy, all this suspicious suspension of publication, this prolonged silence (was it pregnant after all?) in order to master the strange, vast, and intractable field. Then having begun to do so, comes the inevitable realization that the riches they unearthed would not all fit into the prescribed mold. Solution? Like the inspiration, borrowed from the Golden Age: simply multiply the volumes—I, II, III, IV—down the decades.

No, my dear colleagues, it does not follow at all that a happy inspiration from the Golden Age obliges you to be consistent anachronisms, living throwbacks in all respects. In short, the I, II, III, IV solution is not the only one. *Nor* is packing it all willy nilly into Vol. III of the Oxford History. Of course, you have found more than you can get into any one general volume covering the period. I would be disappointed and vastly astonished at any other result. But that is no reason for depriving yourselves of the larger readership awaiting the one general volume. The fact is that you have other readerships for other kinds of volumes awaiting you—elaborations, spin-offs, intensive treatments, chance discoveries, serendipities unlimited. Why not indeed, as you say, "make a career of it"—and without apologies or regrets and with full exploitation of all the discovered treasures of the Inca. Instead of either (1) abandoning half of them as sacrifice to the Oxford one-volume obligation, or (2) following the anachronistic model of the Golden Age and packaging all goodies arbitrarily and inappropriately in uniform volumes under the same title. With all respect to the Golden Age, there is something to be said for present reader-and-publisher realities.

So—the time has come, the Walrus said, to talk of many things (not *one* thing)—of ships and shoes and sealing wax, and cabbages and kings. You admit that by this time you can see the whole scheme, not in detail to be sure, but in broad shape and contour—ready for filling in. You say, too, that at best you are still scarcely within two and a half years of finishing Vol. I of the I, II, III, IV solution. Pause, reconsider, and reflect. Set aside for separate books (small or large, popular or learned, austere monograph or sexy best seller) the several aspects that do not properly belong in the general volume we want. Publish one or two first as appetizers, summarize or refer to in the Oxford volume—in which also you teasingly refer to disclosures and treasure yet to come that will astonish and amaze both multitude and polymath. What a PR scheme—what genius has been lost to that calling in diverting me to scholarship! Yet, withal, I flatter myself that there is sound counsel here and food for thought.

P.S. Another vital use for the scheme is to make the small volumes confute, confound, and confuse your critics—and incidentally to correct unfortunate mistakes. See example of your humble correspondent.

CVWP, 41/491: TCLU

224. To William S. McFeely[199]

SEPTEMBER 26, 1975

[deletion]

Yes, Frankfurter gives me trouble too.[200] Alex gave me trouble for the thirteen years I knew him.[201] Troubles about Justice Black and Warren, about integration, about busing, about populism, about Burke and Paine, about liberalism and conservatism, about free speech and revolution. Troubles, troubles—about virtually every bent and bias that clung

199. William S. McFeely, a graduate student of CVW's at Yale, whose dissertation was published as *Yankee Stepfather: General O. O. Howard and the Freedmen* (New Haven: Yale University Press, 1968).

200. Felix Frankfurter (1882–1965), associate justice of the U.S. Supreme Court (1939–62).

201. That is, Alexander Bickel, who had died of cancer.

to my hair, from quotas to Thomas Jefferson. Maybe I gave him a hit too, but he always gave me more than I gave him—not only more troubles but more ideas, provocation, points of view, insights, reassessments, self-searching, disturbing doubts, and more understanding and respect for my utterly un-Rumanian, unHebraic heritage—which this Hebraic Rumanian immigrant understood and respected much better than did I, direct lineal heir to the whole works. Sometimes I thought I would have hated him—had I not loved him.

P.S. At a dinner in honor of Alex in Washington last week the paradox overwhelmed us all. In paying him tribute and honor Tony Lewis vied with Bob Bork, Justice Stuart with Justice Powell, editor of the New Republic with the ed of Commentary, liberal with conservative, Dem senators with Rep senators, black with white.[202]

CVWP, 35/416: TCLS

225. To John W. Hall[203]

OCTOBER 14, 1975

This is an informal report of your committee, consisting of myself, John Blum, and John Blassingame, instructed to inquire into the qualifications of Professor Herbert Aptheker for appointment to teach a college seminar on W. E. B. DuBois for Davenport College.[204]

The committee concluded that the candidate did not measure up to the standard of scholarship we try to maintain for Yale teachers. None of his work can be said to have achieved distinction and for the most part it is second rate. John Blassingame and I were especially disappointed in the first volume of Aptheker's edition of the DuBois papers. I found it so poor that I felt obliged to resign from his Board of Editorial Advisers, a place I had accepted upon his urging. I was not consulted about the volume published. It contained only a small fraction of the correspondence

202. Anthony Lewis (1927–2013), a journalist who wrote often for the *New York Times*, a liberal; Lewis Franklin Powell Jr. (1907–1998) and Potter Stewart (1915–1985), both associate justices of the U. S. Supreme Court and centrists; Robert Heron Bork (1927–2012), then Solicitor General, a conservative.

203. John Whitney Hall (1916–1997), a historian of Japan and then chair of the Department of History at Yale.

204. John W. Blassingame (1940–2000), an African-American historian of black history who had been on the Yale faculty since 1970 and a doctoral student of CVW's; his dissertation was published as *Black New Orleans, 1860–1880* (Chicago: University of Chicago Press, 1973).

I judged to be essential for inclusion in such an edition. The committee's feeling was that if we could not trust him to edit DuBois' papers—a matter of public record—we were even less able to feel confident of his teaching, of which there would be no public record.

CVWP, 62/746: TCLU

226. To Horace Taft[205]

OCTOBER 30, 1975

Recent experience with the Davenport College Seminar debate suggests to me that it may well be time for a re-examination of the college seminar system, its rules and practices.

One thing that calls for consideration is the multiple requests for sponsorship of instructors nominated from outside the University. After informally sounding out the History Department and receiving a negative response, the Master of Davenport then made formal requests for sponsorship to five departments, including History. Anticipating a negative reply from History, the request could only have a divisive effect, setting up department against department and calling into the question the authority of the department immediately concerned. I believe we should have a rule against such shotgun approaches and fishing expeditions.

In the second place, there is clearly a disagreement about whether to apply a double standard in the matter of college seminars. The responses of the History Department and the Political Science Department to the Davenport request spelled out some of those differences clearly.

One source of confusion in standards seems in need of examination. There are at least two types of college seminars: one where the usual academic standards of scholarship apply, the other where they do not clearly apply. The latter type includes journalists, artists, craftsmen, athletes, politicians, etc. If we could form a separate category for the latter and apply somewhat the scheme of the Chubb Fellowship without formal courses and academic credit, I think we would be spared some of the present confusion.[206]

205. Horace Dwight Taft (1925–1983), a physicist, had been dean of Yale College since 1971; he had also been master of Davenport College (1966–71). He was the grandson of President William Howard Taft.

206. The Chubb fellowship is held at Timothy Dwight College; its holder gives a public lecture, is expected to participate in the life of the college and Yale. In any given academic year,

In view of these and other problems about the college seminar plan, I suggest that you appoint an ad hoc committee to study the matter and report their findings to the College Faculty for consideration.

CVWP, 61/721: TCLU

227. To Horace Taft

DECEMBER 8, 1975

I was pleased, as I am sure you were, that our debate on the Aptheker appointment before the Joint Board of Permanent Officers on Thursday last came off without display of ill temper and unnecessary rending of human tissue. That was attributable in good part, no doubt, to your magisterial manner of presiding.

I must confess, however, that I was puzzled by your statement at the very end of the discussion that—as I understood you—my report to you as chairman of the Committee on Junior Appointments had failed to convey our full objection to this appointment. I am not given to strong language, but when I say, as I did in my report, that specified failings "call into question the scholarly integrity of the work" of a man, it would seem to me that my meaning should have been sufficiently clear to any committee of scholars. I might have said that I questioned his "intellectual honesty," but I prefer that other phrase, and it means the same thing—a charge of dishonesty. In our verbal statements before the Board on Thursday my colleagues and I were repeating those charges and supporting them with evidence from the reviews of the books concerned that were submitted to your committee with my report. I do not see how I could have been misunderstood.

More disturbing for us was the unanimous vote of the Committee on Junior Appointments in favor of the candidate. This vote came in the face of a unanimous report against him from the ad hoc history committee with the strong backing of the History Department. It was accompanied by the gravest of charges made by scholars in the candidate's own field best qualified to pass on his qualifications. Less serious objections,

---

there are several Chubb Fellows, who often come and go briefly; during 1975–76, they included four U.S. senators (Charles McCurdy Mathias, Joseph Biden, Daniel Patrick Moynihan, and David L. Boren), a governor of Connecticut (Ella T. Grasso), a secretary of defense (James R. Schlesinger), and two prime ministers (Mario Soares and Edward Heath).

less strongly phrased, would ordinarily seem sufficient to block an appointment in other disciplines—physics included, one might assume. We can only infer that the appointments committee rejected our opinion in favor of one from a department that could make no claim of authority in the field. Indeed, by the admission of one of that department's members on the floor during debate, no pretense was made of having read the works of the candidate or knowing anything about him. The only evidence in support of the candidate's qualification was an article cited by the chairman of the Political Science Department as appearing in the *Political Science Quarterly*. A thorough search of that journal's files failed to turn up any article by the candidate.

It is my hope that you can suggest ways by which I can reassure my colleagues about the respect that their discipline commands or the seriousness with which their views are taken in quarters other than the Joint Board of Permanent Officers.

CVWP, 85/4: TCLS

228. To the *Yale Daily News*[207]

JANUARY 31, 1976

May I correct a misapprehension that has appeared several times in your columns, most recently in a letter from Professor Herbert Aptheker? This is that the decision against his application for a teaching appointment last fall was based on secret evidence that has been withheld from him and from the public.

There was no secret evidence. It is all public. It consists of the published works of the applicant, as is usually the case with applicants. These books are in the Sterling Library, catalogued and shelved under his name and readily available to readers.

Granting what merit these works possess, those responsible for the decision found that they did not measure up to the standard of scholarship desired for teachers at Yale, where scholarly standards can be applied. That was the reason for the decision, and that alone.

A great many negative decisions are made every term. Hundreds of people apply to teach at Yale and only a handful are appointed. Neither the time nor the taste for debate with the candidates over their scholarly

207. This appeared in the issue of February 2, 1976.

qualifications, such as Mr. Aptheker proposes, really exists. Neither the applications nor the reasons for the decisions regarding them are normally made public. It is to be hoped that this unfortunate exception to the rule will not become a precedent. It might discourage applicants from applying.

The more applications from teachers and students we get the better we like it. We like to think that many more want to come here than we can accept. It gives us a greater range of choice, for one thing.

Most disappointed applicants go about their business with the perfectly plausible consolation that teaching or studying at Yale is not the only possible way to pursue an honorable and rewarding career and that there are other good colleges available, even some good community colleges. A healthy response of this sort is to be encouraged.

CVWP, 85/1: TCLU

229. To Marvin E. Gettleman[208]

FEBRUARY 23, 1976

I was interested in your letter and want to know your thoughts. Do you really think our friend Herbert is that good? I wonder what you have in mind. Certainly not his monograph on slave revolts, or the slighter things on Nat Turner or labor in the ante-bellum South.[209] We may differ on the first volume of his edition of Du Bois, but I think you would have to admit serious shortcomings there. Perhaps I have overlooked something of importance. He has published an awful lot. Of course his collection of documents is useful. But frankly I have to admit to my colleagues that I am unable to come up with anything that I could honestly call first rate.

Surely you do not think of him as belonging in the class of Gene Genovese, whom we have had as a visiting professor and whom I would delight in having as a permanent colleague. Or in the class with E. P. Thompson,

208. Marvin E. Gettleman (b. 1933) taught in the Department of Social Sciences, Polytechnic Institute of Brooklyn; he and CVW had been intermittent correspondents since 1962 and had especially discussed the Vietnam War.

209. Herbert Aptheker, *American Negro Slave Revolts* (New York: Columbia University Press, 1943); idem., *Nat Turner's Slave Rebellion: Together with the Full Text of the So-Called "Confessions" of Nat Turner Made in Prison in 1831* (New York: Humanities Press, 1966); idem., *The Labor Movement in the South During Slavery* (New York: International Publishers, 1954).

whom we have unsuccessfully tried to interest in coming to Yale permanently.[210] Or even Herbert Marcuse, who did teach here in the sixties.[211] It is never easy to find and not always possible to attract talent. And it is not easy to persuade an Ed Morgan or a David Davis or a Peter Gay or a Jack Hexter that they ought to settle for the second rate.[212] You are a serious historian with standards I share. I think you would agree with me that if radical historians get themselves into the position of maintaining that every Marxist scholar is first rate they have painted themselves into a corner. Some Marxists are more equal than others.

But I am always open to persuasion and I think my colleagues are too. We respect evidence. What can you offer? Don't stand on ceremony.

The old crowd at Johns Hopkins is all gone now, but I still remember the place with warmth and affection. And I think you would agree that the new history faculty there is a strong and substantial one. It remains a rather special place.

CVWP, 85/1: TCLU

230. To the National Endowment for the Humanities, Division of Research Grants

FEBRUARY 26, 1976

Perhaps the best clue to the shortcomings of this proposal is a comparison with another NEH project, the papers of Booker T. Washington now being edited by Louis H. Harlan of the University of Maryland. The Washington project, with superior standards of editing, is using ten or more volumes to publish the correspondence and papers of that figure. This project, with inferior standards of editing, covers in one volume the first 66 years of the DuBois correspondence. The inadequacy of that coverage is suggested by the fact that Booker T. Washington was dead

210. Edward P. Thompson (1924–1993), a British social historian and Marxist, best known for *The Making of the English Working Class* (London: Victor Gollancz, 1963).

211. Herbert Marcuse (1898–1979), a German émigré social philosopher and member of the Frankfurt School; he was a scholar of Marx and Hegel and his writings on modern capitalism and mass society were influential in New Left circles in the 1970s. He never had a faculty appointment at Yale but did teach a course on the history of socialism in the spring of 1964.

212. Peter Gay (b. 1923), a historian of modern intellectual culture and author, notably, of *The Enlightenment: An Interpretation*, 2 vols. (New York: Alfred A. Knopf, 1966–69); he had taught at Columbia University (1962–69) before coming to Yale.

before the age of 66. Yet I believe it would be generally agreed that the correspondence of DuBois was more important and more extensive than that of Washington. The one volume edited by Professor Aptheker is a great disappointment to historians who had hoped for an adequate and scholarly edition of these important papers. The review in the *Journal of Southern History* by Professor Clarence Contee of Howard University points out many of the shortcomings of the first volume.[213] Professor Contee is the only reviewer who has a personal acquaintance with the DuBois papers. Under these circumstances I think it would be a mistake to subsidize this project.

CVWP, 85/2: TCLU

231. To Godfrey Lehman[214]

JANUARY 12, 1977

Thank you very much for your letter calling me to task for a reference to our being in the third millennium of the "Christian Era."

I note that your letter was dated January 4, 1977. I presume this date refers to the 1977th year of the Christian era. I am sure that you meant no more offense to me, a non-Christian, than I meant to you.

CVWP, 31/369: TCLU

232. To J. Morgan Kousser[215]

JANUARY 19, 1977

[deletion]

I guess I'm of mixed mind about your maintaining the reputation of being a "thug" as critic, especially since I know you as "the soul of charity and good cheer." You ask if a fair and honest criticism is forbidden in this profession: the answer, of course, is yes. I'm sorry I've neglected your education since you got your degree. If you have any doubts

213. *Journal of Southern History* 40 (August 1974): 498–99; Contee had briefly studied with CVW at Johns Hopkins.

214. An "advertising and promotional counselor" in San Francisco.

215. J. Morgan Kousser (b. 1943), whose Yale dissertation with CVW had been published as *The Shaping of Southern Politics: Suffrage Restriction and the Establishment of the One-Party South, 1880–1910* (New Haven: Yale University Press, 1974); he taught at the California Institute of Technology.

about the taboo on honest criticism, try to find an honest assessment of Aptheker's travesty on the Du Bois correspondence. The only exception is Elliott Rudwick's review in the current issue of the *Journal of Negro History*.[216] I place it on your required reading list.

[deletion]

> CVWP, 31/366: TCLU

233. To Lyman H. Butterfield[217]

FEBRUARY 28, 1977

Many thanks for your encouragement and your helpful response to my questions.[218] About some of the questions you raised, I wanted to think a bit before responding, and I shall take the liberty of raising a few more of my own. I only hope I am not imposing too much on your generosity.

I was greatly relieved to find that you share my views about normalizing punctuation and capitalization. I propose to permit her a few characteristic eccentricities. But since she had *only* capitals for some letters of the alphabet and *mainly* dashes for punctuation, literalism would be absurd. (I also remove quotation marks from indirect quotes and undertake to close unclosed direction quotations.)

Spelling presents more complications. To give concreteness to the problem, I enclose a page listing errors as they occur in random samples of the typed transcript, citing the pages to show frequency. They are not necessarily typical but give you an idea. Typical was her misspelling of words beginning "des": dispite for despite, discribe for describe. She was careless and inconsistent about proper names. Altar was always "alter." She often, though not consistently, made two words of one: "any body," "every thing," "any where." She switched back and forth from English to American spellings. I accept your practice of converting silently transposed letters and obvious slips. Question is: where are the reasonable boundaries of literalism and relative gains of expanding or contracting them?

---

216. *Journal of Negro History* 61 (October 1976): 401–4.

217. Lyman H. Butterfield (1909–1982) was then editor in chief of the Adams Papers, based in the Massachusetts Historical Society.

218. About how to edit and annotate the Mary Chesnut diaries.

I would appreciate your views of retaining ampersands (which she uses with great frequency) or substituting "and." She very often ends sentences with "&c., &c, &c." Could I justify a rule of substituting one "etc."?

I rejoice in your blessing for making all versions of the diary subject to editorial use. There remains many problems of *how*. Some think any passage from versions other than the basic Version III should go into footnotes or appendices. I resist this strongly. Much the greater part of other versions I propose to use are things omitted from Version III, paragraphs, pages, whole incidents. My inclination is to insert them in the appropriate place, set off by   marks   and indicating the source—usually Version I. Then there are deleted identifications: "This gentleman   my husband   was diliberately insulting." "Mrs. Walker is a Montgomery beauty   I find her pretty, silly, and I really believe half crazy   ." "No use to talk to me, Mrs. Toombs said   . If one of them Yankees kills my husband, I'll kill one of them certain and sure'   all the time ridiculing Mrs. Reagan's want of polish and education   ." Should I put these short insertions in the text like this, or in footnotes, is the question.

Critics of a purist persuasion say I am "conflating" versions, a grave editorial offense, they believe. I am imposing my preferences on the author, whose deletions or selections should be respected. Part of my answer is that she presents this as a diary, and I, as an editor, cannot connive in concealments and evasions or misrepresentations. Also, I think the reader should read relevant parts of other versions in their most logical context. As you seem to suggest, I will use other versions, especially Version I "rather liberally *along with* the later literary version."

I understand your discomfort about my use of the word "substituted." There I had in mind a very few instances where later polished versions (IV and V) are clearer and better written than Version III. I had intended footnote explanations. But perhaps I had best drop this idea entirely and stick to insertions.

Your suggestion of displaying at least one passage in several versions is an excellent idea which I adopt with enthusiasm.

You are most kind to invite me to come in for a talk. I shall certainly plan to do that later. In the meantime, if you have any reflections on the questions raised in this letter, I would be most grateful if you shared them with me.

CVWP, 69/93: TCLU

234. To Carl N. Degler

JUNE 14, 1977

The L.S.U. Press (thanks probably to your suggestion) sent me a copy of *Place Over Time*.[219] I have been abroad a month and have not had time since my return for the careful reading it deserves. But a quick one indicates the need for a long talk rather than a hasty letter. I wish we could have had such a talk after your book on *The Other South*, for I believe I could have set you right on my own views and spared you some misconceptions.[220]

On the matter of class domination and racial consensus in the Old South, I am much closer to Fredrickson than to Genovese.[221] I thought I made that clear, among other places in a joint review of George's *Black Image* and Gene's *Red and Black* in the *N.Y. Review*.[222] I pointed out that in his doctrine of class domination Gene "runs into difficulties with the intractable complexities of southern history and American racism" and that the evidence supported George's view of egalitarian racism and the Herrenvolk consensus in the Old South.

I never agreed with Gene that Fitzhugh was representative of the planters' outlook on the Old South's attitudes.[223] I argued with him over the manuscript on that point. You may remember that the title of my introduction to *Cannibals All!* was "George Fitzhugh: *Sui Generis*." In it I say: "Fitzhugh was not typical of anything. Fitzhugh was an individual—*sui generis*. There is scarcely a tag or a generalization or a cliché normally associated with the Old South that would fit him without qualification." I went on to specify agrarianism, free trade, "intraracial egalitarianism," etc. as examples of his deviant views.

---

219. Carl N. Degler, *Place over Time: The Continuity of Southern Distinctiveness* (Baton Rouge: Louisiana State University Press, 1977).

220. Carl N. Degler, *The Other South: Southern Dissenters in the Nineteenth Century* (New York: Harper & Row, 1974).

221. George M. Fredrickson (1934–2008), then teaching at Northwestern University and the author of *The Black Image in the White Mind: The Debate on Afro-American Character and Destiny, 1817–1914* (New York: Harper & Row, 1971), which had argued that the antebellum South had a *Herrenvolk* democracy.

222. CVW, "Our Own Herrenvolk," *New York Review of Books* 17 (12 August 1971): 11–14.

223. Eugene D. Genovese, "The Logical Outcome of the Slaveholders' Philosophy: An Exposition, Interpretation, and Critique of the Social Thought of George Fitzhugh of Port Royal, Virginia," in *The World the Slaveholders Made: Two Essays in Interpretation* (New York: Pantheon Books, 1969), 115–244.

Of course I knew we differed over the discontinuity thesis. There will always be room for honest differences over generalizations like that, but little is gained for the service of Clio by conceding that there is something to be said for both sides in such discussions. Let's put that aside and try to get at the nature of our differences. I have never declared an end to Southern distinctiveness. In fact, for years I have taught a course on it that comes down to the present. I have argued that the Civil War and Reconstruction augmented distinctiveness. But continued distinctiveness does not mean lack of change—drastic and frequent change. China is still distinctive, and so are Russia, France, and Italy. But does that establish unbroken historical continuity? Leaving anthropological constants for the moment to anthropologists, isn't the proper study of history the study of change over time? Granting the reassuring continuity of "place," aren't historians more rightly concerned with "time" and what it does? Or am I still bemused by my month of sailing the Aegean in a small boat with the Warrens? Those *places!* Still there—Delos, Patmos, Samos, Lesbos, Rhodes, Ephesus, Miletus—and I suppose still pretty distinctive, too. But then there is *time,* and what it has done. Maybe the ideal spot for continuing our colloquy on this weighty subject is Thera (Santorini) where we spent a whole delightful week. For there place and time are metaphysically and wildly mixed. As you know, half the island sank 800 meters under the sea in 1500 B.C. and with it Minoan civilization, and the crater is now the harbor. And 500 feet above it and 1000 years later the Greeks built a city that guide books still call "old" Thera. Place Under Time, to borrow a famous title.

CVWP, 15/169: TCLU

235. To Charles Gibson and Kenneth M. Stampp[224]

JULY 20, 1977

I will try to answer the questions you raised in your letter of June 23, but not in the order they appear. Out of long habit, I suppose, I prefer the historical approach. I therefore turn first to your Question 14, as I number them. This inquires about the circumstances and significance of my

224. These were the incumbent presidents of the American Historical Association (Gibson) and the Organization of American Historians (Stampp). Charles Gibson (1920–1985) was a historian of Spain and colonial Spanish America, especially Mexico; he was at the University of Michigan.

joining and later withdrawing from the National Advisory Board of the Du Bois papers project published by the Massachusetts University Press and edited by Herbert Aptheker. In answering the question, I should tell you that I have never made any public reference to my resignation from the board. It is significant, I think, that you apparently learned of it through the violation of confidentiality by some member of one of the committees referred to in another question, that of Davenport College. I now address a committee all of whose members, I assume, are firm in their dedication to our common rule of confidentiality in academic debate and procedure regarding appointments.

My interest in the project arose from my eagerness to gain for qualified scholars access to the huge and rich collection of Du Bois correspondence and papers in Mr. Aptheker's custody and stored in his home. I would guess it is the richest single collection of personal papers on American black history and race relations (not even barring the Booker Washington papers) in existence. It lay near the center of my own research interests and that of many historians. Yet throughout my career and the peak years of interest in black history this gold mine was with rare exceptions not accessible to historians. I could name two important biographical studies of Du Bois and more than a score of monographs that suffered irreparably for lack of access to the Du Bois papers. Several of my own students were handicapped for the same reason. Dissertations went uncompleted, or were finished abortively and inconclusively. Research was stalled in numerous lines.

Critics of Aptheker are unfair in blaming him entirely and calling him a dog-in-the-manger. After all, while he was literary executor of the estate, he was not the owner of the property rights. That was presumably Du Bois's widow. I followed some efforts to solve the problem, notably those of the Harvard University Press, which came near success but foundered over the issue of access to the Du Bois manuscript collection for checking and supervision by the usual type of editorial board.

Aptheker wrote me in January 1971 telling me about his plans for a two-volume (later three-volume) *Selected Correspondence of Du Bois* and asking permission to publish a sort of fan letter I wrote Du Bois in 1938. The ensuing correspondence was quite genial. We shared an admiration for Du Bois, whom I had met long before Aptheker had—in 1931 in fact. I told Aptheker that I had no memories or impressions of value such as he requested but gladly gave him permission to print my letter. I also urged him to find a way of placing the Du Bois collection in a good library, saying the Library of Congress would be ideal but offering to get the Yale Library to open negotiations for the collection. He promised to take this up with Mrs. Du Bois. About his plans for the volumes of correspondence I expressed serious doubt of doing justice to the first sixty-six and most important years of Du Bois's life, down to 1934, in a single volume. He acknowledged this was but a fragment of the mass, but said that the contract with his publisher (then Lippincott) guaranteed the right to publish later a full and complete edition of the correspondence. I replied that I was greatly relieved to hear this and offered to be of what help I could in such an effort and also to help in placing the manuscripts in a good library.

It was not long after this that I received from the director of the University of Massachusetts Press an invitation to join a National Advisory Board for a ten-volume edition of the Du Bois papers to be edited by Mr. Aptheker. The University had purchased or was about to purchase the Du Bois Collection and gave assurance that it would be available to scholars as early as possible. This seemed to be the long-sought solution, though only with Aptheker in charge—take it or leave it. We were assured, however, that regular meetings of the board were to be held; the manuscript sources were to be available for checking; and the Harlan edition of the Booker Washington papers and Boyd edition of the Jefferson papers were mentioned as models. With these understandings, I agreed, after consulting other interested parties, to join the board along with Louis Harlan, John Hope Franklin, Henry Commager, Kenneth Clark, and Charles Wesley.[225]

A further understanding of mine, one that like the others later proved erroneous, was that the bulk of the ten volumes would be devoted to Du Bois correspondence. The Harlan volumes on Washington, I pointed out, planned to use some 80 per cent of the space for that purpose. I shall not attempt to assign responsibility for this misapprehension nor enter into any dispute about who was to blame. The fact is, however, not until August, 1973, did I learn (indirectly) the following: that the manuscripts prepared for the abandoned Lippincott volumes contained the only cor-

225. Kenneth B. Clark (1914–2005), psychologist and social critic, the author of *Dark Ghetto: Dilemmas of Social Power* (New York: Harper & Row, 1965); Charles Harris Wesley (1891–1987), executive director of the Association for the Study of Negro Life and History (1965–72).

respondence to be included in the Massachusetts edition; that the first volume containing all the letters to be published down to 1934 was already in press and due to be released shortly; that the selections for the next two volumes had already been made, and prepared for publishing; that the next seven volumes would contain unpublished or rejected manuscripts, essays, and college papers of Du Bois, but no correspondence; and that while other scholars would eventually be able to examine the manuscripts at the Massachusetts Library (still unavailable for that purpose by recent reports), all publication from them remained restricted to those items authorized by Mrs. Du Bois under Aptheker's editorship.

I immediately wrote the editor that these procedures did not accord at all with my understanding of the project when I joined the Advisory Board, that the board had not met or been consulted or even informed of fundamental decisions and policies. Yet the first volume was about to appear. He then offered to seek the advice of the board about future volumes but asked that I suspend judgment until I received and examined an advance copy of Volume I. I have no record of when I received the volume, but it was early in the fall of 1973. Its faults of editorial judgment and scholarly thoroughness were readily apparent, as were its shortcomings in taste and candor, its striking omissions and unjustifiable inclusions, its lopsided imbalance between the letters to and letters from Du Bois, its lack of discrimination between the significant and the trivial. Too many collections of important and relevant manuscripts were skipped over or superficially sampled. The most appalling neglect was that of the vast archives of the NAACP in the Library of Congress, which contain thousands of letters and documents by and about Du Bois. One searches in vain for expected light on Du Bois as leader of the Niagara Movement, for clarifications of his numerous roles and battles in the NAACP and as editor of *Crisis*, and for his involvement in the Harlem Renaissance. The reader is mystified by the glaring omission of Du Bois's world role in the Pan-African congresses of the 1920's. His ambivalences about organized labor, socialism, and black nationalism are inadequately represented. Then there is the editor's embarrassing proclivity for filling scarce space with meaningless acknowledgements, invitations, etc. from Important People, and his regrettable exclusion of letters about the personal life of the man. It was obvious that the editing of the Du Bois correspondence would have to be done over.

You ask in Question No. 14 about reviews of the book I may have recommended to "interested parties." The only two reviews in learned journals available at the height of the controversy were those in the *Journal of American History* and the *Journal of Southern History*.[226] When asked about reviews, I doubtless mentioned them. You may be sure I took no pleasure in mentioning Sterling Stuckey's uncritical and adulatory review in the JAH, and that I got more satisfaction out of pointing out when asked later reviews that supported my own estimate. I call attention particularly to Elliot Rudwick (*Journal of Negro History*, Oct., 1976, pp. 401–404), who says that ". . . Aptheker, in a capricious editorial blunder that defies scholarly sense—and common sense, devotes the first volume to all the years between 1877 and 1934, and entire second volume to a single decade following mid-1934, after nearly all of Du Bois's major contributions had been completed." Rudwick calls the volume "a woefully inadequate sampling" and concludes that "overall the result is an extraordinary disappointment. Surely Du Bois and the field of black history deserve better." I might also mention the review by David L. Lewis (*American Historical Review*, April, 1977, p. 444) who pronounces the book "a puzzling offering" and declares that "few scholars will choose to rely upon Aptheker's editorial judgment." I also found of interest Marion Kilson's review essay, "Veiling Words" (*Reviews in American History*, December, 1976, pp. 577–581).

You ask, Question 15, if I spelled out my criticism of Aptheker's scholarship when resigning from the board. Yes. I resigned in a letter to the director of the press on January 28, 1974, and a month later explained my reasons in a letter to the editor with a copy to the director. I was not so blunt or so detailed in my criticisms as I have been above, but I plainly said I could not accept his editorial procedures and principles of selection, that I could not approve the proportion of space allotted to the correspondence of the period down to 1934, and that neither the role of the Advisory Board nor the purpose and content of the edition had been in line with my understanding when I agreed to join the board. I also listed seven manuscript collections that I thought he had neglected (oddly omitting the most important, the NAACP archives). Louis Harlan also resigned from the board. I do not know about the other members, but the

226. Sterling Stuckey, in *Journal of American History* 61 (December 1974): 746–47; Clarence G. Contee, in *Journal of Southern History* 43 (May 1977): 320–21.

National Advisory Board seems to have disappeared from the project not long thereafter.

I would not presume to speak for John Blassingame about his citing an earlier book of Aptheker's. He is writing you separately. I believe his reply will adequately answer your question about the implications suggested.

I would caution you, gentlemen, not to draw hasty connections between my account of an experience with the Du Bois Papers project and the later ad hoc committee report you are investigating. You asked me for an account of the former matter and I have given it. But that was *my* experience, not that of my colleagues. What part it played in my own later vote and what relative importance it had I would be hard put to say. The causes of things, as every historian knows, are often complex. One reads many things over the years, and human memory is fallible. Other Aptheker works and criticisms of them surely influenced my estimate of his scholarship. At any rate you may be sure that the appearance of Volume I of the Du Bois correspondence was not my first encounter with Aptheker's scholarship nor the dawn of my first doubts about its qualities.

I return now to your first questions in the order listed:

1. *Question:* Why since the History Department regards the seminars as very important, does it allow small ad hoc committees to make decisions on them?

Answer: I am unable to improve upon, or add anything to, Professor Turner's answer to Question 14 in his letter to Dr. Kirkendall, April 26, 1977.[227] I hope your secretary has received and circulated this letter. I will refer to it hereafter as "Turner to Kirkendall 4/26/77."

2. *Question:* Did your committee ever consider the possibility of sponsoring Aptheker on the same basis as the Political Science Department sponsored him?

Answer: This question is somewhat unclear to me because the Political Science Department sponsored Aptheker twice. I assume the question refers to the second sponsorship, the Political Science Department's motion of April 1976 which explicitly removed Aptheker's candidacy from what you have referred to as the "scholarly category" and placed it in the "non-

227. Henry Ashby Turner Jr. (1932–2008), a historian of modern Germany and chair of the Yale History Department (1976–79).

scholarly." If this assumption is correct the answer is no. For the History Department to have resorted to such a formula would have been disingenuous. It would have amounted to a refusal to accord Aptheker recognition as a professional historian. For the reasons indicated by Professor Turner in his answer to Question 20, (Turner to Kirkendall 4/26/77), our department's position was that Aptheker's candidacy clearly deserved to be judged by professional standards.

3. *Question:* Was there any demand from others in the History Department for discussion of the Aptheker issues in a full department meeting?

Answer: Professor John Hall, then chairman, called such a meeting in March, 1976 with this matter on the agenda, but not in response to a "demand." At the meeting the matter was discussed but no action was taken.

4. *Question:* Were any members of the department publicly critical of the decision not to sponsor him?

Answer: The only instance of which I am aware that might be characterized as public criticism is an undated petition addressed to Dean Horace Taft which bears the names of nine junior members of the department. Whether public or not, it was handed to members of the Joint Boards as they entered the meeting of April of 1976. I enclose a copy. On the reverse side was a statement signed, "Committee to Support the Du Bois Seminar," but that was an undergraduate body I believe. Further light on this question will be found in the second paragraph of Professor Turner's answer to Question 25, in Turner to Kirkendall 4/26/77.

5. *Question:* When did your ad hoc committee cease to exist?

Answer: Clearly, the ad hoc committee functioned down to October 21, 1975, when it made its formal recommendation to Professor Hall, then chairman of the department. In March 1976 Professor Hall again consulted with those who had served on the committee about the Aptheker nomination, which had been re-submitted by Davenport College in unaltered form. It would involve niceties of departmental constitutionality beyond my grasp to determine whether this consultation meant the committee was still formally in existence in the spring of 1976. I can say, however, that in October it was my assumption as chairman of the ad hoc committee that it would cease to exist once it had performed the task for which it was called into being, namely to render a professional judgment on the qualifications of Herbert Aptheker to teach a course for credit at Yale. In all previous cases of negative judgments by such ad hoc committees of the department those judgments had been respected by the nominating colleges, so that the re-submission of the Aptheker nomination to the department by Davenport College was an unprecedented development. The same was necessarily the case with Professor Hall's consultation with the members of the ad hoc committee in March 1976. His action seemed to me the appropriate response to an unprecedented turn of events.

6. *Question:* Could you supply the committee with any additional information on the nature of your presentations before the Davenport College Seminar Committee?

Answer: I assume that "additional information" means additional to that leaked to the press in garbled form and referred to in Turner's answer to Question 18 in Turner to Kirkendall 4/26/77. The word "presentation" exaggerates the nature of my participation at their invitation in an informal discussion with the Davenport College Seminar Committee. Realizing that members of the committee included students as well as faculty, I explained, as I recall, the rules of confidentiality involved, that universities did not make public their reasons for rejecting applicants or publish the evidence on which such decisions were reached, that scores of such rejections were made each term, that we could not make exceptions. I did offer to discuss with the committee any of Aptheker's works they had read. None of the members, faculty or student, professed to have read any at all. I was asked about my experience with the Aptheker edition of the Du Bois correspondence. No members had seen the first volume, but I discussed very briefly my dissatisfaction with it and confirmed the impression of one member that I had resigned from the board. I did not go into the details of the matter related above but spoke in general terms about this and about the standards of scholarship in our department.

7. *Question:* The same question as above about the Junior Appointments Committee.

Answer: Here it is not clear what the information requested is in addition to. I am not aware of any leaks to the press from this committee such as I felt free to correct and comment on in the question about the Davenport College Committee. I would not say I ever made a "presentation" to the Junior Appointments Committee. To the first meeting of the committee I responded by a letter it requested and in the second in person by invitation. In both instances the questions and responses fall under the rules of "University policy and practice" described clearly by Professor Turner's response to Question 19 in Turner to Kirkendall 4/26/77. I can say, however, that I spoke not as a representative of the History Department or of its ad hoc committee but as a scholar in the candidate's field. The questions and answers were of the sort that I and the members of your committee have heard many times as members and referees of university appointment committees throughout their academic careers—the usual questions about a candidate's qualifications as a scholar and teacher. As you might expect, there was interest in what other scholars in the candidate's special fields thought of his work.

8. *Question:* The same question as 6 and 7 about the Joint Boards.

Answer: The reply here is about the same as my answer to Question 7, except what is applicable in my response to the following question, No. 9. Statements in the Joint Boards, apart from "presentations" of candidates by members moving appointments, are in the form of participation in the debate over a motion. Participants in such debates speak as individual "permanent officers of the University" rather than as representatives of departments.

9. *Question:* Is it accurate to define the historians' attack on Aptheker as "massive" and their statements against him as "long, fiery orations?"

Answer: The question leaves unclear what is referred to here, but I shall assume you are inquiring about the meeting of the Joint Boards of Permanent Officers on December 4, 1975, when the Aptheker appointment was rejected. No one who was present at that meeting would, I am confident, characterize anything said there in the terms you cite from unidentified sources. As a witness who was present, I would describe the statements that were made as sober, responsible, factual and relatively brief.

It would be misleading, however, to leave the impression that this tempest of months duration came off without dust and heat. There were plenty of "massive attacks" and "long, fiery orations"—deafening, electronically amplified, elaborately organized, shrewdly planned. But this was all in favor of the Aptheker appointment, not against it. It took one back to piping times of the sixties. Demonstrations, protests, mass meetings, campus rallies with bands and imported speakers including repeated appearances of the disputed candidate himself. There were petitions of more than 2,000 names. Out in the profession a former student of mine on the committee that organized the OAH petition resulting in your present investigation warned me before the spring meeting of 1976 that the movement was mobilized coast to coast. "Massive" and "fiery" indeed!

10. *Question:* Do you agree with those who suggest that the concept of professional confidentiality is rather like the concept of executive privilege?

Answer: The attempt to identify the time-honored rules of confidentiality in academic appointments procedure with the discredited "concept of executive privilege" probably comes from those who have used "cover-up" and "stonewalling" with the same purpose. It would not be worth a reply but for the implication that there is something exceptional or unique about the existence of the rule at Yale or Yale's History Department. We assumed the rule to be common to all reputable colleges and universities. I am sure it prevails at Michigan, Berkeley, Wisconsin, Minnesota, and Indiana. If it is not honored in the institution of the petitioners or anywhere else, we should be informed immediately. The character of our correspondence with such places about appointments and promotions would in that event have to be changed at once. The implications of your committee's report for this issue are of great importance. If it can do only two things, your efforts will be justified: (1) reassert the right of confidentiality in appointment procedures, and (2) discountenance resort to massive organized pressure to force appointments. In these two matters, issues of academic freedom are indeed at stake.

11. *Question:* Why did the historians continue to press the issue after the History Department had made its decision?

Answer: After the History Department made its decision in October, 1975, there were certainly those who would "continue to press the issue," but the pressure, as I have pointed out above, came from supporters of the Aptheker appointment. Those historians and others who opposed the appointment did not generate pressure. They maintained silence or responded to committees and bodies officially charged with advising the University administration about appointments. To ask why historians and others voted as they did is to invite speculation about motives. There is no record, public or private, of how they voted. The few who volunteered their thinking on the matter spoke as individuals, not for "the historians." If you are asking reasons for my vote on an appointment, I must tell you that in my judgment the AHA and the OAH have no right to make such inquiries of their members and will do great harm to the profession by suggesting the existence of such a right.

12. *Question:* How did you and your associates from the History Department represent yourselves at the meeting of the Joint Boards?

Answer: This has already been answered: as permanent officers of the University.

Your letter invites me to submit source materials that might be helpful. I enclose the petition addressed to Dean Taft mentioned in my answer to your Question 4. I will spare you samples of undergraduate journalism, of which I imagine you already have an extensive collection and will assess with due caution. With much hesitation I enclose six copies of the reprint of a five-page article of mine published in *Daedalus* in 1973 under the title "The Erosion of Academic Privileges and Immunities."[228] It contains no reference to the case before you and was written well before the events at issue. I nevertheless hope that the article may suggest a broader context in which these matters may be considered.

CVWP, 43/112: TCLS

236. To William G. Carleton

AUGUST 16, 1977

[deletion]

Since I last wrote I have become more involved and interested in our European travelers and commentators.[229] One learns to skip the Niagara and the Indians, etc. The rewards are many and considerable. Just finished Hall and Martineau: the right & the left of it at the time, and what a pair![230] And what a reading schedule. I was most glad to get your list and compare the checked items. With three exceptions I had all yours on my list of 80 out of some 400 in the Harvard Guide. And odd discoveries: The New Rome (German, laudatory, 1840) and the New Romans

228. CVW, "The Erosion of Academic Privileges and Immunities," *Daedalus* 103 (Fall 1974): 33–37.

229. CVW was beginning to think about—or, rather, to resume thinking about—European perceptions of American society; in 1990, this would eventuate in lectures given at the invitation of the New York Public Library and published as CVW, *The Old World's New World* (New York: Oxford University Press, 1991).

230. Captain Basil Hall, *Travels in North America in the Years 1827 and 1828*, 3 vols. (Edinburgh: Cadell, 1829); Harriet Martineau, *Society in America*, 3 vols. (London: Saunders and Otley, 1837).

(Canadian, defamatory, 1968).[231] Much richer than expected. And even a Brissot or a Chateaubriand can yield nuggets.[232] I am not sure you are right about the comparative amount of European writing on America. Sure, all those Italian travels of Englishmen and Germans. But mainly they were travelling through their classical reading, and scenery, not contemporary Italy as they travelled America. Many of the latter are engaged in political controversy with opponents at home. When did left and right switch American symbols?

All these questions I look forward to discussing with you. Alternative subjects you throw out are all worth while, and many thanks. But they are not so rich and attractive as this one. I will track down the Polish Perspectives article for sure. Also discovered books on Russian and on Italian perspectives on America. Must talk.

CVWP, 11/117: TCLU

231. The former is misdated: see Theodore Poesche, *The New Rome* (New York: G. P. Putnam, 1853); A. W. Purdy, ed., *The New Romans: Candid Canadian Opinions of the U.S.* (New York: St. Martin's Press, 1968).

232. Jacques-Pierre Brissot de Warville, *Nouveau voyage dans les États-Unis de l'Amérique septentrionale: fait en 1788*, 3 vols. (Paris: Buisson, 1791); François-René Chateaubriand, vicomte de, *Voyage en Amérique et en Italie*, 2 vols. (Paris and London: Colburn, 1828).

4

Last Years, 1977–99

237. To Walter Johnson

JUNE 12, 1978

Many thanks for sending me your piece on the Montgomery march. I will search my files before mailing this to see if anything turns up. I remember vaguely having an interview but do not know whether I can find any copy of it.

If Dick Hofstadter wrote anything the two people most likely to know would be either Eric McKitrick of Columbia or Stanley Elkins of Smith.

Since you are sticking to interviews another suggestion may be out of line; that was the speech that Martin Luther King gave at the Montgomery rally in which he quoted me.[1] I don't have a copy but naturally it left an impression. I am sure he did not know I was in the crowd.

CVWP, 28/326: TCLU

238. To Willie Lee Rose

JULY 4, 1980

Although we talked and corresponded a bit about your Oxford inaugural address, I never got to read it until I received the copy you

---

1. On March 25, 1965, in his address at the conclusion of the Montgomery to Selma march, King had discussed the history of segregation and said: "As the noted historian, C. Vann Woodward, in his book, *The Strange Career of Jim Crow,* clearly points out, the segregation of the races was really a political stratagem employed by the emerging Bourbon interests in the South to keep the southern masses divided and southern labor the cheapest in the land."

recently sent me.[2] What a gem! One of your best. It alone would justify the books of essays you are planning. It must be made available to its real public—Americans—for all its legitimate claims on a transnational interest.

For one thing it confirms an old hunch about the blindness of academics (maybe intellectuals generally). Because they were never able to fit these enormous phenomena into their established categories and canons they could never really see, grasp, understand them, comprehend their significance. Bad art plus bad history equals non-events. Embarrassments. Silence. Footnotes, or hasty paragraphs about political significance, media, social history, sociology. Maybe that clown Haley came up with the best caricature of categorization—"faction." Though he may never have appreciated the humor of it.

(Incidentally, *Roots* may turn out to be the most ephemeral of the four.[3] Whatever became of Swahili and dashikis? And by the way, don't miss Leonard Levy's "Prize Story" in the last Reviews of American History on his experience with Pulitzer Prize committees.[4] It confirms my own of several years ago.)

Another hunch that "Race and Region" bears out: to what avail are laborious historical research and sophisticated literary criticism without the gift of humility and imagination to face the wildness and improbability of history? The tag-line of your address captures a profound truth with the simplicity of genius. The good teacher, you say, will be "sufficiently modest to recognize that what is apparent may also be real." I would like to have written that.

CVWP, 47/558: TCLU

2. Willie Lee Rose, *Race and Region in American Historical Fiction: Four Episodes in Popular Culture* (Oxford: Clarendon Press, 1979); this inaugural address as the Harmsworth Professor was twice reprinted; see J. Morgan Kousser and James M. McPherson, eds., *Region, Race, and Reconstruction: Essays in Honor of C. Vann Woodward* (New York: Oxford University Press, 1982), 113–39, and Willie Lee Rose, *Slavery and Freedom*, expanded ed., ed. William W. Freehling (New York: Oxford University Press, 1982), 113–36.

3. Alex Haley, *Roots* (Garden City, NY: Doubleday, 1976).

4. Leonard W. Levy, "Prize Stories," *Reviews in American History* 8 (March 1980): 1–20.

239. To Barbara J. Fields[5]

AUGUST 14, 1980

Many thanks for the information about the Maryland department's vote on the Genovese appointment. All I knew about it was from the two letters in the *Times*, about which I wrote Gene but got no relevant response.[6]

I think now that in the letter Maryland requested I should have suggested to them that Eugene's fantasies are essentially of Sicilian rather than of Muscovite derivation. They probably have about as much practical bearing on American politics as Hatfield fantasies about McCoys, or white Southerners' fantasies about Pickett's charge. The difference is that Gene *will* put them in print now and then as an historical revision of Abe's Second Inaugural or a minority amendment to the Democratic platform. And he *will* dwell fondly on the need for mowing down the most Manly, Moral, Magnificent, etc., etc. specimens of the McCoys among the enemy class.

The sheer bravado of it has a certain appeal, of course. Especially to the young. And you and I know individuals who not only share such arm-chair fantasies, but would eagerly revise the American past and plan the rational future to accommodate the Gulags and lavish liquidations of Josif Dzhugashvili (of whom my spies report only one statue remains standing in the USSR, and that in his home town.)[7] I trust you will join

5. Barbara J. Fields studied with CVW at Yale; her 1978 dissertation would later be published as *Slavery and Freedom on the Middle Ground: Maryland During the Nineteenth Century* (New Haven: Yale University Press, 1985).

6. A subcommittee, chaired by Louis Harlan of the Department of History at the University of Maryland, had recommended that Genovese be appointed to a senior position, but the full department, by a tied vote of 23–23, declined to accept the recommendation. According to a report in the *New York Times*, Harlan had observed that Genovese's Marxism had been "not a negligible issue," while the chair of the department, Emory Evans, declined to comment. Genovese was quoted as saying, "I was told privately that the Red-baiting was outright, flagrant and undisguised." The letter column of the *Times* subsequently published two comments: Edward Magdol, chair of the Department of History at the State University College at Potsdam (New York) deplored "the threat to intellectual freedom"; and Louis M. Greenberg, an associate professor in the Maryland History Department, insisted that the decision had nothing to do with Marxism, but occurred because the department already had "three gifted historians in precisely the same field" as Genovese. See "Prof. Genovese Rejected," *New York Times* (13 June 1980): B5; Edward Magdol, "Marxist Scholars Need Not Apply," *New York Times* (22 June 1980): E20; Louis M. Greenberg, "Historians' Choice," *New York Times* (29 June 1980): E18.

7. Stalin.

me in the hope that such dreams do not become essential credentials of the youthful Left.

I hope Gene will soon find an academic base that suits him better than Rochester. I will do all I can to help. I warned him against Harvard. I only wish he had accepted the Princeton offer and settled down to work there.

[deletion]

CVWP, 18/209: TCLU

240. To Louis D. Rubin Jr.

MARCH 8, 1981

[deletion]

My spies report Kenneth Lynn is doing it for the *Times* and is attacking me for not using the surviving fragment of the original as copy text. Bastard!⁸

LDR, 9/174: ALS

241. To Eugene D. Genovese

APRIL 6, 1981

I have wondered whether to reply and whether anything I said would make any difference. I had feared your long silence was due to your health, but now it seems due more to faltering faith in a friend, or to suspicions of his loyalty, his courage, or his good faith.⁹ These are not

---

8. Kenneth S. Lynn, "The Masterpiece That Became a Hoax," *New York Times Book Review*, 26 April 1981, 3, which was a review of CVW's Chesnut edition.

9. In the fall of 1979 and spring of 1980, the Afro-American Studies program at Harvard had sought to recruit several senior scholars and considered Genovese, who then wished to leave the University of Rochester. Initially, it was announced that Harvard wanted to acquire three historians, but the first appointee—Nathan Huggins of Columbia, due to become chair in the summer of 1980—expressed the view that three was too many and wished, instead, to have appointments in literature and the social sciences. This contributed to derailing any possible Genovese appointment, though it was also the case that Genovese's Marxism occasioned division. A further complication was that sundry Harvard faculty spoke indiscreetly about Genovese having been a "difficult" and "controversial" colleague at Rochester, and that this, too, played a role. There were articles that spoke freely of these matters in the *Harvard Crimson* and *New York Times*, articles which in turn were picked up by the Rochester student newspaper. Understandably, Genovese was offended by, what he took be, personal slanders and thought that CVW had failed to rally to his support, in contradistinction to Genovese's support, when

matters I make it a practice to debate. But you have given me your understanding of my role in the Harvard appointment, and I assume you are willing to hear my account.

My only sources of information about that matter were David Davis and you. David spoke only of his *own* position, and that only because he wanted *you* to know what it was. He mentioned no other individual. I never talked to anybody else—at Harvard or anywhere else about it. I did not see the *Crimson* piece or the *Times* article on which you were quoted. I did hear of a black demonstration at Harvard against you and Levine.[10] I admit that I assumed then that the Harvard blacks, especially the woman professor you would have replaced as head of the department, were responsible for leaking the story to the press.[11] I don't see what motive Rosovsky would have for doing so, but I do see motives of the Afro-American Department.[12] It was then I wrote urging you to keep out of the mess at Harvard. At the same time I offered to write in your behalf if you pursued the matter. I was never asked for a letter by Harvard. Then later you wrote saying you should have listened to me and that you had been made a victim of a campaign of vilification, and you expressed suspicion of John Hope. I had no reason to share that suspicion, and still don't. I did have suspicions of others, but no evidence.

Why didn't I "speak out"? My recent experience with "speaking out" at Yale did not encourage a followup. You have had a rough time. But your integrity has not yet been made the subject of an official investigation by the OAH or the AHA, nor were their official publications filled for month after month with correspondence, committee reports, and counter-reports about your motives, your principles, and your honor. "Confidentiality" was no protection from that campaign of vilification— whose organizers were well-known. Don't worry. I'm not intimidated. I

---

president of the Organization of American Historians, of CVW during the Aptheker affair. Genovese expressed these feelings in a letter to CVW, 21 March 1981.

10. Lawrence W. Levine (1933–2006), then at the University of California-Berkeley, was a historian of black American culture; according to the *New York Times*, he was offered and declined a tenured position in the Afro-American Studies program at Harvard.

11. Eileen Jackson Southern (1920–2002), a musicologist and head of the Harvard Afro-American Studies program (1975–79).

12. Henry Rosovsky (b. 1927), an economist and dean of the Faculty of Arts and Sciences at Harvard (1973–84, 1990–91).

propose to speak out whenever I think it justified and will do any good. I confess some doubts about what good you might have derived from such headlines as: "Yale McCarthyite Wants Red for Harvard." Or, "If one for Harvard, why not one for Yale?"

I cannot believe that your old friends Eric Foner, Anne Lane, Michael Greenberg, or David Davis have betrayed you.[13] I very much hope you will not continue to believe that of them.

I find the following recurrent paragraph in my letters about the professional qualifications of a historian of my acquaintance:

> His standing in the profession is attested, among other ways, by his election as president of the Organization of American Historians. Primarily this was a tribute to his scholarship, but also I think it was testimony of admiration for a man who has repeatedly shown the courage of his convictions. I suspect that this admiration is shared by many historians who do not share those convictions. He in turn has consistently demonstrated his ability to respect, profit from, and work agreeably with scholars who are known to have very different views. I have reason to believe that these qualities were among those acknowledged by the American Academy of Arts and Letters in giving him one of their literary awards a few years ago.

I suppose it is arguable whether such statements are more effective when made in private or in public, but that raises the old question of confidentiality, doesn't it?

CVWP, 21/241: TCLU

242. To David Riesman

JUNE 15, 1981

Our recent ailments recall yours. Shortly after our return from Portugal we were both taken with bronchitis. Then Glenn came down with pneumonia, in the hospital for a spell, back home with an oxygen tank, and still in and out of bed but not yet out of the house. You can see

---

13. Eric Foner (b. 1943), then teaching at City College and the Graduate Center at the City University of New York, was best known for his first book, *Free Soil, Free Labor, Free Men: The Ideology of the Republican Party Before the Civil War* (New York: Oxford University Press, 1970); Ann J. Lane (b. 1931), Genovese's first wife and a historian of slavery and feminism, was then at the Bunting Institute of Radcliffe College; Michael S. Greenberg (b. 1941) completed a Rutgers doctorate on Virginia slaveholders in 1972.

what happened to my schedule and why I have been slow in responding to your fascinating autobiographical writings.[14]

Faced with a choice of a longer or a shorter version, I naturally chose the longer and have read only that—and with what fascination and pleasure! You obviously have the autobiographical gift and talents you should develop. Maybe in a more extended version. I would define the essence of that gift as the ability to evoke from one's personal experience the common experience that brings to selfconsciousness a cohort. I don't really take much stock in age establishing cohorts. Too loose. People live contemporaneously in different periods, filtering the same experiences through different cultural lenses molded in different periods. Few of Byron's contemporaries belonged in his cohort. More of Mark Twain's, to be sure. (Well, didn't mean to get so bloody literary.)

In the formative years you and I were long leagues apart in geography and even culture: Philadelphia and Cambridge—Arkansas and Georgia! Yet cohort cohesion set in early. Earlier than 1932, perhaps, but that was the year of my trip to Russia. Was that your year of pilgrimage or was it '31? Couldn't quite tell. How vividly you evoked that unforgettable, mind-shaping, incredible experience. Neither of us would have been the same person without it. From then on at least I think we were more or less cohorters.

Cohort. Military origin, isn't it? As a word I mean. Odd word for an antiwar generation. Apart from religion, sex, and race—and there was not so much apartheid as might be imagined—my strongest passions of youth were about war. I was a passionate non-interventionist in WWII. Pearl Harbor made me physically as well as emotionally sick. Recovering I joined the navy, but never recovered from the revulsion. So you see you raised a lot of ghosts: Japan, Hopkins, Mexico &c &c &c.
[deletion]

   CVWP, 47/551: TCLU

---

14. Riesman had sent CVW both a long and a short version of what, in the short version, would be published as David Riesman, "A Personal Memoir: My Political Journey," in *Conflict and Consensus: A Festschrift in Honor of Lewis A. Coser*, ed. Walter W. Powell and Richard Robbins (New York: Free Press, 1984), 327–64.

243. To James B. Meriwether[15]

JULY 5, 1981

Many thanks for the 1963 letter you and Thorp wrote about one of Lynn's numerous performances of the sort.[16] I have distributed copies for fellow victims who have written me. He's made a career of it and become a favorite of editors. As I told Henry Smith, scholars have been tolerating a fox in the henhouse. You did not mention the letter of reply by Bill Taylor and Steven Stowe in the *Times* of May 17.[17] I would appreciate your reaction and will send you a copy if you missed it. I still think I was right in maintaining silence.

But I am afraid that is not the end of the matter. For example David Donald in an aside to the review of another book recently remarked that Woodward had destroyed the credibility of Chesnut.[18] He or others will likely carry on the Lynn line in learned journals later. It will not be my scholarship but Chesnut's integrity or that of her book that is at stake. It would be nice if somebody else would carry on the defense. But I am afraid I cannot avoid the responsibility and that continued silence on my part in such circumstances would be misconstrued. So I must reluctantly prepare for the fray—as little ad hominem as possible, preferably no ref. to Lynn, possibly an essay instead of a letter of reply.[19]

In this I must beg your help. The venture will inevitably get me into deeper waters of literary analogy and controversy than I am comfortable

15. James B. Meriwether (1928–2007), a literary scholar who specialized in William Faulkner; he was the McClintock Professor of Southern Letters at the University of South Carolina, as well as director of its Institute for Southern Studies, which had invited CVW to be a visiting professor in order to advance his study of Mary Chesnut.

16. Presumably William W. Thorp (1899–1990), who taught American literature at Princeton until 1967; Meriwether had done his doctoral work at Princeton.

17. A letter to the *New York Times*, in rebuttal of Lynn's review of *Mary Chesnut's Civil War*, had been sent by William R. Taylor (b. 1922), who taught at the State University of New York and was the author of *Cavalier and Yankee: The Old South and American National Character* (New York: Braziller, 1961); he was joined in this effort by his former graduate student Steven M. Stowe (b. 1946), then a visiting assistant professor at New York University. The letter was published in the *New York Times Book Review* (17 May 1981): 10.

18. David Herbert Donald, "Word from the Old South," *New York Times Book Review* (28 June 1981): 3, 23.

19. This would be published as CVW, "Mary Chesnut in Search of Her Genre," *Yale Review* 73 (Winter 1984): 199–209; it was reprinted in CVW, *The Future of the Past* (New York: Oxford University Press, 1989), 250–62.

in. Reviewing the dialogue of our conference in Columbia I find several interesting suggestions you and others made. You mentioned T. E. Lawrence's *Seven Pillars*—which I must follow up—and Defoe and Faulkner. Have you thought of any others? Can you? There must be scores. Is Boswell's *Johnson* and the way he converted his journals into the biography a valid analogy? What about Mark Twain's *Life on the Mississippi?* What other instances of extensively revised and expanded diaries do we have? Another way of putting the question is how many diaries have ever been published without some revision or expansion? If Chesnut is banished, what about all the other memoirs? Does it come down to the word "diary" her publishers stuck her with? Or to readers having been taken in once and being burnt children? Or to the question of whether Chesnut intended to deceive her readers? What about the elaborate distinction she makes between the part of her book that is "memoir" and the part that is not? Creativity or disingenuousness or dishonesty? Or is it for lack of a familiar category for her? I don't think the wholly invented "diary" or "letters" that were "found in the attic" as a medium for fiction are any help at all in the way of classifying Chesnut.

But there must be some valid and persuasive way of defending the integrity of this great document. Have you any more thoughts?

CVWP, 70/100: TCLS

244. To Daniel T. Rodgers[20]

APRIL 12, 1982

I hope it was you to whom I told the calf-weening story, and I think it was, and that you saw the close-up angle from which I saw Odum.[21] Too close to take him in and too close for comfort and trying to keep my distance. With difficulties. When I arrived at Chapel Hill he struck an in loco parentis—but furioso—posture and lectured me sternly when I fell in promptly with the "wrong crowd."

20. Daniel T. Rodgers (b. 1942), who had been CVW's graduate student at Yale, had published his dissertation as *The Work Ethic in Industrial America, 1850–1920* (Chicago: University of Chicago Press, 1978); he was then teaching at Princeton. This is one of a series of letters written by CVW to those who had contributed to CVW's Festschrift.

21. Rodgers's contribution to the Festschrift had been, for the most part, a discussion of Howard Odum: Daniel T. Rodgers, "Regionalism and the Burdens of Progress," in *Region, Race, and Reconstruction*, 3–26.

Well, I had read recently essays on Odum by O'Brien and one by Singal, the latter with some interest, both based on extensive use of Odum papers and others and pretty good.[22] But I should have known. It's not the sources that are used but the eyes that see. Both of those missed (as I had myself) the superb paradox of the progressive leader heroically fighting the rear-guard action of the retreating Confederates, long after the latter had struck their tents and stolen away. Marvelous, and so gently humorous. And the others also missed the comparison with Fitzhugh.

Of course, in the Jim Crow lectures I proclaimed W. G. Sumner my target, but I was shooting at Odum. But I only begin to wonder, after reading you, how much of Odum as compared with the Nashville crowd unconsciously rubbed off on my demonology of the New South. I thought I was doing the impossible—fleeing desperately from both. Yours was a most auspicious opening for the book.

Such ventures are redeemed intellectually (if at all) by a few, usually a very few, contributions that simply have to be cited. One distinctive thing about this particular venture is the remarkable number of such contributions it contains. Things of genuine merit, and some with wit, spirit, style, and grace. They make me prouder of my association with them and with the book. I hope they knew me well enough to realize how much their handsome celebration meant to me, even if I neglected to tell them. At least they knew me well enough not to make speeches at me.
[deletion]

CVWP, 31/366: TCLU

245. To Willie Lee Rose

NOVEMBER 30, 1982

[deletion]

It has been a fall mainly of "activities" more than work—some things I had to do, like the trip to Gainesville, Florida, tomorrow to speak at a memorial service for my dear old friend Bill Carleton, who died last month. Some other sad duties. But other things that I had put off or

---

22. Michael O'Brien, "Howard Odum: The Sociological Vision," in *The Idea of the American South, 1920–1941* (Baltimore, MD: Johns Hopkins University Press, 1979), 29–93; Daniel J. Singal, "Howard W. Odum and Social Science in the South," in *The War Within: From Victorian to Modernist Thought in the South, 1919–1945* (Chapel Hill: University of North Carolina Press, 1982), 115–52.

begged off during Glenn's illness, things that combined duties with some enjoyment, like a paper on Mary C. to the Editors Association in Columbia. Or a paper at the U. of Alabama to launch their semester-long seminar on *The Burden* (imagine that!) which I could not very well turn down. While there Willie Morris came over to take me to Oxford, just for a visit. From there to Memphis for the SHA meeting—and all those people, so many of whose names escaped me and whose faces have changed. Still, I knew more of them than of any other gathering of the size and enjoyed some of them. Especially a sizeable number of old students, some from far back and some recent. They are a rather remarkable group. Bert W-B starred with a paper.[23] I think his book is a major and very difficult achievement and is not likely to get the recognition it deserves.[24] Barbara Fields and Steve Hahn pulled off a tour de force of neo-marxism but did not agree and I had a bit of sport knocking their heads together.[25] Still, they were quite good. All of them asked about you and hoped you would be there. Bill McFeely turned up and so did Sheldon Hackney (full of weighty problems and never showing it). In Philadelphia recently I popped in on the Hackneys for breakfast at their newly remodeled presidential mansion. Amazing pair, really two presidents who are one in the flesh, as the scriptures put it.

To complete my confession of frivolities I must put in the return of the native to Arkansas—for the first time in over a half a century. I had begun to feel I looked like the snob I sometimes am at heart, and that would not do. So this time I accepted an invitation, made an appearance, did my duty, &c &c. And rather glad I did. Feel the better for it, and besides had a good visit with my boyhood friend Dick Huie, the only one I have kept up with—all in a day & night at Little Rock. Vanndale would

23. Bertram Wyatt-Brown gave a paper on "Honor as a Cause of Southern Secession," in a session on "Honor as a Factor in Civil War History"; the other papers were given by Dan T. Carter and Dickson D. Bruce Jr.

24. Bertram Wyatt-Brown, *Southern Honor: Ethics and Behavior in the Old South* (New York: Oxford University Press, 1982), was, in fact, a finalist for both the Pulitzer Prize in History and the American Book Award.

25. They were in a session, chaired by Sheldon Hackney, on "The New South in Comparative Perspective"; Fields's paper was on "Political Sovereignty, State Power, and the Advent of Capitalist Agriculture: The New South in the Modern World," and Hahn's on "Landed Elites and National Consolidation in Post-Emancipation Societies." Hahn (b. 1951) was about to publish his Yale dissertation as *The Roots of Southern Populism: Yeoman Farmers and the Transformation of the Georgia Upcountry, 1850–1890* (New York: Oxford University Press, 1983).

have been too much, and besides no one would have been old enough to know me. Then Thanksgiving with the McFeelys. Liza picked me up for the ride to their place on the Cape and Mary popped over from England (where she had been doing research) to cook the turkey. Liza entertained us with guitar and song—and the wolf did not darken the door. So much for my dissipations.

Susan still buzzing about the Balkans. Joined her sister Martha, an anthropologist researching in Hungary, for a toot through Czechoslovakia and Poland, thence to a conference in Athens.[26] Some women are more liberated than others. Susan's temporarily ends at Christmas when she returns to move into her apartment on Whitney Avenue and face Yale classes next term. I hope for the best for her. I can be sure she will make waves at Yale but whether she will make tenure is the question. She knows the facts of life, however, and is prepared to run the risk. I was relieved to learn that she has called off the visit to India. Maybe she is growing up. It will be good to have her here. And maybe now I won't have to be careful not to defend the Occident vs. the Orient—but there is still Politics to be avoided. We both try to keep the peace.

As you will see I have been mostly running away from loneliness instead of settling in with it as my normal way of life. And embracing it as the scholar's way of work. After Christmas I will indeed settle down to work. Practical problems are adequately solved by resort to a caterer. Not only saves thinking and cooking but most important it saves the abominations of shopping. And saves time I need. Oxford History chapters pour in from various quarters. Most prolifically from Jim McPherson.[27] No McClellan this Jim McP. He pushes on to Richmond hell for leather.

I know you have your reservations about my colleague David Davis, but I am taking the outrageous liberty (don't tell) of clipping off and enclosing the final paragraph of his recent application for another Guggenheim, for which I served as one of the referees. This should put you to shame and suggest in what esteem you are held in some quarters. So there.

CVWP, 47/558: TCLS

---

26. Martha Lampland (b. 1952), who was to get her doctorate in anthropology from the University of Chicago in 1987; she was later to teach at the University of California-San Diego.

27. McPherson was then writing *Battle Cry of Freedom: The Civil War Era* (New York: Oxford University Press, 1988), a volume in the *Oxford History of the United States*.

246. To Robert Penn Warren

APRIL 26, 1983

Back from my tour of the late Confederacy—Chapel Hill to Oxford, Miss., and on to Fayetteville, Ark., all reeling drunk with spring—and found in my mail awaiting *Chief Joseph*, through which I immediately plunged, and for which many thanks.[28] I am your debtor for reflections the poem provoked and I am tempted to inflict a few of them on you.

Historians and poets have been kicking back and forth between them for ages Aristotle's chestnut about there being more truth in poetry than in history (or was it "deeper" truth?)[29] If I remember Burkhardt's gloss on it rightly he said poetry gives us more understanding of human nature than history.[30] Of course there are numerous variations on the theme, but so far as I recall they all in one way or another counterpose the two genres—poetry as compared with history.

But now comes along a poet who puts history and poetry together in one genre, call it historical poetry or poetical history, literally a sandwich of the two with layers of history between layers of poetry, the former represented by authentic documents from cited texts. History in poetry, poetry as history, a real consolidation. Now what happens to Aristotle's old chestnut? Now that we have history as poetry.

I realize of course that you have used the one in the other before—as in *Brother to Dragons*. But I believe never this explicitly. And I suppose there are Latin and maybe Greek precedents, though both were vague on what history was. No vagueness in *Chief Joseph*. Documented. I happen to know some of the sources and some of the characters—O. O. Howard,

28. Robert Penn Warren, *Chief Joseph of the Nez Perce, Who Called Themselves the Nimipu, "the Real People": A Poem* (New York: Random House, 1983). CVW, after speaking at a Tuscaloosa conference, was driven to the University of Arkansas in Fayetteville; along the way, he had revisited two of his childhood places, Vanndale and Morrilton.

29. There are various translations, but the standard Loeb edition has, "Poetry is more philosophical and elevated than history; since poetry relates more of the universal, and history relates particulars." The use of "elevated" here means something of ethical import. See Aristotle, "Poetics," ed. and trans. Stephen Halliwell, in *Aristotle, Poetics / Longinus, On the Sublime / Demetrius, On Style* (Cambridge, MA: Harvard University Press, 1995), 59.

30. Jacob Burckhardt, *Reflections on History* (Indianapolis, IN: Liberty Classics, 1979), 107, has, after quoting the above from Aristotle: "[History] is indebted to poetry for insight into the nature of mankind as a whole; further, for profound light on times and peoples. Poetry, for the historical observer, is the image of the eternal in its temporal and national expression; hence, instructive in all its aspects and, moreover, often the best or only thing to survive."

Miles, Sherman, etc.[31] No poet could have invented that Buffalo Bill circus to Grant's tomb—or would have been believed if he did. It must not
have been easy to bring this off—a one-man creation of an entirely new
genre of literature. Only a poet with history in his bones could have done it.

Thanks again. It was one of the most moving literary experiences I
can remember. Or historical experiences either.

RPW, 82/1612: TLS

247. To James M. McPherson

MAY 28, 1983

I think you would agree that my initial response to your suggestion of
a separate volume on social history for the Oxford History was quite
positive. And Sheldon seemed quite open to the idea.[32] I was especially
aware of the difficulty authors of period volumes would have in doing
justice to the monographic flood generally called "social history," and of
the vulnerability of the series to criticism on that score. Your proposal
struck me as a way out.

Since then I have had an attack of second thoughts and doubts. One
source of them was a talk with Ed Morgan, who is very skeptical and
challenged me to come up with a table of contents. I had to admit that
the "field" was poorly defined, unperiodized, fragmented, and rather
centrifugal. Interdisciplinary interests tend to scatter rather than unite
the components. General treatments resort to historiographical essays. I
can't think of any notable or successful effort of unification. I have not
come up with any historian who could or would attempt one.

I used to tell students sagely that if something happened a history
of it could be written. I guess social history undoubtedly happened, but
I am at some loss about how to get a history of it together. That is, more

31. These are various military figures who appear in Warren's poem, because they were
involved in the U.S. pursuit and semidestruction of the Nez Perce Indians in Oregon in the
1870s: General Oliver Otis Howard, who in 1874 was placed in command of the Department
of the Columbia, which included Oregon; Nelson Appleton Miles (1839–1925), who as a colonel led the 1877 campaign against the Nez Perce; and William Tecumseh Sherman (1820–1891),
the Civil War general who in 1869 succeeded U.S. Grant as commanding general of the U.S.
Army and hence had overall responsibility for the Indian wars.

32. Sheldon Meyer (1926–2006), an executive editor at Oxford University Press in New
York, with a special responsibility for works in American history, including the *Oxford History of
the United States.*

than in discrete monographs addressed to a limited group of professionals, local history, a century or two of marriage ages or family sizes: 4.56
to 3.111 children. Important, to be sure, but. Take one of the richest sub-
fields: demography. Infant mortality, life expectancy, birthrate, contra-
ception, abortion, adolescence, menarchy, premarital childbearing, marriage age, aging, death. Or the proliferating sub-sub-fields: family, death
& dying, sexuality, homosexuality, prostitution. Or the super-sub-fields:
WOMEN, ETHNICS, URBAN, NATIVE AMERICANS. OK, round them all
up. Integrate, periodize, unify, summarize. And THEN the carping critics
will say, What! Nothing on asylums, prisons, crime, religion, &c &c &c!
Pray, what are your thoughts? Have I lapsed into defeatism?

I rejoice at news of drafts of Chapters 7–9 and will await 10 with
them eagerly July 20 and more later from Princeton. Hope I thanked you
for your admirable OAH paper and that you disciplined Mills firmly.[33]

CVWP, 41/494: TCLS

248. To Bertram Wyatt-Brown

MAY 30, 1983

I know perfectly well that the time it took you to write this deeply thoughtful comment on my essay had to be snatched from scores of pressing
demands on your time these days.[34] I appreciate it all the more for what
I know it must have cost you. But mainly I value your criticism for what
it profits me, for its astuteness, for its speaking unrelentingly to the point.
Don't worry about my vanity. I knew I was speaking irresponsibly from
the privileged immunity from a followup critic and that I could revise it
before it got into print. And revise it I shall and extensively—largely in
response to your very helpful criticism. Again, many thanks.

I feel the force of all your points and the necessity of responding to them all in some fashion, whether in agreement, rejection, or
clarification—or retraction. But in general I believe there is credible space
for both these interpretive images—both mine and, what is virtually its
mirror image, yours. Let me enlarge a bit on the apparent paradox.

You may be surprised to hear that I find congenial the very statement

33. That is, Mills Thornton; the OAH was held in Cincinnati in 1983.

34. This would seem to be an early draft of what would be given as the Charles Edmon-
son Historical Lectures at Baylor University in 1984, then as the Fleming Lectures at Louisiana
State University in 1985; with additions, these were published as CVW, *Thinking Back: The Perils
of Writing History* (Baton Rouge: Louisiana State University Press, 1986).

you formulate as "where we differ in essence," namely that "the history of the South, in a political sense, is the history of resistance to *unwanted, uncontrolled* change." I have not thought that through regarding the long period before the critical era of sectional conflict, but with regard to the latter period and afterward I think there is much to be said for your position. I think I could endorse it without much trouble and integrate it with my theme of the orthodoxy of continuity. Does not your thesis go a long way to explain mine? Was it not that very passionate resistance to change that was behind the refusal to acknowledge it and the insistence that nothing had changed and that continuity prevailed—"is now and shall be evermore" World without end?

Of course that applies only to the conservatives—that is, the overwhelming majority of Southerners. Radicals and liberals get into the discussion only at the academic or intellectual level. And their purposes in subscribing to continuity are quite different. For the radicals the object is to demonstrate that whatever change there was is superficial or inconsequential, the old oppression under a new guise, and that the revolution is still to come. For the liberals the objects vary: to make welcome change more acceptable under the guise of continuity, to point up the inadequacy of change and the need for more change, more departure from the despised old order. I should make these contrary objectives more clear. But that did not prevent all three from finding common ground on Continuity.

W. J. Cash is a special case and I must heed your warning about being fair to him. He was certainly no conservative or "true Believer" and qualifies as a skeptic. His assumptions and objectives are not those of Phillips or Mitchell.[35] A Menckenean hillbilly without Mencken's aristocratic pretensions, he yearned for change of a liberal order and lashed his beloved South with scorn for its deluded pretensions of modernity, civility, and decency when in reality it clung blindly to the dreams and myths and values of the old order. But in order to buttress his case for blind continuity he freely used the arguments of Grady, Phillips, and Mitchell supporting the existence and reality of continuity. The continuity was for him not imaginary but real and he did not celebrate but deplored it. He could at the same time deplore the Babbittry and materialism of

35. Broadus Mitchell (1892–1988), an economic historian who was a graduate of the University of South Carolina and had taught at Johns Hopkins (1919–39); his early writings included *The Rise of Cotton Mills in the South* (Baltimore, MD: Johns Hopkins University Press, 1921).

the new order and deride its trick of draping itself in the mantle of the old regime. It is no wonder to me that all three schools of present-day continuity—conservative, radical, and liberal—appeal to his authority and proclaim agreement with him.

I must explore with care your suggestion of difference between mutability and change, "constants within change," and "unmasterable change from alien sources." Here is a dimension of subtlety from which I could profit much. I erred if I gave the impression that I thought history confined to change. In fact I think history inconceivable without continuity—"no continuity, no history." I went perhaps too far in adding the corollary "no change, no history," I most certainly erred in attributing the origins of continuitarian orthodoxy to the founding fathers of the New South. I think they contributed substantially but cannot claim full credit. You are clearly right that the origins were broader and deeper than that. I concede an "affinity" between continuity and distinctiveness, but not Degler's logic in a necessary causal connection. I agree I made too much of Degler but he is a convenient whipping boy. I bow to the implied charge of presentism derived from writing amidst the great hurricane of change.

[deletion]

Informed Mills I now counted two vipers from my nest: Morgan the Terrible, terror of quantifiers, and Mills the Terrible, terror of traditionalists. Also admonished him to reread Riesman.

Peter Gay, coming on strong with first of five volumes of Freudian history, has read your book and I would like to get you together for exchange of views.

CVWP, 63/6: TCLU

249. To Erroll McDonald[36]

JULY 11, 1983

Mr. Henry-Louis Gates of the Yale Afro-American and English departments asks me to write you.[37]

He tells me he has encountered the opinion among publishers that the publication of evidence of racial injustice and abuse in the form of illustrations will tend to encourage racial injustice and abuse.

36. An editor at Random House.
37. Henry Louis Gates Jr. (b. 1950), a scholar of African-American literature.

Let me simply say that I do not follow the logic of this assumption. Much important scholarship in the field of racial relations exposes the existence of injustice and abuse. Surely it cannot be assumed that to expose injustice is to advocate or promote it. To apply that assumption would be to bring to a halt publication of much of value in this field.

I do not know the quality of Mr. Gates' work, but it should not be rejected on the assumption mentioned above.

CVWP, 46/543: TCLU

250. To Virginia Foster Durr

HAMDEN, CT
JANUARY 23, 1984

I was distressed to learn from Lucy of a hard time you have been having but she assures me you have pulled out of it now and are up and about as usual. I went through the cataract ordeal with Glenn—as well as many other physical afflictions—and know how the purely physical can affect the psyche and bring on depression. She fought to keep them apart not very successfully—but it was cancer that got her in the end. But you have a stronger and more indomitable mind and will not let it be victimized by the inevitable bodily ailments that will keep on coming. Let the medicine men do what they can about the body but keep them away from the psyche. You are the best doctor for that. Keep up the fight and help us celebrate many more birthdays.

Bless you and Love

VFD, 1/257: ALS

251. To Virginia Foster Durr

JUNE 4, 1984

In turning up the Salant letter (enclosed), I also reread your sweet letter to me about Glenn and your talks with her.[38] It moves me very deeply and I am so grateful to you. I still love her.

I would gladly have undertaken a foreword to your book, but your

---

38. A copy of Richard S. Salant (of the National News Council) to Norman Dorsen (president of the American Civil Liberties Union Foundation), 3 November 1983, in which Salant discusses his nomination of Durr for the ACLU Medal of Liberty Award.

publisher gave me an absolute deadline that was impossible for me to meet, completely impossible. I do not know why he waited so long to write me.

Here's to reunion at the Vineyard.

VFD, 1/257: ALS

252. To David H. Donald

JUNE 17, 1984

O f course I was delighted to learn of that cryptic reference to me in Thomas Wolfe's notebook. I have no idea how he heard of me.[39] I was a constant reader and admirer of his, but I do not recall ever writing him or recall any mutual friends.

I do remember his visiting Chapel Hill and wanting to meet him.[40] It was before Glenn and I were married and I was in her office in Old South Building when I saw this giant lumbering past her door and recognized him. It would have been a simple thing to step out and offer my hand, and I had a strong impulse to do so and will always regret that I didn't—now more than ever since hearing from you about that note. But my nerve failed me and the opportunity slipped by. He was dead within the year.

It was the same with William Faulkner. I was checking out of the Algonquin Hotel in New York on the way to catch a plane to take up my Harmsworth duties—and scared. Standing in line to pay my bill I found a small man just in front of me. He turned a profile and I immediately recognized him. I could have said I was sorry to have missed him when Jim Silver took me to his house in Oxford, but that I had a good visit with his wife. And that I needed his blessing just now. But no. Again my nerve failed me, and I never met another of my heroes.

I don't think it was because I was scared of them but rather of myself, of not being up to the occasion.

My very best wishes for the Wolfe biography. It is a great and difficult opportunity. I look forward keenly to reading it.

39. CVW had forgotten that, in a letter from Antonina Hansell (April 1938) in New York, she told of having dinner with Wolfe, who spoke of CVW and spending time with Glenn Rainey.

40. The visit was in January 1937; see David Herbert Donald, *Look Homeward: A Life of Thomas Wolfe* (Boston: Little, Brown, 1987), 401–3.

Do give my best to Aida. I have often thought it a pity that you and I do not get together more often than we have in late years.

CVWP, 16/176: TCLU

253. To Jonathan M. Wiener[41]

JANUARY 1, 1985

You got me wrong. I did not say that "anti-Marxism has nothing to do with the campaign against Abraham."[42] How could I? Surely you don't think I am such a simpleton. Of course it does. They gather from all points on the Right to focus on a vulnerable target. What else might one expect? That is not the issue, for we agree about that.

No. What I said was that Abraham's Marxism was not the issue that precipitated his troubles. Why? (1) Knowing he was a Marxist, two experts in the field, Feldman and Joll read his manuscript and recommended its publications.[43] (2) Also aware of his politics, the Princeton Press published his book. (3) Equally informed of his Marxism, Mason of Oxford University reviewed his book quite favorably in the AHR.[44] (4) Quite as well

41. Jonathan M. Wiener had taught at the University of California-Irvine since 1973 and was the author of *Social Origins of the New South: Alabama, 1860–1885* (Baton Rouge: Louisiana State University Press, 1978).

42. In 1983, in part because of predominantly positive reviews of David Abraham, *The Collapse of the Weimar Republic: Political Economy and Crisis* (Princeton, NJ: Princeton University Press, 1981), the Princeton Department of History had recommended that Abraham be tenured, but the administration declined to do so. Some critics—notably Gerald Feldman of Berkeley and Henry A. Turner of Yale—then accused Abraham of deliberately falsifying his evidence in order to validate his Marxist analysis, campaigned to prevent Abraham from getting an academic position, suggested that the University of Chicago rescind Abraham's doctorate, and wanted the press to withdraw the book. After a long and bitter controversy, in which most outsiders concluded that Abraham had been sloppy about his evidence (as he admitted) but not mendacious, and that his critics had been excessively vituperative, Abraham gave up his career as a historian and went to law school. On this, see, especially, Peter Novick, *That Noble Dream: The "Objectivity Question" and the American Historical Profession* (Cambridge: Cambridge University Press, 1988), 612–21, and Jon Wiener, *Historians in Trouble: Plagiarism, Fraud, and Politics in the Ivory Tower* (New York: New Press, 2005), 94–105.

43. Gerald D. Feldman (1937–2007), who had taught at Berkeley since 1962; James B. Joll (1918–1994), who had been Professor of International History at the London School of Economics since 1967.

44. T. W. Mason, review of *Collapse of the Weimar Republic*, in *American Historical Review* 87 (October 1982): 1122–23.

informed of his views as the above, his department at Princeton voted him tenure. You would have to agree that there was no trouble up to that point. And you would have to agree that the trouble came later—and there is no disagreement thus far between us. Only after all the above did Mason retract his endorsement of the book, did Feldman retract his support, and Princeton veto the department vote. These are the facts.

As for choosing or renouncing defenders, I suspect that Abraham shares some of Turner's problems—and also deserves some sympathy. That is, I doubt that Abraham solicited or welcomed front-page defense in *Pravda,* or for that matter support from the old-line American Stalinists that have rallied to his cause. Perhaps you can advise him on how to renounce or disassociate himself from them. I have no advice to offer either camp.

I was pleased to hear that no resolutions on the matter of Abraham were offered at the business meeting of the AHA last week in New York. I very much hope that for the benefit of all concerned that things will quiet down and that you will do what you can to further that end.

CVWP, 59/718: TCLU

254. To James M. McPherson

DECEMBER 4, 1985

A reading of Chapter 7, "The Revolution of 1860" and Chapter 8, "The Counterrevolution of 1861" does not change my conviction that this is fine history and that it is the best account we have of the coming and the course of the American Civil War in comparable space. And I still believe that in the long run your emphasis on the political and military aspects of the period will be justified. Having completed that, you now face the challenge of that introductory chapter or chapters on America at mid-century.

At this juncture I beg you to bear with me while I attempt to change roles and play the devil's advocate for a bit. In that role I am trying to summon up some of the "Yes, buts" of the adversarial critics (not the only ones surely) you may expect to encounter.

I need not remind you that the revolt against "traditional" and "narrative" history, political and military history, has not yet exhausted itself—though I think it shows signs of doing so. But enough of its proponents remain around to ask such questions as: "Yes, but did Americans do nothing between 1848 and 1865 but play politics and wage war? What's new in all this? Isn't it all an old story? Haven't we heard it all before? What was happening in those critical years to immigration, industrialization, urbanization, demography, social mobility, class relations, labor relations, sex relations, Indians, religion, intellectual life, art, medicine, agriculture, foreign trade, railroads, merchant marine, banks?"

Well, I have just taken down the first volume of my old edition of Henry Adams, *History of the United States During* . . . and looked through those opening chapters. I don't propose them as a model. After all, Adams had nine volumes to go and took 184 pages to introduce them. But still, I wonder if there is not an opportunity in what you propose to do of this sort to address some of the social history questions mentioned and anticipate your critics. Somewhere, here or in a Preface, I think you should offer your own measured justification for the emphasis you adopt. But apart from that, on the substantive side, I think you can say a lot in a long chapter on the social history side. You know the stuff or sources of it. Throw in an outrageous and unprovable hypothesis or so to outdo the adversary. It could be one of your most exciting sections. Sure, there was more than politics & battles—for example . . . and let them have it. I hesitate to suggest it, considering space, but you might even think of a concluding chapter, perhaps taking off from Fredrickson's *Inner Civil War*, suggesting new meanings for the central event in American history.[45] Brief but soaring. Henry Redux!
[deletion]

  CVWP, 42/495: TCLS

255. To Charles Grier Sellers

APRIL 6, 1987

It is clear that you are producing a new type of synthesis and applying in mainline history themes and findings heretofore largely confined to monographs and specialized studies.[46] I say let innovation thrive. It is

---

45. George M. Fredrickson, *The Inner Civil War* (New York: Harper & Row, 1965).

46. Sellers was writing the 1815–48 volume for the *Oxford History of the United States*. Later it would be decided, since CVW found the manuscript insufficiently to his taste, that the volume would be published, separately from the series, by Oxford University Press. It appeared as Charles Sellers, *The Market Revolution: Jacksonian America, 1815–1846* (New York: Oxford University Press, 1991), and was very successful.

unthinkable that we stick eternally to old models. I am one to welcome new views and bold experiments, and I wish you the best of luck with yours. Of course innovators must expect hecklers, and you are right to anticipate "hoots from bourgeois historians" who will be at it early and late defending tradition and booing radicalism. I am sure you can take all this in your stride. But you would agree that it is the better part of wisdom to avoid unnecessary vulnerabilities when possible. Anything I offer in the way of suggestions is made with that in mind. Please think of it that way and make what use of it you can.

Characteristic of some chapters—and I am thinking mainly of Chapters One, Two, Nine, and Ten—is a certain tendency toward abstraction. I think this may be due to the contrapuntal structure of your analysis and organization as illustrated in chapter titles such as "Land and Market," "New Light/Moderate Light," "God and Mammon," "Ethos vs. Eros." It also appears in the Manichean dualism in such recurrent counterpoint as: Arminian vs Antinomian, subsistence production vs capitalist production, male egotism vs female altruism, patriarchal vs individualist family, nature's time vs clock time, "a use-value world . . . and God's everyday presence" vs "a market world that takes the competitive ego for human nature and rationality for revelation."

It is not that you fail to endow these Manichean concepts with reified actuality and dramatic vitality. In fact I found myself cheering on the honest antinomian country folk, barefoot and forthright as they are, against the arminian city slickers, applauding the antinomian New Lights and deploring the arminian Moderate Lights. The Market assumes menacing proportions as it "uprooted families, curbed fertility," played hell with "kin-and-neighbor cooperation of use-value production" and sapped "human needs for love and trust." (Chapter Ten, p. 13) Anyway, who can favor Ethos over Eros, or Mammon over God? And it is exciting to view a "*Kulturkampf* between arminian market and antinomian land" as "the decisive struggle over American destiny" (Chap. Two, p. 1) and to watch as this struggle "approached its millennial Armageddon when peace released both capital and the energies mobilized by the Moderate Light." (Chap. Two, p. 56)

It is only that I wish you might endow these titanic forces with a bit more flesh and blood and draw more upon your vast store of concrete events and historic figures from the period 1815–1847 to flesh out the abstractions. Of course you do give us dramatic portraits of Joseph Smith and Charles Finney in the flesh, and you no doubt are right that religious leaders and ideas played a larger role in the history of this period than has been acknowledged.[47] And it is probable that political, economic, and military figures and forces will receive more attention in later chapters to balance off the pages of Todd and Graham on masturbation.[48]

Of course the bourgeois hooters and scoffers are capable of anything. They may even ask if Alcohol was "the self indulgence that the market would no longer tolerate" how is it that Chairman Gorbachev is crusading against booze?[49] Or if "The great American whiskey binge was fed primarily by the anxiety of self-making men," what feeds the Soviet vodka binge? Or perhaps ask what accounts for resurgence of the market, black or red, in China and Russia? And there will no doubt be barbs about "sinful lapse from ancestral virtue" in those store-bought calico frocks and shoes. I am sure you can handle these canards, and put the scoffers down.

I know that you have read Tom Haskell's articles in the AHR because you cite them.[50] Shamelessly capitalistic as he is, I wonder if you have dealt adequately with some of his contentions. I note that (Chap. Nine, p. 16) you concede that businessmen were "pioneers of antislavery and other humanistic reform" and that they "brought a new scrupulosity to new-born commitments." But I wonder what you might say about the following contentions of Haskell (AHR, June, 1985, pp. 549–50): "After nearly two centuries of criticism of market society, it is easy to forget how brutal life could be before the profit motive ruled supreme" and again: "But contrary to romantic folklore, the marketplace is not a Hobbesian war of all against all. Many holds are barred."

The following sentence from page 2 of Chapter Ten is fortunately

---

47. Joseph Smith (1805–1844), founder of the Church of Jesus Christ of Latter-Day Saints, that is, the Mormons; Charles Grandison Finney (1792–1875), evangelist and president of Oberlin College.

48. John Todd (1800–1873) and Sylvester Graham (1794–1851), two ministers who freely offered advice on sexuality to the young; the latter is best known for inventing the graham cracker, a dull biscuit.

49. Mikhail Sergeyevich Gorbachev (b. 1931), general secretary of the Communist Party of the Soviet Union (1985–91), then in the midst of perestroika.

50. Thomas L. Haskell, "Capitalism and the Origins of the Humanitarian Sensibility, Part 1," *American Historical Review* 90 (April 1985): 339–61; idem., "Capitalism and the Origins of the Humanitarian Sensibility, Part 2," *American Historical Review* 90 (June 1985): 547–66.

not characteristic of your prose, but there are a few more like it: "Culturally the Moderate Light consolidated the infrastructure projecting 'middle-class' hegemony across the North."

I hope you will press forward with new chapters and postpone further
revision until after a full draft and respond to a full reading.

CVWP, 42/496: TCLS

256. To George M. Fredrickson

MAY 3, 1987

I have read your letter of April 20 with care and sympathy, and with
some reminiscences of personal experiences and those of others.[51] For
my part, your misgivings recall seizures of doubt that would periodically
overtake me while I was at work on *Origins*, especially before beginning
to write. You are by no means the first among authors of the Oxford
History to be so afflicted. I call it the Series Syndrome—being wedged
in between two other volumes and two dates fixed thereby—a kind of
claustrophobia.

Of course it could be worse than that. If you can seriously consider
the "glorified textbook" as a possible solution, it is well to pull out now
and spare us both embarrassment. I certainly want no such thing and
I don't believe you do either. So I don't consider it a serious alternative. What you intended in the first place is what you should do—not an
expanded textbook or a synthesis of conventional wisdom and received
opinion, but a new vision of a period of crucial importance that has long
been papered over with faded cliches. "The Gilded Age," indeed. We can
start by abandoning that cliche—as well as "The Progressive Era."

Two types of historians: the type who starts with outlines, and the
type willing to wait and see what he finds & thinks. From my prejudiced
point of view they are (1) the type willing to waste time in futile and self-
fulfilling prophesies, and (2) the realist prepared to wait with suspense and
wonder to read what he writes in order to know what he thinks. I suspect
you are proceeding as if you were Type I when you are really Type II (I
hope).

Your period stands out as uniquely abused by subsequent periods
for self-serving purposes—primarily by progressives, reformers, laborites,

51. Fredrickson was writing the 1865–1900 volume of the *Oxford History of the United States*,
but would later pull out of the assignment.

New Dealers, socialists, modernizationists etc. to show how wicked, waste-
ful, selfish, oppressive, corrupt, tasteless, vulgar, ostentations, pretentious,
cruel, racist, greedy glutinous, pot-bellied, obtuse, etc. etc. were those
who are going to be reformed, prohibited, Volsteaded, or wiped out by
Forward Looking, Right Thinking, Progressives of an Enlightened Era.

And who was it pointing the accusing finger? None other than spokesmen of the first half of the 20th century—the brief period in which
more human beings were deliberately slaughtered, starved, exterminated
by their fellowmen than all the victims of all the hordes of barbarians
throughout human history—including the enlightened barbarians of the
nineteenth century. And here we are, a half century later—after being
first to use nuclear weapons in anger and triggering enough more to end
life on the planet—still mouthing these stale cliches about the wickedness
of our grandfathers.

Not that theirs was a golden instead of a gilded age, or that they were
blameless. But I was asked recently to say something quotable for the
press about the present administration's "place in history"—particularly
in the perspective of the incumbent's thirty-nine predecessors. I said
I was sorry, but the old bench-marks of perfidy failed me totally. U. S.
Grant? Boss Tweed? Black Friday? Credit Mobilier? Seward's Icebox?
Grant's Santo Domingo? The Compromise of 1877? Rockefeller's trusts?
Peanuts. Chickenfeed. Childsplay. For Christ sake, here we are awash
in the swill of late empire, the stench overpowering. Hollywood's Imperial President daily informs us who are the modern counterparts of the
Founding Fathers, who are our national heroes, and how to tell them
from common criminals.

The point is our prevailing picture of "The Gilded Age" is preposterous, a howling anachronism. Revision, replacement, vindication, updat-
ing, call it what you will, but it is the most pressing duty facing American
historians. Yes, I know: "If he's so smart, why doesn't he do it himself?"
Well, at least I will say that if I picked any period to do myself it would
be this one. Anyways, not enough time left. What little I have seems taken
up with telling my juniors their duty.

And anyways, what better historian to do this most challenging of
jobs than the author of THE INNER CIVIL WAR? And what other period
in our history had keener intellectuals with insight and wisdom to share
with historians about their own times than Henry Adams, Henry and
William James, Mark Twain, George Santayana, Edith Wharton among

others, or such artists as Ryder, Eakins, Homer, Sullivan, Richardson? Who are their modern counterparts? Andy Warhol? E. L. Doctorow? Gore Vidal? Norman Mailer?

But I must not overdo this. You may be right about your inability to rise to this challenge. I cannot agree, however, to wait a year or more for you to decide again whether to write the book. I would reluctantly discuss the possibility of postponement until you wrote another book, but only with the very firm recommitment to the Oxford History book. I hope you understand why I am obliged to insist on continued commitment or complete withdrawal now. And that even though I know that your withdrawal would be a very severe blow to the whole enterprise. The other authors, even young McGerr, are now writing away.[52] But confidence is a fragile thing, and your resignation could lead to others. Any replacement is difficult.

I will therefore ask you to rethink the questions your letter raised in the context of the thoughts I have expressed. I think you might write your Commonwealth Lecture either as a prospectus or a part of the Oxford volume. The London U. people are accustomed to such conditions. So also the two papers for 1987 and 1988 to which you are committed. These three should make a good start on the book. I never know what comes next until I read my previous paragraph.

CVWP, 42/496: TCLS

257. Richard E. Flathman[53]

MAY 5, 1987

It was most thoughtful of you to send me the copies of your report on Freedom of Expression at Hopkins along with the minority statements. I read them all with care and with memories of our own experiences at Yale with the same problems.

Some of these memories are quite fresh—two of them events of this year. One was over the freedom of a student to satirize homosexuals, crude as the satire was.[54] In this I had a hand in getting the university to

52. Michael E. McGerr (b. 1955) of Indiana University; he was writing the 1900–30 volume, but the book was never to appear in the series.

53. Richard E. Flathman (b. 1934), a political scientist with a special interest in the concepts of individualism, freedom, and democracy.

54. A Yale undergraduate, Wayne C. Dick, had distributed a mock poster entitled "Bad Week '86: Bestiality Awareness Days," sponsored by the "Beastiality [sic] Awareness Alliance

reverse a penalty already imposed. The other arose over protests about South African issues. In the latter the university, I thought wisely, tolerated shanties and loud demonstrations at the ceremony inaugurating President Schmidt.[55] But when demonstrators occupied the university treasurer's office and interfered with freedom of operations they were penalized promptly. I thought the distinction consistent with adopted principles, even though no injury to person or property was inflicted.

I hope your colleagues will resolve their disagreements in due time and that you will be kind enough to send me a copy of the resulting statement of policy.

CVWP, 28/332: TCLU

258. To J. Morgan Kousser

NOVEMBER 16, 1987

I can understand how frustrating it must be to characterize, even to criticize, such a chameleon-like creature as *Strange Career*—which changed with every revision. The original edition, 1955, was addressed almost entirely to the South. Then along came Litwack on the North and I got interested to some extent with that.[56] Then in response to critics I began to offer sundry theories—all of them impressionistic and without benefit of the hard work (and evidence) such as you rely upon in your fascinating "Onward March" paper.

To be as helpful as I can about what I meant: First, about variations in degree and pattern of segregation. My main point in this was that segregation was not a constant, that it had a history, that there had been change, and that the Jim Crow laws constituted an important means of change and were not simply a validation of a long-time status quo. To help make the point I did stress (perhaps overstress) variations in pre-Jim

---

(BAA)—open to all species and orientations." After a formal complaint was made, Dick was informed that, if the allegation was substantiated, he would be guilty of a violation of the regulation against "physical restriction, assault, coercion or intimidation of any member of community." In his defense, Dick cited the 1975 Woodward Report on freedom of speech at Yale, but he was placed on probation and a disciplinary mark placed on his record. Upon appeal, after Woodward had taken up Dick's cause and argued his case before the disciplinary body, Dick's punishment was rescinded.

55. Benno C. Schmidt Jr. (b. 1942), president of Yale (1986–92).

56. Leon F. Litwack, *North of Slavery: The Negro in the Free States, 1790–1860* (Chicago: University of Chicago Press, 1961).

Crow patterns of race relations and degrees of latitude unthinkable later on. I did not mean to suggest there was no segregation prior to the laws, nor that repeal of the laws in early days of their history would have shattered the practice, though repeal might have made the pattern less absolute and uniform.

As for explanatory theories, I relied initially on white class interests and traditions, with moderation associated with conservatives who were too confident of social distance to stoop to physical distance. This is compared with lower-class lack of such confidence. Your own findings about blackbelt initiative in racial aggression did that theory no good. And I never took much stock in liberal or religious ideas and motivation, though I did mention these. Next I cheerfully tried on for size the theories of van den Berghe and Mason—the transition from paternalistic to competitive relations of the races, elaborated by Mason.[57] I still think they are of some help. Still later I leaned more to demographic and sociological theories suggested especially by John Cell.[58] That is that plantation and rural subordination of blacks was vertical, direct, and personal, a means unavailable for subordination in cities. Urban subordination had to be horizontal, indirect, and impersonal—for which the main means was segregation by law. (I would be interested to know if the blackbelt aggression you found was predominantly urban.)

I confess I am a bit doubtful about trying to make the North conform to theories used for the South. What may be useful for the latter may not be for the former. Northern society did not come out of a long tradition of paternalism. So the postwar adjustment represented no great change. Some sort of "competitive" system had existed all along. Nor was there likely to be any transition from a vertical to a horizontal system of domination. Nor were Northern whites accustomed to physical proximity of blacks on a regular basis.

To respond to one question: No, I did not "mean to say that the dominant trend in the post-Reconstruction era was for the races to mix . . ." But I do not believe that there was much immediate white demand to

57. Pierre L. van den Berghe, *Race and Racism: A Comparative Perspective* (New York: Wiley, 1967); John Rex and David Mason, eds., *Theories of Race and Ethnic Relations* (Cambridge: Cambridge University Press, 1986).

58. John W. Cell, *The Highest Stage of White Supremacy: The Origins of Segregation in South Africa and the American South* (Cambridge: Cambridge University Press, 1982).

alter traditional proximities of the races so long as social distance was unquestioned.

I hope you will send me a copy of the missing Figure 1, parts A and B.

Just returned from a pleasant visit in New Orleans with the Southern Historical meeting. Saw many of our old friends. I think they might agree with me in defending the proper-noun status of "South." Or is it a bias of your secretary that denies it a capital?

CVWP, 31/366: TCLU

259. To John Herbert Roper[59]

DECEMBER 1, 1987

What an experience! Thanks to you, I get an Alice-in-Wonderland glimpse from the other side of the looking glass—biography from the outside with me on the inside looking out. Disturbing double-image. Biography is probably best reserved for a posthumous honor—at least from the subject's point of view. And probably from the biographer's as well. At least I was glad to have the subject of the only biography I ever wrote well underground beforehand. (I shudder to think of the litigious consequences otherwise.) Had you waited for the inevitable before publication you would have been spared the quibbles of the sort only the subject is in a position to quib. After all, he was *there* (usually), with whatever dubious authority his to command.

On the other hand, had you taken that precaution and waited for your undertaking to follow that of the undertaker, then I would have been deprived of a rare learning experience. For I think I did learn something about history and the perils of writing it, though I am still groping for words to express what I learned. Something about the fallibility of memory—my own first of all. For instance, you innocently relied on my memory for your list of my Ph.D. students at Hopkins, and I thereby hurt many by forgetting half of them at the moment. So the biggest surprise of all was how much I had forgotten about my own life. But other surprises as well. Not the least of which was waking up in bed with Proust, of all people! (at least it wasn't Pound.)

But the main thing was about the mysteries of memory and the weak

---

59. John Herbert Roper (b. 1948), who taught at Emory and Henry College; he had recently published *C. Vann Woodward, Southerner* (Athens: University of Georgia Press, 1987).

reed it is to lean upon—my own especially. I can only hope that the memory of all those other people you interviewed was more reliable than mine. But I wonder, since theirs often differed from mine and from each other's, and we can't all be right. It puts me in mind of one of my prejudices against modern fashions—this one being Oral History. For what is it but reliance upon the aforementioned reed? Returning to my own experience again, I too interviewed friends and foes of my subject and learned a lot, but it was well I could supplement that with the mountainous files of the Watson Papers. Of course you did make effective use of some collections, and I am not about to suggest you should have taken on the mountainous files of yours truly in the Yale Library. After all, as you emphasize, you were not writing a biography. And to have dug through those six decades or so of letters and manuscripts would have taken years and far more time than the subject could possibly deserve.

Before going any further, I must assure you of my deeply felt appreciation of your investment of time and labor—all those thousands of hours. As a fellow craftsman, I know. It is a unique relationship, that of the biographer and his subject. Come to think of it, no other relationship, apart from that of blood, entails so much time and attention of one human being to the affairs of another. How could I be insensitive to such a tribute? And that regardless of whether the published results be pro or con, positive or negative. Pray you, concede me that much detachment.

Furthermore, I am more struck by the range of opinions, views, and values we share than the differences we have. It would have been unreasonable to expect full agreement and preposterous to expect. Some of our differences give you more difficulty than others and perhaps take more space than they otherwise should. Obviously we do not see eye to eye on the matter of Herbert Aptheker. I am not at all surprised, for I believe a few others disagreed as well. Including, as you point out, 2200 Yale undergraduate petition signers. As you imply, perhaps that many Yalies plus the Political Science Department can't be wrong. I readily admit the possibility of error on my part. For example about questions of proportion in the Aptheker edition of the Du Bois Papers. Maybe Malcolm Call, then ed. of the Mass. U. Press, his boss Ms. Stein, and the good Herbert were right that the first 69 years of Du Bois' life—the years, that is, before his political conversion—could be disposed of in one volume and get on to the important years. But Louis Harlan took 13 large volumes to dispose of the first 59 years of a lesser figure, Booker Washington. And as a fellow member of the Aptheker editorial board Harlan resigned with me on the issue. I could also have been wrong about Yale's standards and Aptheker's scholarship. Since I thought I was right I could hardly have acted otherwise.

On one point I am sure *you* are right—that "considerably less pain for everybody would have ensued if Woodward had simply let Aptheker hold his seminar." (p. 284) Of course the same could have been said of the Free Speech report and fight at Yale—or for that matter any of a score of skirmishes you faithfully chronicle from Arkansas to Emory, to Tech, to Florida, and on to the West Coast and back to Hopkins. You would agree that many academics give high priority to avoidance of pain and controversy and embarrassment. I hope the cynics are not right that academic life has a special attraction for folk of that, shall we say, disposition; but I confess that in sixty-odd years (1926–1987) of academic life it sometimes seemed the cynics had a point. Then I reflect that corporate, bureaucratic, church, and political life may attract even more of the timorous. That has encouraged my failing for controversy in the hope that it may keep the pool of academic life a bit less stagnant and stultifying than the corporate, bureaucratic, church, or political cesspools.

Not that I despair of the academy. There's hope yet. I am amazed at outbursts of virtue of late. For example, the recent vindication of Louis Harlan—in one year elected president of the AHA, the OAH, and the SHA. And Louis hasn't an ounce of political adrenalin or a fashionable opinion to his name. And he was opposed for the AHA election by a pol pro of impeccable fashionability and genitalia, comparable to the present incumbent in that office.

For appraisal of many other things in your fascinating book—historiography, politics, the ephemerality of the Woodwardian canon and its shattering by junior leftists—you must rely on counsel of more detachment than I command. But I do feel obliged to pass on a few notes of omission or error I took as I read. They do not affect your conclusions but make you vulnerable to critics, and you might wish to weed some of them out if there is a revision or reprint:
[deletion][60]

I am surprised at the number of things you found space for and disappointed only in your not being able to include the most absorbing and

60. This is a list of errata.

exciting experience of the 70s and early 80s as member of the International Council on the Future of the University. Especially after I was elected president after the murder of Charles Frankel.[61] This took me to Italy, Germany, England, Sweden, and Portugal, resulted in reports on conditions of the universities in several European countries (at their request), and demonstrated to my great delight that professors in the western world shared a common faith in freedom, wherever.

With your critics I wish you civility, fairness, and absence of mean-spiritedness such as I have had the good luck to enjoy with mine. Please give my best to Rita. I wish I had seen more of both of you in New Orleans.

p.s. Of course you have my consent to add the above to your Roper Papers in the Southern Historical Collection at Chapel Hill.

p.p.s. I had hoped to see you and Rita again at the party of those California junior leftists, whose names I can't seem to remember, at New Orleans, but whose chatter always amuses me.

CVWP, 47/556: TCLS

260. To Various Scholars

OCTOBER 1, 1988

Fritz Stern of Columbia and I have prepared the enclosed statement about the threat to liberal principles and traditions that we see in current political rhetoric.[62] We fear the consequences. I am writing you for both of us.

We are planning to place this as a paid advertisement in the New York Times. We are hoping for a full page in a Sunday edition in October.

We have the agreement of Steven Muller, President of the Johns Hopkins University, Marvin L. Goldberger, Director of the Institute of Advanced Studies, Princeton, and Sheldon Hackney, President of the

---

61. Charles Frankel (1917–1979), the philosopher, who along with his wife was killed by a robber in their home in Bedford Hills, New York.

62. Fritz R. Stern (b. 1926), a historian of modern Germany; he taught at Columbia University (1953–97). The statement was headed "A Reaffirmation of Principles" and began, "Speaking as American citizens and not as party members, we wish to reaffirm America's liberal tradition." The statement's contention was that this tradition was under threat. It was published in the *New York Times* (26 October 1988): A21, and was signed by sixty-three prominent figures.

University of Pennsylvania, to sign with us. May we include you among the signers? We are setting a limit of around 50 signatures. May we have your immediate response? Please send your reply to Fritz Stern, The School of Historical Studies, the Institute for Advanced Study, Princeton, NJ 08540. If you have any question, you can reach Fritz Stern at 609–924–7475, or me at 203–624–4534.

We need to raise $48,000 for the cost of the advertisement. We shall approach a few donor-signers for major contributions, but we need all the help we can get. Above all we need your support.

P.S. Checks should be made out to Fritz Stern or to C. Vann Woodward.

CVWP, 78/40: TCLU

261. To Ken Burns[63]

NOVEMBER 2, 1988

In our three days of refighting the Civil War in New York last week we all doubtless suffered a bit of battle fatigue. One result, I suspect, was that in our concentration on seeking improvements, pointing out flaws, and picking nits, we neglected to mention an underlying consensus. I heard it often between the lines in talk with my colleagues, but mainly it remained an unspoken assumption. That was a feeling of assurance that we were working with artists who shared our concern for the integrity of history and our belief in the profound importance of the Civil War in American history. Only these unspoken beliefs could have taken the time and brought together such scholars as you have collected to assist you in this enterprise.

In the cutting you will have to do, I think you will have to sacrifice much that is good. Some of that will have to come out of Shelby Foote's contribution.[64] I believe that some of McPherson should be retained, but the curious thing is that he never set forth his most important insight regarding the contingency element in the Civil War, the importance of

---

63. Kenneth L. Burns (b. 1953), the documentary filmmaker. His television series *The Civil War* was aired on the Public Broadcasting Service in September 1990. Woodward was an adviser to the series and was filmed, though his appearances ended up on the cutting room floor.

64. Shelby D. Foote Jr. (1916–2005), the Southern novelist and author of *The Civil War, a Narrative* (New York: Random House, 1958–74). In fact, Foote featured very prominently in the film.

chance, the What Ifs, the repeated crises that might have turned out the other way, the perception as well as the reality of suspense and doubt about how it was all going to turn out. Defeat and victory were up for grabs many times and stalemate left open many possibilities. I believe you might consider calling McPherson back in for a brief statement of this thesis. It not only serves the integrity of history but the purposes of drama.

Despite the relief of occasional humor you have from the outset presented the Civil War drama as tragedy—and rightly so, in my opinion. In the final scenes, however, it seems to me you run the risk of depriving the men on whom you have conferred the dignity of tragedy of their honors by turning them into comic foxy grandpas. Marching and ceremony are OK, but not capers and cavorting.

Congratulations on the marvelous progress you have made and good luck with the toughest tasks that lie ahead.

CVWP, 9/99: TCLS

262. To Daniel P. Moynihan[65]

MARCH 31, 1989

Many thanks for the new edition of John Dollard's *Caste and Class* and your splendid Foreword.[66] I had not seen it. The first edition came out the year before my first book appeared (1938) and has been with me ever since. So when I arrived to join the Yale faculty in 1962 the first colleague outside the history department I asked about was John Dollard. I was taken to see his severe, dark-brown, saltbox house but was told he was on leave or ill or inaccessible. Anyway, I never met him and did not know what happened. Whatever it was does not seem to reflect well on the Yale of the fifties. At least Brewster's Yale was different.

So I was all the more moved by your Foreward: one Irishman on another Irishman, both with scholarly and pragmatic concerns for maltreated minorities, particularly the black one. And your reflections on what has happened in "just one-half century from the time Dollard departed Sunflower County"—all the way from lynching-bee Mississippi to Miss Mississippi—boggles credulity.

---

65. Daniel Patrick Moynihan (1927–2003), a scholar of urban life and U.S. senator from New York (1977–2001).

66. John Dollard, *Caste and Class in a Southern Town*, with a foreword by Daniel Patrick Moynihan (Madison: University of Wisconsin Press, 1988).

Maybe our salvation (if any) lies in the very excesses of human variety and change in this country. Think for example (as you undoubtedly have had recent cause to) of the present senior Senator, the present junior Senator, and the present House Minority Whip—all from the state of Georgia.[67]

And then I take a look at the composition of the National Economic Commission, and then read the Washington *Post* articles by George F. Will and yourself—and the mind reels again, and something like hope is reborn.[68] My sincere congratulations on your achievement on the Commission and your composition of its Report. And for a copy of the latter, also many thanks.

You must be aware that a part of your moral constituency resides in the academy, that considerable fraction—I would like to think majority— of it which shares your values. We continue to tell each other how fortunate we are in having someone giving voice to those values in a high and conspicuous place.

CVWP, 36/439: TCLU

263. To Marcus Cunliffe

JULY 2, 1989

It was a natural thing as a newly tapped member of the Cancer Club to reach out to friends with longer membership. I know that I did when I was in your place, and I was glad I did. I think I needed more support, having lost son and wife that way and two of my dearest friends, Dick Hofstadter and Dave Potter. I was particularly interested in those who survived the affliction.

Whether it was when or where it was discovered, mine was apparently beyond reach of therapy you will undergo. It was the knife for me with no delay, and it left me with an eleven-inch incision scar and minus a yard or so of colon. Also with the threat of recurrence. So far, after four years, my luck has held and still holds. Earlier this spring I put luck to test

---

67. These are Sam Nunn (b. 1938), a conservative Democrat; Wyche Fowler (b. 1940), a liberal Democrat; and Newt Gingrich (b. 1943), a conservative Republican.

68. See George F. Will, "The Economic Commission Actually *Did* Something," *Washington Post* (5 March 1989): C7, and Daniel Patrick Moynihan, "Why We Called for a Surplus," *Washington Post* (7 March 1989): A25. The bipartisan National Economic Commission had been established by Congress after the 1987 stock market crash and charged with dealing with the federal government's budgetary deficit; in the event, it could not agree on a plan.

with some six weeks of hard travel in India and returned several pounds lighter but no worse for wear.

I have friends here who are undergoing chemotherapy and have been for some time, one of them for nearly two years, who go about their duties, and few aware of their troubles. You already have all the stoicism and humor you might need, so all I can wish you is as much luck as I had. When and if you feel like it do keep me posted. Later we must find occasion to compare notes and celebrate.

CVWP, 13/147: TCLU

264. To Frank M. Turner[69]

JULY 21, 1989

Many thanks for sending me a copy of the Adair Committee report on free speech. I had not seen it before. It strikes me as a thoughtful addition to our efforts to keep the university faithful to principles we profess. I have kept silent during the committee's deliberations and do not wish to make any public response to it. Such suggestions as I do have are, of course, entirely my own and in no way invoke the authority of the committee I headed twelve years ago.

The most conspicuous difference between free speech problems in 1975 and those of 1989 is that the earlier period found *majority* student opinion offended and at present it is mainly *minority* groups that feel offended by unrestricted speech. The grievances of minorities are usually known as "harassment." That term sometimes includes physical coercion or abuse, but here we are concerned only with verbal or symbolic expression. Many epithets have been coined for opinions and speech held repugnant or offensive. The term "harassment" can be regarded as one of them. The revulsion expressed against the public sentiments of Professor Shockley and General Westmoreland some twenty years ago employed much the same rhetoric of shock and anger as that now used against harassment.[70] The difference is that harassment is felt to violate private

69. Frank M. Turner (1944–2010), a historian of nineteenth-century Britain; he served as provost of Yale (1988–92).

70. General William C. Westmoreland (1914–2005), who commanded U.S. Army forces in Vietnam (1964–68), had had a similar experience in 1972, when he was supposed to speak to the students' Political Union, but encountered students who prevented him from reaching the podium and, he thought, threatened him physically.

rights rather than public principle. Otherwise, it seems to me, the problem is the same—the one as difficult as the other, but no more so.

On questions of symbolic protest and expressions of it, I think we need to work on defining reasonable limits—limits of time, space, and attention. In defending the right to these freedoms of expression, the university is surely not obliged to guarantee an audience for the exhibits—only the right of those who wish to see them to do so. To force attention to such expressions or symbols upon all members of the community all the time—whether by permitting conspicuous and unavoidable place of display, or by assuring indefinite and inviolable tenure of the space preempted—would seem to constitute the violation of the rights of others. It might be though comparable to a policy of protecting free speech exercised over a bullhorn, thus forcing all to hear something whether they wished to or not and at the same denying others the right to be heard.

But please credit me with awareness that it is easier to give such advice than it is to put it into practice in the face of opposition.

CVWP, 61/721: TCLU

265. To Carl N. Degler

NOVEMBER 30, 1990

How right you were in your inscription—that I would be surprised at how much that was close to my interests in your SEARCH OF HUMAN NATURE.[71] Thirteen years your senior, I was educated (college) in the 1920s in the outmoded biology and sociology of the early decades of the century. The full curriculum: all those "instincts," hereditary inferiorities, eugenics, and wrong-headed readings of Darwin. Then off to Columbia (really to see the big city) to earn my fellowship in sociology—which I pursued for some 24 hours and then went to see Professor Franz Boas about becoming an anthropologist. He referred me to his assistant Professor Ruth Somebody who encouraged me [to] seek elsewhere my destiny.[72] Which turned out to be an MA in something called political science. Then back to Georgia Tech teaching freshman English. Still in

71. Degler was about to publish *In Search of Human Nature: The Decline and Revival of Darwinism in American Thought* (New York: Oxford University Press, 1991).

72. Ruth Benedict (1887–1948) had studied with Boas and been on the faculty at Columbia since 1923; when CVW was at Columbia, she was about to publish her most important early work, *Patterns of Culture* (Boston: Houghton Mifflin, 1934).

search of my true calling (after losing my Tech job) I walked a mile down the road from Oxford, (where I had taken refuge in my father's house) to call on Professor Howard Odum, who was visiting his parents in the same village. Odum got me a Rockefeller fellowship at Chapel Hill. But again I turned my back on the sociologists. This time my destiny was self-determined by having written four chapters of a book I managed to sell the history department as a dissertation.

Anyway your account of science in the early decades makes it clear how fortunate I was in not becoming some sort of scientist. Judging from the experience of the leaders in that calling, I would have been destined to be remembered for even more mistakes than I made as a historian. [deletion]

CVWP, 15/169: TCLS

266. To Arthur M. Schlesinger Jr.

FEBRUARY 1, 1991

The Portland papers only arrived a few days ago.[73] I hasten to forward my comments and suggestions in the hope they do not come too late.

I think this spreading development in the public schools must not go unchallenged, and that the sooner and more firmly we speak out in protest the better.

The brief letter of November 13, 1990, signed by you and Diane Ravitch, seems to me to strike the right note.[74] That is, we should begin by acknowledging the neglect of cultural diversity and the place of black people's role in American history. We should also deplore any tendency to exaggerate contributions to western culture made by whites, amounting at times to cultural chauvinism. But if we deplore chauvinism in one race, we do not agree that it can be properly corrected by chauvinism in another. We censure this very common human weakness wherever it is manifest.

73. The Portland, Oregon, school system had authorized the use of "Baseline Essays," intended to promote multiculturalism, in part by contending that Western civilization had roots in sub-Saharan Africa. These essays were attacked in Arthur M. Schlesinger Jr., "The Battle of the Schools," in *The Disuniting of America: Reflections on a Multicultural Society* (New York: W. W. Norton, 1992), 73–99.

74. I have been unable to identify such a letter, but it would seem to have followed upon Ravitch and Schlesinger's "Statement of the Committee of Scholars in Defense of History," published in the *AHA Perspectives* (October 1990); this had been cosigned by twenty-four other scholars, including CVW.

I find manifestations of this tendency in the Afrocentric curricula originating in the Portland public schools and now spread to other cities, including Washington, Atlanta, Indianapolis, and Milwaukee. Authors of the Portland essays range widely for support of their claims of black originality on many aspects of art, architecture, literature, music, mathematics, and the sciences. This results in a good deal of lopsided, erroneous, and unbalanced history. Many of the claims made for priority of black achievements rest upon an identification of black Africans with ancient Egyptians. We do not want to enter into arguments about fields of learning not represented in our committee. However, I have had a talk with my Yale colleague Kelley Simpson, an outstanding Egyptologist, who assures me we would be right in rejecting such claims.[75] He tells me they rest largely on the invasion and conquest of Egypt in the eight and seventh centuries B.C. by black tribesmen from the Sudan. That was, of course, long after the great era of Egyptian civilization. The black tribesmen did return to the Sudan with some arts learned from their invasion and build monuments resembling to some extent their ancient Egyptian models. But that is about the extent of it.

P.S. Do include the point about teaching the children to deny or despise European origins of American civilization.

CVWP, 49/577: TCLU

267. To Arthur M. Schlesinger Jr.

MARCH 1, 1991

I am enormously pleased to hear that you are doing a book on the Afrocentric nonsense. It's a large subject, and the nonsense appears to expand daily (or maybe it's because of black history month). As Anglocentric nonsense diminishes or yields to criticism, the black variety expands and gains immunity from criticism. It is difficult to get white academics, and even more black ones, to speak out. I doubt if you could round up as many signers to a statement on this issue as you did on the other.

But while you are at it I hope it is not too much to suggest that you add a chapter on Gendercentric nonsense and Homophobic nonsense. University curricula are already disgracefully cluttered with such stuff. Let me quote from a letter just received from a one-time colleague I have

75. William Kelly Simpson (b. 1928) had been in Yale's Department of Near Eastern Languages and Civilizations since 1958.

not heard from in twenty years: "At Michigan State I am a minority of one in the department protesting as standard after standard has fallen. Every course must be gender-and-race related; chairs are awarded on the sole ground that the occupant would be a good 'role model' for this or that constituency, etc., etc."

It does seem to me that faculty, students, and courses are becoming as politicized now as fully as they were back in the sixties. Then it was over national issues; now it is over internal issues of race and sex. I hope you will think about connecting the race issues with the others. They are often inseparable, politically allied, and equally harmful.

CVWP, 49/577: TCLU

268. To John Hope Franklin

AUGUST 2, 1991

Your comparison of Booker Washington and Clarence Thomas represents for me the perfect use of historical analogy, history legitimately used to illuminate an ongoing controversy.[76] My congratulations. It is the best thing I have read on that debate.

If I have misused history in another ongoing debate I will count on you to set me right.[77] I have done my best to respond fairly and fully to your letter to the editor. I hope you will write me after you read that in context when it appears in the next issue of the *Review* toward the end of the month. I think I can take anything from you in the way of correction

76. John Hope Franklin, "Booker T. Washington Revisited," *New York Times* (1 August 1991): A21. The context was the controversial nomination of Clarence Thomas (b. 1948) to the Supreme Court; Franklin had argued that Thomas followed the same self-help doctrines as had Washington.

77. CVW had reviewed Dinesh D'Souza, *Illiberal Education: The Politics of Race and Sex on Campus* (New York: Free Press, 1991); see CVW, "Freedom and the Universities," *New York Review of Books* 38 (18 July 1991): 32–37. In the review, he had remarked that Duke University had recruited Franklin as "the best historian in his field." In a letter to the editor (September 26, 1991), Franklin objected to the implication that he was only a historian of black America and said that he had not taught a course on black history for twenty years, but instead had taught Southern history and American constitutional history. In reply, CVW contended that he had meant the best "in any field of history he [Franklin] cultivated," but Franklin was unconvinced by this and found CVW's response to be "slightly patronizing." See John Hope Franklin, *Mirror to America: The Autobiography of John Hope Franklin* (New York: Farrar, Straus and Giroux, 2005), 325–28 (quotation on 327).

or reproval—anything but a break or a cooling in an old and cherished friendship. That I am not prepared to accept.

CVWP, 72/123: TCLU

269. To David F. Mitch[78]

SEPTEMBER 19, 1991

Your dilemma about the abortion issue set me to wondering how to reconcile my position on segregation when I was president of the Southern Historical Association with my position on the Vietnam War when I was president of the American Historical Association. In the first instance in 1952 I backed the cancellation of the annual dinner when the hotel refused to serve black members and bussed members for miles to a hotel that would. In the AHA business meeting over which I presided in 1969 I made it evident that I opposed adoption of resolutions opposing the war in Vietnam. In neither case did I favor politicizing a learned society by adoption of a political platform.

The best I can do toward reconciling my position in 1952 with my position in 1969 is to point out that in the former case the hotel was the aggressor in refusing to serve all members dinner and my obligation was more elemental than political. But in the latter fight, the issue was clearly political. That's the best I can do in the way of reconciling the two actions.

Now the SSHA cannot blame the hotel for the horrors of the state legislature.[79] It meets in Louisiana at a time that coincides with the coming of the primary election in which the free-choice question is a major issue.[80] But for the SSHA to plunge into the primary would seem to me a serious distortion of its purpose and an overt politicization of a learned society.

78. David F. Mitch (b. 1951), an economist at the University of Maryland-Baltimore County.

79. The sixteenth annual meeting of the Social Science History Association was due to be held in New Orleans (31 October–3 November 1991).

80. In the 1991 gubernatorial primary, the incumbent governor, Edwin Edwards (b. 1927), failed to get 50 percent of the vote and so was forced into a runoff with David Duke (b. 1950), a former Grand Wizard of the Ku Klux Klan in Louisiana and a Republican legislator, widely regarded as a racist. Edwards eventually won with 61.2 percent to Duke's 38.8 percent, though the latter carried a majority of the white vote.

I have no right to intervene in your discussion since I am not a member of the SSHA. But I have no objection to your sharing my views with others if that is of any help.

CVWP, 34/404: TCLS

270. To Cushing Strout[81]

NOVEMBER 1, 1991

Many thanks for kind and supportive words about my indiscretions and exchanges in the *New York Review*.[82] There appears to be more serious concern and support for our point of view in the academy at large than I had expected. Letters continue to come in, ninety-odd on last count, the great majority "sound on the goose." Of course it's usually the critics and quibblers who write Letters-to-the-editor and friends who think you are right. But not always—as witness three of the six published letters. Franklin, I am glad to add, came forth eventually with assurances of continued friendship, though his published letter left a contrary impression.

Your own views and mine are so similar on these matters that I am happy to say I can see no difference at all. These include your point about the politicization of everything, the guilt-by-association game, and the polarization between radicals and conservatives that leaves liberals voiceless or pushed into conservative identification. You are right that we should speak out, and I applaud your doing so—as in the items for the Journal of American History and Tikkun.[83] You are heard and your influence will count.

81. Cushing Strout (b. 1923), an American intellectual historian at Cornell University; perhaps best known for *The New Heavens and New Earth: Political Religion in America* (New York: Harper & Row, 1973).

82. Concerning his review of D'Souza.

83. Strout had written in objection to Joan Hedrick's review of his *Making American Tradition: Visions and Revisions from Ben Franklin to Alice Walker* (New Brunswick, NJ: Rutgers University Press, 1990): he had decried her "obligatory references to feminist scholarship and to New Historicists and Deconstructionists, ideologically approved forms of 'the School of Resentment' (Harold Bloom's phrase) in which literary criticism and history are used on behalf of groups perceived to be historical victims." See "Letters to the Editor," *Journal of American History* 78 (September 1991): 763. The reference to *Tikkun* is less clear, but is probably to "Special Focus: The Politics of Racial Identity," *Tikkun* 6 (January–February 1991): 54–70, which contained an article by Gary Peller on "Race Against Integration," with responses by Nathan Glazer, Michael Dyson, and Thomas Byrne Edsall.

I encounter pretty often a disposition to dismiss the extent and importance of the nonsense we deplore. I would like to believe it is on the decline but find too much evidence to the contrary. Witness for example the Hunter College debate (or adoption?) of a required course on gays, women, and blacks, and the same thing at UCLA. And I am sure you could cite many others. Keep it up. Let's not let them get away with it. [deletion]

> CVWP, 52/62: TCLU

271. To Sheldon Hackney

MARCH 23, 1992

I did not encounter Bill or Hillary Clinton while they were students here.[84] Nor, for that matter Gerry Brown, Paul Tsongas, or Garry Hart, nor any of the cast of characters in the Thomas-Hill drama.[85]

But I did meet the governor in Arkansas last year when we were both receiving hon. degrees from the unfamous Henderson State University which I attended for my first two years of college and Clinton never did. I found him most agreeable and knowledgeable and liked him right off and wish him well. I encountered Hillary very briefly when she was employed by the House Judiciary Committee in the Nixon impeachment hearings and I was called in by its counsel John Doar to do the study on misconduct of previous presidents.[86] She would make a super VP, not to mention 1st Lady. I think Clinton can handle this stinker Brown but have no prediction for the November election. Clinton will suffer from lingering Yankee anti-southernism, but not I hope as much as LBJ. I delight in his black vote percentages, South and North, and doubt that Brown can outdo him with them.

Emory does not deserve the opprobrium it gets for suspicion of dis-

84. William Jefferson "Bill" Clinton (b. 1946), then governor of Arkansas, and his wife, Hillary Rodham Clinton (b. 1947).

85. These were all candidates for the Democratic presidential nomination in 1992: Edmund Gerald "Jerry" Brown Jr. (b. 1938), governor of California (1975–83, 2011–present); Paul E. Tsongas (1941–1997), U.S. senator from Massachusetts (1979–85); Gary Hart (b. 1936), U. S. senator from Colorado (1975–87). In the Senate hearings on his nomination, Thomas had been accused of sexual harassment by Anita Hill.

86. John Michael Doar (b. 1921), chief counsel for the U.S. House Committee on the Judiciary during the Watergate hearings and impeachment of Richard Nixon; the book was CVW, ed., *Responses of the Presidents to Charges of Misconduct* (New York: Dell, 1974).

crimination against Betsy F-G for ideological or other reasons.[87] But of course Emory cannot afford to make public the real reason.

Glad to see you doing so well in fund raising efforts. Yale plunges into this shallow water in May. Benno is taking a lot of punishment from the faculty on budget decisions, but I hope and believe he will survive. Showdown with trustees next month.

I still find retirement my favorite university status after fifteen years of it—so long as you can feel a part of the university without being on the payroll. All goes well with me. Look forward to seeing you both on the Vineyard.

CVWP, 24/272: TCLU

272. To Neil Jumonville[88]

JUNE 20, 1992

I am glad to be of what help I can, but my relations with Henry Commager were not as close as you appear to assume. Always cordial, our contacts were largely at history conventions until I became a fellow member of the American Academy and Institute of Arts and Letters. I thought of him as a man with whom I generally agreed on political and social issues, as an able and outspoken writer on these subjects, but not as a historian on the frontiers of scholarship. No Perry Miller, he did not seem deep in archival research as his collaborator Sam Morison, but rather one to keep up with and report the latest findings in new editions of their textbook, or in essays and reviews.

I confess I did not think of my contemporaries in terms of current fashions or categorize them by "schools." Dick Hofstadter, my closest friend in the profession, was tagged with "consensus," and we argued over such issues, but not divisively. I am sure that Dave Potter, another

---

87. Elizabeth Fox-Genovese, then a professor at Emory University and director of its Institute for Women's Studies, was being accused of discrimination by the institute's former assistant director and former Fox-Genovese graduate student, Ginger Gould. Later, in January 1993, Gould would sue for violation of civil rights statutes, requiring that subordinates not be obliged to perform personal services for their superiors. After an extended controversy and many legal maneuvers, in 1996 the case was settled, with Emory paying Gould an undisclosed sum. The case sharply divided opinion.

88. Neil Jumonville, who taught at Florida State University, was working on what would be published as *Henry Steele Commager: Midcentury Liberalism and the History of the Present* (Chapel Hill: University of North Carolina Press, 1999).

close friend, always thought of himself as a historian, though he headed a Social Science department here and wrote some in that field.

One could hardly avoid reference to such concepts as national character, myth, identity, innocence, exceptionalism, etc., when they were in such common use. But I did not think of them as the property of a school, whether American studies or American character. I sought rather consciously (if not always successfully) to avoid being tagged with one of these identifications. But they do admittedly turn up in my writings.

On Commager's *American Mind* I shared the opinion of Hofstadter and may have been influenced by his lack of regard for it.[89] As activist Commager, like many of us, was more a writer than a marcher. I was not much aware of his part in the civil rights movement. My impression is that his "activism" expressed rather than "hurt" his writing. He was certainly one of the elite and may have acted the part, but I would reject the epithet "elitist" for him as rather unfair. I am quite in agreement with you about our current misuse of the term "conservative." As a political identification it would seem to have universally lost its usefulness. It is even used to identify defenders of free speech.

I think your subject is quite worth your time and wish you the best with it. If Commager is to be a central figure, I hope you have access to his correspondence.

CVWP, 27/320: TCLU

273. To Cushing Strout

JULY 6, 1992

You don't say when you are returning from Germany, but I am responding now because your memoir chapter is still fresh in my memory. Let me assure you right off that I have nothing to doubt or to question about your account of Yale in the 1950s. It conforms in general to such impressions as I had formed from a distance and academic gossip. That was a decade that will not go down in the record as the academy's proudest. After all I weathered the period at Johns Hopkins when we had McCarthyites breathing down our neck all the time and my colleague Owen Lattimore was assigned the role of McCarthy's Number One Communist Agent. Our work in his defense prevented the university

89. Henry Steele Commager, *The American Mind: An Interpretation of American Thought and Character Since the 1880's* (New Haven, CT: Yale University Press, 1950).

from firing him, which was a better record than some institutions scored. But it was bad enough throughout the American academic community. I found no reason in those years to be tempted by offers or "approaches" from Wisconsin, Chicago, California, or Cornell. And when George Pierson came to talk Yale to me in 1960 I gave him no encouragement. But he persisted with reinforcements from my friend Red Warren and others who pointed out that though George was Mr. Yale, he had got Ed Morgan, John Blum, and other non-blues and renovated a department. It was not the old blue stagnation, and two of the new ones were already collaborators with me in a text. So I came to Yale in '62. No sooner had I arrived than student activists took over to stop free speech and prevent in succession Gov. Wallace, General Westmoreland, Secretary of State Rodgers, and Professor Shockley of Stanford from speaking. It was the conviction of the student and faculty radicals that they not only had the right but the moral duty to shout down anyone whose views they disapproved—not as McCarthyites but as "radicals." Kingman Brewster asked me to head a committee to report on free speech at Yale and its defense. We did and the Corporation adopted it as university policy and law. It has spared us much trouble since and earned me the name of reactionary. So things were bad at Yale in the 60s & 70s, but perhaps not as bad as things were at Columbia, Harvard, and maybe Cornell. Then came the 80s and 90s and Political Correctness headed not by the students but by faculty. And this latest onslaught, in longer perspective, may turn out to be the worst—worse for being largely a self-imposed censorship—silence disguised as freedom, not saying anything that might conceivably offend anybody. No, I am not subscribing to the opinion of Mr. Justice Scalia.[90] But I am saying it's the defining premise of free speech that offensiveness cannot be a valid reason for censorship. Rather Mr. Justice Holmes' "freedom for the thought we hate."

But I have wandered astray. I doubt you can make anything of all this as regards your chapter. If I can do so myself it would be to suggest that if you could do more to place your account of Yale in the 50s [in] the context of the times and the experience elsewhere it might make your trials seem less unique. As witness Ellen Schrecker's *No Ivory Tower.*[91]

90. Antonin Gregory Scalia (b. 1936), associate justice of the U.S. Supreme Court since 1986.

91. Ellen W. Schrecker, *No Ivory Tower: McCarthyism and the Universities* (New York: Oxford University Press, 1986); CVW had reviewed the book: see "The Siege," *New York Review of Books* 33 (25 September 1986): 3–10.

You are right about prevailing disarray at Yale this year. Like Boris, I was disappointed in Benno Schmidt. I had been in firm alliance with him on all free speech issues. But for all his merits the man lacked diplomacy. And his dean Don Kagan, good friend and admired scholar, was never accused of having any.[92] Root of the trouble was money and the necessity of budget cuts. Faculty refused to admit the fact and Benno failed to prepare or consult them. Again Yale's financial problems were not the worst. Not nearly so bad as those of Columbia or Harvard or others. But again the press sure God was the worst!

You say in a P.S. that you are "doing an essay on Schama." You mean another? I had just read one you did in *History & Theory* with the greatest pleasure, admiration *and* agreement.[93] I thought I had written my congratulations, but I guess I only resolved to do so.

CVWP, 52/62: TCLU

274. To Georges May[94]

NOVEMBER 30, 1992

Please assure the Acting President that while I greatly appreciate his concern for ameliorating the plight of retired members of the faculty, I am at a loss to suggest any way in which he could improve the "quality of life" I presently enjoy from continuing membership in a learned community.[95]

To illustrate these advantages I offer my recent experience with a non-Yale cardiologist who changed my medication and firmly instructed me to continue it the rest of my life and never to combine it with the consumption of alcohol in any form or quantity. He would not listen to reason. For a whole miserable week I complied. It then occurred to me that one advantage of membership in a learned community was the ability to find an authority who supported one's own point of view. With that in mind I made known my problem to certain colleagues. One of them obligingly put me in touch with the Deputy Dean of the Yale Medical

92. Donald Kagan (b. 1932), a historian of ancient Greece, was dean of Yale College (1989–92).

93. Cushing Strout, "Border Crossings: History, Fiction, and Dead Certainties," *History and Theory* 31 (May 1992): 153–62; this was a review of Simon Schama, *Dead Certainties (Unwarranted Speculations)* (New York: Alfred A. Knopf, 1991).

94. Georges May (1921–2003), professor of French at Yale, as well as its provost.

95. That is, Howard Lamar, Yale's acting president after the tenure of Benno Schmidt and before that of Richard Charles Levin (b. 1947).

School, Dr. Lawrence Cohen, who looks a little like Voltaire. He proved to be a sympathetic spirit and a reasonable man. It was his suggestion that it was simpler to change the medication than the man. With such a change I now enjoy my customary martini before dinner and a welcome change in my quality of life.

So long as I am assured membership in such a community and access to its wonderful library I can think of no further amelioration to suggest.

CVWP, 34/400: TCLU

275. To William Phillips and Edith Kurzweil[96]

APRIL 12, 1993

I have run into trouble with the contribution to the symposium on Political Correctness that I agreed to write in response to your kind invitation last month.[97]

I promptly took pains to bring myself up to date by reading whatever I could find that had been published on the subject since I last wrote about it. That included four books and several articles. I found little that was new. But there was much to confirm an early impression that the source of the movement and center of its zealotry lie in the departments and schools of literary studies, especially those scholars devoted to literary criticism and "theoretical perspectives." True, there are other groups involved, but I think they tend to climb on the bandwagon and profit as they may from the attention and concessions gained by the literary theorists.

The theorists have their own vocabulary, one of baffling complexity and confused usage. I have talked and corresponded with some of them and find no two who agree on the meaning of key terms they frequently use and few who define their pedagogical purposes in the same way. Nor could I find among them any disposition to listen to critics outside their own circle.

96. William Phillips (1907–2002), editor and cofounder of the *Partisan Review,* and Edith Kurzweil (b. 1925), who would marry Phillips in 1995 and succeed him as editor.

97. This would appear as ""The Politics of Political Correctness," *Partisan Review* 60 (Fall 1993): 509–737, and be reprinted as William Phillips and Edith Kurzweil, eds., *Our Country, Our Culture: The Politics of Political Correctness* (New York: Partisan Review, 1994); the contributors were Robert Alter, Robert Brustein, Roger Kimball, Hilton Kramer, Mary Lefkowitz, David Lehman, Doris Lessing, Daphne Merkin, Arthur Schlesinger Jr., John Searle, and Helen Vendler.

Of course theirs is not my field, and I am a stranger there. I think that what you need for this assignment is someone who is in the field concerned, one who can speak with authority and command respect. My lack of these qualifications has persuaded me that I should withdraw from this commitment. I make this decision with much difficulty and re-luctance. I have never done such a thing before. But I believe it serves the best interest of the symposium. I hope you will understand.

CVWP, 43/508: TCLU

276. To David Burner[98]

HAMDEN, CT

MAY 17, 1993

Many thanks for sending me a copy of "What happened to New Deal Liberalism?" I think it is what the academy has been waiting for and desperately needing for several years. It makes an original contri-bution to 20th Century American history, to be sure, but the urgent need it really fulfills is first-aid therapy for the illness that has afflicted large and often dominant parts of the American educational system from higher to lower levels.

I admire the way you address the problem directly and effectively and yet without abrasiveness. I find myself in agreement with what you are saying. I did speak briefly to the National Association of Scholars in accepting the Sidney Hook Award.[99] I had misgivings but did it with the hope of helping them shake off the identification as reactionaries and

98. David Burner (1937–2010), a former student of Hofstadter's and a historian of twenti-eth-century America; he was then teaching at SUNY-Stony Brook. He was working on a book, later published as *Making Peace with the 60s* (Princeton, NJ: Princeton University Press, 1996).

99. The National Association of Scholars, founded in 1987, was formally committed to fostering "intellectual freedom" and sustaining "the tradition of reasoned scholarship and civil debate in America's colleges and universities"; in the 1990s, this mainly translated into a hostil-ity toward political correctness and multiculturalism, as well as university "speech codes." Its critics felt the association encouraged surveillance of what faculty said in their teaching. The Sidney Hook Memorial Award—not to be confused with the Sidney Hook Memorial Award given by Phi Beta Kappa—was given by the NAS to those it felt had sustained the association's values and, for the most part, was given to conservatives. The prize honored Sidney Hook (1902–1989), a political philosopher who taught for many years at New York University and was prominent among those American intellectuals who moved from the left in the 1930s to Cold War liberalism, and finally to an ambivalent conservatism; he was prominent as an op-ponent of affirmative action.

accept liberals who share their view of academic freedom. Your tactic of shaming liberals for betraying the New Deal tradition (I do hope you can work into the title the phrase in your letter: "historical roots of PC.") is just right.

You do not mention plans for publication, but I think the essay should be published as soon as possible and in a place that will gain wide attention. One place that strikes me as appropriate would be the Op-Ed page of the New York *Times*. I would be glad to write to Mr. Raines, the editor, urging his personal attention to the piece if you do submit it there. Then there is *The American Scholar*, though it has a much smaller and largely academic readership.

CVWP, 9/97: TCLU

277. To Hillary Rodham Clinton

APRIL 15, 1994

I enclose with this the copy of a letter that my doctor handed me yesterday, one that he had signed, sealed, and addressed to the President. He had hoped that I might deliver his letter in person, but had got the date of the dinner wrong. Such a delivery would have been unlikely anyway. So I am mailing his letter to your husband and taking the liberty of sending the copy to you.

Please let me thank you for the entirely unexpected good fortune and pleasure of your company at the dinner on Monday the 11th. I was enormously pleased that you recalled our first encounter just twenty years ago at the time you were employed by the House Judiciary Committee in the matter of President Nixon's behavior.

With every good wish for you and yours and the many hopes we share for the coming years.

CVWP, 12/129: TCLU

278. To Martin Peretz[100]

MAY 19, 1994

Sorry to have distracted and disturbed an old friend who has enough trouble already. I appreciate all the more the pains you have taken in responding not only with a thoughtful letter but with many pages of

---

100. Martin H. Peretz (b. 1938), editor of the *New Republic*.

excerpts from articles dating back to January. I have read (or re-read) all of them and readily agree that much that is supportive and appreciative of the Clinton administration has appeared in TNR during the first three months of the year (not to mention much before that). It was, in fact, my awareness of this that made me bridle and call you about what seems to me some unfortunate departures, departures I deplore.

I have already mentioned by phone two examples—the pieces by Barnes comparing Nixon and Clinton and the one on "Hillary's Cows," both in the issue before the one dated May 30.[101] Now in the latter issue come two on the Paula Jones issue that I feared and anticipated when I called you, and the main reason I called.[102] It is not so much the one by Kinsley, who weighs the pros and cons and admits the cynicism of Jones and her handlers and his mixed feelings about the probability of the president's lying and getting away with it. It is more the tone, apparent intent, of the editorial following that disturbs me and my expectations of TNR.

But first, I do not expect you to agree with everything that appears in these pages, nor am I saying that you are out to destroy the Clinton presidency. Nor can I expect the editors to maintain silence about a story that is on so many minds and in all the media. And that even though it is grossly distorted and politically exploited by cynical opponents. And further I admit that a president's private life, or that of prominent politicians, has lately surfaced in a way unknown to the presidencies from Woodrow Wilson to Lyndon Johnson, both of whom and all save Coolidge and Nixon who came along between them engaged in adulterous adventures.

Rather for me it is disproportionate weighing of issues, a mistake of allowing personal misconduct of the past to distract attention from momentous issues of the nation's present and future. And further is a failure to consider and confront the alternatives, the political alternatives, that would follow from such a course. I hope you understand, and I suspect you share many of my misgivings.

CVWP, 43/501: TCLU

101. Fred Barnes, "Clinton's the One!" *New Republic* 210 (16 May 1994): 11–12; James K. Glassman, "Hillary's Cows," *New Republic* 210 (16 May 1994): 18–22.

102. Paula Corbin Jones (b. 1966), a former Arkansas state employee who was suing Bill Clinton for sexual harassment, which she claimed had occurred while he was governor in 1991. The suit was never brought to trial, but settled. See Michael Kinsley, "Pants on Fire," *New Republic* 210 (30 May 1994): 6; Douglas G. McGrath, "You Sure Are Cute," *New Republic* 210 (30 May 1994): 11.

279. To F. Dudley Williams

July 5, 1994

First to bring you glad tidings only recently brought to my attention, though you may have already heard. At least I am told they are glad. This is the settlement of the old dispute between our brethren of the Jesuit and those of the Franciscan order as to which of the two was held in highest esteem by the Almighty. The solution was to address a letter to the Deity Himself laying before Him the cases of both orders. It went up through proper channels and the reply came back similarly. It assured both orders that He cherished them equally and forevermore. I have not seen the document myself but it was said to have been signed "God, (S.J.)"—which to me at least raises further questions.

I am most pleased to learn that you devote some of the precious hours of your retirement to works of history. And further that you turn first to those on the Civil War. You were fortunate to hit upon Shelby Foote. Like all my acquaintances he is several years my junior. In fact he and his dear friend Walker Percy were undergraduates while you and I were graduate students at Chapel Hill. I did not meet him until years later but we have now been members of three organizations that meet regularly and I see him quite often and always with pleasure. At one of them that meets in Chattanooga I encountered him on his arrival at the airport and came to full salute: "General," I said, "I regret to report that Chattanooga has fallen."[103] Returning my salute without the slightest change of expression he replied: "What can you expect with a man like Bragg in command." As you know he also writes novels—enough to enable Percy and me to nominate for the Am. Academy of Arts & Letters and get him in.

On the tendency to blame the Russian people for their Bolshevik misfortunes, I beg you to look at the recent work by Richard Pipes, *Russia Under the Bolshevik Regime*.[104] He demonstrates to my satisfaction that not only the Russian peasants but the working class did all they could during their civil war to prevent the take over by the Communists. It fell [to] my pleasure to have the company of Pipes during my second mission to Moscow. (In my first, 1932, I fell under the heel of Inturist, but not in those of 1970 and 1990 when I knew better. I should have warned you before your

103. This would be on the way to a meeting of the Fellowship of Southern Writers, of which CVW and Foote had been among the twenty-one charter members.

104. Richard Pipes, *Russia Under the Bolshevik Regime* (New York: Alfred A. Knopf, 1993).

own mission came about.) My sermons in the latter two were attended largely by the converted, but in the second it was my privilege to attend the first religious service in the cathedral on Red Square in seventy years and to greet the Primate of our Orthodox brethren.

Alas, I share your fears for the fate of our Arkansas president and first lady at the hands of the GOP and other malevolent forces of Satan. Thanks in part to our common origin and a brief meeting in our native state four years ago as well as an encounter with Hillary before their union I received in April an invitation to dinner. A cozy affair of some 170 guests. I was greeted in the receiving line by the first lady with the news that I would find my place card by her own at table 3, and so it proved— to my enormous pleasure.

Yes, here we are closing in on the next century. I am game to see the horrors of the present one out—but not those of next one in.

Thine till then,

CVWP, 60/721: TCLU

280. To John Hope Franklin

OCTOBER 11, 1994

I think we have cause for mutual congratulations and I have been for some time intending to extend mine. I mean, of course, our triumph over the Disney invaders.[105] Not that we can claim all the credit for the embattled historians and other word mongers, but we are due some of it. And I must admit that I find satisfaction in the triumph of words over bucks—even bucks by the billions. Pride of pen, I suppose, if not word processor (though not the latter in my case). Clippings by the score continue to pour in.

Quite apart from that I am reminded of another and sadder experience we have in common by a letter from Ben Wall, who told me of a talk in which you told him of Aurelia's afflictions.[106] Glenn's troubles came back to mind. Hers were different—recurrent depression, once requiring hospitalization. I managed to avoid nursing home solutions. I hope you can do that too. Anyway, remember that my heart is with you.

---

105. The Walt Disney Company had planned to build a historical theme park, entitled "Disney's America," in Haymarket, VA. The scheme was opposed, in part because it would have been too close to the Manassas National Battlefield Park.

106. Aurelia Elizabeth Whittington Franklin (1915–1999) had married Franklin in 1940.

I continue in reasonably good health, good enough to do what I want to do, including managing a big old house and the surrounding woods. I intend to see it out here, and would not want to live anywhere else, having lived here 33 years. Retired from teaching for the last 17 of them, I still enjoy feeling a part of the university. Still more than I can do in service to our common calling. Besides work of my own there is the need for keeping up with old students, many of them gray grandfathers by now, and their continuing flow of books and manuscripts they expect me to read at once and write them sooner. And I take genuine pride in some of their work.

I manage to get back South and touch base every year—part of maintaining my status as exile. Just back from a brief visit to Nashville where Bert Wyatt-Brown and Bill McFeely (do have a look at their latest books) turned up. I have decided not to make the SHA meeting in Louisville but hope we can get together again before long. Maybe in Chicago.

CVWP, 19/222: TCLU

281. To Bertram Wyatt-Brown

OCTOBER 25, 1994

Many thanks for your kind letter bringing me up to date on intellectual life in the South, and for many other things: the Lamar Lecture book, the Skip Stout conference, the Genovese mutterings, the slavery debate, theological controversy, and planter capitalism.[107] You confirm all I suspected. And what a southern renaissance it pictures. Glad especially to hear you let Gene have it in your response. Of course he will get over it. As well as my remark about his friend Pat Robertson.[108] And I agree that it is you and not Genovese or O'Brien who can "really demonstrate the vitality and freshness of the antebellum Southern intellectual tradition." I also agree about slaveholders not being quite so high-

---

107. Bertram Wyatt-Brown, *The Literary Percys: Family History, Gender, and the Southern Imagination* (Athens: University of Georgia Press, 1994). The conference, held at the Louisville Presbyterian Theological Seminary and in part organized by Harry S. Stout (b. 1947), a historian of American religion at Yale, would eventuate in Randall M. Miller, Harry S. Stout, and Charles Reagan Wilson, eds., *Religion and the American Civil War* (New York: Oxford University Press, 1998).

108. Marion Gordon "Pat" Robertson (b. 1930), the Baptist televangelist who had run unsuccessfully for president in 1988.

minded about ugly capitalism and joining up with the blokes themselves after Appomattox.

I would have answered your letters earlier but for seeing you in Nashville and for the fact that I hoped to be able to give you cheering news. Well I waited, because Bob Silvers called and asked what I thought about the *House of Percy*. I said I thought it was an absolute MUST. He wanted to know if I would do it, and I told him I would.[109] I also told him about the Mercer lectures and he said for me to think of including that. You know what I think of the book and I mean to do all I can. It may take some time because of a backing of postponed promises. But you may be sure I will get around to it. Also TNYRB is often slow in publishing what it has on hand. So don't hold your breath. As for the *Times* it is rare that things really good get attention—or a proper reviewer when they do. It's a national embarrassment when compared with the TLS.

Do send me a xerox of your review of Gene's opus in the *London Review of Books* or I might miss it.[110]

CVWP, 61/740: TCLU

282. To Eugene D. Genovese

DECEMBER 3, 1994

The best and certainly the most welcome reading of your recent letter was the interlinear message that, hard as you might try, you really could take no serious offense at my review of your book in the TLS.[111] None intended, of course—only a bit of teasing.

As for your epistolary teasing of me about the recent misfortunes of the Democrats I have no trouble taking it in my stride. Not when it comes from a prophet so disarmingly candid as to admit that he "never dreamed that the Soviet Union would collapse."[112] Starting with the genial admission that in this field we all make mistakes, it is even possible for me to understand your confusion of my fellow Arkansan with such "shamefaced totalitarians" as Mussolini, Mao, Tito, etc., etc. I generously attribute this

---

109. CVW, "We Unhappy Few," *New York Review of Books* 42 (22 June 1995): 32–36.

110. Bertram Wyatt-Brown, "Southern Discomfort," *London Review of Books* 17 (8 June 1995): 27–28, a review of Eugene D. Genovese, *The Southern Tradition: The Achievement and Limitations of an American Conservatism* (Cambridge, MA: Harvard University Press, 1994).

111. CVW, "What the South Can Teach Us," *Times Literary Supplement*, 23 September 1994, 9.

112. Genovese, *Southern Tradition*, 7.

to excessive exposure to the rhetoric of the representative of a neighboring district, Speaker Gingrich.[113]

For the healthy side of Liberalism, who [is] more healthy than Al Gore, Jr.?[114] And while we are on the subject of tags and stereotypes I wonder if you do not at times share my doubts about the continued usefulness of such outworn labels as "Marxists," and "Liberals"—especially in a time when "Conservative" has come to mean Radicals of the Right. And that to the embarrassment of a courageous defender determined to do the right thing about them—come what may.

I agree that we must have it out at future meetings and that the subject offers rich opportunities for the exchange of views—and, let us hope, the meeting of minds. As for the opportunities, you did not mention New Orleans in March. I hope that does not mean I will not see you there. I will make every effort to attend the Tucker meeting in June, but will know more about that when we meet in March.[115] But I better not agree to appear on the program. Surely you can find a better informed commentator on the Weaver paper.[116]

Please tell Betsey that I have endlessly admired her cool and calm in the face of the stupid assault upon her. And please give her my love.

CVWP: 21/241: TCLU

283. To Daniel W. Crofts[117]

JANUARY 6, 1995

All I can offer in print about David Potter is a rather formal tribute reprinted as the final essay in my collection, THE FUTURE OF THE PAST.[118] With only a paragraph or so on LINCOLN AND HIS PARTY it can be of little help, though you might take a look.

113. Gingrich had become speaker of the U.S. House of Representatives in 1995; he represented Georgia's sixth congressional district, which partly included the northern Atlanta suburbs where Genovese lived.

114. Albert A. "Al" Gore Jr. (b. 1948), U.S. vice president (1993–2001).

115. Genovese had been among the founders of the Saint George Tucker Society, a group concerned with fostering Southern studies.

116. Richard Malcolm Weaver Jr. (1910–1963), the Southern conservative intellectual in whom Genovese had an interest.

117. Daniel W. Crofts, an American historian who taught at the College of New Jersey, was working on what would become David M. Potter, *Lincoln and His Party in the Secession Crisis*, introduction by Daniel W. Crofts (1942; Baton Rouge: Louisiana State University Press, 1995).

118. CVW, "David Morris Potter (1910–1971)," in *The Future of the Past* (New York: Oxford University Press, 1989), 353–58.

There were many bonds between us—personal as well as professional. But there were limits on the personal side due to a reticence on his
part, or what I felt to be that.

For example, when Yale invited me up after David's resignation to
talk about my replacing him I am sure David wanted to be helpful and
wanted me to accept the place. But his reasons for leaving were a mystery.
Driving around town with him once I said "David, our tastes are very
similar, and if you don't like Yale it is likely that I won't either. So I would
like to know how you feel about the place." After a moment of silence he
pointed to the traffic signal and said "The stop lights here last too long."
Naturally I dropped the subject. And his colleagues were no help. There
were vague hints that his wife was not happy here, but nothing definite.
Maybe he felt stuck in American Studies.

As for Carleton's idea that Yale had no place for Southern history,
why did they urge me to join them?[119] Yes, I did think of David as a historian of the South. And no, I can't accept "his disenchantment with his
home region" as explanation for turning to LINCOLN AND HIS PARTY.
That was a revision of his dissertation, wasn't it? And in those days professors had a way of assigning subjects for dissertations. And after that
wasn't it natural for the editors of the old American Nation Series to ask
him to write the volume on the coming of the Civil War? To be sure, we
of the South had in those days reason for placing distance between our
views and traditional and current orthodox Southern views. We had several ways of doing this. One might have been turning to national history
to prove our freedom from Southern orthodoxies.
[deletion]

CVWP, 13/145: TCLU

284. To Edward L. Ayers[120]

AUGUST 18, 1995

I have long thought of myself as fortunate, or at least lucky, in the critics I have had. I mean the serious ones with real differences over facts,
interpretations, and basic assumptions of the sort that regularly lead to

---

119. Presumably William G. Carleton, CVW's old friend from Gainesville.

120. Edward L. Ayers (b. 1953), then teaching at the University of Virginia; he had recently published *The Promise of the New South: Life After Reconstruction* (New York: Oxford University Press, 1992), perhaps the most concerted attempt to supplement and/or supersede CVW's
Origins of the New South.

bitter words. Instead they have maintained a high level of civility and—
whatever their gut feelings—minded their manners. And they are by no
means all southern bred. I count some of them my genuine friends to
whom I am much indebted.

But what about critics from generations to come I asked myself sometimes—the ones after four, five, going on six decades, if the old books are
remembered that long. It will be their duty, of course, to point out how
dated, out-of-date, time-ridden, and downright quaint the old boy appears in the up-to-date enlightened present day. Not that I lost much
sleep over it, but occasionally I also wondered about my successors, future
historians who would address the same subjects, periods, events that I had
with new books, ideas, insights, preoccupations to replace the old? What
charity, if any, might I expect at their hands?

Well, with more luck I have lived long enough to read a most reassuring answer from one of them, who had already gained my respect
and admiration, and has now earned my gratitude. That piece of yours,
"Narrating the New South" in the August JSH combines keen insight
with a rare generosity of spirit.[121] Your definition of "open" history writing as "a collaborative, cumulative enterprise" sets the tone. And you
could not have defined more accurately the circumstances explaining and
limiting my own books.

The first one, in 1938, came out of the depths, the Great Depression.
Origins came out of the 40s and 50s when I felt oppressed by the tide of
reactionism and McCarthyism. And the "Consensus" school was gaining
recruits in my own profession. So it was I found Charles Beard, "old hat"
as he was already deemed, the most congenial spirit around. So politics
and economics and the seats of power and oppression and their many
victims became my history subjects. The theme of irony could not have
concealed the underlying indignation and anger. I could not have written
different history in that time. And frankly I am glad I did not try. I thank
you, my friend, for understanding.

CVWP, 5/48: TCLS

---

121. Edward L. Ayers, "Narrating the New South," *Journal of Southern History* 61 (August
1995): 555–66.

285. To Bertram Wyatt-Brown

OCTOBER 2, 1995

[deletion]

On the health record, I am just emerging from a bad scare. A colon-oscopy last Wednesday was followed on Thursday by a report from the doctor that the biopsy indicated a malignancy and his call to my sur-geon (who efficiently removed a yard or so of my colon some ten years ago) but asking me to come in Friday (yesterday) for a followup on the colonoscopy. Sunken in despair and anxiety I did turn up. Prone on the mobile bed and awaiting further rectal exploring, I heard the tele-phone. A long conversation followed. It was the biopsy lab saying there *was* malignancy on the surface of the polyp but further study proved it had not penetrated to the wall of intestine. With that I leaped out of the bed, kissed the nurse, thanked the doctor and emerged in a world more beautiful than I remember it being before. I wish you comparable luck with your own ailments. And, yes, I have comparable problems with coumadin.

[deletion]

> CVWP, 61/740: TCLS

286. To Donald S. Lamm[122]

OCTOBER 21, 1995

The Simpson and Farrakhan TV melodramas, like nothing else since our agreement of last January have focused my thoughts about the Racial Paradoxes project.[123] In the meantime great piles of books, stacks of notes, and daily press clippings have accumulated. And so have addi-tional "paradoxes." A few samples to illustrate:

> The unholy alliance of Southern blacks and Republicans for segregated electoral districts.
> The broken alliance of blacks and Jews and black anti-Semitism.

122. Donald S. Lamm (b. 1931), president of W. W. Norton (1976–94).

123. Orenthal James "O. J." Simpson (b. 1947), the former National Football League star, was tried in Los Angeles and acquitted of the murder of his ex-wife Nicole Brown Simpson and Ronald Goldman on 3 October 1995 after a nine-month trial. The reference to Louis Far-rakhan Muhammad Sr. (b. 1933), leader of the Nation of Islam, is to the "Million Man March" in Washington, DC, on October 16, 1995; Farrakhan had called it to express and convey a more positive image of the black male.

Victory of King for integration and Malcolm X for resegregation in
'65.
Africa, the most *dis*united of continents as model for black unity in US.
Black unity by embracing slaveholders' "one-drop" definition of
"black."
Uses of segregation by black businessmen, black professionals, and
politicians.
Black middle class progress with black underclass deterioration.
Poor blacks less skeptical and more hopeful of future than well-off
blacks.
More disagreement on race issues between black intellectuals than be-
tween blacks and whites.
More paranoidal suspicion of whites among black college educated
than others.

As you see, my paradoxes all seem to have in common some degree of criticism or reproach for blacks. Unwelcome as they must be at
this time, I would not withhold or modify them. I believe they must be
acknowledged and dealt with. Acknowledgement of white injustice and
oppression is unlikely to make the reproaches much more welcome to
blacks. Not when followed by an even more unwelcome degree of candor
about the use of money and race to subvert justice and disgrace trial by
jury. And that followed by more plain speaking about Farrakhan with his
separate black nation in America and his blatant racism.

I know that blacks are divided over these and other issues, but they
are more and more united [against] whites who tell them where they err,
what they think, and what they must and must not do. My own offenses
of this sort would be greeted by black indignation and anger. "This from
Woodward," they would say, "one white southerner we have been taught
to regard as a friend. But look what he is saying now! Can you believe it?"

I have never let hostility to my views stop me from putting them into
print. But this time there are other reasons against intervening in the bitter quarrels and hatreds. For one thing, this time I would not be writing
as a historian with command of the evidence and some standing in a
learned profession. I would be writing essentially as a journalist, match-
ing wits with columnists and pundits who have far more experience and
resources. And I would be depending largely on such scraps of sociology
as I might pick up. But of course I am neither a journalist nor a sociologist. To come forth in either or both roles in such times as these would be
a poor way to end a long career as a historian.

Well, Don, you know the hesitations with which I entered our agreement. I promised to put in a year of serious work on the project with the hope that it would overcome my doubts and speed me on to completion. I am still more than two months short of a full year. They have not, however, resolved the doubts or inspired genuine hope of doing so. I think, therefore, that I should wait no longer to tell you that I must withdraw. Please believe me that I regret very much that this idea did not work out. Be assured also that I greatly appreciate your offer and the confidence it revealed. I will file away my notes and let you know if I change my mind. But this must not inhibit your efforts to find another author for the book.

CVWP, 70/104: TCLU

287. To John Updike

MAY 25, 1996

We seem to share an admirer—if he can be called that.[124] On reading his tribute to you in a recent TLS I was reminded of a shorter one to me and some other "scholar squirrels" which I enclose herewith— for your waste basket.[125] I took some satisfaction in replying to his eight or more columns in a single paragraph. I wish I had followed your example of silent contempt. What an unspeakable skunk this Gore Vidal.

CVWP, 53/638: TCLU

124. The context for this letter is that, in 1987 when reviewing William Safire, *Freedom* (Garden City, NY: Doubleday, 1987), CVW had spoken critically of Gore Vidal, *Lincoln: A Novel* (New York: Random House, 1984). In 1988, there had followed an exchange between Vidal and CVW, which had, in turn, led to other scholars criticizing Vidal and a further riposte from Vidal. In these exchanges, Vidal began to refer, slightingly, to "scholar-squirrels." In time, he would warm to the theme and come to designate CVW as a careerist bureaucrat par excellence, someone interested mainly in the "gravy train" of academe and someone who won a Pulitzer prize only because a colleague (John Morton Blum) was on the Pulitzer committee. See CVW, "Gilding Lincoln's Lily," *New York Review of Books* 34 (24 September 1987): 23–26; CVW and Gore Vidal, "Gore Vidal's Lincoln: An Exchange," *New York Review of Books* 35 (28 April 1988): 56–58; "Vidal's Lincoln: An Exchange," *New York Review of Books* 35 (18 August 1988): 66–69 (with letters from Richard Current, Harold Holzer, and Vidal); Gore Vidal, "Bad History," in *The Last Empire: Essays, 1992–2001* (New York: Doubleday, 2001), 292–93, originally published as Gore Vidal, "Bad History," *Nation* 266 (20 April 1998): 11–15.

125. Gore Vidal, "Rabbit's Own Burrow," *Times Literary Supplement* (26 April 1996): 2–5.

288. To Anne Behrens[126]

[UNDATED, BUT SUMMER 1997]

What a dear you are to write me about the American Scholar essay.[127] I only wish I could say I had been responsible for sending it, but my guess is that you were on a list of PBK members invited to subscribe. I get it for free because I was long ago a member of the editorial board (with a youth named Pat Moynihan).

I too live alone, but still resist retirement homes and still live in the house I bought 36 years ago when I came to Yale. It has four beds and two bathrooms more than I can use, and I rattle around a bit from my study on the first floor to bed on the third floor. I miss the family I bought it for, but I find compensations in both single living and aging. Plus daily walks in the most beautiful city park I know. It has 30 miles of walks and adjoins my lot. No Olympic Mountains, but a volcanic cliff, a tidal basin, a river and waterfall.

Other compensations for staying put is remaining a member of a university community. I retired from the faculty 20 years ago, but am still a member of college fellowships, a club founded in 1830, a faculty dining place. What social life I have centers there with old friends.

I curbed my tourist addiction about ten years ago with a second trip to India and my third to the USSR. But I still yield once in a while to an invitation to a foreign conference. That requires listening to papers I had rather not hear. But the one in August on an island off the coast of Denmark consists of Europeans from all over with papers on—of all subjects—my native region and special field. I did not know they had heard about the South and could not resist. So, off again I go.

CVWP, 7/71: TCLU

126. Anne K. Behrens (1911–2003) had known CVW since the late 1930s, when she wrote an enthusiastic letter about his *Tom Watson:* see Anne Behrens to CVW, 16 July 1938. She was married to Arthur Hilstad Behrens (1910–1991), who worked for many years in the U.S. Patent Office; after his retirement, they had moved to Kitsap County in Washington state.

127. CVW, "The Aging of Democracies," *American Scholar* 66 (Summer 1997): 349–58.

289. To Joel R. Williamson[128]

SEPTEMBER 26, 1997

I am glad to hear of your continued work connecting the arts and writers with history, a work so beautifully illustrated by your *Faulkner*.[129] Keep it up. You and Wyatt-Brown are creating a new field for historians. You may have heard about Bert's next big venture on the revenges of depression among Southern writers from William G. Simms through Faulkner and Styron. You have probably seen some of his essays. The working title for the book is "Melancholy's Children."[130]

I think I told you about the European academic growth of courses on the South I encountered at the Denmark conference.[131] The scholars I questioned for an explanation usually said that it started with popularity of jazz and rap and blacks on the mass level and Elvis combining it all for whites. You know about the Elvis museum somewhere in Norway or Sweden I have never seen, and memorials in marble elsewhere. I had to confess the prevailing snobbery among American academy and that I had never seen nor heard Elvis. If I wrote in support of your project I would say how much I admired your work on Faulkner and encouraged you to continue, but I was ignorant about Presley and scholarship on him. I will surely make the best case I can on those terms, but you must decide. I would urge you to ask support from any European scholars on popular culture that you know.

Here's the story of my nearest contact with Elvis. Years ago Willie Morris picked me up at Jackson to drive me to Oxford to give a lecture. He said we would pass through Tupelo on the way and he had assured people gathering at the Elvis birthplace for his birthday that I would be glad to address them. Hard to tell when Willie was serious. But we pulled

128. Joel R. Williamson (b. 1930), a historian of Southern race relations at the University of North Carolina-Chapel Hill; he is perhaps best known for *The Crucible of Race: Black/White Relations in the American South Since Emancipation* (New York: Oxford University Press, 1984).

129. Joel Williamson, *William Faulkner and Southern History* (New York: Oxford University Press, 1993).

130. Eventually published as Bertram Wyatt-Brown, *Hearts of Darkness: Wellsprings of a Southern Literary Tradition* (Baton Rouge: Louisiana State University Press, 2003).

131. The Southern Studies Forum, created in 1988, is an organization affiliated to the European Association for American Studies; it met in 1997 at the University of Odense on Ærø Island, Denmark.

up at Tupelo and sure enough there was a long line waiting to view the house. I looked at Willie. He grinned and drove on. End of story. [deletion]

  CVWP, 60/726: TCLU

290. To Michael O'Brien

For your collection of Southerners abroad I offer this:[132] Early in 1955, while I was at Johns Hopkins, I received an invitation from the University of Tokyo to teach a class on the South during Reconstruction in the following summer term. In my reply I said I would like to accept their invitation, but added that in view of the probable lack of background I thought it better to make my course treat the South in the Nineteenth Century. Their reply was extremely polite but quite firm in asking that my subject be confined to the South During Reconstruction. With some puzzlement I agreed.

The puzzlement was cleared up shortly after I arrived and reported for duty. By far the most popular movie in town was Gone with the Wind, Japan was under reconstruction by Yankees, and the Japanese identified with the defeated South. Facing a room full of rapt and attentive students, who seemed to understand my American English with Southern accent, I held forth for the term. It was agreed that I give no examination and no grades, but I was asked to wind up with an address to a university-wide audience, which seemed to go off well.

During the term I lunched daily with Japanese colleagues at their faculty dining hall. At lunch toward the end of term I remarked that I read a lot in an English newspaper about anti-American feeling and demonstrations in Tokyo but had not witnessed any and asked where I could find it. Silence, followed by the customary titter covering embarrassment. Then one friend, who later visited me in the states, smiled slowly and said, "My dear colleague, you have been living at the center of it since you have been with us."

  Private Collection: TLS

132. O'Brien was editing a special issue of *Southern Cultures* on how non-Southerners viewed the South; this letter, since it was so brief, was published as CVW, "Haiku," *Southern Cultures* 4 (Winter 1998): 19.

291. To John Morton Blum

JANUARY 12, 1998

This is to put in writing, as you suggested, what I said to you at lunch the other day.

Should the question ever come up about my wishes concerning the nature of any memorial service that might be held for me, you may say that you know my preference was for one of a secular character.

It was the recent memorial for Jack Hall that reminded me of this.

CVWP, 8/81: TCLU

292. To Cushing Strout

JANUARY 19, 1998

Your prospectus on liberalism reminds me of a postponed project of my own, an essay on the mounting meaninglessness of current political terms. A few years ago Gene Genovese asked me to give a name to my political faith. When I replied it was usually called liberalism he said, "Nonsense, you are no liberal. You might say you are a Zen Buddhist." I responded with some similar slur about his professed Southern conservatism.

In fact I think of Gene as a perfect example of present confusion in political terminology, and said as much in a review of his *The Southern Tradition* for the TLS. He has never quite forgiven me. But there he was, comparing the collapse of the USSR with the defeat of the Confederacy, embracing Southern conservatism as the logical refuge for an ex-Communist. Of course he said true conservatives renounced the legacy of racism and added hurriedly that there was some "awkwardness" in its relations with religious fundamentalism, but nevertheless real Southern conservatives have "always criticized capitalism severely." I can only wonder at his finding himself in bed with the Christian Coalition, Pat Buchanan, Newt Gingrich, the Solid Republican South, and sundry conservatives leading us to a reactionary climax of the century.

As for the plight of today's liberals trying to fit their faith into some phase of left-right-center I sometimes despair. No sooner have we placed ourselves as left-of-center than center turns out to be where right was the day before yesterday. And off we go to the brink of reactionism.

But don't share my despair. Do carry on with the Jeffersonian struggle, and I wish you the best.

I applaud your resistance to the eager therapies of the medicoes. I also resist their efforts to persuade me I am a sick man.

I will hope to see you on Jefferson in the *Sewanee Review*.[133]

In your spare time don't miss Peter Gay's *The Pleasure Wars*, fifth and final volume of his *Bourgeois Experience*.[134]

CVWP, 52/62: TCLU

293. To Kenneth C. Barnes[135]

APRIL 29, 1998

Let me thank you first for sending me a copy of your fine new book.[136] And second for your generous references to my work and the way in which you treated it. Yes, I agree that my critics do have a point in saying that I exaggerated the discontinuity between the Old and the New South. But I agree with you that while I erred in a literal sense, I was right in a basic sense about the passing of the planter class from power.

Your book brought home to me as nothing had before how much the historian as generalist writing about *The* Nation or *The* South misses about history in overlooking the particular, the distinctive that local history brings forth. As you know, I grew up in Morrilton, peddled *Time* (at 10c a copy) as a teenager, went to school with whites of all classes, yet never heard of the exodus of blacks from S.C. to the "promised land" of Conway Co., or their attempted back-to-Africa exodus, or their exodus to Oklahoma, or the Holy Ghost Fathers, or the nunnery near the railway station, or the series of politically motivated murders. How's that for the historical awareness of a budding historian?

Your "second civil war for Arkansas, Conway County in particular" seems to have ugly consequences as numerous and extended as the first one. I lived with the immediate descendants of its heroes and villains— the Fizers for example, Poindexter in particular, yet I doubt if they knew

133. Cushing Strout, "The Case of the One-Eyed Pundits and Jeffersonian DNA," *Sewanee Review* 108 (Spring 2000): 248–54.

134. Peter Gay, *The Bourgeois Experience: Victoria to Freud*, 5 vols. (New York: Oxford University Press, 1984–98).

135. A historian at the University of Central Arkansas in Conway.

136. Kenneth C. Barnes, *Who Killed John Clayton? Political Violence and the Emergence of the New South, 1861–1893* (Durham, NC: Duke University Press, 1998).

much more about their forebears than I did.[137] I lived among lynchers, but knew nothing of [the] beginnings of lynching. As for inter-marriage and cohabitation of blacks and whites—unthinkable, Yankee propaganda!

I can think of no other scholarly monograph (and I have read a good many) that moved me so deeply as yours. Of course there were special reasons that I need not enumerate for you and that few other readers will share. But among them are some that I am sure a good many will recognize, the dedicated and thorough work of a true historian.

CVWP, 6/50: TCLU

294. To Henry Ashby Turner

OCTOBER 1, 1999

Many thanks for *Hitler's Thirty Days*.[138] I find it splendidly readable. After a month in the USSR in the summer of 1932 I had a month in Germany, mainly in Berlin, into September. So I was there when Hindenburg publicly rebuked Hitler. And I was assured by the Jewish family with whom I had pension in Berlin that the Nazis would come to nothing—and heard that elsewhere. So I went home with somewhat better hopes for Germany than for Russia—alas! Love to have a talk. Please give me a ring when you are free for lunch.

CVWP, 53/629: ALS

137. The reference here is to Napoleon Bonaparte Fizer (b. ca. 1855), a Methodist preacher who ran on the Union Labor ticket in the Arkansas gubernatorial race of 1890. Barnes had interviewed Fizer's descendant, Poindexter Fiser [*sic*], in Morrilton in 1992, and learned about a lynching whose aftermath CVW himself had witnessed; see Barnes, *Who Killed John Clayton?*, 176–77 n.46. For CVW's experience, see Roper, *Woodward, Southerner*, 16.

138. Henry Ashby Turner, *Hitler's Thirty Days to Power: January 1933* (Reading, MA: Addison-Wesley, 1996).

Acknowledgments

My first thanks must go to Susan Woodward and Sheldon Hackney for encouraging me to undertake this project and offering valuable advice along the way. Next I am under a great obligation to the staff of the Manuscripts and Archives Division of Yale University Library, especially its director, Christine Weideman, and William Massa. Further I need to thank the staff at the other archives I visited: the Southern Historical Collection in the Wilson Library at the University of North Carolina-Chapel Hill; the Rare Book and Manuscript Library of Columbia University; the Beinecke Rare Book and Manuscript Library of Yale University; and, especially, the Manuscripts, Archives, and Rare Book Library of Emory University. For materials sent to me, I am also grateful to the Arthur and Elizabeth Schlesinger Library of the Radcliffe Institute at Harvard University and the Rare Books and Special Collections Library of the University of Rochester. Columbia University and the Beinecke do not require editors to request formal permission to publish copyrighted materials, but the other archives do, so I am pleased to acknowledge that these permissions have been granted.

For funds that helped me to spend time in New Haven and the South, I am under an obligation to the Foreign Travel Fund of the University of Cambridge and to Jesus College, Cambridge. For answering sundry vexatious inquiries, I need to thank Johanna Shields, Jack Roper, Sam Webb, Ann Webb, Ben Johnson, Linda Evans (of the library at Henderson State University), and Steve Hahn, and, for reading a draft of the manuscript with his usual sensitivity and care, Steve Stowe. (The dedication of this book can little repay what I have come to owe him over the years.) In arranging that this book find its way to Yale University Press and casting an eye over the introduction, Andrew Wylie was, as usual, prompt and shrewd. At that press, the manuscript's two anonymous readers gave the edition an unusually thorough scrutiny, which has much improved the text and corrected sundry blunders. But I need most to thank Caitlin Verboon, who generously took time away from her studies at Yale to transcribe most of the letters I have used here and to undertake those miscellaneous research tasks which my distance from Yale rendered difficult to accomplish.

Index

Abernethy, Thomas P., 65, 84

Abolitionists (and antislavery), 102, 133, 152n85, 155–56, 169–70, 199, 223–25, 257, 288n144, 301, 314, 363

Abolitionists (of the 1960s), 139, 279n120

abortion, 381

Abraham, David, 359–60

Adair, Douglass and Virginia, 123n19

Adams, Henry, x, xliv, 23n54, 228, 315, 361, 365

Adams, Herbert Baxter, xliv

Adams, James Truslow, 64

Adams, John, 69n153, 76

Adams, Josephine, 192n177

Adams, L. Sherman, 181

Adorno, Theodor W., 197, 227

Africa, 67, 284, 378n73, 379, 400, 406

African-Americans, xii, xviii, xxxiv, 205, 233–34, 266, 277, 311, 331, 343–45, 356–57. *See also* blacks, colored, Negro

Agnew, Spiro T., 307

Agrarians, Southern, 23n53, 25n63, 133, 62, 64, 70–71, 74–75, 83n178, 141

Ahern, James F., 282

Ahlgren, Elizabeth A., 206

Alabama, xxvn33, xxvii, 62, 103, 120, 122, 183, 217, 219–20, 301, 309: Birmingham, 62; Montgomery, 222, 225, 270, 326, 340; Selma, 270

Alden, John R., 304

Aldrich, Winthrop W., 142–45

Alexander, Hartley B., 88

Alexander, Will W., 10, 199–201: letter to, 94–95

Alexander the Great, 285

Allen, John D., 45, 61

Allen, John M., 119

Alsace-Lorraine, 212

American Academy of Arts and Letters, xxvi, 345, 384

American Academy of Arts and Sciences, xxvi, 26, 311, 313n190

American Association of University Professors, xxv–xxvi, xxviii

American Civil Liberties Union, xxvi, 230, 357n38

American Legion, 62, 96

American Protective Association, 184

American Revolution, xii

Americans for Democratic Action, 185

American Socialist Party, 11, 34n80, 37, 200n192, 234

American Studies, 148, 385, 397

Ames, Adelbert 119

Ames, Nathaniel, 181n146

Annan, Noel, 156

anthropology, 165, 242, 289, 305, 328, 377

Anti-Masons, 184

anti-Semitism, xiii, 226–27

Aptheker, Herbert, xxxiv–xl, 152, 247–48, 252–53, 294, 318–25, 328–38, 344n9, 370–71: letters to, 291–92, 306, 310–11

aristocracy, 156, 309, 355

Aristotle, 7, 352

Arkansas, xi, xvii–xix, xxxix, xlii, 16, 43–44, 54, 74, 81n176, 83, 88, 103, 127n25, 132, 165, 183, 206, 220, 250, 251, 346, 350, 352, 371, 383, 391n102, 393, 395, 406–7: Arkadelphia, xi, 2n2, 13nn31–32, 15n35,

411